The European Wit

The European Witch-Hunt seeks to explain why thousands of people, mostly lower-class women, were deliberately tortured and killed in the name of religion and morality during three centuries of intermittent witch-hunting throughout Europe and North America.

Combining perspectives from history, sociology, psychology and other disciplines, this book provides a comprehensive account of witch-hunting in early modern Europe. Julian Goodare sets out an original interpretation of witch-hunting as an episode of ideologically-driven persecution by the 'godly state' in the era of the Reformation and Counter-Reformation. Full weight is also given to the context of village social relationships, and there is a detailed analysis of gender issues. Witch-hunting was a legal operation, and the courts' rationale for interrogation under torture is explained. Panicking local elites, rather than central governments, were at the forefront of witch-hunting. Further chapters explore folk beliefs about legendary witches, and intellectuals' beliefs about a secret conspiracy of witches in league with the Devil. Witch-hunting eventually declined when the ideological pressure to combat the Devil's allies slackened. A final chapter sets witch-hunting in the context of other episodes of modern persecution.

This book is the ideal resource for students exploring the history of witch-hunting. Its level of detail and use of social theory also make it important for scholars and researchers.

Julian Goodare is Reader in History at the University of Edinburgh. His previous books include *The Government of Scotland, 1560–1625* (2004), and (as editor) *Scottish Witches and Witch-Hunters* (2013). He is Director of the online Survey of Scottish Witchcraft.

'This is a wonderful work, with real pace, clarity and sparkle, which combines excellent scholarship with a full recognition of the emotive quality of the material. It will exactly suit the intelligent, enquiring and thoughtful among students and general readers, and be of real interest and value to scholars.'
Ronald E. Hutton, University of Bristol, UK

'This book excellently presents the different layers of meaning of witchcraft and witch trials all over Europe. Julian Goodare combines a sublime understanding of the topic with a personal interpretation in writing about one of the greatest enigmas in history: Why were so-called witches persecuted by their neighbours as well as by the state? The book provides a most fruitful resource for students and scholars in presenting new research and new perspectives on the history of witchcraft.'
Rita Voltmer, University of Trier, Germany

'Julian Goodare's *The European Witch-Hunt* is a valuable addition to the study of early modern witchcraft and witch-hunting. Goodare devotes extra attention to explaining the mentalities, both illiterate and erudite, that converged to create the stereotype of the witch. His explanations of recurrent themes in ideas about witchcraft will be particularly helpful to students and prepare them for a better understanding of primary texts and more specialized secondary studies.'
Walter Stephens, John Hopkins University, USA

'In this brilliant new book, Julian Goodare draws on a vast range of the most up-to-date scholarship and a variety of different disciplinary perspectives to explain why around 50,000 people, most of them women, were executed for witchcraft in early modern Europe. Goodare explores the beliefs, social and religious tensions, and political and judicial systems that underpinned the identification and persecution of "witches" at both the popular and elite level, encouraging the reader to take early modern ideas about witchcraft seriously, and arguing that early modern European witch-hunting was uniquely characterised by fears on the part of "godly states" about demonic witchcraft. Engagingly and lucidly written, including many detailed examples and case-studies, and with a strong sense of the moral and emotional issues linked to the phenomenon of witch-persecution in both the past and the present, this book will have wide appeal within and outside academia.'
Alison Rowlands, University of Essex, UK

The European Witch-Hunt

Julian Goodare

LONDON AND NEW YORK

First published 2016
by Routledge
2 Park Square, Milton Park, Abingdon, Oxon OX14 4RN

and by Routledge
711 Third Avenue, New York, NY 10017

Routledge is an imprint of the Taylor & Francis Group, an informa business

© 2016 Julian Goodare

The right of Julian Goodare to be identified as author of this work has been asserted by him in accordance with sections 77 and 78 of the Copyright, Designs and Patents Act 1988.

All rights reserved. No part of this book may be reprinted or reproduced or utilised in any form or by any electronic, mechanical, or other means, now known or hereafter invented, including photocopying and recording, or in any information storage or retrieval system, without permission in writing from the publishers.

Trademark notice: Product or corporate names may be trademarks or registered trademarks, and are used only for identification and explanation without intent to infringe.

British Library Cataloguing-in-Publication Data
A catalogue record for this book is available from the British Library

Library of Congress Cataloging-in-Publication Data

Names: Goodare, Julian, author.
Title: The European witch-hunt / Julian Goodare.
Description: London ; New York : Routledge, 2016. |
Includes bibliographical references and index.
Identifiers: LCCN 2015050307|
ISBN 9780415254526 (hardback : alk. paper) |
ISBN 9780415254533 (pbk. : alk. paper) |
ISBN 9781315560458 (ebook)
Subjects: LCSH: Witchcraft—Europe—History. |
Witch hunting—Europe—History. |
Trials (Witchcraft)—Europe—History.
Classification: LCC BF1584.E9 G66 2016 | DDC 133.4/3094—dc23
LC record available at https://lccn.loc.gov/2015050307

ISBN: 978-0-415-25452-6 (hbk)
ISBN: 978-0-415-25453-3 (pbk)
ISBN: 978-1-315-56045-8 (ebk)

Typeset in Sabon
by diacriTech, Chennai

To Malcolm and Duncan

Let my words knit what now we lack
The demon and the heritage
And fancy strapped to logic's rock.
A chastened wantonness, a bit
That sets on song a discipline,
A sensuous austerity.
>Hamish Henderson, *Elegies for the Dead in Cyrenaica* (1948), Prologue (Polygon, 1990). Reproduced with permission.

Contents

Diagrams and illustrations xiii
Preface xv
Acknowledgements xix
Conventions and abbreviations xxi

Introduction: The witch-hunt and you 1

Why the witch-hunt matters 1
Understanding believers in witchcraft 1
Where I stand 3
How do we know about witch-hunting? 6

1 Witchcraft! 9

Introduction 9
The fourfold concept of witchcraft 9
Identifying witches 14
A world of religion and magic 19
Witchcraft and 'superstitious magic' 22
Elite and popular beliefs 24
Understanding 'witch-hunting' 26
The scale of the European witch-hunt 27
Conclusion: Causes of witch-hunting 30

2 Towards witch-hunting 31

Introduction 31
The growth of the idea of persecution 32
Prosecutions before the witch-hunt 35
Political magic in the fourteenth century 36

viii Contents

    Towards a new crime of 'witchcraft', c.1400–1435 39
    The 'new sect' of witches, c.1435–1485 42
    The Malleus Maleficarum *(1486) and village witchcraft 48*
    Conclusion: Witchcraft beliefs come together, 1486–1500 50

3 **Witchcraft and the intellectuals** 55

    Introduction 55
    The cosmos and the cosmic story 55
    Sources of elite witch-beliefs 58
    Natural, supernatural and preternatural 60
    Natural and demonic magic 63
    Distorted echoes of popular belief 64
    Witchcraft as a 'cumulative concept' 65
    Medieval foundations: The Devil 67
    Early developments: The debate on witches' flight, 1440–1580 71
    Later developments: The revival of the sabbat, 1580–1612 73
    The elaborated concept of witchcraft 76
    Varieties of scepticism 79
    Genres of demonology 83
    Conclusion: From demonology to witch-hunting 85

4 **Witches in the community** 88

    Introduction 88
    Trust and distrust 88
    Identifying a witch 91
    Forming a witchcraft reputation: A five-stage model 92
    Quarrels and grievances 94
    Linking a misfortune to witchcraft 96
    Spells and curses 99
    Heightening suspicion 103
    Instant reputation 104
    The search for reconciliation 106
    Living with a witch 110
    Denouncing a witch to the authorities 113
    Conclusion: Neighbourhood quarrels in context 117

5 **Witchcraft and folk belief** 121

    Introduction 121
    The peasant world-view 121

Popular Christianity 126
How folktales structured witchcraft stories 128
Non-human inhabitants of the popular universe 130
Witches in legends and folktales 133
Flying and shape-shifting 136
Shamanistic visionaries and cults 140
Hallucinogenic drugs? 145
Psychological conditions and the 'nightmare experience' 145
Conclusion: Popular beliefs about 'witchcraft' 150

6 Witches and the godly state   155

Introduction 155
The rise of the early modern state 156
The Reformation and Counter-Reformation 157
The divine ruler and the Devil 159
Demonology and the Reformation: Consensus and controversy 162
The godly state and godly discipline 163
The withdrawal of magical services 165
The 'huge mass' of ungodliness revealed 166
The programme of godly discipline unfolds 167
Witch-hunting and other persecutions 170
Religious wars 171
Witch-hunting, colonies and ethnicity 173
Types of state and intensity of witch-hunting 176
Critics and limitations of the godly state 182
Conclusion: Witch-hunting and state formation 183

7 Witches in court   189

Introduction 189
Laws on witchcraft 190
Courts that tried witches 191
State formation and legal developments 192
Initiating prosecutions 193
Deciding on guilt or innocence 194
What happened in court 196
Evidence of guilt 197
Torture 202
Constructing and negotiating confessions 208
Explaining confessions 209

x Contents

    Credibility of confessions 213
    Costs and profits 216
    Executions 217
    Conclusion: A miscarriage of justice? 220

8 **The dynamics of witch-hunting**   225

    Introduction 225
    A political model of witchcraft prosecutions 226
    Witchcraft panics 229
    The scale of panics 233
    What did people do when they panicked? 235
    Chain-reaction witch-hunts 236
    Panics and high politics 238
    Neighbourhood panics 240
    Economic stresses and witch-hunting 241
    Dynamics of panics 244
    Witch-hunters 246
    Witch-hunting from above or below? 249
    Witch-hunting and negotiations of power 253
    Ending a panic 259
    The witch-hunting experience 260
    Conclusion: Social attitudes towards witch-hunting 262

9 **Women, men and witchcraft**   267

    Introduction 267
    A female majority and a male minority 267
    Patriarchy 269
    Misogyny and stereotyping 270
    Stereotypes of female witches 273
    Stereotypes of male witches 277
    Scapegoating and deviance 281
    The godly state and gendered offences 283
    Women, men and magical practice 285
    Gendered patterns of accusation 288
    Men as secondary targets 291
    Children: Victims and victim-witches 292
    Gendered images of witchcraft 295
    Sex with the Devil 298
    Malefices related to sex 304

Demonic possession 306
Witchcraft and gender-related trauma 307
Conclusion: Connecting witches and women 309

10 The end of witch-hunting   317

Introduction 317
Patterns of decline 318
Judicial caution 322
The decline of torture and the death penalty 328
The decline of the godly state 329
The Scientific Revolution 335
Demonology in a sceptical age 339
Open attacks on demonology 343
Witchcraft as fiction 345
Shifting views of witches' malefice 347
Continuing prosecutions for superstitious magic 349
Village witchcraft after witch-hunting 350
Conclusion: How witch-hunting became unnecessary 352

11 Perspectives on the witch-hunt   360

Introduction 360
The witch-hunt as 'European' 361
Perspectives from the liberal tradition 363
Perspectives from the romantic tradition 366
Perspectives from anthropology 370
Perspectives from psychology 372
Global perspectives 375
Modern Western images of witches 382
Conclusion: Power, persecution and the lessons of the witch-hunt 387

Further reading   397
Appendix: Intensity of witch-hunting in Europe   410
Index   414

Diagrams and illustrations

Map

Intensity of witch-hunting in Europe 28

Diagrams

3.1	The demonic witch	77
4.1	The village witch	90
5.1	The folkloric witch	135
5.2	The envisioned witch	149

Illustrations

1.1	Felipa la Calabria, a Sicilian witch, 1624	15
1.2	Three witches burned at Baden, 1574	16
2.1	An early heretical sabbat, c.1467	43
2.2	The *Malleus Maleficarum*, 1486	49
3.1	An elaborate demonic pact, 1634	70
3.2	Witches' sabbat on the Blocksberg, 1668	75
4.1	Magical harm by a witch, c.1489	100
5.1	Nature spirits become demonic, 1555	123
5.2	The nightmare experience, 1608	148
6.1	King James VI interrogates witches, 1590	161
7.1	Torture at Mellingen, 1577	204
8.1	The Bamberg witch house, 1627	234
9.1	Imagining female witches, c.1514	296
9.2	The demonic pact as a narrative, c.1489	300
10.1	Witchcraft is mocked as old-fashioned, 1762	334

Preface

What is a witch? – or is the answer so obvious that the question is not worth asking? I first began working on the project that turned into this book quite a few years ago, when my elder son was three. He found out that I was interested in witches, and I wondered if he would ask me to explain what a witch was. But I soon realised that he already knew.

What this three-year-old 'knew', though, was hard to pin down. Masked older children at the door at Hallowe'en – an old woman in a gingerbread house in a dark wood – the most fearfully memorable character in *The Wizard of Oz*: all were 'witches'. Witches were malevolent (he found the *good* witch in *Oz* hard to credit), they wore pointy hats, they cackled, and they tended to live in the dark. They sometimes ate children. They were 'scary things'. They were not necessarily human – but not definitely non-human either, unlike trolls or dragons. They were changeable, different every time you looked.

And they were fascinating. Witches seem to arise inexorably from our secret fears and fantasies. Many people are attracted to fantasies of amazing magical power, like being able to fly. Fantasies of forbidden sexuality can be scarily potent. Anger and revenge are powerful forces, and may seem like magical forces. If you dream or fantasise about killing your rivals, or your boss, by wicked magic, perhaps you might really do it, or be able to do it, or somehow find yourself doing it? It's hard to think of cursing someone without imagining that this curse might somehow take effect. Magic brings about effects by hidden or unusual means.

If you have fantasies of magical power (even wicked magical power), these don't make you a witch, because you're not evil. (You're not, are you?) Thus you don't see yourself as an enemy of society. But what about other people? Can you be so sure about them? If you dream of harming your rivals by wicked magic, perhaps others might be out to harm *you* by wicked magic? They wouldn't tell you that, of course, so you'll have to think about secret enemies. Fear of secret, harmful magic by other people can seem to make a lot of sense. This book is about a period in history when the fear of secret, harmful magic was real. Witches were other people, and they were out to do all the harm they could.

Meanwhile, in the present century, both my children then moved on to, and beyond, the Harry Potter books, where witches are different again: the concept of a 'witch' is submerged in that of a 'wizard'. Harry Potter's world is a mostly male one, and its so-called 'witches' are essentially wizards who happen to be female. Wizards, and thus witches, are portrayed positively – though magic, as in all such stories, can be used to bad ends as well as good. The Harry Potter series is one of many in which people have told stories of an imagined world in order to compare it with our own. That other world is distinguished from our own by being magical, but its strangeness ultimately directs attention back onto the ordinary humans who encounter it.

Witches have to be female today, but that was not so in early modern times. Witches were mostly female, and many witchcraft beliefs were connected to women; but witches could also be men. About one out of five people executed for witchcraft were men. By contrast, all the people in charge of the courts were men, and most other people convicted of crimes were men. In the witch-hunt, men were doing something unusual in prosecuting mainly women. To a great extent, witch-hunting arose from the fear of secret, harmful magic *by women* – a fear shared by both men and women.

What *would* I say if a three-year-old child asked me what a witch was? I would talk about the folkloric witch: the witch of 'Hansel and Gretel' and 'Rapunzel', the witch who casts wicked spells. I would not discuss the modern suburban witch, practising a benign pagan religion; she or he has little resonance in popular culture, since modern pagans rarely proselytise, and modern Western religion has become a private matter. Nor would I say that witches do not exist. I would no more say to a child that witches do not exist than I would say that stories, dreams or nightmares do not exist. They do.

This book is about witches who both did and did not exist. It is about thousands of people who suffered torture and death. Their existence and suffering were real; yet their crime of 'witchcraft' is by modern Western standards impossible. The book, therefore, is also about the systems of thought and belief that made the crime of witchcraft fearfully *possible* – possible to people as rational and intelligent as ourselves. It is also about the political and judicial structures that enabled these people to act on their fears.

Nowadays we have a wider range of cultural fears, such as fears of aliens, paedophiles or terrorists. Some of these fears are encouraged by politicians, or by commercial popular culture. We shall see that belief in abduction by aliens is the modern cultural form of a sleep disorder that shaped some accusations of witchcraft and witches' own confessions. Nobody can prosecute aliens, but we may ponder the way in which we, or the authorities, respond to some of our other fears. Fear of terrorists (or alleged terrorists) in the modern world has led governments to commit inhuman and unjust acts, some of which may well be compared with the brutalities of witch-hunting.

Witch-hunting may have been brutal, but it was not caused by the 'ignorance' or 'barbarity' of past societies. If any of us were magically transported to live in a seventeenth-century village, we would soon discover that *we* were ignorant; we lack a vast range of complex survival skills that early modern peasants took for granted. In a seventeenth-century university, we would encounter sophisticated knowledge in intellectual disciplines that we, today, have barely heard of. So much for 'ignorance'. As for 'barbarity', are our own times so free of wars, persecution and injustice that we can afford to look down disapprovingly on earlier ages? Perhaps by contemplating the persecutions of the past we may gain some insight into how to treat one another humanely in the present.

This book is a work of synthesis. Nobody could master all the primary sources, or even all the secondary sources, for the European witch-hunt. Beyond my own specialist field, Scotland, I have relied largely on secondary works. Still, I have made direct use of primary sources from many different European countries, and I hope this book has at least something of the character of a work of original scholarship.

Even just in English, the scholarly literature on the European witch-hunt is vast, and growing rapidly. I have drawn on many works in French, notably the publications of a group of scholars at Lausanne, which have greatly advanced our understanding of the earliest witchcraft trials and demonological works. If I had read other languages as well, especially German, Hungarian or some of the Scandinavian languages, I might have been able to present a fuller picture. However, I would either have had to spend several more years researching the book (which would not have pleased my publishers), or I would have had to neglect some of the English-language and French-language material. Germany is significant as the largest European region in which intense witch-hunting occurred. However, current trends in scholarship have urged (partly for this reason) that the European witch-hunt should be treated as a phenomenon of the whole of Europe, not just as Germany writ large. Numerous works of German, Hungarian and Scandinavian scholars have been translated into English, and some of these scholars have even had the kindness (for someone like me) to write in English. Through their works, I hope that Germany, Hungary and Scandinavia – and Spain, Italy, the Netherlands, Poland and Russia – receive full weight in this book.

If my own linguistic abilities have given this book any bias, it is probably towards the region to the west of the Rhine – a string of territories, mostly French-speaking, that were not attached to the French crown. The Spanish Netherlands, Luxembourg, Lorraine, Franche-Comté and western Switzerland saw some witch-hunts that were as intense as those in the adjacent German-speaking lands. But the individual cases I have cited, whether from Valais in Switzerland or Württemberg in south-western Germany, are all intended to be typical examples of European witch-hunting as a whole – or, rather, typical of that aspect of European witch-hunting that the example is intended to illustrate. Numerous examples come from Germany or other central European places with high levels of witch-hunting, but there are also examples from places that produced fewer witches – places as far apart as

Finland, Transylvania and the Canary Islands. In these places, too, witchcraft was important, not least in structuring community interactions.

This book is an analysis of how witch-hunting functioned, and of how people experienced it. It is not a narrative of one persecution after another, nor is it a country-by-country survey. There were many geographical variations in witch-hunting, but I have aimed to show why these variations occurred in the context of Europe as a whole, rather than trudging through the different regions one after another. Many specialists in particular countries will readily be able to see how much I owe to their works. My knowledge of witch-hunting in their country will inevitably be shallower than their own, but I hope that this book may at least enable specialists to situate their detailed knowledge in a wider context. And it may encourage readers encountering the subject for the first time to explore some of the fascinating scholarship from which I myself have drawn. The 'Further Reading' section at the end of this book provides a starting-point for such an exploration.

Historians of witch-hunting should also look beyond works on the history of witch-hunting, if they wish to provide a fully analytical account of their subject. I have drawn on numerous works of broader European history, notably in order to explain dynamics of power both at the village level and at the level of the state. Not only this, but I have used numerous scholarly works that are not 'history' at all. To understand witch-hunting fully requires an understanding of social and psychological processes that can be gained only by engaging directly with other social-science disciplines. In this book, the most notable such disciplines are sociology and psychology, while political science, anthropology, ethnology and law also make appearances. I hope that this book may encourage further such research – research that may become even more interdisciplinary.

Finally, the epigraph to this book comes from the war poetry of the celebrated Scottish folklorist Hamish Henderson (1919–2003). Henderson's 'demon' was not that of early modern times, at least not directly; modern war has its own horrors. But if great poetry is for all time, then the present may illuminate the past; historians in turn may hope to make the past illuminate the present. A 'sensuous austerity' may be what we need for a calm appreciation of the terror inspired by early modern demons and their human allies, the witches. When I met Henderson, towards the end of his life, he told me that he had become interested in some of his own occult experiences. The world is a mysterious place to human beings, partly because our luxuriant imaginations have made it so. Through witches, and through witch-hunters, we may come to a deeper knowledge of ourselves.

Acknowledgements

In the course of writing this book I have been privileged to receive advice, help and inspiration from a wide range of scholars, not all of whom can be mentioned here.

My single greatest debt is to Professor Ronald Hutton, who has encouraged me over many years and who generously read and commented on a draft of the text. I have also benefited considerably from comments on the draft text kindly provided by Dr Rita Voltmer, with whom it has been a pleasure to collaborate on other projects.

Other scholars whom I should mention individually are Dr Willem de Blécourt, with whom I had many productive discussions on anthropological methodology and on the meaning of the witches' sabbat; Professor Richard Bonney, who long ago challenged me to define a 'witch-hunt' more precisely; Professor Stuart Clark, who first encouraged me to undertake research into this topic; Ms Anna Cordey, to whom I owe the concept of 'instant reputation'; Mrs Margaret Dudley, with whom I collaborated in the study of sleep paralysis and its connection to witchcraft; Professor John Henry, a generous and indispensable guide on the Scientific Revolution; Professor Brian P. Levack, author of the single most influential book on the European witch-hunt, and a kind and delightful companion; Professor Mirjam Mencej, who has guided me on human and non-human witches and on the nature of 'belief'; Professor Éva Pócs, from whom I have learned much about nature spirits and popular cults; Dr Jacqueline Simpson, an inspiration on all folkloric matters; Ms Emma Wilby, a pioneer in investigating visionary experience; Professor Liv Helene Willumsen, to whom I owe most of my knowledge of the Finnmark witches, and for whose hospitality in Finnmark I am most grateful; Dr Louise Yeoman, with whom I have had many discussions of early modern spirituality and psychology; and Professor Charles Zika, who has kindly shared his expertise on visual representations of witchcraft.

Collectively, I am grateful to all the students in my honours class on the European witch-hunt, with whom many of the topics in the following pages have been discussed. These discussions have given me many opportunities to develop and refine my ideas. Any shortcomings in what follows are my responsibility alone.

xx *Acknowledgements*

It is a pleasure to acknowledge the way in which the editorial staff at Routledge have maintained a consistent interest in and support for this book over a number of years. The map was drawn by David McCutcheon FBCart.S, for whose skill I am most grateful.

With my wife, Jackie Gulland, a specialist in socio-legal studies, I have had many fascinating discussions – including a continuing discussion about whether this book is a socio-legal study. Finally, I should once more mention our children, Malcolm and Duncan, whose exuberant encounter with the world has enriched my understanding of what it means to be human. This book, on a scarcely exuberant but deeply human topic, is dedicated to them.

Julian Goodare
Edinburgh
December 2015

Publisher's acknowledgements

The publishers would like to thank the following for their permission to reproduce copyright material: Bibliothèque Royale de Belgique; Birlinn Limited; Brepols Publishers; The Trustees of the British Museum; Cambridge University Press; Harvard University Press; Palgrave Macmillan; The United Nations; University of Pennsylvania Press; Centre for Reformation and Renaissance Studies, University of Toronto; Zentralbibliothek, Zurich.

Conventions and abbreviations

There is no single system for rendering foreign personal names from this period into English. There are variant spellings, and even more variation in accents. Modern writers in English sometimes translate first names into English versions. Learned writers of the period sometimes translated their own surnames into Latin, in either the nominative or genitive case. The author of the notorious *Malleus Maleficarum* can have his first name given as Henry or Heinrich, and his surname as Kramer, Krämer, Kremer, Institor or Institoris. I have called him Heinrich Krämer, and have tried to follow the same pattern with other names unless there is a clear consensus on another version.

Names of early modern states, countries or provinces can be tricky. The boundaries of states like 'France' or 'Savoy' were not necessarily the same as modern boundaries. 'Germany' is a particularly difficult term, since it was not a state, and a political idea of 'Germany' barely existed in the early modern period. The region covered by the modern state of Germany was part of the Holy Roman Empire, a loose collection of states of varying size. The Holy Roman Empire had nominal jurisdiction over much of central Europe, including parts of what are today the Netherlands, eastern France, Switzerland, northern Italy, Hungary and southern Poland. When I use the term 'Germany', this denotes the lands in which the German language was spoken. I have also used other geographical expressions within these lands, such as 'Austria', when that allows more precision. Similarly, names like 'Italy' or 'Spain' are geographical and cultural expressions rather than the names of states. I have tried to discuss places in such a way as to make it clear (if the distinction matters) whether the place concerned was a state, a region of some other kind, a town, or a village. Some of the states that I mention have disappeared from modern maps, such as Franche-Comté (now a region of France) and the Palatinate (now Rheinland-Pfalz in Germany). There was political change during the period covered by this book; for instance, the fifteenth-century 'Burgundian Netherlands' (roughly the territory of modern Belgium and the Netherlands) became the 'Spanish Netherlands', and the northern provinces later broke away to form the 'United Netherlands'.

A few words on how I have cited primary sources. The *Malleus Maleficarum* ('Hammer of Witches') is quoted in the translation of Christopher S. Mackay, except that I have translated '*maleficus/malefica, maleficium*' as 'witch, witchcraft' rather than 'sorcerer/sorceress, sorcery'. There are various translations of the *Malleus*, some of which have appeared in different editions; thus it helps to provide references in a form that can be used across as many of these as possible. References are given, first, to Mackay's system of folio numbers (which is consistent across the one-volume and two-volume versions of his work), and then, in brackets, to the alternative system of 'question' numbers, used in the original work and in some other translations. Some other demonological works are cited, first by the page number of the edition I have used, and then by the original chapter or section number in brackets. Throughout the book, translations not otherwise attributed in the works cited are my own.

The following abbreviations are used throughout the reference notes:

Encyclopedia	Richard M. Golden (ed.), *Encyclopedia of Witchcraft: The Western Tradition*, 4 vols. (Santa Barbara, Calif., 2006).
Lea, *Materials*	Henry C. Lea, *Materials Toward a History of Witchcraft*, 3 vols., ed. A. C. Howland (Philadelphia, Pa., 1939).
Malleus	*Hammer of Witches: A Complete Translation of the Malleus Maleficarum*, 2 vols., trans. Christopher S. Mackay (Cambridge, 2009; original publication 1486).

Citations of other works are abbreviated on their second and subsequent mentions in each chapter.

Introduction
The witch-hunt and you

Why the witch-hunt matters

The witch-hunt was a shocking episode in history. Thousands of people all over Europe were deliberately tortured and killed by the authorities, in the name of religion and morality. How could people do such a thing?

This book will try to answer that question. If you already feel shocked by the idea of witch-hunting, maybe your feelings will intensify as you learn about some of the details. But maybe, by the end, you will be less shocked. The things that shock us are surprising things, hard to understand. Yet we *can* understand the witch-hunt if we try. The witches were people much like us; the witch-hunters, too, were people much like us. They had some beliefs and values that we no longer share, but we can reconstruct them. We can recognise witch-hunters and witches as our fellow humans. To explain witch-hunting, to understand it, is to explore the dark side of human nature – our own nature. We don't hunt witches today, at least in Europe, but we do other things that future generations may find just as shocking. This, then, is a book about history, but it is also a small meditation on human nature as we find it today.

Understanding believers in witchcraft

In defining our concepts, including the concept of 'witchcraft', we need to be clear about what kind of definitions we are using. One type of definition is something that we can use today – a definition that belongs to modern intellectual understandings of the world. This means using modern concepts, often derived from the human sciences allied to history – branches of knowledge such as sociology, anthropology or psychology. It is sometimes said that we should not use modern concepts to understand the pre-modern world, because pre-modern people 'thought differently' and did not use our concepts. But this misunderstands the purpose of our concepts. They are *meant* to be used to explain the behaviour of people who are not familiar with them (even today), and to explain these people in their own social setting. Psychologists do not just study people who are familiar with psychology. And seventeenth-century people did not think *that* differently from us; their culture may have been different, but their brains and nervous systems were not.

To the historian, understanding people in their social setting means analysing evidence for what people said and did, and deciding which modern analytical tools to adopt. The concept of 'moral panic', for instance, has been developed by sociologists to explain outbursts of sudden public concern. One famous case study looked at panics about youth gangs and their anti-social behaviour, but sociologists use the concept of 'moral panic' to explain outbursts of public concern about other issues too. As an analytical tool, the concept of 'moral panic' can be used by sociologically-minded historians to explain outbursts of public concern about witchcraft.

A second type of definition is the kind that early modern people themselves used. When they talked of 'magic' or 'religion', or indeed of 'witchcraft', they did not necessarily use these words in the same ways that we do today. This may be because the words have changed, or because the concepts they describe have changed, or both. We have to be clear what we understand by the words we use, but we must also be alert to the meanings of the words used by the people we study. These people, moreover, did not all use words in the same way; educated folk had many ideas that the common people did not share. As historians, we naturally want to understand the definitions used by early modern folk, but we will not automatically regard them as 'correct'. We can interpret contemporary evidence in ways that they could not. Ultimately, the definitions that matter to us are *our* definitions.

We must be clear whether the definitions we use are value-laden. 'Knowledge', for instance, tends to be something we approve of. 'Superstition' is something we disapprove of. 'Belief' lies somewhere in between. We cannot avoid value-laden words entirely, but when we use them we should be as clear as possible about what we are doing. We should be aware, when we speak of witchcraft 'belief', that this word distances us from those who actually held the belief. If we say we 'believe' something, this often means that we are not sure. If we are sure about something, we usually say that we 'know' it. In this sense, most people in early modern Europe did not 'believe' in witches; they *knew* about witches. However, most people today would not agree, so 'belief' is a useful phrase to distance ourselves from early modern 'knowledge'.

One exception to the way in which 'belief' means 'not being sure' comes with Christian religion. Christians are expected to 'believe' in the Christian God, not because they are 'not sure', but because God is held ultimately to be unknowable by mere humans; 'belief' is the best that humans can manage. Early modern Christians were sometimes expected to 'believe' in witches, rather in the way that they were expected to 'believe' in God. This was not because witches were thought to be unknowable, but because everyone was expected to have the same beliefs. Unlike God, witches were perfectly knowable.

'Belief' can also be a problematic term for other reasons. Many people in early modern Europe confessed to being witches; interrogated, they often stated that they had made a pact with the Devil, that they had flown to the witches' sabbat, or that they had harmed their neighbours. Such confessions were usually extracted under torture. Did those who made the confessions 'believe' them? Some, we know, did not; they tried to retract their confessions afterwards, or maintained their innocence in other ways. We shall see, however, that others may have come to 'believe' at least some of what they confessed. A few even confessed voluntarily. Is 'belief' an appropriate word for something that we are likely to see today as a fantasy, perhaps brought on by trauma or mental disturbance? The issue of 'belief' in witchcraft forces us to confront the question of how human beings understand themselves and the world in which they live. If you're a human being, then this book is for you.

Where I stand

It may help if I state that I don't believe in witches in the sense that early modern folk did. The word 'witch' in this book is shorthand for 'someone who was believed at the time to be a witch'. However, that does not entitle me to write about early modern witchcraft beliefs as 'ignorant' or 'superstitious'. Popular witchcraft histories usually do this, sometimes tossing in a few more boo-words like 'bigoted'. Calling witchcraft beliefs 'superstitious' implies that the beliefs were the irrational result of inadequate education – but educated people in early modern times also believed in witchcraft, and a few of them wrote erudite and sophisticated treatises on the subject. Terms like 'ignorant' and 'superstitious' are judgemental; before we can judge, however, we must understand. If we do not, we ourselves are the ignorant ones.

Understanding witchcraft beliefs, or any other beliefs, does not mean that we cannot judge them. We probably think that witch-hunting would be wrong today. One reason we don't hunt witches today, at least in Europe and North America, is that we have *learned better* than to do so. You are reading this book because you want to learn. This book will explain why people believed in witches and why they hunted them, but it will also explain why they eventually learned better. We are not entitled to criticise early modern witch-hunters for not having access to learning that was only produced later. If you or I were in the witch-hunters' position, there is no particular reason to think that we would do better than them.

It is sometimes suggested that this makes all systems of belief equally valid. Thus, we happen to believe in modern science: early modern folk happened to believe in witchcraft. Our beliefs are valid for us: their beliefs were equally valid for them. However, there are problems with this 'relativist' position. It is a product of educated Western thought, so Western relativists may be willing to treat the belief systems of two different tribes as equally valid with each other and with their own beliefs – but the tribespeople themselves will not agree. Relativism also abandons any effort at dialogue with people with whom one disagrees, including non-relativists and indeed witch-hunters. What would a relativist say to the people who are killing witches today in the townships of southern Africa? Would they say, 'Well, I don't believe in witches, but you can believe in them if you like?' Myself, I would seek to understand the witch-hunters, but I would also hope that they would learn better.

These reflections may seem unusually philosophical. Don't worry, this is a book about history, not philosophy; it's a record of past human activities, together with an attempt to explain those activities. History, like philosophy, is a human science. What makes history distinctive is its concern for change over time. The great European witch-hunt, as we shall see, grew and declined over time, and history is the only discipline that can explain that. Historians can also recognise the way in which our own statements belong to a particular historical context. Grand statements about the 'essential meaning' of magic or religion – or witchcraft, for that matter – are beyond my scope. I take history as being one age's record of what it finds significant in another age. A hundred years ago, for instance, people did not find all the same things significant in the seventeenth century that we do today. When they asked themselves questions like 'What is witchcraft?', such a question meant something different to them, and so the answer was different – as it will be again in the future. My statements about the seventeenth century, like those of past and future historians, are as true as I can make them, but they do not aspire to universality; if what I say is true, it is true for today.

History, as a human science, is part of the study of human behaviour. Historians seek to explain past events in terms of human behaviour as this is understood by the human sciences – philosophy, psychology, sociology, economics, anthropology, to name just a few that can stand alongside history itself. All these use empirical evidence – that is, evidence deriving from observation – that would be generally accepted by an educated person. Witchcraft makes this difficult because some of the reported events are so unusual. If I have a document reporting that a witch flew through the air to the witches' sabbat, this is hard to explain in empirical terms: our observations of the human physique tell us that flying is impossible. Could the witch have been doing something 'paranormal' or 'supernatural'? There is no need to jump to this conclusion; there are adequate naturalistic explanations available. It could have been a dream, a fantasy, or simply a misunderstanding or a lie. Historians evaluate their documents: what is the origin of this document? If the document claims to be recording a statement by a witness, then the witness may have said that they saw the witch personally, but in fact have been relying on (and unwittingly distorting) what they were told by someone else. Most reports of witches' flight, in fact, were not based on witness statements but on confessions by witchcraft suspects; confessions could easily be distorted by leading questions, especially if torture was used.

All this is well within the range of normal behaviour as understood by the human sciences.

An educated person in early modern times might have explained a report of flying in similar ways – but they had a further, potentially lethal, possibility. They could say, 'This is a genuine report of someone flying with demonic aid; we know that this is possible because the Bible says that the Devil carried Jesus to the pinnacle of the temple' (Matthew 4:5). However, if I were to say this today, the only people who would believe me would be those who shared a belief in the Devil – and not only that, but a particular view of the Devil's powers, and the authority of the Bible to give us accurate information on the subject. For that reason alone, I'm not going to do so.

This makes my personal beliefs largely irrelevant to my aims in this book. Even if I were a biblical fundamentalist (and I'm not), I would still want to address a general educated audience, and so would present my arguments in terms of empirical evidence and naturalistic assumptions about human behaviour. Actually I'm a Quaker. I do believe that human life has a spiritual dimension. But, for the purposes of historical understanding of witchcraft, I'm an agnostic – someone who has yet to be convinced that there is anything out there that science will never be able to explain. We shall encounter reports of strange happenings in this book, and maybe some 'paranormal' occurrences are lurking in witchcraft trial records; but, if so, I would take these as occurrences that science cannot *yet* explain.

One question that is sometimes asked at this point is: 'Did the witches' magic spells really work?' It is interesting that this question is more common than another one that could equally well be asked: 'Did the Devil really do the things he was said to do?' But my answer to both questions is the same. I have seen no historical evidence that would compel me, as a historian, to accept reports of magical or diabolical feats at face value. We should always seek to explain strange events in terms of things that we do understand. In modern Western society, that primarily means experimentally-based science and empirical, evidence-based research in the humanities.

Believers in magic or the paranormal will thus find no explicit support for their beliefs in this book, though they will find no explicit challenge to them either. Much the same applies to believers in the miracles endorsed by some orthodox religions, with one difference. Believers in the 'paranormal' tend to think of paranormal phenomena in scientific, rather than religious, terms: the phenomena could be explained by science, if only the scientists would admit it or would direct their attention towards it. Perhaps in a few cases they are right, and today's weird phenomenon in the fringe media will become tomorrow's mainstream science. If so, tell me about it tomorrow. In most cases the believers will probably remain tomorrow where they undoubtedly are today: on the fringe, with their status enhanced in their own eyes by communities of fellow believers who reassure one another that they have special knowledge. I'm not going to join them, but I'm not out to prove them wrong. On this subject, again, I'm simply an agnostic: I'm at present unconvinced by claims that magic, or for that matter the Devil or God, operate in the world contrary to the ordinary rules of nature and patterns of human behaviour. Nature, and human behaviour, are complicated enough as they are!

Today, in the West at least, we do not expect everyone to believe the same things. We expect cultural conformity in some fields, but our culture incorporates and even celebrates wide areas of diversity. The idea of a single public religion has largely evaporated, and religious pluralism can be valued for its own sake. Pluralism is less highly valued in the natural or human sciences; if there were three competing explanations for (say) the extinction of the dinosaurs, or the Reformation, we would probably take this as a sign that these events were inadequately understood. We recognise, however, that a full understanding of events is most likely to arise from a free discussion of the alternatives. Not only are there no authorities seeking out and punishing intellectual dissent, but dissent is welcomed as a means to finding the truth.

So you do not have to take my interpretation of the witch-hunt on trust. Naturally I would be pleased if you were persuaded to agree with it, but I hope you will make up your own mind. This does not mean that you (or any other historian) can believe what you like about the witch-hunt, because to be taken seriously by historians you have to be able to cite empirical evidence for your conclusions. I have done my best to indicate what evidence there is for mine.

How do we know about witch-hunting?

What evidence is there, in fact, for the European witch-hunt? Historians rely on primary sources – broadly speaking, documents written at the time. Documents written within living memory, or later copies of documents written at the time (so long as we can be confident from internal evidence that the copying was done accurately), can also be accepted as primary sources. These sources then need to be interpreted by asking questions about them – questions that may be informed by methodologies from other human sciences, like the concept of 'moral panic' mentioned above.

The core primary sources for witch-hunting are records of witchcraft trials. These can be a few lines long, or they can be hundreds of manuscript pages. The briefest records tend to say that such-and-such a person was convicted of witchcraft at a particular place and date. Sometimes no trial records survive, and all we have is a chronicle or other narrative source saying that a witch was executed, or that 'many witches' were executed. The grim human stories behind such brief statements can be hard to grasp, though they are undoubtedly real. More detailed records often include statements by the suspect's neighbours, or records of the suspect's own confession, or both. This material can tell us, not only that a particular witch was executed, but also what the evidence was – *why*, in fact, the person was convicted of witchcraft. This is vital evidence for the historian.

Confessions sometimes included information about flying, about sex with the Devil, about cannibalism, and about visits to other worlds. This material is hard to interpret. Some of it probably came from the interrogators, who could ask suspects leading questions; some of it probably came from the suspects themselves. Witches were usually tried by criminal courts that mainly dealt with other crimes, so the search for witchcraft trials involves sifting through a mass of manuscripts, usually held in local archives, all over Europe.

Some studies have ventured beyond this core evidence, to consider documents that are not about witchcraft at all – for instance, records of other community interactions in places where witchcraft trials occurred. Many of these records are about property, and especially property disputes, since this was the kind of thing that tended to be written down. In them we can sometimes see neighbours arguing, local factions forming, and enmities being created that would eventually feed into witchcraft accusations. The English colonies in North America – which are included in this book, as they were culturally European – made, and preserved, particularly detailed records, from which some influential studies have been written. The famous panic at Salem, Massachusetts, in 1692 forms an important case, though the fact that it was driven by something rather like demonic possession means that it was not entirely typical of the European witch-hunt as a whole.

Many trial records are missing, so no account of the witch-hunt can ever be complete. However, we can often gain some idea of what is missing from what survives. In England, most witches were tried in assize courts – travelling courts that went on 'circuit' round groups of counties. There were six circuits altogether, but records survive for only one, covering five south-eastern counties, and even those are incomplete. The best we can do is to surmise that the others were broadly similar, while being alert to any evidence that might suggest differences. In some cases, there may be records for just part of the process; trial records may be missing, but financial accounts for the costs of executing witches may survive. In some parts of Europe, the records have not yet been fully studied. Most studies of Italian witchcraft, for instance, have used records of church courts or the Inquisition; these courts seem to have taken priority over the secular criminal courts, but we cannot be sure until more research is done in the records of the latter. In Russia, too, we are not sure how many witches were accused – many local archives have not been searched, and the national figures relate just to national archives. However, in the last few decades there has been a great deal of local research on witchcraft trials, and this allows more accurate general conclusions to be drawn.

Another important type of evidence for witch-hunting is demonological writings. The existence of witches was never taken for granted – it had to be proved. From the fifteenth century onwards a series of mainly academic treatises was written to explain what witches were, how they related to the Devil, how they obtained their special powers, how they harmed humanity, and why God permitted all this to happen. These treatises led to intellectual debate, since not everyone agreed. The question of how witches flew through the air, mentioned above, was a key test; if the demonologists could prove that witches could fly, they had a virtually unanswerable case for the reality of witchcraft. In the later part of the witch-hunting period we find more intellectuals criticising witchcraft beliefs. Demonological works do not tell us how much witch-hunting there was, but they are vital for the historian's task of explaining why witch-hunting occurred at all.

Finally, witch-hunting has to be studied in the broader context of European history between about 1400 and 1750 – the period when significant witch-hunting occurred. Let me mention a few of the broader topics that we shall need to discuss. Demonology was bound up with the Renaissance, the Reformation and the Scientific Revolution – three vast and related developments in cultural, religious and intellectual history. The criminal courts that tried witches can be understood only if legal procedure in criminal cases is understood; these courts were also affected by law reform and state formation, so we shall have to glance at those topics. The peasant quarrels that led to witchcraft accusations were part of broader patterns of community interaction. Peasant communities were gripped by vast economic and social forces – in particular, the economic downturn of the sixteenth century, which caused misery and starvation. Witches were mainly women, and this was related to structures of patriarchal power that can be reconstructed from a variety of sources. All this will come into the pages that follow. Although this is a book about 'the European witch-hunt', then, it is also part of a much broader field of historical enquiry. Is it possible to make sense of all this diverse material? Well, we can try.

1 Witchcraft!

> In our times the number of witches and of supporters of the Devil is growing rapidly, so that almost all towns and villages in the whole of Germany, not to mention other people and nations, are full of this vermin. These servants of the Devil not only do harm to the precious crops in the fields which the Lord has made grow through the power of his blessing, but also try to do as much harm as possible through thunder, lightning, showers, hail, storms, frost, flooding, mice, worms, and in many other ways which God is permitting and for which they use the support and help of the Devil.
>
> *Further News of Witches*, Germany, 1590[1]

Introduction

Throughout early modern Europe, people feared witchcraft. However, the 'witchcraft' that they feared was not a single, simple thing, easy to define. Anyone who has heard of an 'essential definition of witchcraft' has been misinformed. There were then, and there still are today, several overlapping definitions of it – and the definitions tended to change over time. Here we need to focus on the definitions that were used in the early modern period. Executions for 'witchcraft' were for that specific crime, and a specific word had to be used – though, as we shall see, not all languages used their word or words for 'witchcraft' in the same way. But the specific crime of 'witchcraft' was built up out of a number of components, which can be analysed separately. There are four main fields into which these components can be grouped.

The fourfold concept of witchcraft

The four fields of the early modern concept of witchcraft were all interlinked, but they can be separated out for analytical purposes. There were different definitions of witchcraft because, although everyone feared witches, they did not all fear them in the same way. In particular, the elite had a more intellectual and theoretical fear, while the common people's fear was more immediate and practical. This provides the basis for two of the fields of the fourfold concept. (There is more about elite and popular beliefs later in this chapter.) The third and fourth fields were less about real witches that were feared, but provided essential background for everyone's witchcraft beliefs.

The first field to be discussed, then, is the *demonic witch* of the elite – the witch who was in league with the Devil. Then comes the *village witch* of the common people – the witch who harmed her or his neighbours. Witchcraft was also a matter of story and legend, so we need a third field: the *folkloric witch*. Finally, witchcraft was sometimes a matter of intense personal experience, with people entering trances and seeing visions. They either encountered witches in nightmare visions, or entered trances and went on spirit-voyages that could make others think that they themselves were witches. The fourth field, therefore, is the witch experienced through trance, dream and nightmare: the *envisioned witch*.

The demonic witch was in league with the Devil. This view of witchcraft saw it essentially as a religious crime – a type of heresy or false belief. The Christian church authorities had been concerned about heresy since the middle ages; they had not usually thought of witchcraft as a heresy, but we shall see in Chapter 2 that they began to change their minds. Combining ideas from various sources, fifteenth-century theologians gradually became convinced that a 'new heresy' had arisen, consisting not of people who worshipped God in the wrong way, but of people who actually worshipped the Devil. They formed a secret, underground sect, who renounced God and promised their souls to the Devil, and gathered at night to perform evil ceremonies in a witches' sabbat.

In Chapter 3, which provides a detailed discussion of the demonic witch, we shall see these ideas becoming elaborated. Witches flew to the sabbat, and the ceremonies included horrific rites: witches had promiscuous sex with the Devil and with one another, they danced naked, and they killed and ate babies and children. Some of these ideas were ancient and stereotypical fantasies of what an evil group would do, much older than the idea of demonic witchcraft. The essence of the demonic witch did not lie in these acts, though; the basic crime was that she or he had promised their soul to the Devil, in a contract known as the 'demonic pact'. The crime of the demonic witch, then, was a thought-crime – the crime of *being* a witch.

The village witch was also an evil figure, but on a smaller scale. Peasants were concerned about their health, their families and their farms, and they feared magical interference with these. Peasants had to work closely with their neighbours, bartering and sharing goods and tools, and this sometimes led to disputes and rivalries. When a peasant suffered a misfortune that was hard to explain, they sometimes feared that a witch had caused it, and they tended to ask themselves whether there was anyone who might have a grudge against them. We shall see in Chapter 4 that village witchcraft was not about threats to society as a whole, nor even (with rare exceptions) about threats to the village as a whole. It was about personal, individual malice. Peasants were likely to ascribe a misfortune to witchcraft if they had quarrelled with a neighbour and believed that the neighbour was out for revenge. They would be particularly likely to do so if the neighbour fitted one of the stereotype images of the witch, with the most common stereotype by far being the quarrelsome older woman – something that we shall examine in Chapter 9. The crime of the village witch, then, consisted in carrying out specific harmful acts – the crime of *performing* witchcraft.

The folkloric witch was a character from stories. These stories were told by villagers, but had their own traditions and their own logic; they did not simply replicate what was known about village witches. The folkloric witch did not live in the village; her residence, if known, was in a remote region, often a forest. She was always female, unlike the demonic witch or the village witch. She was not necessarily a normal human – she was sometimes related to giants or fairies. She was always maleficent; sometimes her evil deeds resembled those of the village witch (killing and injuring livestock, for instance), but she also committed more fantastic malefices, especially the stealing and eating of children. We shall see in Chapter 5 that stories tended to focus on the witch's remarkable powers, especially of magical travel and flight, and of shape-shifting. There was some mention of witches' sabbats, usually large gatherings in remote locations, but witches in most stories were solitary figures. The main non-solitary witches were the product of folkloric multiplication – there might be three witches in a story, rather in the way that there could be three sons or three princesses. The folkloric witch was not necessarily a criminal, and indeed was not necessarily human, but ideas about her fed into ideas about criminal human witches.

Envisioned witches, also discussed in Chapter 5, were of two related types. First, some people had trance experiences in which they felt themselves carried away to distant lands or to other worlds; sometimes they encountered strange beings there. Although such experiences could be traumatic, they could also be empowering; typically the person would gain powers of healing or prophecy. If the authorities came across such a person, they might think that they had found a witch. Second, more directly envisioned witches arose from another type of visionary experience – a nightmare or other traumatic event when the victim believed that the 'spectre' of the witch had appeared in their room and attacked them. Such 'spectral evidence' would be important in some witchcraft trials. Envisioned witches, then, arose from various intense personal experiences, for which 'witchcraft' provided explanations.

A simple comparative view of the demonic witch and the village witch has the authorities believing in the former, and the common people believing in the latter. This is a useful starting point, but it is too simple for our purposes. The authorities *also* believed in the village witch. As for the villagers, they do not seem to have disagreed with what they were told about demonic witches, though they rarely thought demonic witches important. Their idea of the Devil was less frightening, and they were hardly ever interested in conspiracies of multiple witches. Villagers' testimony against witches almost always stressed acts of magical harm by individuals. The demonic witch, by contrast, was rarely thought to act alone, but was usually a member of a group. How much effort the authorities put into identifying the other members of the group might vary, but worship of the Devil was definitely a collective affair.

The demonic witch of the elite and the maleficent witch of the village could be seen as mirroring the two parts of the Ten Commandments, known at the time as the 'two tables'. The first table (the first three or four commandments) consisted of crimes against God, notably worshipping other gods. The second table consisted of crimes against one's neighbour, such as theft, murder or adultery. Broadly speaking, the demonic witch broke the first part of these commandments, while the village witch broke the second part. The elite tended to be concerned with crimes against God; peasants were concerned mainly with harm to society. The elite's concern for society tended to be more symbolic and less practical than the peasants' everyday worries. The peasants' concern about malefice was firmly grounded in real, practical misfortune and tragedy. Sometimes their cattle or children really did die, and it is not surprising that they sometimes blamed witches. By contrast, although the elite imagined that witches were killing unbaptised babies and eating them, these babies never existed at all. The elite did have reasons for their beliefs, but – as we might expect for educated people – these reasons were more complicated. The horrific rites of the witches' sabbat were a symbolic inversion of positive human values: not just bad acts, but the imagined *opposite* of good acts.

In the demonic witchcraft of the elite, witches had no power of their own. They appeared to do extraordinary things, such as causing illness and death, bringing hailstorms, sinking ships, or flying; but it was not actually the witches themselves that performed these acts, it was invisible demons acting on their behalf. Demonologists usually explained that the Devil deceived witches into thinking that they themselves performed the actions. A few suggested or implied that the demons were obliged to carry out the witch's wishes, which made witches seem more fearsome (though this idea was arguably unorthodox). All elite thinkers, however, agreed that the power of witchcraft originated with demons.

In village witchcraft, villagers usually assumed that witches did have inherent power. Witness statements by witches' neighbours rarely discussed this, probably because they took it for granted. Sometimes they said that witches' power was taught to them. Another common idea was that the witch inherited her or his power; typically a daughter was said to have got her witchcraft from her mother. These two ideas combined when a mother was said to have taught her daughter. At any rate, once acquired, the power was always something that the witches themselves possessed. When witches were thought to issue curses or cast secret spells, their victims did not usually think that the power came from any other source than the witch.

This should be qualified, however, because some villagers, when cursing their neighbours, *did* invoke the power of others. Typically their curse was a kind of prayer, publicly calling down the wrath of God on their enemy. They might also invoke the Devil, perhaps asking him to take their enemy away. These curses are not entirely distinct from the idea of the witch's inherent power, because certain people's curses were thought to be more effective (just as certain people's prayers were more often answered). However, people who cursed their neighbours probably did not think that this made them 'witches', even if they thought that the curses took effect.

The power of envisioned witches usually came from outside. People who had visions of fairies or ghosts, and who used these fairies or ghosts in folk healing or fortune-telling, may well have thought that the power came from the fairies or the ghosts. Some people who encountered spirits in trance-voyages thought that they themselves had the power to initiate such voyages. But probably most trance-voyagers were *taken* by their spirit-guide; some, indeed, had no choice about whether they went or not. On the whole, power here rested with the other-world beings – fairies, ghosts or even demons. In this sense, folkloric witchcraft was closer to demonology than village witchcraft was. Indeed, aspects of folkloric witchcraft fed into demonology. When interrogators were told by a witchcraft suspect that they had visited fairyland, the interrogators would tend to assume that the fairies were really demons, and they could use this to enhance their understanding of demons.

Perhaps for this reason, there was no actual conflict between demonic witchcraft and village witchcraft. If an educated priest or pastor explained to the villagers that the power really came from the Devil and his demons, peasants seem to have had no objection to this view. For their own part, educated people seem to have tolerated the beliefs of the uneducated – they simply assumed that they knew better.

Globally, most traditional societies have believed in figures similar to the village witch. The folkloric witch and the envisioned witch, too, are widespread. The demonic witch, however, was unique to early modern Europe. Because demonic witchcraft was collective, this gave the European witch-hunt a uniquely destructive character: witches could readily be multiplied. Although numerous witches were prosecuted as isolated individuals, there were also many panics in which groups of witches were prosecuted. These panics arose largely from elite fears of demonic conspiracy. However, they often involved one of the other types of witch as well. Typically, an individual village witch was identified and arrested, and was interrogated about her or his accomplices. Especially if torture was used, this process could generate names of further witches who could be accused of making a pact with the Devil, attending witches' sabbats, or both. The procedure of the criminal courts will be described in Chapter 7, while the dynamics of witchcraft panics will be explored in Chapter 8. Finally, a global perspective on the European witch-hunt will be outlined in Chapter 11.

Identifying witches

Witches were an enemy within; they were thought to keep themselves secret. Both the authorities and the common folk were aware of other dangerous groups of people, such as Jews or lepers, who were segregated from the community and were feared as perhaps wanting to conspire against it. But Jews and lepers were publicly known to be such. Witches were not publicly known; they could be anyone.

Today we can see that the 'witches' of early modern times were largely imaginary. Except in cases of mental illness, hardly any villager thought that she or he was a 'witch' until they were called that by someone else. However, early modern folk could have what seemed to be good reasons for deciding that someone else was a 'witch'. This could be because of the person's known magical activities – they could have been folk healers or diviners, for instance. Magical practitioners like this were not usually thought of as witches – more often, they helped identify other people as witches; but, if magical practitioners were perceived to have misused their powers to harm people instead of helping them, they could be accused of witchcraft. To villagers, witchcraft was essentially harmful.

The most common way in which villagers came to see someone as a witch was through neighbourhood quarrels that were followed by misfortune. If someone suffered a misfortune that they could not explain through natural causes, they might begin to suspect that the misfortune was the result of a witch's curse. This would lead them to ask themselves: Who might be cursing me? Who have I quarrelled with recently? Who might have a grievance against me? They might consult a magical practitioner at this point, who could guide them to confirm their suspicions. Early modern villages were full of neighbourhood rivalries, and it was easy to think that one's rival was using witchcraft in revenge. This was particularly so because many quarrels involved threats and curses. The misfortune could be interpreted as the curse taking effect. This will be discussed in Chapter 4.

Once a suspected witch was arrested, the authorities' witchcraft beliefs would start to operate. These included a number of ideas that were distinct from popular belief – in particular the idea that a 'witch' was someone who had made a pact with the Devil. Related to this was the idea that witches were collectively worshipping the Devil and carrying out secret rituals – the idea of the witches' sabbat. The authorities often obtained details of this by questioning the suspect, sometimes through leading questions under torture. Witch-hunting thus began in the village, but the major panics, claiming multiple victims, spiralled outwards through the demonic ideas of the elite. Illustration 1.1 is an unusual portrait of an individual Sicilian witch, Felipa la Calabria; it is unusual because most pictures of witches are stereotyped images rather than portraits of real human beings. Illustration 1.2 shows a group of witches being executed during a panic in Baden, Germany. There is further discussion of witchcraft imagery in various chapters below, particularly Chapter 9.

Illustration 1.1 Felipa la Calabria, a Sicilian witch, 1624

This is a rare portrait of an individual witch. Felipa la Calabria, in Sicily, was convicted of witchcraft by the Spanish Inquisition (Sicily was part of the Spanish dominions) and made to do public penance in an *auto da fe*, ceremony of penance, in Palermo on 19 May 1624. The artist Anthony van Dyck was present, and sketched her carrying a candle and wearing a cap illustrating her crime.

The Inquisition, which exercised jurisdiction over Spanish and Italian witchcraft, usually treated it as a penitential matter; there were very few executions. The Inquisition's fearsome popular reputation for witch-hunting is undeserved.

© The Trustees of the British Museum

Illustration 1.2 Three witches burned at Baden, 1574

Most witchcraft executions were by burning. Usually the witch was tied to an upright stake in the centre of the pyre, but here, in Baden, Germany, three witches have been tied to a wooden frame which is being lowered onto the pyre. Note the crowd of spectators; witch-hunting was a popular spectacle, and crowds often attended executions.

The idea of the sabbat – essentially an idea about groups of witches – led to another way in which someone could be identified as a witch: by being named by another confessing witch. If the interrogators thought of witchcraft as a conspiracy, they might well ask witchcraft suspects about their accomplices. When they met the Devil at the sabbat, who else did they see there? Some suspects tried to evade this demand for further names, but others, perhaps with their reluctance having been broken down by torture, were willing to co-operate. They tended to name people who they thought were likely to be witches, often those who fitted one of the stereotypes of what witches were like – older women, for instance.

Interrogation under torture could be a point at which someone might come to believe that they themselves were a witch. The experience of torture might lead them to believe that God had abandoned them. They normally owed their lives to God who watched over them; surely, therefore, the only reason God would allow them to suffer so terribly must be because they deserved it for their sins. This could lead on to the idea that they must indeed be guilty of the sin of witchcraft. However, some of those accused and convicted of witchcraft resisted all efforts at labelling them, and went to their deaths insisting on their innocence – sometimes with moving dignity.

In general, then, the European witch-hunt involved people accusing other people. Hardly any of those who were executed for witchcraft thought that they were witches before they were accused. People hardly ever admitted to demonological witchcraft except under torture, and sometimes not even then. Village witches, too, were usually identified by their neighbours. People might well think to themselves, 'I have the power to curse my neighbours', but the term 'witch' had such negative connotations that they did not identify with it. If you were a 'witch', you were simply evil – and very few people believe that about themselves.

As for folkloric witches, many were not real human beings, as we shall see in Chapter 5. Those who *were* human were all self-identified to the extent that they knew about their relationship with the other world. But, even more than people who cursed their neighbours, the people who visited fairyland or flew out at night did not think that this was 'witchcraft'. Sadly, though, when such a person was arrested and questioned about 'witchcraft', the story they told could well lead the interrogators to believe that they had identified a witch.

Words for witches

The concept of a witch is hard to pin down, and this is reflected in the complex inter-relationships of the words that were used for it. In English, for instance, the word 'witch' comes from the early medieval Old English words '*wicca*' (masculine) and '*wicce*' (feminine), pronounced 'witch-a' and 'witch-eh'. Both meant a witch, and derived from the verb '*wiccian*', to practise harmful magic or divination. (The idea that '*wicca*' meant 'wise one' is erroneous.) In English we also have the terms 'conjuror', 'diviner', 'enchanter/enchantress', 'magician', 'necromancer', 'sorcerer/sorceress', 'warlock' and 'wizard', not to mention the less familiar 'hag', 'sibyl' and 'pythoness'. Each European language had its own range of such terms.

(continued)

Some terms implied that the person must be bad, while others could be used for a person who was either bad or good in different circumstances. In English, a 'witch' was always bad; a 'magician' could be bad or good. Similar distinctions could be drawn in other languages, such as French ('*sorcier/sorcière*' bad, '*magicien/magicienne*' ambivalent) and German ('*Hex/Hexe*' bad, '*Zauberer/Zauberinnen*' ambivalent).

Today we tend to think of a 'witch' as female, and to use other words for men, such as 'warlock'. But, in the early modern period, a 'witch' could be either male or female. That is the way in which the term is used in this book. However, English was unusual in not being a gendered language. Gendered languages, in which all nouns have a gender, operated differently, though the end result was similar. As in the French and German examples above, they tended to have two separate terms for a witch, one masculine and one feminine, showing that they did not think that a witch *had* to be female (or male). This allowed speakers and writers to indicate which gender they had in mind, though this was sometimes obscured by the convention of using a masculine term to embrace both males and females in the plural.

Learned concepts were expressed in Latin. The main Latin words for 'witch' were '*malefica*' (feminine) and '*maleficus*' (masculine), both formed from the medieval Latin word for 'witchcraft' – '*maleficium*'. This originally meant a harmful deed of any kind, but by the middle ages specifically meant harm done by magic. The medieval Latin translation of the Bible used the masculine *maleficus* in Exodus 22:18 ('Thou shalt not suffer a witch to live', in the contemporary English translation). The notorious book *Malleus Maleficarum*, 'Hammer of Witches', used both masculine and feminine forms but showed a strong preference for the feminine – beginning with the title. A few scholars were aware of the original Hebrew and Greek terms used in the Bible; the Hebrew word in Exodus 22:18 was '*mekhashshepheh*', the feminine form of a word meaning 'witch' or 'magician' (it is not clear whether the term was always bad or whether it was ambivalent).

Use of Latin can obscure the vernacular terms used by the common folk. By the early modern period, most court records were kept in the vernacular, but these records may still obscure the way in which people actually spoke of witchcraft. An ethnographic study in the 1970s in the Bocage region of France, where some traditional witchcraft

(continued)

> beliefs continued, found that people usually referred to witchcraft indirectly, using euphemisms: 'that filth' or 'the one who did it' for the witch; 'trick' ('*tour de force*') for spells they cast; 'little father' for an unwitcher; 'what he had to do' for the unwitching ritual.[2] Whatever words we use, there can be a sense in which the reality of witchcraft is always just out of reach.

A world of religion and magic

People felt threatened by witchcraft because they believed in magic. The witches' powers were essentially magical. So what do we mean by magic?

People also felt threatened by witchcraft because they believed in religion. It was Christian religion that told people about the Devil, and it was the Bible that said 'Thou shalt not suffer a witch to live' (Exodus 22:18). So what do we mean by religion?

In defining magic and religion, one question to ask is: Were they the same thing, or different? The religious authorities in early modern Europe would certainly have said that magic was different. At best, they thought, magic was superstitious: at worst, it was demonic. More recent scholars have often been more struck by how much overlap there was between religion and magic. This is because 'magic' has shifted its definition. In Europe, it has usually been defined by disapproving elites. In early modern times, it was mainly defined as *not-religion*, since religious knowledge was considered the highest and most correct form of knowledge. In modern times, however, the dominant form of knowledge is scientific, and 'magic' is mainly defined as *not-science*. Because modern religion can also be seen as not-science, it can appear to be quite similar to magic.

So what do we, today, mean by magic in the early modern period? A modern working definition of early modern magic could run as follows:

> Magic was a set of traditional beliefs and ritual practices that helped people to understand the unusual forces in the world, and to achieve practical ends by seeking to manipulate those forces.

Magic was thus overwhelmingly practical. People cast spells or carried amulets for material reasons. Magic relied primarily on tradition rather than on what we would call science; people believed that it worked, not because its operations could be demonstrated empirically, but because people whom they respected had said that it worked. It was ancient wisdom. In societies where most knowledge is handed down and where ancestors are respected, this is the most powerful way in which any knowledge is validated.

The word 'magic' was originally a pejorative term for practices of which the writer disapproved. It comes from the Latin word '*magia*' (itself deriving from Greek). Early medieval European vernacular languages had no word for it – not because early medieval Europeans did not practise it, but because the common folk did not disapprove of it. Churchmen used the term '*magia*' to condemn popular practices, sometimes seeing them as pagan. The word 'superstition' (Latin *superstitio*) meant something similar: unnecessary (and thus false) Christian belief or practice. There is more on superstition later in this chapter. By the late medieval period, the authorities were well aware that the common folk tended to merge the concepts of 'religion' and 'magic'. Then, in the sixteenth century, the Reformation and Counter-Reformation sharpened the official hostility to magic, and defined a wider range of practices as magical (as we shall see in Chapter 6). The witch-hunt can be seen as a small but dramatic part of a broader official attempt to stamp out popular 'magical' practices in order to promote correct religion.

This brings us back to the question of what we mean by religion. A modern working definition of early modern religion could run as follows:

> Religion was a system of belief in God, and of organised, public rituals, run by a professional staff, designed to propitiate God. This operated for the spiritual and material benefit of believers, and provided believers with an altruistic code of conduct by which they should behave towards other humans.

On this was based an organisation (a church, with a hierarchy and financial resources), a set of collective and individual 'religious' actions (rituals to worship God), and a code of behaviour in society. Organised religion is a product of human culture; different cultures have different religions, and religions change as culture changes. But religion is always organised, and in our period it was very much a public, group affair. Individuals may have been more 'religious' or less 'religious' by the standards of their church, but they had to belong to a church, and their affiliation to that church was part of the public identity that they carried around with them. In modern Western society, by contrast, religion has become a largely private affair and churches have become voluntary associations. Whether you attend a church, or a chess club, is nobody's business but your own.

The differences between early modern magic and religion were thus numerous and complex. Religion offered a universal interpretation of the world. Priests could discuss and explain any natural phenomenon, or any human behaviour, in religious terms. Magic was limited to individual cases, and did not seek to explain the human condition as a whole. Religion was organised, with churches, staff, property, and formal powers over people's lives. Magic, by contrast, was essentially private. It is impossible to imagine a church of magic. Magical practitioners were not organised, and, if they sought to persuade people to believe in magic, this was a matter of attracting business to themselves rather than of attracting converts to the cause. Here again we see magic as seeking immediate, practical benefits.

Religion offered a system of morality, with precepts and rules for how people should treat others. We cannot say that religion was straightforwardly 'good' – outrages and crimes were committed in its name, including (we may well think today) witch-hunting itself; but we can say that it *sought* 'good', trying to show people how they should treat others well. Magic, by contrast, was largely about gaining benefits for oneself – a natural thing for people to want, but morally neutral rather than 'good'. Where early modern religion overlapped with magic, it was in this area: people used religion, in the form of legitimate prayers or other rituals, to gain benefits for themselves.

Some scholars have drawn a different distinction between religion and magic. They have argued that magic is a mechanical process, which is held by its practitioners to work automatically once the correct rituals are performed. The equivalent procedures in religion are uncertain because they rely on petitioning divine forces – God may grant your prayer, or he may not. This is largely correct on early modern religion (though not entirely – the miracle of transubstantiation in the Catholic Mass, when bread and wine became the body and blood of Christ, *was* held to work automatically). However, it is incorrect on early modern magic. When people performed a magical ritual, they *hoped* that it would work, just as they *hoped* that a prayer or other religious ritual would work. They knew, from sad experience, that magic frequently failed. Nor is it correct to say that magic did not use petitioning; plenty of magical rituals petitioned spirits, saints or even God.

Magic today, as we have seen, is usually defined as not-science rather than as not-religion. Educated people today do not usually believe in magic, usually because they think that it is unscientific. The handful of educated believers in magic are usually respectful of science, and try to argue that magic is compatible with it. As a traditional belief system, however, magic is largely incompatible with modern science, which relies on observation and experiment and has no place for tradition. New knowledge constantly supersedes the old. But science was different in early modern times, because it was subordinate to religion – at least until the Scientific Revolution of the seventeenth century, which will be discussed in Chapter 10.

The sharpest distinction between early modern religion and magic, then, is that religion was organised while magic was not. Religion had to be organised, because it was about ideology and morality. Religious authorities needed power, to deal out rewards for correct behaviour and punishments for incorrect behaviour. The power of magic was wielded over things more than over people; magicians did not need to preach or to win converts. Early modern magic occasionally sought to coerce people, as with love magic, in which spells were cast to attract the love of a desired partner. But this did not operate through ideological or political power. Science, too, is, and was then, about power over things, not people; it does not preach. Religion requires a church, but there is no church of magic, and no church of science.

Why, though, were the religious authorities so hostile to magic? Paradoxically, it was because of the area in which magic had most similarities to religion. Let us recall that in our working definitions of magic and religion, both could offer material benefits – and sometimes in strikingly similar ways. Churchmen objected to magic because it was a rival.

This rivalry intensified in the late middle ages. The late medieval church offered a large repertoire of material benefits, such as rituals to bless growing crops, in ways that looked very similar to magic. So they had to police the boundaries carefully, upholding authorised 'religious' rituals but criticising or suppressing unauthorised 'magical' ones. A debate on how best to do this was already running in the late medieval church, but accelerated in the sixteenth century. Part of the movement we know as the Reformation – though this aspect of it occurred in both Protestant and Catholic countries – was an attempt to purge official religion of magical practices that had come to seem illegitimate. The result was a dramatic growth in official disapproval of magic. This was connected with a growth in disapproval of witches, since witches were imagined as practising magic. We shall see in Chapter 6 that the Reformation gave the authorities more power to supervise and control the lives of the common people. Unlike late-medieval churchmen, they had more opportunities to put their hostility to magic into practice.

Witchcraft and 'superstitious magic'

As well as the serious crime of witchcraft which is the main subject of this book, the authorities perceived various other magical beliefs and practices around it. They perceived a serious problem of people engaging in 'witchcraft', and, around it, a milder but more widespread problem of people engaging in 'superstition'. Witchcraft, they thought, was a particularly serious variety of 'superstition', or 'superstitious magic'.

'Superstition' is a difficult and much misunderstood term. Today, when people talk of a 'superstition', they usually mean a belief or ritual that they regard as irrational – a belief in lucky or unlucky numbers, for instance. The point to note is that 'superstition' is not an objective word to describe a given belief; it is a pejorative term used by one person to criticise a second person's ignorant beliefs. People rarely apply the term to themselves; someone who believes in a lucky number is likely to say, 'I'm not superstitious, but I do have a lucky number'. It tends to be the beliefs of the uneducated that are called superstitious by the educated; studying mathematics leads to a better way of understanding numbers. We can wish that people were better educated, but, if we are trying to explain people's beliefs, we should do so using neutral rather than pejorative language. I have read many students' essays saying that early modern European beliefs were 'superstitious'; that tells me that the student doesn't share those beliefs, but it doesn't help me, or the student, to understand the beliefs. As historians, we don't have to share the beliefs of the people we study, but we should try to understand why people's beliefs made sense to them. Calling these beliefs 'superstitious' is thus misguided.

In early modern times, the term 'superstition' was similar, in that it was pejorative. However, there were some important differences. The term was used by the educated to describe popular beliefs or rituals of which they disapproved. These could be pre-Christian survivals, or medieval practices that had been superseded by the Protestant Reformation or by parallel movements of Catholic reform. Sometimes these were seen as harmless or silly, like modern superstitions; but not always. The word 'superstition', as we have seen, literally meant an unnecessary extra belief. Such a belief was essentially *false*. Instead of being false and silly, early modern superstitions could be false and dangerous. False beliefs about Christianity could even be heresy – a serious crime.

The term 'superstition' operated similarly to the term 'witchcraft' in that it was normally applied to other people's behaviour. We can see today that witchcraft was imaginary, while magic was real; nobody practised 'witchcraft', but people did really carry out magical rituals, mainly with benevolent intent. But nobody called themselves 'superstitious'. In this book I will use the term 'superstitious magic', like the term 'witchcraft', to describe what one person at the time thought about another person at the time. I am not saying that anyone *really was* superstitious, nor am I saying that anyone *really was* a witch. The term 'superstitious magic' is thus shorthand for 'beliefs and practices that someone at the time (probably a member of the elite) thought to be superstitious magic'.

The actual practice of superstitious magic was common, and indeed normal, in pre-industrial society. Its patterns of belief and practice thus validated belief in serious witchcraft. The fact that many people practised benign or harmless magic made it easier to believe that some people might practise harmful magic. And occasionally the line between superstitious magic and witchcraft was crossed. Superstitious magic was reinterpreted as something more serious, or was simply prosecuted more intensely in its own right. Practitioners of benevolent magic might then find themselves in trouble as witches.

Some contemporary thinkers were keen to blur the distinction between superstitious magic and witchcraft. Jacob van Hoogstraten, in Cologne, Germany, in 1510, wrote a treatise on the seriousness of consulting magical practitioners: 'Magicians [*magi*]' – by which he meant magical practitioners – 'are generally referred to as witches [*malefici*] on account of the extent of their misdeeds'.[3] Johannes Geiler, preaching on witchcraft in Strasbourg, Alsace, in 1509, demanded punishment for '*beneficia*' – good deeds done by magic.[4] William Perkins, writing in England in the 1590s, even declared that 'death therefore is the just and deserved portion of the good witch'.[5] Perkins was extreme. Most writers who called benevolent practices 'witchcraft' were using an emotive term to highlight the offences and argue that they should be taken more seriously.

Overall, the dividing line between superstitious magic and witchcraft remained intact. Moralising polemicists might call magical practices 'witchcraft', but the courts did not normally prosecute the practitioners as witches. The elite did not see superstitious magic as being seriously demonic; if they saw the Devil as behind it, that was only because the Devil was behind all human sin in some way. Practitioners of superstitious magic were not thought to make a demonic pact. As for villagers, they simply saw superstitious magic as helpful, not maleficent, and probably did not use the word 'witchcraft' for it at all.

What of the practitioners of magic themselves? We should not call them superstitious, but what should we call them? Surprisingly, there is no universally-recognised term for such people in modern English; in this book I call them 'magical practitioners'. The term 'white witches' is sometimes found, but it was not a common contemporary term, and it also suggests false parallels between 'witches' and magical practitioners. Another possible term is 'folk healers', since much of their business concerned healing; but they also provided other services, such as fortune-telling, or finding lost or stolen goods. Some magical 'charms' were uncomplicated rituals that anyone could perform; others were more powerful, and restricted to professionals with special gifts. Magical practitioners were often called 'cunning folk' in England, and some historians have adopted this term, but it is cumbersome, lacking both a verbal form and a gender-neutral singular form. Hence my preference for 'magical practitioners'. There is more about magical practitioners in Chapter 4.

Ideas about superstitious magic also featured in the folkloric imagination. Many folktales and ballads involved magic; some of these 'fairy-tales' are still told today. In early modern times they were not primarily children's stories; the magic in them, and the magical beings in them, were real. A particular story about fairies or trolls might be fiction, but there was no sense that fairies or trolls were anything but real. The all-pervasive character of early modern magical beliefs is striking; no wonder that people believed in witches.

Elite and popular beliefs

The social structure of early modern Europe was complex, with people's social position being defined not just by class but also by status, gender, education and other things. For many purposes, however, this can be simplified. Belief in witches can be divided, broadly, into 'elite' and 'popular' beliefs – though the difference between the two was not absolute.

Beliefs of the 'elite' were heavily influenced by intellectuals – those with access to the latest ideas, usually with a university or equivalent education. In the late middle ages these were mostly churchmen, and intellectual knowledge (outside specialised areas like medicine and law) was mainly deployed for religious purposes. With the Renaissance, in the fifteenth and sixteenth centuries, learning broadened its social scope and purpose. More laymen became literate, and by the seventeenth century most leading intellectuals were laymen. Religious concerns continued, but the increasing willingness of intellectuals to approach knowledge of the world in non-theological ways would contribute to the decline of witchcraft belief, as we shall see in Chapter 10. Whether churchmen or laymen, therefore, one can discuss 'intellectuals' as those who created and disseminated the most sophisticated knowledge.

The 'elite', however, was a broader group than the intellectuals: it included the political rulers themselves and social groups attached to them. Rulers included not just kings and great nobles but also local landlords, who often 'ruled' their tenants directly using their own seigneurial courts. Political rulers did not have to receive an academic education themselves; it was almost unheard of for kings to attend a university. Instead, rulers hired whatever talent they required. They employed painters and sculptors to decorate their *châteaux*, poets to sing their praises, churchmen to pray for them, and lawyers to maintain their property rights. Works of political theory were mostly written to uphold the power of these same rulers. (Similarly, modern rulers' power may be underpinned by computers and the media, but rulers themselves are not usually computer programmers or journalists.) So the political 'elite' shared a common culture with the intellectuals: the intellectuals created the culture, but the rulers commissioned it and benefited from it.

The term 'elite' can also be defined in terms of who it leaves out. The main exclusion is ordinary working people, who had little or no formal education. Women are harder to classify than men, because the system was created by and for men. Wives and daughters of elite men usually received little more than a decorative education in such things as music and needlework. Unlike the common people, however, they moved in elite circles and shared in benefits brought by membership of the elite. Ultimately, therefore, the term 'popular beliefs' means the beliefs of the common people – those who worked for a living, and were often not far from the margins of subsistence.

These two systems of belief were distinct, but not wholly separate. There were two reasons for them to connect. One was that some important people were on the boundary between the two. Parish priests, for instance, were often poorly educated and shared most of the culture of the common people, although in the course of the early modern period they were increasingly expected to distance themselves from their parishioners and to adopt elite values. Another connection between elite and popular belief was simply that *all* members of the elite shared much of the culture of the people, simply adding their own specialised interests to this. They participated in popular festivities, at least in the early part of our period, and listened to folktales. They believed that the common folk were 'superstitious', and to that extent they held themselves aloof, but one can find nobles and propertied folk employing magical practitioners in ways that university-educated intellectuals would themselves have disapproved of. The concepts of 'elite' and 'popular' belief, though essential, denote the ends of a spectrum rather than two wholly separate belief systems.

Understanding 'witch-hunting'

What do we mean by a witch-*hunt*? The term has become conventional in witchcraft scholarship in the English language. There is one curious exception: in studying England itself, a generation of scholars has assiduously avoided it, and the prosecution of English witches tends to be called 'witchcraft prosecution', or even (misleadingly) 'witchcraft'. It is true that 'witch-hunting' was not a contemporary term in English, but the contemporary term 'witch-finding' meant the same thing: the discovery and prosecution of hidden witches. Today, we can speak of a European 'witch-hunt' because the authorities did not just prosecute witches who were somehow already known; they searched them out. Indeed, unwittingly, they *created* witches in the process of searching them out.

It could be argued that prosecution of individual witches, already identified by their neighbours before the courts became involved, was not 'witch-*hunting*'. Well, perhaps. But we should think about how the neighbours identified a witch. Witches were believed to be ordinary people, or at least to look and behave like ordinary people; they did not identify themselves publicly. They were secret enemies. In that sense, finding a witch was indeed a process of hunting for a witch.

What alternative terms might historians use instead of 'witch-hunt'? 'Witch craze' was common at one time, but tends to imply some kind of psychological derangement, and has fallen out of favour. 'Witch hysteria' suffers from a similar problem. 'Witch panic' is useful, and we shall see in Chapter 8 that the sociological concept of a 'panic' is a useful tool for explaining episodes of serial prosecution. The term 'Burning Times' was fashionable among the neo-pagan movement in the late twentieth century, but has declined with the recognition that the witches of the early modern period were not pagans; this will be discussed in Chapter 11. That chapter will also discuss some of the modern meanings of the term 'witch-hunt' – terms that sometimes carry more connotations of irrationality than would be justified for the prosecution of early modern witches. Finally, one possible term is the undramatic 'witchcraft prosecution'; this is often useful, but ultimately fails to capture the sense in which, even for contemporaries, witchcraft was not just another crime to deal with. It was a dramatic, shocking and controversial business.

It is sometimes argued that the witch-hunt was not a singular thing because it happened only in some places and not others. However, this is false. Carried to its logical conclusion, it would imply that witch-hunting could only have been a single thing if it had occurred in every town, every village and every street. There certainly were individual 'witch-hunts' (plural) in the sense of definable episodes of prosecution, each typically involving a single court and a single group of interlinked suspects. But, when we find similar episodes of prosecution scattered widely across Europe, we are entitled to conclude that there was an overarching pattern. Although each individual episode had its own uniqueness, it also shared common features with other episodes, and we can analyse them collectively as having been caused by broad developments that were important throughout Europe.

Moreover, people at the time thought that witchcraft was a single phenomenon, and that efforts to eradicate witchcraft should be made all over Europe. Many works of demonology were written in Latin, the common language of European intellectuals, and these same works were read in the same way all over Europe. This differentiates witch-hunting from some other common phenomena of early modern Europe, such as peasant revolts. Historians can discuss the common features of peasant revolts in different places and times, but nobody at the time thought that there was just one peasant revolt. With the witch-hunt, they did. This will be discussed further in Chapter 11.

The scale of the European witch-hunt

How many witches were executed? This question has always attracted historians' interest. Past estimates were often wildly exaggerated, with a figure of nine million being widely circulated for much of the twentieth century. In the last thirty years or so, the most common estimates have come down from about 100,000 to about 40,000, before rising again to a current consensus of about 50,000 executions. In order to understand the witch-hunt fully, we should remember that beyond these 50,000 there were many more people imprisoned or formally accused but for whom there was some other outcome – sometimes acquittal, or a non-capital sentence like banishment. Some cases ended in escape, or death or suicide in prison, or the case being dropped for some reason. These cases would probably add at least another 50,000 people who were labelled in some official way as 'witches'. Those who had witchcraft reputations in their community but who were never brought to trial are unquantifiable at present, but for some purposes we would also want to include such people in any count of early modern 'witches'.

A figure of 50,000 executions means little on its own. How did it relate to the population at the time? Some outline statistics can help to answer this question. Significant numbers of witches were executed from about 1400 to about 1750, 350 years altogether, so that is about 143 executions per year on average. Let us take the population of Christian Europe (excluding the Ottoman Empire, where no witches were executed) as about 100 million – a figure that would be roughly correct for 1600. From these figures the death rate from witchcraft executions can be established as 0.00143 executions per year per 1,000 of population. The death rate from all causes was about 40 deaths per year per 1,000 of population, so we can conclude that one in

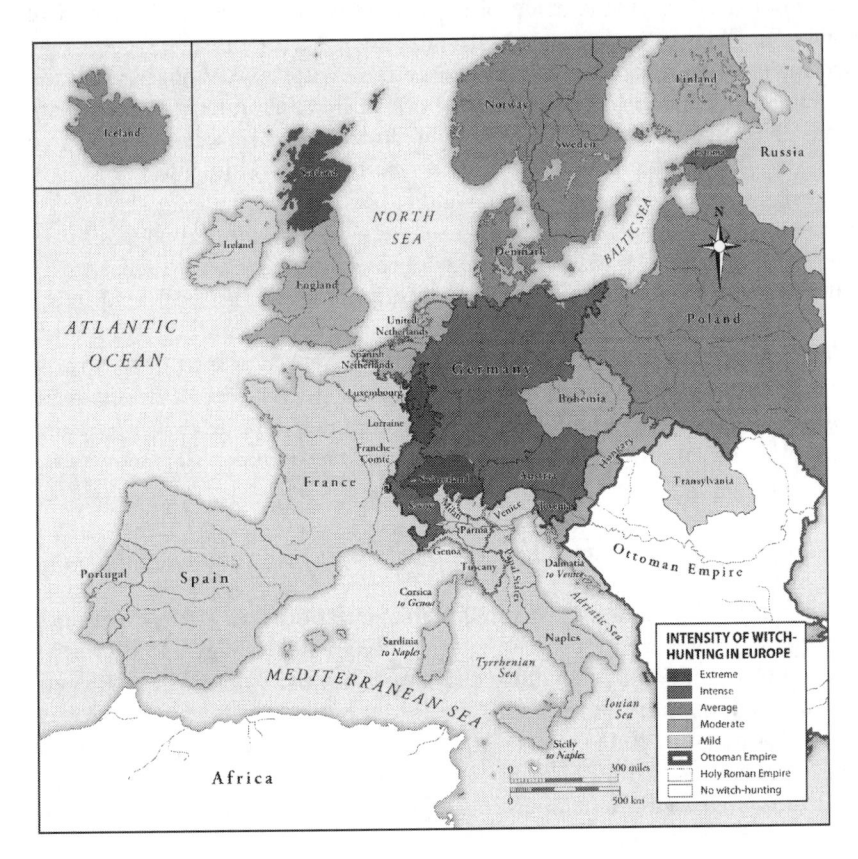

Map Intensity of witch-hunting in Europe

every 28,000 deaths in early modern Europe was caused by execution for witchcraft. This is in the same range as the death rate from air accidents today, which in Britain amounts to one in every 16,500 deaths. Air accidents are a rare, if newsworthy, cause of death; motor vehicle accidents are over 70 times more common (one in every 230 deaths). Witchcraft executions, similarly, were rare but newsworthy.

The crude figure of one in every 28,000 deaths is an average, concealing wide variations in time and space. As for variations in time, quite possibly half the executions were concentrated in the most intense half-century, from about 1580 to about 1630. On that basis, for most of the period 1400–1750 Europe's witchcraft death rate was one in every 48,000 deaths; but, for the period 1580–1630, witchcraft executions accounted for one in every 8,000 deaths – six times more intense.

There were also variations in intensity of prosecution in different places in Europe. The map, 'Intensity of Witch-Hunting in Europe', shows the scale of witchcraft executions, per head of population, in different European states and regions. There are five categories, from 'Mild' to 'Extreme'. The political boundaries of Europe are shown as they stood in about 1600. 'Germany' is shown as a single unit, although it was politically fragmented; the fragmentations are too complex to represent, and there are no readily-available statistics for witch-hunting in each small princely state. As it is, 'Germany' as a whole comes into the 'Intense' category; if the region could have been broken down, quite a few German states would have been added to the map's 'Extreme' category, while others would have moved to a lower classification. Ideally one would want to show regional variations in the other large states too, such as France and Spain. 'Spain' was another politically-divided state, although under one king. Spanish witch-hunting occurred almost entirely in the northern parts. The data are recorded state by state, and so have to be presented using contemporary political boundaries. This has some historical validity, since states had distinct laws and judicial practices, but any suggestion that prosecutions were determined entirely by states would be misleading. An ideal map would plot each individual execution at its exact location, showing a precise regional distribution. The data on which the map is based are tabulated and further analysed in the Appendix at the end of this book.

The most striking pattern shown in the map is the concentration of witch-hunting in west-central Europe. About two-thirds of the executions were concentrated in the German-speaking lands ('Germany', Austria, and part of Luxembourg and Switzerland), with only one-fifth of the population. However, language itself does not seem to have been crucial. French-speaking Lorraine, adjacent to this region, was also one of the 'Extreme' witch-hunting states, with Franche-Comté and Savoy not far behind. Within Germany itself, the most intense prosecutions occurred in the west and south, a region adjacent to Lorraine, Franche-Comté and Switzerland. This area around the river Rhine can be seen as a single west-central heartland of European witch-hunting.

Beyond this west-central heartland, patterns varied. Much of northern Europe saw considerable witch-hunting, with Scotland one of the few 'Extreme' states. By contrast, the kingdom of France saw only 'Mild' witch-hunting (at least per head of population – France was heavily populated), as did Spain and the Italian states. It is often said that English witch-hunting was unusually mild, which is not entirely wrong, but the statistics place it in the 'Moderate' category, with more witches than France per head of population. The Ottoman Empire extended far into south-eastern Europe, populated by Christians but ruled by Muslim sultans. The Ottomans did not allow any witch-hunting. Finally, not shown on the map, there were transatlantic colonies, particularly those of Spain, Portugal and England; there was some witch-hunting in the English colonies. It is sometimes suggested that smaller states prosecuted witches more intensely; this possibly misleading idea, along with other geographical patterns, will be discussed in Chapter 6. Broader patterns of witch-hunting, including the influence of different social and political groups within the state, will be discussed in Chapter 8.

Conclusion: Causes of witch-hunting

At the heart of this book, then, are the 50,000 or so people who were executed for witchcraft in early modern Europe. The book's central question is: why were these people executed? In answering this question, we shall have to spend a good deal of time investigating witchcraft beliefs, since it was obviously essential for Europeans to believe in witches in order to hunt them. But it was possible to believe in witches without hunting them, so we shall have to distinguish between beliefs and hunts. Witch beliefs were arguably an essential precondition for witch-hunting, rather than a determining cause.

This should be evident from chronology. The common people can be shown to have believed in witches, in some form, for most of European history, from the early middle ages until the nineteenth century or even the twentieth. Witch-hunting, however, was specific to a much shorter period, beginning gradually in the years after 1400, reaching a climax in the half-century 1580–1630, and then slowly fading away, ceasing everywhere by about 1750. What changed – first to cause prosecutions to rise, and then to cause them to decline?

Another way of looking at this is to consider geography rather than chronology. Geographically, the idea of the village witch has been much more widely spread than the idea of the demonic witch. Most traditional societies, all over the world, have believed in the idea of humans who can secretly wreak magical harm. The folkloric witch, too, is a global figure. The demonic witch, by contrast, was tied into a great deal of elite knowledge that was specific to one place – Europe – and one time – the early modern period. Beyond that, it does not feature. This book, then, is a study of that one place, and one time, when witch-hunting was intense and dramatic.

But, in order to make sense of this, we need first to turn to the medieval roots of European witch-belief and even witch-hunting. That will be the subject of the next chapter.

Notes

1 Quoted in Hartmut Lehmann, 'The persecution of witches as restoration of order: the case of Germany, 1590s–1650s', *Central European History*, 21 (1988), 107–21, at p. 112. Reproduced with permission of Cambridge University Press.
2 Jeanne Favret-Saada, *Deadly Words: Witchcraft in the Bocage*, trans. Catherine Cullen (Cambridge, 1980), 98–9.
3 Quoted in Marcel Gielis, 'The Netherlandic theologians' view of witchcraft', in Marijke Gijswijt-Hofstra and Willem Frijhoff (eds.), *Witchcraft in the Netherlands from the Fourteenth to the Twentieth Century*, trans. Rachel M. J. van der Wilden-Fall (Rotterdam, 1991), 37–52, at p. 47.
4 Rita Voltmer, 'Du discours à l'allégorie: Représentations de la superstition, de la magie et de la sorcellerie dans les sermons de Johannes Geiler de Kaysersberg', in Antoine Follain and Maryse Simon (eds.), *Sorcellerie savante et mentalités populaires* (Strasbourg, 2013), 45–88, at p. 51.
5 Quoted in *Encyclopedia*, iii, 891.

2 Towards witch-hunting

> We have recently and sadly heard that some Christians and perfidious Jews within the boundaries of your jurisdiction have founded new sects and perform rites that are repugnant to the Christian religion. They also often teach hidden doctrines, preaching and affirming them. And we have also heard that there are within the boundaries of your jurisdiction many Christians and Jews who are sorcerers, diviners, invokers of demons, enchanters, conjurors, superstitious people, augurs, practitioners of nefarious and forbidden arts, and that all of these stain and pervert the Christian people, or at least the simpler-minded of them.
>
> Pope Alexander V to the inquisitor Ponce Feugeyron, 1409[1]

Introduction

There is a popular view of witch-hunting as 'medieval'. People see the middle ages as a 'barbarous' time, with fierce barons tyrannising over downtrodden peasants. Those who objected were thrown into castle dungeons or became heroic forest outlaws. It is all too easy to imagine witches being tortured in those dungeons. Yet there was actually very little witch-hunting in the middle ages. The vast majority of witches were executed in the sixteenth and seventeenth centuries – the age of Leonardo da Vinci, Shakespeare, Galileo and Newton. Why then, and not before?

Answers to this question will emerge gradually as this book proceeds, but part of the answer is that the early modern period (the sixteenth to eighteenth centuries) was an age of state formation. Witch-hunting was a judicial operation requiring state power, and there was not much *state* power in the middle ages (partly because so much power was exercised by those fierce barons). But, if we look back far enough, there was a previous age of state power in Europe – the Roman Empire – and there were occasional witch-hunts then. In particular there were at least three panics in Roman Italy between 184 and 153 BCE. Much less is known about these panics than about the early modern ones, but there were similarities. Torture was used to gain confessions; groups, not just individuals, were prosecuted; and those executed seem to have been mainly women. The numbers executed seem to have run into the hundreds, or even thousands (though the reported numbers may be exaggerated). There were also differences between these ancient panics and the early modern ones, mainly in the nature of the crime. The ancient Roman prosecutions were for *'veneficium'*, a word meaning not only 'harmful magic' but also 'poisoning', and the panics were connected with epidemics of disease. The executed women were thus blamed for spreading disease by magical means. This is different from the later age of European witch-hunting; epidemics of disease in early modern Europe were not blamed on witches. Instead, early modern witchcraft was rooted in everyday village quarrels. The great European witch-hunt very much belonged to its own place and time, but, as the Roman panics show, it was neither wholly unique nor wholly unprecedented. In this chapter we shall examine its medieval roots.

The growth of the idea of persecution

European society in the first millennium CE was to a great extent tribal, even within the Roman Empire; certainly, after the empire's fall, the early medieval period was dominated by tribes. Religion, too, was thus tribal. A tribe would have a keen loyalty to its gods, but would recognise that other tribes could have different gods. There might be tribal warfare, but there was no persecution for believing in the wrong gods. This was so even once the European tribes – perhaps we should start to call them peoples – became Christians and adhered nominally to the same god. Local loyalties continued, expressed in cults of local saints. Local bishops ruled their dioceses as the heirs and successors of these saints, and there were few institutional structures to supervise them.

Early Christianity even tended to discourage witchcraft beliefs. After the fall of Rome, some pagan societies made laws against witchcraft, sometimes mentioning a stereotype of a maleficent female witch. Little is known about these laws, and they probably derive more from Roman models than from indigenous folk belief, but they do indicate some kind of official belief in witchcraft. However, there were also several early Christian laws against witchcraft prosecution, or against calling someone a witch. These Christian authorities regarded witchcraft belief (whatever that meant) as something surviving from paganism, and thus inherently false and superstitious.

Early Christianity also had an intolerant streak. As soon as it spread beyond the Jews, it began to see itself as a universal religion. The Christian god was no longer the tribal god of the Jews, but the only real god; no other gods could be tolerated. Conversions to Christianity were often initiated by kings or lords, who forced the conversion of their peoples and suppressed pagan temples. However, this intolerance was not focused on individuals; it was mainly a matter of replacing the old collective religion with a new collective religion. It was hard to imagine individual deviants from the collective religion, if only because individual believers were not expected to have detailed knowledge of what beliefs were correct or incorrect. Groups of pagans survived in the late Roman Empire after it became Christian (fourth and fifth centuries CE), but when pagans were persecuted it was by deprivation of civil rights. Pagans were not treated as criminals, and certainly not put to death – at least not until the early Byzantine period, when pagans were killed during the sixth century.

Christianity developed an increasingly precise set of official beliefs, under the influence of Greek philosophy. The nature of the Trinity was particularly controversial: God had a threefold nature as Father, Son and Holy Spirit, but what exactly did this mean? Were there three gods, or only one? From the second to the fifth centuries CE, a series of church councils debated these issues and defined a series of 'heresies' – incorrect Christian beliefs. In 325 CE, the Council of Nicaea decreed that the three 'persons' of the Trinity were equally divine. The followers of Arius, who had argued that full divinity was possessed only by the Father, were outvoted; their belief became the heresy of 'Arianism'. As intellectual theology became more complex, the list of notional 'heresies' grew. Actual heretics, however, declined in number as the Catholic church gradually imposed a theological consensus. The last Arian church accepted Catholicism in 589 CE. There was little or no persecution in western Europe for the next four hundred years.

Meanwhile, systems of political authority arose that were more integrated and no longer tribal. The papacy began to co-ordinate the Christian churches more closely. In about 1000 CE the frontier of settlement in western Europe finally closed, and a more unified seigneurial economy emerged. The common people became a homogeneous class of serfs, subject to territorial lords. Instead of arbitrary tribute, systems of customary law emerged to regulate lords' demands for rents, services and taxes. A thin network of towns and long-distance trade was created. An even thinner network of scholars emerged – at first mainly in monasteries, but in the twelfth century the first universities were founded. Theology became more sophisticated still, and the discovery of Arab scholarship stimulated an interest in the study of the natural world.

The eleventh century set some precedents in persecution. There was the first-ever execution of a group of heretics – in 1022 at Orleans, France, though this does not seem to have set a precedent. There was the first mass killing of Jews – in 1063 in Spain. Even more dramatically, there was the First Crusade against the Muslim occupation of Palestine, from 1095 onwards. A schism between the western (Roman Catholic) and eastern (Orthodox) churches became formalised in 1054; it was mainly a dispute about authority rather than false belief, but it underlined the position of the church as an official body with powers and doctrines that should not be questioned.

The twelfth century saw the development of what has been called a 'persecuting society'. Intolerance became official, and the authorities started to seek out deviants. Moreover, real heresy arose in this century with the Cathars and Waldensians, who came into open conflict with papal authority. Heretics can be seen as part of a diverse movement for church reform and evangelical revival; if people seeking 'reform' overstepped doctrinal boundaries they could be defined as 'heretics', while more prudent reformers remained doctrinally orthodox. In the late twelfth century, the Catholic church moved beyond reacting to individual attacks on it, and started to organise to defend orthodoxy. The pope sent an envoy to the Toulouse region of France (a Cathar stronghold) in 1178, with orders to work with local bishops in identifying heretics: they were to 'give us in writing the names of everyone they knew who had been or might in future become members or accomplices of heresy, and to leave out nobody at all for love or money'.[2] It was the first-ever *hunt* for false believers.

Once the church was familiar with the idea that there were heretics about, it started to elaborate its ideas of what heretics were like. Real heretics tended to consist of a charismatic leader and a handful of local followers, but, when the authorities uncovered such a group, they tended to assume that it was the tip of an iceberg. They feared that heretics formed an international conspiracy with a coherent set of beliefs. Thus, although real heretics were scattered and diverse, a unified myth was created from them. At the same time, persecutions began of other groups who had previously been tolerated: particularly Jews, and also lepers and male homosexuals.

The myth of the wicked heretical organisation came to include horrifying details of what heretics did in secret. The two main accusations were that they practised sex orgies, and that they ritually killed and ate babies. This was not because any real heretics did any such thing, but because the authorities thought that heretics were wicked, and they fantasised that these were the kind of things that wicked people would do. The secret orgies presumably arose from the frustrations of medieval clergymen, who were all supposed to be celibate. In today's permissive society, it may be necessary to emphasise just how shocking the idea of sex orgies was. We can readily find the idea of killing and eating babies repellent; to the medieval mind, the idea of orgies was also repellent. Actually these ideas were not new; they can be traced back to accusations made by the ancient Roman authorities against the early Christians. Medieval Christian writers thus picked up some of their ideas about heretics' horrifying rites from a deeply ironic source: they came from earlier Christian writers denying pagan accusations that *Christians* practised horrifying rites.[3]

A more unified and powerful church could orchestrate the persecution of heretics, create institutions to sustain persecution, and persuade people that persecution was desirable. The key persecuting institution was the Inquisition, which emerged gradually during the thirteenth century. Particular inquisitors were appointed from time to time for particular places, initially with no permanent bureaucracy. Inquisitors were judges who held special church courts to punish people for a single offence: heresy. Heresy was defined as the public avowal of false beliefs, and persistence in the error after a bishop or other official had corrected it. In practice, Cathar and Waldensian heretics were identified not by their individual beliefs but by their association with other Cathars and Waldensians. Inquisitors gathered evidence of this from witnesses and from interrogation of suspects, sometimes under torture. The aim was to get heretics to recant their false beliefs and to reaffirm orthodoxy. They could then be made to do penance – anything from a series of visits to churches to ruinously expensive pilgrimages. Heretics who refused to recant were handed over to the secular authorities to be burned to death. This was a small minority, but here we are tracing the growth of the *idea* of persecution, and the idea that people *could* be burned to death for an ecclesiastical offence was important.

The fourteenth century was a time of turmoil and disaster, with famines and epidemics. It is sometimes thought that the Black Death of the 1340s was connected with the growth of witch-hunting, but the link is indirect at best. The Black Death, Europe's worst-ever natural disaster, saw millions of deaths, perhaps a quarter of the population. But it was not blamed on witches. In a few places, plague was blamed on conspiracies of Jews or lepers. Jews or lepers were a different kind of threat from witches, living in separate, visible communities; the threat from them was a threat from outside. Witches, when they later developed as enemies of society, lived in ordinary communities and were outwardly indistinguishable from non-witches. They were an enemy within. If the Black Death contributed anything to the witch-hunt, it may have heightened the fear of conspiracy in general.

Prosecutions before the witch-hunt

The 'witchcraft' that was prosecuted in the early modern period had a number of components. One way of tracing the medieval antecedents of the great witch-hunt is to look at earlier prosecutions for offences like witchcraft. There were some relevant prosecutions in the middle ages, which are sometimes called 'witchcraft prosecutions', but almost all of them were either for harmful magic (with little or no suggestion of demonic conspiracy) or for demonic conspiracy (with little or no suggestion of harmful magic). Most of the prosecutions were of elite men; the authorities did not think that peasant women might be dangerous witches. And the prosecutions for demonic conspiracy were all for 'heresy', which before the fifteenth century had connotations that tended to move it away from 'witchcraft' as that would later be understood. Usually the prosecutors were looking for an identifiable heresy like Waldensianism. Such prosecutions could not lead to panics over village witchcraft. So, although the full image of the witch had not yet coalesced, its components were taking shape. In this section we shall examine how this happened in some key instances.

Prosecutions for harmful magic occurred sporadically throughout the middle ages. These were almost all of individuals, not of conspiratorial groups, and the offenders were not thought to be heretical or to have carried out horrifying rites. Different terms were used in different regions, even though court records were almost all in Latin. A practitioner of harmful magic in one place might be called a '*maleficus*', which would later be the standard early modern term for a witch. In other places, however, such practitioners were called by terms like '*magus*' (magician), '*sortilegus*' (sorcerer), '*tempestarius*' (storm-raiser), '*phitonissa*' (pythoness), '*venefica*' (poisoner), '*incantatrix*' (enchantress) or '*striga*' (with no direct English equivalent).[4] (The first four of these terms were masculine, while the last four were feminine; this varied with the sex of the practitioner.) This profusion of terms indicates that the learned classes of Europe had no sense that a single category of 'witches' was in existence. Nor did elites think that 'witches', or anything like them, operated in groups; law codes occasionally mentioned '*malefici*', or other witch-like terms, but always as isolated individuals.

This does not mean that magic was not around; it mainly means that elites were not interested in it. Most of the magic actually practised (as we shall see in Chapter 4) was of an everyday kind, which did not involve conspiring with demons or deviating from the correct form of Christianity – the things that worried the authorities. Overwhelmingly, indeed, magic was not harmful but beneficial (though beneficial acts could generate the idea of harmful ones, as we shall also see in Chapter 4). Bernard Gui wrote a standard inquisitors' manual in the 1320s. He described 'sorcery' as involving everyday rituals like healing by incantations, finding lost or stolen goods, or love-magic – largely beneficial services that magical practitioners provided to their clients. However, although such magic was common, few inquisitors prosecuted it. Gui himself tried over 1,000 cases, but none involved magic. At this time, the Inquisition's concern with 'sorcery' was theoretical rather than real.

Political magic in the fourteenth century

Some rulers began to worry in the early fourteenth century about magical threats to their authority. These threats might or might not involve demons, but they certainly involved elite men rather than villagers. Some of the threats were imaginary, but still generated prosecutions. Some related to French and papal political instability – several French kings, and Pope John XXII (reigned 1316–34), feared attack by magical practitioners.

The most feared form of political magic was necromancy. Necromancy, both real and imagined, grew from the late twelfth century onwards. It was a particular form of magic carried out by learned men, mainly priests. It was based on the church's ritual for 'exorcising' demons – commanding demons to depart from a human who was being plagued by them. Ingenious and disobedient priests worked out that the ritual of exorcism, which was basically about controlling demons, could be adapted to command demons to do other things; finding treasure and seducing women were popular things that demons could help with. The term 'necromancy', which had originally meant divination with the aid of spirits of the dead, came to be applied to these adapted rituals, carried out by summoning and commanding demons. Such rituals required a knowledge of Latin formulae. Orthodox churchmen condemned necromancy, but late medieval Europe was full of impoverished priests, unemployed or only partly employed, and it was impossible to police them all. Critics of necromancy claimed that necromancers could only summon and employ a demon if they made a pact with the demon. The idea of a pact with a demon, or with the Devil himself, would be crucial to the later idea of witchcraft, and it came from this source.

Political magic, or at least the idea of it, became hugely important with the destruction of the Knights Templar, by Philip IV of France, between 1307 and 1314. The Templars were a large international crusading organisation. Their headquarters was in Paris, but they were subject to nobody except (nominally) the pope. They had amassed great wealth by using their privileged position to build up a banking and trading business, but by 1307 they were not doing much actual crusading. The Christians had lost Acre, their last Palestinian outpost, in 1291, and the Templars were doing nothing to recover it. Philip IV (reigned 1285–1314) was an ambitious and aggressive king who in 1307 was in deep money trouble. His attack on the Templars was linked to his financial desperation, though he was deeply pious in his own way and probably persuaded himself that the charges against them were true. The attack was masterminded by his cynical adviser Guillaume de Nogaret, who probably did not.

At any rate, beginning on 14 September 1307, Templars all over France were suddenly arrested. They were accused of carrying out horrifying secret rites involving homosexuality, denial of Christ and worship of an idol. Later, with the aid of confessions, further charges were added, notably that the Templars gave allegiance to the Devil in the form of a giant cat, and that they anointed their idol with the fat of babies that they had killed and roasted. There was no truth in the accusations, but confessions were rapidly extracted under torture. Once this process began, those Templars who maintained their innocence began to seem even more heinous for refusing to admit to the order's depravity. The order of the Knights Templar was duly suppressed with the pope's aid (the pope at that time was politically dependent on the French king). The order's wealth was officially transferred to another crusading order, the Knights Hospitaller, but within France much of it disappeared into the royal coffers. The accusations against the Templars drew on ancient stereotypes of heretical evil; they were certainly not about 'witchcraft', but they were very much about demonic conspiracy.

The crushing of the Templars, which echoed all over Europe, had a tiny and virtually unnoticed sequel in Ireland that is nevertheless of interest to those studying witchcraft. This was the prosecution of Alice Kyteler, a wealthy matriarch, and her associates, in Kilkenny in 1324. Richard Ledrede, bishop of Ossory, who led the prosecution, had been at the papal court in Avignon during the Templars' prosecution, and no doubt brought ideas from there. He was supported by Kyteler's stepchildren, who were at odds with her about property, and who accused her of having killed her three previous husbands by magic. Ledrede's central charges were that Kyteler and associates had conducted magical rites with a demon, which sounds like the Templars. What makes the case more like a later witchcraft one was that harmful magic was also mentioned (the killing of the husbands, and also causing sexual impotence), and that most of those accused were women. Kyteler fled, but one of her servants, Petronilla of Meath, confessed under torture and was executed.

The Kyteler case (from its outcome we might call it the Petronilla case) attracted no attention at the time, but it has interested historians because it appears to show, in 1324, that it was at least possible to have a witchcraft case that looks as though it could have occurred at the height of the later witch-hunts, say in 1624. It does not have all the elements of the demonic witchcraft stereotype that had become familiar three centuries later, but, even in 1624, not all individual cases had every single element. The Kyteler case included heresy, demonic rites, harmful magic and conspiracy; it did not have the demonic pact, or flying, and not much importance was given to the harmful magic. It put women in the foreground, unlike most medieval accusations of heresy which were directed at men.

Some features of the Kyteler case make it more typical of 1324 than of 1624. The actual crime was defined as 'various heresies' rather than 'witchcraft' (so it is not certain that we should call Kyteler and Petronilla 'witches'). The word 'sorcery' also appeared in the narrative of the crimes, but only as a description of the kind of heresy it was.[5] The offenders were seen essentially as heretics who had carried out demonic rites. Thus, if the case had spiralled out further, the authorities would have been looking for more people who had participated in demonic rites, not for more practitioners of harmful magic. Finally, the case was part of a struggle for political power, with the bishop, Ledrede, using it against his rival, the seneschal of Kilkenny. Ledrede was not interested in regulating peasants' lives, and would not have been likely to start the kind of witchcraft panic that became common in the early modern period. Women were involved only because Kyteler was a member of the elite; this was not about village magic.

The Kyteler case, then, is the exception that proves the rule. It brought together several things that the middle ages normally kept separate. We do not normally find prosecutions for demonic conspiracy that also involved harmful magic before the fifteenth century. The case was to some extent a fortuitous combination of elements in the aftermath of the Templars' destruction – harmful magic and demonic conspiracy. If this 1324 case does show something relevant to 1624, though, it shows that it was *possible* to combine these elements.

Let us take stock of the general situation in about 1400. The idea that wicked heretics might conspire against Christian society was well established, though not all the ideas of conspiracy were the same as the ideas that would come to be used in the witch-hunts. The allegation of horrifying secret rites would come in time to be used against witches – it was in some ways an all-purpose set of ideas that could be applied to any evil group. The idea that the Inquisition could prosecute wicked anti-Christian conspirators was also well established. Although the Inquisition itself would not be responsible for more than a tiny proportion of the later witchcraft prosecutions, it did kick-start the process in the fifteenth century. But, in 1400, several developments were still in the future. In particular, because there had been no more cases like Kyteler's, nobody was concerned that practitioners of harmful magic might be heretics, or that heretics might be practitioners of harmful magic. The secular criminal courts, which would prosecute most of the early modern witches, had not yet become interested in harmful magic among the common folk. The crime of 'witchcraft', as the early modern period would know it, had not yet been invented.

Towards a new crime of 'witchcraft', c.1400–1435

The pace of prosecutions accelerated in the early fifteenth century. Until about 1435, most prosecutions continued to be either for harmful magic or for demonic conspiracy, but the two elements started to overlap, and new ideas entered the mix. In the years around 1400 there was another outburst of accusations of magical conspiracy at the French court, and Jean Gerson, an influential Paris theologian, wrote forcefully against those harnessing demonic forces. He also, separately, denounced 'old women sorceresses', though he said little about what he thought these might be.[6] Gradually, the idea of a new and more distinct crime of 'witchcraft' would emerge in this period, at least among elites in certain areas. Initially this was a localised phenomenon, mainly in and around the region of the western Alps – the French-speaking parts of Switzerland and neighbouring provinces. It would take a long time for it to spread to the rest of Europe. And large-scale witch-hunting would not occur for another century and a half.

Before considering the western Alps, though, we should glance at a group of cases in central Italy, mostly in 1427, provoked by a charismatic preacher, Bernadino of Siena. Like Ledrede in Ireland a century earlier, Bernadino brought together several things that had usually been kept separate. He had a fairly clear concept of 'witchcraft', though he used various different words for it. Witches were old women who made a pact with the Devil and killed and ate children. They also committed other less important malefices. Bernadino thus had some idea of harmful magic; he did not focus on the everyday malefices that concerned peasants, but he did at least identify the witch as an old woman – something that peasants did more readily than churchmen concerned with heresy. He also had some idea of demonic conspiracy, foregrounding the demonic pact and thinking of witches in the plural, but his ideas on witches' meetings remained undeveloped. He mobilised people in several towns to denounce witches, though they took some persuading. A handful of executions resulted, but usually the authorities prevented any action being taken.[7] One remarkable trial influenced by Bernadino occurred at Todi in 1428, in which Matteuccia di Francesco was made to confess to transforming herself into a fly and sucking children's blood. She also flew to nocturnal meetings of witches.[8] Some of these ideas seem folkloric (and will be discussed as such in Chapter 5), but the fact that Matteuccia was said to have worked with a demon was ominous. Connections were gradually being made between the various components of witchcraft belief.

The western Alps was the cradle of the new combined witchcraft belief. This region included the western part of what is now Switzerland, which in the early fifteenth century consisted of a number of largely independent cantons. The region also included the duchy of Savoy, a medium-sized state to the south of present-day Switzerland, comprising not only present-day Savoy (now in France) but also Piedmont (now in Italy). Finally, the region included the province of Dauphiné, which in the early fifteenth century had recently been acquired by the French crown. Most of the people in this region spoke French, but their neighbours in central Switzerland and northern Italy spoke German and Italian; it was a cultural crossroads.

In Savoy itself, the duke, Amadeus VIII, was reorganising and extending his dominions. This led to a prominent case of political necromancy. In 1417, a dramatic pair of trials was held: Jean Lageret, a wealthy former councillor of the duke, and Michael Dishypatos, a Greek physician and astrologer, were accused of magically plotting to gain influence at the duke's court. Tortured, they confessed to having made statuettes to summon demons to aid them in this. Lageret was executed.[9] This necromancy episode may have contributed to the inclusion of 'sorcery' in a new Savoyard law code of 1430, though this still used traditional language.

Heresy was also rife in the area, and most of the witch-related ideas arose in connection with this. The church had various new heresies to worry about in the early fifteenth century. The Lollard movement had arisen in England, and in Bohemia there were Hussites. In the western Alps, the actual heretics were traditional ones: Waldensians, who had grass-roots support in many rural communities.

It is sometimes assumed that witches were invented, whereas heretics were real. However, this is too simple. As well as real heretics, there were also heretics who were manufactured in the process of hostile interrogation, much as witches would later be. The authorities did not always understand the unusual beliefs they came across. When the English authorities encountered a man who believed that the sun and moon were gods, they put him down as a Lollard.[10] Some heretics existed wholly in the imaginations of orthodox but fearful churchmen, who wrote tracts denouncing deviant but imaginary activities. Heresy, after all, was defined not by the heretic but by the orthodox. Most of those labelled as 'heretics' either did not realise that they were unorthodox, or saw themselves as loyal critics of an unfortunately misguided establishment that would shortly come round to their views. The fifteenth-century establishment, however, was busily imagining new heresies.

One example of this came as early as 1409, when a papal rescript (quoted at the head of this chapter) was issued to the inquisitor Ponce Feugeyron in the French Alps and Savoy. It mentioned that innumerable Jews and Christians had 'founded new sects' and were performing hidden and repugnant rites that seem to have been connected with magical practices, especially necromancy. The rescript may well have been requested and even drafted by Feugeyron himself. It was reissued to him in 1418 and 1434. What it meant is not entirely clear, but Feugeyron was evidently worried about heresies proliferating in his region.

Feugeyron was an individual, despite his broad jurisdiction, and there were limits to what one man could achieve. What was needed was an organisation. In parts of the western Alps, especially Piedmont, standing organisations of inquisitors were established at this time to combat the Waldensian problem. Feugeyron may have played a co-ordinating role for them, but local inquisitors like Ulric de Torrenté in Lausanne were at the heart of the process of imagining the 'new sect'.[11] Indeed, the 'sect' of witches was not the only sect that they invented; they also produced an imaginary sect of 'Luciferians'.

Meanwhile, the local Waldensians, although they were not imaginary, had been developing some unusual characteristics. Waldensianism had begun as a conventional movement for 'reform' of Christianity, with its 'heresy' consisting mainly of refusal of papal authority. In the early fifteenth century, however, the Waldensian leaders in the western Alps, the 'brothers', had gained remarkable powers in the eyes of their peasant followers. They could visit heaven or hell, and meet angels or God or the souls of the dead. Some of the 'brothers' were believed to fly out with dead souls and visit houses at night. These abilities could give them powers of healing or prophecy. If such Waldensians were arrested and tortured, their confessions could take on a witch-like quality.[12] In parts of French-speaking Switzerland from about 1430, witches became known as '*Vaudoises*', a word usually meaning 'Waldensians' but which could also mean 'inhabitants of the canton of Vaud' (in western Switzerland). The word was also used sometimes to mean 'heretics' in general. There was thus confusion about the idea of '*Vaudoises*', made worse when French-speaking officials in Fribourg (a canton adjacent to Vaud) prosecuted German-speaking peasants.

In the late 1420s and early 1430s there were several large-scale panics centred on the Valais, a Swiss canton part of which had recently been acquired by the duke of Savoy. These were trials of '*Vaudoises*', described as heretical conspirators who caused illness and death, who caused men to be impotent and women to be infertile, and who damaged crops. Torture was used, and large numbers of executions occurred, though we do not know how many. Hans Fründ, who reported on these trials (see the text box 'The writers on the "new sect"'), first mentioned one hundred executions, then two hundred. Medieval statistics were often vague and exaggerated, and these numbers should not be taken literally. What we can see, though, is that the idea of '*Vaudoises*' had been attached to this new sect, which was now recognised as separate from the Waldensians. The 'new sect' did not yet have a name of its own, but it was about to acquire one.

The 'new sect' of witches, *c.*1435–1485

During the 1430s, several writers in or near the western Alps became convinced that a 'new sect' of heretics had arisen. Existing heresies were mostly about worshipping God in the wrong way, but this group consisted of people – mainly women – who deliberately worshipped the Devil. To be sure, all heresies were inspired by the Devil, but this new sect of heretics seemed to be particularly shocking in giving allegiance to the Devil directly. Moreover, the sect carried out appallingly gruesome and obscene rites. And this new sect consisted of 'witches'.

The five writers who first articulated the idea of the 'new sect' are listed in the text box 'The writers on the "new sect"' (pp. 47–8). Two were churchmen – a theologian (Johannes Nider) and an inquisitor (Ponce Feugeyron). Two were laymen – a judge (Claude Tholosan) and a town chronicler (Hans Fründ). The fifth, Martin Le Franc, was a poet and administrator, nominally a churchman. Whatever their background, they all thought in religious terms and were concerned about heresy. Some of them may have known each other or been influenced by each other's work; Nider mentioned talking to an unnamed inquisitor who sounds like Feugeyron. They are important because they all show that the idea of a 'new sect' had arisen. Not only that, but collectively these five writers display a remarkably consistent picture of the sect.[13]

All five writers thought that they were dealing with an organised group, describing the group's arrangements for secrecy and discipline. The witches met the Devil at night, and kissed him or made sacrifices to him in a witches' sabbat (usually called a 'synagogue'), as in Illustration 2.1. The Devil taught them various harmful acts. The witches killed babies and children while sleeping, most often other people's children but sometimes their own. After the children were buried, they dug up the bodies, brought them to the sabbat and ate them. Usually they also made magic potions from their fat. These tales of infanticide and cannibalism were borrowed wholesale from previous accusations against other heretics. Most of the writers also wrote that the witches engaged in sexual orgies. Renunciation of Christianity, and sometimes attacks on Christianity (such as trampling on the cross), were also described. These accusations came from similar sources.

Illustration 2.1 An early heretical sabbat, *c.*1467

Witches worship a demon in the form of a goat, while others fly overhead on demons in the shape of fantastic beasts. The witches are described as '*Vaudoises*', a word usually meaning 'Waldensian' heretics. At this early date, witches were thought to be an underground sect of heretics rather like the Waldensians. Versions of the demon-worshipping stereotype were applied to numerous heretical groups.

Johannes Tinctoris, *Tractatus de secta Vaudensium* ['Tract Concerning the *Vaudois* Sect'], manuscript, *c.*1467. Bibliothèque Royale de Belgique, Bruxelles, MS 11209, fo. 3.

© Copyright Royal Library of Belgium.

Since the Waldensians were in the news, the 'new sect' writers seem to have borrowed various ideas from what inquisitors thought about Waldensians. However, nobody thought that Waldensians simply *were* witches. The general idea was that a new sect had arisen that was *rather like* the Waldensians. After all, the authorities already thought they knew what Waldensians were like. The connection with the Waldensians should not be over-stressed; Nider, the most important of the 'new sect' writers, never mentioned them. And the 'new sect' writers borrowed ideas from other sources too. They usually described witches' meetings as 'synagogues', a term borrowed from Judaism. Again, they already thought they knew what Jews were like, and did not think that Jews were witches either. Something of the way in which they understood these terms can be glimpsed from a witchcraft trial in the region in 1448 in which the accused, Pierre Munier, was said to be one of the 'new Waldensian heretics' (*'hereticorum modernorum Valdensium'*).[14]

The 'new sect' writers described the Devil instructing his witches in magical techniques. The idea of instruction in magic is an important clue. This 'new sect' was imagined as a conspiracy of peasants practising harmful magic, but with demons involved. In imagining the relationship between the peasants and the demons, the 'new sect' writers drew on the main model that they knew for relationships between humans and demons: the model of necromancy. It was necromancers who were believed to summon demons and make pacts with demons. However, necromancy involved Latin rituals, to which peasants had no access; so the 'new sect' writers had to work out where the peasants' knowledge came from. They concluded that this knowledge must come from instruction by the Devil.[15]

Women were prominent as members of the 'new sect'. This was novel; in a patriarchal age, heresies were usually thought to be led by men. Nider's account in particular was vehemently anti-women; much of the misogynistic material that later attained prominence in the *Malleus Maleficarum* (1486) derived originally from him. Nider's critique of women included a general objection to sexuality. He was interested in church 'reform', which in this period often meant trying to stop priests taking concubines; he extended his denunciation of priests' sexual activity to a general denunciation of women. He was uninterested in ordinary peasant women, but he did object to women in politics, in particular Joan of Arc, the French military leader who had been executed by the English in 1431. Joan's execution had been for 'heresy', but in Nider's view this had a demonic element.

Not all the 'new sect' writers stressed women, but only one, Tholosan, ignored the issue. Fründ and Feugeyron specified that the sect consisted of both men and women, which was almost as effective as Nider in drawing attention to women and in undermining patriarchal assumptions. Finally, Le Franc's account of the sect concentrated on women, though he mentioned that it contained a few men. This new interest in women connected with popular belief, and may have been influenced by popular belief.

Bernadino, as we have seen, stressed women witches, indeed old women, and it was these whom the common folk tended to imagine as practitioners of harmful magic. The 'new sect' writers had moved beyond the stereotype of heresies run by men, and had imagined a heretical sect in which women were important.

Another way in which the 'new sect' writers responded to popular concerns was in weather magic. Most of the writers said that the witches caused hailstorms. Weather magic was an ancient popular belief. Hailstorms were particularly common in Alpine regions, and were the most feared type of bad weather there. Apart from cannibalistic infanticide, storm-bringing was the main type of harmful magic said to be committed by the 'new sect'. Otherwise, though, the motif of harmful magic was virtually absent from the five writers' works – a significant omission, as we shall see.

Finally, the witches' ability to fly was important. Four of the five 'new sect' writers said that witches flew, often to the sabbat. The one who omitted this point, Nider, was influential in other respects but did not prevent witches' flight becoming a standard part of later accounts of witches. Fründ's witches flew on chairs from one mountaintop to another. They visited cellars and drank wine which they then magically restored. Tholosan's witches flew on sticks and animals. Le Franc described a recent 'synagogue' in Italy attended by ten thousand women who had worshipped the Devil in the form of a goat. His manuscript included an illustration of two witches flying – one on a broomstick, the other on an ordinary stick.

All these ideas about the new sect of heretical witches might have remained as local traditions, if it had not been for the Council of Basel. This was a council of leading churchmen from all over Catholic Christendom, which met in the Swiss town of Basel from 1431 to 1437. Johannes Nider, one of the 'new sect' writers, was a prominent member of the council. He may well have met some of the other writers there (Le Franc certainly attended), but what is more important is that churchmen from the rest of Europe had the opportunity to discuss the problem of the 'new sect', and some of them probably took ideas about it home with them. The ideas seem already to have reached Lyon, the Alpine region's gateway to France, in the late 1430s.[16]

The 'new sect' needed a name, and the name needed to be disseminated. Language is relevant here. Three of the 'new sect' writers used Latin; of these, Feugeyron wrote of '*heretici*' ('heretics'), but Nider and Tholosan called the sect '*malefici*' ('witches'), and Nider's work was particularly influential. Most of the discussion, and most of the executions so far, had been in French-speaking regions. Le Franc, writing in French, used both '*Vaudoises*' ('Waldensians') and the longer-lasting '*sorcières*' ('witches'). Germans, too, soon picked up on what was going on. A new word, '*hex*', had already appeared in the late fourteenth century in Schaffhausen, a German-speaking canton of Switzerland; Fründ, the only 'new sect' writer to write in German, used the terms '*Hexsen*' and '*Zauberern*' ('witches' and 'magicians'). The new word then spread into Germany itself, in the form '*Hexerei*', which soon became a standard German term for 'witchcraft' (though the term '*Zauberern*' was never abandoned). This helped others to recognise that the new sect was a sect of 'witches', with a clear word for them both in Latin and in the vernacular. As the new ideas spread into Germany, the idea that the sect consisted mainly of women also became clearer. A copy of the *Errores Gazariorum* made in the Palatinate in the 1450s feminised most of the pronouns.[17]

The 'new sect' writers did not clearly connect the sect's demonic rites with the harmful magic believed in by peasants. In the period that followed (from the 1440s to the 1470s), one of the few writers to make this connection was Nicolas Jacquier, a French Dominican inquisitor. He wrote his *Flagellum Haereticorum Fascinariorum* ('Scourge of Heretical Enchanters') in 1458, to prove the reality of the witches' sect – or even two sects, since he wrote of the sects of 'witches' ('*malefici*') and of 'enchanters' ('*fascinarii*') as if the 'enchanters' were a separate group, or possibly a more wicked subgroup within the 'witches'.[18] He wrote mainly about the horrifying rites of the sabbat, but he did discuss harmful magic.

In this period, then, writers on the emerging demonology concentrated on the horrifying rites of the sabbat – or the 'synagogue', as they still usually called it. They aimed, not just to describe the new sect, but to explain it with more theological sophistication, especially about the powers of demons. As they did so, they stirred up debates – but they usually won the debates, by force in one celebrated case. A French monk and theologian, Guillaume Adeline, challenged the new demonology in 1452 by preaching that the witches' sabbat was merely an illusion, but he was arrested by the local bishop in Evreux, and forced to confess to witchcraft himself. According to Adeline's confession, it was the Devil who had ordered him to preach that witchcraft was an illusion. Imprisoned for life, Adeline died four years later. His case was often cited to prove the reality of the witches' sect.[19]

Meanwhile, most late fifteenth-century witchcraft trials were still for harmful magic alone, but an increasing number were for demonic conspiracy as well, and they attracted more attention than before. Jeannette de Sala de Juxue, in Gascony, western France, as early as 1450, gave a detailed demonic confession with hardly any mention of harmful magic.[20] The interrogators of Antoine Rose, in Savoy in 1477, questioned her in detail about whether she attended church.[21] This shows that they were thinking of witchcraft as demonic conspiracy, but doing so very much in a 'heretical' model. Churchmen thinking about heretics often asked themselves how secretive the heretics were. Some 'sects', they thought, acted more openly than others. Did the heretics attend church (perhaps hypocritically), or did they withdraw openly from the church as part of the process of setting up their own 'sect'? This question would lose prominence in later witchcraft trials. Once the idea of witchcraft was uncoupled from the idea of heresy, those prosecuting witches simply thought that they were prosecuting witches. In 1477, witch-hunting was still to a great extent heretic-hunting.

The idea of demonic conspiracy also meant that the late fifteenth century had more multiple witch trials than ever before. Particularly notorious was a panic in Arras, in the Burgundian Netherlands, between 1459 and 1460, influenced by Jacquier's recent demonological treatise. It led to numerous trials, twelve executions, and recriminations afterwards. Only one of the witches was charged with harmful magic, and the charges were largely about collective worship of the Devil. The accusers claimed that one-third of Christians were secretly witches – another example of exaggerated statistics, or exaggerated anger and fear, or both.[22] Overall, trials were particularly frequent in 1455–60 and in 1480–85. This may allow the *Malleus Maleficarum* to be seen as a culmination of previous trials – on several of which it drew. At any rate, it is now time to turn to the *Malleus* itself.

The writers on the 'new sect'

Five early writers described a 'new sect' of heretical witches. They are listed here in rough chronological order, but their texts cannot all be dated precisely, nor is it clear whether they influenced each other directly. This was before the invention of printing, but writings circulated in manuscript; some of these texts survive in several copies. Whether these writers were in contact with one another or not, they were expressing similar concepts. Clearly, new ideas about a 'new sect' were developing and circulating in the western Alps.

c.1430–35: *Hans Fründ*, chronicler of Lucerne, Switzerland. He wrote a report of recent witchcraft trials in the Valais, a nearby Swiss canton, that took place from 1428 onwards. The trials seem to have been traditional ones for harmful magic, but Fründ's report elaborated them to produce an account of a demonic sect conducting horrifying rites.

c.1435–37: *Ponce Feugeyron*, Franciscan inquisitor in western Alps and Savoy area from 1409 onwards. He is the most likely author of the anonymous tract *Errores Gazariorum* ('The Errors of the Heretics'). A revised version of the *Errores* was written in or after 1438, adding an account of a trial of that date.

1436: *Claude Tholosan*, secular magistrate of Briançon, Dauphiné, France. He wrote *Ut Magorum et Maleficorum Errores* ('The Errors of the Magicians and Witches'). Tholosan had tried and executed people whom he considered to be members of a new 'sect of diabolical witches'. Most were women.

(*continued*)

> c.1436–37: *Johannes Nider*, Dominican prior at Basel, Switzerland. He wrote *Formicarius* ('The Ants' Nest'), a satirical, moralising view of human society. One of the five sections of this work was devoted to the witchcraft sect. Nider's work was particularly influential.
>
> c.1440–42: *Martin Le Franc*, French poet and humanist, secretary to the duke of Savoy. He wrote *Le Champion des Dames* ('The Defender of Ladies'). This long poem, a literary exercise, had a section attacking women who became witches.

The *Malleus Maleficarum* (1486) and village witchcraft

Few books in history can have provoked such strongly-contrasted modern responses as the *Malleus Maleficarum* ('Hammer of Witches'). Its erudite but eccentric translator in 1928, Montague Summers, proclaimed it one of the great books of Western civilisation. Some feminists have denounced it as a blatantly misogynistic tract responsible for the deaths of millions (or at any rate thousands) of women. Some postmodernists have commended its intellectual rigour, no doubt with coolly detached irony. Other scholars have pointed to its internal weaknesses and inconsistencies. To put the *Malleus* into its own context, we must remember to treat it as a work of theology by a fifteenth-century German Dominican friar, Heinrich Krämer, who was angry at being rebuffed in prosecuting some local witches in Innsbruck.

The *Malleus* is indeed an important work, a constant presence in the intellectual atmosphere of the great early modern witch-hunts. It was never entirely superseded by later demonologies; while its current relevance declined as later works appeared, its venerable authority actually grew. It took advantage of the new technology of printing, as can be seen in Illustration 2.2. It was repeatedly reprinted from 1486, when it first appeared, up to 1669. But it was a work of its time and place, not a generalised totem to stand for the whole of witch-hunting. Thus its true importance can emerge. Its authorship has been ambiguous; sixteenth-century editions attributed it jointly to Heinrich Krämer and Jacob Sprenger, but it now seems more likely that it was Krämer's work alone. The *Malleus* will be discussed further in later chapters of this book, especially on intellectual witch-belief (Chapter 3), witchcraft trial procedure (Chapter 7) and women (Chapter 9); here we need to look at the way in which it marked a new stage in the growth of fifteenth-century beliefs.

The *Malleus* is not a masterpiece of detailed logical argument, but it is a competent work and its message to readers is clear. Witches are real people who cause real harm of various kinds; their power derives from the agency of a powerful Devil and demons, with whom witches enter into a real agreement – the demonic pact; and all this can be explained in theological

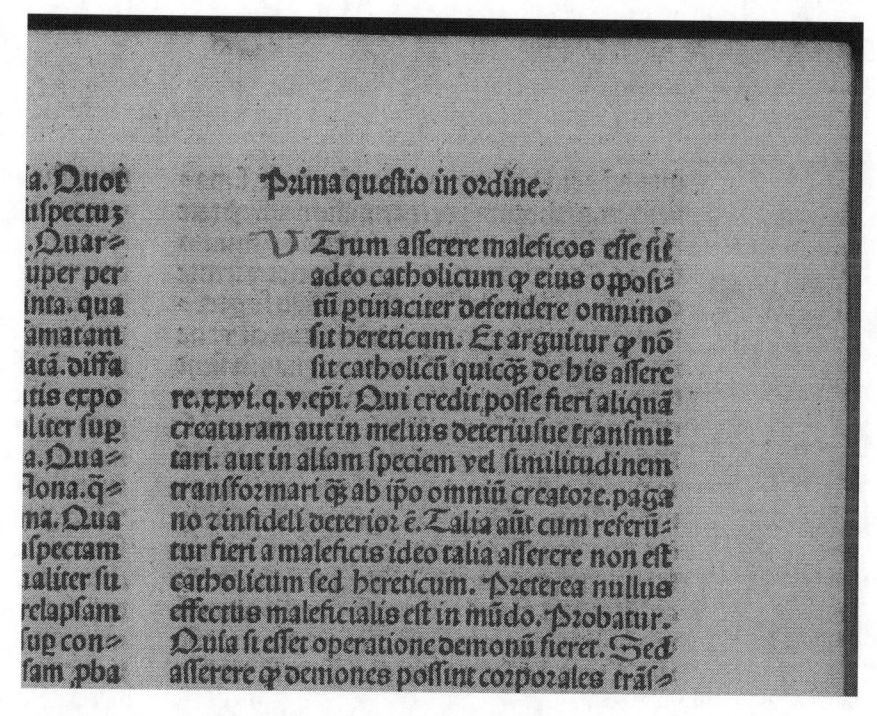

Illustration 2.2 The *Malleus Maleficarum*, 1486
This is the beginning of the main text of the first edition of the most influential demonological book. In the early years of printing, books were printed to look like manuscripts. A space has been left for a hand-coloured initial letter. The text begins: 'Prima questio in ordine. [V]trum asserere maleficos esse sit adeo catholicum ...' ('First question in order. Whether it is Catholic to assert that witches exist ...'). The *Malleus Maleficarum* was often reprinted, with the last edition appearing in 1669.

© Edinburgh University Library, Special Collections Department. Shelfmark Ic.54, folio 5r.

terms, since it occurs with the permission (but not the active agency) of God. Witchcraft is heresy and thus can be punished by the Inquisition, but it should also be punished by the ordinary church courts (here Krämer was getting back at the bishop who had overruled him in Innsbruck) and, because of the harm it causes, by the secular courts too. One of the reasons the *Malleus* was to become notorious was that it incorporated a detailed procedural manual for how a witchcraft trial should be conducted, how evidence should be gathered, and how interrogation and (if necessary) torture should be carried out.

Previous theologians had usually seen witchcraft as a heresy, and had imagined an underground sect of Devil-worshippers. Krämer did not deny any of this, but, rather than dwelling on it, he grounded witchcraft in the actual beliefs and practices of individual peasants. Quarrels led to curses, and, when someone who had been cursed suffered a misfortune, they interpreted this as the curse in action, and decided that their antagonist must be a witch. This led to the concept of witches as female – something much more familiar in the village world of maleficent cursing than in the erudite clerical world of struggle against heresy.

The *Malleus* said very little about the witches' sabbat. This was novel and important. Some historians have treated the failure to discuss the sabbat as an oversight, a weakness in the argument, but it was arguably a strength. The 'new sect' writers had emphasised lurid Devil-worshipping sabbats, but this had not led to the discovery of significant numbers of actual attenders of such sabbats – no doubt because such sabbats were imaginary. By contrast, those who sought the witches described by the *Malleus* would readily find them in any European village. For two centuries after 1486, witch-hunters often did just that.

The *Malleus* was not actually against the sabbat. Once it had established a basic conceptual framework for village witchcraft, therefore, prosecutors who knew about the sabbat from other sources could bring it into the trials they conducted. The sabbat could produce chain-reaction trials, in which the first witch named others who had attended. After the *Malleus*, chain-reaction trials could now be more firmly grounded in village witchcraft; the first witch would be someone identified as a witch by her or his neighbours. Such witches were easy to find, unlike the heretical witches imagined by earlier demonologists.

The *Malleus* was one of the last works to endorse the idea of a 'new sect'. By now the sect was not so new, and the idea of its recent origin had become less important. Krämer nevertheless followed Nider, arguing that modern witchcraft had emerged in about 1400. He added that there had been a few witches before, but it was unclear whether they had had pleasurable, willing sex with demons, as modern ones usually did.[23] Krämer might have preferred to argue more firmly that witches had always existed, but he was probably reluctant to challenge Nider.

Conclusion: Witchcraft beliefs come together, 1486–1500

A number of historians have argued that a single concept of witchcraft emerged in the fifteenth century from a 'fusion' or 'amalgam' of different motifs. This is an important topic, so it is worrying to find that there is little agreement and much vagueness as to exactly what motifs were 'fused' and how. It is even slightly worrying to find that there is hardly any actual controversy about the topic; instead, different scholars seem to have been developing their ideas in isolation. Given the lack of resulting agreement, surely we have here a problem that we ought to be trying to solve? What seems to have happened is that some excellent surveys of fifteenth-century beliefs by early scholars appeared to be comprehensive, leading more recent scholars to try to fill in some details and to amend parts of the picture. However, they have not all been trying to solve the same 'problem', and nobody has pointed out that the profusion of detailed studies (many of which are excellent in themselves) has created contradictions and inconsistencies. We need a new synthesis. What follows will attempt to provide one, at least in outline.

To illustrate the problem in more detail, let me mention some of the key motifs. Witches' flight has been seen to be important; so has the witches' sabbat. The demonic pact was clearly relevant to the way in which 'witchcraft' came to be conceived as heretical; the demonic pact is a motif in itself, and so is heresy. Finally, these elite concepts seem to have been brought into some relationship with village malefice, so malefice is also a relevant motif. But what were the 'fused' motifs? Flight plus sabbat? Pact plus sabbat? Flight plus malefice? Pact plus malefice? Heresy plus sabbat? Heresy plus pact? Heresy plus malefice? All the above ideas have been proposed by different scholars. So has the idea that the whole 'fusion' involved components of the sabbat.[24] Not all of these ideas can be wholly right. There is also the question of whose 'fusion' it was. These ideas of 'fused' belief are intellectual ones, but not all historians make this clear. The common folk, as we shall see in Chapter 4, continued to think of witchcraft largely as malefice.

We should begin by recognising that the question has been badly framed. Scholars have tended to see the question as being 'What motifs were fused to create the new concept of witchcraft?', but arguably 'fusion' is the wrong metaphor. Motifs like pact and sabbat continued to be distinct, even if they were both connected with witchcraft. I suggest that we should think of a 'combined concept' of witchcraft rather than a 'fusion'.

We should also think more carefully about chronology. Perhaps there was more than one period during which connections were made between different motifs. And perhaps some motifs needed to be downgraded if the new package was to become workable and convincing. Actually this is one topic on which there has been at least a little debate, with some recent scholars arguing that relationships between different motifs were different at different times and in different places. Things were more complicated than we thought. There is, nevertheless, a possible solution to the problem.

The solution is to recognise that the combined concept of witchcraft emerged in two stages, with the key periods being the 1430s and the 1480s. The first stage was the 'new sect' period. Here the key concepts to be combined were the demonic pact (from necromancy), the idea of conspiracy (from defining witchcraft as a heresy), the idea of horrifying rites (from stories told of existing heretics), the idea of flight (from folklore), and the idea that witches were peasant women (from village witchcraft beliefs). This was a remarkable and ominous intellectual breakthrough.

But a second stage was necessary before large-scale witch-hunting could become possible. The 'new sect' writers emphasised horrifying rites, and thus created an idea of a 'witches' sabbat'; but, because these rites were imaginary, it was hard to find people who practised them. Nobody who really knew their local heretics, or their local village witches, would believe that they took part in nocturnal orgies or infanticide. Such rituals could be imposed only by powerful outsiders who could torture people into confessions – and this was unlikely to occur often, or to attract local support. Until a tangible link was made with well-known magical practices, prosecutions for horrifying rites would remain rare.

This link was made in the second stage, with the *Malleus Maleficarum* in 1486. The *Malleus* ignored the witches' sabbat, and focused instead on village quarrels and harmful magic. Its witches certainly made a demonic pact, but the *Malleus* presented them as the kind of people who could be found in real villages. It is true that harmful magic was largely imaginary too, but, unlike the imaginary horrifying rites, villagers believed in it. Villagers identified witches as people who engaged in quarrels and curses – curses which their neighbours interpreted as harmful magic.

The *Malleus* also uncoupled the link with a definite, organised 'sect' that looked and behaved like other heretical groups. Such a 'sect' was hard to identify in real villages, since village witches were not thought to hold meetings. Instead of telling people to prosecute a sect of heretics who were called witches, the *Malleus* told them to prosecute witches. Witches were still acknowledged to be heretical, but their heresy remained important mainly because it gave inquisitors jurisdiction over them – and the *Malleus* also argued that other courts should prosecute them as well. The vast majority of early modern witches would in fact be prosecuted by secular criminal courts. Here, harmful magic was important, because this was readily recognised as a secular crime. Probably the elite still *cared* more about demonic conspiracy than about harmful magic. But they could now see that they would find witches among villagers who were accused of harmful magic by their neighbours.

The basic combination of concepts, therefore, was the elite combining harmful magic with demonic conspiracy. It was not a 'fusion', because these concepts remained separately identifiable, but they were both attached to the combined concept of 'witchcraft'. Now, whenever a case of harmful magic was discovered, someone in authority might well think that it also involved demonic conspiracy. And, whenever a case of demonic conspiracy was discovered, someone in authority might well think that it also involved harmful magic. And they would assume that it was a case of 'witchcraft', with that single, powerful term replacing the profusion of different medieval terms.

Even after 1486, there was still much variety in what was meant by 'witchcraft'. There were two main reasons for this. One is that the combination of harmful magic with demonic conspiracy was an elite matter only; most peasants still thought mainly or solely of harmful magic. They had no actual objection to the idea of demonic conspiracy, but the idea did not guide their actions. For there to be significant witch-hunting at all, harmful magic was essential in order to get peasants to identify witches. But, for there to be really large-scale witch-hunting, chain-reaction hunts had to be possible, and this required the idea of a conspiracy of groups of witches. The Devil was necessary to this because elites assumed that he was behind wicked conspiracies.

The other reason for the variety of 'witchcraft' beliefs is that even the elites of early modern Europe thought about demonic conspiracy in different ways. It should never be assumed that there was any monolithic 'witches' sabbat' to which everyone subscribed. There was agreement, at the most broad, general level, that witches were linked with the Devil. However, the more we examine the details of witches' dealings with the Devil, the more variety we find. This will be discussed in Chapter 3.

It can even be argued that the 'witches' sabbat' was not essential to the new concept of witchcraft. Historians who have tried to explain the emergence of the demonic witch stereotype by reference to the sabbat have arguably been looking in the wrong place. Of course, if there was a demonic conspiracy, witches would be assumed to hold meetings with each other and with the Devil. But the content of the meetings – whether the witches killed or ate babies, for instance, or whether they kissed the Devil's anus or trampled on the cross – was less important. The idea of the 'witches' sabbat' was not so much a single coherent concept as a loose bundle of motifs tied together by the basic idea that witches conspired together with the Devil. Some regions had some parts of the bundle, other regions had other parts. This, too, will be considered in Chapter 3.

The present chapter has had a mainly narrative structure, telling the story of witchcraft beliefs from the early middle ages until about 1500. In the story so far, only modest numbers of witches have been executed, but all the elements of demonic witchcraft belief are now in place. Large-scale witch-hunting would begin in the sixteenth century. However, it is neither practical nor enlightening to continue in narrative mode, telling the story of one prosecution after another. There will be some narrative in the rest of this book, but it will not predominate. Deeper understanding of the European witch-hunt can be achieved through thematic analysis. The first theme, the subject of the next chapter, will be the demonic witch of the intellectuals.

Notes

1 Alan C. Kors and Edward Peters (eds.), *Witchcraft in Europe, 400–1700: A Documentary History* (2nd edn., Pennsylvania, Pa., 2000), 153. Reproduced with permission of University of Pennsylvania Press.
2 Quoted in Robert I. Moore, *The Formation of a Persecuting Society: Power and Deviance in Western Europe, 950–1250* (Oxford, 1987), 26.
3 Norman Cohn, *Europe's Inner Demons: The Demonization of Christians in Medieval Christendom* (3rd edn., Chicago, Ill., 2000).

4 Wolfgang Behringer, *Witches and Witch-Hunts: A Global History* (Cambridge, 2004), 53–5. The term '*striga*' is discussed in Chapter 3 below.
5 *A Contemporary Narrative of the Proceedings Against Dame Alice Kyteler*, ed. Thomas Wright (Camden Society, 1843), 1.
6 Quoted in Michael D. Bailey, *Fearful Spirits, Reasoned Follies: The Boundaries of Superstition in Late Medieval Europe* (Ithaca, NY, 2013), 143.
7 Franco Mormando, *The Preacher's Demons: Bernadino of Siena and the Social Underworld of Early Renaissance Italy* (Chicago, Ill., 1999).
8 Domenico Mammoli (ed.), *The Record of the Trial and Condemnation of a Witch, Matteuccia di Francesco, at Todi, 20 March 1428* (Rome: Res Tudertinae 14, 1972).
9 Jonathan Harris, 'Byzantine medicine and medical practitioners in the West: the case of Michael Dishypatos', *Revue des Etudes Byzantines*, 54 (1996), 201–20.
10 Jeremy Catto, 'Dissidents in an age of faith? Wyclif and the Lollards', *History Today*, 37:11 (Nov. 1987), 46–52, at p. 52.
11 Bernard Andenmatten and Kathrin Utz Tremp, 'De l'hérésie à la sorcellerie: l'inquisiteur Ulric de Torrenté OP (vers 1420–1455) et l'affermissement de l'inquisition en Suisse romande', *Zeitschrift für schweizerische Kirchengeschichte / Revue d'histoire ecclésiastique suisse*, 86 (1992), 69–119.
12 Wolfgang Behringer, 'Detecting the ultimate conspiracy, or how Waldensians became witches', in Barry Coward and Julian Swann (eds.), *Conspiracies and Conspiracy Theory in Early Modern Europe* (Aldershot, 2004), 13–34.
13 Martine Ostorero, Agostino Paravicini Bagliani and Kathrin Utz Tremp (eds.), *L'imaginaire du sabbat: Edition critique des textes les plus anciens (1430 c.–1440 c.)* (Lausanne, 1999).
14 Martine Ostorero, *'Folâtrer avec les démons': Sabbat et chasse aux sorciers à Vevey (1448)* (2nd edn., Lausanne, 2008), 174–8, 274.
15 Michael Bailey, 'The medieval concept of the witches' sabbath', *Exemplaria*, 8 (1996), 419–39.
16 Franck Mercier, 'La vauderie de Lyon a-t-elle eu lieu? Un essai de recontextualisation (Lyon, vers 1430–1440?)', in Martine Ostorero, Georg Modestin and Kathrin Utz Tremp (eds.), *Chasses aux sorcières et démonologie: Entre discours et pratiques (XIVe–XVIIe siècles)* (Firenze, 2010), 27–44.
17 Martine Ostorero and Kathrin Utz Tremp (eds.), *Inquisition et sorcellerie en Suisse romande: Le registre Ac 29 des Archives cantonales vaudoises (1438–1528)* (Lausanne, 2007), 496.
18 Martine Ostorero, *Le diable au sabbat: Littérature démonologique et sorcellerie (1440–1460)* (Firenze, 2011), 453–6.
19 Martine Ostorero, 'Un prédicateur au cachot: Guillaume Adeline et le sabbat', *Médiévales*, 44 (printemps 2003), 73–96.
20 François Bordes, *Sorciers et sorcières: Procès de sorcellerie en Gascogne et pays Basque* (Toulouse, 1999), 85.
21 Lea, *Materials*, i, 240.
22 Franck Mercier, *La Vauderie d'Arras: Une chasse aux sorcières à l'automne du Moyen Âge* (Rennes, 2006).
23 *Malleus*, 108A–B (II.i.4). The older translation of Montague Summers, 'about 1400 years before the Incarnation of Our Lord' (i.e. 1400 BCE), is incorrect.
24 For a thoughtful discussion along these lines see Robin Briggs, *Witches and Neighbours: The Social and Cultural Context of European Witchcraft* (2nd edn., Oxford, 2002), 25–32.

3 Witchcraft and the intellectuals

> But to attract them [the witches] more readily to this renunciation and false adoration, the Devil usually makes them touch a book containing some obscure writings. ... Often this adoration occurs as they kneel down; and since (books tell us) at the sabbath everything is backwards and done the wrong way, sometimes they adore him with their backs turned toward him, sometimes with their feet pointing upwards, after lighting some candle made of very black wax on his middle horn.
>
> Pierre de Lancre, France, 1612[1]

Introduction

How did European intellectuals know about witchcraft? By 1612, when Pierre de Lancre wrote the book from which the above quotation comes, they had developed a detailed and sophisticated model of witchcraft. Lancre indicated how this had come about when he mentioned that 'books tell us'. Scholars like Lancre himself worked out the details of this. Their intellectual project has come to be known as 'demonology'; it was about the relationship between witches and demons, but demons' powers and purpose were at the heart of it. Demonology made sense only as part of a broader picture, so this chapter will start with some of the big issues that concerned early modern intellectuals.

The cosmos and the cosmic story

Educated people in early modern Europe lived in a fragile world, delicately poised between two towering cosmic realms: heaven and hell. Heaven, the realm of God, was above the planets, sun, moon and stars. The earth was fixed at the centre of the universe, with the other heavenly bodies all orbiting round it. This might have been problematic, because the Polish astronomer Nicholas Copernicus argued in 1543 that the movements of the planets were best explained by seeing them and the earth as orbiting the sun. However, this sun-centred view gained few adherents for over a century, and theologians were generally the last to adopt it. It made more sense, theologically, to retain a traditional view of the cosmos with a stationary earth at the centre. Sun, moon and five visible planets moved round the earth, attached to transparent crystal spheres called 'orbs'; above them was a sphere with stars on it, which also moved round. Just above the sphere of stars was a fixed sphere which controlled the rotation of all those inside it. With the earth surrounded by a sphere of stars (rather like the dome of a modern planetarium), this provided a physical place for heaven beyond. As for hell, this was the fiery realm of the Devil deep within the earth.

In heaven lived God and his angels. For Catholics, the Virgin Mary was also important, as the symbolic 'Queen of Heaven'. Heaven was also the abode of the souls of human beings who had gone there after they had died. God himself was subdivided into three – the Father, the Son (who had lived as a man, Jesus, and redeemed human sinfulness by his sacrificial death) and the Holy Spirit. God could be thought of as being in heaven, as the opening words of the Lord's Prayer attested ('Our Father, which art in heaven'). But God, a creator and eternal being, could also be seen as separate from the world he had created – to which heaven and its other inhabitants all belonged. Heaven was thus given two levels, with God himself in the upper one and the angels and saved souls in the lower one. God's own domain was sometimes seen as a heavenly city, while the abode of the saved souls was a garden, a restored Eden. The prospect of getting to heaven was a key motivating force for human behaviour.

Hell was inhabited by the Devil and subordinate demons, who were all angels who had rebelled against God and been cast out of heaven. The fact that the Devil was an angel was important to demonology, since the question of witches' powers would depend ultimately on the powers of the Devil. The basic idea of the Devil as the personification of evil was simple, but his exact role and purposes could be debated; how much power did he have against God, for instance? In hell, demons tormented the souls of humans who had been sent there, instead of to heaven, when they died. However, the Devil and demons spent much of their time at or near the surface of the earth. Often they were in the air, either high up, or flying around invisibly just above people's heads. In the human world, their aim was to win souls for themselves and to inflict evil on humanity.

The fragile human world was thus a battleground for a furious struggle between good and evil forces. The struggle was fought out in the world as a whole, and also within each individual soul as God and the Devil battled for people's allegiance. This struggle encouraged a 'providential' world-view, in which God was seen as taking an active interest in human affairs and those of the natural world. God often intervened in the world through his 'divine providence'. This allowed the Devil and demons, similarly, to be conceived as constantly active and interventionist. It may help to think of demonologists as being constantly surprised at each new turn of events, with the workings of the natural world being often upset by unpredictable interventions from either God or the Devil.

This cosmic battle was part of a scheme involving the past and the future. This scheme operated both at the level of individuals and at the level of the cosmos as a whole. Any educated person who thought about witches had to consider their place in the cosmic story. We saw in Chapter 2 that fifteenth-century witches came to be seen as a 'new sect', a heresy distinct from ancient heresies. This idea faded away during the sixteenth century; but, during that century, as large-scale witch-hunting got under way, people noticed that witches were more common than they had been before. Demonologists sometimes tried to explain the rise of witches as a part of cosmic history, as we shall see.

For individuals, the future meant that they were bound to die and to go either to heaven or to hell. Their past was relevant here because their social identity – noble, burgess or peasant – was constituted by their ancestry. In the next world they could expect to join their ancestors. Heaven contained the souls of those ancestors who had been saved – though many Catholics had first to pass through purgatory, a kind of antechamber to heaven where people's sins were 'purged' away through torments. Hell was the destination of the souls of the damned. It was a hot, dark, gloomy realm where demons inflicted perpetual torments. Death was ever-present to early modern people; they often had to think about their future destiny, and such thoughts dominated the daily lives of particularly religious individuals.

Most people evidently hoped that they would be saved. We do not know how often or how deeply they worried about this; those who kept spiritual diaries often recorded worries or even despair about salvation, but this was probably untypical. Catholics could worry about how long they would spend in purgatory rather than about whether they would make it to heaven at all, though purgatory did not exist for Protestants.

The salvation or damnation of individuals was only a small part of a vast cosmic story. In the long timeline envisaged by theologians, human society itself was a mere interlude between the Creation of the world and the Second Coming of Christ. God alone was eternal, with no beginning or end. The angels (including the Devil and his demons) were immortal, but they had a definite beginning: they had been created by God, along with the world, a few thousand years ago. The Devil had begun as the most powerful angel, but had led a rebellion against God, whereupon he and his followers were cast out of heaven. God then created the first humans, Adam and Eve, but they were tempted to sin by the Devil. This 'original sin', transmitted to their descendants, left all humans inherently vulnerable to temptation by the Devil. Witches were those humans who succumbed most completely to this temptation, and were key allies of the Devil in his struggle to ruin the human race.

Eventually, in the Christian cosmic story, the Devil was doomed to defeat. At the Second Coming of Christ, he would be chained and Christ would rule for a thousand years. At the end of this 'millennium' period, the Devil would briefly be unchained and would overrun most of the earth until his armies were destroyed by fire from heaven. The Last Judgement would occur, and the world would end. The Second Coming was often thought to be imminent, and biblical scholars deployed the latest mathematical techniques to work out when it would occur. The Scottish Protestant inventor of logarithms, John Napier of Merchiston, calculated a detailed chronology of the future in 1593, predicting that the papacy would be overthrown in about 1639; thereafter the ruins of Rome would be inhabited only by demons until the final ending of the world in 1786. The bitter religious wars of the sixteenth and early seventeenth centuries made it easy to believe that the world was approaching its end. The Bible warned that the Devil would rage when he saw the Second Coming approaching, and that 'lying wonders' would arise (2 Thessalonians 2). This passage was often cited to explain the rise in witchcraft: there were more witches because the Devil was making supreme, last-ditch efforts to recruit them and send them to harm humanity. The witchcraft threat was part of a grand cosmic design.

Sources of elite witch-beliefs

How did early modern intellectuals know about witchcraft, or indeed about heaven and hell? It is worth paying close attention to this question, since popular accounts of the witch-hunt often dismiss witchcraft belief as 'ignorant'. On the contrary, witchcraft rested on deep foundations of knowledge. Study of witchcraft, and of the demons who activated it, was at the cutting edge of an expanding and sophisticated area of research in the fifteenth and sixteenth centuries, when the concept of witchcraft was formulated in a way that would enable witch-hunting to spread. Rejection of witchcraft belief, by contrast, would have threatened some of the foundations of orthodox Christianity – as demonologists often pointed out.

We thus need to understand how knowledge was created and transmitted by late medieval and early modern intellectuals. The 'scholastic' method of study, taught in universities, began with close reading of an authoritative text. Questions were then asked about the text, and these were answered in strict logical form. This was rather like students today, reading textbooks and then writing essays, but essay writing is more effective at transmitting existing knowledge than at creating new knowledge. Creating knowledge today means going beyond the textbook; sometimes it even means challenging the textbook. The scholastic method was used both for the transmission and for the creation of knowledge, and was arguably less successful in the latter function. Creation of new scholastic knowledge mainly involved *elaborating* the text. Medieval scholars were extraordinarily versatile and ingenious at this; using their texts as foundations they constructed vast cathedrals of philosophy, sometimes with multiple levels of reality, that have never been surpassed in sophistication.

There was, however, little freedom in scholasticism to question the text itself. Students writing essays today can often find books propounding different interpretations, and so can criticise one book by means of another. Moreover, the 'authority' of each book stands no higher than that of its human author. By contrast, the authoritative texts that were studied in late medieval times were all assumed to be compatible with one another, and were thus ultimately beyond criticism. What made them all authoritative was the sanction of God. Theology, which addressed religious questions directly, was the highest form of intellectual enquiry. Moreover, no other discipline was entirely separate from theology, and all knowledge required the sanction of God – which, in practice, meant the church.

The most authoritative text to be studied scholastically was of course the Bible. As the divinely-inspired 'word of God', the Bible carried vast authority; but it did not stand alone. Every other authoritative text was also in some sense sanctioned by God. The Bible itself, as scholars knew, was a loose compilation of disparate 'books' written over a long period. As well as the sixty-six 'canonical' books of the Old and New Testaments, there were the 'Apocrypha', fifteen books of lesser authority but often included in the Bible. Further 'apocryphal' writings, by Jews or early Christians, were excluded from the Bible but still recognised as important. Another class of authoritative texts was the theological and devotional works of the early medieval 'Fathers' or 'Doctors' of the Christian church, especially the systematic theologian St Augustine (354–430 CE). As ancient and respected authorities, and as saints, the church Fathers were almost beyond challenge. By a 'doctrine of authority', statements made by such authoritative writers automatically carried more weight than statements made by people with lesser reputations; thus the demonologist Ulrich Müller in 1489 mentioned 'the judgement of the Doctors, before whose superior opinion I must submit myself'.[2] New saints were periodically recognised by the Catholic church, and stories of their lives and achievements, often including miracles, provided a further source of divinely-sanctioned knowledge.

So educated sixteenth-century people were just as good at logical reasoning as we are today – probably better, since all university students studied logic as a formal subject. For instance, because the Bible called the Devil 'the prince of the power of the air' (Ephesians 2:2), they reasoned that this must make the air the natural habitat of demons. But people did not have access to as much accumulated knowledge as we do now. Astronomy has shown that the heavenly bodies obey the same physical laws that operate on earth. Biology and palaeontology have shown that biblical accounts of the Creation and the Flood do not match the scientific evidence. Textual analysis of the Bible itself has undermined the idea that the Old Testament is a uniformly accurate historical record; its earlier books have been revealed as essentially mythology. Early modern thinkers had none of this accumulated knowledge. What they did have was the centuries-old and highly successful scholastic tradition. They had no reason to doubt the accuracy of the Bible and their other texts, and every reason to think them authoritative.

Logical thinking often involves dividing things up and classifying them. In late medieval and early modern times, one tool for this was 'inversion': dividing things into two opposite concepts, with one conceived as the 'inverse' of the other. In theology, the basic opposition was between God and the Devil. Inversion enabled thinkers to imagine a diabolical anti-religion by taking specific components of Christianity and inverting them in order to make them the way that the Devil was assumed to have them. Thus, because Christianity initiated its members through the ritual of baptism, it was logical to infer that the Devil would initiate his witches in a kind of anti-baptism. We shall return to this when we look at some of the details of demonology.

Pre-modern thinkers also tended to build up knowledge through accretion of attractive and meaningful stories. The pelican was believed for centuries to feed its young with blood pecked from its own breast – a memorable image of parental self-sacrifice. Nobody who repeated the story felt a need to check whether pelicans really did peck their breasts, nor could they have given any evidence for the truth of the story other than previous writers' authority. In 1646 Sir Thomas Browne questioned the story, pointing out that ancient Egyptians had told a similar story of the vulture; this, plus the fact that the tip of the pelican's beak is red, probably explains the story's origin. Many early modern witchcraft beliefs were equally traditional. This should not surprise us; how many of us today could readily provide evidence for such well-known scientific 'facts' as ocean tides being caused by the moon? Among the general public, this 'fact' is just as much a traditional belief as the story of the pelican. Nevertheless, traditional or not, early modern demonological beliefs assembled themselves into a pattern that was all too credible.

Natural, supernatural and preternatural

Witches had remarkable powers. They could accomplish amazing feats that were hard to explain by ordinary understandings of the natural world – or so said the demonologists. This had to be proved at the boundary between the everyday world and the world of demonic power. Theology could contribute to this, but it was also essential to study the natural world. To prove the existence of witches, demonologists set out to prove that their remarkable deeds were not 'natural' – or, at least, not fully 'natural'. So they had to define the boundaries of what was 'natural'.

When studying the natural world, most thinkers turned ultimately to the writings of Aristotle (384–322 BCE), a Greek philosopher who had provided a comprehensive view of the natural sciences. Aristotle's system of metaphysics explained the nature of reality, and provided a toolbox of logical procedures by which to analyse ideas on this and other subjects. Aristotle was of course a pagan, but during the middle ages his works had been translated and received into the Christian intellectual tradition. St Thomas Aquinas (1224–74), one of the most influential medieval thinkers, had persuasively synthesised Aristotelian science and Christian theology. Aquinas brought together faith and reason in a way that would be supreme until the Renaissance, and rarely challenged even then – though the Renaissance did set in motion undercurrents of intellectual scepticism, as we shall see. And, as we shall also see, Aquinas had said a good deal about demons.

How could witches' remarkable feats be explained in Aristotelian terms? Aristotle had laid down that there were four 'elements' – earth, air, water and fire – and four 'qualities' that each element could possess – hot, cold, wet and dry. All ordinary workings of nature used some combination of these, in an elaborate system of rules; there were 'affinities' and 'correspondences' between different bodies and elements. Flames, for instance, went up because they 'sought' the fiery bodies of the heavens, while solid bodies went down because they 'sought' the earth. The topography of heaven and hell, with its concentric spheres, was essentially Aristotelian. However, some phenomena were hard to explain in ordinary Aristotelian terms; the behaviour of magnets or poisons, for instance, could not be explained by their qualities. Aristotelian thinkers thus extended their system, reasoning that, as well as 'manifest' (open) qualities, objects could also have 'occult' (hidden) qualities. The 'occult', by its 'hidden' nature, was harder to explain, but that made it an intellectual challenge that the natural philosopher sought to solve.

These rules could be used to explain all regular natural occurrences, at least in principle. However, there were also occasions where the rules appeared to be broken. Some of these were miracles; the Bible described the sun standing still in the sky, or people being raised from the dead. Miracles were 'supernatural' – above nature – and were wrought solely by God, who was outside the world that he had created and could break its rules if he wished. But there were many other unusual events that were not considered to be miracles. For instance, the sun, moon and planets were normally the only heavenly bodies that moved, but occasionally there were also comets. These exceptional events were called 'preternatural' – beyond *ordinary* nature. They were still caused by other created bodies rather than directly by God – but, with many preternatural events, there was a strong chance that they were caused by demons.

The concept of a preternatural event came to be crucial to demonology. When witches inflicted strange illnesses, or when they flew through the air, or when they transformed themselves into animals (either in reality or as an illusion of the senses), they were doing something preternatural. Or, rather, a demon was doing it on their behalf. It is important to remember that the line the demonologists were drawing here was not between the 'natural' and the 'supernatural' – all demons' activities were natural, because demons themselves were natural, having been created by God along with the rest of the world. The 'preternatural' was a subcategory within the broader category of 'natural'. To some extent the demonologists were drawing a line between the 'manifest' and 'occult' qualities in nature – demons tended to use occult forces, though they did not have to. Occult forces were still natural; the term 'occult' had not yet acquired its sinister modern associations. The 'preternatural' and the 'occult' thus largely overlapped in practice. Demonologists were interested in 'preternatural' events because these, although still natural, were often demonic. Ultimately, though, the line that the demonologists were attempting to draw was between *those events that were caused by demons* and those that were not.

Demonologists' works were thus a kind of scientific enquiry. They were not scientific in the modern sense of relying on observation and experiment, since most of their work involved scholastic reasoning. (A tradition of alleged experiments with flying witches is discussed in the text box 'Experiments with witches?', p. 73.) But they were trying to 'explain the unexplained', and to extend the boundaries of knowledge, much as a modern scientist might do. They were not content to say that an event was 'preternatural', since that was to say little more than that it was hard to explain. They wanted to know the details – even if this led to the appalling revelation of the scale of demonic intervention in the world.

Demonologists could not usually perform experiments with witches, but they could gather data through witches' confessions. Some demonologists who were also witch-hunters presented their involvement in trials almost as a research project. By interrogating witchcraft suspects they could learn about the activities of witches and the powers of demons. Henri Boguet, a judge in Franche-Comté, drew extensively on cases from his own court when he published his *Discours des Sorciers* ('Discourse on Witches', 1602). He was particularly interested in witches who confessed to being werewolves, and complained that two of them had been 'hurried too quickly to their execution' before he could interview them to gather the details.[3]

Once they had gathered their data, the demonologists had to build a systematic argument from it. Sometimes their information was fragmentary, but, like many intellectuals, they did their best to extract significance from it and to find patterns in it. Nicolas Rémy studied a number of witchcraft confessions from Lorraine in the 1590s, and found one witch who said that the Devil at the sabbat made the witches report what harm they had committed. Rémy found this story attractive, and in his book he wrote that witches' reports to the Devil were standard practice.[4] Such details could also lead to debate. Pierre de Lancre reckoned that the confessions he had gathered in Labourd, France, provided valuable data on the Devil's mark. Lambert Daneau and Jean Bodin had previously written that the Devil marked only those witches of whose allegiance he was unsure. Lancre, however, argued against this, citing the fact that some of his greatest witches had marks, sometimes more than one.[5] With such debates, demonology thus became a field of expanding intellectual enquiry.

Natural and demonic magic

Modern scientists usually carry out experiments, but demonologists did not learn about magic through experiments. Partly this was because 'magic' was a pejorative term, defined by its critics (as we saw in Chapter 1). There was one much-repeated story of an experiment with a flying witch, but the experiment itself never seems to have occurred (see the text box 'Experiments with witches?'). A few unusual intellectuals did use magic in their research, but they hesitated to call it magic, knowing that this might attract criticism. They themselves felt that they were pursuing a legitimate enquiry into the workings of the natural, created world. If they could work out enough about the correspondences between different kinds of matter, they would be able to perform more complex operations on these, and learn more about what we would call science. A few such intellectuals, notably Cornelius Agrippa (1486–1535), did call their activities 'magic', but they defined this as a legitimate combination of natural philosophy, mathematics and theology. Even then, they attracted little support, so strong was the hostility to magic.

One reason why mainstream intellectuals were hostile to magic was that there was a potential shortcut to acquiring the magician's complex knowledge. Instead of educating himself in the detailed workings of the natural world, the magician might be able to summon assistance in the form of a spirit. This might be either the ghost of some learned human from the past, or an angel, or – more worryingly – a demon. The Devil and his demons were not only very clever but also very experienced; they had been around since the beginning of the world, and possessed detailed knowledge of its workings. If a magician could summon the aid of a demon, he might be able to achieve remarkable things.

So it is no wonder that churchmen were often suspicious of magic. They tended to think that much or all of it came from demons. Some of the magicians – both real, and imagined by their critics – were necromancers. These, as we saw in Chapter 2, used magical rituals to summon and control demons, but orthodox critics claimed that the demons were deceiving the necromancers and only pretending to be controlled. Critics also objected that necromancy involved making a pact with the demon.

Intellectual demons also entered the imaginations of orthodox thinkers through the Renaissance scholarly movement known as Neoplatonism. This originated when a collection of ancient philosophical and magical ideas became fashionable among some thinkers of the fifteenth and early sixteenth centuries. The first was Marsilio Ficino (1433–99), an authority on the pagan Greek philosopher Plato and his early-Christian successor Plotinus. Ficino sought to integrate Plato's philosophy with Christian theology; the term 'Neoplatonism' implied a renewal of Plato's ideas. This became more demonic when Ficino began to study the Greek writings ascribed to 'Hermes Trismegistos' ('Thrice-Honoured Hermes'), who was believed to have been an Egyptian sage contemporary with Moses and possessed of occult knowledge. These 'Hermetic' writings, on astrology and allied magical subjects, had actually been produced by several anonymous scholars in the second and third centuries CE, but Ficino thought that they were much older. The Hermetic writings' supposed connection with Moses seemed to offer the prospect of direct divine revelation. Ficino thus developed a view of the cosmos as inhabited by magical forces which could be understood and exploited. He drew down influences from the stars by musical incantations.

Neoplatonists, unlike Aristotelians, blurred the distinction between mind and matter. They saw everything in the universe as animated by spirits which influenced one another through a complicated (though harmonious) pattern of sympathies and antipathies. A leading branch of Neoplatonism was astrology – the idea that the heavenly bodies all had special properties that influenced life on earth. These spiritual forces followed laws which, in principle, it should be possible to observe and harness. Another branch of Neoplatonism was alchemy, attempting to use spiritual forces to change base metal into gold. (The alchemists, incidentally, were among the few thinkers who actually conducted experiments, though only in this limited field.) However, Neoplatonism was never entirely orthodox. The Neoplatonists' investigations into spiritual forces, indeed, horrified some orthodox Aristotelians, who thought that they were summoning up demons.

Neoplatonism declined in the seventeenth century; the false dating of the Hermetic writings was exposed in 1614. However, the Neoplatonists' ideas merged into further anti-Aristotelian trends. One enduring legacy of theirs was a belief that human beings had remarkable intellectual resources which could be applied to the understanding of the natural world. They were not fully 'scientific' in the sense of testing hypotheses by observation and experiment, but they helped to inspire the Scientific Revolution of the seventeenth century – of which more in Chapter 10.

Distorted echoes of popular belief

Through witches' confessions, then, demonologists assembled data on witches' nature and activities, with which to extend the framework of the knowledge they gained from scholastic theology. Confessions, negotiated between suspect and interrogator, tended to contain a mixture of popular and elite beliefs. Chapter 5 will try to give an accurate account of popular beliefs, as far as these can be reconstructed from surviving elite sources. However, in understanding the European witch-hunt, we also need to understand what the elite *thought* that the common folk believed. Even if the authorities' ideas about popular belief were incorrect, these ideas may still have shaped witch-hunting.

A number of late medieval writers described '*lamiae*': beings that flew out at night, entered houses through cracks, and killed and ate children. 'Lamia' was originally the name of a legendary queen of Libya, who killed children in some classical stories. In due course, *'lamia'* came to be a Latin word for a nocturnal being that could be translated as 'witch' (as could other Latin words for such beings, *'stria'* and *'masca'*), but it was far from clear that *lamiae* were human. As we shall see in Chapter 5, peasants probably did not believe in *lamiae* as such, but several things that they did believe in could be reinterpreted as *lamiae* – the Wild Hunt, or fairy cults, for instance. *Lamiae* and *striae* were sometimes said to kill people and then restore them to life for a short period – for instance by taking out the person's heart and replacing it with a wooden or straw heart. This sounds like an echo of the folk tradition of dark shamanism, also to be discussed in Chapter 5.

The word *'stria'* connects these ideas with ancient literature describing the classical Roman *strix*. The classical *strix* was a legendary female creature, resembling an owl, which flew at night, ate children and drank their blood. It was mainly, perhaps wholly, fictional. The name of the *strix* became *'striga'* or *'stria'* (plural *'striae'*) in medieval Latin, and even transferred itself to the vernacular Italian word for a witch, *'strega'*. Early in the middle ages, *striae* came to be seen as malevolent women rather than birds, which may indicate that the word was now being used to translate vernacular terms for malevolent women. However, a connection with popular belief is hard to establish. Several medieval law codes prescribed punishments for anyone calling a woman a *'stria'*. At first sight this seems to tell us that the common folk believed in *striae*, but the evidence is not so clear. Law codes are not actual trial records, and we do not know whether their authors had ever come across anyone calling anyone else a *'stria'* (or, more likely, a vernacular word translated as *'stria'*). One code, the Law of the Salian Franks (*c.*500 CE), prescribed a fine for any *stria* who was proved to have eaten someone.[6] It seems clear that the code's author would not have come across this actual crime, and this law may well be a misunderstanding of a classical source. It is possible that 'eating' was understood metaphorically (causing someone to waste away), but this illustrates how difficult these law codes are to interpret.

Overall, the connections between this material and popular belief were remote. Stories of *lamiae* and *striae* lost their prominence in demonologies of the sixteenth and seventeenth centuries; writers in these periods were more confident that they knew what witches were like. Some writers still used the words *'lamiae'* and *'striae'*, but they no longer treated them as distinct beings, still less as non-human beings; instead, *lamiae* and *striae* were simply 'witches'.

Witchcraft as a 'cumulative concept'

The pioneering witchcraft scholar Joseph Hansen proposed in 1901 the idea of a 'cumulative concept' of witchcraft, developing gradually during the late middle ages. This idea was an important breakthrough at the time, and has been repeated in most later works. Hansen realised that 'witchcraft' was not a single thing in itself. Various components had to be created, and to combine, before people could start prosecuting witches in significant numbers. Thought of in this way, the witchcraft concept is rather like a snowball rolling downhill, gathering new layers and becoming larger. This is part of how the developing concept of witchcraft should be understood, but not the whole of it. The concept of witchcraft did indeed 'develop', but it was not simply a matter of taking an 'incomplete' concept and adding new components until it became 'complete'. Sometimes it was a matter of combining existing elements in new patterns, and occasionally of removing or downgrading inappropriate ones.

To the extent that the 'cumulative concept' existed, it should be identified firmly as an intellectual idea. We shall see in Chapter 5 that there is little or no evidence that popular belief developed in a 'cumulative' way. Popular belief never needed to be systematic. Elite beliefs did aspire to be systematic; people expected inconsistencies to be ironed out by intellectual debate and enquiry. Some debate continued right through the witch-hunting period, but the broad outlines of witchcraft did come more or less to be agreed.

The conventional story of the 'cumulative concept' of witchcraft usually reaches a climax with the *Malleus Maleficarum* (1486), by which time the idea of the witch was complete, and serious witch-hunting was ready to begin. The assumption is that previous ideas of witchcraft had been incomplete, but now at last the final component was added. This, however, is not how the *Malleus* should be seen. The vital clue is the witches' sabbat, which had usually been prominent in earlier accounts of witchcraft, but about which the *Malleus* said hardly anything. Did its author, Heinrich Krämer, simply forget to discuss the sabbat? As we saw in Chapter 2, it is more likely that he downgraded it because he had not found it useful in the identification and prosecution of actual witches. The *Malleus* did indeed put the idea of witchcraft on a new, more systematic and more threatening basis, but this was because of ideas on witches' malefice that it took from popular belief. To do so, it had to detach the idea of witchcraft from earlier ideas about the sabbat that had more to do with heresy than with peasant malefice. The witches' sabbat later revived in sixteenth-century demonology, but in new ways. Unlike the ineffective medieval idea of the sabbat, these new ideas would be compatible with ideas about witches' malefice – ideas that were grounded both in the *Malleus* and in popular belief. What the *Malleus* did was to combine witches' malefice, or harmful magic, with theological ideas about demons.

If there was a 'cumulative' intellectual concept of witchcraft, then, it involved two different types of combination of ideas. The first and most basic combination was the one that we saw at the end of Chapter 2: the combination of *demonic conspiracy* and *harmful magic* under the single name of 'witchcraft'. This enabled intellectuals to believe that peasant women, often identified by their neighbours as practitioners of harmful magic, had also engaged in demonic conspiracy, and were thus 'witches' in this new sense.

Witchcraft and the intellectuals 67

They were no longer silly old women, but a secret organisation dedicated to the overthrow of Christian society.

Beyond this basic idea, the second level of the 'cumulative' concept consisted of the combined details of what witches did as members of their organisation. This did not develop like a snowball rolling downhill; it was more like a menu from which different thinkers could select or emphasise different options. The 'witches' sabbat', at which witches gathered with the Devil, was a common idea, but it could be understood in various ways.

Demonological ideas thus became coherent and mainstream with the *Malleus Maleficarum* in 1486. However, demonology continued to evolve for about another century and a half, until Pierre de Lancre in 1612, the last important writer of systematic demonology. After Lancre, little more was added to demonology, but it retained at least some significance and vitality for another century or so. The *Malleus* itself followed an earlier formative phase, discussed in Chapter 2, in which a group of writers in the 1430s developed the idea of a 'new sect' of heretical 'witches' gathering to carry out horrifying rites. It also drew on writers of the next generation, the 1440s and 1450s, who placed the 'new sect' more clearly within the framework of systematic theology. Instead of merely describing the sect, they delved into demonic theory and explained how witches and demons operated in theoretical terms.

Intellectual development implies debate, as new ideas were aired, tested and argued over. After the *Malleus*, writers first debated witches' flight, and then returned to the idea of the witches' sabbat. Subsequent sections of this chapter will trace these debates. First, however, we need to draw out some of the basic ideas about the Devil and the demonic pact, showing in more detail how ideas about the Devil's role fitted into Christian theology.

Medieval foundations: The Devil

The Devil and demons were fundamental to the cumulative concept of witchcraft. The basic idea of the Devil had been developed in the medieval period. The great medieval theologians had known little or nothing about witches, but they had provided the materials with which later demonologists could build an account of the relationship between the Devil and the witches. Here we need to begin with the Bible, because all medieval and early modern theologians had to think about this basic text and what it could tell them.

The Bible said a certain amount about the Devil, but not enough to provide a complete account of his nature and powers. Old Testament Judaism had been strongly monotheistic, with everything flowing from one God. There was little room for a Devil when God dealt out rewards and punished sins directly. The Old Testament contained five mentions of a *'satan'* (a Hebrew word meaning 'accuser' or 'adversary'), three of these in the story of Job where a being called 'Satan' suggested to God the idea of testing Job's faith through suffering, and then went and inflicted the suffering on him. The New Testament had more, with Jesus himself encountering the Devil, and with several other demons being mentioned. This allowed information about the Devil to be read back into the Old Testament too. For instance, the Old Testament did not say that the 'serpent' that tempted Eve in the Garden of Eden had been the Devil, but this was a logical elaboration of the story in Genesis. Using the scholastic method, early modern scholars did not have the option of considering the story of the Garden of Eden as an ancient Jewish myth, told by people who knew nothing of demonology. They had to treat the biblical text as the timeless and direct word of God – a firm foundation on which to build the latest knowledge.

There was even less in the Bible about witches, but there was just enough to support an argument that witches existed. The relevant texts were all in the Old Testament, separate from the material about the Devil which was largely in the New Testament. The Bible did not explain what witches did or even what they were, but it did at least give a memorably clear and direct statement about what should be done with them: 'Thou shalt not suffer a witch to live' (Exodus 22:18). This was the English translation; in the sixteenth century the Bible was translated into all the main vernacular languages, making it widely accessible (see the text box 'Words for witches' in Chapter 1, pp. 17–9). Scholars occasionally discussed the accuracy of the translation, and critics of witch-hunting tried to undermine it; but, for most educated people, there was no doubt. The Bible confirmed that 'witches' existed, and that they should die. And, if it did not explain what witches did or what they were, that meant that finding these things out was an important intellectual project.

The basic idea of the Devil had been worked out in the early middle ages by St Augustine, who developed Christian ideas in a systematic form that remained largely unchallenged thereafter. He established what Christians should believe about demons: they were really fallen angels, and the Devil was their leader. Augustine also established that the pagan gods (still widely worshipped in his time) were really demons. Augustine reasoned that, like angels, demons must be immortal and have remarkable powers. They were spirits with no physical bodies, but could make themselves imitation bodies out of condensed air. This allowed them to assume any shape, or to travel at great speed.

Demons could not perform actual miracles – these were reserved to God; but they could perform 'wonders' that mere humans would find hard to distinguish from miracles. One much-discussed biblical example was the contest between Aaron and Pharaoh's magicians, in which both sides turned their rods into serpents, and Aaron's serpent ate up the magicians' serpents (Exodus 7:8-12). Theologians reasoned that the magicians' serpents must have been demonic illusions. Demons could not create life, but could appear to do so by creating illusions, or by speeding up the generation of existing seeds. Augustine discussed demons' knowledge of the future, saying that demons did not have true foreknowledge (which was possessed only by

God), but that they were highly skilled in making deductions from their long experience and wide knowledge.

One of Augustine's most important contributions to demonology, and indeed to Christian theology generally, was to develop the concept of divine permission. God and the Devil were not equals, for God was greater and had in fact created the Devil. God had not *willed* the Devil to be evil; he had simply *permitted* him to become so. God was all-powerful ('almighty'), but allowed the beings he created some freedom. The same argument explained the 'fall' of Adam and Eve; God had not created them sinful, but they sinned through their own free will. The concept of divine permission was vital to demonology. The *Malleus Maleficarum* established this in the very first paragraph of its introduction, mentioning 'the three elements that co-operate to bring about witchcraft, namely, the demon, the witch and the permission of God'.[7] God permitted the Devil to afflict humans because he was angry at human sinfulness. This enabled demonologists to understand God's purpose in allowing witchcraft, and gave them a moral and evangelical message that they sought to spread widely. It is our fault that there are so many witches, they proclaimed, because, if we were better Christians, God would not permit the Devil to afflict us. In the meantime, of course, while humans remained sinful, the demonologists could stress the Devil's powers and activities, and their own importance in bringing this to light.

The powers of demons, though still with no relationship to witchcraft, became clearer with the work of William of Auvergne (d. 1249) and St Thomas Aquinas in the thirteenth century. They systematised existing theology, and showed how it could be reconciled with the knowledge of the natural world that was emerging from Aristotle's newly-rediscovered works. Aquinas produced a model of demons as contrary to human society, and thus as essentially disordered. However, they were ordered enough to be able to co-operate with each other, not out of a love of order but out of a common hatred of humans.

As to demons' place in the natural world, William and Aquinas confirmed that demons were pure spirits, and pointed out some logical inferences from this. Their counterfeit bodies would be unable to perform certain functions – notably eating, drinking and sexual intercourse. But there were many medieval stories of sex between demons and humans that had produced children (as well as an obscure biblical passage on the subject, Genesis 6:1-4), so they reasoned that a demon would be able to assume a female body (a 'succubus'), have sex with a man and capture his sperm, then change to a male body (an 'incubus') and have sex with a woman – impregnating her with the captured sperm. Aquinas was not sure that this really happened, but he said that *if* the stories about demonic offspring were true, this would be the explanation. Both William and Aquinas also pointed out that the resulting child would be fully human; half-human, half-demon beings were a logical impossibility. This conclusion was a small triumph of scholastic reasoning, achieved without any need to examine empirical evidence.

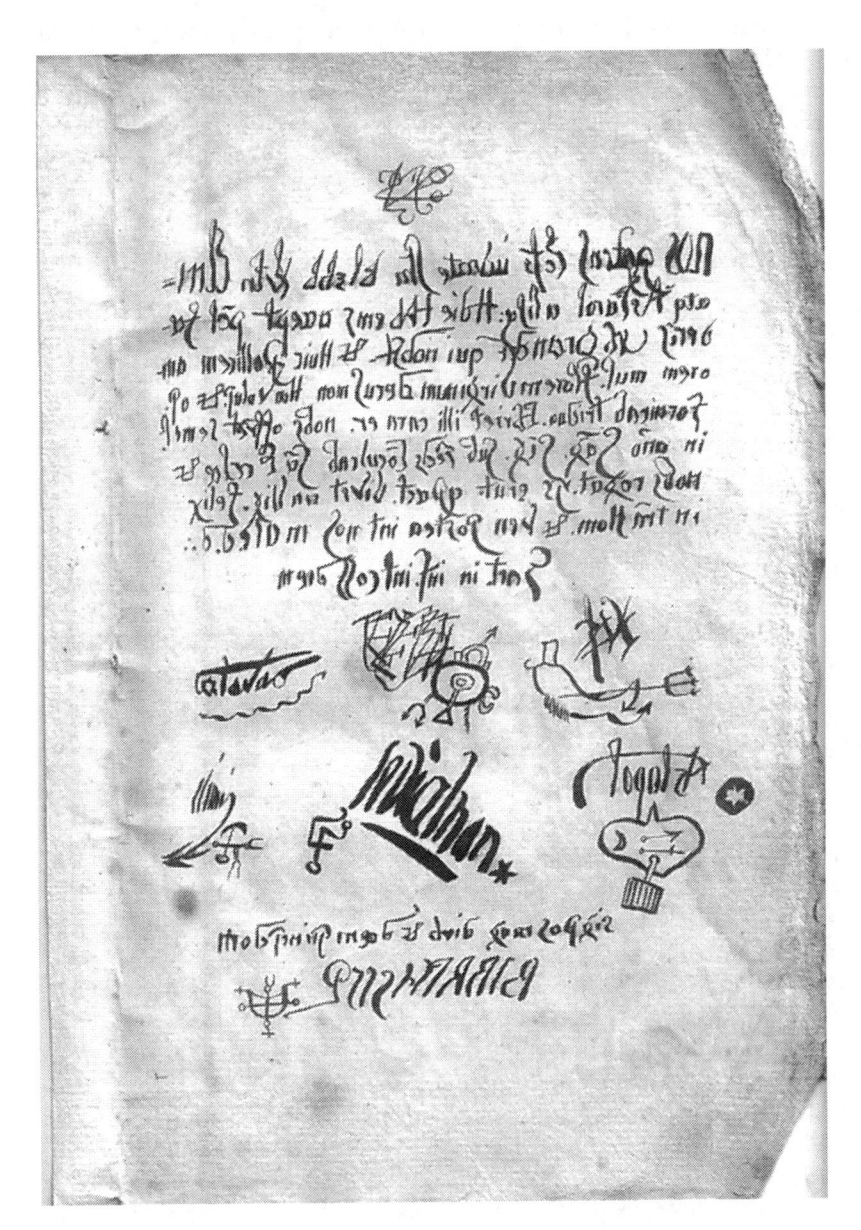

Illustration 3.1 An elaborate demonic pact, 1634

This written demonic pact was produced by the prosecutors at the trial of Urbain Grandier, executed for bewitching the nuns of Loudun, France, in 1634. The text, in Latin, is in mirror-writing, because demons were thought to do things backwards. Grandier's name ('Urb. Grand'') appears in the third line. The signatures, mostly not in mirror-writing but highly contorted, are by various demons, beginning with Satanas (centre left), then Beelzebub, Lefr, Elimi, Leviathan, Astaroth and Baalberith. This document represents the fruit of deep research into the names and habits of demons.

Aquinas developed two concepts of the demonic pact: an explicit and an implicit pact. In an explicit pact, the human appealed explicitly and directly to a demon. In an implicit pact, the human used a ritual that could only be effective through demonic help; this constituted a pact if the demon responded. Such rituals could include necromancy or other forms of divination, or casting spells. The ritual itself did not accomplish the desired result – it merely communicated with the demon, who did the real work. To Aquinas, even an 'explicit pact' was not an actual formally-negotiated agreement with the demon that took place at a particular moment; rather it was an understanding that certain ritual practices carried particular meanings. Aquinas, of course, was not thinking of witches. Later demonologists relied on his work but simplified it, concentrating on the explicit pact and interpreting it as a formally-negotiated agreement. Interrogators of witchcraft suspects often demanded details of when the suspect had met the Devil, and of how the pact had been agreed. Literate suspects could even be imagined to have made a pact in writing, and such documents were occasionally produced in court, as with the case of Urbain Grandier (see Illustration 3.1).

Early developments: The debate on witches' flight, 1440–1580

Once this groundwork had been laid, the first phase of demonological debate focused on witches' flight. The issue of flight could be a test case for the existence of witches. By the late fifteenth century, it had become clear that a group known as 'witches' existed, or at least was alleged to exist. The subsequent debate featured greater clarity about witches than before, identification of them as peasant women carrying out ordinary malefices, and detachment from heretical models. This debate began before the publication of the *Malleus* in 1486, but the *Malleus* played an important role in it. The key question was whether witches could fly.

The debate revolved around an ancient document: a medieval church decree, called the Canon *Episcopi*, that seemed to denounce belief in witches' flight as false and superstitious. The Canon *Episcopi* had been written in *c*.900 CE, but in our period it was thought to have been issued by an early council of the Christian church in 314 CE, and held high authority. (The word 'Canon' meant 'law', while '*Episcopi*', 'Bishops', was the first word of the main text.) Flying was the witches' most dramatic activity, so a statement that flying was impossible came close to saying that witches did not exist. And, if that statement was an authoritative law of the church, it could not be contradicted or ignored. It thus carried the potential to destroy intellectual witch belief. In the late fifteenth and early sixteenth centuries, the central task of the demonologist was to neutralise the Canon *Episcopi*.

The Canon *Episcopi* denounced a belief, which it said was held by some wicked women, that they travelled out at night, flying or riding on animals, in the company of the pagan goddess Diana. Such a belief, said the Canon, was a culpable illusion caused by the Devil, since bodily

72 Witchcraft and the intellectuals

flight was impossible. Today we can see that these women must have been members of a shamanistic cult of magical practitioners; several such cults will be discussed in Chapter 5. We can also see that the author of the Canon knew nothing of witches. But late medieval demonologists did not know this; they thought that the Canon was about flying witches, and that it could perhaps be interpreted as saying that flying witches did not exist.

Three arguments were used to get round the Canon *Episcopi*. One was to say that the Canon condemned only belief in Diana while flying, not belief in flying itself. This argument never became common, perhaps because it obviously twisted the words of the Canon. A second was to say that flying witches were a new sect which had arisen since the Canon was written, so that the Canon was irrelevant to them. This argument worked in the early fifteenth century, when all writers on witchcraft agreed that witches were a new sect – but, even by the later fifteenth century, the idea of a new sect was fading. The third argument, therefore, was to agree with the Canon that women flew in their imaginations – but to say that only *some* women did so, while other women flew bodily. The *Malleus* argued this third point strongly, and it became standard.

Demonologists seem to have been willing to accept the idea of bodily flight, and to overlook weaknesses in the argument. Heinrich Krämer, author of the *Malleus*, interrogated a suspect and reported that she had confessed that witches could fly either bodily or in their imaginations. It was vital to Krämer to prove this, so the woman's confession was highly convenient to him; indeed, he probably shaped it through leading questions. Unfortunately, if Krämer's theory were true, it would be more logical to assume that those witches who flew in their imaginations would believe that they were flying bodily – certainly this is what the tradition of experiments with witches implied (see the text box 'Experiments with witches?' on this). Thus, no witch who fitted Krämer's theory should have been able to confess to it. In his eagerness to gain corroborating evidence, Krämer forgot this logical flaw. Nor was he alone: Pierre de Lancre in 1612 related an equivalent story from confessions that he had obtained.[8]

On the whole, then, the *Malleus* tradition of circumventing the Canon *Episcopi* became mainstream. However, it was not universally accepted. Although Krämer was an inquisitor, the Inquisition itself was often sceptical. In 1526 the Spanish Inquisition held a conference of ten senior inquisitors to discuss witchcraft, concentrating on the issue of witches' flight. A discussion paper was submitted to the conference, arguing that witches did not exist because the acts they allegedly committed, especially flying, were impossible. The conference rejected this radical scepticism, but it did not reach a clear conclusion. Six of the inquisitors decided that witches flew bodily to the sabbat, as the *Malleus* had argued. The other four concluded that they flew only in their imaginations, as the Canon *Episcopi* had said – but, again following the Canon, this was still a matter for inquisitors since it involved backsliding from the faith. Later in this chapter we shall look at scepticism in more detail, but radical scepticism of the kind that denied the existence of witches had become almost impossible to sustain.

> ### Experiments with witches?
>
> As part of the debate on flying, a tradition arose of telling stories about experiments with flying witches. The story related that the experimenter – often a priest or judge – invited a self-identified 'witch' – always an old woman – to demonstrate how she flew. The witch conducted a ritual (sometimes she stripped naked and anointed her body with a flying ointment) which caused her to go into a trance overnight. In the morning she awoke and told of where she had travelled – but the experimenter proved to her that she, or at any rate her body, had been in the room all the time. Most of the writers relating this story said that they had heard it from the experimenter, or from someone who knew the experimenter – the classic 'friend of a friend' who originates urban legends today. Occasionally, writers said that they themselves had carried out the experiment. However, it is more likely that no experiments ever occurred, and that the story was simply repeated from earlier writers, as with the story of the pelican mentioned above.
>
> The flying experiment made an attractive story because it showed that elite men understood witches' flight better than peasant women. Ironically, most of the elite men wanted to prove the reality of witches' flight, and the story did not directly help them to do that. Still, it helped them to show respect for the Canon *Episcopi*, which was required from participants on all sides of the debate. Martin Delrio in 1599–1600 added an ingenious twist: the Devil had invented illusory flight in order to deceive humankind into believing that there were no witches.

Later developments: The revival of the sabbat, 1580–1612

The debate about witches' flight fed into the next phase of demonological development, in which the focus was on the witches' sabbat. This made sense, since flying witches were clearly going somewhere. Their destination, it could now be seen, was the place where they gathered to worship the Devil, so it was important to establish more about this. Late sixteenth-century authors virtually reinvented the witches' sabbat. An earlier, heretical sabbat had been discussed in the fifteenth century, but the debate on flight, and the loss of interest in heresy, had obscured it. As we saw in the last chapter, the *Malleus* had sidelined the sabbat, and in 1509 the sabbat was still barely in evidence in the demonological sermons of Johannes Geiler.[9] Later in the sixteenth century, a new sabbat emerged, now as a more elaborate idea. In its most elaborate form, indeed, it was a Catholic idea.

The new phase began in 1580 with Jean Bodin's book *Démonomanie* ('Demon-mania'). This was one of the most successful demonological works ever, going through at least twenty-three editions. Written in French, it was translated into Latin, German and Italian. Bodin, a lawyer, took a legal and political view of witchcraft as treason against God. He provided no set-piece description of the sabbat, but his chapters on flight, shape-shifting and sex between witches and demons contained a great deal about witches' meetings and what happened at them. Bodin's view proved influential, and later demonologists needed to do little more than develop his promptings.

Bodin tried to do for shape-shifting what the *Malleus* had done for flight. Pointing out that the limits of the Devil's power were unknown, he argued that, if the Devil could enable people to fly, he could also transform people into animals. However, the idea of real, physical shape-shifting never caught on. Later demonologists almost always specified that shape-shifting was an illusion caused by the Devil's power over the mind. Witches themselves were led to believe that they had turned into (say) a cat, while onlookers were also led to see a cat, but their physical body did not change. The reason, usually given without supporting argument, was that God would not permit the Devil to interfere with people's physical shape or size. Demonologists did not need to believe in real shape-shifting; illusory shape-shifting was perfectly acceptable, and never undermined demonology in the way that illusory flight had threatened to do.

With the acceleration of witch-hunting in the late sixteenth century, demonologists had a wealth of new material to draw on. Witches' confessions, relating their personal experience of the Devil, were evidently well suited to the purpose of demonology. Peter Binsfeld in 1589 developed Bodin's themes further. By 1595, Nicolas Rémy could give a coherent and detailed account of the sabbat, which became further elaborated with Delrio in 1599–1600. The new-style sabbats were also depicted in art, for the first time, in the 1590s. Until then, witches had been depicted singly, or in twos and threes. Now there were crowds of witches with multiple activities and prominent demons, as in Illustration 3.2.

The method of 'inversion' allowed new ideas to be developed by inverting existing ones. The sabbat was sometimes conceived as a parody of a Christian church service, with the witches performing disgusting rituals of 'worship' such as kissing the Devil's anus, and behaving in a disorderly and irreverent way. Another idea about the sabbat treated it as a parodic 'inversion' of a feast or party, with the witches sharing foul food and drink, or dancing naked and back to back instead of face to face. The sabbat could also use inversion of political models. Johann Fischart, who made an adapted German translation of Bodin, called the sabbat a '*Hexenreichstag*' ('witches' parliament').[10] Rémy saw it as an inverted feudal ceremony, with the Devil as feudal lord.

Other kinds of sabbat relied less on inversion. Some writers called it the 'race' ('*cursus*'), thinking of the witches' meeting not as a stationary

Illustration 3.2 Witches' sabbat on the Blocksberg, 1668

This witches' sabbat, on a mountain in central Germany, shows the fully-developed intellectual idea of the sabbat, involving large numbers of witches and various activities. In the centre, a witch worships the Devil, in the form of a goat, by kissing his anus. A procession of witches and demons circles the mountain, with music and dancing. Some of the witches are naked. A witch stirs a cauldron, preparing harmful potions, surrounded by magical animals (centre right). Witches fly on goats (top; one has fallen off) or on a forked cooking-stick (bottom left). A demon defecates into a cauldron (bottom). A demon and a witch make love (bottom right). The caption, '*Bloks-Bergs Verrichtung*', means 'Blocksberg Performance'.

gathering but as a collective flight or journey. Others called it the 'game' ('*ludus*'), borrowing a term from visionary folkloric cults who sometimes used this word for their spirit voyages (on which more in Chapter 5). Early modern witches were always assumed to have a relationship of some kind with the Devil, and to perform harmful magic of some kind, but there were many different ways in which the details could be understood. It should be remembered that the term 'witches' sabbat', though historians have adopted it for convenience, was far from universal at the time, and the concept was not entirely homogeneous either.

The new-style sabbats also drew on older beliefs. Most of the fifteenth-century ideas of horrifying rites were now revived. The Devil often had sex with the witches, and sometimes there were indiscriminate sexual orgies. Babies were killed and eaten, or dug up from graves and eaten, or their fat was used to make demonic ointments. These infanticidal stories were hardly ever connected with real, named babies. Peasants sometimes feared that witches would kill their babies, but they did not fear that their babies' bodies would be taken to the sabbat for ritual use. The sabbat was an elite fantasy.

In theory there was no reason why the Devil should not use witches to inflict well-recognised diseases or other ordinary misfortunes on people. In practice, most intellectuals preferred to ignore this possibility. If they admitted that witches could be behind *any* misfortune, no matter what, they risked abandoning any sense that humans could recognise witchcraft as a distinct phenomenon. For the common folk, this was not a problem; as we shall see in Chapter 4, it was the witch's vengefulness that enabled them to distinguish witch-inflicted misfortunes from other misfortunes, and they could identify the vengefulness directly, from the witch's own quarrelsome behaviour. However, the intellectuals' theory of how witchcraft was identified relied on preternatural feats accomplished by demons, not on village quarrels.

The elaborated concept of witchcraft

At this point it may help to summarise the components of demonological witchcraft, as they finally came together around 1600. It could be called the 'cumulative concept' of witchcraft, but calling it the 'elaborated concept' may call attention more clearly to the fact that it was a late development.[11] The earlier, crucial stages, discussed in Chapter 2, were to identify 'witches' as a heretical sect, and then to combine harmful magic with demonic conspiracy at the time of the *Malleus Maleficarum*. That basic combination allowed people to identify 'witches' more clearly than before, and to find them in ordinary villages; that was enough to facilitate witch-hunting. In the course of the sixteenth century, ideas of witches were not only clarified but also elaborated. More details of the picture were filled in, until the elaborated concept looked something like the following summary. A diagrammatic version of the elaborated concept is shown in Diagram 3.1.

Witchcraft and the intellectuals 77

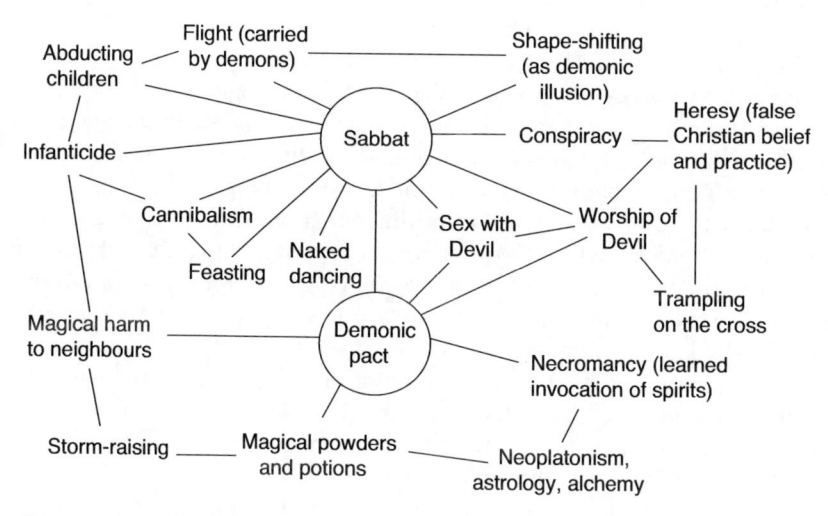

Diagram 3.1 The demonic witch

First, witches existed – or, to put this in the way that demonologists wished it to be understood, it was *necessary to believe* that witches existed. It was important that witches were mainly women, though it was usually noted that there were also some men. Discussion on witches' motives reached no consensus – lust or anger were the main ideas – but there was no doubt that they were wicked. Witches entered deliberately into a formal agreement with the Devil, by which they gained harmful powers in return for transferring their allegiance from God to the Devil. The Devil was enabled to do this, and everything else, by the permission of God, who permitted witchcraft and other afflictions through his anger at human sinfulness. The Devil often made deceitful promises to witches or gave them deceitful rewards, such as money that turned to leaves or dung. The Devil sealed the demonic pact by giving witches a mark on their bodies – either a skin blemish or an insensitive spot. This initiated the individual witch into a broader conspiracy. The idea of 'heresy' faded from view in most later demonologies; the idea was never contradicted, but witches, although still conspiratorial, no longer needed to be a heretical sect. Witches were simply witches.

Witches were thus enabled by the Devil to exercise harmful powers. Accounts of these powers varied. The everyday harmful magic feared by peasants also featured in many demonologies, but demonologists often stressed more unusual and collective malefices. Raising of storms, especially hailstorms, featured more in demonologies than in actual trials. The same applies to interference with sexual intercourse. As well as committing everyday malefices, witches also committed further harm at the sabbat, as we shall see.

The sabbat was usually reached by flight, and details were usually given as to how witches flew. Vehicles for flight were often specified (forked cooking-stick, broomstick, demonic animal); even more common were accounts of ointments or spells for flight. Witches might be transformed into animals, either for flight or for other purposes; this shape-shifting was a demonic illusion, but it was such a convincing illusion (both to the witch and to others) that it emphasised demonic power and ingenuity.

The sabbat itself could be at a named destination, often a mountain or sometimes a meadow. Sabbats were almost always at night, which was associated with evil and death. The Devil would be present, as, often, would be other demons. The central point of the sabbat was worship of the Devil, sometimes by kissing his anus; attacks on Christianity were also common, such as desecration of the host or trampling the cross. These motifs are a reminder that elaborate sabbats were often Catholic. The Devil sometimes preached to the witches, though the fifteenth-century idea of instruction in magical techniques was less prominent later.

The sabbat was often linked with malefice, though rarely of the everyday kind feared by villagers. Demonologists described witches working at the sabbat to prepare ointments or powders for future malefices. Planning of these malefices could be discussed, while the Devil sometimes received reports of harm done. He might discipline witches, for instance beating those who had not committed enough malefices. Since ointments for malefice were often made from children's body parts, the sabbat also saw the killing of babies and children. The origin of these children was often vague. A few demonologists explained that they were either the witches' own children, or others that had been abducted to the sabbat; however, these were never traced back to real children. Hailstorms were another stereotypical element of collective malefice; many demonologies described hailstorms, and illustrators often depicted witches collectively brewing hailstorms, but most of these hailstorms remained imaginary. Intellectual discussion of such malefices occurred, not in response to real harm, but as an attempt to answer the intellectual question 'What happens at the sabbat?'

Cannibalistic feasts were a common feature of sabbats, at least in southern Europe. Other food at the feasts was usually disgusting, and often omitted bread and salt (which had Christian associations). Northern European sabbats tended to emphasise dancing – often in an inverted way, back to back or even upside down, and often with the dancers naked. The idea of nakedness was connected with the idea of sexual activity, and intercourse often happened at the sabbat – either between the Devil and individual female witches, or in the form of indiscriminate sexual orgies.

Finally, one common occurrence at sabbats – at least it was a common story about them – was that a non-witch intruder would mention the name of God and cause the whole assembly to vanish. Sometimes the intruder was left stranded in a remote location. Unlike most components of the sabbat, the idea of the non-witch intruder came from folklore, in which the key point was the breach of a taboo. Demonologists adopted the idea because it fitted into their broader framework of the relative powers of the Devil and God.

Varieties of scepticism

Demonological ideas were mainstream from about 1450 onwards, and until about 1650 they could readily surmount open challenges to them. But there were always currents of scepticism. The existence of witches could never be taken for granted. Most 'sceptical' arguments were expressed by writers who generally accepted the existence of witches, but some writers criticised ideas of witches on a broader front. Before about 1650, very few attacked the whole of demonology. Piecemeal attacks by handfuls of critics on various aspects of demonology may even have stimulated orthodox demonologists to develop more persuasive ideas. Overall, demonology in the fifteenth and sixteenth centuries was a cutting-edge intellectual topic, expanding in sophistication. Debate on it took various forms and examined various themes, and it is useful to look at each of these 'sceptical' themes in turn – first looking at the way in which scepticism was structured by the Renaissance.

The Renaissance brought new artistic and intellectual ideas – including new ideas about magic. It was a time of confident intellectual discovery, partly based on classical learning. People thought that they could discover new things from a closer study of ancient authors. It was realised that Aristotle was not the only ancient philosopher to have studied the natural world, and that other philosophers had other theories. The Copernican, sun-centred view of the cosmos began to gain credibility in the seventeenth century when its proponents argued that it had been put forward by the ancient Greek thinker Epicurus (c.341–270 BCE).

People also thought that they could discover new things *directly*, rather than picking up where the last late-medieval thinker left off. Thinkers in the Renaissance no longer assumed that their immediate forebears must have been wiser than they were. Some Renaissance scholars, like Erasmus (1466–1536), were quite rude about their immediate forebears. New currents of thought were in motion, and these had the potential to undercut traditional ideas – including demonology to the extent that it was regarded as a traditional idea.

Scepticism was not a dominant way of thinking during the Renaissance. Many intellectuals were theologians, who were required to accept large quantities of dogma without question. Thinkers enquiring into the natural world tended either to accept orthodox Aristotelianism, or to be magicians. Still, there were particular Renaissance lines of scepticism that questioned received authority. Aristotelianism still reigned, but not without challenge. Pierre de la Ramée (1515–72) made a radical attack on Aristotle.

By contrast, Aristotle's own ideas were mobilised in a sceptical way by Pietro Pomponazzi (1462–1525). He was a fully Aristotelian philosopher – indeed more deeply Aristotelian than most thinkers of his day, who used Aristotle in a conventional way. He argued persuasively that Aristotle's own philosophy did not support the existence of demons, challenging the way in which Aquinas had Christianised Aristotle's ideas. Pomponazzi argued that a true Aristotelian should seek to explain reports of witches' malefice as having non-demonic causes. His book on this, *De Naturalium Effectuum Causis* ('The Causes of Effects in Nature'), was published posthumously in 1567. Pomponazzi had few direct disciples, but his erudite arguments could not be ignored.

One characteristically Renaissance line of scepticism was linguistic. With growing scholarly interest in the ancient languages, some sceptics refused to take the Old Testament references to 'witches' at face value. Several authors including Weyer and Scot (on whom more in a moment) proposed alternative translations of the Hebrew word used in Exodus 22:18; they usually argued that it really meant 'poisoner'. In the fifteenth century this would no doubt have been met with the reply that witches were a new sect, but, by the sixteenth century, demonologists preferred to regard witches as having always existed, and sought to use the Bible to support their position. Lengthy linguistic arguments thus ensued.

Another line of Renaissance scepticism was philosophical. Thinkers seized on the newly-rediscovered ideas of the ancient Greek philosopher Pyrrho (*c*.365–275 BCE), who had argued that nothing could be known for certain and that all statements about the world contained an element of doubt. This was attractive to Protestants, happy to separate faith and reason, who could use 'Pyrrhonian' scepticism to undermine Catholic claims to infallible truth. Some non-dogmatic Catholics also espoused it since it pointed to the advantages of a quiet life. Pyrrhonian scepticism could be corrosive to religious dogma of any kind – and demonology was particularly vulnerable to it. Demonology extended religious dogma beyond the core doctrines of Christianity, demanding that people accept *as absolute truth* that witches flew, that they raised storms, and so forth. Demonology also demanded that people should be so sure about this that they would be prepared to burn witches at the stake. Yet the idea that anything could be an absolute truth was specifically what the Pyrrhonians denied, and burning witches at the stake was hardly seeking a quiet life. The best-known Pyrrhonian sceptic was the celebrated French essayist Michel de Montaigne (1533–92), with his famous doubting question, '*Que sais-je?*' ('What do I know?'). Montaigne kept his remarks about witchcraft brief, probably for the sake of a quiet life, but he made it plain that he disapproved of witch-hunting and that he interpreted witchcraft in medical rather than criminal terms.

This leads on to the issue of medical scepticism. Once demonologists began to use witches' confessions as evidence for witchcraft, it was open to sceptics to argue on medical grounds that the witches were deluded and that their confessions should not be believed. An early instance of such an argument came from the distinguished Italian lawyer Andrea Alciati, who in

1544 remarked in a much-quoted essay that witches whom he had encountered should have been given medical treatment rather than being executed. In 1563 the medical argument was expounded at much greater length by the Dutch physician Johann Weyer, in a book called *De Praestigiis Daemonum* ('The Devil's Tricks'). Witches were not really evil, but were tricked by the Devil. Typically they were old women suffering from 'melancholy', a medical condition loosely comparable to what today is called depression. They wished to do harm but were incapable of actually doing so, and should receive medical treatment rather than punishment.

Weyer's arguments were much discussed, and his book was a bestseller, but he attracted little support. Another physician, Thomas Erastus, countered in 1571 that melancholy produced visions that varied randomly, whereas the witches' confessions were homogeneous. Weyer had also left himself vulnerable by arguing that the witches were still guilty of making an agreement with the Devil, and still wished to do harm – which might be thought to differ little from the standard demonological position that witches' malefices were worked on their behalf by a demon. Bodin in particular attacked Weyer mercilessly on these grounds. The debate on Weyer's arguments contributed to the revival of demonology in the late sixteenth century. Weyer's name became that of a notorious defender of witches, repeatedly denounced for the next century or so.

Another line of scepticism may be called 'evangelical'. The usual version of the argument was linked with the evangelical drive to spread correct Christianity to the masses, which will be discussed further in Chapter 6. Priests and pastors warned the common people to turn to God for protection, and not to consult magical practitioners. By extension, Protestant pastors in particular often warned people not to blame witches for their misfortunes; misfortunes often came from God, rather than witches, as punishments for sin or as tests of one's faith. These arguments did not deny the existence of witches, but they reduced their importance.

Some evangelical arguments were particularly associated with Catholics, who were also concerned to eradicate 'superstition' in the sixteenth century. Pedro Ciruelo's *Treatise Reproving All Superstitions and Forms of Witchcraft* (1530) was influential in Spain, repeatedly reprinted for a century. Ciruelo condemned necromancy, lot-casting, divination by omens or dreams, charms to acquire riches or success, magical healing, and many other such practices. He also condemned witchcraft, but the general thrust of his attack was against magical practitioners, and witches were only a minor part of his and others' drive to reform popular Catholic Christianity.

A more radical version of evangelical scepticism was propounded in England by Reginald Scot in 1584, in his book *The Discoverie of Witchcraft*. This did deny the existence of witches. Scot, taking a familiar Protestant argument but pushing it further than most, dismissed witch-belief as a remnant of Catholic superstition. Drawing on Weyer and Pomponazzi, Scot argued that the Devil, as a spirit, simply could not affect the physical world, and was sometimes little more than a metaphor. Scot treated all 'preternatural' events as simply natural, and witches as silly old women who should not be taken seriously. These arguments struck at the very roots of demonology. Scot was certainly denounced, as Weyer had been, but he was harder to refute. Perhaps the simplest counterargument, made by William Perkins in the 1590s, was to observe that God was also a spirit but could still affect the physical world. Scot's influence is hard to assess. He wrote in English, an unfamiliar language on the Continent; however, his book was translated into Dutch in 1609 and seems to have been influential in the Netherlands at least.

A final strand of scepticism can be mentioned briefly here; it will receive fuller discussion in Chapter 6. This was what can be called *'politique'* scepticism. As a reaction to the religious wars of the sixteenth century, a strand of conciliatory political thought arose whose supporters were often called *'politiques'* ('pragmatists'). These thinkers argued that the troubled times called for religious reconciliation, not dogmatic partisanship. The Pyrrhonian sceptics like Montaigne, mentioned above, tended to be *politiques*. Demonology, by contrast, encouraged a dogmatic view of the world.

The need to believe

Demonologists' own arguments about witchcraft always had the possibility of scepticism built into them. Henri Boguet opened his 1602 treatise as follows: 'It is astonishing that there should still be found to-day people who do not believe that there are witches. For my part I suspect that the truth is that such people really believe in their hearts, but will not admit it.'[12] Boguet wanted his readers to conclude that belief in witchcraft was normal, because the evidence was so strong. He can, however, be read as meaning that belief in witchcraft was contested or difficult. It is hard to imagine anyone in 1602 writing, 'It is astonishing that there should still be found to-day people who do not believe in horses'. The existence of horses did not have to be argued for: the existence of witches did.

This was because the demonologists placed the existence of witches in a similar conceptual category to the existence of God: it was a matter of faith. They thought of their faith as something that was not only true, but also *had to be believed*. Theologians did not debate seriously whether God existed or not, but they were adept at logical arguments proving that he existed, and it bothered them that others might not believe. The existence of horses did not have to be argued for, *not* because horses were obvious, but because theologians did not care whether people believed in horses or not. With witches, they did care. The existence of witches might or might not be obvious, but it *had to be believed*.

Genres of demonology

The peak period for witch-hunting was the age of the Baroque in art and literature – an age of lush imagery. Baroque religion, especially in Catholic countries, promoted elaborate visions of heaven and hell, and emphasised the details of human depravity. Demonologists were intensely concerned with human depravity. They also made a powerful appeal to the imagination, and any attempt to understand the cultural impact of witchcraft must take into account the various genres in which witchcraft ideas were expressed. It makes sense to concentrate on books of 'demonology' that were recognised at the time to be important, but part of these books' importance is that their ideas spread into other intellectual and cultural forums. Although demonology was at heart a scholarly enterprise, it was also expressed in culture, literature and art.[13]

The most recognisable works of 'demonology' themselves took various forms. The most characteristic format for early demonological works was the scholastic treatise. Works like the *Malleus* tended to grind through proposition and counter-proposition in a way that can disorientate modern readers unfamiliar with the scholastic method. Other writers used a dialogue format, almost like the script of a play, with two or more speakers. This was a more accessible and literary genre, favoured by Renaissance humanists, which allowed discussion of different views without the rigidity of the scholastic format. Some demonological works took the form of personal accounts, often based on the evidence of specific trials or groups of trials. Larger works using trial evidence tended to become encyclopedic collections of anecdotal material. Later authors like Francesco Maria Guaccio (1608) collected and recycled cases from previous authors. This encyclopedic genre would continue beyond the era of systematic demonology, feeding into the seventeenth-century attempt to gather credible empirical data, which will be discussed in Chapter 10.

Individual works could possess several of these features. In contrast to the encyclopedic mode of writing, yet sometimes co-existing with it in the same work, was the polemical mode. Many demonologists were sharply argumentative, aiming their polemics at various targets. Early writers usually wrote against heretics, but, as time went on, the targets shifted. Some later writers attacked witchcraft sceptics, others targeted popular superstition and ignorance. After the Reformation, some demonological works were anti-Protestant, others anti-Catholic. Finally, demonologies could contain practical manuals on prosecution procedure. From the *Malleus* onwards, it was common for works of systematic demonology to have a final chapter, or even several chapters, demanding rigorous punishment for witches and describing how judges should proceed in witchcraft cases.

Witchcraft is always and everywhere about stories people tell – and good stories carry their own meanings and even truth. The people of our period understood a great deal of their world by means of stories that they might agree, on one level, were untrue. For instance, as Christians, they knew that the classical gods were not real, but they often depicted and discussed them in art and literature. Renaissance thinkers entered so deeply into the classical world that classical stories possessed high authority for them. They found classical texts full of material on magic, prophecy, divination and transformation, which they incorporated into their own world-view. There were not many classical witches, but there were enough for this purpose. The most famous classical witch was Circe, who transformed Odysseus's companions into pigs in Homer's *Odyssey*. The *Odyssey* was a story – but Circe was often thought to be real, and was solemnly cited as a witch in numerous demonologies.

Even stories that were manifestly fiction could be influential, such as *Celestina* by Ferdinando de Rojas (1499), which has been claimed as the first European novel. Celestina was an elderly prostitute, procuress and magical practitioner, an expert in love-magic. She could conjure up demons and concoct powerful potions. Whether she was intended to be a 'witch' in the demonological sense is debatable, but her story, and many others like it, provided part of the cultural context in which witchcraft came to be discussed.

People could certainly draw a line between fact and fiction when it mattered to them, but sometimes the line was hard to draw. An actor in Avignon, France, in 1470, had to summon a demon on stage. He took the precaution in advance of registering a legal statement that he did not mean it – in case the Devil really came to claim him.[14] At the other, incautious extreme, an English witch pamphlet of 1592 was presented as factual, but drew wholesale on a recent comic play.[15] This may be seen as dishonest, but it is perhaps little more than the standard willingness of demonologists – or any intellectuals of the time – to believe and to retell specific stories when they carried plausible cultural meanings and fitted into an existing intellectual framework.

Demonologies thus blurred the boundaries between fact and fiction. Pierre de Lancre, in his elaborate accounts of the sabbat, strove for sensational literary effect as much as for academic accuracy.[16] Even the *Malleus*, dry treatise though it was overall, included entertaining stories. For instance, 'a certain saintly man' found the Devil preaching in a church and denouncing people's sins. The saintly man asked the Devil after the sermon why he did this. The Devil replied, 'Well, I tell the truth, because I know that when they listen to the Word but do not act on it, God is more offended and my profit increased.'[17] This story seems to be a kind of fable. It would have made a good anecdote for a popular preacher – and the author, a Dominican friar, was a preacher by profession.

The blurring of fact and fiction was notable in the visual arts. Hardly any images of witches were actual portraits of real people (Illustration 1.1 above is a rare exception). Pictures were generally no closer to reality than what we might today call 'reconstructions'. These reconstruction efforts drew on academic learning, but they were also imaginative – often primarily imaginative. Illustration 3.2, showing a witches' sabbat, was published in a book that was mainly a literary exercise by a professional writer, Johann Praetorius. The word 'infotainment' was coined only in the late twentieth century, but it could well be used to describe many demonological works.

Conclusion: From demonology to witch-hunting

Later chapters of this book will discuss the spread of witchcraft trials. A concluding question for the present chapter is: What was the relationship between demonological books and witchcraft trials? Did the books stimulate the trials, or were the books written after the trials as a kind of retrospective justification? The simplest answer is that both of these ideas are correct in some cases. Some demonologies were written by witchcraft judges, in order to share and disseminate their experiences, to promote their own importance, or to justify their conduct in the face of criticism. The *Malleus Maleficarum* was one such work, with its author, Heinrich Krämer, having been frustrated in attempting to prosecute witches at Innsbruck, Austria, in 1485. Some other demonologists, too, had been involved in controversial trials, such as King James VI of Scotland (in the 1590s) and Pierre de Lancre in France (in 1609), and had scores to settle with their critics.

However, even if demonologies were written after trials, they could still stimulate further trials. The publication of the *Malleus* in 1486 was followed by an eighty-year lull in witch-hunting; but when witch-hunting finally took off, in the late sixteenth century, the *Malleus* was rapidly reprinted and took a natural role as an important witch-hunting manual. It remained the most commonly cited demonological work among Catholics in south Germany in the early seventeenth century. Peter Binsfeld (1589) and Martin Delrio (1599–1600) were also used, but they in any case followed a broadly similar line to the *Malleus*. Both demonologies and confessions gradually gained in detail. In the 1590s, in the early years of confessions to the witches' sabbat in Bamberg and Würzburg, the sabbats that were described were still sketchy; only later did they become elaborate.[18]

The relationship between the trials and the demonologies was thus mutually reinforcing. This can be illustrated from the way in which Binsfeld's demonological ideas may well have provided a starting point for the elaborate confession of Jean Delvaulx, a monk from the prince-bishopric of Liège, Germany, in 1595–97. Delvaulx confessed to witnessing a hierarchy of demons at the sabbat, presided over by Beelzebub with two assistants, Leviathan and Astaroth. Binsfeld was interested in this; he had devised a classification of demons, with principal demons in charge of each of the seven deadly sins. Binsfeld had also been involved in the prosecution of Diederich Flade and others at Trier, the neighbouring prince-bishopric to Liège, in 1589, and Delvaulx mentioned having seen Flade at the sabbat.[19] Delvaulx' trial in turn fed into the work of the learned Jesuit Martin Delrio, who used a number of examples from it. However, Delrio was unusually detached from recent trials, determined to press home the argument that witches were nothing new, but had existed in all times and at all places. He had edited Seneca's tragedies, and the 'witch' with whom he was most intimately familiar was the classical Medea from the story of Jason and the Argonauts. Nevertheless, he filled his three-volume book, *Disquisitiones Magicae* ('Disquisitions on Magic', 1599–1600), with practical as well as theoretical material. It became perhaps the most influential demonology of the seventeenth century, often reprinted up to 1755.[20]

Although demonologies influenced trials, they did not become known everywhere. They certainly spread widely, aided by the use of Latin as a common language of learning. Most demonologies were written in Latin or translated into Latin. Some were also translated into vernacular languages, which no doubt helped their spread, but they could spread without translation; the *Malleus* itself was translated only into Polish. Demonology stopped, however, at the eastern boundaries of Latin Christendom. The Orthodox churches, which did not use Latin and whose theologians were not university-educated, were little affected by it. Russia had trials for harmful magic but did not combine harmful magic with demonic conspiracy, while Greece and the Balkan states were occupied by the Ottoman Empire, whose Muslim rulers did not allow any witch-hunting.

In many places even within Latin Christendom, some components of demonic witchcraft remained unknown. The elaborate sabbat of the later demonologists seems to have been particularly restricted. In most of Denmark and Norway, for instance, witchcraft prosecutions were largely for malefice, with a basic demonic pact but little more. In one part of Norway – Finnmark, in the far north – a more elaborate demonic sabbat occurred, with witches flying to large gatherings where they danced, feasted and worshipped the Devil. This was evidently imported from Scotland, where demonology was well known. A Scotsman, John Cunningham, was appointed governor of Finnmark in 1619, and demonic elements appeared in trials from 1620 onwards. Even in Finnmark, the demonic sabbat had a notable gap: sex with the Devil was entirely absent. This element of demonology was standard in Scotland, but was somehow mislaid in transit to Finnmark.[21]

Still, ideas did spread widely. It is sometimes said that the witches' sabbat was not known in England, but this is misleading. The sabbat was rarely mentioned in trials, because English law, unusually, required proof of specific magical harm; evidence of attending a sabbat was useless in court. Yet, although English demonological writers certainly spent longer on matters relevant to their own law, they were quite willing to discuss flight and other aspects of sabbat belief. The physician William Drage in 1665 cited Weyer, Bodin, Rémy and others, as well as English case studies, to prove witches' flight.[22] Overall, then, sabbats, and other aspects of elaborated demonology, were particularly important in those countries and periods where intense serial witch-hunts occurred. For most of Europe, most of the time, witches were prosecuted one by one – a topic to be considered in the next chapter. Here the sabbat was less crucial, but demonological ideas still validated the idea of witchcraft as a whole.

Notes

1. Pierre de Lancre, *On the Inconstancy of Witches: Pierre de Lancre's Tableau de l'inconstance des mauvais anges et demons (1612)*, ed. and trans. Harriet Stone and Gerhild Scholz Williams (Turnhout, 2006), 99 (II.i.14). Reproduced with permission of Brepols Publishers.
2. Ulric Molitor (Müller), *Des sorcières et des devineresses*, trans. Emile Nourry (Paris, 1926), 79 (ch. 14).
3. Henri Boguet, *An Examen of Witches*, trans. E. A. Ashwin, ed. Montague Summers (London, 1929), 138.
4. Nicolas Remy, *Demonolatry*, trans. E. A. Ashwin, ed. Montague Summers (London, 1930), 68 (I.22).
5. Lancre, *On the Inconstancy of Witches*, 205–6 (III.ii.5).
6. Valerie I. J. Flint, *The Rise of Magic in Early Medieval Europe* (Oxford, 1993), 297.
7. *Malleus*, 3A (introduction to I.i).
8. *Malleus*, 105A–B (II.i.3); Lancre, *On the Inconstancy of Witches*, 115–16 (II.i.5).
9. Rita Voltmer, 'Du discours à l'allégorie: Représentations de la superstition, de la magie et de la sorcellerie dans les sermons de Johannes Geiler de Kaysersberg', in Antoine Follain and Maryse Simon (eds.), *Sorcellerie savante et mentalités populaires* (Strasbourg, 2013), 45–88, at p. 67.
10. Gerhild S. Williams, *Defining Dominion: The Discourses of Magic and Witchcraft in Early Modern France and Germany* (Ann Arbor, Mich., 1995), 68.
11. Wolfgang Behringer, *Witchcraft Persecutions in Bavaria*, trans. J. C. Grayson and David Lederer (Cambridge, 1997), 13–15.
12. Boguet, *Examen*, p. xvii.
13. Lyndal Roper, 'Witchcraft and the Western imagination', *Transactions of the Royal Historical Society*, 6th series, 16 (2006), 117–42.
14. Richard Kieckhefer (ed.), *Forbidden Rites: A Necromancer's Manual of the Fifteenth Century* (University Park, Pa., 1997), 16.
15. Marion Gibson (ed.), *Women and Witchcraft in Popular Literature, c.1560–1715* (Aldershot, 2007), p. xvii.
16. Nicole Jacques-Chaquin, 'La fable sorcière, ou *le labyrinthe des enchantements*', *Littératures classiques*, 25 (1995), 87–96.
17. *Malleus*, 125B–C (II.i.9).
18. Robert Walinski-Kiehl, 'La chasse aux sorcières et le sabbat des sorcières dans les évêchés de Bamberg et Würzburg (vers 1590–vers 1630)', in Nicole Jacques-Chaquin and Maxime Préaud (eds.), *Le sabbat des sorciers en Europe (XVe–XVIIIe siècles)* (Grenoble, 1993), 213–25, at p. 217.
19. Lea, *Materials*, iii, 1223.
20. Jan Machielsen, *Martin Delrio: Demonology and Scholarship in the Counter-Reformation* (Oxford, 2015).
21. Liv Helene Willumsen, 'Exporting the Devil across the North Sea: John Cunningham and the Finnmark witch-hunt', in Julian Goodare (ed.), *Scottish Witches and Witch-Hunters* (Basingstoke, 2013), 49–66.
22. William Drage, *Daimonomageia* (London, 1665), 8–9.

4 Witches in the community

> The poore old witch, pined with hunger, goeth abroad unto some of her neighbours, and there begge a little milke which is denied. Shee threatneth that she will be even with them. Home shee returneth in great fury, cursing, and raging, Forth shee calleth her spirite, and willeth him to plague such a man. Away goeth hee. Within few howres after the man is in such torment, that he can not tell what hee may doe. Hee doth thinke himselfe unhappy that he was so foolish to displease her.
>
> George Gifford, England, 1587[1]

Introduction

When the common folk thought of witchcraft, they mainly thought of everyday magical harm. Deaths and illnesses of humans and animals needed to be explained, and witchcraft was one of the possible explanations, though not the only one. How did people decide whether a particular misfortune had been caused by witchcraft? How did they identify the witch responsible? And what action did they then take? We may think that peasants demanded the prosecution of witches; sometimes they did, but often, as we shall see, they did not. Community relationships were a complex business, and it will be the task of this chapter to reconstruct them.

Trust and distrust

The early modern village was a close-knit community in which everyone knew everyone else's strengths and weaknesses. The same few hundred people, or few dozen, usually lived and worked together all their lives. Much of their farming was done collectively. Each peasant household had its own crop-growing land, but decisions about what to grow were made collectively. Ploughs and plough animals were shared. The village's cattle were herded together.

Peasants thus had to co-operate for survival. If one family was negligent, others might suffer. If one family experienced misfortune, such as the loss of animals or crops, then neighbours might be the family's only hope against starvation. People had a strong sense of duty to those in need: You should help the needy, because next time it could be you. They also had a strong sense that their neighbours should be trusted, because cooperation can only work if there is trust. But they knew that not everyone was trustworthy. There was always the possibility that people might not be what they seemed to be on the surface.

Life was not always grim. There were popular festivities – Christmas, midsummer, weddings, even funerals. There was an escapist culture – songs and stories about heroes and villains, about romance and glamour. But misfortune was never far away. Farm animals could die; able-bodied adults could fall ill and be unable to work; butter could refuse to churn; crops could be harmed in the fields by drought, frost or rain, or once harvested they could rot in the barn or be eaten by rats. When these disasters struck, people needed explanations. Witchcraft was not the only possible explanation, but for some types of misfortune it was an attractive one.

These economic anxieties deepened in the sixteenth century. Europe's population grew, perhaps by as much as 50 per cent, between 1450 and 1600. To feed these increased numbers, peasant landholdings were often subdivided, driving each family closer to the margin of subsistence. Some people were forced off the land altogether, becoming vagrants and beggars. Hillsides and other marginal lands were ploughed up in desperation, though crops grown on such land were particularly likely to fail. Famines had been rare in the late middle ages, because land was abundant; now, harvest failures led periodically to mass starvation.

It can be imagined that peasants' magical beliefs and concerns were all about 'fertility'. This was certainly important, but the term 'fertility' does not encompass the whole of the material concerns of the common people. Witches were feared in towns as well as in the countryside; there they interfered with other economic activities, like brewing or cloth manufacture. Finally, in town and country alike, people needed to come to terms with death. Death was common and immediate. Each year, per head of population, about three times more people died in early modern times than die today. Instead of dying in old age, when people's lives can be seen as completed by 'retirement', they often died young. And they died visibly in the community, not segregated in hospitals and nursing homes. Explanations for death were badly needed.

People did not despair in the face of these anxieties; they took action. They worked hard, of course, to maximise production; but they also took ritual and magical actions that gave their work meaning and offered them hope of success. They prayed for health and prosperity. They studied signs and portents. They resorted to protective magic – spells to keep them safe from witchcraft and other harm – and to counter-magic – spells to identify a witch or to counter-attack against her or him. Simple spells could be practised by anyone, while more elaborate and powerful ones were available from specialist magical practitioners. Diagram 4.1 shows a framework within which villagers could think about magical harm and how to deal with it.

Witches in the community

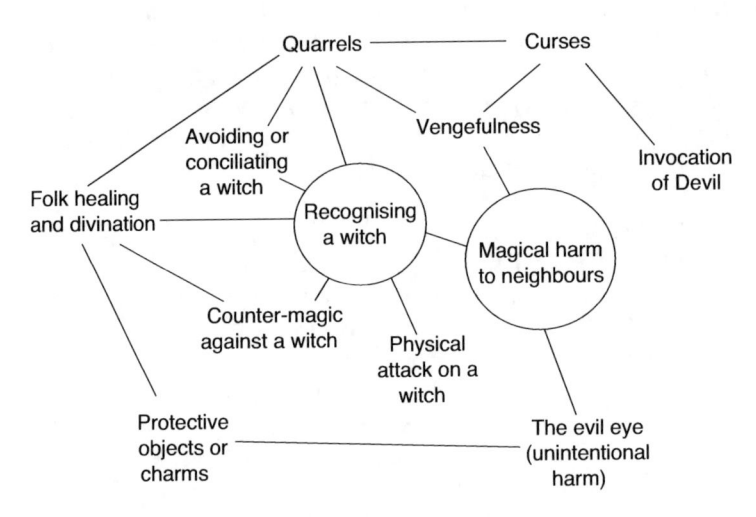

```
                    Quarrels ──────── Curses
                   /    /              /
                  /    /              /
          Avoiding or    Vengefulness
          conciliating                  Invocation
            a witch                     of Devil
Folk healing      ┌─────────┐
and divination────│Recognising│
                  │ a witch  │──── Magical harm
                  └─────────┘       to neighbours
                  /    \
          Counter-magic  \
          against a witch  Physical
              /            attack on a
             /              witch
     Protective                      The evil eye
     objects or ─────────────────── (unintentional
      charms                              harm)
```

Diagram 4.1 The village witch

Making sense of misfortune

One important function of witchcraft as a belief system is to explain human misfortune. Most traditional societies have believed in witchcraft or something like it, and have used it for this purpose. However, there are also alternative ways of explaining misfortune:

- Divine punishment, for sin or for breaking a taboo.
- Fate – often personified as an inscrutable god or goddess.
- Evil or angry demons.
- Evil or angry ancestor-spirits.

Compared with these alternatives, witchcraft belief has several advantages:

- It allows blame to be allocated to someone else. The idea that your misfortune was divine punishment, by contrast, implies that *you* are to blame.
- It allows a coherent story to be told about the misfortune. Fate is arbitrary and inexplicable, but witchcraft can be explained, for instance as the witch's malicious revenge after some earlier quarrel.
- It provides a clear course of action. You cannot prosecute a demon or a ghost (though you may be able to banish it through ritual), but you can prosecute a witch, or negotiate with her or him.

(continued)

Witchcraft, and the traditional alternatives to it, are all personal explanations. They involve deliberate acts by a human or a non-human being. By contrast, modern explanations tend to be impersonal. Misfortune is seen as occurring through some scientifically-explicable cause (such as a virus), or by chance (which can be analysed mathematically using probability theory). Traditional societies rarely believe in 'chance' events; everything has a cause. Today, the concept of an 'act of God' is still used in insurance, but it denotes an unpredictable natural disaster, not a deliberate act. The idea of deliberate, magical harm, which was central to witchcraft, has been banished by science. For many misfortunes today, the victims still search for someone to blame, or even someone to prosecute. But the victim of mugging, or of medical negligence, does not usually think that the person who harmed them did so out of personal malice. In a mass society, we no longer know our enemies personally.

Identifying a witch

Witches were thought of as an enemy within. They appeared to be ordinary members of the community, pretending to be good Christians, and not admitting openly to being witches. They cast their spells in secret. This internal danger was different from dangers that were seen as originating outside the community: wolves in the forests, fairies in the hills.

People sought to trust their neighbours, but sometimes found it hard to do so. This can be illustrated by the use of food and drink to structure neighbourhood relations. Gifts of food were important to hospitality and friendship, and villagers gave each other many such gifts. If you ate someone else's food, this showed that you trusted them – because, although they could have poisoned it, you were demonstrating that you thought they would not have done so. But there were limits to trust. People who accepted gifts of bread from neighbours sometimes threw bits to their chickens first, as a precaution. Even husbands and wives sometimes suspected each other of poison. Since poisons were often thought of as magical, the fear of poison was closely linked to the fear of witchcraft. And, since it was women who prepared food, this was a fear of *female* witchcraft; there is more about this in Chapter 9.

Witches, then, were secret – so that the question of how to identify them was crucial to the way in which villagers thought about them, as Diagram 4.1 shows. There were various methods of identification, but one basic fact distinguished witches from other villagers: Witches were angry and vengeful. They quarrelled openly with their neighbours, and hit back at perceived enemies. Vengefulness was a basic quality of the village witch. But even vengefulness was not enough in itself to generate a witchcraft reputation; further elements were required.

Forming a witchcraft reputation: A five-stage model

If a neighbourhood quarrel was going to lead to an accusation of witchcraft, it would pass through a number of stages. Let us trace the structure of a conflict between two neighbours, knowing in advance that it will lead to one of the parties to the conflict being perceived as a witch. While dividing the conflict into five stages for analytical purposes, we can recognise that some of the stages might take place concurrently. We should also note that there was nothing inevitable about these five stages; there were exit points and alternative options at every stage.

In the first stage, conflict would probably begin over something material. Somebody borrowed a pot and did not return it when asked; somebody allowed their cattle to eat their neighbour's hay; somebody refused to lend a pot to somebody. The two parties to the interaction thus acquired divergent material interests, and divergent views on their interests.

The second stage would be an analysis, by the neighbours, of the perceived rights and wrongs of this conflict of interest. This could begin at any time after the issue arose. Neighbours would in principle have felt able to say which of the two parties was in the wrong – though they might not always have agreed, and the messy realities of the conflict would often mean that there was some right and some wrong on both sides. The identity of the future witch would not be crucial to this; as we shall see in a moment, the witch could be the one who was in the wrong, but also (and perhaps more often) the one who was in the right.

The third stage (often beginning at the same time as the second stage, or even before) would consist of what the two parties said to one another about the conflict of interest. People knew that they should stick up for their interests; if anyone failed to do so, other people might learn that it was easy to take advantage of them. Concepts of honour and shame made it important not to be seen to be in the wrong. So there would probably be an angry confrontation. Either party, or both, might issue any of three related types of utterance: *insults*, *threats* and *curses*. Insults could include 'You thief!' or 'You witch!'; threats could include statements along the lines of 'You will regret this!'; while curses could include phrases like 'May the Devil drag your soul through hell!' Curses tended to incorporate threats. Can we see yet which of the parties is going to become the witch? It was preferable not to be called a witch, of course, but insults (including 'You witch!') were probably not crucial in themselves. It was threats and curses that were dangerous; the person who made them could well be a witch.

These quarrels were not, therefore, 'witchcraft quarrels'; they were quarrels about something else, not about witchcraft. Quite possibly, this third stage might pass without anyone mentioning witchcraft or even thinking seriously about it. But a seed had been sown, and, in the right conditions, it could germinate.

For the fourth stage, we have to wait and see what happens next. In witchcraft cases, what would typically happen is that a misfortune occurred to one of the parties in the quarrel. They became ill, perhaps, or their cattle died. To be more precise, we should say that a misfortune occurred *and was seen as significant*. It would be interpreted as the result of a spell (or a curse) by the witch, who was taking revenge. We shall come back to the question of what gave the misfortune significance. Just now, it is enough to note that this stage involved at least one misfortune that might have been attributable to witchcraft.

The fifth stage would be an attempt by one or both parties to present themselves publicly, to their neighbours, as the wronged victim of an aggressive spell or curse. At the third stage, let us recall, both parties could have been making threats or curses; afterwards, they and the neighbours would have to discuss which of the threats or curses had mattered. In principle, the party who had suffered a misfortune would be the one claiming to be the victim; not only had there been a curse, but *it had taken effect*. In practice, once you had connected up your opponent's curse with your own misfortune, it sometimes required skill and influence to persuade your neighbours to recognise the connection. Richer peasants, who possessed more influence in the village, have sometimes been found doing this more successfully than poorer neighbours. We shall come back to the question of relationships between richer and poorer neighbours.

The point about influence in the village should be noted. So far this five-stage pattern has been presented as a conflict between individuals, but people were rarely complete 'individuals' in early modern Europe. They had friends and kinsfolk to whom they had obligations, and who were expected to take their part. Sometimes this could divide a village into factions, making quarrels more destructive. However, friends and kinsfolk could also play a restraining role, discouraging the anti-social escalation of quarrels and trying to arrange reconciliations. Reconciliations were crucial, as we shall see.

This five-stage pattern may seem convincing in showing that someone was a witch, but, in many cases, and probably most, it was no more than suggestive. Witches in court sometimes faced long lists of accusations by neighbours, each of which contained its own version of the five-stage quarrel-plus-misfortune pattern. This indicates that a single quarrel followed by misfortune might be significant, but would not usually lead neighbours to see a person as a witch. What seems to have happened is that neighbours gradually perceived a pattern of *repeated* quarrels, and *repeated* misfortune. In some cases in Jersey, Channel Islands, there were sixty or even eighty witnesses testifying against the accused.[2] This shows that people did not always prosecute witches straight away; it also suggests that they did not necessarily perceive the person to be a witch straight away. One question that we shall come back to is: how soon did they begin to perceive the pattern, and, in particular, did they reinterpret earlier events once they did so? At any rate, we can say confidently that neighbours identified witches by a pattern of repeated quarrels followed by repeated misfortune.

One of the questions that could be asked in future research is: was there anything different about the first quarrel? Once that occurred, neighbours might have been more willing to accept subsequent misfortunes as having been linked to quarrels and thus having been due to the person's witchcraft, but, by definition, the first quarrel would involve someone to whom no suspicion attached. One might also ask: was there anything different about the *last*, most recent, quarrel? This could well have been the one that landed the witch in court, as we shall see.

Quarrels and grievances

In the quarrel, the witch might well have a justifiable grievance. This takes us back to the second stage: who was in the wrong? When the cattle ate the neighbour's hay, the owner of the cattle may well have been perceived as being in the wrong. Yet the person who got into trouble could well be the one whose hay was eaten – if they threatened or cursed the owner of the cattle, who then suffered a related misfortune.

It could even make more sense for the witch to be seen to have a justifiable grievance than an unjustifiable one. Anyone could understand that having a justifiable grievance would generate a desire for revenge. To some extent, what people objected to was *disproportionate* revenge – witches killing livestock, or even killing people, in revenge for trivial slights. It would be interesting to know how far villagers were willing to tolerate revenge that was proportionate. People who were believed to be witches were often tolerated by their communities for long periods. Would villagers have said that it was all right for a witch to take magical revenge, so long as they kept it within reasonable bounds? Or would they have objected to *any* exercise of magical revenge? It is hard to know. Unfortunately, witches' revenge – as it was perceived – was often outrageously disproportionate.

In general, accusers were ordinary villagers who accused other ordinary villagers on the same social level as themselves. There was no general pattern in which the rich accused the poor, or *vice versa*. The average witch, and the average accuser, were both settled members of the community, not marginal beggars. But within this broad and general pattern there were some distinct sub-patterns involving distinct types of quarrel.

One notable pattern involved the rich, or at least the less poor, making witchcraft accusations against the very poor. The pattern would begin when a beggar came to the door of a more prosperous villager asking for a handout, and the villager refused to give them one. After this, the villager suffered a misfortune, and assumed that this was the beggar getting their revenge by magical means. The villager was particularly likely to suspect this if they themselves felt guilty for having turned the beggar away; they had, after all, flouted conventions of neighbourliness, and the beggar could be seen as having an understandable grievance. Sometimes the beggar expressed the grievance openly – they cursed or threatened the villager as they departed. Sometimes they simply went away muttering to themselves. It is easy to see how the villager might become anxious at this. Such an encounter was described by George Gifford in the quotation at the head of this chapter.

This 'refusal-guilt syndrome', as it has been called, is found in numerous English witchcraft cases. It was originally identified by Keith Thomas and Alan Macfarlane, who argued that it was linked to the English development of organised poor relief in the late sixteenth century. The idea was that a villager who refused charity to a beggar was endorsing a new individualistic or capitalistic economic attitude: people no longer felt a need to help their neighbours, and expected the state to provide for the poor. This idea probably retains validity in some cases, but as a general interpretation it has been undermined by the realisation that the refusal-guilt syndrome was not unique to England, nor was it new in the late sixteenth century. It can be found in many Continental cases too, including some in the fifteenth century, where a link to the emergence of capitalism is most unlikely. The refusal-guilt syndrome is mainly a notable type of the quarrelsome interaction that was likely to lead to witchcraft accusations.

People believed that witches were motivated by vengeance. This is worth noting, since, in principle, people could have used magical powers for other purposes – profit, for instance. There are occasional hints of a profit motive. In fifteenth-century Gelderland, Netherlands, women were sometimes prosecuted for being 'milk witches', magically stealing others' milk. Usually they were fined or banished, though there were one or two executions.[3] Milk-stealing was known all over Europe, but was rare in witchcraft accusations. A profit motive is clearer with the occasional accusations of witchcraft against people who were seen to prosper uncannily. There was even a university student in Finland whose apparently effortless success in learning languages was attributed to demonic aid in 1661.[4] But cases of unusual prosperity were highly exceptional, and mostly male; the virtually-universal motive of female witches, and the normal motive of male witches, was vengeance.

So far we have been discussing quarrels as if each quarrel was an isolated occurrence. However, some serious quarrels gave rise to long-running enmities. These were feuds. Feuds tended to be carried out between families, often extended families, and to be led by male household heads who organised their followers in occasional acts of tit-for-tat violence against the rival family. Feuds occurred among the elite as well as among villagers, and at least in the early part of our period they could be bloody affairs with vengeance killings. Feuds among the common folk were less lethal, but probably just as bitter. What was the relationship between feuds and witchcraft?

Feuds did not usually give rise to witchcraft accusations – but then, neither did many other quarrels. Because feuds were orchestrated by men, they were usually thought to involve physical violence rather than magic. But if an uncanny misfortune occurred to someone who was involved in a feud with another family, he (or, less often, she) could easily believe that someone from that other family had caused it through witchcraft. In Burg, Saxony, in Germany, several witchcraft executions took place in 1617–20, but the main agitation was directed against two highly placed women, Margarete Knadel and Anna Eggers, wives of two prominent town officials with numerous enemies. Despite all efforts, Knadel's and Eggers's friends and relations manipulated the law in their favour, and they survived.[5] In the panic in Salem, Massachusetts, in 1692, members of one village faction accused members of the other faction. Feuds could also occur between individual ordinary villagers. In Bettenfeld, Germany, in 1652, Leonhard Gackstatt accused Margaretha Horn of being a witch and of magically infesting his house with fleas, during a feud between the two households that had continued for over a decade.[6]

What happened if an insult, or a threat, or a curse, was not seen to have been followed by a misfortune? The five-stage model would halt at the third stage, and witchcraft would not be suspected. One or both parties to the quarrel could still get into trouble, though. Women who quarrelled publicly could be prosecuted, usually in the church courts, for 'scolding' – a minor offence punishable by some form of public penance or humiliation. 'Scolds' can be seen as potential witches. They cursed or threatened, but, so long as their adversaries did not suffer a misfortune, they would not be thought to be witches. As for insults ('You witch!'), we shall see that these could be met by prosecutions for slander.

Linking a misfortune to witchcraft

Since many misfortunes were not attributed to witchcraft, we should ask: what was different about those that were? This takes us back to the fourth and fifth stages: the occurrence of a significant misfortune, and the discussion in the community about its relationship to witchcraft. How did people decide whether a given misfortune had been caused by witchcraft? They could do so in three main ways.

First, witchcraft could be identified though a connection between the nature of the misfortune and the topic of the previous quarrel. If the quarrel had been about someone's cattle eating someone else's hay, then a misfortune to the cattle might be seen as significant. This would be even more likely if the owner of the hay had directly cursed or threatened the cattle.

Second, witchcraft could be identified in the nature of the misfortune itself – an inexplicable event that was regarded as not 'natural' and thus attributed to magical causes. Usually this would be a strange illness, either human or animal. The issue of witches bringing magical illness and death features so heavily in the European witch-hunt that it is worth investigating it in some detail. One preliminary point is that villagers were usually interested in whether an illness was 'natural' or 'unnatural' (or sometimes 'supernatural'). Intellectuals, as we saw in the previous chapter, sometimes used a threefold categorisation of 'natural', 'preternatural' and 'supernatural', but the common folk did not. In Venice, not only the common folk but also the religious authorities divided unusual events into only two categories, 'natural' and 'unnatural', with the latter being a synonym for 'supernatural'.[7]

Although people often said that a particular medical condition was 'unnatural', research has not so far identified a clear pattern in illnesses attributed to witchcraft. Witches' malefices were often active and sudden, or dramatic in other ways. Crops were ravaged by hail, rather than failing to thrive through drought or lack of sunlight; hailstorms could also seem dramatically purposeful in attacking small areas. Animals that sickened and died suffered obvious pain, which was easier to attribute to witches; the deaths of plants were not as distressing or shocking, even though plants might be just as important for human survival. Not all shocking misfortunes were sudden, however. Slow, wasting diseases, or conditions that disabled without killing, were also distressing in their own way. Mental illnesses were also relevant; witches could be accused of causing someone to be 'frenzied' or 'distracted in their wits'. It is often hard to tell, from contemporary accounts, what a given illness was in modern medical terms.

Interest in the 'unnaturalness' of a disease was often strongest when magical practitioners (or even, occasionally, professional physicians) were involved. If they diagnosed bewitchment, they were likely to stress this issue. In favour of the idea of 'unnatural' diseases is the fact that some well-recognised diseases were rarely if ever attributed to witchcraft. Bubonic plague was feared throughout the early modern period, but was almost never blamed on witchcraft. The exception was an unusual series of panics, mostly around Geneva, Switzerland, when groups of people were accused of spreading plague by means of demonic 'grease'. Usually, plague was plague, and needed no further explanation. This might suggest that a witchcraft-induced disease had to have an unusual set of symptoms, one that had no 'natural' explanation. Contemporaries sometimes discussed the symptoms of witch-induced diseases in this way, but two English commentators illustrate how little consensus there was: George Gifford said that slow, wasting diseases were most likely to be witch-induced, while Matthew Hopkins stressed diseases that struck suddenly.[8]

The 'unnaturalness' of a disease ultimately lay, not in its symptoms, but in its aetiology – the way in which it was held to have been caused. This in turn was often diagnosed, not from the symptoms themselves, but from the way in which the symptoms responded to treatment. A folk healer or physician was most likely to diagnose bewitchment when the patient failed to recover after the usual treatment. Professional physicians in the sixteenth century began to doubt the universal explanations for disease offered by their medieval and classical predecessors, leaving more room for unexplained (and thus possibly diabolical) illnesses.[9] And bewitchment formed a useful explanation for any unsuccessful healer to offer to a client.

A third way to link a misfortune to an earlier quarrel, and thus to a curse, was to decide that the misfortune had followed soon after the quarrel. Victims and witnesses testifying about a quarrel often said that the misfortune had occurred only days later, or even hours later. It is easy to imagine that this could have been exaggerated with hindsight. Many testimonies were given years after the events occurred. Victims brooding on their sufferings in the meantime, and pondering witchcraft as an explanation, could easily have persuaded themselves that the misfortune had followed more closely after the quarrel than it had really done. Isobel Young, in East Barns, Scotland, in 1629, was accused of having transferred an illness from George Smith to William Smith, but her defence counsel objected that two years had intervened between the two illnesses.[10] Any aspect of victims' testimony may have been exaggerated, but this is an area where exaggeration would have been particularly easy. And there could be even more basic uncertainty about the quarrel thought to have caused the misfortune. A boatswain in Öland, Sweden, in 1670, initially blamed his illness on the witchcraft of Nils Mjölnare, with whom he had quarrelled. Questioned further, however, the boatswain admitted that he was not sure who had inflicted the illness, since he had previously quarrelled with some people in Småland and it could have been they who had caused his illness.[11]

Sometimes the misfortune was not obviously connected to the quarrel, and yet was still blamed on a witch. A perfectly ordinary, if tragic, event could still be attributed to witchcraft if there was a suspect who could be perceived as having a motive to cause it. Accusations that a witch caused business failure, or general loss of prosperity, often fell into this category; such a failure was less likely to match up precisely with a witch's curse, or to be obviously 'unnatural' or sudden. Still, the process of generating suspicion worked in a way that seemed logical to the neighbours. Not all misfortunes were blamed on witchcraft, even after quarrels; those that were blamed on witchcraft were those that seemed to have a clear and logical link to the prior quarrel.

It would be interesting to carry out a study of the scale of witches' malefice. Historians have paid little attention to this, which is perhaps surprising; witches could be seen by contemporaries as wreaking a trail of destruction through their communities. Malefices ranged widely, but, taking only killings of humans, these were common complaints against witches. The number of people believed to have been killed by witches may well have exceeded the number of witches killed. In the val de Lièpvre, Alsace, 40 named witches were prosecuted and 27 executed; in total they were said to have caused the deaths of 54 people (of whom 35 were children).[12] These deaths seem to have been real; by contrast, during some serial witch-hunts, witches were interrogated and made to confess to malefices that had little or no basis in community reputation. On the other hand, many deaths were probably attributed to 'witches' who were never prosecuted. At any rate, when misfortune occurred to villagers, witchcraft was a common explanation.

Spells and curses

How were witches' spells actually thought to operate? This issue was usually left in the background of peasant accusations, without being articulated clearly. People did not say, 'I know that I was bewitched because I saw the witch carrying out such-and-such a spell.' They assumed that witchcraft operated secretly – an assumption that was built into the logic of identifying a witch. As a result there are very few illustrations of witches carrying out spells, though Illustration 4.1 is a rare example of an artist attempting to depict a harmful spell symbolically. However, people did sometimes think that they could associate a suspected witch's known actions with their witchcraft. Often this may have been with hindsight: an innocent-seeming or everyday event took on a new significance once it was thought of as 'something that had been done by a possible witch just before a misfortune occurred'. Some people thought that it was important that they had been touched by a witch. Witches intruding on private spaces in houses were felt to be doing something threatening. Many bewitchments were attributed to eating or drinking something provided by the witch.

The most prominent type of publicly-performed witchcraft action was the curse. Spells may have been secret, but curses were all too public. This is one area where villagers felt themselves on firm ground in identifying witch-like behaviour. Verbal curses were particularly common; the victim of the curse may have thought that the words they heard spoken were in themselves the operative formula for the spell, or they may have thought that the witch, having expressed her anger, went home and performed the spell in secret. As well as words, curses could take the form of symbolic actions. In Württemberg, Catharina Ada stood next to her victim and silently tore a loaf of bread in half; Agnes Langjahr placed three eggs on her victim's bed.[13] Victims recognised that such an action had magical force, and was aimed at them. Then there was the so-called 'evil eye': witches were sometimes believed to send out harmful emanations from their eyes, so an angry look might be important. Some spells were believed to use physical objects – stirring water to make storms, or sticking pins in a wax or wooden image to cause illness or death. Some people did do such things, but the point here is that villagers believed that this was the kind of thing that a witch might do.

Physical witchcraft objects were sometimes mentioned in accusations, or even occasionally produced in court. These included ointments or powders for spells or for flying, or wax images for image-magic. In Venice in 1552, a housemaid called Lugrezia was accused of placing a long list of objects in a mattress: 'bones of the dead, human nails ... seeds of different kinds of

Illustration 4.1 Magical harm by a witch, *c.*1489

A witch casts a spell on a man's foot. The bow and arrow are not real (note that the arrow is reversed); they represent the artist's attempt to create a visual metaphor for magical harm. The common folk mostly imagined individual witches harming individual neighbours. Because the spells were carried out in secret, identifying the witch was a challenge.

By permission of University of Glasgow Special Collections.

plants, coals and a small head which appears to be that of a human body, and teeth of the dead and other suchlike witchcraft materials'.[14]

Some of these objects were probably genuine. Just as some people really did curse their neighbours verbally, other people really did practise image-magic against them. All societies contain criminals; in a witch-believing society, some people behaved like witches to pursue criminal ends. However, it is usually hard to be sure about this in individual cases, because the evidence tends to be contaminated, and there are other possible explanations for the objects produced or mentioned in court. Some were probably concocted by malicious or attention-seeking accusers, either in cold blood or to sustain a case that seemed to be going badly. When a suspicious wax image was discovered, there were rarely independent witnesses present. Accusers sometimes said that they immediately burned the magical objects that they found; perhaps they did, but such claims are hard to evaluate. In a notorious case in Logroño, Spain, in 1611, several suspects were threatened with burning if they did not produce jars of ointment, and they duly concocted ointments using ingredients like pork fat and soot.[15]

Some of these spells and curses – or what their victims perceived as spells and curses – probably took effect. People believed that spells and curses could harm them, and the stress of this could cause a range of physical illnesses. Edward Bever has examined psychological and medical studies of 'somatoform disorders' – in which the mind creates or exaggerates physical symptoms – and 'stress-related disorders' – in which people under stress develop physical symptoms.[16] Somatoform disorders are not well understood, but examples would be convulsions or loss of speech with no detectable physical basis; psychiatrists today can sometimes identify non-physical causes for these. Stress as a cause of physical symptoms is well known; most headaches are due to stress, for instance. Studies of 'voodoo death' have shown that some people who believe that they have been cursed do in fact die – apparently of heart failure. Something like this probably happened sometimes in early modern Europe.

Bever himself argues that this shows witchcraft to have been a 'reality', but this argument should be treated cautiously. Not every person who cursed their antagonists really expected that their curse would take effect. Some curses were uttered in the heat of the moment. Some were imagined by the victim. And very few of the people who uttered curses thought that this made them 'witches'. Moreover, Bever's theory works best for human illness, but many misfortunes attributed to witchcraft involved animal illness; others involved crop failure or business failure. It is implausible to suggest that crops really withered because they had been cursed. Ultimately we should recognise that most of the misfortunes attributed to witches were just that – misfortunes. Life in early modern times was hard and uncertain, and things often went wrong. People wanted explanations, and witchcraft was a possible explanation.

Magical practitioners

Magical practitioners did not usually describe their powers as 'magical'. They tended to use less provocative words like 'lucky' or 'blessed', or described themselves as having a 'skill' or a 'craft'. They did not make the source of their powers clear to their clients; for many, it was probably not clear to themselves. Magical 'spells' overlapped with recipes for cooking, in which one was simply expected to perform mechanical operations with ingredients. Some books included both spells and recipes. Spells also overlapped with prayers; most magical practitioners invoked God or the saints in some way. Nevertheless, 'magic' is a helpful term to use about them today, signalling that their practices involved more than the material world but were distinct from official religion.

Magical practices used three main principles. First, *contact*: using something that had been in contact with the person or thing being operated on. Second, *similarity*: using something that was like the person or thing, or represented the person or thing (this is sometimes called 'sympathetic magic'). Third, *contrast*: using something that was different from, or opposite to, the person or thing. Magical practices could also be categorised by technique. They could use words, numbers, objects, properties (like colour), times or places. Verbal formulas, or 'charms', were particularly important. These rituals and techniques sometimes invoked Christian beings in non-approved ways, or invoked non-Christian beings like fairies. The belief system that supported magical practitioners also supported belief in witchcraft. Indeed, magical practitioners sometimes diagnosed witchcraft as a cause of their clients' illness or other problem.

People expected magical practitioners to act for the good of their clients – to adhere to a professional code of conduct, we might say. But their special powers made them dangerous. As an Italian proverb said, 'Who knows how to heal, also knows how to harm'.[17] Human illnesses were sometimes removed by being transferred magically to a dog or other animal, which would be expected to die; such procedures could give rise to belief in hostile transfers of illness. Magical practitioners were normally trusted, but those who quarrelled with clients or neighbours could come to be seen as using their powers for bad ends, and could develop a witchcraft reputation. In the county of Essex, England, research has identified 41 magical practitioners, of whom four were accused of witchcraft – a far higher rate of accusation than for the general population, in Essex or anywhere.[18] These statistics are

(continued)

> merely indicative, but it does seem as though witch-hunting created a distinct occupational hazard for magical practitioners.
>
> Magical practitioners thus played two direct roles in the witch-hunt: they might identify witches, or might be accused of witchcraft themselves. But the most important role that magical practitioners played in the witch-hunt was an indirect one. By making beneficent magic an everyday reality, they encouraged people to believe that harmful magic would also be practised.

Heightening suspicion

Once a quarrel had been followed by misfortune, and people had begun to think about witchcraft, suspicion of the person concerned was heightened. People were more careful when they dealt with them, and paid closer attention to their behaviour. Other types of interaction with them would also come under scrutiny, as well as quarrels. Almost any non-standard encounter with someone suspected of witchcraft, if followed by a misfortune, could be attributed to witchcraft. In Aberdeenshire, Scotland, in 1597, John Burnett encountered the midwife Margaret Bain in the street, and he thought that she mumbled something as he passed, instead of giving him a friendly greeting. When he later fell terminally ill, he blamed his illness on her witchcraft.[19]

Vengefulness seems normally to have been expressed openly, and witches were normal in this respect. When they were angry, they were expected to show it. However, villagers knew that enmities could be secret; being a witch was itself something secret. There was sometimes an idea of witches who smiled in public while plotting revenge in secret. A few witches gained a reputation for vengefulness by *not* quarrelling openly about some issue that they had with their neighbours. They were perceived as storing up their resentment. Probably this was more likely to be perceived once suspicion had already begun.

Suspicion could sometimes be heightened if a suspected witch was seen as too *friendly*. Friendliness was not in itself a sign of witchcraft, but, if you already suspected someone of witchcraft, to have them constantly calling at your house could make you wonder whether they were up to no good in their busybodying. Some witnesses testifying against witches said that the person had called at their house in a friendly way, and then a misfortune had occurred. Such a misfortune would not have been attributed to witchcraft if the visitor had not had a reputation, but, if they already had one, then the reputation could be heightened. Some regions had a taboo against praising babies or children (it was tempting fate to say that a baby looked healthy); if an ordinary person broke this taboo it might not matter, but, if a suspected witch did so, it could be interpreted as a hostile spell. A particularly tragic aspect of such friendly visits and friendly remarks is that the suspected witch may often have been trying to *remove* their reputation and to initiate a reconciliation ritual. We shall come back to reconciliation rituals.

Instant reputation

The idea of the gradual development of a reputation for witchcraft is well established in scholarship, and no doubt formed a familiar pattern in many villages. Because it was a familiar pattern, however, it could be generated artificially. Some people had real witchcraft reputations going back many years: other people were suddenly given reputations that appeared to go back many years, but which were really new. We are looking at the concept of instant reputation.

In this concept, a person starts with no reputation for witchcraft, but then a misfortune occurs to one of their neighbours, who attributes it to that person's witchcraft. Instant reputation enters when people start discussing the person, and reinterpret one or more earlier events. At the time of those earlier events, nobody had said that they were due to witchcraft, but, in the light of this new misfortune, they decide that the previous occurrences had been witchcraft too. The crucial reinterpretation occurs when they decide that they had thought *at the time* that the previous occurrences were witchcraft. When they go off to court, therefore, they will testify to a series of occurrences that were all due to witchcraft. The court record will make it appear as if the reputation began with the earliest of these occurrences, but actually it will have begun only with the most recent one. Instant reputation may have been quite a common pattern, but it is hard to say how common, since proving it in individual cases is often difficult.

One case where instant reputation seems likely is that of Chatrina Blankenstein, from a village near Naumburg, Germany, in 1676. She was arrested following the death of a baby who had eaten some jam that she had supplied. This was a familiar type of misfortune triggering an accusation. But there was then an additional accusation concerning an earlier event: the town tax-collector testified that he had previously collected some taxes from her and on reaching home had found the money 7 halfpence short. Clearly, he now thought that the discrepancy had been due to witchcraft – but there was no suggestion that he had said so at the time, and it is quite possible that he had not *thought* so at the time. Blankenstein's defence insisted that she was of 'unblemished reputation' at the time of her arrest, indicating that nobody had called her a witch before the incident with the jam. The incident with the taxes thus seems to have been reinterpreted after it occurred.[20] In an even clearer case, in Reillon, Lorraine, in 1604, Claude Dieudegnon accused Nicolas Raimbault of having killed two horses and a cow by witchcraft, but added, 'at the time of the said disasters he did not think of the accused at all, and it was only since hearing of his evil fame that he had become of that opinion'.[21]

Reinterpretation could also occur through hearing news of other witches. In Bouvignies, Spanish Netherlands, during a witchcraft panic in 1679, Marie-Anne Dufosset was one of those accused. Her neighbour, Marie Deffontaines, testified that 'she had had no suspicion that the said Marie-Anne Dufosset had bewitched her child until people had spoken of witches', but that, 'since that time, remembering that she had begged to hold her child, she had begun to fear that there had been some malefice done by the said Marie-Anne'.[22] Thus a reputation could be generated by a panic.

Scholars have generally accepted that it often took quite a few suspicious incidents before a person's neighbours decided that they were a witch – and we should think about what that means. It probably means that the earliest incidents were not attributed to witchcraft at the time – not conclusively, and perhaps not at all. Once a witch appeared in court, her or his reputation might appear from the court records to be based on a series of incidents stretching back twenty years; but we should not conclude from this that their neighbours had assumed them to be a witch for twenty years. Quite possibly they had not thought this for the first five, ten or even nineteen years. The incidents during that period were reinterpreted later, in the light of the community's subsequent decision that the person was a witch. That subsequent decision might well involve some rethinking of earlier events.

Villagers liked the idea of a reputation stretching back in time, but the amount of time could be vague. Trial records usually obscure this vagueness, so that many historians relying on these records have stated confidently that a given witch's reputation went back to the earliest recorded incident at a precisely-specified date. This confident precision is probably unjustified, as can be seen from the records of an enquiry into witchcraft suspects in Peney, near Geneva, in 1530. Here the villagers were asked, not only about specific incidents, but also about the length of the suspect's reputation in the community – and they completely failed to agree. Thus, Richard de Tembley testified 'that he had heard the infamy of heresy [i.e. witchcraft] spread against Jacques Condurier alias Chaillot since two years ago and since then continually, being the period during which he had heard that Jacques was defamed of the said crime of heresy'. Eleven villagers made statements about the length of Condurier's reputation, of whom de Tembley was the only one to say it was two years. Two said it was three years, two said four years, two said six years, two said eight years and two said twelve years. The pattern was similar with the other Peney suspects.[23] In Mayen, Germany, in 1590, a woman testified that she had suspected Diederich Inich of having been a witch for forty years – even though he was only twenty-five years old![24] Perhaps she was thinking of his family's reputation. Villagers looking back at a witch's past reputation did so with more creativity than historical accuracy.

All this indicates that we should not think of a 'witchcraft reputation' as something that arose inexorably among a suspected witch's neighbours, becoming steadily stronger with each quarrel. This 'building' of a reputation is to some extent an artefact of our evidence; this mostly comes from trial documents, which usually present the reputation as being at its height. Closer inspection shows that many reputations fluctuated, and people were willing to forgive and forget. In one Lorraine case, a man accused a woman of witchcraft – but later, after she was acquitted, he offered to marry her! She declined the offer, but it looks as though she had escaped from her community reputation as well as from the court.[25] We now need to look at how witchcraft reputations could be brought to an end.

The search for reconciliation

Quarrels were disruptive and troublesome. Openly-expressed hostility between two villagers was against their own interests. It was also against the interests of their friends and kinsfolk, and indeed of the whole village. After a quarrel, people wanted reconciliation. This was not easy, because the original issues that had given rise to the quarrel might be continuing, and the witch's magical vengeance (as the misfortune was by now perceived) had made things worse. The initial quarrel might well be followed by others. But people on both sides of the quarrel knew that an eventual reconciliation was the ideal solution.

Reconciliation rituals are crucial – and fascinating. During quarrels, friends and kinsfolk of the quarrelling parties sometimes urged restraint or offered to mediate. This is an area where the study of feuds is relevant; feuds, too, were envisaged as requiring eventual reconciliation. What were the dynamics of the reconciliation of a quarrel in which witchcraft was thought to be involved? Two related patterns may be suggested: one in which the reconciliation was initiated by the victim of witchcraft, and one in which it was initiated by the witchcraft suspect.

Reconciliations were often initiated by a person who was thought to have been made ill by a witch's curse. They would approach the suspected witch in a friendly manner and ask formally for their health to be restored, often adding a religious phrase such as 'for God's sake'. The request might be more indirect, simply asking the suspected witch to comment on the illness. The suspected witch's reaction was vital. The most socially acceptable response was a friendly one: to wish the person good health, perhaps adding a religious blessing. Once the two parties had both expressed friendship to the other, they were (or hoped to be) reconciled. Such a reconciliation could be cemented by the two parties drinking together or sharing food.

There was a difficulty in such a reconciliation, which had to be overcome. As many suspected witches recognised, it was difficult to express the friendly response that was being demanded of them without also admitting prior guilt, at least implicitly. If the ill person recovered, that could be attributed to the witch lifting the curse. Nevertheless, suspects often, perhaps usually, responded in the expected, neighbourly way. The ill person helped them to do this by showing that they were not demanding an explicit admission of guilt. Instead, both parties kept discussion of the cause of the illness at a hypothetical level. The ill person refrained from saying directly that the curse had caused the illness, and the suspected witch refrained from saying directly that they were lifting the curse. In 1594 in a village near Siena, Italy, a mother named Alessandra suspected that an elderly magical practitioner, Angelica, had bewitched her baby daughter. She brought the baby to Angelica, who unswaddled her, stretched her limbs and handed her back, saying that she would not die of her illness.[26] The implicit assumption seems to have been: *if* there had been a curse, and *if* this had caused the illness, then it was being removed. What was made explicit was that the two parties were restoring a friendly relationship.

Did a successful reconciliation mean that the suspect was no longer a witch? Quite possibly it did. Peasants did not think of witchcraft primarily as the ongoing state of 'being a witch'; they thought of witchcraft as the exercise of magical harm on specific occasions. A person might have caused magical harm to their neighbours, but they could also stop doing so, and return to being a trusted member of the community. An analogy with other offences may help to clarify this. Someone might have assaulted a neighbour with a stick, but they might afterwards make it up with their neighbour. Over time, the villagers might decide that the offence was in the past and that the person could be trusted again – even if they still had a stick in their house. Someone who had committed magical harm could in principle do so again, just as someone who had committed assault with a stick could in principle do so again; but they could demonstrate, by their good relationship with their neighbours, that they were not going to do so.

So witchcraft suspects were encouraged to admit their witchcraft, at least implicitly, in return for a reconciliation. They were aided by the other party to the quarrel, who indicated in advance that they were willing to forgive, rather than pursuing the accusation of witchcraft. There was also a negative incentive for the witchcraft suspect to co-operate when asked to restore an ill person's health. Their main alternative option was to deny responsibility for the illness, and thus in effect to refuse the proffered reconciliation. That might be a clearer assertion of innocence, but it could be seen as hostile and un-neighbourly behaviour – the kind of behaviour often attributed to witches. And, if their protestations of innocence were not believed, they were probably in more trouble than before.

That witchcraft suspects often wanted reconciliations is shown by the fact that they sometimes initiated reconciliation rituals themselves. They would visit the alleged victim in a friendly way, perhaps offering food or drink. Someone who was offered a gift of food or drink was expected to accept it – that was the neighbourly thing to do. Here it was the victim's response that was vital. If they refused the proffered gift, they were being hostile and could be blamed for any continuation of the quarrel. But, if they accepted it, they were agreeing to restore neighbourly relations. Sharing food or drink offered by a suspected witch was particularly constructive because, by doing so, they were showing that they did not think that the suspect was out to poison them magically. They were also proving to themselves that the food or drink had not been poisoned, simply by consuming it. Many victims seem to have cheered up, or even to have recovered their health, after this ritual of reconciliation.

Magical practitioners sometimes encouraged reconciliation rituals in order to benefit the health of a client. They might identify a witch who was held to be responsible for their client's illness, but they did not usually want to initiate a witchcraft trial, which might lead the authorities to enquire into their own magical practices as well as the witchcraft. Instead they often advised the client to seek reconciliation, and prescribed rituals for this. Chonrad Stoeckhlin, the shamanistic magical practitioner discussed in the next chapter, advised a client that he had been bewitched by Anna Enzensbergerin. He advised that 'he should go to her, Anna, and ask for her help, three times in the name of God and the Last Judgment, and then she would be compelled to help. Which happened just as he had expected.'[27]

Reconciliations were not guaranteed to succeed. If a suspected witch provocatively offered gifts to someone, and if a further misfortune occurred, that misfortune could well be attributed to the witch's interference. If the victim did *not* recover after eating the witch's food, or if they got worse, that would be further evidence of guilt. In some cases, therefore, the reconciliation ritual actually damaged the suspect's reputation in the long run; further misfortunes occurred, or the implicit admission of guilt was used against them in a later court case, or both. But this was not how the reconciliation ritual was expected to be used, and most such rituals did not lead to an immediate court case. In fact, the reconciliation ritual should be seen as an *alternative* to a court case. The reconciliation was meant to be real and lasting.

It is easy to read the records of witchcraft trials, or the books written by some historians about these, and to conclude that a quarrel followed by misfortune would normally lead to a witchcraft trial. However, reconciliation rituals show that this is a fundamental misunderstanding. The *normal* outcome was that a quarrel followed by misfortune would lead to reconciliation. It is true that we know about reconciliation rituals largely from witchcraft trial records, but this does not mean that reconciliation rituals were normally followed by witchcraft trials. We have to work with the trial records because they are our main form of evidence. If there was a trial, people wrote down the previous reconciliations as part of the narrative of how the witch's reputation had developed. Most of these reconciliations were successful at the time – they did not lead to an immediate trial. Often the trial records show the suspected witch living for many years alongside her or his neighbours, more or less harmoniously. If it had not been for some later incident (often shortly before the trial), they would have never have been prosecuted, and nothing would have been written down.

A more confrontational way out of a witchcraft-related quarrel was for the person who had been called a witch to prosecute their opponent for slander. This was quite common, and indeed possibly more common than actual witchcraft trials. Slander cases were usually heard in church courts, not the criminal courts in which witches were prosecuted; studies of church court records have revealed a good deal about witchcraft. In records of slander prosecutions, for instance, we often find further evidence of prior reconciliation rituals. However, for the person who had been called a witch, the point of a slander prosecution was to win their case. The person complaining of bewitchment would then be expected to stop complaining, having been found to be in the wrong. Slander prosecutions may have helped to discourage accusations of witchcraft, but they also shaped and formalised witchcraft belief. The existence of the possibility of a slander prosecution meant that people had to think carefully about witchcraft: they should not call someone a witch *unless they had good evidence*.

A few prosecutions for slander went horribly wrong when neighbours rallied to support the person complaining of bewitchment, and to add their own complaints. This could lead, not only to the alleged witch losing their slander case, but also to a witchcraft prosecution in a criminal court. Grace Sherwood, in the English colony of Virginia in 1698, complained that Elizabeth Barnes 'had wronged and abused the said Grace in her good name and reputation saying the said Grace came to her one night and rid [i.e. rode] her and went out of the key hole or crack of the door like a black Catt'. Sherwood demanded that Barnes pay £100 damages – but the jury found in Barnes's favour. Sherwood herself was then prosecuted for witchcraft, though not until 1705 (and she seems to have been acquitted).[28] Such cases seem to have been rare, presumably because people did not initiate prosecutions for slander unless they were confident of winning.

Another way for witchcraft suspects to vindicate themselves was to demand to undergo some kind of trial, confident of their innocence. Typically this would not be a legal trial but a community ritual. The so-called swimming test, where suspects were dropped into water to see whether they floated, could be such a ritual; some suspects demanded to undergo it, evidently believing that they would be vindicated and that this would silence the rumours against them. Like a slander prosecution, this could go badly wrong, but it must sometimes have succeeded. In the late seventeenth and early eighteenth centuries, the civic weighing house of Oudewater, Netherlands, offered a service weighing people: they could (for a fee) be issued with a certificate that their weight was normal for their height and girth. This implied that they were not too light, as witches were believed to be. Most of the customers came from regions where the swimming test was recognised. They were unlikely to face prosecution at this late date, and they probably wanted their certificates to counter neighbourhood gossip.[29]

In a pattern diametrically opposed to that of the reconciliation ritual, some suspected witches deliberately accentuated their quarrels and curses. They let it be known that their curses took effect, and thus implicitly encouraged their neighbours to think that they were witches. This pattern was a possible (though not essential) part of the 'refusal-guilt syndrome' described earlier in this chapter. Some of these 'witches' may simply have been naturally quarrelsome and malicious, and may have come to believe in their powers by seeing misfortunes happen to people whom they had cursed. Others, though, seem to have been poor and marginal members of the community, who cultivated a witchcraft reputation in a desperate struggle for survival. It probably worked sometimes, since (as we shall see) neighbours sometimes tried to appease and conciliate people whom they thought of as angry witches. But such people were dicing with death.

This leads on to the issue of 'witches' involving themselves in criminal activities. In a sense, of course, contemporaries thought that all witches' activities were criminal; but there does seem to have been a distinct category of 'witches' who were consulted by other people with a criminal intent. After all, people in early modern Europe believed that curses worked; and some people, then as now, were criminals, willing to harm others in order to achieve their desired ends. It would make sense to expect that some early modern criminals would use magic as a weapon.

Evidence for deliberately criminal 'witches' is not extensive, but there is some. Books of necromancy often included spells to injure or kill people. Some magical practitioners offered a service in harming as well as healing. A Russian *koldun* (magical practitioner) could use the following formula for 'sending spells on the wind' on behalf of a client. The *koldun* stood with the wind blowing towards his victim, took from the client a handful of earth, snow or dust, threw it into the wind, and recited: 'Kulla, Kulla! Blind [victim's name], black, blue, brown, red eyes. Blow up his belly larger than a charcoal pit, dry up his body thinner than the meadow grass, kill him quicker than a viper.'[30] Although Russian *kolduny* mainly practised healing and other beneficial magic, they were thought to be dangerous, and their powers may have been seen to derive more directly from the Devil than those of their counterparts elsewhere. Whether people who provided spells or poisons for murder plots thought of themselves as 'witches' is unclear, but it seems likely that their clients thought of them as 'witches', and they may have encouraged their clients in this belief. Thus the main evidence we have for such people – as for almost all of those convicted of witchcraft – is that 'witch' was what others called them.

Living with a witch

Villagers had various strategies for coping with someone whom they believed or suspected to be a witch. They did not immediately go off to court and demand that the witch be burned at the stake. There has, in fact, been debate about the extent to which neighbours initiated prosecutions; we shall come back to this. But, having identified a witch in the village, neighbours normally thought that they had to live with that person. How did they cope?

One straightforward approach to the problem was in fact a non-approach to the witch: a strategy of avoidance. Villagers would try not to work with the witch, not to give them anything, and not to accept anything from them. This was not very neighbourly, but it may often have succeeded in preventing further conflict. Not all witchcraft suspects accepted being avoided, and they might initiate a reconciliation ritual with someone whom they had offended, perhaps by provocatively offering gifts. But people who were more widely suspected may have found it hard to decide where to begin their reconciliation attempts. Some suspected witches thus found themselves ostracised for long periods.

An alternative approach, more neighbourly, was conciliation and appeasement of the witch. The witch was a powerful and dangerous person in the community; it was wise to treat her or him with respect. Rather than quarrel with a known witch, some people gave way. They aided a witch, or granted their requests. Sometimes they did so even if the requests were unreasonable. This was why it could be advantageous for really poor people to cultivate a witchcraft reputation: they could use it to gain handouts. However, even those who had acquired their reputation unintentionally might still benefit from it in this way. Conciliation and appeasement can be seen as similar to reconciliation rituals (and could certainly lead to reconciliation rituals), but there were some differences. Conciliation and appeasement was a continuing attitude, not a distinct event. It was also less sincere than a reconciliation ritual, since it involved regularly being nice to someone whom you did not like or trust. Reconciliation rituals were intended to restore real trust.

Witches had magical power, but, in coping with them, another strategy was to meet their magical power with opposite magical power. The church would probably disapprove if it found out, but peasants saw magic in a utilitarian light: it could be used for good ends as well as bad. Two types of magic could be used against witches: protective magic and counter-magic. Counter-magic can be further subdivided into divinatory magic, and magic that counter-attacked against the witch.

Protective magic involved rituals, words or objects that would protect one's household or one's animals or crops against witchcraft. Such magic could be carried out by anyone, with no need for specialist advice. Sometimes it was a community matter. On St John's Eve, 23 June, about the time of the summer solstice, people lit bonfires and kept them burning through the short hours of darkness, in the belief that this would banish demons. Protective magic did not usually need to be directed against a particular witch, and could act as a kind of general insurance policy. People who feared the enmity of a particular witch had a pressing motive to employ protective magic, but it seems to have been normal in village life. There could always be witches about, even if you were not aware of having quarrelled with one.

There was also protective magic against *unintentional* witchcraft. Belief in the unintentional bewitching effect of the 'evil eye' was widespread in Europe. Vision was often believed to be an active process; it worked by emitting a substance from the eye that was reflected back from the object being viewed, rather like radar waves. The 'evil eye' was thus a look that harmed the person being looked at. It was set off by the looker's feelings of jealousy or envy, with the actual effect on the victim being either intended or unintended by the looker. Mothers with babies were thought to be especially at risk; not only were babies fragile and vulnerable, but mothers' fertility might attract the jealousy or envy of infertile women. Preventative measures included amulets, protective symbols painted on roofs, an iron nail above a baby's cot, or an iron horseshoe outside the door. Beliefs about the evil eye fed into some accusations of magical harm.

One possible protection against witchcraft was to lead a godly life. Numerous witches, when interrogated about their malefices, described occasions on which they had been foiled by the devout faith of their intended victim. There was clearly a popular belief in divine protection for the godly. Demonological writers, too, tended to advise that people should turn to God for protection – though writers who stressed the Devil's independent power might suggest that he particularly relished assaulting the godly. In practice, godly members of the community were pulled in different directions. They might hope that their prayers and devotions would protect them, but this hope was undermined by their heightened sense of the dangers of witchcraft. Orthodox devotional practice stressed the sinfulness of the believer and his or her difficulty in escaping the Devil's temptations and assaults. The cosmic struggle between God and the Devil was also a war within many a troubled individual conscience. Witch-hunting, for devout Christians, offered a way of shifting blame for sin away from themselves and onto an external enemy.

As well as protective magic, there was counter-magic. This was more active. There were divinatory spells and rituals that could identify a witch, and even magical counter-attacks against witches. Some of these were elaborate and demanding, and the bewitched person would need to employ a specialist magical practitioner. As to identifying the witch, usually they already had their own suspicions, being aware that their misfortune had been preceded by a quarrel with that person. Magical practitioners knew how to make the most of this, and guided the client towards the answer that they wanted to hear. One well-known method of divination was by the sieve and shears: typically the sieve was balanced on the upturned point of the shears, and would 'turn' when the correct answer was given. No doubt, if the ritual gave the 'correct' (expected) answer, this confirmed both the client and the practitioner in believing in the practitioner's powers.

Why did clients want to be told that a particular person had bewitched them? Occasionally they wanted evidence for a court case, but this was rare. Sometimes they wanted a diagnosis of their condition, just as some people today visit doctors in order to be told what is wrong with them. There was also a good deal of folkloric interest in identifying witches, as we shall see in the next chapter. Sometimes, of course, they wanted the magical practitioner to cure them. It was here that reconciliation rituals could enter, since many cures included following a reconciliation ritual in a prescribed manner. One common reason to consult a magical practitioner about bewitchment was to put pressure on the witch to lift the curse. If a suspected witch knew that their neighbour had visited a magical practitioner, this would show them that the neighbour was serious about the problem. This too pointed towards a future reconciliation ritual.

Counter-magic also included magical practices that might actually harm the witch, though these may have been rarer. One ritual, known as 'scratching' the witch, or 'scoring above the breath', was based on a belief that drawing blood from a witch's forehead would cancel their spell. It could be a licence for an essentially physical assault. Assaults on witches, and even lynchings, occurred occasionally, but they were rare – and could be punished by the authorities. Normally, people lived with witches. And, on the rare occasions when people's patience ran out, they did not normally take vigilante action; they denounced the witch to the criminal courts.

It should be stressed that such denunciations seem to have been uncommon. Some neighbours, far from denouncing known witches, aided and protected them. In Peney, Switzerland, Pierre Ballini was suspected of witchcraft, and Jean Besançon persuaded Conrad de Trembley to warn him to flee to avoid arrest, saying that 'if he was taken, he would inculpate many men'. Besançon was clearly worried that he himself would be among the next to be accused. Indeed the affair came out ten years later, in 1530, during Besançon's own trial – but, had it not been for this, it would not have been recorded. At the time, de Trembley, who was not under suspicion, had co-operated with Ballini and Besançon in avoiding a trial.[31] A wish to keep the courts out of the villagers' business may have been common. But, for reasons that will need further exploration in later chapters of this book, many witches did find themselves in court, and villagers sometimes played a role in this.

Denouncing a witch to the authorities

There were thus several approaches that neighbours could take to witches, most of which involved living with the witch somehow. We now arrive at the option that is perhaps historically most significant, and certainly most dramatic: the option of initiating a formal legal prosecution. As we have seen by now, a legal prosecution can be regarded as an aberration from the community's point of view – a *failure* of the normal community-based methods of coping with a witch.

The question of how witches actually arrived in court is surprisingly neglected, or perhaps surprisingly difficult to say anything definite about. We mainly know about witchcraft from court records, which rarely explain how the person came to be arrested and charged; instead they focus on the evidence for the crime itself. We sometimes catch glimpses of suspected witches trying to persuade their neighbours not to report them to the authorities; several such cases have been found in Rothenburg ob der Tauber, Germany.[32] At any rate, in searching for the formal denunciation, we are typically looking at a shift from female quarrels to male courts.

A prosecution was a risky business, beyond the villagers' control. Peasants may have been deferential to their lords, but they knew that their lords' interests differed from their own. Once the authorities started enquiring into village affairs, they might upset a number of established informal arrangements. The impression is that it may have needed a more wealthy or influential member of the community to take the initiative. A celebrated English study found a pattern in which misfortunes occurring to women were handled by the community, but, when a subsequent misfortune occurred to a propertied man, he would launch a prosecution and marshal the women to support it.[33] In Russia, prosecutions had to be initiated by a written petition to the tsar, a major challenge in a country with a very low level of literacy.[34]

Some governments had officials whose job was to investigate unusual human deaths. This role in the region of Langenburg, Germany, was held by the town steward. When the steward investigated the sudden death of Anna Fessler in 1672, Fessler's husband told him that she had been poisoned or bewitched by Anna Schmeig.[35] This led to Schmeig's prosecution – but, if Schmeig had been suspected merely of causing human illness or damage to animals, there would have been no town steward investigating her activities.

The town of Ortebello, Italy, provides a case study of denunciations. An inquisitor, Francesco Pedrosa, took up residence in the town in 1648, and issued a public demand for heresies and magical practices to be reported to him. During the next eighteen months, over a hundred people were denounced to him, including some witches. Pedrosa prosecuted about twenty of these people, though only a handful were convicted, and none were executed. After this initial flood, the number of denunciations slowed to a trickle, and no witches were denounced after 1656. The number of people with witchcraft reputations was limited.[36]

In a context of general fear of witchcraft, some accusations were bound to be fraudulent. In Hougham, England, in 1651, Thomas Hogbin accused Helen Dadd of bewitching his three-year-old son to death; Dadd was executed. Later, however, witnesses testified that Hogbin himself had caused the boy's death by kicking him and beating him with a rake.[37] It is unclear whether Hogbin was simply trying to shift blame away from himself, or whether he also had a grievance against Dadd. This case is reminiscent of today's popular idea that a witchcraft accusation was a means of 'getting rid of anyone you didn't like' (which will be discussed in Chapter 11). However, there could be fraudulent accusations of any crime, and there is no reason to think that witchcraft was particularly prone to them. Most accusations were undoubtedly sincere.

Neighbours' statements in evidence were often cautious and oblique. Typically, the neighbour described a quarrel, described a misfortune that followed, and then stopped. They did not use the word 'witch', nor did they say explicitly that the misfortune was caused by the person with whom they had quarrelled. They left it to the court to join up the dots. This may have been through mistrust of the court; if the court acquitted, then the villagers could find themselves having to live with an angry and vengeful witch who was now even angrier and more vengeful. On the other hand, perhaps people *trusted* the court and felt that it was the court's job, not theirs, to join up the dots. Another consideration is that the penalty for witchcraft was so severe. Would you want to be responsible for having had someone burned at the stake? By leaving it to others to join up the dots, the neighbour could avoid feeling responsible for the outcome.

Neighbours tended to abandon their usual caution when it came to reporting deathbed speeches. People sometimes died believing themselves to have been bewitched, naming the guilty party, and demanding that action be taken against them. The heirs and kinsfolk of the dying person, hearing their demand, might well feel bound in honour to prosecute the witch. Deathbed speeches made good evidence, because people were thought particularly trustworthy when facing death. But it was also convenient for the surviving relatives to stress, or even exaggerate, the speech – because it saved them from having to accuse the witch themselves. If so, this may help us to see their usual failure to join up the dots as a piece of self-protection, rather than as a genuine reluctance to prosecute – at least in cases of witches who had caused human deaths.

Once the idea of witchcraft had been mentioned during village quarrels, the possibility of a trial was often present in the background. In Berry, France, in 1583, Romble Lymousin testified that, three years ago, he had fallen ill after a quarrel with Marin Semellé about some wheat. He sent his brother to fetch Semellé, and told him 'that he had bewitched him and given him his illness when he touched him on the left shoulder, and that, if he did not lift the illness and cure him, he would send his brother to the lord to complain of him'. Semellé replied that they should eat together, which they did, and a reconciliation ensued. Presumably nothing more would have been heard of the incident had it not been for the fact that

Semellé's mother was prosecuted for witchcraft three years later, whereupon he was dragged in also; but the threat of prosecution had already been issued.[38]

Why, then, were witches denounced to the authorities after many years with a reputation? What changed? One possibility is that people's patience simply ran out, and they decided that enough was enough. The latest malefice may not have been any worse than the previous ones, but it was the last straw. In other cases, however, the latest malefice seems to have been distinctive. Sometimes the harm done was unusually serious – the death of a human rather than an animal, say. Sometimes the victim was an unusually powerful person – a leader of the village, or even a member of the propertied elite – or an unusually determined person.

Something may also have occurred to reduce the peasants' fears of the witch. One likely possibility is news of successful witchcraft prosecutions nearby. If people saw other prosecutions leading to executions, they would be more willing to denounce their own witch. This is probably one reason why we find witches with long-standing reputations being prosecuted in panic years. There were also some panics in which villagers themselves took the lead in demanding that the authorities prosecute the local witches. These panics, which occurred mainly in the Rhine-Moselle region of western Germany, will be discussed in Chapter 8.

In some cases, the initiative in prosecution lay with the authorities themselves rather than the peasants. Again this was more likely in chain-reaction panics, when the authorities had available to them names of witches that had been given by previous witches under interrogation. These issues, too, are discussed in Chapter 8.

From belief to action

It is possible to speak of a general level of intensity of witchcraft belief, and even to imagine that the intensity would be measurable statistically. That is what opinion polls measure today. In predicting the proportion of the population who will vote for a given party in a future election, pollsters are measuring, not only how many people prefer that party, but what proportion of them will translate their preferences into action by actually going out and voting. The relevant question for early modern Europe is: how many people, at any given date, were prepared to translate their witchcraft beliefs into action by going out and participating in the prosecution of a witch? We cannot of course conduct an actual poll on this, but we can recognise that the opinions that such a poll would have measured did exist. Variations in the strength of these opinions are likely to have contributed to the varying intensity of witch-hunting.

(continued)

There are several questions we would want to ask if we were doing an opinion survey of early modern Europe. They might include:

- Do you believe in witches?
- Is it likely that there are any witches in your village?
- What would you do if you thought that there was a witch in your village?
  - Complain to the authorities?
  - Use counter-magic to attack the witch?
  - Use protective magic to defend yourself?
  - Avoid the witch?
  - Conciliate the witch?
  - Do nothing?

Some of these questions would have yes/no answers, while others would be more about intensity of response. 'Is it likely that there are any witches in your village?', for instance, might have the possible answers 'Very likely', 'Fairly likely', 'Fairly unlikely' and 'Very unlikely'.

The intensity of attitudes would affect people's choice of action if they suspected witchcraft. It would also affect how likely they were to take action. Finally, it would affect their standards of proof. If you saw a malevolent cat in a dream, how sure would you be that it was the suspected witch in feline form? Would your own feeling that it was the witch convince you, or would you need further evidence? The question of intensity of attitudes would apply also to the judge or priest to whom you reported your dream. Some judges might be satisfied with your sense that the cat was actually the witch, while others would probe sceptically for alternative explanations and would send you away if you could not convince them. Sometimes this would make the difference between prosecuting the witch and not doing so, or between a guilty and a not guilty verdict.

Conclusion: Neighbourhood quarrels in context

For a witch's neighbours, denouncing them to the courts was usually a last resort. We know of many cases in which the suspect had had many other types of interaction with their neighbours before they were prosecuted. Still, the option of prosecution certainly existed, at least during the period of witch-hunting, and the option – with or without the neighbours' encouragement – was taken often enough to generate thousands of prosecutions and executions.

Neighbourhood quarrels, however much they contributed to the prosecution of many or even most individual witches, cannot be regarded as a general cause of the wave of prosecutions that swept over early modern Europe. Such tensions probably long predated the period of witch-hunting, and certainly continued long after it. One cannot explain a change by a constant – and neighbourhood tensions, however crucial, were a constant. They are thus best seen as a necessary precondition for witch-hunting rather than as a precipitating cause of the upsurge of prosecutions in the sixteenth century. Without such quarrels, witches could not have been prosecuted in anything like the numbers that they were, yet the sixteenth-century upsurge of prosecutions has to be explained by distinct sixteenth-century developments. Later chapters of this book, especially Chapter 6, will address this issue.

In the meantime it is worth asking how many witches were executed as a result of neighbourhood animosities. This question still awaits its historian. We can reconstruct many reputations, but the partial nature of the records tends to make it difficult to say that a given witch did *not* have a reputation. We can, however, identify many witches who were denounced to the authorities, not by neighbours, but by other confessing witches in chain-reaction panics. My own estimate – merely an educated guess – is that neighbourhood animosities played a role in no more than a large minority of the total of about 50,000 who were executed in the course of the European witch-hunt. Probably more executions were generated by mass panics (to be discussed in Chapter 8) than by neighbours. However, the mass panics were relatively restricted in space and time, whereas neighbourhood tensions existed all over early modern Europe, even in places and times with little witch-hunting. Most places, most of the time, had *few* witchcraft trials; not many could say with confidence that they had *none*. The lurking possibility of witchcraft trials thus played an important role in structuring and constraining neighbourhood relations all over Europe during this significant period of history. Before our period, and again after it, the neighbours had similar beliefs about witches, but were restricted to non-judicial options. Whether the absence of the prosecution option made the relationships between witches and their neighbours more rancorous, or less rancorous, would be hard to say.

Notes

1 George Gifford, *A Discourse of the Subtill Practises of Devilles by Witches and Sorcerers* (London, 1587), sig. G3.
2 G. R. Balleine, 'Witch trials in Jersey', *Société jersiaise: bulletin annuel*, 13 (1939), 379–98, at p. 388.
3 Hans de Waardt and Willem de Blécourt, '"It is no sin to put an evil person to death": judicial proceedings concerning witchcraft during the reign of Duke Charles of Gelderland', in Marijke Gijswijt-Hofstra and Willem Frijhoff (eds.), *Witchcraft in the Netherlands from the Fourteenth to the Twentieth Century*, trans. Rachel M. J. van der Wilden-Fall (Rotterdam, 1991), 66–78, at pp. 68–9.

4 Antero Heikkinen and Timo Kervinen, 'Finland: the male domination', in Bengt Ankarloo and Gustav Henningsen (eds.), *Early Modern European Witchcraft: Centres and Peripheries* (Oxford, 1991), 319–38, at p. 327.
5 Bob Scribner, 'Witchcraft and judgement in Reformation Germany', *History Today*, 40:4 (April 1990), 12–19, at pp. 17–19.
6 Alison Rowlands, *Witchcraft Narratives in Germany: Rothenburg, 1561–1652* (Manchester, 2003), 181.
7 Jonathan Seitz, *Witchcraft and Inquisition in Early Modern Venice* (Cambridge, 2011), 12–13, 20–1.
8 Alan Macfarlane, *Witchcraft in Tudor and Stuart England* (London, 1970), 182.
9 Leland L. Estes, 'The medical origins of the European witch craze: a hypothesis', *Journal of Social History*, 17 (1983–84), 271–84.
10 *Selected Justiciary Cases, 1624–1650*, 3 vols., eds. Stair I. Gillon and J. Irvine Smith (Edinburgh: Stair Society, 1954–74), i, 103.
11 Per Sörlin, 'Witchcraft and causal links: accounts of maleficent witchcraft in the Göta high court in the fifteenth and sixteenth centuries', *Arv: Nordic Yearbook of Folklore*, 62 (2006), 51–80, at p. 70.
12 Maryse Simon, *Les affaires de sorcellerie dans le val de Lièpvre (XVIe et XVIIe siècles)* ([Strasbourg:] Publications de la Société Savante d'Alsace, 2006), 21, 22, 43, 162.
13 Edward Bever, 'Witchcraft fears and psychosocial factors in disease', *Journal of Interdisciplinary History*, 30 (2000), 573–90, at pp. 585, 589.
14 Ruth Martin, *Witchcraft and the Inquisition in Venice, 1550–1650* (Oxford, 1989), 193.
15 Gustav Henningsen, *The Witches' Advocate: Basque Witchcraft and the Spanish Inquisition, 1609–1614* (Reno, Nev., 1980), 297–300.
16 Edward Bever, *The Realities of Witchcraft and Popular Magic in Early Modern Europe: Culture, Cognition and Everyday Life* (Basingstoke, 2008).
17 Quoted in Mary R. O'Neil, 'Missing footprints: maleficium in Modena', *Acta Ethnographica Hungarica*, 37 (1991–92), 123–42, at p. 131.
18 Macfarlane, *Witchcraft in Tudor and Stuart England*, 8, 127–8.
19 Julian Goodare, 'The Aberdeenshire witchcraft panic of 1597', *Northern Scotland*, 21 (2001), 17–37, at p. 31.
20 Lea, *Materials*, iii, 1241–2.
21 Robin Briggs, *Witches and Neighbours: The Social and Cultural Context of European Witchcraft* (2nd edn., Oxford, 2002), 120.
22 Quoted in Robert Muchembled (ed.), *La sorcière au village (XVe au XVIIIe siècle)* (Paris, 1979), 128.
23 Sophie Simon, *'Si je le veux, il mourra!' Maléfices et sorcellerie dans la campagne genevoise (1497–1530)* (Lausanne, 2007), 190–241, 277–80.
24 Johannes Dillinger, *Evil People: A Comparative Study of Witch Hunts in Swabian Austria and the Electorate of Trier*, trans. Laura Stokes (Charlottesville, Va., 2009), 80.
25 Briggs, *Witches and Neighbours*, 269.
26 Oscar Di Simplicio, 'Giandomenico Fei, the only male witch: a Tuscan or an Italian anomaly?', in Alison Rowlands (ed.), *Witchcraft and Masculinities in Early Modern Europe* (Basingstoke, 2009), 121–48, at p. 135.
27 Wolfgang Behringer, *Shaman of Oberstdorf: Chonrad Stoeckhlin and the Phantoms of the Night*, trans. H. C. Erik Midelfort (Charlottesville, Va., 1998), 85.
28 'Grace Sherwood, the Virginia Witch', ed. Edward W. James, *William and Mary Quarterly*, 3 (1894–95), pp. 96–101, 190–2, 242–5; 4 (1895–96), pp. 18–22; quotation at vol. 3, p. 100.

29 Hans de Waardt, 'Prosecution or defense: procedural possibilities following a witchcraft accusation in the province of Holland before 1800', in Gijswijt-Hofstra and Frijhoff (eds.), *Witchcraft in the Netherlands*, 79–90, at pp. 86–9.
30 Quoted in W. J. Ryan, 'Eclecticism in the Russian charm tradition', in Jonathan Roper (ed.), *Charms and Charming in Europe* (Basingstoke, 2004), 113–26, at p. 117.
31 Simon, *'Si je le veux, il mourra!'*, 232–3.
32 Rowlands, *Witchcraft Narratives*, 42.
33 Clive Holmes, 'Women: witnesses and witches', *Past and Present*, 140 (Aug. 1993), 45–78.
34 Valerie Kivelson, *Desperate Magic: The Moral Economy of Witchcraft in Seventeenth-Century Russia* (Ithaca, NY, 2013), 236–43.
35 Thomas Robisheaux, *The Last Witch of Langenburg: Murder in a German Village* (New York, 2009), 39–41.
36 Louise Nyholm Kallestrup, *Agents of Witchcraft in Early Modern Italy and Denmark* (Basingstoke, 2015), 67, 78–9.
37 Malcolm Gaskill, 'Witchcraft in early modern Kent: stereotypes and the background to accusations', in Jonathan Barry, Marianne Hester and Gareth Roberts (eds.), *Witchcraft in Early Modern Europe* (Cambridge, 1996), 257–87, at p. 283.
38 Nicole Jacques-Chaquin and Maxime Préaud (eds.), *Les sorciers du carroi de Marlou: Un procès de sorcellerie en Berry (1582–1583)* (Grenoble, 1996), 128–9, 135.

5 Witchcraft and folk belief

> O see not ye yon narrow road,
>   So thick beset wi thorns and briers?
> That is the path of righteousness,
>   Tho after it but few enquires.
>
> And see not ye yon braid braid road,
>   That lies across yon lillie leven?
> That is the path of wickedness,
>   Tho some call it the road to heaven.
>
> And see not ye that bonny road,
>   Which winds about the fernie brae?
> That is the road to fair Elfland,
>   Where you and I this night maun gae.
>
> The Ballad of Thomas the Rhymer (Scottish traditional)[1]

Introduction

What did ordinary people know about witches? For them, even more than for intellectuals, witchcraft was part of an imaginative world – a world of stories, songs and fantasy, and in some cases, a world of visionary experience that took them far from their mundane lives. To be sure, peasants also had practical concerns about the danger of harmful magic, as we saw in the last chapter. The present chapter, however, will explore a wider and deeper world of magic and culture.

The peasant world-view

Ordinary people in early modern Europe lived in a magical world. The magical powers wielded by witches were just a small part of a wide interplay of hidden forces. We may think of these forces as 'natural' processes – the cycle of the seasons, with sowing and harvesting; the raising and slaughtering of livestock; the seeking of fish in lakes, rivers and seas; the human life-cycle itself, with the forming of relationships, and the conception, bearing and nurturing of children – but the wonder and even awe that these powerful forces could inspire meant that they were far from ordinary. Life and death were indeed magical. Peasants needed to understand these forces in meaningful ways, and to feel that they could act to protect their families and livelihoods from unpredictable harm.

Life was not always hard, but it was unpredictable. Crops might be damaged by rain, drought or storms, or might fail to ripen in a cooler summer. Fish might shift their habitat. Farm animals were vulnerable to harsh weather or to disease, and their suffering could be visibly distressing. Human illnesses and deaths, especially the illnesses and deaths of children, were even more harrowing.

At the heart of all magical beliefs lies the fear of the unpredictable and the uncontrollable. Today we can forecast the weather, and retreat from it into heated or air-conditioned houses. We expect global markets and technology to fill our supermarket shelves with food, no matter what problems our local farmers may face. And we have health services, welfare services and insurance policies that we hope will protect us from modern life's tribulations. Early modern people had none of this security.

Peasants thus needed to be able to understand and interpret their uncertainties and insecurities – to give their worries a meaning that allowed them to cope with them. These meanings provided people with recognisable and reassuring actions to take. To do this, they interpreted the world as governed by various spirit beings. Instead of abstract 'nature', they thought of nature *spirits*. Instead of the blank absence of death, they thought of the *spirits* of the dead. And, in order to understand these spirits, they told stories about them.

These stories gave symbolic structure to the world. They showed how it was divided into cultivated places – villages and farmlands – and wild places – hills, forests and lakes. Even towns were not far from wild places, and town walls and gates symbolically kept the wildness out. The wild places were the haunt of nature spirits. Wells and springs were often located in these wild places, and journeys to them were magical rituals. Churchyards were connected to heaven and hell, the ultimate destinations of the spirits of the dead. In this way, what the authorities thought of as 'religion' was included in this magical world, so that journeys to wells and springs became pilgrimages. Cultivated places became safer and more homely when the wild places were populated with magical beings. The dangers could be thought of as coming from an external force.

The changing seasons had rituals attached to them. Winter was cold and dark: people wanted celebrations that would bring light and warmth. In spring they wanted symbols of rebirth, growth and renewal. In summer they wanted to make the most of the sunlight and warmth for outdoor celebrations. Autumn brought harvest and plenty, but also the end of the growing season. Leaves turned brown and died; some farm animals were deliberately slaughtered because they could not be maintained over the winter. Seeing things die in the natural world turned people's thoughts towards death, and perhaps towards the otherworld.

One way in which early modern people understood their world, then, was to populate it with a variety of remarkable non-human beings – ghosts, revenants, fairies and giants, to mention just a few. Peasants' stories were never about beings that were agreed to be wholly fictional, like today's cartoon superheroes; there was assumed to be some reality to them. A particular story about fairies might be just a story, but there was no doubt about the reality of fairies in general. Some people even had special relationships with beings such as fairies – either as individuals, or even as members of groups with shared beliefs and ritual practices. These popular beliefs and practices were not usually about witchcraft directly, but they contributed to the development of stereotypes of witchcraft, and also influenced individual trials. Stories about witchcraft drew heavily on folk belief.

The belief in fairies provides an example of how this tended to happen. A suspected witch, interrogated about her relationship with the Devil, might know more about fairies than about the Devil, and might talk about fairies in answer to questions about the Devil. The interrogators would assume that the fairies were really demons. Educated people did not usually believe in fairies, but they certainly believed in demons, and knew that demons were deceptive and dangerous. They would not be surprised to find demons deceiving an uneducated witch into believing that they were fairies. Illustration 5.1, showing a 'Dance of the Elves' in which the elves are depicted as demons, shows popular beliefs becoming demonised.

Illustration 5.1 Nature spirits become demonic, 1555

This is a 'Dance of the Elves', illustrating Scandinavian folk belief, from a 'History of the Northern Peoples' by Olaus Magnus. The 'elves' look rather like classical satyrs, presumably because the artist knew more about classical satyrs than about elves – but they also look rather like demons. The rise of demonology led educated people to explain the nature spirits of popular belief as demons.

Ideas of the witches' sabbat were often influenced by folk belief. As we saw in Chapter 3, demonologists tended to envisage the witches' worship of the Devil as a parody of orthodox Christian worship of God. But, when they interrogated witchcraft suspects, this was not really what they found. The common folk did not worship the Devil, nor did they believe that anyone else worshipped the Devil. Instead, they believed in a lot of other things that were less obviously wicked, but sometimes much stranger. Interrogators and demonologists had to try to fit this folkloric material into their preconceptions. This chapter will thus try to reconstruct the popular beliefs that witchcraft suspects brought into the torture chamber – often to be reinterpreted there as demonic.

There are two principal difficulties with this exercise in reconstruction. The first concerns the source material for popular belief. Our sources were all written by members of the elite, who may have distorted or misunderstood what they were told. While the common folk knew little of educated beliefs, the elite did know a good deal of popular beliefs, often learned from their servants (particularly during their own childhood). However, the elite seem usually to have been unfamiliar with the most bizarre and exotic material discussed in the present chapter. Either they were never told about this material, or else they dismissed it as vulgar superstition in which they need take no interest.

Members of the elite would be particularly likely to distort or misunderstand what peasants told them if they thought that the peasants were themselves ignorant of the true nature of the beings they described. Here it can be useful to distinguish between statements in confessions and statements in neighbours' accusations. Both arose from popular belief, and both might be shaped by leading questions, but their perspectives were different. Confessions tend to contain more folkloric material, because suspects often *had* to say something about otherworldly beings when they were interrogated coercively about the Devil. Neighbours, by contrast, were not expected to have met the Devil, and were usually asked about everyday magical harm. Confessions, therefore, tend to go deeper into folkloric belief and experience – but they have to be read carefully, because the interrogators often shaped the material to fit demonological assumptions. Demonological works themselves, restricted by the need for correct theology and elaborated by their authors' own imaginations, are even more untrustworthy as sources of folklore.

Fortunately some interrogators, interviewing people on suspicion of witchcraft or heresy, were either not seeking an immediate conviction or else were genuinely unsure what to make of the outlandish stories they were being told, and so recorded some valuable folkloric material without much apparent attempt to adapt it to their own preconceptions. Moreover, some confessions diverge so widely from demonological stereotypes that it is clear that they represent the suspects' real belief or experience. There is also some medieval evidence, which is less contaminated by demonological stereotypes, though it may pose its own problems of interpretation. The richest material has been found only in a few areas, so there are problems in deciding how far it can be applied to Europe as a whole. But the *clearly* regional patterns are few, and it seems evident that witches' confessions and neighbours' accusations all over Europe were affected in some way by folkloric beliefs. The attempt to reconstruct this folklore must be made.

The second difficulty with this folkloric material is simply that it is hard to interpret, even today. In this chapter we shall encounter people with some very strange beliefs. They believed, apparently genuinely, that they had met fairies, or had flown out at night, or had made voyages in spirit while their bodies remained behind. We may well ask: what was really going on here? There may or may not be answers to these questions, but one thing is certain: the process of seeking the answers takes us to the limits of what it means to be human.

'Paganism' and animism

Popular witch beliefs are sometimes said to have been 'pagan', or to have originated with 'paganism'. However, this idea is rarely helpful. There were hardly any pagans in early modern Europe. Paganism in ancient times had meant the organised, public worship of various pagan gods (Celtic, Germanic or Roman); such worship was long dead. Most Europeans had been converted to Christianity over a thousand years before the early modern period. By then only a few tribal peoples were still pagan, like the Sámi people in northern Scandinavia. They were on the fringes of European society rather than full members of it. Even more marginal were the non-Christian peoples of the Spanish and Portuguese empires outside Europe. Within Europe there were some Jews and Muslims, but they were in a class of their own, usually tolerated officially by the Christian states in which they lived, and certainly not 'pagan'.

Although there was no survival *of* paganism, there were survivals *from* paganism. These were mostly beliefs and practices carried out by individuals, such as healing charms. Most such charms had been Christianised, and people who used them cannot have known their pagan origins. There were also occasional group rituals. The authorities sometimes feared anti-Christian cults and societies (not all of which really existed outside their own fantastic fears), but they thought of such cults as heretical, not as pagan. In the 1920s, the eccentric folklorist Margaret Murray popularised the idea that early modern

(continued)

witches were members of a pagan cult that had survived underground since pre-Christian times, but this idea has long been discredited (it will be discussed further in Chapter 11). The common folk in early modern Europe thought of themselves as Christians.

Some of the beliefs and rituals that have been called 'pagan survivals' are better understood as instances of folkloric animism – the idea that plants, rivers, hills, and other features and attributes of the natural world had their own personalities. Fairies, for instance, were basically nature spirits. This idea was as current in the seventeenth century as it had been in the seventh century; it was simply a popular idea, and does not have to be considered a 'survival' of something earlier. All organised religions have had to come to terms with animism in some way.

Popular Christianity

If fairies were important folkloric figures, so were saints and angels, and so was the Virgin Mary. Christian belief and ritual formed an important component of folklore. Christianity was basically an organised religion, defined and controlled by the intellectual and political elite, but it had won universal acceptance among the common folk. There was a tradition of popular cynicism about priests, who rarely lived up to the high standards proclaimed by the Church, but most 'anticlericalism' was basically religious – it expressed a desire for good priests. People saw their world in a way that was structured by Christianity. They asked God's blessing on their work. They expressed morality in Christian terms. They dated events with reference to religious festivals. They hoped to go to heaven when they died, and thought of meeting their ancestors there.

Although we do not know how often most people attended church, it is clear that enough of them attended often enough to learn basic ideas of Christianity. God, who was good, had created the world and still ruled over it; Jesus, his son, had 'saved' the human race by his death. God could grant people, not only spiritual benefits like salvation, but also material benefits like good health, a good harvest or a good husband. Catholics asked saints, or the Virgin Mary, to approach God on their behalf; the authorities in Protestant countries tried to discourage this but found it an uphill struggle, since people often wanted to believe in intermediate, intercessory beings with their own personalities. Indeed the Catholic church sometimes worried that people were praying to the saints themselves, which was not strictly correct. Popular Christianity was sometimes unorthodox, but it was a living force.

Many Christian characters thus passed into folklore. There were folktales about saints – indeed many official lives of medieval saints, written by monks, had an essentially folkloric structure. There were folktales about the Virgin Mary, such as the 'Cherry Tree Carol', still well known today.

There were folktales about angels. Above all, there were folktales about the Devil.

Because God was considered to be good, another religious being was needed to represent and explain evil. This was of course the Devil. The common folk were just as familiar with the basic Christian idea of the Devil as they were with God. Wall paintings in late medieval churches often depicted the Devil and demons, sometimes dragging human souls into the fearsome mouth of hell. There were 'mystery plays' (meaning 'religious' plays), organised by the church with popular participation, in which the Devil and other demons often appeared.

The common folk were thus well aware of the basic opposition between God and the Devil. They also knew that witches were in some sense connected to the Devil. They may have had only a rudimentary idea of the demonic pact, but it was a Christian commonplace that evil came from the Devil, and popular witches were certainly evil. Flying witches were believed to fall to the ground if they named God or made the sign of the cross. The Sicilian *donas de fuera* ('ladies from outside'), a fairy cult that we shall meet again shortly, refused to mention Jesus in their meetings.

The folkloric Devil, although clearly evil, was not terrifying. In mystery plays he was often a figure of fun, trying to make trouble but getting his comeuppance at the end. In folktales the Devil was often an adversary to the peasant hero in riddles and verbal tricks – in which the peasant usually outwitted him. Many witches' confessions illustrate the limited powers of the folkloric Devil. One Scottish witch in 1659, Janet Wood, related that she had asked the Devil to take revenge on an English soldier who had stolen her malt; the Devil replied that the man had returned to England and was now beyond his reach.[2] Popular Christian rituals could also overcome the Devil. A Swiss witch, Pierre Chavaz, confessed in 1448 that he had been unable to make hail near the village of Sainte-Croix because the church bells rang.[3]

There were popular ideas about the demonic pact. People were initiated into Christianity through baptism, so it was natural to assume that the Devil would initiate witches through a similar ritual. This idea could be elaborated theologically, but the basics of it were equally accessible to the common folk. Parents wanted their children baptised as soon as possible after birth, believing that the child could not enter heaven without this. Witchcraft suspects, asked about demonic baptism, could produce folkloric elaborations on it, such as the idea that demonic baptism had to occur three times. Elaborations of the demonic pact involved telling a *story* about it, usually about the development of the suspect's personal relationship with the Devil – a story that often culminated in sex. As we shall see in Chapter 9, these stories were essentially women's stories, and functioned as versions of the courtship narratives that interested women.

Our period was one of religious 'reformation'. In both Protestant and Catholic countries, the authorities tried to inculcate new orthodoxies among the common folk. This will be discussed further in Chapter 6, but here we may ask: what was the effect of the new preaching and catechising on popular beliefs about the Devil? How much did ordinary folk learn about the terrifying Devil of elite belief, who was out to destroy humankind – in alliance with witches? How much, in short, did people learn about elite demonology?

Answers to this question are not straightforward. It is clear that the common folk did not simply switch from folkloric beliefs to demonological ones; popular ideas about the Devil are found just as readily at the end of our period as at the beginning. But people might well have learned *something* from a century or two of preaching, not to mention the dissemination of demonological information in reports of witchcraft trials themselves. Seventeenth-century witchcraft confessions are usually far longer and more detailed about the Devil than fifteenth-century ones; this is due mainly to greater elite interest and habits of record-keeping (other court records also expanded), but it may also indicate that more seventeenth-century peasants possessed detailed information about the Devil.

How folktales structured witchcraft stories

Witchcraft confessions were basically *narratives*, told chronologically, with a beginning, a middle and an end. People were familiar with this structure from folktales, and the way in which they constructed their confessions about witchcraft could resemble the way in which folktales were constructed. Suspects were often asked, not just about whether they had a pact with the Devil, but about *how* they had come to make a pact with the Devil – and, in response, they had to tell a story about this. The story that they narrated typically began with a setting in space and time, and continued with an encounter between the narrator and a person who initially appeared to be human. The setting could include a reason for the narrator to have a problem or to expect a visitor. The narrator and the stranger then established some kind of a relationship with each other – for women, this could be a sexual relationship. But then the Devil revealed himself openly, or else the narrator noticed something demonic – a cloven hoof, a tail, horns, or a wooden hand. It was a powerful and dramatic *dénouement* to a story.

Many such stories were extracted under torture, but some were told voluntarily. In southern Italy in 1745, Antonia Macarella told a neighbour a remarkable tale about how she had encountered the Devil. A love affair that she had been having with a man had recently ended, and she was walking outside the town, despondent about this, when someone called out to her. She thought it was her lover, but it turned out to be the Devil. He led her to a place where the earth opened up, and they went inside. She found three mounds of gold and silver, and hoped to carry them off, but a fierce image warned her that she would accomplish this only if she carried away all the treasure at once. Realising that this was impossible, she dropped the treasure she was carrying and fled. This story was told as factual, and Macarella herself may have believed it, but it is so similar in content to a folktale – with the earth opening up, the three treasures, the impossible task – that her knowledge of such tales surely shaped it.[4]

Today, we think of a 'folktale' as something told by the common people. But members of the elite also told stories about witches that were basically folktales, and their tale motifs circulated and shaped new tales. This can be illustrated by a tale related by the German lawyer Johann Georg Godelmann in 1591. This had supposedly happened to a student in Martin Luther's time, the early sixteenth century. The student was studying in Wittenberg, Luther's university, and he made a pact with the Devil, written in his blood, in order to have money always in his purse. However, he was moved to repent by hearing Luther preach, and Luther organised public prayers that forced the Devil to surrender the writing.[5] Godelmann's story of the student was basically a Protestant adaptation of the medieval legend of Theophilus, who had been said to have made a pact with the Devil in order to gain promotion in the church. On Theophilus' repentance, it had been the Virgin Mary who forced the Devil to return the written pact to him. There had indeed been such a student in Wittenberg, named Valerius Glöckner – but Luther's own story of him ended with Glöckner's repentance.[6] Godelmann, or his informant, reshaped and elaborated the story using similar motifs to that of Theophilus. Nor was he alone, since the Catholic demonologist Martin Delrio related a 'completely reliable anecdote' from Italy, also based on the Theophilus legend.[7] Godelmann's story of the student was credible and effective because, like the story of Theophilus, it was a good *story*, with strong characters and motives, clear and dramatic narrative, and a useful moral.

Today, we also think of a 'folktale' as something told to children. In early modern times, children were certainly told stories, but so were adults. We know little about whether children's stories were different, but they were probably influential; some adults' memoirs allude to what they were told as children. The fact that a story was principally told to children did not in itself lessen its status as 'true'.

The 'truth' of a folkloric narrative was rarely absolute and taken for granted. Rather, it was something to be assessed in the light of experience and knowledge. If you heard that a woman in your village had transformed herself into a hare, you would ask yourself questions about whether this was likely to be true. Is my informant a trustworthy person? Is that woman known to have a magical reputation? Was the sighting of the hare linked to some other unusual event? Depending on your answers to these questions, you might decide that the story of the woman's transformation was true, or that it was false. However, you would not dismiss the story as false, as most people would today, simply on the grounds that such transformations were impossible. In early modern Europe, you would know that such transformations were possible.

Non-human inhabitants of the popular universe

Let us take a tour of the popular universe, to learn more about the non-human beings with whom the common folk shared their lives. We have already noted popular Christianity's good beings – God, Jesus, saints, angels, Virgin Mary – and its bad beings – the Devil and demons. But there were numerous other beings, and they were not thought of in distinct compartments separate from Christianity. People were not taught about fairies in church, and much of what was 'known' about such beings came from folktales – but popular Christianity also operated in folkloric ways. We shall see that some people also had visionary experiences in which these non-human beings, and the worlds in which they lived, became vividly real.

Fairies were probably the most important group of non-human beings. They went under various names in different languages, such as elves or pixies in English; some other beings that we might think of as different, such as goblins and trolls, were much the same type of beings as fairies. Fairies lived in another world, though this was rarely precisely identified; it was sometimes an alternative to heaven or hell, as with the ballad of Thomas the Rhymer quoted at the head of this chapter. In practice you were likely to encounter fairies in wild places – mountains, forests, lakes. They had their own society, with a king and queen.

Fairies were often benevolent, but they could also cause harm, and they were not trusted. They were sometimes called the 'good people' to conciliate them. Fairies sometimes stole babies, leaving a 'changeling' in place of the human baby. This fake infant would demand large quantities of food but would remain thin, ill-nourished and miserable. It is easy to see how such beliefs could thrive among inexperienced and desperate parents. Changeling beliefs provide an example of elite misinterpretation: the *Malleus Maleficarum* attributed changelings to demons.[8]

There were two possibly contradictory aspects to the relationship between fairy belief and witch-hunting. The main point is that witchcraft suspects, when interrogated about the Devil, sometimes talked about fairies instead. Today we can see this as evidence (if we needed it) that these suspects were not really witches. The interrogators, however, assumed that the fairies were demons, and so were enabled to continue the prosecution. Fairy belief and witch belief were, in this respect, mutually supportive. However, there is also the issue of fairies causing misfortune. If a peasant suffered a misfortune and blamed it on fairies, then that misfortune was not going to be blamed on a witch. Fairy belief and witch belief were, in this respect, mutually exclusive alternatives.

Was misfortune blamed on fairies often enough to prevent a significant amount of witch-hunting? Answers to this question are bound to be tentative, because of the nature of the evidence. Fairies could not be arrested and brought to court. If any particular misfortune was blamed on fairies, not only would it not generate a witchcraft trial, but it would probably not generate any written evidence at all. Fairy belief may well have damped down the intensity of European witch-hunting, but this idea would be impossible to quantify. The same applies to the related idea that more misfortune had been blamed on fairies in the middle ages, thus helping to explain why few witches were prosecuted in that period.

The best way to tackle these questions is probably regional. One case study has argued that in the nineteenth century (when we at last have good evidence from folklorists), Irish people did blame misfortune on fairies, while rural English people were still blaming witches in a way familiar to early modernists.[9] This might help to explain why there were virtually no witchcraft cases among Gaelic-speaking Irish Catholics, and only a handful even among the seventeenth-century Protestant settlers in Ireland. Other explanations are unfortunately possible, notably the reluctance of Irish Catholics to denounce their neighbours to Protestant courts run by the English-controlled government (which will be discussed in Chapter 6). Still, the idea that attributing misfortune to fairies could have averted witch-hunting in some regions is thought-provoking.

Witches in some regions had small, demonic animal companions. This was often a toad, lizard or cat that lived with the witch and sometimes committed malefice on the witch's behalf. This belief was found mainly in Hungary and England; in Hungary the animal was called a *lidérc*, in England it was called a familiar. Today, at least in English-speaking countries, the witch's cat has become established in the popular imagery of witchcraft (a subject to which we shall return in Chapter 11). The animal 'familiar' in this sense was uncommon in most of Europe, though occasional examples can be found quite widely scattered – in Lorraine, Venice, Navarre and Poland, for instance. By contrast, even in Hungary and England, witches did not have to have familiars. The Hungarian *lidérc* was often a lizard or chicken; the English familiar was often a toad or a cat, or sometimes a fantasy animal. A few familiars were insects, which may be connected with shamanistic beliefs in spirit flight; such beliefs sometimes included the idea that the spirit left the body in the form of an insect.

Belief in animal familiars should be understood in a broader context of belief in spirit companions. The word 'familiar' came from the biblical phrase 'familiar spirit', understood to mean a demon assigned personally to the witch. The idea of a personal demon was quite common, so the English and Hungarians were simply imagining such a demon as a small animal. In northern Germany, witches could work their malefices by sending small demonic creatures called '*Holden*' or '*Elben*' to lodge themselves in their victims' bodies.[10] In Denmark, some female witches were thought to make a pact with a personal demon called a '*dreng*' (servant boy); after the pact, the demon became a dog or other animal and was sent out to enter houses and bewitch victims.[11] A personal demon called a '*kikimora*', sent by a witch to afflict a victim, was found in Russia.[12] Future research may show the animal familiar as more closely linked in to broader patterns of belief.

The idea of 'fate' could become personified in order to explain the mysteries of life and death. In central and south-eastern Europe there were 'fate women' or 'night goddesses' – goddesses or demons associated both with fertility and with death. The medieval Scottish 'weird sisters' were similar; Shakespeare converted them into witches in *Macbeth* (*c.*1606), but in the earlier Scottish story of Macbeth they were a distinct group of non-human beings who governed people's fates. The Scots word 'weird' (deriving from Anglo-Saxon '*wyrd*') meant 'fate'; the word's adoption into standard English, with its modern meaning, began only with Shakespeare's play.

Ghosts were important. Death was intimately familiar to pre-industrial Europeans; they saw people die, at all ages, in their own or neighbours' houses. They had to think about what was going on, and what these people's destiny might be. People also recognised a continuing connection with their ancestors, who formed part of their own identity in a way that is hard for today's individualistic world to recapture. People's status often depended on their ancestors' status. Recent ancestors can be seen as a kind of age-group, exercising a continuing influence on the lives of the living.

So it is not surprising that dead people were sometimes encountered, as ghosts, by the living. They could not do so officially; theology usually taught that the soul departed immediately from the body on death – to heaven, hell or (for Catholics) purgatory – and could not return without a miracle. However, popular belief saw the spirits of the dead as able to linger in and around their bodies for some time, haunting the people they had known. As well as possession by demons (which will be discussed in Chapter 9), there existed a popular belief in 'ghostly possession', in which wandering ghosts could take over people's bodies. Ghosts were unwelcome. Sometimes they were pitied – the ghost needed help to get to heaven, its rightful home – but often they were feared. People took precautions like opening a window in the death-room to enable the soul to depart. One reason churchyards were walled was to prevent anything getting out of them.

It was usually the dead person's spirit that returned, but sometimes it was their physical body, in which case they could be called a 'revenant'. Revenants seem mainly to have been known in northern Europe. Similar to revenants, if more specialised, were vampires – animated corpses that returned for the specific purpose of attacking the living and drinking their blood. Vampire belief was mainly held in south-eastern Europe. Vampires, like revenants, were always other people – nobody believed themselves to be vampires. Countermeasures against vampires involved digging up corpses and piercing them with poles.

Ghosts could also wander the earth in troops. There was a group of stories about this, usually known today as the 'Wild Hunt'. People told stories of encounters with a procession of wandering ghosts, sometimes led by a mysterious character called Hellequin. Sometimes the ghosts had died prematurely in battle, and perhaps were compelled to wander the earth until their allotted span of years was concluded. The tradition is clearest in northern France, though it was also found in Germany and other places. How much of it was folkloric is unclear, since some of the writers reporting it drew more from each other than from the common folk, but some connection with popular belief seems likely. Some writers condemned the popular belief as a demonic illusion.[13] The Wild Hunt supplied some imagery for the early modern Devil, if not for the idea of the sabbat itself.[14] The Lorraine demonologist Nicolas Rémy, in 1595, recalled childhood stories about dancing hobgoblins called the 'Helequin family'.[15] Rémy's hobgoblins may have been closer to fairies than ghosts. Fragments of the Wild Hunt may also have surfaced in witches' confessions.[16]

Witches in legends and folktales

This book is focused on real, human 'witches' who were put to death for their alleged crimes. However, folklore also contained 'witches' of its own, who were not always the same as real, human ones. In themselves, these folkloric witches might not concern us; but there was some overlap or cross-fertilisation. As a result, some distinctive motifs from folklore found their way into neighbours' accusations and into the confessions of witchcraft suspects.

A schematic analysis of the folkloric 'witch' indicates that there were two related but often distinct types: the witch of legend and the witch of the folktale.[17] There was some overlap between these, but, broadly, 'legends' were stories that were taken to be straightforwardly true, while folktales were seen as fictional. Even fictional stories were true to the reality of their tellers in some way, just as a 'fictional' novel today may be set in the 'real' world and offer insights into 'real' life. Legends and folktales both tended to involve magic, but that did not make them 'unreal'; people believed that magic was real. Let us take the legendary witch and the folktale witch in turn.

The legendary witch had several links with the demonological witch and the village witch. She was connected with the Devil, from whom her powers derived. Witches in legends could be plural, and could fly to witch mountains like the Blocksberg in Germany. Like the village witch, the legendary witch had a range of evil powers: stealing milk and butter, harming livestock, and weather magic such as storm-raising.

Beliefs about the legendary witch have sometimes led historians to conclude that, before the witch-hunts began, there was already a fully-formed set of popular beliefs about an identifiable 'witches' sabbat'. However, this conclusion is at least partially misleading. Peasants believed that legendary witches existed, but they did not believe that such witches lived in their own villages. They did not even believe that they were necessarily human, though they could have been humans who lived in some other perhaps magical place. The legendary witch's place of residence was usually left vague.

The folktale witch, by contrast, was not linked with the Devil; her powers were innate. She was always solitary. Like the legendary witch, she lived outside the village, but she tended to live in an identifiable remote place, such as a forest. She was even less obviously human; she might have iron teeth or feeble red eyes, or be bulletproof. Although she had remarkable and perhaps terrifying powers, these were not necessarily the same as the powers attributed to demonic or village witches; they could include, for instance, the power to turn people to stone. Among her malefices, she might have a habit of stealing children and sometimes eating them. Some demonic human witches were also said to do this, but under the different circumstances of the witches' sabbat. Both the legendary witch and the folktale witch were almost always female, though a few folktales also included male warlocks.

This can be illustrated with a Russian case study. Russia was little touched by western European demonology until the eighteenth or even nineteenth centuries, so folk beliefs on witchcraft emerge more clearly. There were two related kinds of witch in Russian folklore: the '*ved'ma*' and the '*baba-iaga*'. The *ved'ma*, like the legendary witch, was more often thought to be human, though stories featuring such a character often emphasised fantastical elements. The *baba-iaga*, like the folktale witch, was a more monstrous character, clearly different from a human being, who changed her shape and enticed and ate children. She might, however, have a more or less human daughter, whom the hero could rescue in an escape featuring a magical contest.[18] A folktale witch in the Ukraine was sometimes called a '*zirokhvatka*', star-grasper, because stories told that she had the habit of stealing stars and the moon in order to interfere with Christian holy days.[19]

One feared type of legendary witch was the bloodsucking night witch – or, rather, night witches, for they were usually plural. They were distantly related to elite beliefs in *lamiae* and *striae*, discussed in Chapter 3. In fifteenth-century Italy, witches who sucked children's blood were sometimes thought to be human, and seem to have been distinct from the emerging idea of the demonic witch who abducted babies to the sabbat.[20] In the Canary Islands, claims that unnamed 'witches' had sucked the blood of newborn babies were recorded from the sixteenth to the eighteenth centuries; these 'witches' may not have been human.[21]

More research is thus needed on overlaps and distinctions between human witches and non-human witches. When the seventeenth-century Polish lexicographer Grzegorz Knapiusz studied the vernacular term '*przypołudnica*', normally meaning 'noon-tide demon', he linked it with '*czarownica*' ('witch'), '*wiedma*' ('hag', evidently related to the Russian *ved'ma*) and '*latawica*' ('flying demon' or 'succubus').[22] Was the 'witch' here a human being? More broadly, did those who used these words draw a clear distinction between those beings that were human and those that were not?

Some stories about folktale witches focused on how the witch was overcome or thwarted. She might be defeated by counter-magic, by protective magic, by physical attack, or by outwitting her in the knowledge of her limitations – for instance, her powers might not work at a crossroads. Antoine Rose, a confessing witch in Savoy in 1477, related how another witch was thwarted by physical means: 'she had tried to take a son of Michel Rose by night and would have done so, had not Michel wounded her in the arm'.[23] As well as stories of overcoming witches, there were stories of simply recognising them – usually connected with their powers of shape-shifting. A particularly common tale told how a cat had its paw cut off, whereupon a woman was found without a hand and discovered to be a witch. Versions of this tale occasionally surfaced in witchcraft trials, but it surely originated in folklore. Then there was the tale of the man who married a female water-spirit and had children with her, but she returned to the sea after he breached a taboo. The demonologist Ulrich Müller related this tale as factual in 1489, gravely explaining that the woman and her children must really have been demons.[24]

There has been less research on folkloric witches than on real, human witches. It is thus unclear how far the legendary witch and folktale witch were distinct in practice. A schematic way in which their attributes can be connected is shown in Diagram 5.1. The issue of the witch's powers was central, with the witch being able to perform various fantastic feats that were sometimes distantly related either to the demonic witch or to the village witch. However, the idea of a battle of wits between the folkloric witch and her human victim was often important, with the contest being played out in different ways from those between village witches and their neighbours. Further important ideas about folkloric witches concerned their powers of flight and shape-shifting – motifs to which we now turn.

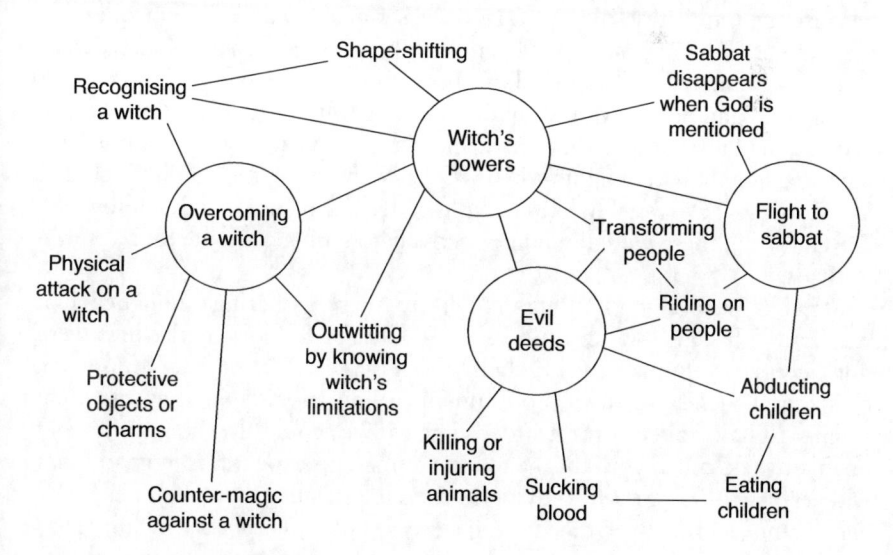

Diagram 5.1 The folkloric witch

Flying and shape-shifting

Popular beliefs about legendary witches sometimes included the idea that witches gathered in remote places, especially on mountains. In the fifteenth and sixteenth centuries the most famous of these was the Heuberg, in the Swabian Alps in south Germany. In the seventeenth century the Blocksberg or Brocken, in the Harz Mountains in central Germany, also became well known (see Illustration 3.2 above). The most famous Scandinavian witch mountain was Blåkulla ('Blue Hill') in Sweden, sometimes identified with the island of Blå Jungfrun, though the word probably originated in Germany as the name of an imagined place. Another Scandinavian witch mountain, Domen, in northern Norway, was a real mountain, said to be the entrance to hell. Hungary too had a real mountain for its witches, Saint-Gellert near Buda. Poland and Russia, by contrast, had 'Bald Mountain', an imagined place that could be identified with any nearby hill. As for southern Europe, Portugal had a witch venue in the city of Lisbon itself, the Val de Cavalinhos. Italy had a particularly famous place for witches to meet: a walnut tree said to be found at Benevento near Naples. Matteuccia di Francesco, who was executed for witchcraft in Todi, Italy, at the early date of 1428, confessed that she had flown on a goat to a witches' sabbat at the walnut tree of Benevento.[25]

Sometimes the destination of flying witches was less prominent than the journey. Belief in flight may well have originated as a belief about legendary, non-human witches, but humans could tell stories about how they joined such flights or rides. Several people from the Venetian countryside claimed to have gone out '*in strighozzo*', a phrase meaning something like 'going witching'; how they should be understood is not entirely clear, partly because the Inquisition did not take them seriously and so did not question them in detail.[26] They may have been describing a cult such as those we shall meet in a moment, or they may have been telling stories.

Witches' gatherings were sometimes linked to the seasons. The folkloric calendar had a strongly annual rhythm, with particular days or periods having ritual significance. Nights when witches were thought to gather included St Walpurgis Eve (30 April), St John's Eve (23 June) and Hallowe'en (31 October); these were linked respectively to spring, summer and autumn festivals.

Witches were always thought to fly to these gatherings, and belief in witches' flight was important in itself. Witches at folkloric gatherings were not necessarily human, and beliefs about witches' flight may thus have transferred themselves from non-human to human witches. Peasants seem usually to have taken it for granted that witches could fly, though they did not always do much with this belief. In German interrogations, it is odd that witches usually confessed to flying to the sabbat, since they often described it as being held in the immediate neighbourhood. The belief in flight has been argued to be essential to enable interrogators to explain large sabbats at long distances, but evidence for a need to explain this seems to be lacking. Witches' flight occurred in confessions, not because the interrogators wanted to explain large gatherings at long distances, but because flight was itself an important ingredient in witchcraft beliefs.

Methods of flight varied. Witches often had vehicles for flight – especially forked cooking-sticks, used in Germany. Witches also flew on broomsticks, plain sticks, straws, stools, demonic animals (especially goats), or simply by their own power. Some flew in animal form. A few transformed other (innocent) humans into animals and rode on them. The idea of *multiple* vehicles for flight was important, with groups of flying witches sometimes using a variety of different vehicles. Flight rarely if ever involved high altitudes. The Spanish witch Lauria de Pavia said that she and her company flew at a height of six *palmas* (half a metre) over the ground.[27] People seem to have thought of 'flight' as swift, horizontal movement, like riding a horse but more so. Such magical means of transport led Françoise Perroz, in Quingey, Franche-Comté, in 1657, to be accused of crossing the flooded river Loue 'without getting at all wet', which must have been 'by the intervention and aid of the demon'.[28] These ideas about the mechanics of flight were incorporated into demonology, but mostly originated in folklore.

Another distinct idea was the flying person who inadvertently mentioned God or Jesus, whereupon the Devil let them fall to earth. In some stories this person was a witch, in others it was someone who had gone along with the witches out of curiosity. Similarly, there was a motif of the person at the sabbat who inadvertently mentioned God or Jesus, whereupon the demonic feast disappeared and the person was left alone in the wilderness. Some demonologists repeated these stories, but they originated as folklore about groups of legendary witches.

Such ideas may have been very old, though the medieval sources are fragmentary. In a few late-medieval Swiss trials, the accused were said to have ridden on wolves. This seems to have been a popular rather than elite idea, as the accusations did not involve the Devil. There was no suggestion that they were werewolves, nor that the wolves were demons.[29] In the Scandinavian sagas, too, witches' riding was most often on a wolf. In a Swedish law code of the early thirteenth century, it was a calumny to say of a woman that she had been seen flying at the equinox, riding on a magical gate and with loose hair like a troll. It is hard to know what to do with such fragments of information; they surely indicate important beliefs, but, like the stories of *lamiae* discussed in Chapter 3, the beliefs may have become distorted. The earliest Swedish flight beliefs are probably about flight by trolls rather than humans.[30]

Related to flight was the folkloric idea of shape-shifting – of a human changing into an animal. This often came up in confessions, and was occasionally mentioned in neighbours' statements. Courts usually accepted shape-shifting reports as proof of guilt. Demonologists tended to warn that animal transformations were demonic illusions rather than physical realities, as we saw in Chapter 3, but demonic illusions still connected the witch with the Devil. The most common animals for witches to change into were cats and hares, animals with rich folkloric associations. Pre-industrial cats were not pets but working animals, living in the barn rather than the house, on the boundary between the domestic and the wild. Although they were small, their behaviour was clearly predatory, and also unpredictable. Cats were also seen as nocturnal, as were witches. To be thought of as a cat was to be thought of as wild and dangerous. Hares, better known than rabbits before modern times, were also unpredictable but were thought of not as predators but as prey – and as difficult to catch, because they ran so fast. It seems to have been mainly women who transformed themselves into hares. To be thought of as a hare was to be thought of as someone who was skilled at evading one's enemies.

Witches were also said to change into various other animals. Dogs were fairly common, though more witches may have seen the Devil as a dog than became dogs themselves. Various birds and insects were also mentioned; birds were presumably evoked by the idea of flying witches, while insects may have been connected to the belief that the spirit might leave the body in the form of an insect (as mentioned above in the discussion of familiars). Some Norwegian witches confessed to changing into whales in order to sink ships; whale transformations had also been mentioned in a medieval Icelandic saga. Transformation into horses was mentioned in stories that associated it with the idea of being 'shod' as a horse and controlled by another being – a being that became the Devil in confessions. The Devil, too, tended to transform into animals familiar in the locality concerned; in the Canary Islands he sometimes appeared as a camel.[31]

Finally, werewolves – humans who changed into wolves and attacked people violently – carried out a distinctive type of shape-shifting. They attracted particular elite attention because they were mentioned in classical literature, and much or most of the werewolf material in trials probably originated with the elite.[32] A folk belief in werewolves nevertheless existed in a few scattered places, notably Franche-Comté. Wolves were dangerous predators, and the idea of a human who became a magical wolf could be seen as similar to the idea of a human who became a witch. A handful of werewolf trials occurred in the sixteenth century; these increasingly became assimilated to witchcraft trials, with the suspects being accused of making pacts with the Devil and behaving in other witch-like ways.

The witches' ride and the cover illustration

This book's cover shows an airborne witches' ride. It is a detail from a painting of 1528, 'Melancholy', by the German artist Lucas Cranach the Elder. 'Melancholy' was a technical term that did not

(continued)

simply mean sadness; it also meant openness to the Devil's trickery. A melancholic person was particularly imaginative and liable to see strange visions. The witches' ride in the painting is a demonic vision seen by the painting's central character, a young woman who personifies 'Melancholy'.

There are eight witches and one demon in the witches' ride. The demon is a composite beast (apparently part pig, part toad), like some of the well-known demons depicted by Cranach's older contemporary Hieronymus Bosch. The demon is nearest to the centre of the group and may well be the leader. All the witches are naked women – a reference to the elite idea that flying witches had to strip naked and anoint their bodies with a magical ointment, though Cranach, like commercial artists working for a male audience today, presumably also had more mundane reasons for wanting to depict naked women. But, while such illustrations today are all of young women, two of Cranach's are clearly *old* women, and a third may also be old. Two of these women wear headscarves or hoods, their only garments. The loose, flying hair of the other women is either a sign of unbridled sexuality, or a sign of a witch's power, or both. Sexuality, but more specifically masculine sexuality, is also alluded to by a flying cock, a symbol of the mercenary soldier as sexual predator.

The riders are mounted on various animals. The demon rides a horse, which may indicate that he is in charge, since a horse was a higher-status animal; he also appears to be controlling his mount, whereas some of the women are mere passengers on theirs. There are also a boar, a cow (carrying two women), a bull, a giant cat, a deer and two goats. The cat is a domestic cat rather than a lion, despite its size; it alludes to an idea by medieval churchmen that some heretics worshipped a demon in the form of a giant cat. The goat was similar; Waldensian heretics had been accused of worshipping the Devil in the form of a goat.

Two witches carry banners, with pictures of toads (magical animals) and a serpent (associated with the Devil). Several carry sticks, one at least of which is the forked cooking-stick associated with German witches; one of the banners is mounted on a forked stick (more clearly seen in a sixteenth-century copy of the painting). Two witches at the bottom are engaged in some kind of ritual combat, while a companion, with her fingers in her mouth, appears to be whistling – normally something done only by men. Overall, Cranach's 'Melancholy' warns that witchcraft is linked to unbridled female sexuality.

Shamanistic visionaries and cults

The early modern cosmos, then, contained magical beings and other worlds – and this was not just a matter of stories. Some people had visionary experiences in which they felt that they actually encountered these beings and visited these worlds. Some visionary experiences were unique to the individual concerned, while others were shared and could be replicated. Traditions arose of encounters with spirit beings. When these traditions took shape as distinct visionary and ritual practices among certain individuals, they may be called 'cults' – a sometimes difficult term that will be further discussed below, as will the equally difficult term 'shamanistic'.

The authorities took a disapproving view of most visionary activities. They were well aware of one way in which people could form relationships with non-human beings: people could become witches and make a pact with the Devil. Indeed historians mainly know about visionaries because some of them came to the authorities' attention on suspicion of witchcraft. Some of the visionaries' activities provided material for demonologists. In order to open up the subject of visionaries, it may help to begin with one well-documented example.

Chonrad Stoeckhlin, in Oberstdorf, Austria, made a pact with a friend in 1578: whichever of them died first would return and tell the other about the afterlife. The friend then died – and Stoeckhlin began to see visions of him. Further visions followed, especially a vision of an angel clad in white; the angel summoned Stoeckhlin to follow him, which he did. Stoeckhlin soon found himself entering trances and taking part in spirit flights, guided by the angel. He visited heaven and purgatory. He also encountered various folkloric beings, including the 'night phantoms' who played unearthly music; they seem to have been wandering ghosts, perhaps connected with the Wild Hunt. Stoeckhlin used this experience to become a magical practitioner, helping clients with various problems. He also acted as a folk prophet, exhorting people to reform their lives. His troubles began when he accused people of bewitching some of his clients, and his name came to the authorities' attention at the time of a witchcraft panic. Stoeckhlin was executed for witchcraft in 1587.[33]

This experience, and others like it, can be interpreted by relating it to worldwide traditions of shamanism. Shamans have been important as part of the public culture of numerous tribal peoples, particularly in Siberia (where the word 'shaman' originates) and among North American Indians. But the heart of shamanism is the visionary experience of meeting spirits and visiting other worlds, and it is hard to believe that this is culture-specific. If you experience a vision of another world, you will populate that world with beings from your own culture, whether these are angels, fairies, ghosts or (nowadays) aliens; but the journey arises within your own psyche. Visionary experience is probably a universal aspect of the human condition.

Chonrad Stoeckhlin was not fully a 'shaman' in the sense of enacting public performances of the trances that led to his spirit voyages. However, he made clear to his clients that he was using his spirit guide and spirit voyages in his work. The same can be said of the cults that we shall examine in a moment. Here they are called 'shamanistic' in the hope that this will be understood to be a broader term than the strict 'shamanic'. In early modern Europe, shamans as public performers of trance rituals were found only among the Sámi people in northern Scandinavia. Visionaries like Stoeckhlin, who undertook their spirit voyages in private, were the European norm. Such spirit voyages were certainly strange and exotic, and to a great extent folkloric, but there were also orthodox Christian visionary traditions, with famous practitioners like St Teresa of Ávila (1515–82). Stoeckhlin himself thought he was being a good Christian, though the authorities disagreed. He was not the only shamanistic visionary to be prosecuted as a witch, but the most important contribution that shamanistic traditions made to European witchcraft was not to furnish witches, but to furnish ideas about witchcraft. We shall now examine some of these ideas, focusing on popular traditions that formed themselves more or less concretely into cults.

Women flying out at night were known in various places in medieval Europe, and contributed to the idea of the witches' ride. Women who believed that they followed the goddess Diana were denounced by the tenth-century Canon *Episcopi*, as we saw in Chapter 3. There is a good deal of *elite* evidence for this, most of it denouncing the popular belief as a wicked and ignorant superstition. However, there is independent evidence indicating that the Canon *Episcopi* and related writings had some real connection to popular belief. Some people, mainly women, really did envisage themselves as flying out at night, often in the company of a magical female being or a group of non-human beings. These non-human beings were often fairies, so we may speak of 'fairy cults', while recognising that the term 'fairies' here is shorthand for various magical beings.

In their nocturnal voyages, the fairy-like beings and their female leader were joined by human followers, who went into trances and saw visions of the adventure. The whole procession would visit houses, often bringing prosperity. They would celebrate, with dancing and feasting. The feasting included drinking the contents of wine cellars and then magically restoring them, and eating whole animals and then resuscitating them from the bones and skin. The resuscitation of animals was a worldwide myth. The idea of eating and drinking one's fill was a compelling one for pre-industrial folk, who were often hungry at certain seasons.

Detailed documentation exists for one fairy cult: the Sicilian *'donas de fuera'* ('ladies from outside').[34] These 'ladies' (as they were usually known, though a few were men) gave detailed accounts to shocked but fascinated sixteenth-century inquisitors, describing how they travelled out at night in spirit to take part in celebratory gatherings with a remarkable group of fairy beings led by a queen. The *donas de fuera* thus believed that they were taking part, in spirit, in a group activity, while their bodies remained behind in their own beds. Indeed it was these non-human beings who were primarily called *'donas de fuera'* (a term that could simply mean 'fairies'), but some of the human members of the cult also adopted this name for themselves.

The human members of the cult, who experienced all this in their states of trance, felt that their visions made them special people with special powers. They used their powers for healing and divination. However, the *donas de fuera* incorporated both positive and negative values within their cult. The human members of the cult were beneficent magical practitioners, but the spirit *donas*, as fairies, held the ambivalent morality characteristic of most fairies, and could cause harm. The human members of the cult sometimes advised people that their illnesses or other troubles were caused by their having inadvertently offended the spirit *donas*, and enacted rituals to placate the spirits.

Reports of fairy cults are sometimes found in writings by churchmen denouncing them. This evidence needs to be treated with caution; some clerics imagined superstitions and heresies lurking behind every bush. The leader of the cult is particularly enigmatic. In elite writings she usually had a classical or biblical name, like Diana (a Roman goddess), Herodias (wife of the biblical Herod Antipas) or Abundia (medieval Latin for 'abundance'). These names probably did not originate with the common folk, but at least some were taken up by them; the vernacular Romanian word for 'fairy' was 'zână', derived from 'Diana'. The leader of the *donas de fuera*, by contrast, was given various non-specific names like 'the Eastern lady' or 'the wise sibyl'.

We do not know how common fairy cults were. Until recently such cults were known only in Italy: the Sicilian *donas de fuera*, and various individuals in northern Italy who also reported relationships with fairy-type superhuman females. Another cult of this type has recently been discovered in a very different part of Europe, the Scottish cult of the 'seely wights'. This, too, was a fairy-type cult; the phrase 'seely wights', which was also used as a euphemism for fairies, meant 'blessed beings' or 'magical beings'.[35] The evidence for the cult is fragmentary, and Scotland and Italy are far apart; further fairy cults may await discovery, or may simply have vanished from the records. The fact that these cults used well-known folkloric motifs, such as nocturnal visits to houses or magically resuscitating animals, suggests that fairy cults may have been widespread.

Another group of shamanistic cults can be described under the label of 'warrior shamanism'. These cults also involved humans flying out at night, in a state of trance, but their activities were different. Instead of flying out to celebrate, they flew out to take part in nocturnal battles. The best-known warrior cult, the *benandanti* ('good walkers') of Friuli, north-eastern Italy, flew out four times a year. Members of the cult entered trances and flew out at night in spirit to conduct battles with 'witches', wielding fennel stalks against the witches' sorghum stalks. The outcomes of these battles determined the fertility of the fields. As with the *donas de fuera*, the *benandanti* were usually magical practitioners in their everyday lives – curing the bewitched, identifying witches and carrying out counter-magic against witches. Particularly full evidence survives for them, so that we know of details such as the fact that each *benandante* was born wrapped in the caul (amniotic sac). People born with the caul have been believed to have special powers in many cultures; the caul could symbolise an external soul or guardian spirit. There was also an initiation rite of some kind when a *benandante* reached adulthood.[36]

The *benandanti* were similar to other warrior cults, for which less evidence survives. Those found so far were mostly in south-eastern Europe, notably the Hungarian *táltos*, the Slovenian *kresniki*, and the Serbian *zduhačs*. When the *kresniki* flew out to fight the witches, they transformed themselves into dogs, horses or giants.[37] Friuli, the region of the *benandanti*, was quite near these places, especially Slovenia. Traces of warrior shamanism have also been found further north, in Latvia, with 'werewolves' reporting that they travelled out in spirit to battle with witches.[38] This makes a regional pattern harder to perceive.

Some warrior shaman beliefs were linked with beliefs about legendary or folktale witches. Those who fought witches, like the *benandanti*, seem to have imagined their opponents as magical, non-human witches rather than as ordinary humans. One *benandante* claimed that he could recognise witches, especially those who ate children. He clearly did not have the usual village witch in mind. At least one warrior cult was linked with fairies: the Croatian *vilenicas*, who in this respect resembled the *donas de fuera* and the seely wights.[39] There was also a masculine tradition of visits to the 'Venusberg', a legendary Italian mountain haunt of a 'sibyl' who sounds like a leader of a fairy cult. However, this was at least partly a literary tradition, and a link with direct visionary experience is harder to establish.[40]

People who have visionary experiences usually use them for good, but not always. Tribal shamans normally provide a public service, but in Amazonia they may also harm people, in practices known as 'dark shamanism'. Some dark shamans send spirits to kill enemies of the tribe, which is a kind of public service – but they may also harm members of their own tribe. Typically these dark shamans are acting as the agents of fate. One such cult has been found in Europe – the *mazzeri* of Corsica, which was researched in the 1950s. Possibly it existed already in our period, but the point is that similar cultural practices may have occurred in various places. In their trances the *mazzeri* would fly out and feel compelled to kill an animal that they saw below them; they would then recognise the 'animal' as a human neighbour, or even a relative, who would subsequently die. The *mazzeri* were not morally responsible for these killings; their vision meant that it was the person's fated time to die.[41] There may well be parallels with early modern magical practitioners, who were sometimes asked, not so much to cure someone's illness, as to predict whether they would live or die, or even to hasten the person's fate whatever that might be. There is also the remarkable case of Isobel Gowdie, from Auldearn, Scotland, in 1662, which looks very like dark shamanism. Gowdie confessed in detail to joining envisioned flights in which she and her companions were impelled to shoot people with 'elf-arrows' – neolithic arrowheads, which were believed to be fairy artefacts.[42] Such beliefs and experiences may have fed into some witches' confessions, and further research may be able to disentangle them from more conventional demonological material.

These beliefs and practices are often called 'cults' by those who study them, but this term requires qualification. The term 'cult' tends to draw attention to the more exotic aspects of visionary traditions, notably their spirit voyages with non-human beings; indeed a narrow usage of the term 'cult' might restrict it to groups who actually worshipped such beings, which would disqualify most if not all of the groups we are discussing. It thus seems helpful to extend the term to wider visionary traditions with distinct identities, but certain caveats should be noted. The *benandanti* envisioned themselves flying out together, but did not hold collective meetings in their everyday lives. Instead they all took part, individually, in an activity that was known to them all because they talked to each other from time to time. Most of them were magical practitioners, so their spirit voyages became known to their clients also. They should be thought of as rather like what contemporaries called 'crafts' – skilled, specialised occupations like blacksmith or midwife. Practitioners of 'crafts' learned their skill from another individual, and shared a common identity, but did not meet for group activities unless required to do so by institutional regulations. Thinking of the 'craft' aspects of visionary practices may remind us not to neglect their less exotic aspects.

The gender profiles of these cults are interesting. The fairy cults seem to have been mostly women, and were sometimes described as if they were entirely women. The name '*donas de fuera*' exemplifies this, though there were a few men in this cult and may have been in others too. The pattern was reversed in the warrior cults; these were mostly men, though apparently not all men. Much less is known of dark shamanistic cults. The Corsican *mazzeri* included both men and women, but it is not known whether this specific cult dated back to early modern times.

Visionary beliefs, practices and cults were clearly important to early modern ideas of witchcraft, influencing demonological ideas and also being embedded in broader popular discourses of magic. Many of the details are obscure or controversial or both. Older studies tended to argue for ancient folkloric roots of all these beliefs, perceiving interconnections and common patterns across much of Europe and throughout many centuries or even millennia. Recent scholarship has tended to problematise this, to see more separation between various different traditions, and to perceive influences running both ways between elite and popular culture. This will be discussed further in Chapter 11. Here we should conclude by recognising that witchcraft beliefs were influenced, not just by actual visionaries, but also by *ideas* about visionaries. The Canon *Episcopi*, written in the Rhineland in the tenth century, may well indicate that there was such a cult there, though the idea that it was a cult of Diana may be an elite rationalisation.

But the circulation of stories about visionaries added depth and credibility to witchcraft ideas generally.

Hallucinogenic drugs?

It has occasionally been suggested that hallucinogenic drugs might lie behind some of the reports of witches' strange behaviour, especially flight and shape-shifting. However, the evidence for this is weak. Drugs that could induce hallucinations were theoretically available in early modern Europe: bufotenin from the skin of toads, and scopolamine and atropine from the related plants henbane and deadly nightshade. These drugs would have been difficult to take in practice; toads, henbane and deadly nightshade also contained lethal poisons, while the drugs themselves were far from harmless. Some demonologists were nevertheless aware of their hallucinogenic effects, and even stated that witches used these drugs. But it is hard to take these reports literally, since they were at least partially constructed, not from direct observation, but from classical models and through use of deductive reasoning about what was theoretically possible.

The best-known European shamanistic cults are well enough documented for us to be able to answer the question of whether they used hallucinogenic drugs. The answer is that they did not – though it remains unclear how their trance experiences originated, or how much control they had over them. It is in the shamanistic cults, if anywhere, that drugs might be relevant to early modern witchcraft in any systematic way, and this negative finding should be enough to dispose of the idea that witchcraft beliefs were 'caused' by drug-taking. Even flying and shape-shifting can be explained without the need to resort to the hypothesis that drugs were involved; psychological studies of hallucinations can take us some way into this, as we shall see in a moment.

It remains possible that a few individual witches had really taken hallucinogenic drugs, voluntarily or involuntarily (though no firmly-documented instances have yet been found). However, this possibility should be treated in the same way as the much better documented fact that a few individual witches had really attempted to make pacts with the Devil: neither was integral to the idea of witchcraft, or even important to it. A few demonologists believed that witches used drugs, while most of them believed that witches made pacts with the Devil; but there is no need to connect either belief with contemporary reality. The idea that witches used drugs is to some extent a modern myth, and will be discussed as such in Chapter 11.

Psychological conditions and the 'nightmare experience'

A few contemporaries tried to explain witchcraft as a delusion caused by witches' 'melancholy' – their term for what they perceived as a medical condition. This is no longer regarded as adequate, but, if we sifted through the evidence from witchcraft records looking for medical or psychological conditions recognised today, what would we find? It is difficult to diagnose such conditions at a distance of hundreds of years, since symptoms were recorded according to contemporary, not modern, categories; but this difficulty presents itself, in some way or other, in most historical work, and is not insuperable in principle. Historians and epidemiologists have thought it worthwhile to diagnose the cause of the fourteenth-century Black Death, for instance; recent DNA-based studies have confirmed the theory that the disease was bubonic plague, caused by the bacterium *Yersinia pestis*. Can we diagnose medical or psychological conditions, either in witches themselves, or in their accusers?

Medical conditions are those in which there is an observable, physical cause for the symptoms. Psychological conditions are those in which the cause of the symptoms is taken to be located in the brain (where there may or may not be an observable condition). An example would be the distinction between fits caused by epilepsy (a medical condition) and fits caused by conversion disorder (a psychological condition). Here we are mainly looking at what seem to be psychological conditions. To begin with there are hallucinations, which are quite common. Mostly they are aural; about 5 per cent of the population today hear imaginary voices or other sounds. Visual hallucinations, in which people see imaginary objects, also occur. The imagined objects are usually modifications of existing ones; thus it is possible to glimpse some movement and to decide that it was a cat. A few people, however, genuinely 'see' things that are not there at all – usually a single object (or, often, a person) superimposed on a real background. The word 'imaginary' should not be misunderstood; to people who hear voices, the voices are real, even though they know that nobody else can hear them.

Witches reported having sex with the Devil; neighbours reported being assaulted by the witch, often at night. Could there be a medical or psychological condition that might lie behind these strange reports? Unlikely though it may seem, there is indeed such a condition.[43]

Sleep paralysis is a disorder experienced by perhaps a quarter of people at some time in their lives. Typically they are just falling asleep or are just waking up. They believe that they are awake, are aware of their surroundings and can look about – but they cannot move or speak, because their bodies are still 'asleep'. They feel themselves becoming heavier, their hearts race and they have difficulty breathing. They feel anxiety or terror. A large minority of those experiencing sleep paralysis hear strange sounds (such as buzzing or heavy footsteps), see strange visions (such as lights, animals or demons) or feel strange presences assaulting them. The whole experience lasts from a few seconds to several minutes, but can seem much longer. Although the sleep paralysis experience is physically harmless, it can be utterly terrifying to the helpless and bewildered sufferer.

Sleep paralysis is not well known, even today, and sufferers make sense of their experiences in culture-specific terms, 'seeing' the kinds of intruders that they believe in. Today, some turn to the belief in 'abduction by aliens', which is essentially a modern folk belief – and it provides clues to the beliefs of earlier ages. People's accounts of alien abduction are usually produced with the help of therapists who believe in alien abduction themselves, using techniques like hypnosis or guided imagery to 'recover' what the therapist calls 'repressed memories'. Under the therapist's guidance, the subject's vivid but fragmentary experience of sleep paralysis is transformed into a detailed and convincing-looking narrative, complete with recognisable aliens and spaceships. In psychological terms, these are 'false memories' which the therapist has unwittingly implanted in the subject. This is fairly easy to do for many people, particularly those who have elaborate fantasies, as we shall see when interrogation is discussed further in Chapter 7.

The nearest equivalent to the therapist for the early modern witchcraft suspect was the interrogator. We tend to think of interrogators as hostile to the suspects, but some interrogators, at least some of the time, behaved in a sympathetic manner towards them, encouraging them to 'repent'. Witchcraft suspects were often questioned intensely, and leading questions were used; this is likely to have produced similar effects to the therapists who implant false memories. Moreover, sleep paralysis can be brought on by deprivation of sleep, to which witchcraft suspects were sometimes subjected.

Early modern folk knew nothing of aliens; what they believed in was the 'night-mare', a terrifying experience, sometimes thought of as a female non-human entity, that laid on people's chests at night and tried to crush them. (This should be distinguished from what we usually call a 'nightmare' today; physiologically, this is an ordinary anxiety dream.) The early modern 'night-mare' did not have to be a distinct being; people often attributed 'night-mare' experiences to witches or demons. Neighbours' testimonies against witches sometimes described the witch as visiting them in their beds, sometimes also as pressing on their chests (a rationalisation of the breathlessness common in sleep paralysis). A nocturnal visitation by three witches is depicted in Illustration 5.2. Some neighbours reported being pressed by a cat; witches were reputed to transform themselves into cats, and cats were known to lie on people in their beds. The belief that witches 'pressed' their victims in bed was well known, found not only in the testimony of victims (sleep paralysis sufferers), but also in confessions of witches who allegedly carried out the pressing.

Some women sleep paralysis sufferers report experiences resembling sexual assault. This probably contributed to the medieval and early modern belief in the 'incubus' and 'succubus'. The incubus was a male demon that had intercourse with women in their sleep; it was thought to be a particular problem in nunneries. The succubus, a female demon that had intercourse with men, was rarely heard of in practice, and may have been invented for the sake of symmetry. Both incubi and succubi were sometimes regarded as equivalent to the 'night-mare'. To the extent that incubi were regarded as demons, they may have been alternatives to the idea of assault by a witch, but there was some confusion and flexibility about these experiences. If the sleep paralysis experience was interpreted as demonic possession, this in turn could be attributed to a witch.

Illustration 5.2 The nightmare experience, 1608

A sleeping woman experiences a vision of being assaulted by three witches. Sleep paralysis, a medical condition sometimes known as the 'nightmare experience', caused people to see terrifying visions that they interpreted as witches or demons. This woman is seeing witches, so she is a victim of witchcraft; sometimes people saw demons, which might lead them to think that they were witches themselves. The witches do not look very terrifying in this woodcut, published in Francesco Guaccio's *Compendium Maleficarum*, but two of them carry jars of ointment that identify them as witches.

© De Agostini Picture Library/Getty Images

Sleep paralysis may also have something to tell us about witches' flight. Although the experience of being pressed is a common symptom of sleep paralysis, a few sufferers instead experience floating, flying or spinning. A yet smaller number have out-of-body experiences, floating above their beds and looking down on their own bodies. Unlike the terrifying intruders, some of these flights are experienced as positive and even blissful. Some of the people who believed that they had travelled with the fairies were probably sufferers from sleep paralysis, though it is unlikely that they all were.

The idea that some people joined nocturnal processions with non-human beings was widespread. Sleep paralysis seems to have been behind a second popular idea about nocturnal witches (that is, legendary or folkloric witches), related yet distinct. The main idea arose from the visionary experience of people who believed themselves to have flown or travelled out. But some people believed that they had been *visited* by nocturnal witches, or feared that they might be visited by them. In Hungary, there was a name for such witches: '*mora* witches'. Many victims witnessed an apparition of a *mora* witch – a person known to them, but (it was believed) appearing to them in a second, physical body. A *mora* witch could enter a house through a keyhole, or could appear and disappear. One was said to have 'formed herself at the fire', while another flew through the window 'in a night-going manner'.[44] Sometimes the victim was the only person able to see the *mora* witch. To the extent that the *mora* witch was a known neighbour, she (and it was always she) was related to the community witch whom we examined in the last chapter. She was also an individual, rather than a member of a group such as a fairy cult. Unlike the community witch, however, the *mora* witch was not primarily a worker of malefice – at least not of ordinary malefice; if she committed harm it was in abducting the victim to an imagined witches' sabbat.[45] The *mora* witch was a regional elaboration of the widespread idea of the nocturnal visit by a witch.

Finally, therefore, sleep paralysis could lead people to believe that they had been abducted to a witches' sabbat. In Kiskunhalas, Hungary, in 1747, Anna Hös reported that her husband woke up terrified, 'lying there stiff, barely drawing breath', and then cried out, 'My Lord Jesus help me! Oh! fiery witches took me to Máramos and they put six hundredweight of salt on me.'[46] The inability to move, the breathlessness and the visions all mark this as a case of sleep paralysis – but the content of Hös's husband's visions was culture-specific. Sleep paralysis, which is not culture-specific, can hardly 'explain' the cultural content of witchcraft beliefs, but it provided early modern folk with material with which to articulate and validate those beliefs.

The structure of beliefs about witches and envisioned experience is illustrated in Diagram 5.2. This diagram is in two largely separate parts: the trance experience (positive) and the nightmare experience (frightening).

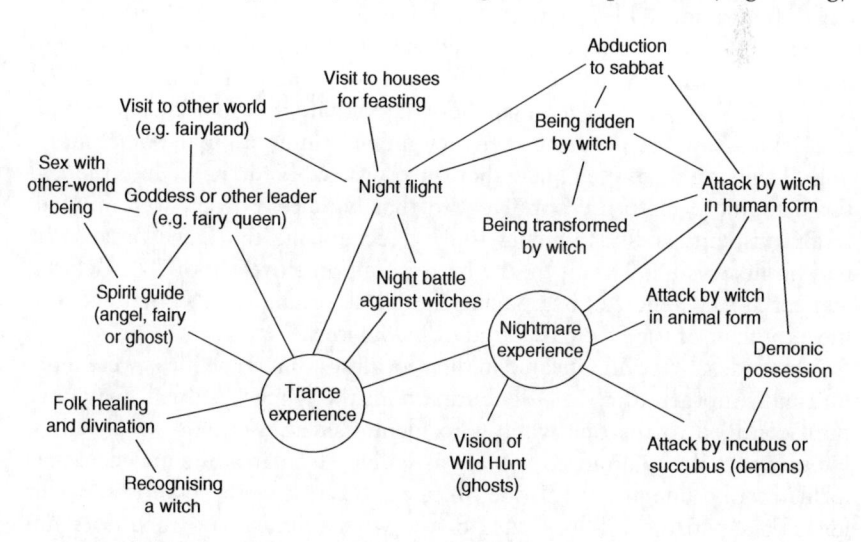

Diagram 5.2 The envisioned witch

Shamanistic visionaries had trance experiences, and should be distinguished from witchcraft victims who had nightmare experiences stemming from sleep paralysis. There are connections between the two, notably in the shared motif of night flight. Some witches' confessions were based on the nightmare experience (it was not just something for victims of witchcraft), which provides another link between these two modes of experience.

Conclusion: Popular beliefs about 'witchcraft'

This chapter has tried to place popular ideas about 'witchcraft' in a broader context. In trying to understand witches, people drew on various ideas that were not specifically about 'witchcraft' – ideas about fairies, ghosts and other beings, for instance. But, if they were going to initiate a witch-hunt, the common folk had to identify people as 'witches', and that required them to have ideas specifically about 'witchcraft'. We saw in Chapter 3 how intellectual ideas of witchcraft developed, and how various concepts were combined in the late middle ages to produce a more elaborate and threatening picture of the witch. Were there similar patterns in popular ideas? The answer is yes and no.

On the one hand, we can break down the popular idea of witchcraft into its component parts, and analyse the parts separately – much as has been done for demonological witchcraft. On the other hand, we do not find a similar pattern of development over time, starting with a few simple medieval ideas and ending with an elaborate set of ideas in the seventeenth century. Popular belief constantly renewed itself, but did not develop in a linear fashion.

Popular ideas of witchcraft tended to consist of a few simple and widespread ideas, and a large number of local variations or elaborations. The demonic pact is an example of a simple, widespread idea; here are some local elaborations. In Offenburg, in Baden, Germany, numerous witches confessed that when they made a pact with the Devil, he gave them a magical 'switch' (whip) which could kill a person or animal with one blow.[47] In Finnmark, Norway, several witches related that, after making a pact with the Devil, they first tried out their new power on an animal, sometimes a dog. If the dog died, they knew that the power worked.[48] This motif linked the demonic pact to the popular idea that witches' powers were limited. In Braunsberg, Prussia, witches told of recognising the Devil because he had no nostrils – a variant on the more common cloven hoof.[49] In Geneva, Switzerland, witches told of paying the Devil an annual tax; they seem to have thought of the Devil as a kind of feudal lord.[50]

These ideas were all repeated in their localities, but some ideas were more unusual. Another story in Offenburg, about the witches' sabbat, may have been confined to the one witch who mentioned it, Urban Byser in 1575. He said that if one hundred witches assembled to plan some malefice, they all had to be unanimous; if one objected, the rest were powerless.[51] This idea, linked to the folkloric idea of the witch's limited powers, does not seem to have been mentioned by any other witches, nor was it taken up by demonologists. Some ideas concerning malefice at the sabbat were well developed in Lorraine, where most sabbats included the planning of crop destruction by hail. Confessions there often told stories about the poor and the rich arguing; poor witches claimed that they had objected to damaging crops in ways that would cause hardship. Such stories may have been encouraged by interrogators, but interrogators are unlikely to have originated them.

Popular beliefs about the witches' sabbat were not necessarily important or deeply-felt. If early modern villagers genuinely believed that witches met together at night to conduct horrific rituals – or even just to dance and sing – then why does such a belief hardly ever seem to surface in neighbours' accusations? Sabbat beliefs are reported largely in suspects' confessions, while neighbours overwhelmingly assumed that the witch who had bewitched them was a solitary individual. Yet, in thinking about the person they were accusing, the neighbours were thinking that this person was a 'witch', and they must have wondered whether this witch did other things that 'witches' were said to do. Did they assume that she or he went to the sabbat as part of a witch's normal activities?

Neighbours almost never reported witnessing sabbats. There could be several reasons for this, quite apart from the reason we may consider most important today (that sabbats never occurred). There was an interesting episode when a passing traveller saw some women dancing around a fire near Neuchâtel, Switzerland, in 1582. He reported them as witches, thus triggering a witchcraft panic. The story was soon embellished with prints showing the traveller pursued by the Devil, but this was not part of the original report.[52] The point about this apparently real gathering is that it was *different* from the fantastic gatherings described by confessing witches. The same applies to a more fantastic tale told by a man in the Canary Islands in 1589: he saw ten women at midnight, nine dressed in white and one in black, with a goat – behind which they tried to hide when they saw him.[53] The goat was a recognised demonic animal, but otherwise this story was not very like the usual witches' sabbat. And such stories were very rare.

Thus, neighbours were probably not worried by the idea of the witches' sabbat. As the previous chapter showed, they were largely worried by individual village witches and the harm that they could cause. If neighbours took the sabbat seriously when considering their village witch, they might also have discussed who this witch's accomplices were. However, they did not. One can see reputations spreading from one individual to another, usually within families (as when a daughter was believed to learn witchcraft from her mother), but this is not the same as neighbours assuming that witches carried out collective rituals. Unlike the keenly-felt malefice of the individual witch, the sabbat was not an immediate part of the neighbours' experience.

152 Witchcraft and folk belief

This suggests that people's 'belief' in the sabbat was at least partly hypothetical and even semi-fictional. They thought of the witches' sabbat as something to tell stories about – stories about legendary witches, not real village witches. The fact that some children *were* eloquent about the sabbat when accusing witches may even indicate that the sabbat was more important as a realm of children's stories. In some areas, the belief grew up that witches transported children to the sabbat during the night. Children would wake in the morning and report that they had been taken to the sabbat. There were two major panics in areas where adults persuaded themselves that such sabbats were real: in the Basque country of Navarre and south-west France (*c*.1608–12), and in Sweden (1668–76, discussed in Chapter 8).

The witches' sabbat, therefore, was at best a remote belief to most early modern villagers. And, if this is true of witches' neighbours, it is surely also true of witches themselves. Before they were accused and interrogated, witches were ordinary villagers with the ordinary folk culture of the village. It was the interrogation process itself that forced the accused witches to convert their occasionally childish stories into something more sinister.

Notes

1 'Thomas Rymer', in Francis J. Child, *English and Scottish Popular Ballads*, 5 vols. (Boston, Mass., 1884), no. 37 (vol. i, p. 324).
2 Christina Larner, *Enemies of God: The Witch-Hunt in Scotland* (London, 1981), 156.
3 Martine Ostorero and Kathrin Utz Tremp (eds.), *Inquisition et sorcellerie en Suisse romande: Le registre Ac 29 des Archives cantonales vaudoises (1438–1528)* (Lausanne, 2007), 56–7.
4 David Gentilcore, *From Bishop to Witch: The System of the Sacred in Early Modern Terra d'Otranto* (Manchester, 1992), 250–1.
5 Lea, *Materials*, ii, 766.
6 E. M. Butler, *Ritual Magic* (Cambridge, 1949), 214–15.
7 Martín Del Rio, *Investigations into Magic*, trans. P. G. Maxwell-Stuart (Manchester, 2000), 266–7.
8 *Malleus*, 182D-183A (II.ii.8).
9 Richard P. Jenkins, 'Witches and fairies: supernatural aggression and deviance among the Irish peasantry', in Peter Narváez (ed.), *The Good People: New Fairylore Essays* (Lexington, Ky., 1991), 302–35.
10 *The Trial of Tempel Anneke: Records of a Witchcraft Trial in Brunswick, Germany, 1663*, ed. Peter A. Morton, trans. Barbara Dähms (Toronto, 2005), pp. xxxix–xl.
11 Louise Nyholm Kallestrup, 'Women, witches and the town courts of Ribe', in Marianna G. Muravyeva and Raisa Maria Toivo (eds.), *Gender in Late Medieval and Early Modern Europe* (New York, 2013), 122–36, at pp. 130–2.
12 Valerie Kivelson, *Desperate Magic: The Moral Economy of Witchcraft in Seventeenth-Century Russia* (Ithaca, NY, 2013), 72–4.
13 Ronald Hutton, 'The Wild Hunt and the witches' sabbath', *Folklore*, 125 (2014), 161–78.
14 Karin Ueltschi, *La Mesnie Hellequin en conte et en rime: mémoire mythique et poétique de la recomposition* (Paris, 2008), 527–42.

15 Nicolas Remy, *Demonolatry*, trans. E. A. Ashwin, ed. Montague Summers (London, 1930), 28–9 (I.8).
16 Julian Goodare, 'Scottish witchcraft in its European context', in Julian Goodare, Lauren Martin and Joyce Miller (eds.), *Witchcraft and Belief in Early Modern Scotland* (Basingstoke, 2008), 26–50, at pp. 32–3.
17 Lutz Röhrich, *Folktales and Reality*, trans. Peter Tokofsky (3rd edn., Bloomington, Ind., 1991), 17–18.
18 W. F. Ryan, *The Bathhouse at Midnight: An Historical Survey of Magic and Divination in Russia* (Stroud, 1999), 78–82; Lesia Mouchketique, 'Les croyances démonologiques du folklore de la contrée limitrophe de l'Ukraine et de la Hongrie', *Acta Ethnographica Hungarica*, 37 (1991–92), 201–13.
19 *Encyclopedia*, iv, 1139.
20 Richard Kieckhefer, 'Avenging the blood of children: anxiety over child victims and the origins of the European witch trials', in Alberto Ferreiro (ed.), *The Devil, Heresy and Witchcraft in the Middle Ages* (Leiden, 1998), 91–109.
21 Francisco Fajardo Spinola, 'Des vols et assemblées des sorcières dans les documents de l'Inquisition canarienne', in Nicole Jacques-Chaquin and Maxime Préaud (eds.), *Le sabbat des sorciers en Europe (XVe–XVIIIe siècles)* (Grenoble, 1993), 299–315, at p. 304.
22 Michael Ostling, *Between the Devil and the Host: Imagining Witchcraft in Early Modern Poland* (Oxford, 2011), 25–6.
23 Lea, *Materials*, i, 239.
24 Ulric Molitor (Müller), *Des sorcières et des devineresses*, trans. Emile Nourry (Paris, 1926), 39–40, 77 (chs. 7, 13).
25 Domenico Mammoli (ed.), *The Record of the Trial and Condemnation of a Witch, Matteuccia di Francesco, at Todi, 20 March 1428* (Rome: Res Tudertinae 14, 1972), 36–8.
26 Ruth Martin, *Witchcraft and the Inquisition in Venice, 1550–1650* (Oxford, 1989), 209–10.
27 Gustav Henningsen, 'The witches' flying and the Spanish inquisitors, or how to explain (away) the impossible', *Folklore*, 120 (2009), 57–74, at p. 62.
28 Francis Bavoux, *La sorcellerie en Franche-Comté (Pays de Quingey)* (Monaco, 1954), 159.
29 Richard Kieckhefer, *European Witch Trials: Their Foundations in Popular and Learned Culture, 1300–1500* (London, 1976), 31, 71–2.
30 Bengt Ankarloo, 'Blakulla, ou le sabbat des sorciers scandinaves', in Jacques-Chaquin and Préaud (eds.), *Le sabbat des sorciers*, 251–8, at p. 252.
31 Fajardo, 'Des vols et assemblées des sorcières dans les documents de l'Inquisition canarienne', 302.
32 Rita Voltmer, 'The judges' lore? The politico-religious concept of metamorphosis in the peripheries of western Europe', in Willem de Blécourt (ed.), *Werewolf Histories* (Basingstoke, 2015), 159–84.
33 Wolfgang Behringer, *Shaman of Oberstdorf: Chonrad Stoeckhlin and the Phantoms of the Night*, trans. H. C. Erik Midelfort (Charlottesville, Va., 1998).
34 Gustav Henningsen, '"The ladies from outside": an archaic pattern of the witches' sabbath', in Bengt Ankarloo and Gustav Henningsen (eds.), *Early Modern European Witchcraft: Centres and Peripheries* (Oxford, 1991), 191–215.
35 Julian Goodare, 'The cult of the seely wights in Scotland', *Folklore*, 123 (2012), 198–219.
36 Carlo Ginzburg, *The Night Battles: Witchcraft and Agrarian Cults in the Sixteenth and Seventeenth Centuries*, trans. John and Anne Tedeschi (Baltimore, Md., 1983).
37 Gábor Klaniczay, 'Shamanistic elements in central European witchcraft', in his *The Uses of Supernatural Power: The Transformation of Popular Religion in Medieval and Early-Modern Europe* (Princeton, NJ, 1990), 129–50.

38 Willem de Blécourt, 'A journey to hell: reconsidering the Livonian "werewolf"', *Magic, Ritual, and Witchcraft*, 2 (2007), 49–67.
39 Zoran Čiča, '*Vilenica* and *Vilenjak*: bearers of an extinct fairy cult', *Narodna Umjetnost: Croatian Journal of Ethnology and Folklore Research*, 39 (2002), 31–63.
40 Marina Warner, *From the Beast to the Blonde: On Fairy Tales and their Tellers* (London, 1994), 3–10; Giovanni Kral, 'Il viaggio de Zuan delle Piatte al Monte della Sibilla', in Ottavio Besomi and Carlo Caruso (eds.), *Cultura d'elite e cultura popolare nell'arco alpino fra Cinque e Seicento* (Basel, 1995), 393–431 (I am grateful to Mick Swithinbank for a translation of this paper).
41 Dorothy Carrington, *The Dream-Hunters of Corsica* (London, 1995).
42 Emma Wilby, *The Visions of Isobel Gowdie: Magic, Witchcraft and Dark Shamanism in Seventeenth-Century Scotland* (Brighton, 2010).
43 Owen Davies, 'The nightmare experience, sleep paralysis, and witchcraft accusations', *Folklore*, 114 (2003), 181–203; Margaret Dudley and Julian Goodare, 'Outside in or inside out: sleep paralysis and Scottish witchcraft', in Julian Goodare (ed.), *Scottish Witches and Witch-Hunters* (Basingstoke, 2013), 121–39.
44 Éva Pócs, *Between the Living and the Dead: A Perspective on Witches and Seers in the Early Modern Age*, trans. Szilvia Rédey and Michael Webb (Budapest, 1999), 38, 46.
45 Gábor Klaniczay, 'Le sabbat raconté par les témoins des procès de sorcellerie en Hongrie', in Jacques-Chaquin and Préaud (eds.), *Le sabbat des sorciers*, 227–46, at pp. 231–3.
46 Quoted in Pócs, *Between the Living and the Dead*, 73.
47 Lea, *Materials*, iii, 1141.
48 Liv Helene Willumsen, *Witchcraft Trials in Finnmark, Northern Norway*, trans. Katjana Edwardsen (Bergen, 2010), 14.
49 *Encyclopedia*, iii, 939.
50 E. W. Monter, 'Witchcraft in Geneva, 1537–1662', *Journal of Modern History*, 43 (1971), 179–204, at pp. 195–6.
51 Lea, *Materials*, iii, 1141.
52 E. William Monter, *Witchcraft in France and Switzerland: The Borderlands during the Reformation* (Ithaca, NY, 1976), 92–3.
53 Fajardo, 'Des vols et assemblées des sorcières dans les documents de l'Inquisition canarienne', 307.

6 Witches and the godly state

> It is not within the power of princes to pardon a crime that the law of God punishes with death, such as the crimes of witchcraft. Moreover, princes do a great offence to God to pardon such horrible wickednesses committed directly against His majesty, since the smallest prince avenges his injuries with capital punishment. So those who let witches escape or who do not carry out their punishment with utmost rigour, can be assured that they will be abandoned by God to the mercy of witches. And the country which tolerates them will be struck by plagues, famines, and wars – but those who take vengeance against them will be blessed by God, and will bring an end to His wrath.
>
> Jean Bodin, France, 1580[1]

Introduction

Witch-hunting was an exercise in state power. A handful of witches were lynched by their neighbours, but they were highly exceptional. The vast majority of witches were given a regular criminal trial by the state authorities. If convicted, they were executed by the state authorities. Who, therefore, were these authorities? Answering this question may offer the prospect of establishing responsibility for the witch-hunts. Of course, identifying the rulers of states will not in itself explain *why* these rulers executed witches, and we may find that rulers acted because of other pressures on them; but these other pressures certainly acted *through* states and rulers.

This was the period of the Protestant Reformation and the Catholic Counter-Reformation, acting both against each other and in parallel with each other. Working through the authorities of the state, these 'reform' movements transformed the way in which the authorities interacted with the common people, and made new demands on the common people. Many studies focus on the differences between Protestants and Catholics, but witch-hunting was promoted by both sides, and we shall often have to focus on their similarities. These two vast movements, locked in combat, needed both to assert their godliness and to stamp out ungodliness. One thing they had in common was a view of witches as ungodly. The godly state could well be a witch-hunting state. This was especially so since the 'godly state' was really a *process* rather than a static entity – a process of striving after godliness, and of using state authority to enforce godliness.

Those who 'ruled' ranged from kings and princes at the top, down to the judges, clerks and messengers of local courts at the sharp end of governing. One fruitful line of enquiry has focused on local courts and how much autonomy they possessed; local courts could be caught up in witch-hunting fervour, while central courts sometimes restrained them if they could. Not all 'rulers', central or local, behaved in the same way; some encouraged executions, while others discouraged them. A comparative approach may thus prove illuminating.

The rise of the early modern state

Europe in the early modern period had about twenty times as many states as it has today. There were some large kingdoms, such as France and Poland; other regions, notably Germany and Italy, were divided into hundreds of often tiny principalities. States differed in type as well as size. Territorial kingdoms and dukedoms formed the most common type, but there were also independent cities with corporate governing councils, or prince-bishoprics ruled by bishops elected by their cathedral clergy. In Germany and much of central Europe, the Holy Roman Emperor claimed ultimate authority, even though the princes within the Empire's boundaries often behaved as if they were independent. The pope, based in Rome, claimed spiritual authority over the whole of western Christendom, and rulers of Catholic states sometimes had to defer to him. To the extent that witchcraft was a spiritual crime, this could be important.

State power increased in the sixteenth century. Royal armies multiplied in size, and were equipped with the latest artillery and handguns. A new art of naval warfare developed. This was accompanied by the growth of formal diplomacy, with new procedures for resident ambassadors and international treaties. Within each state, new, bureaucratic institutions were created, staffed by legally-trained office-holders. These office-holders were nominally dependent on the crown, but were also members or clients of noble families – an illustration of the way in which nobles were becoming integrated into the state's service. Nobles ceased to have private armies, and instead acted as officers in royal armies. Thus, even within the smaller German and Italian states, rulers were consolidating their power. Central rulers sought to enhance their authority at the expense of local privileges, creating unified, territorially-sovereign states to replace the interlocking hierarchies of medieval power.

This sometimes led to instability. Demands for higher taxes could lead to tax revolts, and occasionally to civil wars. The trend towards governmental centralisation tended to promote absolute monarchy, but the religious conflicts of the Reformation era raised the stakes, sometimes encouraging contrary trends. Some religious movements, seeking to change a state's religion in opposition to the monarch's wishes, attempted to mobilise nobles through local or national representative assemblies. Proponents of absolute monarchy clashed with proponents of constitutional or limited monarchy – in learned treatises, in courts and assemblies, and sometimes on the battlefield. Demonology was connected with the ideology of absolute monarchy, as we shall see.

Because of these conflicts, religious and political commentators often felt themselves to be living in times of 'instability' or 'disorder' – or even in the last days of the world before the Second Coming of Christ. It was believed that the Devil would rage in these days, as we saw in Chapter 3. There was a desperate need for 'order', of a kind that only rulers could provide. And not just any rulers, but godly rulers. Early modern government was not just a matter of reconciling the material interests of lobby groups. The problems of the state were caused by human immorality and wickedness, and, ultimately, by the Devil. People appealed to rulers to wield their power against disorder and demonic ungodliness.

The Reformation and Counter-Reformation

Scholars who have expected witchcraft prosecutions to be caused by new ideas about witchcraft have sometimes been puzzled at the apparently delayed rise in prosecutions – beginning no earlier than the late sixteenth century. After all, the *Malleus Maleficarum* had expressed many of the new ideas in 1486. If ideas were the crucial cause of trials, then the trials should have begun eighty or a hundred years earlier. What was new? There are several answers to this, but the most important answer is the Reformation and Counter-Reformation.

The Reformation was the movement by Protestants to create new 'reformed' churches with new forms of correct belief. Particularly important was the belief that Christians were saved solely by their faith in God (faith that they were enabled to hold because of God's grace conferred on them). The Counter-Reformation was the movement by Catholics to 'reform' their own churches in response. Catholics would discard inappropriate beliefs and practices (including some criticised by Protestants), but would also reaffirm the belief that Christians were saved in part through the power of priests to absolve people of their sins. Protestant and Catholic doctrines of salvation were thus incompatible, and Protestants rejected the authority of the pope. There followed a fierce struggle whereby each side tried to defeat the other – by preaching and propaganda, by intellectual argument, by political manoeuvre, and often, ultimately, by warfare.

At the heart of both the Reformation and the Counter-Reformation was a desire for religious 'reform': to rid the Christian church of corruption and abuses, to create a purer and more authentic faith, and to spread that faith to the people. This partly sprang from the Renaissance, a movement seeking to break with the intellectual and cultural traditions of the middle ages and to draw inspiration from a deeper understanding of antiquity. Scholars sought to return to the first principles of Christianity and to ask themselves intellectual questions about it: what the Bible really meant, and what the early Christian church had really practised. One sensational example came in 1440, when the Renaissance scholar Lorenzo Valla demonstrated that the 'Donation of Constantine', the document by which the popes claimed that the Roman emperor Constantine had granted them secular authority, was a forgery.

Demands for 'reform' led to controversy, and to challenges to authority. The first reforming leader, Martin Luther (1483–1546), did not intend to create a breakaway Protestant church, but to reform the entire Catholic church from within. He defied the pope's authority, but he hoped that future popes would come round to his views. They never did, but Luther instead achieved political success in the 1520s because many German princes saw advantages in asserting control over the church in their territories. This led to warfare between states, and also to political instability within states.

Protestantism thus became a political movement, with a programme of action. There were aristocratic leaders, committed activists at lower social levels, intellectuals justifying the demands ideologically, and pamphleteers and printers distributing propaganda. The movement sought political power with which to implement its ideas of 'reform'. Gradually, a similar Catholic political movement arose. This did not aim to preserve the status quo, but to achieve Catholic 'reform'. The Jesuit order, launched in 1540, was an influential activist organisation for this movement, while there were also aristocratic political leaders. This Catholic movement spread a Counter-Reformation message in Catholic countries and agitated politically in Protestant countries.

The early years of the Reformation, from about 1520 to about 1560, were taken up with political struggle between the religious movements. Activists focused on winning the political allegiance of kings and princes – either peacefully, or through warfare, uprising and *coup d'état*. Protestants won political power in much of northern Europe: most of north Germany, then Scandinavia, the Baltic states, England and Scotland. Catholics managed to retain the allegiance of most of southern Europe, especially Spain and Italy. The lands in between – France, Switzerland, the Netherlands, south Germany, Hungary and Poland – formed a complex and shifting battleground. There were various religious wars, especially in Germany.

Throughout these struggles, the energies of reformers and their opponents were devoted to winning and keeping political control. The allegiances that mattered were those of rulers and elites. In the early sixteenth century, Catholic states executed many Protestant activists, while Protestant states executed many Catholic activists. The common folk, including witches, were not a priority. There were not yet many executions of witches – but a precedent was being set in state-sponsored religious persecution.

Gradually, during the 1550s and 1560s, conversions slowed and patterns of religious allegiance stabilised. It became clear that the Protestant states were going to stay Protestant, while the remaining Catholic states were going to stay Catholic, at least for the time being. Nobody was happy with this division in Christendom, and each side continued to struggle against the other, but no immediate victory was in sight for either side. It was like a transition from free-flowing field warfare to static trench warfare.

This period of trench warfare, lasting broadly from about 1560 to 1650, was the peak period for witch-hunting. Rulers sought to consolidate their power within their territories, and their national churches sought to entrench their orthodox message among the common people. Rulers needed, more than ever, to prove that they and their states were godly. Godliness was not just important, as it had been in the middle ages; it was *contested*. As part of the process of inculcating the details of correct Christianity, the authorities had to investigate, and stamp out, ungodliness in all its forms.

The divine ruler and the Devil

Throughout these struggles, theologians and religious propagandists appealed to kings and princes, praising their godliness and calling on them to suppress ungodliness. Kings and princes were expected to prove their godliness. Reforming preachers reminded everyone about godly Old Testament kings like Josiah, who had banished 'the workers with familiar spirits, and the wizards, and the images, and the idols, and all the abominations that were spied in the land of Judah and in Jerusalem' (2 Kings 23:24). Appeals to rulers emphasised the rulers' authority. More importantly, they presented rulers' authority as being divine. Witch-hunting was part of the contest between the divine ruler, seeking godly order, and the Devil, seeking ungodly disorder.

Christian theology had deep reservoirs of respect for authority. Renewed study of the Bible led theologians to emphasise a famous passage in it, Romans 13, which began: 'Let every soul be subject unto the higher powers. For there is no power but of God: the powers that be are ordained of God.' This praise for the 'powers that be' continued by stressing the ruler's capacity and indeed duty to punish wrongdoers: 'For he is the minister of God to thee for good. But if thou do that which is evil, be afraid: for he beareth not the sword in vain: for he is the minister of God, a revenger to execute wrath upon him that doeth evil.' This passage was endlessly quoted and expounded in the sixteenth century. The 'sword' of the ruler's justice became a constantly-repeated metaphor. Indeed, with the death penalty so prominent, it was more than a metaphor.

Political ideology met godliness in the doctrine of the divine right of kings. This was developed by sixteenth-century thinkers in response to civil and international wars, succession disputes and religious struggles that threatened to destroy political society and to bring anarchy. The need to restore and maintain order was desperate. The best guarantee of order was for everyone to agree to respect and obey the king, and to put the choice of king beyond dispute. The king was held to have been chosen by God – 'by the grace of God' was the formal phrase. The present king represented a legitimate dynasty that God had appointed in the distant past and that could not be changed or resisted by humans. This ideology was presented as a divine command rather than being argued pragmatically, but it gained support and credibility because it seemed to work in practice.

A godly prince or king was thus, in a real sense, divine. He had special powers. His divine authority was exactly what was needed to counter the rising tide of anarchy and disorder. God was on the side of legitimate authority. Several demonologists wrote that witches lost their powers when lawfully imprisoned, because the judges were the agents of God. Given that much of the anarchy and disorder was inspired by the Devil, the divine king and his agents formed the *only* earthly power who could credibly counter it. The European witch-hunt, from this point of view, was a contest between the Devil and the divine kings of Europe.

The ultimate divine king was probably the king of France, who bore the title 'Most Christian King'. He possessed the near-miraculous power to cure scrofula, a skin disease called the 'king's evil', simply by touching the patient – a power he shared only with the king of England (and with seventh sons). He was not only crowned, but also anointed with holy oil. Several other kings were anointed, but the French holy oil was believed to have been brought directly from heaven. Even the Holy Roman Emperor, sometimes called the 'lord of the world', did not have all these sacred attributes. Yet there was nothing exotic about the king of France; *all* rulers were divine in some sense. Not just all the kings and princes, but also all the judges in the courts, were the 'powers that be' as Romans 13 described them.

Witches were almost necessary enemies of a godly king, and could be used to demonstrate a king's godliness. When the witches of North Berwick conspired against James VI of Scotland in 1590, the Devil told them that 'the king is the greatest enemy he hath in the world' – or so said a pamphlet about the panic.[2] Being singled out for attack by the Devil was quite a compliment to the king. Illustration 6.1 was published in the pamphlet, *Newes from Scotland*, to show James interrogating some of the witches. James, an intellectual as well as a king, was inspired to write a book about witches, *Daemonologie* (1597). He also wrote about the divine right of kings, which to him was another aspect of divine rulership.

There was an alternative to the divine right of kings: the political ideology of constitutionalism. This was based on the idea that authority

Illustration 6.1 King James VI interrogates witches, 1590

The king (seated, right), accompanied by a standing courtier and an official with a stick, interrogates four suspects during the North Berwick witchcraft panic in Scotland. Although this was a stock image that had been published before, it underlined the king's authority when it was used to represent the king in the English pamphlet *Newes from Scotland*. James VI later published a book about witchcraft, *Daemonologie* (1597), emphasising the lawful power that a divinely-sanctioned king wielded over ungodly witches.

© Private Collection/Getty Images

arose from the political community instead of descending from the monarch. Typically it was argued that the monarch's powers were limited by parliament, or that he was obliged to take his nobles' advice, or even that he could be assassinated if he ruled unjustly. Constitutionalist ideas appealed to divine authority, but less directly than the divine right of kings; they owed more to secular classical republicanism. Such ideas were less successful than divine-right ones, at least before the late seventeenth century, but they may have played a role in limiting the witch-hunt in some places. However, the constitutionalist challenge also made supporters of divine right even more determined to demonstrate their correctness.

Demonology and the Reformation: Consensus and controversy

Did the battling religions accuse one another of witchcraft? On the whole, the answer is no – or, at least, not directly. Protestants did not directly prosecute Catholics as witches, and Catholics did not directly prosecute Protestants as witches. Each denomination regarded the other as evil, and indeed as being inspired by the Devil, but they understood perfectly well that their denominational rivals were not witches.

Witches were in fact of concern to both sides, and in similar ways. The core demonological doctrines were largely bipartisan, and were well known to be so. Protestants continued to use pre-Reformation demonological works like the *Malleus Maleficarum*, while both Protestant and Catholic demonologists routinely cited works from the other side as being authoritative. The French book *Démonomanie* by the Catholic Jean Bodin was translated into Latin by a Dutch Protestant, and into German by a German Protestant. The two sides could also co-operate over witchcraft prosecutions. The Catholic senate of Savoy wrote to the Protestant authorities of nearby Geneva in 1578, warning them about three Genevans who had been cited as accomplices in a recent trial of some Savoy witches.[3]

Nevertheless, Reformation controversies were deep and bitter. Committed activists were prepared to die for their faith. More relevantly for the present study, they were also prepared to kill for their faith. To convinced Catholics, Luther and his allies were a deadly threat to Christian souls, leading people astray on a path leading to their own damnation; the Lutheran heresy had to be stopped, at any cost. To convinced Protestants, the pope and his allies were a corrupt conspiracy that had blinded people to the truth for centuries, clinging to power because they profited from false doctrine; the papacy had to be destroyed, at any cost. Confident that they were carrying out God's will, militants on both sides waged unremitting war – spiritual war and actual war – against the enemies of godliness as they saw it.

The Reformation thus stimulated demonological debate, as each side sought to use demonology to prove its own superiority and to score points off the other side. The Catholic Martin Delrio wrote in 1600 that 'Nothing has spread magic more quickly or copiously in Scotland, England, France, and Belgium than Calvinism'.[4] Friedrich Förner, a leading Catholic witch-hunter in Bamberg, Germany, made a different debating point by arguing that the Devil would not bother recruiting Protestants as witches – he had already gained their souls. Equally partisan arguments emerged from the Protestant side. A Dutch Protestant demanded in 1556: 'what difference is there between these sorcerers who make an evil spirit enter a crystal, or on their fingernail, or some in a mirror, when you [Catholic priests] will conjure

Christ to enter into a piece of bread'?[5] The ritual of the Catholic mass was thus denounced as ritual magic; Catholic priests were 'conjurers', the pope was 'the witch of the world', and so forth.

Witches, and even the Devil himself, could be found testifying to the superior merits of one faith over the other. In 1551, two witches in Bregenz, a Catholic town in south Germany, confessed that the Devil had told them that demons preferred Protestantism – much to the annoyance of a pastor in the nearby Protestant town of Lindau.[6] In an example from the other side, the Protestant Thomas Cooper, in England in 1617, wrote that the Devil insisted on witches undergoing a second, diabolical baptism, 'as if outward baptism made a Christian, and nothing else'.[7] Protestants claimed that God allowed people to be saved without baptism, while Catholics insisted that baptism was essential. According to Cooper, the Devil, by insisting that his own anti-baptism ceremony was essential, was craftily promoting a Catholic view of ordinary baptism.

The witches' sabbat was of particular interest to Catholics after the Reformation. When Protestants rejected traditional rituals, the Catholic response was to emphasise many such rituals and to give them new, more sophisticated meanings. Protestants denied that the bread and wine in the communion service were really transformed into the body and blood of Christ – so Catholics laid fresh emphasis on this transformation, focusing on the 'host', the consecrated bread. Catholic demonologists seized on stories of witches desecrating hosts, producing a stream of stories in which the pierced or trampled host reacted by revealing its sacred nature – usually it bled, spoke or even became an actual child. These stories were largely borrowed from stories that had been told about medieval Jews, who had also been accused of desecrating hosts; but now they served a new purpose as part of the Counter-Reformation struggle.

Sometimes, only total religious purity would do. There was a belief, for instance, that witches were unable to recite the Lord's Prayer with complete accuracy. Françoise Secretain, a witch tried in Franche-Comté by the demonologist Henri Boguet in 1598, 'was always talking of God, of the Virgin Mary, and of the Holy Saints of Paradise'. She recited faultless prayers from her rosary beads – but the interrogators found that the cross of the rosary was defective. Boguet added that 'nearly all the rosaries of those who have been executed in this place have been examined and have been found to be without a Cross, or at least to be defective in some detail of the Cross, as in one of the arms or some other particular'.[8] Even the tiniest imperfection could be a sign that the Devil was at work.

The godly state and godly discipline

The ideal of the godly state took shape in the late sixteenth century, during the period of trench warfare between the deadlocked faiths. In an ideal godly state, rulers and people were all doctrinally orthodox and adhered to high moral standards. Rulers, from kings at the top to the judges and clerks of local courts at the bottom, used their authority to encourage godliness and to suppress ungodliness. Witchcraft was in some ways the ultimate ungodliness, and godly rulers were not going to tolerate it.

This phase of the Reformation and Counter-Reformation would thus be particularly significant for witch-hunting. The religious movements on both sides had to put their godly visions into practice. The initial conversion of a prince to Protestantism was one thing, but it was another thing to find a Protestant pastor for each parish church, and an even bigger challenge for the pastors to change the way in which ordinary people worshipped and behaved. The states that remained Catholic faced a similar challenge; they could not continue with the old ways, but had to spread a 'reformed' Catholic message throughout their churches and congregations. This phase would last throughout the late sixteenth and early seventeenth centuries – the peak period for witch-hunting. Religious 'reform' and witch-hunting were closely connected.

Reformers on both sides sought to spread their message to the masses. To the extent that Protestantism required a sophisticated intellectual understanding of the Bible, it was obviously not going to succeed in the short term; most people were not even literate. Protestants did their best to extend education, and they eventually made the Bible a widely-read book. Catholics too encouraged literacy, but also used images and ritual objects (like rosary beads) to spread their message of how the details of correct religion should be practised. Their ultimate vision remained an unfulfilled long-term goal on both sides, but we need to concentrate on the fact that a vast programme of evangelisation and education was undertaken in pursuit of that goal. The programme has even been described as 'Christianisation'. Much of it involved encouraging people to scrutinise their own consciences more closely, in order to avoid sin. This could make people feel guilty for their sins, but such feelings could be projected psychologically onto others: it was *other* people who were sinful and wicked. Such wicked people could include witches.

The godly programme was not just educational; it was also about coercion, and stamping out false belief and incorrect practice. It thus required courts to enforce it. The Protestants either established new local courts or revitalised existing ones in order to supervise people's faith and morals. Many Lutheran states established so-called 'marriage courts', initially to regulate marriage but usually taking on other business to do with morality – dealing with sexual sins like fornication and prostitution, and also other offences like blasphemy. In Calvinist states, following a version of Protestantism inspired by John Calvin (1509–64), these new courts were called 'consistories' and were particularly powerful. 'Discipline' became a reforming goal.

The Catholic church responded swiftly to the Protestant example. In some places, Catholics already had an institution for suppressing false belief: the Inquisition. The Inquisition was in fact discredited in Germany and Switzerland and had to withdraw, while it had never been allowed in France, where Catholic kings resisted papal interference. But the Inquisition was upgraded in the sixteenth century in the Catholic heartlands, Italy, Spain and Portugal – controlled in the latter two places by kings rather than the pope. As for Germany, princes who embraced the Counter-Reformation could upgrade the regular church courts, run by bishops, in order to combat ungodliness.

The Counter-Reformation reaffirmed the role of the parish priest in hearing people's confession of their sins – something that Protestants had rejected. Every Catholic was now expected to go to confession at least once a year. Priests also developed a new line of questioning in the confessional. Instead of simply asking about a person's sinful acts, they now probed the person's internal moral state. Rather than relying on people's sense of shame for their public behaviour, they fostered a sense of guilt for their internal feelings of sinfulness. Meanwhile, shame remained important because the results of the sinful acts – such as illegitimate children born from fornication – attracted more attention than before. This was a society increasingly aware that sin was a public problem.

The essence of the campaign for godly discipline was that all individuals were personally responsible for their salvation. People could no longer leave the village priest to take care of the eternal verities while they got on with making a living. In places where the campaign was active, it could create a climate comparable to the totalitarian regimes of more modern times: the authorities demanded active ideological commitment from everyone. In this highly-charged atmosphere, people who were thought to have the wrong beliefs were vulnerable. The authorities were not simply waiting until somebody complained; they were seeking out opportunities to exercise their authority. Witch-hunting would usually begin with a complaint against an individual who had been identified in the community as a witch. But the process so often included a deliberate search for further names that it fully deserves the name of witch-*hunt*.

The withdrawal of magical services

In the late middle ages, priests provided many magical services. Some of these services were recognised officially by the church, others were technically illegitimate, but there was often little effort to police the line between the two. Further services were provided by unofficial magical practitioners; they have been studied more in the early modern period, partly with the aid of evidence generated by witchcraft trials, but there is no reason to think that magical practitioners were fundamentally different before the trials began.

Priests' magical services operated in the area where religion overlapped with magic, as we saw in Chapter 1: people using religion, or magic, to gain material benefits for themselves, as opposed to seeking salvation for themselves, praying for others, or obtaining guidance about ethical conduct. People wanted good health and cures for illness, for themselves, their families, and their farm animals. They wanted sunshine to ripen their crops, and rain to hydrate them. They wanted safety in childbirth, and magical protection (in the form of baptism) for their newborn babies. The late medieval church provided services for all these things, fostering a comforting relationship between priests and people.

The Reformation and Counter-Reformation changed this relationship drastically. Protestant pastors withdrew wholesale from the field of magic, refusing to bless crops or heal illnesses using ritual. They remained willing to offer prayers for some material purposes, but prayers, though often welcome, did not satisfy demand in the way that had been done by such things as holy water, candles, or masses celebrated for specific material ends. The Catholic church also sought to withdraw its priests from this field; it remained willing to offer 'sacramentals' in more limited circumstances, but it scrutinised the boundaries of legitimacy more carefully.

Meanwhile, the common people's demand for magical services remained high. Some people no doubt accepted the official line that magic should be shunned, but they were probably a small minority. So the withdrawal of official magical services opened up a wider field for unofficial magical practitioners to meet the demand. In the present state of research we do not know whether magical practitioners' business actually increased in the sixteenth century, but we can gain a general sense that trade was brisk.

When people realised that their church was withdrawing their magical protection, this may well have made them anxious. Levels of anxiety are inherently hard to document, but it is at least plausible to suggest that if late medieval folk were confident that their church protected them against witchcraft, they would have been less likely to attribute a misfortune to witchcraft. Early modern folk, if they felt more vulnerable, may have been more ready to blame witches for their misfortunes.

The withdrawal of official magical services also clarified the authorities' position that magic was illegitimate. Protestant pastors preached against magic, and Catholic priests considered carefully whether a particular use of holy water was legitimate or magical. Official disapproval led to some prosecutions of magical practitioners, but most such practitioners seem to have been secure, because their communities supported them. Nevertheless, the authorities and the common folk no longer shared the same understanding of magical practice.

The 'huge mass' of ungodliness revealed

The authorities also began to realise that quite a few people's beliefs and practices were seriously ungodly. Laurence Chaderton, in Protestant England in 1584, asked how it was that in a supposedly Christian country there should be such a huge mass of old and stinking works, of conjuring, witchcraft, sorcery, charming, blaspheming the holy name of God, swearing and forswearing, profaning of the Lord's Sabbaths, disobedience to superiors, contempt to inferiors, murder, manslaughter, robberies, adultery, fornication, covenant-breakers, false witness bearing, liars, with all kinds of unmerciful dealing with one another.[9]

This was indeed a 'huge mass' of ungodliness, much of it consisting of breaches of the Ten Commandments. Chaderton was against witchcraft, but he had a much broader agenda.

Catholics, too, realised that traditional beliefs and practices were no longer enough. The prince-archbishop of Trier, Germany, in 1590, issued a decree stepping up religious instruction of the people, saying that several witches had confessed that they would not have made a demonic pact if they had received correct instruction.[10] In Poland in 1717, the evangelical priest Stanisław Brzeżański complained that peasants 'have become so un-used to the Lord's Church, that they have nearly turned back into pagans'.[11] Brzeżański interpreted popular ungodliness to mean that religious standards had declined, but his statement tells us at least as much about his own higher expectations.

To many authorities, the extent of popular ungodliness seems to have been a new discovery. Until they began their campaign of preaching and education, reforming authorities did not realise how limited people's understanding of correct religion was, nor did they understand the magical practices in which they had hitherto taken little interest. In 1563, just three years after Scotland became officially Protestant, those in charge of the new church were confused about the difference between magical practitioners and witches. The witchcraft act passed in that year treated 'witches' as practitioners with clients, rather than as conspiratorial enemies of society.[12] The reformers believed that there was a lot of witchcraft and ungodliness about, but they were hazy about the details. Once they established courts for godly discipline, they would learn more.

The programme of godly discipline unfolds

Witch-hunting thus makes most sense when it is set in the context of a broader programme of godly discipline. There were several aspects to this programme. The regular criminal courts, those that could impose the death penalty for serious crimes, broadened their remit to include crimes against God as well as crimes against ordinary humans. Then, both these courts and the courts of the church became more concerned with 'superstition' – incorrect Christian belief and practice, plus magic. Finally, popular festivities that conflicted with godliness needed to be reformed or suppressed.

First, then, the regular criminal courts expanded their field of operation, as we shall see in more detail in Chapter 7. In some ways these courts were already agents for enforcing a moral code. Most of the crimes that they tried were breaches of the Ten Commandments as well as of a specific criminal law. This became more important when churches, both Protestant and Catholic, increasingly adopted the Ten Commandments as a moral code. The late medieval church had more often stressed the Seven Deadly Sins, which were mainly offences against the community. The Ten Commandments included community offences too, but began with offences against God, especially 'idolatry' – the worship of false gods. Offences against God thus began to come into a similar conceptual category to traditional offences against the community like theft or murder.

Crime also became popular news in the sixteenth century. Criminals were expected to admit their guilt, and to express repentance on the scaffold. With the introduction and spread of printing, criminals' edifying final speeches (often fictitious) began to be published widely. Broadside ballads about criminals were also printed. Like media reporting of crime today, this satisfied a need for the moral code to be confirmed, but also provided entertainment and titillation. Beginning in the late sixteenth century, the Devil was brought into the picture, especially in Germany, with the mass marketing of a new genre of pamphlets called 'Devil books', short, entertaining stories linking the Devil with everyday sins like drunkenness. Pamphlets about witchcraft cases were thus part of a wider genre. But public executions of witches drove home a much more specifically Christian message than public executions of, say, thieves. Witchcraft news was important godly news.

News was not just printed. Church sermons were built by reformers into a vital medium for news and information – vital because they reached beyond the literate minority. Late medieval parish priests had rarely preached, and sermons had been usually heard only in towns where there were preaching friars. In the sixteenth century, first Protestants and then Catholics raised educational standards of parish priests so that they could deliver informative sermons spreading Christian messages. How many of these sermons discussed witchcraft is not known, but some certainly did. In Rottenburg, Germany, in 1594, a priest demanded witchcraft trials from the pulpit shortly before a panic broke out.[13]

When considering people's actual behaviour, it is not helpful to compare witchcraft 'crime' rates with other crime rates, since witches arrived in court differently from conventional criminals. Most of those convicted of conventional crimes had probably committed the acts of which they were accused, even if they did not always see their acts in quite the way that the court saw them. Convicted witches, by contrast, had rarely committed acts of witchcraft.

However, when considering the attitudes of the authorities, then placing witchcraft in the context of other crimes is exactly what we need to do. The authorities thought that they needed to stamp out crime and ungodliness, which took various forms. Witchcraft was one form, but there could well be others. States seeking godliness tended to crack down on a wider range of crimes, and to treat the prosecution of crime as a more public matter rather than leaving victims to lead prosecutions. Because this relates to the role of courts, it will be discussed further in Chapter 7.

As well as serious crimes, agencies of the godly state started to concern themselves with lesser 'superstitions'. These mainly consisted of beliefs and practices that reformers were no longer willing to tolerate. In Protestant states, 'superstitions' included surviving Catholic practices like praying to saints or making the sign of the cross – carried out either deliberately by loyal Catholics, or inadvertently by people who had not yet learned that such practices were no longer tolerated. In Catholic states, 'superstitions' typically meant unreformed Catholic practices like asking saints for the wrong things or making the sign of the cross incorrectly. In both Protestant and Catholic states, 'superstitions' also included popular magical practices, which had never been fully orthodox but which now came under closer scrutiny. Authorities looking for 'superstitions' were not always expecting to come across witchcraft, which was a less common but more serious offence – but, if there was any witchcraft about, they were probably going to pounce on it if they found it.

This can be demonstrated particularly well for the duchy of Württemberg, Germany, where the rates of prosecution for witchcraft and for beneficent magic ('superstition') have been compared. The two offences increased together in the 1570s, and continued to be correlated with each other, rising and falling together, until the 1680s, when they diverged. Witchcraft prosecutions declined, but prosecutions for beneficent magic rose, peaking in the 1740s.[14] The period after the 1680s was one of decline for witch-hunting, as we shall see in Chapter 10, but, before then, these Württemberg statistics display the godly state in action.

This can be taken further by looking at an individual case from Modena, Italy. In 1599, the magical practitioner Diamente de Bisa found herself in an inquisitorial court after a child that she was trying to heal died. The child's mother, 'frightened' by de Bisa's demeanour and her warnings to tell nobody about the incident, denounced her to the Inquisition for having killed the child. The court ascertained that de Bisa had the 'nickname' of '*la strega*' (the witch), and that she had previously been warned to stop her practice of 'superstitious medications'. But the court did not think that she was a witch, and it sentenced her merely to a year's penance for 'superstitious medications'.[15] Few witches were executed in Italy (and only one in Modena), but the crackdown on 'superstition' was widespread. In the right (or wrong) circumstances, an attack on 'superstition' could be accompanied by, or could escalate into, a witch-hunt.

The attack on 'superstition' went hand in hand with an attack on 'disorder'. Reformers set out to suppress ungodly popular festivities, or to purify them of their ungodly elements. Folk dancing was attacked because it encouraged sexual licentiousness. Carnival, the season of festivity that preceded Lent, encouraged violence. Charivari – publicly mocking cuckolds or ill-matched married couples – was an affront to the sanctity of marriage. Christmas, a time of disorderly festivity, had to be reformed or even (for some Calvinists) stamped out altogether. For a Catholic example, we are told that Maximilian, duke of Bavaria, whom we shall meet again shortly, prohibited 'magic, masquerades, short dresses, mixed bathing, fortune-telling, excessive eating and drinking, and "shameful" language at weddings'.[16] The witch-hunt was part of a much broader campaign.

Witch-hunting and other persecutions

Godly states could take different routes to godliness, not all of which entailed prosecuting witches. There were many forms of ungodliness, and different states had different campaign priorities. Were these campaigns alternatives to witch-hunting, or supplements to it? Here we shall consider various persecutions of organised dissident groups. Some of these groups were real, while others, like witches themselves, were imaginary.

One significant persecution was that of the Anabaptists. These were radical reformers who emerged alongside orthodox Protestants in the early sixteenth century. They were inspired by Protestantism, but made more far-reaching demands; in particular, they rejected infant baptism. The Anabaptists mounted a populist challenge to established regimes, but unlike orthodox Protestants they never succeeded in allying themselves with kings and princes, and did not establish their own states. They were persecuted in both Catholic and Protestant states.

Anabaptists, like witches, were seen as being in league with the Devil. Their rejection of orthodox baptism was presented as an attack on the sacraments, especially by Catholics. This was similar to the way in which witches were thought to trample on consecrated hosts. Anabaptists were also thought of as an underground conspiracy, as were witches. Even so, people never thought that Anabaptists *were* witches. From this point of view, their persecution was similar to that of the Waldensian heretics in the fifteenth century, discussed in Chapter 2.

Prosecutions of Anabaptists and prosecutions of witches were, to some extent, alternatives. Few authorities pursued both at the same time, though some alternated between them. There was a general shift away from Anabaptists and towards witches, hinging on the decades around 1560. The city of Bruges, in the Spanish Netherlands, prosecuted mainly Anabaptists in the early sixteenth century, but also a few witches (and others, such as necromancers and an alchemist). Prosecutions of Anabaptists ceased in Bruges after 1573, whereupon the number of witch trials grew until there was a small panic there in 1596.[17]

This is not to argue that the shift from Anabaptists to witches was a general cause of witch-hunting. Anabaptists were numerous in only a few areas – Switzerland, south-western Germany and the Netherlands. Most places that prosecuted witches had never seen any Anabaptists. Rather, we should see the prosecutions of both groups as part of a broader pattern of enforcement of orthodoxy by the godly state. Since Anabaptists tended to be committed activists, the shift from prosecuting them to prosecuting witches was also part of the general shift from field warfare to trench warfare in the broader Reformation struggle. In the former phase, activists were targeted; in the latter phase, the focus shifted to ungodliness among ordinary parishioners.

A smaller but revealing instance of elite concern with organised dissident movements came during the English Revolution of the 1640s, when various radical religious groups arose. Shocked conservatives denounced the provocative activities of real sects like the Quakers, but in their fear and hatred the conservatives also created at least one imaginary sect, the 'Adamites'. Members of this sect supposedly worshipped naked, in imitation of Adam and Eve. Hostile pamphleteers were soon writing that the Adamites indulged in indiscriminate sex orgies – an echo of the shocking rites of which medieval heretics had been accused, and of which witches were still accused.[18] If it was possible to imagine a sect of Adamites, it was possible to imagine a sect of witches. And more English witches were prosecuted in the 1640s than in any other decade.

There were Jewish communities in several parts of Europe, and these were sometimes persecuted, officially or unofficially, by the Christians who surrounded them. Since medieval times there had been a tradition of accusing Jews of ritual crimes against Christians. The main accusations were that they abducted and killed children (the so-called 'blood libel'), and that they stole consecrated hosts in order to mutilate them. Accusations that Jews mutilated hosts were similar to accusations that witches did so. In Poland, there was an upsurge of anti-Jewish protest and official persecution in the 1650s and 1660s, shortly before the main upsurge of witch-hunting in the country. In Portugal, the Inquisition pressed hard on the so-called '*conversos*', Jews who had been forced to convert to Christianity and whose conversion was thought to be insincere. Possibly for that reason, witches were never a priority in Portugal. The Spanish Inquisition had its own *conversos* to deal with, and also the 'Moriscos', forcibly-converted Muslims. Witch-hunting often occurred as part of a state's struggle against ungodliness, but the hunt for ungodliness in Portugal and Spain could proceed without witches.

Religious wars

The religious wars of the early modern period helped to enhance state authority, as states mobilised and organised for war; but they also caused political instability and human suffering. As well as wars between Catholic and Protestant states, there were civil wars between Catholic and Protestant factions in a single state. Sometimes, especially in the politically-fragmented areas of Germany, religious wars could be a bit of both. In the long run, the two sides would fight each other to a standstill; but, until then, so long as each side hoped to defeat the other, religious wars were always going to recur.

There were various phases of religious wars. From the 1520s to 1555 there were wars in Germany at the time of Protestant expansion. From the 1560s to 1648 there were wars in the Netherlands, partly a war of independence by the northern provinces against Spanish rule, but partly religious. From 1562 to 1596, France experienced intermittent civil wars on religious grounds. From 1609, religious conflicts resumed in parts of Germany. Even in times of peace, there were often political struggles that were expected to lead to wars, or political pressures for countries to become involved in neighbours' wars. Spain and England both intervened militarily in the French Wars of Religion.

Finally there was the Thirty Years' War of 1618–48, a titanic struggle that engulfed most of the states of western and central Europe. Much of it was fought in the German territories, but Spain, France, Italy, the Netherlands, Switzerland, Hungary and Scandinavia were also dragged in. The Thirty Years' War is little known in the English-speaking world, perhaps because England itself was little involved, but it was the bloodiest and most wide-ranging war in Europe before 1914, with a death toll exceeding that of the Napoleonic wars. And it was fought largely, or at least ostensibly, on religious grounds.

The immediate pressures of fighting a war tended to discourage witch-hunting, at least in the theatre of war itself. When armies were on the march in a territory, regular courts tended not to sit. If a foreign army occupied a territory, the occupying authorities tended not to be interested in witches among their conquered peoples. But these immediate pressures affected only a few territories at a time. Most territories, most of the time, felt the stresses even of the Thirty Years' War from a distance that left their state institutions intact. Zeal for their religious cause could lead such states to pursue godliness intensely.

The stresses of war could also disrupt existing institutions in a way that could facilitate witch-hunting. England's biggest witchcraft panic, in 1645–47 in East Anglia, occurred in the later stages of the English Civil War. The assize courts that normally exercised a cautious jurisdiction over witchcraft were in abeyance, and the territory instead established a special court that could pursue witches without the usual restraints. Special witchcraft courts were established by some German states in the early seventeenth century, not always directly connected to warfare but with the broader religious struggle very much in mind.

There were many ways in which warfare could be practised and experienced. People whose countries fought wars experienced military recruitment and taxation, both socially stressful. When hostile armies passed through a territory, people experienced requisitioning, pillage, killings, flight of refugees, epidemics of disease, and large-scale disruption to economic and social life. The Thirty Years' War was more destructive than later wars because states mobilised huge armies but had not yet developed sophisticated supply mechanisms, so that armies devastated the countryside through which they passed. Finally, the ideological effects of warfare need to be considered: propaganda, stereotyping of the enemy, and the encouragement of black-and-white world-views. For religious wars, these effects were particularly important. Godly states often needed to prove that they were wholly virtuous. If they were wholly virtuous, and their enemies were wholly evil, then the enemies could be extirpated without mercy. All too often, those enemies included witches.

Witch-hunting, colonies and ethnicity

During the sixteenth and seventeenth centuries, some European states extended their authority in a strikingly new way: they established colonies beyond Europe, especially in newly-discovered America. These colonies gave Europeans control over new subject populations, about whom the Europeans initially knew little. Could this colonial encounter give rise to accusations of witchcraft?

There were few witchcraft executions in Europe's colonies, but the colonial encounter nevertheless shaped witch-hunting in important ways. To begin with, demonologists gained information about demons and their relationships with humans. As colonists and explorers encountered the peoples of the New World, they took particular interest in these peoples' religious rites, assuming that their gods were really demons. Such demons, and the sabbat-like rites with which they were allegedly worshipped, found their way into several demonologies. An 'Island of Demons', off the coast of Labrador, appeared on numerous sixteenth-century maps, including that of Gerhard Mercator. Readers of demonological works were thus encouraged to see Europe as an expanding Christian stronghold, surrounded by other global regions still under the dominion of the Devil.[19]

Renaissance scholars connected the 'paganism' of colonised peoples with ancient classical paganism, with which they were already familiar. Portuguese Jesuits tried to make sense of native Brazilian rites, not only in terms of the witches' sabbat, but also of the ancient Roman bacchanalia, a festival that was believed to have involved drunkenness and sexual licence.[20] Bodin, as well as using classical parallels, interpreted native American rites in terms of the wicked idolaters of the Old Testament.[21] Images of demonic witches as cannibals resembled images of native Americans as cannibals (a reminder, incidentally, that most accusations of cannibalism have been colonial inventions).[22] Fifteenth-century witches had often been interpreted as being like heretical groups such as the Waldensians: sixteenth-century witches were often interpreted as being like colonised peoples.

Colonial witchcraft ideas could then be re-imported to Europe. Pierre de Lancre, in the Basque country of south-western France in 1612, had a notably global vision. He noted that Basque fishermen crossed the Atlantic to fish near Newfoundland, and this set him thinking about demons that they might have brought back with them. He reasoned that, now that the global preaching of Christianity had reached 'the Indies, Japan, and other places', demons were being chased out of these places – and the Basque fishermen were bringing these demons back to infest their homeland.[23] One of the possessed nuns of Loudun, France, in 1633, was said to have spoken in the language of the Tupí Indians of Brazil.[24] In eighteenth-century Portugal, four of the country's six witchcraft cases had Brazilian connections.[25]

What of actual witchcraft accusations in the colonies? The earliest and most populous colonies were those of Spain and Portugal. The rulers of Spanish America certainly saw the Devil everywhere.[26] But jurisdiction over witchcraft in these colonies, as in the home countries, was exercised by the Inquisition, which firmly restrained witchcraft prosecutions. In the Spanish colonies (Mexico, Central America and Peru), the Inquisition seems to have executed no witches at all. There may have been two executions for witchcraft by the secular authorities in Peru in 1610, but this was exceptional.[27] In Portuguese Brazil, too, no executions occurred. Those convicted of witchcraft by the Brazilian Inquisition were all sent to Portugal; typically they were whipped and ritually humiliated before being banished or sent to the galleys.[28]

During the sixteenth century, colonists started enslaving African people and transporting them to the New World. The Spanish authorities worried more about witchcraft among these Africans. There was a small panic in 1620 in New Granada (present-day Colombia) when five slaves were arrested for witchcraft. Under torture, four made demonic confessions. Most of the content of these must have been supplied through leading questions, since the suspects did not all speak Spanish and can have known little of demonology. The confessions prominently featured killing of people by sucking their blood, perhaps because the inquisitors regarded the Africans as cannibals. An inquisitor wrote that 'these lands are widely infested with male and female witches and specially the mines of Zaragoza and its surroundings', adding that the witches 'destroy the fruits of the earth and impede the mining of gold'. Further prosecutions followed for the next two decades, though the convicted witches were punished only by terms of imprisonment; there were no executions.[29]

Native Americans did believe in 'witchcraft' in the global sense of magical harm – 'village witchcraft' as it has been called in this book. But they did not complain about it to the authorities, because the colonial masters' relationship with their conquered peoples was different from their relationship with their peasant tenants back home. Both existed to be exploited, but peasants generally respected their 'lord' and regarded his rule over them as legitimate. Maintenance of such a relationship required give and take on both sides, so the lord had to display interest in his peasants' concerns. The colonised peoples, by contrast, were usually ruled by force alone. If one Inca person bewitched another Inca person, they knew that the colonial authorities would not be interested.

As for witch-hunting in the English colonies, this displayed some differences, as well as similarities. The Spaniards and Portuguese ruled their conquered peoples from fortified towns, but the English sought land for settlement, and drove out the indigenous people rather than ruling over them. Colonists in New England thus lived near to dispossessed native Americans who, they saw, had good reason to hate them, as well as worshipping demons. At the time of the Salem panic of 1692, several of those involved in the panic had been caught up in recent 'Indian wars'. Cotton Mather looked back on the panic itself as a 'prodigious war, made by the *spirits* of the *invisible world* upon the people of New-England', and reflected 'that this inexplicable war might have some of its original [i.e. its cause] among the Indians, whose chief sagamores are well known unto some of our captives to have been horrid *sorcerers*, and hellish *conjurors*, and such as conversed with *demons*'.[30] The idea that the state must enforce godliness on its people was here supplemented by a related idea: the state must protect its people from external ungodliness.

While this external demonic threat sharpened fears of witchcraft, actual witchcraft cases in New England occurred within the colonist community, not among native Americans. Here the English colonists were behaving more like their Spanish and Portuguese counterparts. In Bermuda, too, all the accused witches were Europeans. Bermuda had no indigenous population, but it did have African slaves, and none of them were accused of witchcraft; even bewitchings of African slaves were rare.[31] In colonial Ireland, similarly, witch-hunting occurred largely within the 'new English' colonist community (see the text box 'Case study: Ireland', pp. 181–2).

Within Europe itself, there emerged a quasi-colonial idea of the witch as a member of an external and distrusted ethnic group. This was distinct from the village witch, who was usually considered an enemy within the village. The witch as ethnic 'other' was not entirely new, since a tendency to label distrusted groups as magical existed already in the middle ages. Late medieval Italians regarded Tatar and African slaves as particularly likely to practise harmful magic.[32] But the early modern idea of witchcraft, together with colonial expansion, made ethnic labelling of witches important.

Exotic peoples could be imagined as a site for witchcraft. In Poland, people said that there were more witches to the east – in Russia, an exotic land for the Poles.[33] In fact there were many more in Germany, to the west. Such exotic, external witchcraft could be brought into the community

176 *Witches and the godly state*

by distrusted outsiders. In Russia, many witches were members of ethnic minorities, described as Mordvins, Tatars, Poles, Lithuanians, Cherkes, or simply 'foreigners'; they were usually accused of bewitching ethnic Russians.[34] The exotic outsiders could be imaginary, as when witchcraft in Lancashire, England, was attributed in 1612 to 'Mother Grady', a vaguely-identified Welsh witch from Penmaenmawr, 'a great mountain in Wales'.[35] The Swedes saw their neighbours, the Finns, as an exotic ethnic group who were particularly likely to be witches – even in the New World. The two witchcraft accusations that occurred in New Sweden, the seventeenth-century colony on the Delaware, were against 'Lasse the Finn' and 'Karin the Finnish woman'.[36] In New Sweden we thus see both the English colonial pattern – with witchcraft accusations occurring within the settler community – and the idea of witches among other ethnic groups.

Overall, then, European understandings of witchcraft and the Devil were affected by the encounter with the New World. Europeans discovered new aspects of diabolism in the world beyond their shores, but their spectacular conquests in America gave them an aggressive confidence that they could triumph over the Devil. This aggressive confidence was a significant dimension of the godly state.

Types of state and intensity of witch-hunting

When discussing the role of states in witch-hunting, historians have often been interested in two points about Germany. First, the German-speaking lands were divided into many small states; second, these lands were the scene of particularly intense witch-hunting. Indeed, even within Germany, it seems to have been one of the most fragmented regions – the west and south-west – that prosecuted the most witches. Could the size of states be related to the intensity of witch-hunting?

The hypothesis that the small German states prosecuted more witches *because they were small* has been discussed in various ways. One related idea is that it was not so much the smallness of a state that was important, but its degree of centralisation: in this idea, states prosecuted witches *because they were decentralised*. Perhaps related to this is the idea that small states, and perhaps other states, were weaker and thus unable to resist popular pressure for prosecutions. In this version of the idea, states prosecuted witches *because they were weak*. The idea of small, decentralised and weak states has gained a good deal of currency, and needs careful attention.

The hypothesis has not been proven statistically, and probably could never be so proven; the data are not robust, and there are too many other variables. But, perhaps for that very reason, the hypothesis is an interesting case study of historical causation, illustrating the attractions and complexities of what is sometimes called 'multivariate analysis' – analysis of an effect that appears to have had multiple causes acting in different ways. Nobody has plotted all the known executions on a map of Europe, in a way that might allow statistical analysis. Most maps provide only impressionistic data, based on 'hotspots', 'sustained persecutions' or other such non-statistical concepts. There have been partial attempts to tabulate execution rates *per capita* in different states, but until these tabulations are complete it will not be possible to analyse them statistically. Not all states have received equal historical attention, and the data from different states are not always standardised (many statistics are for executions, but some also include deaths in prison, and others count witchcraft 'cases' whatever the outcome). And loss of records means that the data can never be complete.

Historians have sometimes been tempted to argue the hypothesis by concentrating on the states at the top of a hypothetical league table – those that hunted witches most intensely *per capita*. It can seem persuasive to say something like, 'All the top ten witch-hunting states were small, therefore small states hunted witches more intensely.' But this will not do. The top of the league table is dominated by small states mainly because small states vastly outnumbered large ones. If someone were to compile a list of states that prosecuted no witches at all, that list too would be dominated by small states.

There are in fact two reasons why the top of the league table is dominated by small states. The first is that panics in larger states usually occurred in individual regions rather than in the state as a whole. There was a panic in the Labourd region of France in 1609, making this region a witch-hunting hotspot. If the Labourd panic had occurred in the nearby small state of Navarre, we might have thought that it confirmed the hypothesis about small states. Yet the high figures for Labourd are instead swallowed up in the figures for France, which are much lower overall. Thus, in large states, witch-hunting patterns were often regional rather than national.

A second reason for small states to produce dramatic statistics is that small states were likely to deviate further from the average than large ones – in both directions. The German-speaking lands, overall, had three times as many executions *per capita* as the European average, which is striking; but Germany was such a large part of Europe that it could not possibly have had 60 times the European average. A small region could; Finnmark, Norway's northernmost county, did indeed have 60 times the European average of executions *per capita*. We should not be comparing Germany with Finnmark. Similarly, at the lower end of the league table, numerous small states executed no witches at all, but no regions the size of Germany executed no witches. Statistics can be misleading if we do not compare like with like.

The argument about different types of state should ideally be formulated with exactitude. In some versions of the argument, as we have seen, the distinction is between large states and small ones. In other versions, it is between 'centralised' states and 'decentralised' ones. In yet others, it is between 'strong' states and 'weak' ones. None of these distinctions can be drawn with precision. Even distinguishing large states from small ones is not simple: what was a 'state'? The kingdom of Poland incorporated the grand duchy of Lithuania, which was partly governed separately: do we count Poland-Lithuania as one state or two? The cantons of the Swiss Confederation were internally autonomous: was the Swiss Confederation a 'state', or was each canton a 'state'? As to 'centralised' and 'decentralised' states, was France centralised because royal officials all theoretically answered to the king, or decentralised because several provinces had assemblies with special privileges? In small states, the 'central' ruler could be so close to his subjects that he looks more like a 'local' ruler. Finally, what do we mean by a 'strong' state? Successful wars? Political stability? High taxes *per capita*? A large bureaucracy? Commercial prosperity? Conquest of overseas colonies? Some states were 'strong' by some of these criteria, and 'weak' by others.

These three variables – size, centralisation and strength – did not always match up in consistent ways. France and England were large and strong; Poland and Russia were large and weak. Savoy, the Rhine Palatinate and the Swiss Confederation were small and strong; the small and weak states were very numerous but have mostly been wiped off the map. Savoy was centralised, the Swiss Confederation and the United Netherlands were decentralised. Among the large and weak states, Poland was decentralised, but Russia was centralised. Was it mainly size, or centralisation, or strength, that affected witch-hunting?

To carry conviction, the hypothesis about small states ought to be applicable anywhere in Europe – yet it has never been applied in detail outside Germany. Italy, in particular, had a number of small states, like the republic of Lucca or the duchy of Modena, yet not one of them experienced panics on anything like the German scale. Italy, like Germany, was familiar with demonology (one demonologist, Bartolomeo della Spina, was a Modena inquisitor), but did not apply it.

Despite these difficulties, the hypothesis about small states does seem to have some validity, at least in some places. The main place for it was southern and western Germany. Some of the larger states in that region, like Württemberg and Bavaria, did prosecute fewer witches *per capita* than many of the smaller states around them. Again it must be stressed that this is merely an impression, and has not been proven statistically. Any statistical analysis of the region would be hampered, not only by the conceptual problems already mentioned (separating out size from strength and centralisation), and by patchy data, but also by the region's modest size. Even one unusual case would skew the statistics. A further problem would be where to draw a line round the region to analyse. For instance, should we include Cologne, a sizeable state with intense prosecutions? Future research may solve these problems. In the meantime, the statements that previous scholars have made about small states should be regarded as no more than impressionistic.

The small-states hypothesis is complicated in south-western Germany by an alternative hypothesis that may be called the core-periphery pattern. Regions often learned about witch-hunting from neighbouring regions, so that one can sometimes see witch-hunting spreading from one place to another. We might expect witch-hunting to be most intense in the core area that initiated it, and then gradually to weaken as its ripples spread outwards to the periphery. The combined concept of witchcraft, as we saw in Chapter 2, first arose in the French-speaking part of the western Alps, but the idea soon took root in nearby south-western Germany. Perhaps south-western Germany would have been a core witch-hunting region whatever kind of states it had. Witch-hunting then seems to have spread outwards gradually; broadly, it occurred later in eastern Germany than in western Germany, and later still in Poland. It seems to have spread more readily among linguistic networks. Beyond eastern Germany there were further German-speaking enclaves, and these regions probably executed more witches than the surrounding Slavic populations.

The core-periphery pattern, like the hypothesis about small states, is a broad and impressionistic generalisation. One problem with such generalisations is that they are difficult to disprove in the present state of our knowledge. Once we have witchcraft executions accurately mapped, and tabulated chronologically, we will be able to analyse them with more precision. The basic difficulty of multivariate analysis will remain – how can we analyse an effect that had multiple causes? – but we will at least be able to leave the present era of vague speculation behind.

These remarks may seem discouraging, so I should conclude on a more positive note by suggesting a more fruitful approach to the subject. Within states, what kind of people took the initiative in witch-hunting? Those who have argued that small states (or weak states, or decentralised states) prosecuted more witches have usually explained this by reference to some kind of popular demand for witch-hunting. Courts that were under the firm control of a distant central ruler were less likely to be caught up in panics. This is an important point, but it raises a range of questions – including how far there was, in fact, popular demand for witch-hunting. Perhaps there was such demand in Germany (or parts of Germany) but not in Italy? These questions feed into a broader question of whether the initiative for prosecutions came from above or from below – bearing in mind that this may not be a simple question. Were local elites 'above' or 'below'? Nevertheless, questions about where the initiative lay for prosecutions arguably get us closer to explaining witch-hunting than questions about types of state. We shall examine these more fruitful questions in Chapter 8.

Case study: The German prince-bishoprics

One remarkable category of states seeking godliness was found among the Catholic prince-bishoprics of the Holy Roman Empire.[37] There were six notorious prince-bishoprics – Bamberg, Cologne, Eichstätt, Mainz, Trier and Würzburg – plus the connected prince-abbacy of Ellwangen. Between them they executed about 6,500 witches, an appreciable proportion of Europe's total of about 50,000. These executions mostly fell between 1581 and 1634, with a peak in the late 1620s.

The prince-bishops were secular rulers as well as ecclesiastical ones. From the late sixteenth century onwards, they sought to 'reform' their provinces in a Catholic direction. Most of the prince-bishops who ruled these seven states in this period were militant Catholics, obsessed with sin and with the Counter-Reformation struggle. Philipp Adolf von Ehrenberg, bishop of Würzburg, declared in 1627 that God intended to destroy Würzburg as he had Sodom and Gomorrah, because of its witches. Executing the witches was urgently necessary to avert God's wrath.

Was there a link with state formation? The prince-bishops' power was limited in some ways. They did not inherit their positions, but were elected by the members of their cathedral chapter – the dozen or so 'canons' who formed a kind of management committee for the cathedral. These canons were usually members of local noble families, and the bishops could not easily remove them – some could even be Protestants. Some of the bishops' territories consisted of scattered parcels of land rather than cohesive political communities. They could not build strong states – but they could try. Bamberg and Würzburg tried particularly hard. The central courts were given more power, and were staffed by professional lawyers. New laws were passed to curb popular ungodliness. Taxes were increased. They both built special 'witch houses', prisons to expedite the trials; Bamberg's prison is shown in Illustration 8.1 below. Most of the seven states achieved their spectacular execution rates by establishing special 'witch commissions' to carry out trials, often with ruthless determination. In Ellwangen, every single suspect either confessed or died under torture.

By contrast, some of the prince-bishoprics, notably Mainz and Trier, were politically disorganised, and their witch-hunting cannot be explained as efforts at state formation. Prosecutions in Cologne started from below in 1626, with popular demand for punishment of witches who had caused storms. When the archbishop appointed

(*continued*)

witch commissioners to take control of an existing process, the commissioners got out of hand, claiming about 2,000 lives. Ultimately these prince-bishoprics exemplify a commitment to militant godliness, and to witch-hunting as a means of demonstrating this.

Ellwangen, as a small prince-abbacy, was unusual, since the Empire's prince-abbacies were usually less ambitious politically than the prince-bishoprics, and most prosecuted few witches. Another smaller but even more striking parallel to Ellwangen was the abbey of St Maximin, whose prince-abbots vigilantly asserted their independent rule over a tiny territory of about 2,200 inhabitants. In a panic between 1586 and 1596, St Maximin executed at least 400 witches.[38] To demonstrate their Counter-Reformation godliness, the abbots were prepared to wipe out a fifth of the population. Their officials also compiled a register of over a thousand further people, including many in neighbouring territories, who had been named as witches in the trials. They clearly had something they wanted to prove.

Case study: Ireland

Ireland, where there was hardly any witch-hunting, forms an illuminating test case.[39] Ireland was ruled by England, more or less as a colony. After the Reformation, there were three groups of people in Ireland: the majority 'native Irish', Gaelic-speaking, who remained Catholic; the 'old English', descendants of medieval English colonists, who also remained Catholic; and the 'new English', privileged Protestant settlers who arrived in the sixteenth and seventeenth centuries (many in fact from Scotland). Almost all of Ireland's witchcraft cases occurred among the small new English minority. The most prominent case, a panic in Islandmagee in 1711, resembled recent Scottish cases involving demonic possession, as well as the much-publicised case in Salem, Massachusetts, in 1692 – all of which were also Protestant. The Catholic majority in Ireland produced almost no witches. Why?

The main answer to this question is the failure of the Irish Reformation. The official Protestant church in Ireland, controlled by the English government, was inadequately funded and had few Gaelic-speaking preachers; the native Irish and old English were neither coerced nor persuaded into Protestantism. Irish peasants willingly

(continued)

used the criminal courts in cases of theft or assault; if they had wished to prosecute their neighbours for witchcraft, they could have done so. The main explanation for the absence of witchcraft cases among the Catholic Irish, then, is that the Protestant authorities failed to establish a foothold in Catholic communities. When the authorities demanded godly behaviour from the Irish, the latter either refused to listen, or – because of the linguistic divide – they did not understand.

Critics and limitations of the godly state

It should not be assumed that all rulers tried hard to make their states 'godly' in the sense that this chapter has been using the term. Of course, nobody said, or even thought, that they preferred the state to be 'ungodly'. But there were many rulers, at every level, who did not make godliness a priority, or who sought a different kind of godliness.

Opponents of the 'godly' reform movement thus existed throughout our period. This should be distinguished from the growth of seventeenth-century intellectual scepticism that would later undermine witch-belief (for which see Chapter 10). Earlier opposition often came from conservatives (whether Protestant or Catholic) who were satisfied with moderate 'reform' and saw no need for unsettlingly militant action. 'Reform' measures also had to overcome vested interests. Funding for new, 'reforming' church institutions often had to be obtained by dispossessing unreformed institutions, which might be politically well connected. Catholic priests were often reluctant to give up their concubines, while many lay people resented enforcement of rules on sexual morality. The attack on popular festivity was particularly often resisted, and not only by the common folk; many members of the elite also enjoyed such festivity. Satisfied with the status quo, the cathedral clergy of Saragossa advised their Madrid agent in 1576 that there was no need to mention witchcraft to the higher authorities: there were no witches in the entire archdiocese.[40]

Several demonologists expressed frustration at those who disagreed with them, with Bodin in particular denouncing judges for ridiculing witchcraft beliefs. In late sixteenth-century France, caught up in religious civil wars, Bodin supported the militant Catholic League, but most of the judges took the royalist side. Typically these judges were described as '*politiques*', meaning 'pragmatists'. This was largely a term of abuse (it could be coupled with 'atheists'), but the attitudes it described were real. When militant Catholics opposed royal authority, royal authority could turn against them. The Jesuits were expelled from France in 1594 for supporting the opposition to Henry IV.

One case study illustrates the godly state and its limitations particularly vividly. The government of the duchy of Bavaria experienced a protracted debate about witches between 1591 and about 1630.[41] The dukes, Wilhelm V (ruled 1579–97) and Maximilian I (ruled 1597–1651), were committed to the Counter-Reformation, but also sought political stability and political control of the church. On the ducal council, rival factions of *'zelanti'* ('zealots') and *'politici'* ('pragmatists') struggled to dominate policy on witch-hunting. The zealots staged periodic show trials, but on the whole the pragmatists were able to curb their efforts, aided by cautious legal advice from the university of Ingolstadt. The zealots marshalled the support of several Jesuits, including the demonologist Martin Delrio, but the pragmatists had their own influential Jesuit, Adam Tanner. In 1613 the pragmatists even managed to secure the execution of a witch-hunting judge, Gottfried Sattler, for misconduct. Quite a few witches were executed in Bavaria, but nothing like as many as in nearby prince-bishoprics.

Conclusion: Witch-hunting and state formation

The European witch-hunt can be seen as an episode in the formation of modern states. Witch-hunting and state formation were both complex phenomena in themselves, and the relationship between the two was also complex, but, during the early modern period, the existence of relationships between the two is surely clear. Broadly speaking, those who wanted godly states wanted witch-free states. Overall, though, some aspects of early modern state formation encouraged witch-hunting, while other aspects discouraged it.

In studying 'state *formation*', we are dealing with processes, not static situations. It is not enough to say that godly states imposed order, while witches were ungodly and disorderly. The states that prosecuted witches were not the states that simply *were* godly or orderly; they were the states that were *engaged in a process of seeking* godliness or order. They might be at different stages of the process, or might be achieving different degrees of success in the process.

Partly this is because of the complexities of state formation, with some of the processes entailing what might be called negative feedback. Rulers pursued policies that we can describe as 'state formation' partly to combat the prevailing 'disorder' of the period. Yet it was the voracious demands of the emerging states, and their incessant wars with each other, that caused much of the 'disorder' in the first place. Strong states required money, and taxes increased hugely during this period – but taxes could lead to resentment or even revolt, a clear example of negative feedback. The usual solution to revolts against taxation was repression, requiring more state machinery and more taxation; sometimes this worked, but not always. Attempts to 'reform' any given institution, from a craft guild to a ruler's council, could stir up opposition from vested interests. State formation was a struggle, and some of the witch-hunting states seem to have been those that participated actively but with less success in the struggle.

The question of success can be pursued further by asking: was the godly state, overall, a success? In the long run, probably not. The common folk were never persuaded, as a whole, to abandon all their 'superstitious' beliefs and practices. After the Reformation and Counter-Reformation came the eighteenth-century Enlightenment, and the goals that states set themselves became less coercively evangelical. The divine right of kings lost its commanding ideological position even earlier, in the middle years of the seventeenth century.

At the time of the witch-hunts, though, this long-term failure was still in the future. Preaching, catechising, educating, printing godly tracts, organising godly rituals and ceremonies, making godly rules and regulations, creating godly institutions both charitable and penal: these things were done by rulers and religious movements in the expectation of success. At the time, they had an enormous effect on people's daily lives. The links between the godly state and the witch-hunts are complex and often indirect, and not all of the links even operated in the same way; on the whole the project to create godly states encouraged witch-hunting, but some aspects of the project discouraged it or led in other directions entirely.

To this extent we should see the godly state as an essential background factor rather than a determining cause of specific witchcraft trials or even specific witchcraft panics. Still, unlike other background factors – peasant quarrels and curses, for instance – the project to create godly states was chronologically coterminous with witch-hunting; the two rose and fell together. In this cautious sense, therefore, we can interpret the Reformation and Counter-Reformation, and the political developments that accompanied them, as important causes of the European witch-hunt.

Early modern witchcraft was clearly an ideological crime, linked to political ideology through the doctrine of the divine right of kings. Because divine right was an ideology of state formation, this can lead to crude suggestions that state formation encouraged witch-hunting. In the crudest formulation of this view, early modern states prosecuted witches to demonstrate, and to legitimise, their power. Rulers would seek to impress their subjects by taking tough action against the perceived threat of witches. There is a little truth in this, but it can all too easily mislead. Divine-right rulers did not say to themselves, 'I'm going to prosecute witches in order to impress my subjects'; they prosecuted witches because they believed that it was their God-given duty to do so. Impressing the subjects was a secondary aim at most.

As for the subjects, they were sometimes impressed by witch-hunting, but not always. Witch-hunting could enhance state authority, but it could sometimes cause political turbulence and instability. Godly zealots, who saw themselves as a crusading minority struggling against the sins of the world, were quite prepared to promote witch-hunting even if it was unpopular. Witch-hunting by a political faction might worsen political divisions instead of uniting people in support of their ruler. Witchcraft panics often led to lower standards of evidence, as we shall see in Chapter 8; people might look back on the trials and decide that they had been miscarriages of justice. The collapse of a witchcraft panic might discredit those who had promoted it.

One aspect of state formation certainly tended to restrict witch-hunting. This was when rulers, seeking to build a more orderly state, centralised and professionalised their courts. Such courts would be likely to insist on higher standards of evidence, and would be less likely to engage in panics. Not all professional jurists were against witch-hunting; some demonologists were professional jurists themselves. But, when we find witch-hunting being reduced or discouraged in the later part of our period, we often find professional jurists at work, as we shall see in Chapter 10.

Godly rulers wanted to stamp out a wide range of offences, but their priorities varied. Pressure for godliness sometimes caused other prosecutions *as well as* witch-hunting, while, at other times or in other places, pressure for godliness caused other prosecutions *instead of* witch-hunting. A full understanding of this will be reached once research has established, not only more precise contours of witch-hunting, but also more precise contours of prosecution of other offences. In the meantime, though, we can gain through case studies a sense of how each of these processes operated. Broadly speaking, in Italy, the alternative offences prevented witchcraft from becoming important; in Germany, the alternative offences complemented witchcraft and confirmed its importance.

The other offences prosecuted by godly states might be classified under three headings: other moral crimes, other conspiracies, and other superstitious magic. Witch-hunting was related to the prosecution of other moral crimes because their incidence tended to rise and fall together. Paradoxically, witch-hunting was related to persecutions of other conspiratorial groups (real or imagined) for the opposite reason: witch-hunting tended *not* to occur together with these other persecutions. However, in both cases, we are seeing witch-hunting in the context of other actions that could be taken by a godly state. A godly state was unlikely to undertake more than one headline-grabbing persecution at once, so authorities who were bothered by Jews or Anabaptists would be unlikely to undertake a major persecution of witches. But routine moral offences could be pursued together. A push for prosecution of routine offences would be likely to bring in some witches as well as some sexual offenders.

As for the role of the godly state in prosecuting other superstitious magic, there were two main aspects to this, pointing in different directions as far as the study of witch-hunting is concerned. The first is that if an offence was treated as superstitious magic, then the offender would not be executed. Every time the authorities, faced with a given offender, punished them with fines or penances, that was potentially a missed opportunity to prosecute them for actual witchcraft. Prosecutions for superstitious magic may have saved many people's lives.

The second aspect, however, is that the godly state's search for superstitious magical offenders was a broad one. In the process of looking for such offenders, they mostly found mild offenders, and did not execute them. Many German states that hunted witches also prosecuted people for '*Zauberei*' (magic) or '*Segensprechen*' (casting charms); this was *additional* to their witch-hunting, an extended aspect of their godly programme. Moreover, their search sometimes turned up serious offenders as well as mild ones. If the authorities had not been concerned about godliness, they would not have been searching at all.

Finally, then, one conclusion that can surely be reached with confidence is that states and rulers that had *no* concern for godliness were unlikely to prosecute witches in any numbers, and sometimes did not prosecute them at all. Fear and hatred were stirred up by the struggles over the Reformation and Counter-Reformation. Without this, the early modern period might well have experienced no more than the handfuls of prosecutions for harmful magic that had occurred during the middle ages.

Notes

1 Jean Bodin, *On the Demon-mania of Witches*, trans. Randy A. Scott, ed. Jonathan L. Pearl (Toronto, 1995), 218 (IV.5). Reproduced with permission of The Centre for Reformation and Renaissance Studies, University of Toronto
2 Quoted in Lawrence Normand and Gareth Roberts (eds.), *Witchcraft in Early Modern Scotland: James VI's Demonology and the North Berwick Witches* (Exeter, 2000), 315.
3 E. William Monter, *Witchcraft in France and Switzerland: The Borderlands during the Reformation* (Ithaca, NY, 1976), 108–9.
4 Martín Del Rio, *Investigations into Magic*, trans. P. G. Maxwell-Stuart (Manchester, 2000), 28.
5 Quoted in Gary K. Waite, *Eradicating the Devil's Minions: Anabaptists and Witches in Reformation Europe, 1525–1600* (Toronto, 2007), 59.
6 Waite, *Eradicating the Devil's Minions*, 188–9.
7 Quoted in Stuart Clark, 'Protestant demonology: sin, superstition, and society (*c*.1520–*c*.1630)', in Bengt Ankarloo and Gustav Henningsen (eds.), *Early Modern European Witchcraft: Centres and Peripheries* (Oxford, 1991), 46–81, at p. 58.
8 Henri Boguet, *An Examen of Witches*, trans. E. A. Ashwin, ed. Montague Summers (London, 1929), 4, 120.
9 Quoted in Patrick Collinson, *The Religion of Protestants: The Church in English Society, 1559–1625* (Oxford, 1982), 151.
10 Johannes Dillinger, *Evil People: A Comparative Study of Witch Hunts in Swabian Austria and the Electorate of Trier*, trans. Laura Stokes (Charlottesville, Va., 2009), 76.
11 Quoted in Michael Ostling, *Between the Devil and the Host: Imagining Witchcraft in Early Modern Poland* (Oxford, 2011), 184.
12 Julian Goodare, 'The Scottish witchcraft act', *Church History*, 74 (2005), 39–67.
13 Dillinger, *Evil People*, 103.

14 Edward Bever, *The Realities of Witchcraft and Popular Magic in Early Modern Europe: Culture, Cognition and Everyday Life* (Basingstoke, 2008), 379.
15 Mary O'Neil, 'Magical healing, love magic, and the Inquisition in late sixteenth century Modena', in Stephen Haliczar (ed.), *Inquisition and Society in Early Modern Europe* (London, 1987), 88–114, at pp. 95–7.
16 Peter Burke, *Popular Culture in Early Modern Europe* (3rd edn., Farnham, 2009), 306. For a longer list see Wolfgang Behringer, *Witchcraft Persecutions in Bavaria*, trans. J. C. Grayson and David Lederer (Cambridge, 1997), 107–8.
17 Waite, *Eradicating the Devil's Minions*, 106–8.
18 David Cressy, 'The Adamites exposed: naked radicals in the English Revolution', in his *Agnes Bowker's Cat: Travesties and Transgressions in Tudor and Stuart England* (Oxford, 2000), 251–80.
19 Grégoire Holtz and Thibaut Maus de Rolley (eds.), *Voyager avec le diable: Voyages réels, voyages imaginaires et discours démonologiques (XVe–XVIIe siècles)* (Paris, 2008).
20 Laura de Mello e Souza, 'Autour d'une ellipse: le sabbat dans le monde luso-brésilien de l'Ancien Régime', in Nicole Jacques-Chaquin and Maxime Préaud (eds.), *Le sabbat des sorciers en Europe (XVe–XVIIIe siècles)* (Grenoble, 1993), 331–43.
21 Bodin, *Demon-mania*, 63–4 (I.3).
22 Charles Zika, 'Les parties du corps, Saturne et le cannibalisme: représentations visuelles des assemblées des sorcières au XVIe siècle', in Jacques-Chaquin and Préaud (eds.), *Le sabbat des sorciers*, 389–418.
23 Pierre de Lancre, *On the Inconstancy of Witches: Pierre de Lancre's Tableau de l'inconstance des mauvais anges et demons (1612)*, ed. and trans. Harriet Stone and Gerhild Scholz Williams (Turnhout, 2006), 58–60 (I.ii.8–9).
24 Grégoire Holtz, 'Démonologues et voyageurs: le démon de l'analogie', in Holtz and Maus de Rolley (eds.), *Voyager avec le diable*, 165–81, at p. 165.
25 de Mello e Souza, 'Autour d'une ellipse', 337–8.
26 Kenneth Mills, '*Demonios* within and without: Hieronymites and the Devil in the early modern Hispanic world', in Fernando Cervantes and Andrew Redden (eds.), *Angels, Demons and the New World* (Cambridge, 2013), 40–68.
27 Andrew Redden, *Diabolism in Colonial Peru, 1560–1750* (London, 2008), 96.
28 Laura de Mello e Souza, *The Devil and the Land of the Holy Cross: Witchcraft, Slavery, and Popular Religion in Colonial Brazil*, trans. Diane Grosklaus Whitty (Austin, Tex., 2003), 215–16.
29 Heather Rachelle White, 'Between the Devil and the Inquisition: African slaves and the witchcraft trials in Cartagena de Indies', *The North Star: A Journal of African American Religious History*, 8 (2005), 1–15 (quotation at p. 2).
30 Quoted in Emerson W. Baker, *A Storm of Witchcraft: The Salem Trials and the American Experience* (Oxford, 2015), 106.
31 Virginia Bernhard, 'Religion, politics, and witchcraft in Bermuda, 1651–55', *William and Mary Quarterly*, 67 (2010), 677–708.
32 Michael D. Bailey, 'Nocturnal journeys and ritual dances in Bernardino of Siena', *Magic, Ritual, and Witchcraft*, 8 (2013), 4–17, at p. 11.
33 Wanda Wyporska, *Witchcraft in Early Modern Poland, 1500–1800* (Basingstoke, 2013), 140.
34 Polina Melik Simonian, 'Following the traces of xenophobia in Muscovite witchcraft investigation records', in Gábor Klaniczay and Éva Pócs (eds.), *Witchcraft Mythologies and Persecutions* (Budapest, 2008), 197–212.
35 Richard Suggett, 'Witchcraft dynamics in early modern Wales', in Michael Roberts and Simone Clarke (eds.), *Women and Gender in Early Modern Wales* (Cardiff, 2000), 75–103, at p. 76.

188   Witches and the godly state

36 Amandus Johnson, *The Swedish Settlements on the Delaware, 1638–1664*, 2 vols. (New York, 1911), ii, 544–5.
37 *Encyclopedia*, iv, 1217–19.
38 *Encyclopedia*, iv, 1082–3.
39 E. C. Lapoint, 'Irish immunity to witch-hunting, 1534–1711', *Eire-Ireland*, 27 (1992), 76–92.
40 María Tausiet, *Urban Magic in Early Modern Spain: Abracadabra Omnipotens*, trans. Susannah Howe (Basingstoke, 2014), 20.
41 Behringer, *Witchcraft Persecutions in Bavaria*, 230–310.

7 Witches in court

> Concerning sufficient indication of witchcraft.
> When someone offers to impart witchcraft to other people, or threatens to bewitch someone and such befalls the threatened person, and the aforesaid person otherwise has associated with men or women witches, or has employed suspicious things, gestures, words, and signs such as characterize witchcraft, and when, further, the said person has a bad reputation of similar sort, then that constitutes a legally sufficient indication of witchcraft and is adequate basis upon which to examine under torture.
>
> Section 44 of the *Carolina* criminal code of the Holy Roman Empire, 1532[1]

Introduction

Witchcraft was a crime. Being a witch, or committing acts of witchcraft, were not just about being morally wrong, or deviant, or odd, or evil. Witchcraft was a *crime* – a serious offence that was defined by the law and enforced in courts of law. The question of whether someone was a witch or not was decided, ultimately, by courts of law, and it was these courts that ordered guilty witches to be punished.

We thus need to understand how crimes were dealt with in early modern Europe. Criminal courts existed, but no professional police forces. Rural courts were mostly run by local noblemen – men who wielded political and even military power, as well as judicial power. Urban courts were run by town councils, mostly controlled by an urban elite of merchants and other businessmen. Some courts, at least in more centralised states, operated under commission from the king, duke or other ruler; such courts might still be staffed by local noblemen, but could be more answerable to the central government. Many local courts were effectively autonomous, but sometimes there were central appeal courts that exercised some kind of supervision. These courts were all secular. There were also ecclesiastical courts, which sometimes contributed to witch-hunting, though usually indirectly.

When treating witchcraft as a crime, we have to be careful how far we treat it as an ordinary crime. People convicted of ordinary crimes like theft, or even serious crimes like murder, may well have really committed those crimes; but we can hardly argue that all those people burned at the stake for witchcraft were guilty as charged, and that their prosecutions thus represent the normal operations of the criminal justice system. There was indeed a sense at the time that witchcraft was an 'extraordinary' crime. Still, unless we grasp the outlines of European criminal procedure, we will not understand the European witch-hunt.

Laws on witchcraft

Courts applied the law. As well as criminal law, there was also civil law (governing interpersonal disputes on matters like property). Often there were separate courts for civil matters. It is the criminal courts and the criminal law that concern us. What, in particular, was the criminal law on witchcraft? This question is surprisingly difficult to answer in detail, but, fortunately, a detailed answer is rarely required. Many early modern crimes were crimes, not because a lawmaker had decreed that they were crimes, but because tradition recognised them as crimes. This is what is meant, even today, by the British and American concept of 'common law'. In most of Europe, courts recognised that witchcraft, or something like it, was a traditional crime.

As witch-hunting gained momentum in the sixteenth century, some states did pass new laws against witchcraft, usually attempting to clarify the law rather than change it. These laws could be seen as a consequence rather than as a cause of an increased desire to prosecute witches, but, once in place, they usually made prosecutions easier. In the Holy Roman Empire, the *Constitutio criminalis Carolina* ('criminal code of Charles') was issued in the name of the Emperor Charles V in 1532. It was often simply called the *Carolina* code. It applied to the Empire but was influential all over Europe. It was followed by other similar codes, for instance in France (1537) and Spain (1567). The *Carolina* code made clear that witchcraft was a criminal offence, defining it as harmful magic, and gave some procedural details of how to prosecute witches.

Laws specified various penalties for crime. Imprisonment, a familiar penalty today, was hardly ever used – it was too expensive to keep criminals locked up. Prisons, if they existed at all, were centres of pre-trial investigation. Various punishments were used instead. There were physical punishments – whipping, branding or public humiliation; there was banishment from the locality; there were fines; and, quite often, there was the death penalty. Death was the usual penalty for serious crime, including the crime of witchcraft.

Witchcraft was also, of course, a religious offence. This was important, but only indirectly so. Courts did not recognise Exodus 22:18 ('Thou shalt not suffer a witch to live') as a directly binding law; there were many obscure laws in the Old Testament that were not considered binding on

Christians. But, as the 'law of God', the Old Testament carried moral force. More directly legal force was carried by 'canon law', a body of written medieval laws regulating the church. Canon law included the law of marriage, and various matters concerning church property and moral conduct; it also influenced criminal procedure more generally.

Courts that tried witches

Just as there were both secular and ecclesiastical laws, there were secular and ecclesiastical courts. In the localities, secular criminal courts were controlled either by the local lord in rural areas, or by the king or other ruler, or by a combination of the two. Urban secular courts were controlled by town councils. There might be a right of appeal, or at least mechanisms for supervision, by a central court, typically that of the king, or of the emperor in the Holy Roman Empire. Later in this chapter we will need to concentrate on the secular criminal courts, because it was they that executed the great majority of witches. However, their activities need to be seen in the context of the ecclesiastical courts – both the regular church courts, and the courts of the Inquisition. We saw in Chapter 6 that the ecclesiastical courts grew in importance in the Reformation era.

Regular church courts in Catholic areas were usually controlled by the bishop. Supervision of them, if any, was exercised by the archbishop and ultimately the pope. Churchmen were forbidden to shed blood, so church courts could not exercise the death penalty, but they could hand convicted criminals over to the secular authorities on the understanding that the latter would carry out the execution. In practice this happened rarely. Most punishments by church courts were mild: penances (ritual actions like fasting or pilgrimage) or small fines. Their main aims were rehabilitation and reconciliation, rather than retribution against the offender.

Very few church courts, Catholic or Protestant, prosecuted witches. They were relevant to the witch-hunt, however, in three ways. First, their activities reminded everyone of the importance of godliness and moral conduct, and of the need to avoid 'superstitious' practices. As long as this was important, witchcraft was also important. Second, they could hear cases of slander, in which a person could complain that a neighbour had called them a witch, and demand the neighbour's punishment. Prosecutions for slander, as we saw in Chapter 4, helped to limit witchcraft accusations, but also gave structure to the ideas behind these accusations and sometimes encouraged them. Third, church courts could prosecute a crime that *might* be seen as witchcraft, but instead the court could call it something else – typically 'magic' or 'superstition'. Such 'superstition' was discussed in Chapter 1. Probably many people escaped prosecution for witchcraft because the church court punished them for a 'superstitious' act but avoided using the word 'witchcraft'. Again, though, this to some extent provided a framework for witchcraft prosecutions rather than preventing them altogether.

In some Catholic areas there were also courts of the Inquisition. These existed to punish just one crime: heresy. We saw in Chapter 2 that witchcraft came to be recognised as heresy in the fifteenth century, which meant that the Inquisition's courts began to deal with it. After the Reformation, the Inquisition ceased to operate outside Italy, Spain and Portugal, but branches of the Inquisition continued to operate in those areas, and largely retained control of witchcraft cases. Like the regular church courts, the Inquisition could not execute anyone itself, but it usually had no difficulty in getting secular authorities to do so on its behalf.

The Inquisition was a punitive institution, but it generally aimed to reconcile sinners to the church. It recognised a variety of magical crimes, rather than just one crime of 'witchcraft'. In the Roman Inquisition, the branch which operated in most of Italy, these crimes were *'magia'* (magic), *'maleficio'* (malefice or harmful magic), *'stregoneria diabolica'* (diabolical witchcraft) and *'negromanzia'* (necromancy). Of these, *'stregoneria diabolica'* was the closest to witchcraft as other courts understood it. But the existence of the other related crimes meant that offences were rarely placed in this category – and the other categories were mostly seen as milder. Moreover, the Inquisition had several possible verdicts; in between 'guilty' and 'not guilty' of heresy, suspects could be said to be under 'vehement suspicion' or 'light suspicion' of heresy, so that few received the 'guilty' verdicts that alone could place a suspect at risk of execution (and then only for a repeat offence). Those who confessed their sins and displayed penitence were usually given mild punishments that were supposed to rehabilitate them. Illustration 1.1 above shows a convicted witch in Sicily being given such a punishment. Only the tiny minority who remained 'unrepentant' were executed.

Parts of eastern Europe, particularly the Balkans and Russia, adhered to the Orthodox church. This had church courts similar to those of Catholics and Protestants, though there was no Inquisition. The Balkan states, ruled by the Ottoman Empire, were allowed to practise Christianity but prevented by their Muslim overlords from hunting witches. In Russia, cases of magical harm usually went before the church courts, to be punished by penances and excommunication. In western and central Europe, witch-hunting may have been more important because witchcraft was prosecuted before the secular criminal courts. It is on these courts that we now need to focus.

State formation and legal developments

During the fifteenth century, standards of proof were lowered in many criminal courts. Medieval courts had protected the interests of propertied suspects – sometimes they just needed to swear an oath of innocence to be automatically acquitted – but now courts were keen to achieve convictions. Jurists became more concerned about crimes committed secretly or at night, and allowed a wider range of evidence into such trials. Courts had not previously allowed the testimony of poor people or 'infamous' people (those with previous convictions or in degrading occupations like prostitution), because the poor could be threatened or bribed, and the 'infamous' could easily lie. Now their testimony was allowed.[2] This made prosecution easier for numerous crimes. As to witchcraft, a concern with secret crimes was important, for witchcraft was notoriously a secret crime.

The number of executions for crime overall rose strongly in the sixteenth century, and public executions for crime became more elaborate and ritualised. The sixteenth and seventeenth centuries were not just the peak period for witch-hunting; they were the peak period for executions of criminals as a whole.[3] The authorities put steadily-increasing administrative effort into detecting and punishing crime. Fifteenth-century court records were usually brief: a page or two on each case, or just a few lines saying that such a witch had been convicted. By the later seventeenth century, a witchcraft case could generate dozens or even hundreds of pages of evidence and other paperwork, as the court authorities summoned and re-summoned witnesses, corresponded with neighbouring towns and consulted university law faculties, as well as repeatedly interrogating the suspect.

The increase in the numbers of executed criminals went alongside an increase in the numbers of different crimes. Many newly-created or newly-important crimes were public, victimless crimes. Traditional crimes almost all had individual victims; criminal procedure meant the victim of theft or assault, or the surviving relatives of a victim of murder, complaining to the courts and seeking 'justice' against the person who had wronged them. The only significant victimless crime in medieval Europe was counterfeiting of coinage. But, in the fifteenth and sixteenth centuries, the idea grew up that the state should prosecute a criminal even if there was no aggrieved victim – and the number of victimless crimes rose sharply.

Several case studies have indicated that witch-hunting was part of a broader picture of criminal prosecution. In Paris, France, levels of witchcraft accusations rose and fell together with levels of accusations of adultery, sodomy, incest and infanticide – and none of these crimes would have been considered to have 'victims' in medieval times. Similarly, witchcraft trials in several Swiss towns tended to cluster in the same years as trials for sodomy. Here, in order to understand 'witch-hunting', we should be trying to understand this broader attack on ungodliness, and the role of the godly state as the authority that could bring order.

Initiating prosecutions

We now need to look in more detail at how crimes were reported, investigated and prosecuted. From now on, this chapter will focus mainly on the secular criminal courts.

There were two basic ways in which suspected criminals could be brought into court: accusatory and inquisitorial. In the accusatory system, the victim of crime reported the crime and led the prosecution; the judge simply presided over the dispute between victim and suspect. In the inquisitorial system, the judge initiated prosecutions, and could prosecute even if there was no complaint from a victim. The concept of 'inquisitorial' procedure, meaning procedure in which the judge took the initiative in 'inquiring' into the crime, should not be confused with the special ecclesiastical courts known as the 'Inquisition'. The 'Inquisition' was 'inquisitorial', but many secular courts were also 'inquisitorial'. In practice, many courts operated with a mixture of these two systems; sometimes victims took the initiative, sometimes judges did. And even inquisitorial courts had to get their information from somewhere; if the victim did not report the crime, someone else had to do so.

The difference between accusatory and inquisitorial procedure was partly about how cases arrived in court, but also affected what happened in court and the kinds of evidence that would be used. Accusatory procedure ensured that there would be evidence for the prosecution – the evidence of the victim; an inquisitorial judge, by contrast, might be able to gather his own evidence, or might have to do so. With witchcraft cases, this might mean that courts using accusatory procedure would rely on testimony from victims, which would tend to be about village witchcraft, malefice and specific harm done by individuals. Courts using inquisitorial procedure might concentrate more on demonic witchcraft, interrogating suspects and gathering confessions to the demonic pact and witches' sabbat. But this mention of interrogations and confessions is running ahead of the story.

Deciding on guilt or innocence

There were two main systems for deciding on guilt or innocence in serious crimes: the customary system and the Roman system. As a broad generalisation, versions of the customary system were used in the British Isles, Scandinavia, Poland, Russia and Hungary, while much of Germany, France, Italy and Spain used the Roman system – so called because it was based on the law of the ancient Roman Empire. Procedure in any one country sometimes incorporated elements of both systems, and there were local variations, but it is important to begin by outlining the principles of each system. One difference was that the customary system was 'accusatory', while the Roman system was 'inquisitorial', as those terms were defined above. But the most important difference concerned the way that the verdict was reached.

In the customary system, the decision on guilt or innocence was made by a jury of the suspect's neighbours. The judge presided over the trial, and passed sentence if the jury convicted the suspect, but the actual verdict was the responsibility of the jury. People trusted this system because the members of the jury, even if they did not know about the actual crime, did know something about the suspect and the locality. They were supposed to be respectable, propertied men, and it was clear that they would have to live with the results of their decision, along with the families of the suspect and of the victim. For the sake of their own reputations, they would try to make a fair decision.

In the Roman system, by contrast, there was no jury. The judge not only presided over the trial, but also supervised the investigation into the crime beforehand – and he made the decision on guilt or innocence himself. People recognised that this system had some advantages over the customary one: judges were less open to bribery, intimidation and favouritism than juries, and knew more about the law. But the Roman system placed a heavy burden of responsibility on the judge, and there was a risk that he might misuse his power or simply make mistakes. So the system had strict rules about evidence. A suspect could be convicted of a crime only if there were two witnesses to the actual crime, or if the suspect confessed credibly to having committed the crime. Two witnesses to the actual crime meant what it said; if two witnesses saw a man running from a house in which a victim had been stabbed to death, that was not enough. If one witness saw the actual stabbing, that was not enough either. If there were two witnesses but one was a woman, that was not enough either; women were not usually accepted as witnesses. Roman-law courts therefore had frequent recourse to the suspect's confession – the 'queen of proofs', as confession was sometimes called. And if the suspect did not confess voluntarily, then, so long as there was *some* evidence against the suspect, the court could use torture to obtain a confession.

The Roman system thus placed its emphasis on the suspect's confession, and on torture. The customary system, by contrast, placed its emphasis on the suspect's reputation in their community. Some countries using the customary system allowed torture, others did not; in particular, torture was rare in England, and not used in witchcraft cases. Overall, neither system was obviously 'better' or 'worse' by the standards of its time. The English might pride themselves on not using torture, but their juries could convict a suspect on indirect or hearsay evidence – less evidence, in fact, than would even allow a Roman-law court to authorise torture. For witchcraft trials, the Roman system's reliance on confessions had greater potential for facilitating panics; it was confession evidence that would allow single cases to spiral outwards into chain-reaction panics, as suspects named further names in their confessions. However, the customary system *could* use confessions, and countries with that system were quite capable of having witchcraft panics if conditions were right.

To write of the Roman and customary 'systems' may make them seem more systematic than they really were. To some extent these 'systems' are abstractions created by legal historians in order to analyse the principles involved. Most criminal courts operated with at least some elements of both systems; probably few ordinary judges recognised a firm distinction between them. Poland's courts, for instance, were probably more customary than Roman, but can be regarded as a kind of hybrid. They had two lay 'assessors', rather like jurymen, to assist the judge; the decision on guilt or innocence was made by all three, so that the assessors could outvote the judge if they thought he was being unfair. In Denmark and Norway, courts used juries to decide on guilt or innocence – the distinguishing feature of the customary system – and so did not need confessions for this purpose. But torture could be applied *after* conviction, to obtain further information about the crime – including information about accomplices. In Luxembourg, the judge decided on guilt or innocence – the distinguishing feature of the Roman system – but the village mayor and aldermen gathered initial evidence and played a filtering role.[4] Many German courts also had 'aldermen', operating effectively as a jury. Numerous jurisdictions had other officials besides the judge, such as a public prosecutor, exercising responsibility for parts of the process.

These 'systems' also experienced change over time. The customary system was an older one, and the Roman system had grown up gradually in the middle ages to replace it in many places. This is sometimes described as the 'reception' of Roman law, with jurists rediscovering the legal principles of the Roman Empire. Canon law, the law of the church mentioned earlier, was also based on Roman-law principles; the Roman system itself is sometimes called the 'Roman-canon' system. The reception of Roman law began in the twelfth century, but, in Germany, with its political fragmentation, more of the transition to the Roman system occurred much later. Some of the transition occurred in the fifteenth century, while many German states may not have reached the transition until after the witch-hunting period was over. The German combination of uncertain procedural rules and political fragmentation could provide the preconditions, at least, for unrestricted witch-hunting.

What happened in court

Most of the work of a criminal trial was done before the formal court hearing. Evidence was gathered in advance, sometimes while the suspect was in prison. Neighbours' written statements were compiled, or suspects themselves were interrogated (perhaps under torture). In a Roman-law court, all this was part of the trial procedure itself, while a customary-law court treated the gathering of evidence as a pre-trial procedure, but the results were similar. During this process, supporters of the prosecution and supporters of the suspect might both lobby the court, trying to influence the judge in their favour. A criminal trial was to some extent a ritualised contest between the suspect's supporters and the accuser's supporters. The suspect might object to witnesses, or to aspects of procedure. Suspects were not usually represented by lawyers, but they could call on friends and relatives to help them.[5] The support of a woman's husband – if in fact he decided to support her – could count for a good deal; this will be discussed in Chapter 9.

With all this work done in advance, the trial hearing itself might not take long – less than a day, or even just a few minutes. There might be an official prosecutor, but defence lawyers were rare. Many trials were conducted informally. At the trial of Anne Bodenham in Salisbury, England, in 1653, 'the spectators made such a noise that the judge could not hear the prisoner nor the prisoner the judge, but the words were handed from one to the other by Mr R. Chandler, and sometimes not truly reported'.[6] The casual nature of some proceedings is illustrated in an order to the courts of Hohenberg, Austria, that witchcraft trials should be held one at a time – clearly the judges had been processing cases in batches.[7] At the end of the trial hearing, the judge or jury would announce their verdict: guilty or not guilty.

Not all witches were found guilty, but they often were. If they were convicted, the next stage would be for sentence to be passed. There was often a pause between verdict and sentence, forming another opportunity for interested parties to lobby the court. The judge might decide on the sentence himself, but many German courts had to report their verdicts to the city council or the territorial ruler for sentencing; these too could be lobbied. For most crimes, respectable, well-connected criminals received light sentences or pardons, having demonstrated repentance; the rigours of the law were reserved for the lower orders. To some extent this happened in witchcraft cases too, but the shocking nature of the crime of witchcraft sometimes prompted courts to severity. Courts that treated witchcraft as an 'exceptional crime' (for which see the text box 'Witchcraft: An exceptional crime?') sought to show no mercy to witches. At any rate, execution was the usual punishment for a guilty witch. Executions themselves will be considered later in this chapter; at this stage, we need to probe the question of evidence in more detail.

Evidence of guilt

Courts used various types of evidence to establish guilt. For present purposes the different types can be placed in three broad categories: neighbours' testimony, the suspect's confession, and various supplementary types of often physical evidence. These were used in slightly different ways by customary-law and Roman-law courts, but an overall pattern can nevertheless be discerned.

Neighbours' testimony, first of all, can be subdivided into different types. The testimony of actual witnesses to the crime, theoretically valued by Roman-law courts, played hardly any practical part in witchcraft trials.

More important was the testimony of victims of the crime: people who had been harmed by the witch's malefice. This was theoretically distinct from witness testimony, since witnesses were supposed to be impartial (suspects were sometimes allowed to object to witnesses who were their enemies), whereas victims could present themselves openly as having quarrelled with the suspect. Victims' testimony was important in many cases. Courts were often more interested in the fact of the quarrel, establishing the suspect's malicious and vengeful nature, than in the credibility of the harm that had supposedly followed.

Testimony about specific harm done tended to shade off into testimony about a suspect's general reputation – something that carried legal weight, especially in customary-law courts. Statements by neighbours that a suspect was generally reputed to be a witch would not usually be accepted on their own, but could supplement statements about specific harm. Neighbours' testimony like this, recorded by many courts, has enabled historians to reconstruct the process of forming reputations that was discussed in Chapter 4. Such evidence could be given in the form of written depositions presented to the court, or orally in the court itself, or both.

There has been a good deal of discussion of the contamination of suspects' testimony by leading questions and torture. It is perhaps surprising that more attention has not been paid to the possible contamination of witnesses' testimony. Witnesses, obviously, were not tortured, but they were just as likely to be asked leading questions in ways that might undermine the validity of their memories. This is a topic on which more research is needed, probably applying the psychological theory of memory that will be discussed below.

After neighbours' testimony, the second type of evidence was confessions by suspects – often extracted under torture. Torture itself will be discussed later in this chapter, but here it is important to note that confession evidence often painted a different picture of witchcraft from neighbours' evidence. Neighbours thought of village witchcraft, with the central aspects being vengefulness and harm done. Confessions, given in response to questions from educated interrogators, tended to present a picture of demonic witchcraft, with the central aspects being the demonic pact and the witches' sabbat. These concepts of village witchcraft and demonic witchcraft, though distinct, were compatible with one another. Confessions could also include statements about harm done. One of the most important points for the dynamics of witch-hunting was that confessions could name other witches, sometimes in large numbers – something that neighbours' evidence hardly ever did.

These two types of evidence – neighbours' statements and confessions – were the most common, and indeed the most normal kind of evidence; courts used them for other crimes too. In some witchcraft cases, however, courts also used other more unusual types of evidence. These mostly involved detecting some aspect of the physical manifestation of the Devil's role in the world. Such evidence was rarely used alone, but could be combined with neighbours' statements or confessions in order to build up a case.

The Devil's mark was a common type of evidence. Although most ideas about the Devil came from elite demonology, the idea that witches had a distinguishing mark probably originated as a folk belief. Demonologists elaborated the idea because they were interested in the demonic pact, the key fact about the demonic witch. The idea was that the Devil gave witches a mark when they made the pact, as a parody of Christian baptism. One common type of Devil's mark was a skin blemish, identified by sight. There was also a belief that witches had a mark in their eyes, visible only to other witches. A few confessing witches claimed the ability to identify such marks; as star witnesses they occasionally generated large numbers of accusations. This mark in the eyes may have been a folk belief, but there was also an elite idea (going back to classical times) that there were women with double pupils who could inflict the evil eye.[8] A further kind of Devil's mark, found mainly in England and its colonies, was a teat that witches were believed to use to suckle their animal familiars. These different types of mark were not always distinguished precisely; when a suspect simply confessed to having a mark, its nature could be left vague.

A further and notorious kind of mark was an insensitive spot on the skin, identified by pricking with pins. During panics, a few prickers acquired enough expertise to become professionals, charging for their services. Pricking was not technically torture; torture aimed to inflict pain in order to achieve a confession, while pricking aimed to show that *no* pain was inflicted when the pin was inserted in the right spot. Nevertheless, pricking was a coercive and humiliating process. Some suspects broke down and confessed their guilt once they were told that a Devil's mark had been found.

Another notorious type of evidence was the so-called 'swimming test', in which suspects were dropped into water to see whether they floated. Witches were supposed to float, as they were rejected by the water, the element used in baptism. Suspects had a rope tied to them – the idea that the innocent were drowned is a modern myth – but, in practice, most suspects who were 'swum' were deemed to have floated. The swimming test was based on a folk memory of the early medieval 'ordeals', long abandoned by the courts, in which suspects had been subjected to tests in which God was supposed to reveal the guilty party. The test was revived, specifically for witches, in many countries during the early modern witch-hunts. Probably most countries north of the Alps saw at least some use of it. The most influential demonologists all rejected the swimming test, however, and it never became wholly standard. As with pricking, the swimming test could lead to confessions; suspects' resistance sometimes broke down after they were told that they had floated.

The swimming test was fairly common in England; it was usually carried out as an informal pre-trial procedure, but its evidence could be used in court. It spread to England's colonies, being used in 1651 on the first witch to be executed in Bermuda, Jean Gardiner, who 'did swyme like a corke and could not sinke'. In another case from the same panic in Bermuda, John Middleton was subjected to the test and floated, whereupon he confessed that he now knew he was a witch although 'he knew yt not before'.[9] The common expression that the suspect floated 'like a cork' may well indicate more precision in the process than really existed; the onlookers, seeing someone struggling in the water, made their decision as to whether the person was 'floating' or 'sinking' based on what they wished or expected to see. Usually they were perceived to have floated. In Łobżenica, Poland, in 1692, the landlord experimented by swimming some people known to be innocent. They floated – which was not supposed to happen; so the experiment was ignored.[10] In some cases, very little can have been seen. Numerous suspects were subjected to the swimming test in Vardø, in the far north of Norway – even in the winter, when in this Arctic region there was no daylight at all. They were all declared to have floated in the icy waters.[11]

Items of witchcraft equipment, such as magical ointments or wax figures, were sometimes used as evidence. The idea of wax figures for image-magic was widespread; ointments may have been more dependent on demonological ideas. Ointments or wax figures were usually mentioned in confessions, or less often in neighbours' accusations, rather than being actually produced in court. The defective rosaries that attracted suspicion in Franche-Comté (as we saw in Chapter 6) were possessions of the witch, but conceptually were more like the witch's mark than witchcraft equipment. Defective rosaries expressed the idea that the Devil sought to imitate God, or God's creations, but could not achieve a perfect imitation. The Devil's own bodily abnormalities, described in many confessions, expressed a similar idea.

Physical evidence about harm done to neighbours was sometimes cited in court to supplement the neighbours' own statements. In cases of human illness or death, this might involve a professional person, such as a physician, examining the victim's body and testifying that their illness was 'not natural'. Such examinations were rare, but occurred in some seventeenth-century German cases. In Venice, Italy, physicians were often called in by the Inquisition to testify about magical harm.

Behavioural evidence was sometimes used. It was widely believed that witches were unable to shed tears, so allegations that a suspect had not shed tears in certain circumstances (under torture, for instance) could be used against them. Another type of behavioural evidence, occasionally mentioned, was an inability to recite the Creed or the Lord's Prayer correctly. This again was linked to the idea that the Devil could not produce a perfect imitation of God's creatures, as well as reflecting the campaigns for godliness that demanded that people learn these texts. A third type of behavioural evidence was sometimes found in neighbours' testimony, when neighbours reported, not specific harm to themselves, but unusual behaviour – often linked explicitly or implicitly to storm-raising. In Bazuel, Spanish Netherlands, in 1621, Antoine Nicaise testified that he had seen Marie Lanechin, at dawn, 'all dishevelled and with loose hair'; the implication was that she had been casting a spell.[12]

During the seventeenth century there came to be increasing interest in 'spectral evidence' – testimony that the 'spectre' of the suspect had appeared to the victim. This was particularly important in cases of demonic possession or its analogues, such as that at Salem, Massachusetts, in which victims accused witches of sending their 'spectre' to torment them. Another kind of spectral evidence was given by children who accused witches of having abducted them to the sabbat, as in the Swedish panic discussed in Chapter 8; such abductions were assumed to take place in spirit. Spectral evidence could thus be thought of as a special type of evidence of malefice, with ordinary misfortunes replaced by more exotic ones.

In interpreting evidence like this, people often saw what they wished to see. At Bury St Edmunds, England, in 1662, the court conducted a test to see if two accused women were really causing a girl to have fits when they touched her, as she claimed. The girl was blindfolded, and then touched, not by either of the women, but by someone else – and she still fell into a fit. Many of the onlookers declared that the women must be innocent, but the prosecution produced some twisted reasoning about the fits not being counterfeited. This, along with other evidence, convinced the jury.[13] As well as self-deception, there were no doubt instances of deliberate fraud. In Salem, one of the girls accusing Sarah Good claimed that Good's spectre had stabbed her, and produced the tip of a knife. However, a man present testified that he had broken the knife the day before in the girl's presence, and produced the rest of the knife. This did not discredit the girl's testimony; the judges merely warned her to tell the truth from now on.[14]

One final type of evidence should be mentioned: the testimony of another confessing witch saying that the suspect had been seen at the sabbat. This leads back to confession evidence, but in this case the confession was being used differently: instead of just showing that the confessing suspect was guilty, it showed that someone else was also guilty. As we shall see in Chapter 8, this type of evidence was used mainly in panics. When a confessing witch named other names, this was rarely sufficient on its own to convict these other people, but it could be sufficient evidence to arrest them and torture them into confessing themselves. This type of evidence, like all the supplementary types, was thus used mainly in the times and places when witch-hunting became severe enough to lead to panics.

Witchcraft: An exceptional crime?

The concept of an 'exceptional crime' or 'excepted crime' ('*crimen exceptum*' in Latin) affected some witchcraft trials, particularly in some Roman-law courts. The concept derived from ancient Roman law, which stated that some crimes were so serious, and so hard to prove, that special procedures should be used in prosecuting them. There was no precise agreement on what these procedures should be, but, typically, rules protecting suspects could be lifted, a wider range of prosecution witnesses could be heard, and torture could be used more freely. Roman law also stated that an exceptional crime should never be pardoned.

Several demonologies, from the *Malleus Maleficarum* onwards, argued that witchcraft was an exceptional crime. Bodin wrote: 'Since the proof of such wickednesses is so hidden and so difficult, no one would ever be accused or punished out of a million witches if parties were governed, as in an ordinary trial, by a lack of proof.'[15] What this meant in practice was not always clear. Courts were not always guided by demonologists in their procedures, nor did they record clearly when they were treating witchcraft as an exceptional crime (or indeed when they were not). However, courts did often disregard the rules in witchcraft cases – particularly the rules concerning torture. Such intensifications of prosecution occurred in some customary-law courts as well as Roman-law ones.

From the late sixteenth century onwards, the idea of witchcraft as an exceptional crime came to be a point of attack by critics of trials' excesses. The argument tended to run: it is obvious that witchcraft trial procedure is excessive, because the courts are treating witchcraft as an exceptional crime. Friedrich Spee, the sharpest critic of excessive trial procedure, took a different line; he began by *agreeing* that witchcraft was an exceptional crime, but emptied this of its substance by going on to argue that courts should still seek justice and truth. This will be discussed further in Chapter 10.

Torture

In principle, torture was not mindless cruelty. Judicial torture was not a punishment, but a means of eliciting the truth from a suspect who might be guilty or innocent. Confessions were expected to be true. Interrogators knew well that suspects might 'confess' falsely, in order to stop the pain of torture; thus they sought more than simply an admission of guilt. 'Yes, I'm a witch, stop torturing me' was not in itself a credible confession. A credible confession was one that revealed information that only a guilty person would know. A suspected thief would not be asked simply whether he had stolen the goods; he would be asked where he had hidden the stolen goods. The idea was that an innocent person would know nothing of the crime and would thus be unable to reveal true information about it. With suspected witches, this could be problematic, as we shall see.

The most common form of torture was the strappado (see Illustration 7.1). The suspect's hands were tied behind them, and they were hauled into the air by a rope tied to the hands and passed over a beam in the ceiling. The pain could be intensified by lifting them and letting them fall with a jerk, or by attaching weights to the feet, or simply by letting them hang for longer. In Luxeuil, Franche-Comté, in 1529, the stone attached to the feet of Desle la Mansenée weighed 50 pounds; she confessed immediately afterwards.[16] Another common torture was the leg brace, in which the calves were crushed between metal plates. The rack and thumbscrew, familiar in modern imagery of torture, were sometimes used. One distinctive type of torture was sleep deprivation, often for a period such as forty hours.

There was probably a good deal of sadism and cruelty in practice. The *Malleus* warned that torturers should act 'without joy, as if they are upset'.[17] Suspects' words during torture were rarely recorded, but we have the following exception, from Pere Torrent in Barcelona, Spain:

> My lord, I haven't been any such thing of this. For the love of God don't make me say what I am not.... Ai, Mother of God! I haven't been any such thing! Don't torture me! ... Mother of God of the rosary, help me! ai, ai, ai! I'm dying! My heart is breaking! My chest is giving! I haven't been any such thing!

Eventually he confessed.[18] Martin Delrio advised that torturers should avoid inflicting permanent injury, but that 'laceration of the flesh, breakage of bones and muscles, and a not inconsiderable dislocation or rupture of joints and bones are scarcely avoidable during torture'. He added that sleep deprivation was 'the best and safest method'; not only did it avoid physical injury, but it was also highly effective in obtaining confessions.[19]

There were several formal rules restricting torture. Before torture could be allowed at all, it had to be clear that a specific crime had in fact been committed. There had also to be strong circumstantial evidence that the suspect was guilty of it. Here the idea of 'half proof' was sometimes used; thus, if two witnesses to the crime were sufficient for conviction, one witness was sufficient for torture. Then there must be no other means available for getting at the truth. Torture could be authorised only by

Illustration 7.1 Torture at Mellingen, 1577

A mother and daughter, suspected of witchcraft, are tortured by the strappado at Mellingen, Switzerland. The daughter is hoisted into the air by her arms, while the mother (left) waits to be tortured in turn. Weights are available on the floor for attaching to the suspects' feet to increase the pain.

Johann Jakob Wick, *Sammlung von Nachrichten zur Zeitgeschichte*, 1560–87, F. 12–35 (24 vols.), F. 26, fo. 226r. Zentralbibliothek, Zurich.

Reproduced with permission of Zentralbibliothek, Zurich.

the judge, and sometimes the judge had to be present in person; some writers said that a physician should also be present. Once torture had been authorised, there were also restrictions on how it could be applied. Leading questions must not be asked. Torture must not be excessive, nor cause permanent injury. It must be administered only on one occasion; thus a suspect who refused to confess under torture had to be acquitted. Finally, any confession obtained under torture must be freely repeated later by the suspect in court – though a suspect who refused to do so could be tortured again.

Unfortunately, these rules were often disregarded by criminal courts – and not just in witchcraft cases. Torture was often used without definite evidence; suspects were tortured repeatedly; leading questions were used; and sometimes torture did injure or kill. The rules, indeed, may have existed in order to provide overall legitimacy for torture, rather than being actually followed. We are told that the councillors of Rothenburg ob der Tauber, Germany, never treated witchcraft as an exceptional crime, and were always scrupulous about procedures. But even in Rothenburg, nine of the town's forty-one witchcraft suspects were tortured – and torture was applied up to five times.[20]

One significant bending of the rules concerned the issue of when torture could be authorised in the first place. The traditional rule, endorsed by the *Carolina* code, was that of 'half proof', usually meaning one witness to the crime instead of two. In chain-reaction witchcraft trials, many courts interpreted this to mean that torture could be authorised if there was one *denunciation* of the suspect by a previous confessing witch. This could lead to rapid escalation of a panic; if one witch named several suspects, they could all be hauled in and tortured straight away. Yet it went completely against the spirit of the *Carolina*, for a denunciation by a criminal (who was by definition 'infamous' and untrustworthy) was quite different from a report by an impartial eyewitness.

It is hard to say how common torture was. A few courts meticulously recorded details of torture, particularly in the seventeenth century when record-keeping was more extensive. Many others did not write down anything about torture, probably because they saw no practical use for doing so. With these courts we rely on other sources, such as chronicles or correspondence, to tell us that torture was practised. The vagaries of record-keeping are shown in the case of Suzanne Gaudry, from Rieux, France, in 1652. She confessed various details of witchcraft: she had entered the Devil's service 25 years ago, she had been to the sabbat, and so on. A month later she retracted everything: 'what she has said was done so by force'. Only after this was it formally recorded that she was tortured – but it sounds as though she had been tortured before.[21]

Official torture may have been the tip of an iceberg, in the sense that many more suspects had pressure placed on them by being ill-treated in custody. A German tract of 1626, the *Malleus Judicum* ('Judges' Hammer'), described harrowing prison conditions for suspected witches: prisons with no light or heat, infested by vermin, with prisoners kept in their own filth, in chains.[22] In Venice, prisoners were usually held in such conditions for months before the Inquisition was ready to interrogate them; no wonder they were desperate.[23] Some suspects in Salem 'would not confess any thing till they tyed them Neck and Heels, till the Blood was ready to come out of their Noses'.[24] Rape of female prisoners by gaolers was sometimes reported, and may have been common. All this is important to the European witch-hunt in several ways, but the most relevant point here is that prison brutality put pressure on suspects to confess.

As with modern atrocities, euphemisms were often used for torture, a common euphemism being 'putting to the question'; compare this with the modern phrases 'third degree' or 'moderate physical pressure'. Also, courts sometimes recorded that suspects had made their confessions 'freely' or 'willingly'. Such words should not necessarily be taken at face value, and may even represent deliberate denials that torture had occurred. Friedrich Spee alleged that some tortures were concealed in this way.[25] Bodill Danielsdatter, in Finnmark, Norway, in 1652, made an informal confession but refused to repeat it in court, and was therefore tortured. Brought back to court, it was recorded that 'she willingly upholds her first confession'.[26] If a court record says that a confession was given 'willingly', we cannot use this to prove that it means the opposite, but we should be suspicious. At the other extreme, some critics of witch-hunting alleged large-scale and indiscriminate torture; some of these accounts may be exaggerated too. Ultimately, therefore, we cannot produce statistics for the incidence or intensity of torture in the European witch-hunt, but, when we find people confessing to witchcraft, we should take torture to be the most likely explanation for why they did so. Torture does not explain the content of suspects' confessions, but it is the best single explanation for why suspects confessed.

Torture usually succeeded in getting suspects to confess, though not always. One extreme case was that of Maria Holl, in Nördlingen, Germany, in 1594, who survived sixty-two sessions of torture without confessing, and had to be released. Her endurance contributed to the collapse of the witchcraft panic in the town.[27] Maria Holl deserves to be remembered, but she was hardly typical. We have some statistics from Lorraine about torture's effectiveness. Of 276 people who got as far as the torture chamber, 60 (22 per cent) refused to confess even after torture.[28] A confession rate of 78 per cent is still far higher than it would have been without torture. In Jersey, Channel Islands, torture was not used – and the confession rate was only 10 per cent (6 out of 66).[29] Of course, informal pressure that fell short of official 'torture' could have been used in both Lorraine and Jersey. Some of the Lorraine witches confessed in the torture chamber with only the threat of torture. Fear of torture even led to suicides in prison, such as that of Treyn Hupricht in Luxembourg in 1620; the judges noted frustratedly that this had prevented them reaching a verdict in her case.[30]

Remembering Maria Holl's sixty-two sessions of torture, we should bear in mind that intensity of torture varied. Some courts observed the rule that there should be only one session of torture. The *parlement* of Rouen, the court governing Normandy, France, was one of them; it sent several suspected witches to be tortured, but almost all withstood the single torture session, which was presumably less intense than some. They were then released, sometimes after a period of imprisonment.[31] In Italy, the Venetian Inquisition was even more cautious; it insisted on first establishing that a specific crime had been committed before it would authorise torture, with the result that most witchcraft investigations fizzled out before interrogation and there were no convictions at all.[32] However, places with more intense witch-hunting had no such inhibitions, and used torture freely. They sometimes followed the recommendation of the *Malleus Maleficarum* that, because torture should not be 'repeated', a second or further session of torture should be called a 'continuation'.[33]

Successfully withstanding torture without confessing ought to have confirmed a person's innocence, but it did not always do this. Sometimes suspects who had withstood torture were banished. And being freed after torture was not necessarily the end of a suspect's problems, as in the case of Isabeau Wilverdange, a 65-year-old widow from Houffalize, Luxembourg, in 1678. She refused to confess after being tortured over a period of three months in prison, in the winter with no fire, and eventually had to be freed. But she was too badly injured to walk, and her niece had to carry her on her back to her own house, where she was

> so torn and dislocated in her body, that she can neither move, walk nor leave her bed, and is distressed and afflicted by reason of the long cold and imprisonment that she has endured; her feet are frozen and almost rotted; the nails are falling from her toes and fingers; she has extraordinary swellings on her arms, and is unable to raise them to her head; and she is not only afflicted in all parts of her body, but also finds herself despoiled of all her small goods, movable and immovable, because the officers of justice have sold them to pay the costs they claim.[34]

Torture could sometimes get out of hand entirely. In Szeged, Hungary, the authorities had something to prove in 1728; the imperial army had only recently recaptured the town from the Ottoman Turks. Witch-hunting had not been allowed under the Ottomans' Muslim regime, so it was perhaps natural that the new Christian authorities would want to prosecute some witches. But they had no experience of how to do it. The first three suspects were subjected to the swimming test by being tied up and thrown into the River Tisza – in which they drowned. This was not supposed to happen; the suspects should have had a rope tied to them, so that if they were innocent, and sank, they could be pulled out. The three were nevertheless declared innocent. The next three suspects were tortured – and all died under the torture. This was declared to have been the work of another witch, but what we seem to see here is zealous and callous incompetence.[35] In another such case, in Luxembourg in 1622, Isabeau Frérot died during torture, and the local authorities reported that the Devil had killed her.[36]

Constructing and negotiating confessions

The confession was typically expected to contain individual detail about places and times, motives for entering the Devil's service, activities at the witches' sabbat, and malefices committed; it had also to be refined for theological correctness. Some detailed confessions furnished raw data for demonologists on the powers and activities of demons. Confessions were often polished and elaborated over several sessions of interrogation, with the interrogators asking further questions, and the suspect changing or adding to their story each time. The interrogators had up to three aims here. First, they wanted the suspect to create a coherent story, since this made the confession convincing. Second, they often wanted the suspect to confess all that they knew. Third, they often wanted the suspect to express repentance for their crime. Here, interrogation and confession were comparable with the Christian practice of confession of one's sins to the priest – a process that was supposed to be redemptive.[37]

The demonic pact was central to most confessions. This was usually understood as an agreement made between witch and Devil at a specific place and time. To make a confession to such a pact credible, many interrogators demanded additional details, especially concerning the witch's motive for entering the pact. Such details often came from folklore, as we saw in Chapter 5. Boguet recognised the importance of the witch's story, focusing on the moment 'when they are alone and in despair or misery because of hunger or some disaster' at which the Devil was able to seduce them.[38] The witch's 'despair' at this moment often had a gendered element; this will be discussed further in Chapter 9.

As well as the demonic pact, suspects often had to confess to committing malefice. Here, they often entered a kind of negotiation with their interrogators about how far their confessions would go. Ann Käserin, in Eichstätt, Germany, in 1629, initially denied everything, but broke down under torture and began to give the answers that her interrogators wanted. Even then, however, she carefully limited her guilt. She admitted that she had often prayed to the Devil, but insisted that she had never spat at nor blasphemed the Virgin Mary. She had killed a cow, but had never injured men. This limited confession allowed her to retain a small part of her previous identity as an innocent person. Many interrogators took advantage of a limited confession, stopping when they had enough material for a conviction. Eichstätt, however, was in the grip of a witchcraft panic, and the interrogators pressed on. At a later session, with more torture, Käserin was made to confess to killing several people including her own daughter. Asked about damage to crops, she admitted to having made mists, hail and snails – but, still trying to salvage her own self-respect, she denied having made rain.[39] Desle la Mansenée, mentioned earlier, limited her guilt in a different way: she had carried out malefice with demonic powder, but last Easter she had attended church and had burned her boxes of powder and the stick on which she had flown.[40]

The witches' sabbat was another vital part of demonology, and suspects were often expected to confess to some kind of collective gathering. Most gave a predominantly festive and cheerful account of the sabbat: there was feasting, with good food and drink, and dancing. The interrogators in Eichstätt, guided by a standardised questionnaire, searched constantly for demonic details; the suspects were willing to acknowledge that the Devil had been present, but did not produce more than a perfunctory account of any horrifying or demonic rituals.[41] Elsewhere in south Germany, interrogators were more successful in obtaining confessions to cannibalism – perhaps the rigid questionnaire format was not the most effective – but the sabbat, as a whole, remained festive and cheerful.[42] More research is needed as to which aspects of confessions arose through different interrogation practices, and which represent regional variations in popular culture.

Some suspects told stories of fairies or other folkloric beings – and these stories are unlikely to have been imposed by the interrogators. As we saw in Chapter 5, they arose from popular culture, told by people who knew more about fairies or ghosts than they did about demons. Interrogators did not usually believe in fairies, but they did believe in demons, so they assumed that they understood the nature of these beings better than the suspects themselves. Some of this folkloric material may have originated in suspects' dreams. Orthodox theologians thought that dreams could not give reliable information, so, if such confessions were believed, the dreams were likely to be recorded as waking visions. And some people may indeed have experienced waking visions. Psychologists regard certain people as 'fantasy-prone': such people imagine various events and conditions in such a way that they seem vividly real, and find it difficult to distinguish between fantasy and reality. While fantasy-proneness is part of the general human condition, the actual content of people's fantasies is culture-specific.[43]

Explaining confessions

It is reasonable to assume that most witchcraft suspects knew, before the interrogation began, that they had not carried out the acts of which they were accused. They knew that they had not made a pact with the Devil, neither had they attended a witches' sabbat nor cast spells to harm anyone by magic. Many suspects had probably done nothing at all along those lines. Others had engaged in some kind of magical activity that could be reinterpreted as witchcraft, but they too knew at the start that they were not witches. If they were innocent, how did they come to confess? To say that they did so under torture is a large part of the answer, but we need to probe this further – beginning with the psychological theory of 'false confession'.

Psychologists studying false confessions tend to divide them into three types: voluntary, pressured-compliant, and pressured-internalised.[44] Voluntary false confessions are usually prompted either by psychological disturbance or by a desire to shield someone else; both of these can be found in witchcraft cases, but were probably rare. The 'pressure' associated with most false confessions usually came from judicial torture or other ill-treatment. The difference between 'compliant' and 'internalised' confessions, though, is important. Suspects who make pressured-compliant confessions are largely agreeing with suggestions put to them by the interrogator; they never entirely believe their own confessions, and tend to retract them later. By contrast, suspects who make pressured-internalised confessions really come to believe that they are guilty. These three types of confession need to be examined in more detail.

To take voluntary false confession first: such confessions today are sometimes given to shield someone else. Helen Guthrie, in Forfar, Scotland, in 1661, made several elaborate confessions, naming many other witches and claiming to be able to recognise witches by their faces. One name that Guthrie never mentioned, though, was that of her daughter, Isobel Hewat; she seems to have been pointing the finger in all directions in a desperate attempt to direct attention away from her daughter. Alas, Hewat was also arrested, and confessed that she and her mother were both witches.[45]

Even Guthrie's confession was probably not entirely voluntary, though she steered it in a direction of her own choosing. Really voluntary confessions, where people turned themselves in to the authorities, were unlikely to lead to prosecution. A woman in Stockholm, Sweden, confessed voluntarily in 1596 that she was 'of the bad sort riding to Blåkulla' (the legendary Swedish witch mountain) and that she had 'had intercourse with the Devil'. The court did not believe her; she was 'admonished to tell the truth and to refrain from lies and deceptions'.[46] They may well have thought that she had mental health problems, and people with such problems did not make credible witches. Witches were thought to be bad, not mad: criminal, not insane.

Most confessions probably fell into the second, 'pressured-compliant', category. The straightforward reason for these is the intuitively obvious one: the pain of torture was unendurable, and suspects felt themselves obliged to invent material in order to stop the pain. Johannes Junius, in Bamberg, Germany, in 1627, vividly described this in a letter he smuggled out of prison to his daughter:

> And then came also – God in highest Heaven have mercy – the executioner, and put the thumb-screws on me, both hands bound together,

so that the blood ran out at the nails and everywhere, so that for four weeks I could not use my hands, as you can see from the writing ... Thereafter they first stripped me, bound my hands behind me, and drew me up in the torture. Then I thought heaven and earth were at an end; eight times did they draw me up and let me fall, so that I suffered terrible agony.[47]

Well aware of torture's power to coerce, Pierre Chavaz from Vuiteboeuf, Switzerland, in 1448 offered sarcastically to confess when threatened with it: 'I will say whatever you want. I will say that I ate children, and that I did all the harm that you wish.' He evidently knew what his interrogators would want to hear – eating babies was a common detail in early Swiss confessions.[48] The repeated interrogations common in panics are indicators of false confession. Study of modern criminal confessions shows that most genuine confessions are given in the first few minutes of interrogation. Suspected witches, by contrast, often maintained their innocence for some time before confessing.

Sometimes, in a confession record, we can see how the suspect was forced to invent material – and we can even see where it came from. Laura de Adamo, in Francavilla Fontana, Italy, in 1678, confessed that the demons she had seen at the sabbat 'resembled the figures of demons painted in the picture and church of St Anthony Abbot in this town'.[49] Evidently de Adamo knew little of demons, and thus relied on the only images she knew: the local church paintings. Many other details came from the everyday world. Lorenz Perauer, in Carinthia, Austria, in 1653, was a poor farm servant; it was credible, both to himself and to his interrogators, for him to confess that he had been given only a little to drink at the sabbat, while others had received large amounts of wine.[50] Cosme, a freed mulatto slave in the Canary Islands in 1573, confessed under torture that he had flown to the 'sandpits of hell'; he later said that these had been the sand dunes at the edge of the town.[51]

Another reason why people make pressured-compliant confessions today is to escape from the stress of interrogation. Being in custody is stressful in itself, and being questioned about crime adds to the pressure. Interrogators routinely remind suspects that the easiest way to end the stress and unpleasantness is to confess. Some suspects naively assume that, because they are innocent, a confession can do them no harm. This assumption may be particularly common for people on the autistic spectrum, who have difficulty in distinguishing between their own perceptions and those of others; they may think that, because they themselves know they are innocent, the interrogator knows that too. This would be unlikely to show up in witchcraft trial records, but we can recognise that it probably happened.

The third type of false confession, the 'pressured-internalised', was that in which suspects came actually to believe in their guilt. Such confessions, which include some of the most remarkable and the most tragic, occurred through the creation of false memories. Psychologists distinguish between 'episodic memory', which records the experience of specific events, and 'semantic memory', which records broader general knowledge. Our 'memories', as we call them, are formed by combining these two types. 'Episodic' memories of specific events can unwittingly become distorted to fit with preconceived ideas from the semantic memory, so that people 'remember' what they expected to experience, or what their general knowledge tells them it would have made sense for them to experience, rather than what they actually experienced. This confusion can occur when the person's memory of the event is first encoded by the brain, or it can arise later in the course of questioning.[52] It is particularly likely for memory to become distorted in retrospect, with 'false memories' being unwittingly implanted by questioners. Numerous psychological experiments have demonstrated how false memories can be created through leading questions. In one experiment, young adults who had visited Disneyland as children were led to 'remember' having encountered Bugs Bunny there, although Bugs is not a Disney character.[53]

Thus, under the pressure of hostile interrogation, some suspects lost confidence in their memories and created false memories instead. The interrogators were confident and powerful; perhaps they were right? Susanna Dietherich, from Neuerburg, Germany, in 1627, initially denied everything, but began to confess under torture – and to seek advice from her interrogators. Having confessed to attending one sabbat, she asked whether it could have been possible for her to have attended another one without knowing it.[54] An even more poignant example is María de Yriarte, from the Spanish Basque country. She was arrested in February 1609, was interrogated repeatedly, and by April or May broke down and confessed. She claimed to have murdered five children, and begged the inquisitors not to tell anyone, for, if this became known, she would be damned. She was obviously confused by this stage. Later she offered another confession in which the number of child murders went up to nine. She said that her mother and sister (who were also in custody) had taken no part in the murders – but she added that, if they themselves had confessed to taking part, she was willing to confirm that they had done so. She was evidently trying to co-operate, and even to anticipate the things her interrogators might want her to say.[55]

Some suspects eventually came to see the interrogators as protective figures who would look after them, and became eager to co-operate with them. Confession can be therapeutic. Part of the purpose of gaining a confession from a witch was to induce the witch to 'repent'. This functioned as a distant echo of Catholic penitential practice, in which all parishioners were supposed to confess their sins to the parish priest, to repent, and to receive forgiveness. A confessing witch would not be forgiven by the court – on the contrary, confession would usually lead to execution. But the interrogator could encourage the witch to think that God would be merciful to them, and that confession and repentance could enable them to go to heaven. Some confessing witches thanked their torturers.

Pious suspects might remember the story of Jesus's sufferings before his execution, and conclude that their own sufferings must have been sent by God to punish them for their sins. Not for their witchcraft – such suspects tended to insist on their innocence. Instead they confessed to various minor sins which, they felt, had led to their punishment. This echoed the expected structure of criminals' scaffold testimony; criminals, as we shall see, were supposed to die penitently and to express repentance for their sins.

Finally, some suspects, even if they had been forced to confess under torture, retracted their confessions and consistently insisted that they had been forced to make them. Sometimes they went to their deaths protesting their innocence. Magdalena Weixler, in Ellwangen, Germany, in 1614, wrote to her husband from prison:

> I know that my innocence will come to light, even if I do not live to see it. I would not be concerned that I must die, if it were not for my poor children; but if it must be so, may God give me the grace that I may endure it with patience.[56]

If Maria Holl deserves to be remembered because she survived, perhaps Magdalena Weixler deserves to be remembered because, like thousands of other tortured witches, she did not.

Credibility of confessions

Why were witches' confessions believed, even when they had been extracted under torture? People knew then, just as well as they do today, that torture could cause suspects to confess falsely. However, they also believed that torture could reveal the truth. Jeannette Anyo, in Lausanne, Switzerland, in 1461, was ordered that 'you must be submitted to the corporal question and tortured until the truth bursts forth from your mouth'.[57] How did the interrogators know whether a confession was 'the truth'? Let us recall that a credible confession required the suspect to reveal information that only a guilty person would know. How could the court verify this? In a theft case, it might be possible to check where the stolen goods were hidden, but the crime of witchcraft was not usually expected to generate tangible evidence. Spells were usually performed in private, rarely using physical equipment. Meetings with the Devil left no tangible evidence behind. How could an interrogator, not knowing whether the suspect was guilty or not, question the suspect in such a way that he would be able to distinguish between the answers of a guilty person and the answers of an innocent one?

Interrogators addressed this challenge by focusing on the fact that a guilty witch had a particular past; they would have a story to tell about what they had done. Interrogations thus sought to elicit credible *stories* about witchcraft from suspects. In particular, suspects were questioned about their relationship with the Devil. A story about this had to be constructed that was credible both to the accused witch and to the interrogators. The idea was that an innocent person, who had had no dealings with the Devil, would be unable to tell a story about such dealings.

Unfortunately, a good deal of information about the Devil was available in the public domain, so that anyone who knew about the Devil might be able to construct a credible, though false, confession. The major demonologists never confronted this problem outright; those who discussed interrogation and confession in detail always assumed that interrogators were dealing with guilty witches. Legally-trained demonologists generally argued more like prosecuting lawyers than like impartial judges.[58] Presumably they recognised that they had to work with the confessions they had, or else abandon the whole project of prosecuting witches. They usually assumed that God would not permit an innocent person to confess. Martin Delrio argued that God had more power over judges than the Devil had over witches.[59] Adam Tanner, criticising the excesses of torture in 1617, felt it necessary to argue against the idea that God would always protect the innocent: had God not permitted the martyrdom of early Christians?[60] Spee criticised Binsfeld and Delrio for arguing that God would protect the innocent.[61]

Some courts seem to have felt that they were upholding judicial standards by seeking especially detailed confessions – far more than the minimum necessary for conviction. An innocent person might know some details about the Devil, but surely only a guilty person would be able to produce a confession running to thousands of words? During the period of intense witch-hunting, demonologists often pointed to the growing piles of confessions, containing consistently similar details, as evidence that the confessions simply must be true. Obtaining such confessions also justified further torture: if torture produced results in the form of credible confessions, it must be working. Alas, it seems that a combination of folklore and leading questions could readily produce such confessions.

One theological complication was that the Devil might intervene in the interrogation process – either strengthening his witches so that they did not confess, or planting false evidence that would cause innocent people to be accused. Demonologists usually avoided the idea of false evidence, perhaps fearing that it would undermine the prosecution of witches; deliberate searches for false evidence would have been likely to operate in favour of the accused. By contrast, several demonologists argued that the Devil would intervene to prevent witches confessing; sometimes this point was used to justify harsher tortures. In principle, both of these demonic interventions might have been equally likely (or equally unlikely, given the theory of divine permission that underpinned the whole theology of the Devil); it is thus noteworthy that demonologists spent longer discussing the idea that encouraged more torture and more prosecutions.

Sometimes, interrogators did check a suspect's story. In Württemberg, Germany, in 1683, a thirteen-year-old girl, Anna Catharina Weissenbühler, confessed voluntarily to visiting witches' sabbats and performing various other acts. One of her claims was that she had taken wine from a barrel in the cellar of the mayor of Gerlingen. Officials consulted the mayor and found that he had had no barrels of wine in his cellar. The case was dropped.[62] However, other checks were less rigorous. An early case that helped to shape later demonology was the prosecution of a man called Scaedeli by the judge Peter of Bern in the western Alps in the 1390s. Accused of causing sterility in a peasant family, Scaedeli confessed under torture to burying a lizard under their doorstep. The judge had the doorstep dug up, but nothing was found – whereupon he concluded that the lizard must have rotted away. To us it may seem more likely that Scaedeli had been forced to invent the story.[63] Similarly, Ann Käserin, mentioned earlier, confessed to flying on a forked stick, which flew when a flying-ointment given her by the Devil was applied. The stick, she said, was in her kitchen, and there were three pots of ointment hidden in her house. A search was made by a physician, who found two pots, one empty, and the other containing a hard, black substance. No stick was found. This seems dubious, but it was enough for a conviction.[64]

Another kind of check could be made, not with the physical evidence, but with the theoretical correctness of the evidence. Caterina Patrimia, in Oria, Italy, in 1704, confessed to having made a demonic pact that would cease at the end of ten years. An inquisitor declared that this was theologically impossible – the pact had to be permanent – and the case was dropped.[65] Related to this, the internal consistency of the confession could be scrutinised. Ana Perdomo, a black slave in the Canary Islands, confessed in 1580 that she had sucked a girl's blood, but did not know whether it was from the arms or the legs. Her confession was dismissed as due to 'fear and ignorance'.[66] These suspects seem to have been fortunate in their interrogators.

Much of the material in confessions came from leading questions, in which the interrogators themselves fed the suspects the details that they wanted. It is easy with hindsight to see that leading questions could distort confessions, but inexperienced interrogators at the time probably did not realise how far they were doing this. Leading questions have been found to be common even in modern police interrogations – more common than written interrogation records suggest, and more common than the interrogators themselves believe. Claude Bochet, in Lausanne in 1479, confessed that the Devil had twice given him five sous, 'but he did not know what had become of that money'.[67] Evidently the interrogators were searching for the answer that the money had turned to leaves or dung, though in this case they dropped the matter when Bochet failed to take the hint. In the seventeenth century, several jurisdictions circulated lists of standard questions. Even when we do not have a record of the questions, we can sometimes see from the stereotyped answers that standard questions must have been used. In the Basque region of Spain, several witches confessed that they were accompanied to the sabbat by 'dressed toads', toads with human faces and clothes.[68] This may have originated as a folk belief, but seems to have been adopted and systematised by the interrogators.

Some records of questioning also show that the interrogators presupposed guilt. Consider this, from the interrogation of Sarah Good, in Salem, in 1692. She was accused of bewitching ('tormenting') several children, who were brought before her. Some of the discussion between her and the two interrogators, John Hathorne and Jonathan Curran, went as follows:

> Q. Sarah Good, do you not see now what you have done? Why do you not tell us the truth? Why do you thus torment these poor children?
> A. I do not torment them.
> Q. Who do you employ then?
> A. I employ nobody. I scorn it.
> Q. How came they thus tormented?
> A. What do I know? You bring others here and now you charge me with it.

Sarah Good was a difficult person to interrogate. At the end of the record, the interrogators noted: 'Her answers were in a very wicked, spiteful manner, reflecting and retorting against the authority with base and abusive words, and many lies she was taken in.'[69] Certainly she did not give the interrogators the answers they were hoping for. Despite this, Hathorne and Curran's questions show that they had difficulty imagining the possibility that she might be innocent. We shall return to this question when we examine how far the witch-hunt was a miscarriage of justice.

Costs and profits

Witchcraft prosecutions could be expensive. Costs included the fees of the court officials and gaolers. Elite judges usually had salaries, paid separately, but there might be a specialist torturer or pricker. If legal advice was sought, that would be particularly costly. When it came to executions, burning witches on a specially-built pyre (on which more in a moment) was an expensive method of killing. Those who profited, such as the torturers and lawyers, were not usually in charge of prosecutions, so they could not encourage prosecutions directly for financial gain. Those who had encouraged the prosecutions were usually left to pay the bills. In Quiévy, Spanish Netherlands, in 1664–65, eight witchcraft trials cost 1,702 florins. The village community had to pay half of this, equivalent to the price of 65 cattle, and the central government paid the rest.[70]

Were the courts after the witches' property? In most cases they were not. Most witches had little or no property, and the costs of holding their trials were likely to be more than their property was worth. The authorities generally spent time and money on prosecuting witches, because they thought that it was important to do so. This needs to be stressed, because there is a popular myth today (discussed further in Chapter 11) that witch-hunting was deliberately carried out for profit.

Several jurisdictions confiscated at least some of the property of at least some of the witches they executed. In the Holy Roman Empire, the *Carolina* code was unclear on this point, but several states interpreted it to mean that confiscations were allowed. Most confiscations were partial, with officials apportioning money among surviving relatives and taking a share typically equivalent to that of one of the surviving children. And confiscations usually applied only to movable property rather than inherited lands. Some of the confiscated property was used to pay for the trial, but, if the witch had property, there was often a profit.[71]

However, the idea that there was any general property motive for witch-hunting surely vanishes when we recognise that most witch-hunting states never confiscated any witches' property. There is no suggestion that the pattern of witch-hunting was any different in the states that did. Even when property was confiscated, it usually went to the ruler or his local agents; neither those who made the initial accusation, nor those who conducted the trial, were likely to benefit. Rulers sometimes allocated profits to 'pious uses' like schools and hospitals. Finally, even when the property benefit was clear, it was not necessarily an important motive. In Eichstätt in 1627, after ten years of intense prosecutions, the citizens of the town complained to the prince-bishop, Johann Christoph von Westerstetten, about confiscations of property of rich witches. Westerstetten had personally encouraged the trials, and he gained considerable financial benefit from them. However, there is no doubt that his motive for the prosecutions was overwhelmingly religious – he was a militant promoter of the Counter-Reformation.[72]

Executions

Convicted witches were usually executed by burning. Typically the witch was tied to an upright stake on top of a pyre, which was then set alight. Many witches were burned alive, though in some places it was usual to strangle the witch to death before lighting the pyre; this was considered more merciful. Instead of a stake, a few authorities tied the witch to the top of a ladder-like structure at the side of the pyre; ropes were then used to lower this into the flames once the pyre was lit (see Illustration 1.2). Others put the witch into a small wooden hut on top of the pyre, in which they might be fortunate enough to suffocate from smoke before the flames reached them. During panics, one pyre could be used for several witches.

The pyre was meant to reduce the body completely to ashes, a process that might take four or five hours. It thus had to be large. Contemporary illustrations, seeking to foreground the witch, usually depict improbably small pyres; modern experiments (using dead animals, not live humans) have used a pyre about the height of a person. Six cartloads of wood were required to burn Sybille Goura in Vevey, Switzerland, in 1441.[73] The pyre had to be built mainly of heavy, slow-burning fuels: large logs if these were available, or, in some places, peat or coal. Light fuels like brushwood were also needed to get the fire going. The stake itself, set into the ground and with the pyre constructed round it, had to be a sizeable piece of timber, the cost of which was sometimes itemised separately in the accounts. In Goura's case, an iron chain was also purchased to tie her to the stake; this was no doubt more effective than a rope which would be likely to burn. The pyre required careful construction, otherwise it might collapse during the burning process; some illustrations show a framework round the pyre. The right weather conditions had to be chosen, as rain or wind could extinguish it. On a windy day it was best not to stand downwind of the pyre, as the wind could carry smoke and even molten fat.

By burning the witch's body, the authorities were denying them anything resembling a Christian burial. Ordinary criminals might be buried in unconsecrated ground, which was bad enough, but witches were not buried at all. Most people hoped that, after their own burial, they would eventually be bodily resurrected in heaven; denial of burial was deeply upsetting. From a theological point of view, denial of burial did not prevent the witch from getting to heaven (and the damned, too, were to be bodily resurrected in hell), but it did symbolise the unlikelihood of their doing so. The destruction of the witch's body removed them from normal community processes, even after death.

Some witches, whose crimes were considered especially shocking, were publicly subjected to additional torments before they were burned. Jean Grelant, one of a group of witches in Chamonix, Switzerland, in 1462, had confessed to trampling the consecrated host (the body of Christ) under his foot; he was stripped naked, had his foot cut off, and was made to kiss the ground three times.[74] Walpurga Hausmännin, a midwife convicted of witchcraft in Dillingen, Germany, in 1587, had confessed to killing several babies. She was carried round the town in a cart, which paused at five different places where parts of her body were torn by red-hot tongs; then her right hand was cut off; finally she was burned alive.[75]

In a few places, witches were hanged like ordinary criminals – notably England and its colonies, and Aragon and Catalonia. Other execution methods, such as beheading or drowning, were used in some places. Local variation in small jurisdictions is illustrated in the Channel Islands. In Jersey, witches were first hanged and then their dead bodies burned; in Guernsey, they were burned at the stake, alive in at least some cases.[76] Overall, burning was by far the most common execution method, and universally recognised – even in England, where Joan Flower in 1619 told a neighbour that her familiars had promised her that she should not be hanged or burned.[77]

Authorities often encouraged condemned witches to 'repent' before their execution. In the Holy Roman Empire, the *Carolina* code required convicted criminals to be given three days' grace before execution, to reflect on their crimes and their spiritual state. In the case of witches, their 'repentance' might be held to cancel the demonic pact. They were still executed for their crime, but they could now hope for salvation. Witches who 'repented' – that is, confessed sincerely and expressed sorrow – could also act as star witnesses in chain-reaction hunts, as we shall see in Chapter 8.

Executions were almost always in public, and normally attracted crowds. Crowds of thousands, and even tens of thousands, are occasionally mentioned. Executions were tense and exciting theatrical moments. Would the condemned person make a good death? Would they admit their crimes and express repentance? Would they forgive the executioner? Would the executioner succeed in killing the person in the expected way, without bungling or nerves or mess? Executions for witchcraft could also be educational events, with the witch's confession being read out to the crowd. This was an important way for people to learn what witches did.

Ordinary folk in early modern Europe were usually deferential to their rulers – though never uncritically subservient – and were rarely sympathetic to criminals being executed. Two categories of criminals who might expect the crowd's sympathy were young women executed for infanticide, and political rebels executed for challenging unpopular regimes. Witches being executed did not receive so much sympathy. Outside the major panics, most people seem to have had no doubts that the witches being executed were guilty – and witchcraft was a shockingly anti-social crime. Witches being burned might suffer terribly, but they deserved it.

The pain and suffering involved in executions could constitute a therapeutic process for the spectators. People knew that, if they were good Christians, they should repent of their sins. 'Penance' could involve suffering, but could lead to redemption – a feeling of being cleansed of one's sins and of repairing one's relationship with the community and God. Criminals, who had sinned badly, could also repent movingly at the point of their execution. By displaying remorse and repentance, and by accepting the pain and suffering of execution, they could be seen to die as noble martyrs. Preachers stressed the cleansing effects of suffering, comparing it to Jesus's suffering on the cross. Executions were stage-managed to display reconciliation and to present the suffering as purposeful; for instance, the executioner and the criminal were supposed to forgive each other. Through pain, the criminal's sins were cleansed away and the community was purified.[78] This applied in principle to all executions for crime, but burnings of witches provided particularly satisfying spectacles from this point of view.

Crowds might occasionally be hostile to the authorities if injustice was suspected. Spee wrote that many witches who had been tortured were 'so ripped and torn that when they were to be executed the executioner did not dare to bare their shoulders, as is customary, lest the populace become enraged at such a cruel sight'.[79] Pierre de Lancre and his fellow commissioners had difficulty executing a group of witches in the Labourd region of France in 1609: 'there was such unrest and such a great crowd that the order and safety needed for the executions could not be assured'. Angry people threatened the condemned witches on their way to the stake, trying to get them to withdraw accusations that they had made against others. 'The executioner, the trumpeter, the sergeant, the interpreters [needed in this Basque-speaking area], and the clerks of the court were so afraid that we could barely make them proceed with the execution of anyone else, except by force.'[80] People's hostility may have stemmed from the fear that they themselves would be accused next, but this in itself illustrates their lack of trust in Lancre's commissioners. Witch-hunting was a dramatic and sometimes frightening process.

Conclusion: A miscarriage of justice?

How far was the witch-hunt a miscarriage of justice? This is a crucial question, but not an easy one to answer. We may think that early modern courts did not meet today's standards of justice, but that is irrelevant; witchcraft is not a crime today, and early modern courts cannot be blamed for not meeting standards from another era. For historians to say 'This was a miscarriage of justice', we would want to show that *by the courts' own standards*, it would have been 'just' for them to have acquitted the accused witches instead of convicting them. Quite a few witch trials were indeed criticised at the time as being unjust, especially in the later stages of witch-hunting – but how do we know whether the critics were more 'correct' in absolute terms than the judges? We may well ponder whether it is possible to make an absolutely, objectively correct assessment of a controversial decision even by a modern court.

One argument for saying that the courts were wrong to convict witches *by their own standards* would be to point out that many trials did not follow the formal rules on torture. This is not a decisive argument, since not all societies follow their own formal rules, but it is suggestive. The contemporary critics of excessive torture are clear witnesses to the judicial standards that they, at least, preferred. Ultimately we may be able to say about a witch trial only that some people supported the conviction and that others opposed it. We may be able to reach some assessment of which side had more public credibility at the time, but that is not the same as being able to say for certain which side was 'right'. A miscarriage of justice, then? Yes, to the extent that some people thought so. And, if others did not, we should do our best to understand why they did not.

Even without labelling the prosecutions a 'miscarriage of justice' in contemporary terms, we as historians can say that the prosecutors created their witches in the process of interrogation. Most of these prosecutors probably did not realise just how far they were distorting the evidence through torture, or contaminating the evidence by asking leading questions. However, it is likely that some of them did realise the problem, yet persisted in their abusive behaviour. As far as we can tell, this was not usually because they were trying deceitfully to secure the conviction of someone they knew privately to be innocent. If prosecutors deliberately distorted the evidence, they usually believed that the suspect was guilty, but were worried that the existing evidence would be insufficient – so they manufactured some more. When this happens in modern police forces it is sometimes called 'noble cause perjury'; police officers behave dishonestly in order to secure a conviction that they believe is for the public good. In a time of panic about witchcraft, it is easy to see how this could get out of hand and lead to the condemnation of many innocent people. The next chapter will look in more detail at witchcraft panics, and how panics fit into a broader picture of the dynamics of witch-hunting.

Notes

1 Quoted in John H. Langbein, *Prosecuting Crime in the Renaissance: England, Germany, France* (Cambridge, Mass., 1974), 279. Copyright © 1974 by the President and Fellows of Harvard College.
2 Trevor Dean, *Crime in Medieval Europe, 1200-1550* (Harlow, 2001), 17.
3 Richard van Dülmen, *Theatre of Horror: Crime and Punishment in Early Modern Germany*, trans. Elisabeth Neu (Cambridge, 1990), 82–5, 139–45.
4 Marie-Sylvie Dupont-Bouchat, Willem Frijhoff and Robert Muchembled, *Prophètes et sorciers dans les Pays-bas, XVIe–XVIIIe siècle* (Paris, 1978), 102–3.
5 Maria R. Boes, *Crime and Punishment in Early Modern Germany: Courts and Adjudicatory Practices in Frankfurt am Main, 1562–1696* (Farnham, 2013), 49.
6 Quoted in C. L'Estrange Ewen, *Witchcraft and Demonianism* (London, 1933), 125.
7 Johannes Dillinger, *Evil People: A Comparative Study of Witch Hunts in Swabian Austria and the Electorate of Trier*, trans. Laura Stokes (Charlottesville, Va., 2009), 169.
8 Béatrice Delaurenti, 'Femmes enchanteresses: figures féminines dans le discours savant sur les pratiques incantatoires au Moyen Âge', in Anna Caiozzo and Nathalie Ernoult (eds.), *Femmes médiatrices et ambivalentes: Mythes et imaginaires* (Paris, 2012), 215–26, at p. 219.
9 Quoted in Virginia Bernhard, 'Religion, politics, and witchcraft in Bermuda, 1651–55', *William and Mary Quarterly*, 67 (2010), 677–708, at pp. 693, 699.
10 Michael Ostling, *Between the Devil and the Host: Imagining Witchcraft in Early Modern Poland* (Oxford, 2011), 69.
11 Liv Helene Willumsen, *Witchcraft Trials in Finnmark, Northern Norway*, trans. Katjana Edwardsen (Bergen, 2010), 15–16.
12 Quoted in Robert Muchembled, *Sorcières, justice et société aux 16e et 17e siècles* (Paris, 1987), 137.
13 Gilbert Geis and Ivan Bunn, *A Trial of Witches: A Seventeenth-Century Witchcraft Prosecution* (London, 1997), 224–5.
14 Bernard Rosenthal, *Salem Story: Reading the Witch Trials of 1692* (Cambridge, 1993), 93–4.

15 Jean Bodin, *On the Demon-mania of Witches*, trans. Randy A. Scott, ed. Jonathan L. Pearl (Toronto, 1995), 218 (IV.5).
16 Francis Bavoux, *Hantises et diableries dans la terre abbatiale de Luxeuil: D'un procès de l'Inquisition (1529) à l'épidémie démoniaque de 1628–1630* (Monaco, 1956), 36–7.
17 *Malleus*, 212A (III.15).
18 Gunnar W. Knutsen, *Servants of Satan and Masters of Demons: The Spanish Inquisition's Trials for Superstition, Valencia and Barcelona, 1478–1700* (Turnhout, 2009), 109.
19 Martín Del Rio, *Investigations into Magic*, trans. P. G. Maxwell-Stuart (Manchester, 2000), 215–16.
20 Alison Rowlands, *Witchcraft Narratives in Germany: Rothenburg, 1561–1652* (Manchester, 2003), 30–3.
21 Alan C. Kors and Edward Peters (eds.), *Witchcraft in Europe, 400–1700: A Documentary History* (2nd edn., Pennsylvania, Pa., 2000), 359–67.
22 Lea, *Materials*, ii, 694.
23 Ruth Martin, *Witchcraft and the Inquisition in Venice, 1550–1650* (Oxford, 1989), 27–9.
24 Robert Calef, *More Wonders of the Invisible World* (London, 1700), 105.
25 Friedrich Spee von Langenfeld, *Cautio Criminalis, or a Book on Witch Trials*, trans. Marcus Hellyer (Charlottesville, Va., 2003; orig. 1631), 77.
26 Willumsen, *Witchcraft Trials in Finnmark*, 107–8.
27 Lyndal Roper, *Witch Craze: Terror and Fantasy in Baroque Germany* (New Haven, Conn., 2004), 75.
28 Robin Briggs, *The Witches of Lorraine* (Oxford, 2007), 72–3.
29 G. R. Balleine, 'Witch trials in Jersey', *Société jersiaise: bulletin annuel*, 13 (1939), 379–98, at p. 386.
30 Dupont-Bouchat et al., *Prophètes et sorciers dans les Pays-bas*, 106.
31 William Monter, 'Toads and eucharists: the male witches of Normandy, 1564–1660', *French Historical Studies*, 20 (1997), 563–95, at pp. 586–7.
32 Jonathan Seitz, '"The root is hidden and the material uncertain": the challenges of prosecuting witchcraft in early modern Venice', *Renaissance Quarterly*, 62 (2009), 102–33.
33 *Malleus*, 212D (III.15).
34 Quoted in Dupont-Bouchat et al., *Prophètes et sorciers dans les Pays-bas*, 110.
35 István Petrovics, 'Witch-hunt in Szeged in the early eighteenth century', in Blanka Szeghyová (ed.), *The Role of Magic in the Past: Learned and Popular Magic, Popular Beliefs and Diversity of Attitudes* (Bratislava, 2005), 108–16, at p. 114.
36 Dupont-Bouchat et al., *Prophètes et sorciers dans les Pays-bas*, 107.
37 Cf. Michel Foucault, *Wrong-Doing, Truth-Telling: The Function of Avowal in Justice*, eds. Fabienne Brion and Bernard E. Harcourt, trans. Stephen W. Sawyer (Chicago, Ill., 2014), 205–10 and *passim*.
38 Henri Boguet, *An Examen of Witches*, trans. E. A. Ashwin, ed. Montague Summers (London, 1929), 21.
39 Lea, *Materials*, iii, 1138–9.
40 Bavoux, *Hantises et diableries*, 40–1.
41 Jonathan B. Durrant, *Witchcraft, Gender and Society in Early Modern Germany* (Leiden, 2007), 70–3.
42 Roper, *Witch Craze*, 69–81, 104–23.
43 Gisli H. Gudjonsson, *The Psychology of Interrogations and Confessions: A Handbook* (Chichester, 2003), 227.
44 Gudjonsson, *Psychology of Interrogations and Confessions*, 211–12.
45 Joseph Anderson (ed.), 'The confessions of the Forfar witches (1661)', *Proceedings of the Society of Antiquaries of Scotland*, 22 (1887–88), 241–62.

46 Bengt Ankarloo, 'Sweden: the mass burnings (1668–76)', in Bengt Ankarloo and Gustav Henningsen (eds.), *Early Modern European Witchcraft: Centres and Peripheries* (Oxford, 1991), 285–318, at p. 289.
47 Kors and Peters (eds.), *Witchcraft in Europe*, 351.
48 Quoted in Martine Ostorero and Kathrin Utz Tremp (eds.), *Inquisition et sorcellerie en Suisse romande: Le registre Ac 29 des Archives cantonales vaudoises (1438–1528)* (Lausanne, 2007), 46–9.
49 Quoted in David Gentilcore, *From Bishop to Witch: The System of the Sacred in Early Modern Terra d'Otranto* (Manchester, 1992), 244.
50 Rolf Schulte, *Man as Witch: Male Witches in Central Europe*, trans. Linda Froome-Döring (Basingstoke, 2009), 227.
51 Francisco Fajardo Spinola, 'Des vols et assemblées des sorcières dans les documents de l'Inquisition canarienne', in Nicole Jacques-Chaquin and Maxime Préaud (eds.), *Le sabbat des sorciers en Europe (XVe–XVIIIe siècles)* (Grenoble, 1993), 299–315, at pp. 301–2.
52 Gillian Cohen, 'Human memory in the real world', in Anthony Heaton-Armstrong, Eric Shepherd and David Wolchover (eds.), *Analysing Witness Testimony: A Guide for Legal Practitioners and Other Professionals* (London, 1999), 3–18.
53 Kathryn A. Braun, Rhiannon Ellis and Elizabeth F. Loftus, 'Make my memory: how advertising can change our memories of the past', *Psychology & Marketing*, 19 (2002), 1–23; Elizabeth Loftus, 'Our changeable memories: legal and practical implications', *Nature Reviews Neuroscience*, 4 (2003), 231–4.
54 Lea, *Materials*, iii, 1199.
55 Gustav Henningsen, *The Witches' Advocate: Basque Witchcraft and the Spanish Inquisition, 1609–1614* (Reno, Nev., 1980), 63–4.
56 Quoted in H. C. Erik Midelfort, *Witch-Hunting in Southwestern Germany, 1562–1684* (Stanford, Calif., 1972), 190.
57 Quoted in Georg Modestin, *Le diable chez l'évêque: Chasse aux sorciers dans le diocèse de Lausanne (vers 1460)* (Lausanne, 1999), 271.
58 Ian Maclean, 'La doctrine de la preuve dans les procès intentés contre les sorciers en Lorraine et en Franche-Comté autour de 1600', in Jean-Paul Pittion (ed.), *Droit et justice dans l'Europe de la Renaissance* (Paris, 2009), 177–95.
59 Del Rio, *Investigations into Magic*, 214.
60 Lea, *Materials*, ii, 649.
61 Spee, *Cautio Criminalis*, 36–8.
62 David Sabean, *Power in the Blood: Popular Culture and Village Discourse in Early Modern Germany* (Cambridge, 1984), 105.
63 Martine Ostorero, Agostino Paravicini Bagliani and Kathrin Utz Tremp (eds.), *L'imaginaire du sabbat: Edition critique des textes les plus anciens (1430 c.–1440 c.)* (Lausanne, 1999), 152–3.
64 Lea, *Materials*, iii, 1138.
65 Gentilcore, *From Bishop to Witch*, 254.
66 Fajardo, 'Des vols et assemblées des sorcières dans les documents de l'Inquisition canarienne', 302–3.
67 Quoted in Eva Maier, *Trente ans avec le diable: Une nouvelle chasse aux sorciers sur la Riviera lémanique (1477–1484)* (Lausanne, 1996), 182–3.
68 Gustav Henningsen (ed.), *The Salazar Documents: Inquisitor Alonso de Salazar Frías and Others on the Basque Witch Persecution* (Leiden, 2004), 116–18, 152.
69 Paul Boyer and Stephen Nissenbaum (eds.), *Salem-Village Witchcraft: A Documentary Record of Local Conflict in Colonial New England* (2nd edn., Boston, Mass., 1993), 6–7.
70 Muchembled, *Sorcières, justice et société*, 147.
71 Midelfort, *Witch-Hunting in Southwestern Germany*, 164–78.

224 Witches in court

72 Durrant, *Witchcraft, Gender and Society*, 41.
73 Ostorero and Utz Tremp (eds.), *Inquisition et sorcellerie en Suisse romande*, 420.
74 Carine Dunand, *Des montagnards endiablés: Chasse aux sorciers dans la vallée de Chamonix (1458–1462)* (Lausanne, 2009), 150–3, 164–5.
75 E. William Monter (ed.), *European Witchcraft* (New York, 1969), 81.
76 Balleine, 'Witch trials in Jersey', 388.
77 Gregory Durston, *Witchcraft and Witch Trials: A History of English Witchcraft and its Legal Perspectives, 1542 to 1736* (Chichester, 2000), 425–7.
78 Mitchell B. Merback, *The Thief, the Cross and the Wheel: Pain and the Spectacle of Punishment in Medieval and Renaissance Europe* (London, 1999), ch. 4.
79 Spee, *Cautio Criminalis*, 76.
80 Pierre de Lancre, *On the Inconstancy of Witches: Pierre de Lancre's Tableau de l'inconstance des mauvais anges et demons (1612)*, ed. and trans. Harriet Stone and Gerhild Scholz Williams (Turnhout, 2006), 138 (II.iii.6).

8 The dynamics of witch-hunting

> In the twenty-eighth burning ... six persons: Mistress Knertzin, a butcher; Babel Schütz, a blind girl; Schwartz, a canon from the village of Hach; another canon executed at 5 o'clock in the morning and burnt with Mistress Bar; Ehling, vicar; Bernhard Mark, vicar at the cathedral was burnt alive.
>
> In the twenty-ninth burning, seven persons: A baker; the innkeeper (the keeper of the Klingen Inn); the reeve of Mergelsheim; the bakerwoman from the Ochsentor; the plump noblewoman; a clerical doctor by the name of Meyer from the village of Hach; and a nobleman called Junker Fleischmann. A canon from Hach was also secretly executed at about the same hour and burnt with Mistress Bar, Paulus Vecker. Since then there have been two burnings.
>
> Dated 16th Feb. 1629. But there have been many different burnings since.
>
> Chronicle of Würzburg, Germany, 2 February and 16 February 1629[1]

Introduction

Much of the discussion of witchcraft prosecution focuses on individual cases. Witches were all individuals, and they almost all received their own trials, even when many prosecutions were occurring together. But, as well as individual prosecutions, there were many panics in which witches were prosecuted in short bursts and in large numbers. We cannot understand the great European witch-hunt unless we understand these more intense episodes of prosecution – both in themselves, and in their relationship to individual trials.

In general, regions with mild witch-hunting tended to confine themselves to individual prosecutions, whereas countries with more intense witch-hunting had individual prosecutions but *also* had panics. The duchy of Lorraine, unusually, had intense witch-hunting that consisted almost entirely of individual cases in its French-speaking regions. The prince-bishopric of Eichstätt, another place that hunted witches intensely, was more typical of the places that did so: most of its witches were identified in chain-reaction hunts and had no prior reputation in the community. Large-scale witch-hunting generally involved panics.

A typical panic began when one witch, who might well have been identified by neighbours using the mechanisms discussed in Chapter 4, was interrogated by members of the elite who were preoccupied with conspiratorial, demonic witchcraft. This witch was induced to confess that she or he had attended a witches' sabbat with a number of others, whereupon these others were hauled in and made to confess under torture that they had also attended the sabbat. This pattern of demonic witchcraft was not closely tied in to popular belief.

Both in panics and in individual prosecutions, dealing with witches involved interactions and negotiations between the common folk and the elite – and indeed between various different popular and elite interests. Study of these interactions has led to debate as to responsibility for witch-hunting: was it 'from above' or 'from below'? This debate, as we shall see, has been rather more fruitful than the debate on different types of state (discussed in Chapter 6), but it is not a simple matter.

This chapter will begin with a model setting out the stages of decision-making through which a witchcraft prosecution had to pass in order to succeed. The model applies principally and initially to individual prosecutions, taking in decision-making within the community as well as within the courts. Some of the processes were different in panics, since the formation of a community reputation was no longer always needed. Later sections of the chapter will look in more detail at panics.

A political model of witchcraft prosecutions

The prosecution of witches was an exercise in power. As such, it needs to be analysed from a political perspective. It might be thought that witch-hunting was only 'political' when it involved political leaders like kings and princes, or political theorists like Jean Bodin. But village quarrels, negotiations and attempts at reconciliation were also exercises in power, and thus also political at a village level. All witchcraft prosecutions were political.

'Politics' is classically defined as a process of decision-making by negotiation and compromise among interest groups. If one interest group regularly takes everything for itself and gives the others nothing, that is not politics; however, this is very rare. Usually it is possible to identify an element of negotiation even in the most uncompromising decisions. A political model of witchcraft prosecutions needs to identify these negotiations, and to specify the interest groups that took part.

Executing someone, especially for a crime like witchcraft, might be seen as utterly final and uncompromising. However, this depends on how the decision was reached. An uncompromising solution to a problem may represent a decision that in itself is of a yes/no kind, where no middle way is available. The 'uncompromising' solution is still a political decision if the decision-makers take the interests of both sides into account, and if they adapt their decision-making to the circumstances of the individual case. It may also be possible to interpret a decision to execute a witch as a failure of previous attempts at compromise.

The dynamics of witch-hunting 227

The course of each individual witchcraft trial can be seen as a negotiated process, in which prosecution and defence manoeuvred for success over a number of stages. The following five-stage model shows how a witchcraft prosecution could begin, and how the process could be continued through to the execution of the witch. This model applies in the first instance to individual trials rather than panics, but it can also be used to shed light on how panics arose from individual trials. For completeness, the model takes the process through to a decision to execute the witch (at the fifth stage), but it will be seen that there were alternative decisions and exit points at every stage. At different stages, different interest groups might become involved, influencing decisions in favour of the prosecution or the defence. These decisions were truly matters of life and death.

At the first stage, people decided that an unsanctioned and deviant act had recently occurred, and that a witch was to blame for it. Witchcraft was a sensational and complicated crime, and much of what has been written about it – including much of the present book – has been about what witches were thought to be like and how they were identified by their neighbours. Here, however, we have to move on to the other four stages.

At the second stage, people decided that the witch should be prosecuted. Prosecuting a witch was a separate decision from identifying a witch; many people who had been identified as witches by their neighbours were never prosecuted. So far everything had happened within the community, but, at this stage, one or more representatives of the community had to request that the criminal court become involved.

At the third stage, someone responded to the community's request by deciding to hold a criminal trial. In most countries the judge would be formally responsible for this; in practice he might delegate the task to the clerk of the court, but would retain control of overall policy on such decision-making. We know less about this stage than about others, even though it was a crucial moment of transition when proceedings moved from the community into the realm of the authorities.

The two last stages were also the authorities' responsibility. At the fourth stage, the court declared a verdict deciding that the alleged witch was guilty – a decision made either by the judge or by the jury, depending on the type of court, as we saw in Chapter 7. Finally, at the fifth stage, the judge or the higher authorities passed sentence, deciding that the guilty witch should be punished with death. In some courts, this decision might be reached gradually, with a judge's initial decision being subject to central confirmation or even, occasionally, appeal.

These five stages represented hurdles that a prosecution had to overcome. If the prosecution fell at any stage, the witch would not be executed. Each of the stages, or hurdles, could be considered as a political negotiation. These negotiations were not simply about abstract justice or injustice; they were about satisfying the needs of concrete interest groups. These needs could well include a wish for justice to be done, but people's 'interests' were influenced by many factors: family honour, material benefit, a wish to please patrons or clients, or a wish to support godly reform, not to mention (for the accused witch personally) sheer survival.

At the first stage, the decision to call someone a witch was an exercise of ideological power within the community. If the alleged witch's friends were more influential, neighbours would tend to believe them rather than the accuser. Such cases sometimes emerged as slander prosecutions, but many more must simply have been dropped. The outcome of community discussion in these cases was that the accused person was not a witch after all.

If the case proceeded to the second stage, the decision to seek a prosecution against the alleged witch probably involved community leaders or power-brokers who could negotiate with the authorities. Then, at the third stage, the judge's decision whether to hold a criminal trial would be influenced partly by the strength of the community leaders' evidence, but also by how strongly the judge himself felt about the issue of witchcraft. This was a 'political' decision in a broader sense, since a keen witch-hunter would take into account the interests of the movement for godly reform.

At the fourth stage, the trial itself was open to influence from interest groups in the community. Neighbours' testimony about the alleged witch's reputation was formally about evidence of specific events, but it also functioned to enable the judge or jury to gauge the strength of community feeling in the case. Similarly, at the fifth stage, the sentencing decision was also open to influence from interest groups in the community. The convicted witch's friends and relations might lobby for a pardon, or a non-capital sentence, rather than execution.

So, if witch-hunting was an exercise in power, it was not simply a matter of 'powerful' people imposing their will on 'powerless' ones. The use of power had to be negotiated. Some people were certainly more powerful than others, but their power stemmed from an ability to carry others with them when they took action – an ability that could not be taken for granted. Even when they took apparently 'uncompromising' decisions, like executing a witch, they had to be seen to be open to compromise in principle.

Multiple trials could involve a further kind of compromise: finding some witches guilty and others innocent. Even in panics there were usually some acquittals. Convicting only nine out of ten accused witches might be seen as a compromise. The essence of this political model, though, is not so much the compromise nature of the outcome as the process of negotiation by which the outcome was reached.

We thus need to take into account the contribution made to these negotiations by each social and governmental level. As well as the ordinary folk, we need to understand the local elites, the national rulers and administrators, and the intelligentsia – the university teachers and clergymen who advised on witchcraft trials and shaped the ideas that occurred in them. Each of these groups had its own political interests deriving from its specific social position. But each group was also internally divided: villager against rival villager, rival political factions at local and national level, Protestant against Catholic, religious militant against pragmatist, and so on. No wonder it is hard to identify the socio-political 'causes' of witch-hunting when there were so many different ways in which these interest groups could co-operate or compete.

Witchcraft panics

Political negotiations over witchcraft prosecutions were particularly tense, and particularly complicated, during panics. The concept of a witchcraft 'panic' is vital for the understanding of witch-hunting, so it is surprising that so little trouble has been taken to define one. Perhaps people feel that they can recognise a panic when they see one. If so, this may help to show that 'panic' is a useful concept, but, for our purposes, a clear definition is needed.

Panics can be identified through a combination of statistics and historical narrative. Statistics may seem to be the most reliable indicators, but they have serious limitations. One influential work suggests that a 'panic' might be defined as 'ten deaths for witchcraft at one place in one year'.[2] However, this raises numerous problems. We cannot be sure that when people prosecuted eleven witches in one year (perhaps one per month), they did so in a mood of panic. Nor can we be sure that when they prosecuted nine (perhaps in a single episode), this was done in a spirit of calm deliberation. This is before we even begin to discuss what is meant by a 'place' – ten deaths per year in one street, or in one village, or in one province or country? And should the statistics take account of deaths in prison before trial, or acquittals? Statistics are useful in identifying sudden leaps in numbers of cases, and can show that such leaps accounted for a high proportion of all cases, but they are not simple. And statistics cannot explain what a panic actually *was*. As we shall see, a panic was not ultimately about numbers, but about a state of mind.

We can get nearer to understanding panics by historical narrative. Many studies of individual panics involve a narrative of how prosecutions suddenly rose and declined in a particular place. Such a study may show, not just that there were (say) eleven cases in one year, but that, when one woman was arrested, she made a demonic confession and named ten other people as having attended a witches' sabbat. Because they were panicking, the authorities believed this confession and arrested the other ten people – even though these people had no community reputation. A study that reveals this may also reveal who was in charge of the prosecutions, and may even give a sense of whether the prosecutions were motivated by unusual religious zeal or by political or social instability. The basic idea of a panic here is that it manifested itself in a number of linked cases forming a chain reaction. It is not just about whether there were nine cases or eleven, but about whether the nine, or the eleven, were linked together in a single, continuous story. Historical narrative can identify the chain and its links, and may well show that the authorities were taking a sudden, unusual interest in witch-hunting.

At the root of a panic, then, was a state of mind. People were angry, or fearful, or both, and came to feel that witchcraft was a more serious threat than usual. It might be a threat to the whole community (rather than to an individual household); it might be a threat to a member of the elite; or it might be a threat to fundamental religious or social values at a time when these values were particularly important or contested. Such a threat could not credibly be mounted by one witch, and so people imagined a group of witches behind it, or even a growing conspiracy. Intellectuals, who regarded the Devil as the real power behind the witch, had to bear in mind that the Devil's theoretical powers were the same whatever the number of witches. But intellectuals, as we saw in Chapter 3, were particularly prone to seeing witchcraft as a conspiracy, because they tended to think of it as an organised anti-religion. They could see an increase in numbers of witches as evidence of the Devil's growing influence. In Italy, Bartolomeo della Spina feared in 1523 that witches would soon outnumber faithful Christians.[3] No wonder such a conspiracy scared them – and angered them.

Fear and anger are linked by what psychologists call the 'fight or flight response', in which a perceived external threat triggers an interlocking series of reactions, the 'defence cascade'. The person focuses their attention on the threat and prepares either to run away, to freeze (delaying the reaction until more is known) or to attack in self-defence. Compared with other animals, humans are particularly prone to continue acting with increased arousal even after the threat is past.[4] Moreover, although many psychological studies of this concern immediate reactions (how do people react within seconds of seeing a snake or a gun?), it has also been shown that people with a history of exposure to violent crime or similar trauma react more strongly to perceived threats.[5] These moods of anger and fear were prominent in witchcraft panics.

It may seem unusual to emphasise people's emotions and thoughts in this way. As historians, we are not directly interested in people's thoughts; we are interested in the actions that they undertake as a result of their thoughts (if only because thoughts without actions leave no trace in the historical record). The fact that people were angry and fearful about witches is not as significant as the fact that they killed other people for being witches. But the anger and fear were surely real, and surely contributed to the killings. If we understand that, we may be able to understand the distinctive actions that people took when they began to feel that witchcraft was a particularly serious and immediate threat. The *ultimate* definition of a panic is that it occurred when people were 'panicking' – that is, that their state of mind was unusual. But the *immediate* definition of a panic is that people took unusual actions when they panicked. Historically, we can identify panics by the unusual actions of those who panicked.

Could it be argued that even the existence of a chain-reaction hunt might not prove the existence of a mood of panic? Hypothetically, one witch might readily have named ten accomplices, giving so much circumstantial detail that there seemed little alternative but to arrest the ten people named, even without the anger and fear that panics generated among prosecutors. However, there is little or no evidence that this ever actually happened. Interrogators often rejected or ignored unwelcome accusations when it suited them. They had no need to initiate a chain-reaction hunt unless they wanted to – unless they were panicking, in fact. The exception to this was when the courts were faced with *popular* demand for prosecutions – those west German cases in which, as we shall see, peasants experienced poor harvests and demanded punishment for the witches responsible. Some judges were keen to join in such prosecutions, but others seem to have complied out of fear that the alternative would be lynchings and the loss of the judges' own credibility and control of the situation. Although the judges may not have been panicking in these cases, the peasants certainly were. The theory of panic does not mean that *everyone* was panicking.

Panicking is irrational behaviour. It is important to note this, and also important to note that it does not in itself tell us anything about the crime of witchcraft as such. Today, many people assume that because witchcraft is 'not real', *any* prosecution of it must have been irrational. This is not particularly helpful in explaining witch-hunting, because early modern people had – by their standards – quite good reasons for thinking that witchcraft was real. But people can panic just as much about real crimes as about unreal ones. Today, for example, child abuse or terrorism are real, but actions to deal with them may be taken in a mood of panic. The authorities may accuse some people of child abuse or terrorism when the evidence, on rational reflection, would be considered to be insufficient. The equivalent question to ask about an episode of witch-hunting, therefore, is: was the evidence against these witches sufficient by contemporary standards? If it was not, and if the witches were nevertheless convicted, this is an indication that the convictions were obtained in a mood of panic. In this sense, then, *some* witches were prosecuted in a mood of panic, but not all. With hindsight we may regard *all* the evidence against witches as unconvincing, but we can recognise that at least some of it looked convincing at the time. When people panicked, they were more active in prosecuting witches, and were more readily convinced even by limited evidence.

How much direct evidence do we have for people's psychological states in early modern Europe? Most of what was written down was formal and businesslike. Occasionally we find direct evidence that people were going out of their way to hunt witches. During the Scottish witchcraft panic of 1597, it was reported that 'the king has his mind only bent on the examination and trial of sorcerers', and that 'hereat all estates are grieved and specially the church'.[6] Clearly, James VI was pursuing witches in an unusually active and perhaps obsessive way, and was not carrying everyone with him. Even this evidence does not tell us exactly what James's motives were, but it does show that he was more serious about witch-hunting than many others around him. In the terms used here, he was 'panicking'.

Evidence like this, about the witch-hunters' intentions, is rare. More often, all we have is the record of a sudden jump in the number of linked witchcraft trials. Here we have to be more cautious, but it is usually reasonable to infer that the jump was the result of a 'panic' – people taking extraordinary measures to deal with witchcraft. If we can see that they were doing something distinctive, then the best explanation we have is that they were panicking.

Models of panic

In studying witchcraft panics, we are studying collective behaviour. A classic sociological study by Neil Smelser defines a 'panic' as 'a collective flight based on a hysterical belief'.[7] Such a panic is not caused by problems of individual psychology – it occurs among groups of people who are, in a social-scientific sense, 'normal'. Smelser sees panic as occurring when there is an immediate threat, when people can communicate their fears to one another, and when the precise dimensions of the threat are unknown or unseen. The precipitating cause is the sight of a few people fleeing. Smelser's examples are mostly drawn from the battlefield or the stock exchange, but there is much in this for witchcraft historians to ponder.

Smelser also discusses what he calls the 'craze' – similar to a panic, but involving a rush towards something instead of away from it. Perhaps those who hunted witches were moving irrationally *towards* them, rather than fleeing them? Elements of this can be found in witchcraft panics, but on the whole it is better to see 'panic', and not 'craze', as the correct social-scientific concept. Those who hunted witches were not irrationally endorsing some positive idea: they were irrationally trying to save themselves, and their community, from a threat that they feared. The fact that their fear led them to react with anger and aggression, rather than flight, is not surprising; where would you go to escape from witches?

These ideas gain support from another classic of sociology: Stanley Cohen's study of 'moral panics'.[8] His panics are similar to Smelser's, but they involve, not a 'flight', but an organised attack on what is felt to be a new or unusually threatening form of 'deviant' behaviour. Cohen's fieldwork was done in communities responding to alleged threats from youth gangs, but the model he developed is readily applicable to communities responding to alleged threats from witches. Cohen's 'moral panic' begins with a dramatic event or series of related events that are perceived as challenging social norms. Public fear and anger at this is mobilised and orchestrated by one or more 'moral entrepreneurs' – self-appointed spokespeople who circulate news and demand action from the authorities. They discover evidence of further deviant behaviour, sometimes by re-labelling existing behaviour that had previously passed without comment, and claim that this new deviance represents a threat to society. The 'control culture' of police, courts and legislators is mobilised, a crackdown on the deviant behaviour is announced, the deviance ceases to be newsworthy, and the panic subsides.

The scale of panics

In defining a panic, one question is how to define *one* panic and to separate it from others. There are two types of distinction to draw here: distinctions of time, and of place. The problem of distinctions of time can be illustrated by asking: if the same place had two peaks of prosecution five years apart, is that two panics or one? The answer is: if historical narrative can establish continuity of action between the two peaks, then it can be considered as a single panic. Continuity might be established if the same authorities were involved and if some of the witches in the second wave of prosecution had earlier been named in the first wave. A related question can be asked about distinctions of place. If two villages five miles apart had panics at the same time, is that two panics or one? If it was the same authorities carrying out both prosecutions, or if suspects from one village named people in the other, it might well be considered as a single panic. A 'larger' panic in the sense of one that involved larger numbers could thus cover a larger area, or it could be one that was very intense in a small area.

The smallest possible panic was arguably the prosecution of two linked people. One typical pattern was the prosecution of an older woman followed by the prosecution of her daughter. The popular idea that witchcraft could be learned or inherited placed such daughters in peril, and they could be accused even if they had little or no reputation for independent malefice. Agnes Waterhouse, in Chelmsford, England, confessed in 1566 to having committed numerous malefices with the aid of a demonic familiar, a cat or toad called 'Satan'. Her daughter, Joan Waterhouse, was then arrested; she confessed merely to having scared someone with her mother's familiar (which she described as a dog). In the end only Agnes was executed.[9] It was a 'panic' when the prosecutors came to feel that there was more than one witch involved at one time; among other things, this could lead to mothers and daughters being prosecuted *together*. Usually it was the mothers who were named first. The fact that many daughters were prosecuted with little or no independent reputation underlines the fact that judicial standards were lower for them than for the first suspects to be identified – something that the panic model would predict.

Could individual witches, too, have been prosecuted in a mood of panic? Yes, possibly. Witchcraft was, after all, a very serious crime; even one case of witchcraft could have been considered shocking, and the basis of the definition of panic is not 'multiple cases' but 'the taking of unusual measures'. However, most individual trial records do not provide any evidence for or against the idea, making it difficult to do more than speculate about it. The mechanisms for identifying and prosecuting an individual witch did not require any heightened sense of the importance of witchcraft. Investigations sometimes seem to have been undertaken in a straightforward way, as for any other crime. Some individual cases even seem to display a reluctance to prosecute; neighbours were willing to let grievances fester for years before they would initiate judicial action. Individual prosecutions were unusual

234 *The dynamics of witch-hunting*

events, but they should be distinguished from panics, which were more unusual still.

At the other extreme from the very small panic, some panics grew without stopping until they reached colossal proportions. These included the panics in the German prince-bishoprics, discussed in Chapter 6, and the Swedish panic of the late seventeenth century, discussed later in this chapter. At the height of the panic in Bamberg, one of the prince-bishoprics, a special 'witch house' was built to facilitate the prosecutions, shown in Illustration 8.1. Major panics were terrifyingly intense; news of them spread all over Europe, and they continued to be discussed for many years afterwards.

Illustration 8.1 The Bamberg witch house, 1627

Witchcraft panics in Bamberg, Germany, became so intense that the prince-bishop, Johann Georg II Fuchs von Dornheim, had a special prison built for detaining, interrogating and torturing suspected witches. There was accommodation for about 30 suspects. Large panics were sometimes constrained by the limits of prison capacity.

© INTERFOTO / Sammlung Rauch / Mary Evans

What did people do when they panicked?

To say that people were 'panicking', then, is to say that they had come to believe that witchcraft should be taken exceptionally seriously, and that they were acting on that belief. When people panicked, they decided to take extraordinary measures. So what exactly did they do? They could take any, or all, of three related courses of action.

First, they could simply move witch-hunting up their agenda. They spent more time on it, doing more of the things that they had occasionally done in non-panic times, but essentially doing the same *sort* of things. This would mean that witches with long-established reputations would suddenly find themselves in court, not because of something they had recently done, but because the authorities' interest in them had grown. During a witchcraft panic, the first targets were often the village witches with established reputations, who otherwise might have escaped prosecution. This could be because the authorities were working harder on village witchcraft, or because the witch's neighbours at last overcame their reluctance to denounce her or him. This raises the question of whether it was the authorities, or the neighbours, who were panicking; usually it was the authorities, as we shall see.

Second, the authorities could do some new things – things that they might not have done at all in non-panic periods. This might include torturing suspected witches, or asking for names of accomplices when they interrogated them. This would be likely to lead to the prosecution of people with no established reputations for witchcraft, who by definition were not at risk of being accused of witchcraft by their neighbours. Another new thing that people could do if they were panicking was to shift the emphasis from individual malefice to the demonic pact, which was another way of broadening the hunt beyond individual suspects with established reputations.

Third, the authorities could lower their judicial standards, giving more credence to prosecution evidence and less to defence evidence. This would lead people to be convicted on less evidence than usual. If the panic was to be kept going, it had to be fed with more convictions; this would prove to the witch-hunters themselves, as well as to onlookers who might otherwise doubt them, that the witch threat was really serious. Acquittals usually slowed the momentum of a panic, and could easily bring it to a complete halt. The lowering of judicial standards could occur in numerous ways, as discussed in Chapter 7, but the single most important one was to carry out unrestricted torture.

Most of the things that people did when they panicked, therefore, were likely to lead to chain-reaction witch-hunts. They no longer prosecuted witches simply as isolated individuals, even large numbers of such individuals. Instead they used each witch to lead them to further witches. In practice, then, the single best defining evidence for a 'panic' is a chain-reaction witch-hunt, in which one witch named others who were then accused in their turn. We should remember that the chain reaction did not *constitute* the panic;

the panic was constituted by a state of mind in which people were especially angry, or scared, or both, about witchcraft. But the likely historical result of a mood of panic was a chain-reaction hunt.

Chain-reaction witch-hunts

The pointing finger, with one witch accusing someone else of witchcraft, is a powerful image to evoke a mood of witch-hunting. One trial clerk, in Switzerland, actually drew a pointing finger in the margin of a witch's confession to indicate the names of the *'complices'* (accomplices).[10] The basic idea of chain-reaction witch-hunts may be easy to grasp, but such hunts could develop in various different ways. Any one chain might have different types of links. There might also be more than one linked 'chain'.

The most familiar type of link in the chain was the witchcraft suspect who named names of other suspects under interrogation. This would typically be because the interrogators feared a witchcraft conspiracy and so pressed for other names. The easiest way for a suspect to provide such names was to say who else they had seen at the witches' sabbat – the familiar gathering of conspiratorial witches. Some suspects tried to sidestep the question 'Who did you see at the sabbat?', knowing that giving names could lead to more deaths. They replied that they had not been able to recognise people because it had been too dark, or because the other participants had been disguised, or because their own eyesight was poor. Sometimes they named people who were already dead. However, for many interrogators, this was not enough, and, with the aid of torture, they could usually force the suspect to give them the kind of names that they wanted. Ursula Funk in Eichstätt was questioned every day from 5 to 10 October and again from 15 to 17 October 1626; on each occasion she had to give more names. Another Eichstätt suspect, Valtin Langg in 1617, eventually named 237 accomplices.[11]

There were five types of names that a suspect could produce. First, they could name people who already had a reputation for witchcraft. Second, they could name people who fitted a witchcraft stereotype – especially an older woman, or possibly a magical practitioner. (There is more about stereotypes in Chapter 9.) Third, they could name ordinary people who were well known to them – members of their social circle, or even their own family. Fourth, they could name prominent names – members of the local elite, perhaps clergymen or political figures or their wives. Fifth, they could name names virtually at random. Any of these types of names could be produced, either on the suspects' own initiative, or in response to guidance and suggestions from the interrogators; occasionally, indeed, the interrogators even suggested specific names.

These five types of names may represent an escalating trend in severity of prosecution. A suspect who knew of one or two witches with established reputations would tend to name them first; some interrogators would be satisfied by this. If more names were required, suspects would name people who seemed likely to be witches. If the interrogators pressed for still more names, suspects would move on to people known to them – neighbours, members of their extended family, or people with whom they worked or traded. At the fourth stage, there was probably always a temptation to name members of the local elite, because these were well-known names that would come readily to suspects' minds. At the fifth stage, any names would do. Few individual suspects would follow this fivefold scheme precisely – these were, after all, desperate, bewildered people suffering intense pain. But patterns would emerge when considering large numbers of names provided by large numbers of suspects.

Larger numbers of names probably came from the third category (people well known to the suspect) rather than the fourth (members of the elite), simply because the third category would contain the largest numbers of names. Elite people were a small group. This is what we find in one well-studied group of suspects in an intense panic, the Eichstätt witches. There seem to have been few people with witchcraft reputations in Eichstätt, so, while the suspects named some older women and some priests (female and male stereotypes), most of the suspects named their associates – often specifying how they knew them. One consequence of this was that women usually named other women and men named other men, because this was how social networks functioned in early modern times; this will be discussed further in Chapter 9.

Accusations against members of the elite were particularly provocative. How would the interrogators react to a suspect who named one of their betters? They had a particularly strong tendency to disbelieve such accusations. Twenty-two Eichstätt witches denounced the secretary to the town council, Paul Gabler, as a witch, but the authorities never took this seriously.[12] On occasions where such accusations were believed, this could lead to a factional witch-hunt involving high-level politics – on which more in a moment.

As a suspect named more and more names, they would tend to do so more and more at random. It is hard to show exactly how random a given list of names was, though Johannes Junius in Bamberg, discussed in Chapter 7, described how he was forced to name names with little regard for his connection with them, or for the likelihood of whether the persons concerned might be guilty. The torturer told him to think about each street in the town and name some names from each. Interrogators did not usually want names clearly given at random; the names had to be credible. Junius's names were credible only because Bamberg was in the grip of one of Europe's most intense panics. His torturer was simply cynical, but the prince-bishop and his commissioners were surely sincere in their belief in a widespread conspiracy.

Some suspects named people with whom they themselves had quarrelled, which can look like a deliberate attempt to drag down their enemies. Interrogators sometimes rejected names of known enemies for this reason.

However, quarrelsomeness was a stereotypical witchcraft characteristic, so the suspects could really have come to believe (especially under torture) that their quarrelsome enemies were witches, and the interrogators could have shared this belief. Names that were both offered and accepted represent the outcome of a negotiation between the suspect and the interrogators.

A star witness – a witch who claimed the ability to detect other witches – could greatly aid a witch-hunter in fostering a chain-reaction panic. In Navarre, Spain, in 1525–26, two girls aged 9 and 11 claimed to be witches and to be able to identify witches through a mark in their left eye. Several hundred suspects were arrested, and, although there were few executions in the end, this episode formed Spain's largest sixteenth-century panic. It is not entirely clear who selected the suspects, although it was not the girls themselves. In principle we should distinguish between star witnesses who named names, and star witnesses who confirmed the guilt of people selected by others. However, there could be overlap between these two patterns, with negotiation between the star witness and the authorities; either the authorities might suggest names to the witness, or they might take up only some of the names supplied by the witness.

A distinctive kind of chain-reaction hunt could develop in cases of demonic possession. Here the names were given, not by the witchcraft suspect, but by the victim or victims of demonic possession. Most witchcraft victims believed that their misfortune was due to just one witch, but victims of possession could name many witches. Typically they began by accusing one witch, or a small number, but might broaden out their accusations if encouraged to do so. Just as with the names given by witchcraft suspects themselves, therefore, this process might well be influenced by interrogators. The pointing finger could be manipulated by those directing the panic.

Panics and high politics

It was argued above that all witch-hunting was 'political' in the sense that it all involved the exercise of power. However, some panics were also 'political' in a narrower sense: they were linked with open struggles for political power over issues that went beyond witchcraft. National panics, in particular, were exercises of power, in which the ruler or rulers of a state took dramatic action to eradicate the witchcraft threat. Were the prosecutions the ruler's own idea, or was the ruler responding to pressure from elsewhere – and, if so, from where?

Many such panics were controversial. Some people in power supported prosecutions; others were reluctant or even downright hostile. The prince-bishopric of Bamberg, between 1610 and 1628, experienced a prolonged political struggle between two factions. One faction, led by the suffragan (deputy) bishop, Friedrich Förner, favoured Counter-Reformation zeal, including witch-hunting; the other faction, led by the chancellor, Georg Haan, took a more pragmatic line. An initial bout of witch-hunting began in

1612, but Haan curtailed it in 1618 by cutting the budget of the witch commissioners. However, this was at the opening of the Thirty Years' War, and the Catholic League of the Empire installed a new, zealous bishop in 1622. Förner's faction increased their influence, and in 1628 got Haan himself, and his entire family, burned as witches.[13] It was during this panic that the Bamberg witch house (Illustration 8.1) was built and that Johannes Junius was executed. In another, later example, Transylvania had a witchcraft panic in 1679–86 that was led by the ruling prince himself, Mihály Apafy. Thirteen of the twenty-five accused were noblewomen, and the principal witch, Zsuasanna Vitéz, was the wife of the prince's defeated rival Pál Béldy.[14]

Factional panics were sometimes linked to the fear of magic in princely courts, where rulers could become convinced that their enemies were using necromancy against them. This fear mainly involved elite men rather than the lower-class women who were the most common witches in the early modern period. Court necromancy, as we saw in Chapter 2, has been more studied in the late middle ages, but the pattern of political magic certainly continued as long as the end of the sixteenth century, and in eastern Europe perhaps longer. In Russia, there were panics involving alleged magical conspiracies against various tsars.

Related to witch-hunts involving internal political factions, there could be witch-hunts involving territorial rivals. In areas of Germany where territories were fragmented and boundaries intricate, two rival lords might claim jurisdiction over a locality. One way for a lord to establish that a particular village belonged to him, and not to his rival, was to hold a court for the village. Witchcraft cases, because they could be easily fomented, were a good type of case to bring before such a court. The village faction who supported the lord's claim could encourage the prosecution of a witch – perhaps someone associated with a rival faction. Such cases may seem cynical, but the participants may well have believed that the person concerned was a witch. As will be discussed further in Chapter 9, people have a propensity to believe that their personal or group enemies are wicked people, or members of a wicked group.

A few panics began with the trial of a prominent person. In the prince-bishopric of Cologne, Germany, the execution of Katharina Henot, a member of the elite, was so dramatic that it inaugurated a panic that ran from 1627 to 1630.[15] Other panics moved *towards* a prominent person. The panic in Trier, Germany, in 1587–89, began with lower-class people, but saw accusations gradually building towards the town's bailiff, Diederich Flade, executed in 1589. The so-called North Berwick panic in Scotland in 1590–91 began with a servant maid, Geillis Duncan, but, within weeks, suspects' confessions were being shaped to implicate the king's cousin, the earl of Bothwell. Unlike Flade, however, Bothwell evaded trial until 1593, by which time the panic had subsided, and he was acquitted.

The North Berwick panic also illustrates the complex dynamics that multiple interrogations and trials could set in motion. The king was interested in

Bothwell's possible complicity, but the ninth earl of Angus became interested in the suspicious death of his own predecessor (a distant cousin) in 1588. He noticed early in 1591 that some of the emerging witchcraft suspects had previously been consulted by the eighth earl's widow, Jean Lyon. He began assembling evidence against her, but Lyon escaped a formal accusation when the ninth earl himself died suddenly in June 1591.[16]

Witch-hunting could be promoted by a new political regime. In an age when political authority was said to come from God, rulers had to say, and even believe, that God had chosen them to rule. For some rulers, godly behaviour was important. A new regime might well feel more godly than its predecessor, or want to present itself as such, and prosecuting witches could be a way of showing godliness. The regime might also feel insecure and vulnerable, heightening its sensitivity to the idea of demonic conspiracy. The Swiss territory of Prättigau had a sudden outburst of witch-hunting, with over a hundred trials, when it became independent of Austrian control in 1648.[17] The Navarre panic of 1525–26, discussed above, occurred during Navarre's annexation to the crown of Spain, and may belong in this category.

If new and insecure regimes were particularly prone to witchcraft panics, this may be connected with another pattern, in which a suspension of normal forms of authority could leave room for a panic. The panic of 1645–47 in East Anglia, the largest to occur in England, broke out during the English Civil War. The regular assize courts had been suspended, and office-holders with exceptional religious zeal had come to the fore. The Salem panic in Massachusetts was similar, being conducted by a special court during the suspension of the regular courts.

Factional panics could thus occur in localities as well as at the centre. One example is the panic led by Gerhard de Horst, provost of Bitbourg-Echternach, Luxembourg, between 1587 and 1599. At least thirty witches were executed, and Horst claimed that there were over 1,500 witches in the locality. His prosecutions were linked to his feud with a local administrator and financier, Johann Schweistal. Horst got several witches to name Schweisdal as an accomplice, and even to claim that Schweistal was out to destroy him personally by magic. Schweistal fought back successfully, however, informing the ducal council of alleged financial corruption by Horst.[18] Witches' confessions formed a weapon in this struggle between rival elite factions.

Neighbourhood panics

A notable contrast to the pattern of elite-driven panics occurred in the Rhine-Moselle region of western Germany. These were panics of ordinary people. Peasants became convinced that witches were attacking, not specific individuals against whom they bore a grudge, but the entire community. Typically they believed that the grape harvest was being damaged by storms, frost or other bad weather brought by witches. Such local disasters were too serious to be blamed on one witch, and the panicking peasants sought action on a larger scale. They formed committees to drive witch-hunting forward. They collected subscriptions, commissioned legal advice, arrested suspects and lobbied lords' courts to carry out formal prosecutions. Occasionally they carried out their own tortures; even more occasionally, if the courts refused to prosecute, they lynched the witches themselves. Well-established state structures would not allow such committees, which threatened to usurp official power, but small and weak jurisdictions in this politically-fragmented area of Germany were sometimes forced to co-operate with witch-hunting committees for considerable periods.

These committees were almost always made up of richer peasants – the village elite. This is an important point that will be discussed further below. A committee tended also to be controlled by a faction within the village, which demanded allegiance to itself in the name of the greater good. Committees took oaths of solidarity, sometimes on a knife driven into a table. This could be a divisive process. If rival villagers displayed reluctance or resistance, the committee could attack them as witches. Village witch-hunting using these committees could thus produce miniature versions of the factional witchcraft panics discussed above.

One reason for the emergence of these committees in this part of Germany may be found in the extreme vulnerability of the grape harvest to bad weather. Hailstorms could destroy every single grape within minutes, and such storms could give rise to extreme fear. Finally, there was the simple fact that western Germany was the heartland of intense witchcraft prosecution by state authorities – perhaps two-thirds of all those executed in Europe were German-speaking. If Germany saw intense prosecution of witches by state authorities, perhaps it is natural also to find at least some instances of intense fear and hatred of witches by their neighbours.

Economic stresses and witch-hunting

Together, population pressure and climatic deterioration made peasant life more difficult just at the time when prosecutions of witches were rising – the late sixteenth and early seventeenth centuries. There was surely a connection, but what exactly was it? There can be a temptation to write glibly of witches being blamed for 'crop failures', but most witches were not in fact blamed for crop failures, and peasants' economic problems ranged well beyond crop failures. More precise analysis is required.

There are two ways in which the harsh economic picture can be related to witch-hunting. The first, more general approach is to say that, with more widespread hardship, there were probably more individual misfortunes for which people needed explanations. An increase in malnutrition, for instance, would lead more people to die prematurely. This might be expected to cause more accusations of village witches, of the kind that were discussed in Chapter 4 above. It is hard to see how an increase in village misfortunes could be quantified, but we can surely recognise that it is likely to have had some effect on long-term trends in witch-hunting. It is suggestive, for instance, that the statistical relationship between the number of witchcraft cases and the level of wheat prices was quite close between about 1550 and 1650.[19] Economic problems thus probably made village witchcraft more serious.

The second, more specific approach is to focus on harvest failures, and to argue that storms that destroyed harvests were blamed on witches. Wolfgang Behringer, in particular, has developed this idea into what can appear to be the single most important cause of witch-hunting.[20] According to this argument, peasants demanded the prosecution of witches who had destroyed the crops through hailstorms. This is convincing in the cases of neighbourhood panic discussed above, but does not seem to have been a general cause of witch-hunting beyond western Germany.

One problem with climatic explanations for witch-hunting is that much of the evidence is indirect. Correlations do not in themselves prove causal relationships. A correlation between 'crop failures' or 'famines' and witch-hunting may be evidence only of a rise in individual, village misfortune rather than collective misfortune. Or it may not be evidence of anything at all; the relevant 'correlations' all fall short of statistical significance. Behringer has more than once cited an apparent correlation between famines and witch-hunting in Scotland, but no Scottish evidence has yet been found actually connecting the two. King James VI, in his book *Daemonologie* (1597), gave a conventional account of witches' storm-bringing powers, but this was a theoretical matter. Neither he, nor anyone else in Scotland, stated that witches' storms had harmed actual crops or caused actual famines. When Scottish trial records mentioned malefices, these were individual rather than collective.[21] Indeed it was normal throughout Europe for witches to be accused of weather magic by the authorities, and not by neighbours. Reyne Percheval, in the Cambrésis, Spanish Netherlands, in 1599, confessed to having used toads' venom to make a dense rain that could rot apples and pears, but this motif occurred only in her confession; her neighbours spoke instead of everyday malefices.[22]

However, storm-bringing witches had a broader importance, precisely because of this demonological element. Members of the elite could be just as concerned about them as the common folk. In Swabia, Germany, a destructive storm in 1562 led the *minister* of Esslingen, not the peasants, to demand punishment of witches.[23] Other magical attacks on farming also concerned the authorities. The Bamberg panic of 1626-32, with at least 630 suspects, was prompted by a frost that destroyed the grape harvest, and a petition against witches who were blamed. However, the authorities shaped the panic and rapidly escalated it in their own direction.[24] In the Champagne-Ardennes region of France, in 1587, an epidemic of livestock deaths was blamed on witches by evangelical preachers of the Counter-Reformation.[25]

Storm-bringing was also a subject of demonological debate. Pedro Ciruelo, in Spain in 1530, went against the demonological trend by arguing that thunderstorms normally had natural causes. He argued that storms occurred mainly in spring and summer, whereas if demons could bring them they would do so at any season.[26] In 1532, the governing body of the Spanish Inquisition warned a local inquisitor in Navarre that damage to grapes or other crops from the weather could have natural causes and should not necessarily be blamed on witches.[27] Perhaps the inquisitor was responding to popular demand for prosecution, but this is not certain; what is certain is that storm-bringing mattered to *him*.

Thus, if members of the elite were worried about witches' crop destruction, this would affect their actions. Rulers could have a paternal concern for their subjects. Clergymen could see the hand of God in natural disasters of all kinds – either through direct divine action, or through God permitting witches to afflict communities for their sinfulness. However, rulers or clergymen needed to uphold their elite status by distancing themselves from the practicalities of labouring in the fields. If they took initiatives against witches damaging crops, they would be likely to legitimise their actions by saying that they were responding to peasant demand. Thus, some of the peasants who allegedly complained about crop damage may have been as imaginary as the babies allegedly eaten at the sabbat. Yet, even though some of the witches' storms raged only within the demonologist's study, witches' storms still contributed to witch-hunting ideology.

The peasant economy and the Little Ice Age

The later sixteenth and early seventeenth centuries were not only the peak period for witch-hunting; they were also a particularly harsh period for the peasant economy. Land had been abundant in Europe for two hundred years, since the Black Death of the 1340s, but, in the sixteenth century, population levels rose steadily, and it became difficult to feed the increased numbers from the available land. Peasant families subdivided their farms. Marginal, poor-quality land was ploughed up in desperation, although crops grown on such land were more likely to fail.

Meanwhile, the climate deteriorated. Climate is a complex issue, requiring us to consider slow, long-term trends along with dramatic, short-term fluctuations. A period of global cooling began around 1570, with Alpine glaciers advancing. This colder episode, a phase of the longer early modern cool period now dubbed the 'Little Ice Age', lasted until about 1630. It was exacerbated by major volcanic eruptions,

(continued)

spreading atmospheric dust that blocked sunlight. Such eruptions occurred in 1580, 1586, 1593, 1595 and 1600 – the largest-ever concentration of volcanic disasters in such a short period. Some may have been as bad as the better-documented eruption of Tambora, in April 1815, which would cause 1816 to become notorious as the 'year without a summer'. There were also other years of short-term disaster, with 1626 in particular being as bad as 1816 in northern and central Europe.[28]

Bad weather affected the productivity of early modern farming in various ways. Grain crops suffered from colder springs or from wetter summers or autumns. Dairy cattle suffered from cold at any season, or from wetter summers. Grapes suffered from late frosts in spring, or from wetter summers, or from colder autumns, or – dramatically – from hailstorms in summer or autumn. Overall, people in the late sixteenth and early seventeenth centuries were poorer than before, and with fewer resources to fall back on if disaster were to strike.

Dynamics of panics

Tracing the origin of panics is difficult. People did not sit down in a meeting and say to one another, 'Let's abandon all restraint and plunge into a frenzy of reckless accusations'. Still less did they then write this in the minutes of the meeting, for historians to use as evidence. Historical narrative often shows a gradual slide into panic, with one or two cases, then three or four, then a larger number. Sometimes there are more sudden and distinct initiatives, such as the establishment of a special commission, but the usual pattern seems to have been for panics to arise gradually.

Some panics seem to have been set off by official law-enforcement initiatives. In the duchy of Bouillon, Luxembourg, in 1622, the public prosecutor sent a questionnaire to all villages: 'Who are those noted for witchcraft, why do people have a bad opinion of them, whether they have used threats, harming people or animals, or whether anyone has accused them, how many times and with what evidence?' This questionnaire may not have been issued in a mood of panic, but in one village, Sugny, it produced three trials. Five more trials from Sugny followed in 1626 and three in 1630.[29]

Panics often had a high proportion of executions, with few acquittals. In the long-running panic in Eichstätt between 1617 and 1631, 240 suspects were named to the authorities and 182 arrested. Of those arrested, 175 were executed and only one seems to have been released (two died in prison, one died under torture, one was sentenced to house arrest and died in 1644, and the fate of two is unknown).[30] In this panic, accusation almost always led to execution.

The dynamics of witch-hunting 245

Sometimes, however, there were large-scale prosecutions with few executions or even none. The Salem panic, in which 19 witches were executed, is an example; over a hundred suspects were imprisoned and many more were named, most of whom were never brought to trial. In the late 1430s, the prior and inquisitor of Lyon, France, were frustrated in prosecuting witches at a time when neither the civic authorities nor the French crown were keen to do so. The prior and inquisitor panicked, but their efforts were blocked, and few or no executions resulted. The civic authorities sought political stability in the aftermath of a local revolt, and seem to have feared that witch-hunting would destabilise their fragile authority.[31] This still qualifies as a 'panic' in the terms used here, because it was a chain-reaction hunt in which the local prosecutors panicked. This is another reason for rejecting any definition of a 'panic' that relies on numbers of executions.

Quite a few places had just one panic. This may mean that the authorities had learned from their experience, and avoided having any more. These could include panics that were brought to a halt deliberately, either by the authorities in charge themselves, or by the intervention of a higher power such as the prince or a central court. However, other places had repeated panics. Rottenburg, Germany, had panics in 1595–96, 1599–1602, and 1605.[32] These authorities were not really learning a lesson – or, if they were, the lesson was that chain-reaction witchcraft trials were a *good* thing to have.

Panics could spread though the transmission of news of witch-hunting. Germany, the region with some of the heaviest witch-hunting, also had the most developed printing industry. From 1533 onwards, a distinct genre of newsletters about witchcraft trials began to be printed – single sheets or pamphlets, often with illustrations. Their numbers continued to grow until the 1620s, when once-off newsletters began to be replaced by early periodical newspapers. These too reported witchcraft trials, though by the late seventeenth century they more often adopted a sceptical tone towards 'superstition', including traditional witchcraft beliefs.[33]

People could thus learn about panics, both in a positive and negative sense, not only from panics in their own country but also from those in neighbouring states. In Germany, the Wiesensteig panic of 1562 is often cited as a harbinger of later and bigger panics. It was also discussed as an example of high-handed procedure – a lesson in what to avoid.[34] However, this seems to have been unusual, at least before the later seventeenth century. Most witchcraft prosecutions were not perceived at the time as dire warnings of what to avoid. News reports of executions were either positive or neutrally descriptive. That being so, these witchcraft prosecutions can be seen as educational events; they gave experience, both to the prosecutors themselves and to those who heard the news. Thus, the Trier panic of the 1580s was reported in shocked but approving terms by the tutor of the sons of the duke of Bavaria:

> What we hear of these vicious witches here borders on the unbelievable. Everywhere around here we see almost more stakes from burned

witches than green trees. Like the heads of the hydra, more witches always grow back.[35]

A witchcraft panic was often a shocking matter, but people tended to be shocked by the witches, rather than by the prosecution. By means of a panic, people *learned* about the witchcraft threat, and they *learned* about how to combat it.

There is a tension between the view of large panics as dysfunctional – indicating some kind of social strain – and the view of individual prosecutions as functional, restoring harmony in a village disrupted by quarrels. Both these views may be valid in some cases, but, if so, we have to work out how they related to one another. One problem is that large panics occurred in societies that also had individual prosecutions. The solution to this might be to say that although an individual prosecution could promote harmony, it might not be enough to remove all the strains being faced in that society. However, we should not necessarily assume that an individual prosecution was functional; as we saw in Chapter 4, such prosecutions often represented the failure of normal processes of community reconciliation. Perhaps individual prosecutions were somewhat dysfunctional, panics even more so. And there was probably a shift over time. As we shall see in Chapter 10, later panics more often attracted criticism and were more often followed by recriminations.

Witch-hunters

It is possible, at least in theory, to distinguish 'witch-hunters' in an active sense from those who took part in prosecutions dutifully. The witch-hunters, in this active sense, were those who were panicking and taking active measures as a result. Let us recall that 'panic' is a state of mind, but is identifiable historically through people's unusual actions – in particular, chain-reaction witch-hunting. What kind of people, therefore, were actually responsible for chain-reaction witch-hunting?

Panicking central rulers were unusual, but some can be found. Charles, duke of Gelderland, announced in 1514 that he intended to suppress all 'devil worship and witchcraft' in his domains.[36] The governor general of the Spanish Netherlands, in 1592, issued an order that judges should 'proceed rigorously' against witches 'by the most severe and exemplary punishments'; there was a threat that judges who were remiss in this duty would themselves be punished. The order was reissued in 1606.[37] Even kings could panic; this was rarer still, but could promote witch-hunting with particular effect. Christian IV, king of Denmark, in 1626 wrote to his chancellor about witches: 'We have unfortunately far too many of these creatures, and it is desirable that they be thoroughly swept away once and for all, so that the house is free of this filth.'[38]

Local witch-hunters were much more common, and probably more typical of the European witch-hunt as a whole. Charles Van der Camere, lieutenant of the castellany of Bouchain, Spanish Netherlands, wrote in 1612:

> This district is strangely infected by persons abandoned and enthralled to the Devil, of all ages and of either sex, so that in the past two years I have convicted more than eighty in this town and in six villages, besides a great many suspect and banished and fourteen others now prisoners.[39]

In Schongau, Bavaria, in 1589–90, there was a major witch-hunt connected with weather magic. Four years later, the weather had returned to normal, and the proud county judge proposed to erect a monument to his own success.[40] Even governmental assemblies could panic. The estates of Béarn, France, complained of witches in 1594: 'the dangerous and pernicious vermin of the said crime swarm and increase from day to day'.[41] The *parlement* of Dôle, Franche-Comté, in 1629, sounded a similar note of panic: 'The evil grows every day, and this unfortunate rabble goes swarming everywhere'.[42]

Stanley Cohen's model of 'moral panics', as we saw earlier, stresses 'moral entrepreneurs' – people with no official position, who take the lead in publicising the offence, organising popular opposition to it and demanding action from the authorities. One notorious example was the minor gentleman Matthew Hopkins, self-styled 'witch-finder general' during the panic of 1645–47 in East Anglia, England. Hopkins was not a judge or government official, but promoted himself as a kind of consultant to witch-hunting courts. He succeeded in orchestrating a panic with several hundred victims. Those with no official role may have found it harder to exercise influence in areas of the Continent where the inquisitorial system of criminal justice (discussed in Chapter 7) placed so much authority with the judge. However, the politically-fragmented territories of western Germany offered opportunities for moral entrepreneurs. The lawyer Johann Möden made a career as a witchcraft specialist in the early seventeenth century, offering his services to various courts in and around Cologne, and taking part in hundreds of witchcraft trials.[43] It was often people like Möden who provided a link whereby the peasant witch-hunting committees of this region could gain access to the courts. And judges themselves could be active witch-hunters; two who publicised their own role by writing books were Nicolas Rémy in Lorraine, and Henri Boguet in Franche-Comté.

A pattern has been identified in England whereby it was often a man from the local elite who took the initiative to bring a case to the authorities' attention. At this point, he would seek out other people – typically lower-class women – who had other, longer-standing grievances against the suspect. One such woman was Elizabeth Field, brought in to testify against Jane Wenham at the latter's celebrated trial at Hertford assizes in 1712. When Field testified that her child had died nine years earlier, the judge asked her why she had not brought a prosecution at the time. She replied that 'she was a poor woman, and the child had no friends'; she appeared now, 'the opportunity presenting itself'.[44] Field's 'opportunity' was clearly provided by several elite men who had orchestrated Wenham's trial. There are issues of gender here that will be discussed in Chapter 9, but here we should note the issue of class.

There may be a distinction between 'witch-hunters' who organised trials, and 'witch-hunters' who took the lead in testifying against witches. The accusers of five witches in Bazuel, Spanish Netherlands, between 1599 and 1627, have been studied in detail.[45] Many were ordinary villagers, but some stand out as members of the village elite. The six witnesses against Reyne Percheval in 1599 included two aldermen of the village, both of whom testified about other people's misfortunes rather than their own. One of the others, Pierre Wattelier, was a young thatcher who complained about the death of a cow. Wattelier seems an ordinary villager – but he was probably well off, since by 1627 he had become an alderman. On that occasion he testified that Pasquette Barra had caused his son to become ill, and had caused the death of the son of another alderman. Members of the village elite were more likely to be among the accusers, and some may have been serial accusers.

Thus, just as communities could accumulate knowledge of witch-hunting, individuals could do so too, and could learn to be witch-hunters. One example is Claude Burritaz, a local notary (legally-trained scribe) in the canton of Vaud, Switzerland. His first recorded encounter with witchcraft was in 1448, when it was his duty to act as the scribe for three witchcraft trials. He then acted as a prosecution witness in a trial of 1461, and finally became a leading prosecutor in a trial of 1465.[46] At this early date, information about witchcraft may well have been rare, so Burritaz's learning process is particularly noteworthy, but a process of sharing and spreading information can surely be seen at work in any panic. Many panics involved serial witch-hunters, usually members of the local elite who promoted one prosecution after another. We shall come back to the role of local elites.

Some of the people whom we see as committed 'witch-hunters' were really committed reformers on a broader scale. The issues of godly 'reform', both Protestant and Catholic, came to the fore during the sixteenth century, as we saw in Chapter 6; individuals who espoused 'reform' could thus be keen prosecutors of witches as well as keen promoters of other forms of godliness. Such people can be found even in the fifteenth century, like Georges de Saluces, bishop of Lausanne in the 1440s, who banned profane activities from churches, pressed his parish clergymen to raise their standards of pastoral care, segregated Jews, and issued ordinances against card-playing and blasphemy. Saluces certainly encouraged several witchcraft trials, but he was much more than simply a 'witch-hunter'.[47]

Because active witch-hunters were unusual, sometimes they visibly failed to carry people with them. In some cases, local witch-hunters were restrained by higher authorities. In 1605, a local court convicted Françoise Le Poyne, from Alençon, Normandy, but she appealed to the *parlement* of Rouen, which overturned her conviction because the judge had improperly ordered local priests to make public appeals for information against her.[48] In Dornhan, Württemberg, in 1608, a local constable initiated a chain-reaction hunt using torture, and the husband of one of the suspects complained, 'It seems as if the constable's private obsession has taken over this place'.[49] Active witch-hunters could well be seen as people with private obsessions.

Did people take the law into their own hands? Witch lynchings by ordinary folk were very rare in most places, but there were quite a few places where they did occur from time to time. Information is patchy, but significant numbers of lynchings occurred in France, Denmark and Poland.[50] If someone killed a witch without legal sanction, the question arose of how the authorities should treat them. In the Spanish Netherlands, they were usually convicted of murder, but then pardoned.[51] These pardons indicate that the authorities had at least some willingness to accept popular initiatives against witches. Indeed, extra-judicial killings may well be one of the best indicators of popular demand – and such killings continued sporadically beyond the era of legal executions. However, most witch-hunts proceeded without such killings. To the question of whether there was, in fact, popular demand for witch-hunting, and of where the initiative lay in prosecution, we now turn.

Witch-hunting from above or below?

In studying witch-hunting and analysing the responsibility for it, one of the most important and keenly-debated questions has been which socio-political groups bore the greatest responsibility. Did witch-hunting come from 'above' or 'below'? This question is related to the issue of what kind of 'witchcraft' was being prosecuted, since Europe's elites tended to be more concerned about demonic witchcraft, while the common folk were more concerned about village witchcraft. However, the relationships between social groups, and the subdivisions within such groups, were complex, and there were many different patterns of witchcraft prosecution – in different countries, or even at different periods within the same country. Can a broad pattern be discerned?

There has been a vogue lately for studies to emphasise the extent to which prosecutions were driven by some kind of popular demand. The best of such studies represent major achievements of witchcraft scholarship. On the other hand, this has sometimes given the impression that *most* or even *all* witch-hunting was caused by popular demand, relegating other factors to the margins. So long as the fashion has been to lay the emphasis on popular demand, it has been difficult to gain a balanced view of all the factors at work. Here, then, I will begin with the conclusions of three of the most influential recent scholars on this topic.

Robin Briggs concludes that 'Village and small-town witchcraft was the basic type, the everyday reality around which everything else was built.

The more exotic variants which so often confuse our understanding – possession cases, intense short-term persecutions, witch-finding, lycanthropy, vampirism – were secondary elaborations.'[52] Brian Levack, first mentioning that studies of England have long shown that 'the pressure to prosecute came from the witches' neighbours', continues that also on the Continent, 'in most cases the original pressure to prosecute came, just as in England, from the common people'.[53] Levack, however, does not give a determining role to the common people. He adds: 'Even when the original impetus to prosecute had come from below, the way in which hunts developed was determined mainly from above. The common people played only a supporting role, by testifying against those implicated in the process and maintaining a popular mood that was conducive to witch-hunting.'[54] Finally, William Monter also endorses the idea of witch-hunting from below in a qualified way, but he qualifies it differently: 'the impulse to hunt witches came primarily from beneath, from prominent people in local villages'.[55] He thus differentiates the common folk into ordinary villagers and 'prominent' villagers.

The present analysis will attempt to build on these interpretations. Briggs is valuable in reminding us that village accusations of witchcraft were geographically much more widespread than panics; he has also done more than anyone to elucidate witchcraft dynamics within villages. However, his dismissal of 'intense short-term persecutions' (panics) is surely unfortunate, failing to take into account the large numbers of executions that panics generated – in villages as much as in towns. Probably a majority of Europe's witches were executed in chain-reaction trials rather than as isolated individuals. Levack helpfully draws attention to the different interests involved in a witchcraft prosecution – something that the present chapter has taken further in its five-stage political model above. And Monter takes us into village society itself, drawing attention to the way in which inequalities in power and status among villagers were relevant to the dynamics of forming witchcraft reputations and demanding prosecutions.

In addition to this, the present analysis will take into account a point also made by Briggs and developed further in Chapter 4. Ordinary villagers, having identified a witch, normally negotiated with her or him, seeking reconciliation and rehabilitation rather than prosecution.[56] Executing a witch was a *failure* of normal community processes.

In order to understand how the 'elite' and the 'common people' related to each other over witch-hunting, it helps to think about how they related to each other more generally. Under what circumstances did rulers have to take account of the interests of those whom they ruled? Indeed, how did different groups of elite rulers relate to each other? There has been discussion, for instance, of the relative contributions of 'central' and 'local' rulers. The role of large or small states is sometimes discussed in this context, though this turns out to be a less helpful question, as we saw in Chapter 6. As for the common folk, they were not a homogeneous group either, and growing social differentiation during the early modern period may have changed their relationship with the elite. The existence of middling groups – which is vitally important, as we shall see – means that even the 'above or below?' question will need some reframing before it can be answered satisfactorily.

Let us now look in more detail at the different socio-political groups. The 'above' and 'below' correspond broadly to the 'elite' and the 'common people' – the two broad groups whose socio-political interests need consideration. But both groups need to be broken down further. Some particularly important groups, as we shall see, were somewhere in the middle.

The 'elite' can broadly be divided into central rulers and local rulers. Central rulers included kings and princes and their councillors. Local rulers included noblemen and other landlords, and town councillors. Church authorities had their own institutions complementing secular ones, both central and local. Finally, universities and the world of learning provided an intellectual elite able to discuss demonological ideas in theological or legal detail.

Among the common people, the sixteenth and seventeenth centuries saw the growth of social differentiation within the village. In the late middle ages, most householders had been peasants holding similar amounts of land – an amount that could be farmed by a family and could support a family. The sixteenth-century economic downturn led this group slowly to differentiate itself into three. Ordinary peasants continued as a group, though they were poorer than before. Below them, a new group of cottagers and beggars arose – people who had lost out in the competition for landholdings. Above the ordinary peasants, also, there was a tendency for a small group of richer peasants to arise, known as 'yeomen' in England, '*laboureurs*' in France and '*Vollbauer*' in Germany. These people not only had more land and wealth, they had more power – informal influence in the village, and connections with the formal machinery of government.

The poorest group, below the peasants, were the cottagers and beggars. Cottagers had a house but little land for farming, and subsisted on casual paid work; if this failed, they would turn to begging. Like the richer peasants, these very poor people were a new phenomenon of the sixteenth century, a product of social differentiation. Beggars caused a good deal of official worry. There were panics in several states about conspiratorial beggars as arsonists. Usually the fear was that the beggars had been recruited by agents of an enemy country in order to spread fires.[57] There were also occasional panics over 'plague-spreaders', people accused during plague epidemics of conspiring to spread the disease. Those accused tended to be the 'cleansers' who dealt with dead bodies and infected houses, downtrodden menial workers who often undertook the task reluctantly.[58] Fear of the poor, and of social instability and unrest, often lay behind the authorities' initiatives to impose 'order' in the sixteenth and seventeenth centuries, and helped to legitimise the movement for a godly state.

Villages usually had some form of political organisation, which they needed in order to make collective decisions on farming, and to articulate their relationships with their lords.[59] Crop rotations and animal herding had to be planned collectively. Sometimes this village organisation was formal, with villages having charters, seals and officials. The officials in charge of their day-to-day decision-making, such as aldermen or bailiffs, were sometimes selected by the lord, sometimes by the villagers, but often by negotiation between the two. Thus, the villagers might propose three candidates from whom the lord would select one, or the lord might propose one candidate whom the villagers could accept or reject. These officials, who were usually rich peasants, functioned as intermediaries between villagers and lord.

The expansion of state authority meant an expansion *into the village*. Rich peasants were crucial in this, not because they necessarily sided with the elite, but because they provided links between the elite and the common folk. Medieval villages had been closed systems. Now, however, there were more laws and more taxes. Villagers had to accept regular visits, not just from their lords' representatives, but from rulers' tax-collectors and other officials. Several countries saw a long-term shift in local office-holding from officers representing the community to officers representing the king or central state. This is well documented in England, France and Italy. An apparently contrasting trend occurred in Germany, where peasants gained more control over appointments; however, this was at the cost of recognising the legitimacy of the offices concerned. The overall effect was the same: the state gained more of a foothold in the village.

The Reformation added a religious element to these trends. The parish priest was a key figure connecting the common people to the organisation of the church. In the late middle ages the parish priest was little more than a peasant, often illiterate, with no more education than would enable him to recite the Latin formulas of the mass. During the late sixteenth and early seventeenth centuries, first in Protestant and then in Catholic countries, parish priests' income and status were raised; the job now attracted educated men whose social and cultural affinities were with the elite.

Early modern Europe was a mainly rural society, but villages were also linked to towns, and this raises two issues. First, village witch-hunting might have been affected by the villagers' connections to towns, trade and communications networks. Second, we need to look at witch-hunting in towns themselves. In market towns, wider networks of peasants could form. Buying and selling took place in towns, as did military recruiting. Urban merchants could be intermediaries for peasant negotiations with outsiders, as could lawyers or priests. As for witchcraft trials, most witches were villagers, but they were usually taken to towns for trial, since the criminal courts were based there.

How often were town-dwellers themselves prosecuted for witchcraft? Here, a distinction needs to be drawn between towns of different sizes. Taking the largest ones first, every one of Europe's really large cities had an extremely low rate of witchcraft prosecutions. Some of these cities were in countries that themselves prosecuted few witches, such as Paris in France or Naples in Italy. But even Nuremberg escaped significant witch-hunting, though it was at the centre of Franconia, one of the German regions with intense witch-hunts.[60] In medium-sized towns, the pattern may well have been similar, though studies are more scattered. In Geneva, a Swiss city-state with a rural hinterland, the countryside produced *per capita* about six times as many witches as the city itself.[61] For Saragossa, capital of Aragon, we know that numerous rural witchcraft suspects fled to the city and successfully avoided prosecution.[62] Witch-hunting was definitely not a large-city phenomenon, and sizeable towns did not usually encourage it either.

Small towns may well have been different. A study of towns in Scotland has shown that the largest town, Edinburgh, produced relatively few witches for its population – one-seventh of the Scottish average, the same pattern as that seen in Geneva. But small towns in Scotland, with populations of under 2,000, produced many *more* witches – three times the Scottish average.[63] Some medium-sized and small towns experienced significant panics, and the largest panics (though these were rare) may even have been more intense in such towns than in the countryside.

Urban witch-hunting raises two issues of social structure: the distinctive nature of urban authority, and the distinctive nature of the urban community. Towns were more intensely governed. Town councils supervised the inhabitants closely, and there were more rules to follow than in the countryside. There was nothing like the traditional closed village, in which the peasants regulated their own lives and kept outside interference to a minimum.

The urban community contained more social stratification. Merchants and craftsmen had special privileges of trade and manufacturing, though some were richer and others poorer. They were the only town-dwellers who were as much in control of their daily lives as a peasant who farmed his own holding of land. Below the merchants and craftsmen, socially, were wage-labourers and apprentices – usually the majority of the urban population. Some urban societies may have been more mobile or anonymous or both, making it harder for long-term witchcraft reputations to form. Urban misfortunes, not involving farming, may have been harder to interpret as having been caused by witchcraft. More research is needed on these possibilities. However, we now need to analyse the ways in which the different social groups related to each other.

Witch-hunting and negotiations of power

In considering relationships between those 'above' and those 'below' – or indeed between those in the middle and those above or below *them* – we are looking at negotiations of power. Specifically, we are looking at cultural aspects of unequal power relationships. What happens, culturally, when a dominant group tries to exert power over a subordinate group?

The ideas of the dominant group have clarity, coherence and credibility. Members of the subordinate group may be uncomfortable with the ideas, but no clear or coherent alternative presents itself to them. In the negotiations, both sides can have influence, but it can still be seen as a one-way process, in which the possessors of cultural authority exert their influence to persuade the subordinate people of the correctness of their views. Sometimes early modern rulers could enforce laws in full, while at other times they were flexible in implementing them. Sometimes, too, they responded to popular demand. This is how governments legitimise their power: they identify an issue of concern, and they provide a solution – a solution that they control.

Historians of the Reformation and Counter-Reformation have sometimes stressed the failures and limitations of the reform process, pointing out that evangelisation did not succeed in the evangelists' own terms. But evangelisation still wrought massive changes. The common people of Protestant England and Catholic France may not have internalised the details of the new theology, but they did know that they were on one side, and that their enemies lay on the other side of the Channel. When the English authorities executed the Catholic Mary Queen of Scots in 1587, there were mass demonstrations of sorrow in Paris, and mass demonstrations of joy in London. This kind of popular mobilisation in support of a godly cause could easily feed into attacks on other forms of ungodliness, including witchcraft.

Witch-hunts tended to involve opening up the community to the influence of higher powers. In Ireland, as we saw in Chapter 6, this failed because Catholic peasants would not take witchcraft cases to the Protestant-dominated courts. A comparative study of three provinces in the Spanish Netherlands argues that one province, Artois, had villages that were cohesive and resistant to state interference, while the other two, Flanders and Hainaut, had unstable village communities that could be more easily penetrated by officials and their ideas. Flanders and Hainaut had much more severe witch-hunts.[64] In this sense, although at least some witchcraft beliefs and ritual practices were a functional part of community life, a witch-*hunt* was not; it marked a *failure* of community life. Usually it also marked an intrusion of the power of the state, though the popular panics in the Rhine-Moselle region instead produced locally-driven factionalism and chaos.

Russia provides another illuminating case. Russian witch-hunting grew in the seventeenth century along with the expansion of a centrally-controlled bureaucracy. Witchcraft prosecutions were centrally authorised (in theory by the tsar personally), and witchcraft was treated politically like treason. Yet cases were initiated individually by written complaints from wronged neighbours, or from informers who discovered suspicious magical grasses, roots or written spells. Most of these people, both accusers and accused, were humble, but the need to attract the authorities' attention – and to do it in writing – had a filtering effect. Accusers and accused were mostly men, cases connected to high politics were disproportionately prominent, and there was a high acquittal rate.[65] The process of negotiating power emerges clearly even in this notoriously autocratic state.

There were thus many dimensions to witch-hunting, and simplistic explanations for it are bound to fail. Robin Briggs, who is committed to the view that communities were responsible for witch-hunting, argues that if states had been serious about witch-hunting, there would have been much more of it than there was.[66] This is illogical. It could equally be argued that if *communities* had been serious about witch-hunting, there would have been much more of it than there was. The scale of witch-hunting cannot be used as evidence for community or state responsibility.

Much of what has been written to explain witch-hunting has been simply about 'accusations'. However, we do not just need to explain 'accusations', we need to explain prosecutions and convictions. The five-stage political model of decision-making in prosecutions, discussed above, allows us to get beyond the idea of a single operative cause for witch-hunting. Conditions had to be right at each stage. A prosecution originating in the community had to have the right support within the community but also the right links to the authorities, and the right support from the authorities themselves. The idea that prosecutions 'originated' in the community can thus be accepted, while detaching it from the simplistic idea that community processes were the single operative cause. The idea that prosecutions 'originated' in the community may even be little more than a truism: all witchcraft suspects were members of communities.

The idea that ordinary people could have been the most important witch-hunters, when considered along with the rising and falling chronology of prosecutions, implies that we should accept one of two ideas. Either ordinary people changed in some significant way during the sixteenth century, so that they began to demand witch-hunting for the first time, or else there were elite developments that enabled an underlying popular demand for witch-hunting to come to the surface for the first time. How credible is either of these ideas?

The idea of popular demand being new is credible in the Rhine-Moselle region of western Germany, where there seems to have been an intensification, if no more, of popular demand for the punishment of storm-bringing witches. But the broader outlines of European popular culture did not change anything like so much or so quickly. Everyday village quarrels had probably been occurring for centuries before witch-hunting began. It is true that we know about them only during the witch-hunting period, but that is because they are revealed to us only by witchcraft trial records; nobody has ever suggested that medieval villages did not have similar quarrels. There may have been more quarrels, or at least more misfortunes, with the sixteenth-century economic downturn, but surely not *that* many more. The witch-hunting of the late sixteenth century cannot be explained by a rise in village quarrels.

Part of the difficulty lies with phrases like 'the impulse to hunt witches' or 'the original pressure to prosecute'. Such phrases can easily give the impression that they are identifying the *decisive* or *real* cause of witch-hunting – but such an impression is inherently misleading, because there was no single, decisive cause of witch-hunting. The execution of a witch was the culmination of a series of events, of which a neighbour's complaint was only one. Why single out the neighbour's complaint as decisive? In some cases, even before the neighbour complained, the future witch had herself (or himself) taken significant action by behaving like a witch, quarrelling or cursing. Should we assign responsibility for the witch-hunt to the witches themselves? This, surely, would be going too far.

The foregoing analysis shows that the rise of witch-hunting in the later sixteenth century was a dynamic process, and needs to be explained by social change. An analysis of this can be carried out at different levels of social stratification. Which social groups operated, or developed, in ways that would facilitate witch-hunting?

Beginning, then, with ordinary villagers: there is, in fact, little evidence of change in everyday village quarrels and misfortunes. There may have been more misfortunes with the economic downturn, but this has not been proved. In any case it cannot explain the sheer novelty of witch-hunting; witch-hunting was a new phenomenon in most places in the sixteenth century, not an increase in an existing phenomenon. A further reason for rejecting the idea that ordinary peasants formed a dynamic element in the process is that peasants, in dealing with village witches, usually continued to seek reconciliation rather than prosecution.

Dynamic elements can be found instead at a slightly higher social level: among the rich peasants and local elites. To take rich peasants first: they emerged as a larger, more distinct and more influential social group at this time. Crucially, they were also connected more closely than before with the local propertied elites just above them. Rich peasants remained within the village, and, as village leaders, usually sought to articulate the interests of ordinary villagers as well as their own. They also shared the same beliefs about village witches. But rich peasants' interests were not identical to those of ordinary peasants, and their connections to local propertied elites could open up the village to influences from outside – influences that could include demonology.

Local propertied elites, just above the rich peasants, also formed a dynamic social level. They became more educated than before, with the spread of printing and literacy giving them access to new ideologies. These ideologies included the Reformation and Counter-Reformation, and, by extension from these, a new fear of the Devil. Local elites were particularly likely to contain members who would seek to build godly states. The expansion of state authority – a distinctively dynamic feature of this period – created many new local institutions, staffed of course by these same local elites. It is at this social level, therefore, that we find the dynamic mainspring of most witch-hunting.

However, local elites rarely acted entirely alone. Not only did they relate closely to the rich peasants below them: they also sought guidance from, and were regulated by, elites at higher social levels. As lesser officials, they were often answerable to higher officials in the state. As lesser landed proprietors, they were usually linked to the clientage networks of greater nobles. Early modern governments might seem bureaucratic, but their bureaucracies were staffed by men who owed their positions to the favour of aristocratic patrons. Shared aristocratic values and ambitions created networks of patronage and clientage linking each locality to the royal or princely court. Such a network could form a far more effective check on the activities of a local judge – should it be thought that such a check might be needed – than the formal mechanisms of appeal or bureaucratic supervision.

Thus we come to the role of higher elites. The landed estates of great aristocrats spread throughout most early modern states. In Germany, aristocrats might themselves be territorial princes; elsewhere, they gathered at royal courts and counselled kings. As patronage-brokers they linked centre and localities. They were enmeshed in state formation, occupying the high offices of the developing states, commanding the state's armies and benefiting from its taxes. Aristocrats had many calls on their attention, and few of them displayed much interest in witch-hunting – though their interest might spring dramatically to life if a panic reached higher social levels, or if their faction was actively supporting the Reformation or Counter-Reformation. They were more often involved in warfare and diplomacy than local elites; in the sixteenth and early seventeenth centuries, warfare and diplomacy often had a religious dimension.

Aristocrats were concerned about social stability. Witchcraft panics could upset this, but most panics were seen as witch problems rather than social stability problems, at least until the later seventeenth century. It could nevertheless be the aristocrats' job to sort out problems when miscarriages of justice were alleged – allegations which tended to emerge as political controversies. Otherwise, they were happy to leave local elites to sort out local problems – including most cases of witchcraft.

To the extent that we can identify a mainspring of witch-hunting in sociopolitical terms, therefore, we can locate it among local propertied elites. How does this relate to the earlier question of whether witch-hunting came from 'above' or 'below'? The answer is that it was partly from both, and partly from neither alone. Witch-hunting came from 'below' in the sense that it was not directed by central rulers; it was low-level law enforcement of the kind that was usually left to local elites. But witch-hunting also came from 'above' in the sense that most of it did not arise from the common people themselves. The common people saw it being directed by their own social superiors. Local propertied elites, those just above the villagers but with connections to richer members of village society, were more responsible for witch-hunting than any other social group.

Case study: The great Swedish panic

The great Swedish witchcraft panic of 1668–76 is a well-documented episode that attracted international attention.[67] The panic had three characteristics that were common in late episodes: elaborate procedures, a prominent role for children, and a modest execution rate. About two hundred were executed, from among many more who were accused. The panic was driven by children in the northern coastal provinces of Sweden, declaring that witches had taken them in their sleep to Blåkulla, the legendary witch mountain. Initial demands for prosecution came from leading peasants or their pastors. Accusations spread from parish to parish, month by month, along communication routes. Beginning in 1668, the panic proceeded intermittently at first, with bursts of cases every year or two, but the numbers continued to increase. Slowly but surely the panic travelled like a wave across large tracts of countryside. Eight years later, it was still on the move.

The Swedish criminal justice system was centrally supervised and bureaucratic. The government sent out a series of special commissions to gather evidence and hold trials. Reports had to be sent to the central appeal court, which usually upheld convictions. Unusually, torture was rare, because the children's denunciations sufficed. In a distorted version of Roman criminal procedure (in which two witnesses were necessary for conviction), children were treated as fractions of a witness – a 14-year-old was half a witness, a 5-year-old was a tenth. Children could testify against numerous witches, so the necessary numbers were readily assembled. Some children were taken to special 'wake-houses', to protect them from further abduction by keeping them awake. Here they devised stories of Blåkulla together. Those who failed to produce appropriate stories were deemed to be 'liars', while most of the children were assumed to be incapable of deceit. A polarised view of good versus evil, characteristic of panics, comes through clearly in this assumption of children's innocence.

In the later stages, some of the children were taken to 'wake-houses' in Stockholm, the capital. Their trances and visions became public spectacles, and witchcraft cases began in the capital itself as well as the northern provinces. In 1676, however, the children suddenly and unexpectedly announced that their stories of Blåkulla were all make-believe. The panic juddered rapidly to a halt. All the suspects currently in prison were released, and a handful of the most notorious child accusers were themselves executed. The central government, which

(continued)

> had initially promoted the panic, had learned its lesson. When another Blåkulla-related panic broke out in western Sweden in the 1720s, local courts convicted the witches but the court of appeal overturned all the convictions.

Ending a panic

Panicking was an unusual state of mind. People in early modern Europe had lives to get on with, and they did not usually regard dealing with the witchcraft threat as the most important thing in their lives. For this reason, panics were important events, but also rare events. For this reason, too, panics did not just rise and spread: they also died away.

The evidence for the ending of a panic is often indirect and allusive. If people did not write down at the start of a panic, 'Let's abandon all restraint and plunge into a frenzy of reckless accusations', neither did they write down at the end, 'We now realise that we've been panicking and executing innocent people, so we're going to stop.' The end of a panic often seems to be a silent anticlimax: the flood of witchcraft trials simply declines to a trickle and then ceases.

In principle, all witchcraft cases could have been taken further than they were. Any accused person *could* have been asked about more accomplices and *could* have provided more names; any acquittal *could* have been a conviction; and so on. This is so even for the large panics, since all of them stopped eventually. A few large panics, indeed, seem to have been limited mainly by the capacity of the prisons and the availability of expert torturers; without these infrastructural constraints, even more witches could have been executed. Overall, though, to explain the ending of panics we need to return to the five-stage political model with which this chapter began. Seeing the stages as hurdles for a prosecution to surmount, we can also see that it was usually difficult to surmount them. Prosecutions could fail through active opposition, but also through powerful interest groups becoming indifferent. The exhaustion of the original energy and excitement of the prosecutors – or of the interest groups who backed them – would lead to a panic dying away naturally.

Some panics did not die away naturally. Instead they came to a sudden end when miscarriages of justice were exposed, or when a political group opposed to the trials gained the upper hand in the state. The fact that not everyone panicked during a 'witchcraft panic' helps to explain how the panic came to an end. During the panics, some of those who kept their heads could see what was going on – and they sometimes protested. For panics centred in towns, there could be worries about trade, since merchants might avoid a town in the grip of a witchcraft panic. Uncomfortable lessons could be learned from panics. There could be recriminations afterwards, with the recent trials being criticised. Criticisms were likely to focus on excesses and scandals, rather than attacking the principle of witchcraft prosecution or the idea that witches existed, but such criticisms could still undermine the credibility of witch-hunting. We shall see in Chapter 10 that recriminations after panics played an important role in the decline of European witch-hunting.

In the aftermath of a panic, the central authorities sometimes issued regulations to govern witchcraft prosecutions in the future. This may seem like a process of limiting prosecutions – and, in the later stages of witch-hunting, this is indeed what it became. But not all such regulations simply limited panics; they could also legitimise witch-hunting by providing improved procedures for it. At the end of a panic in Vaud, Switzerland, in 1600, the central authorities in Bern issued an edict requiring testimonies from no fewer than three witches in order to convict a suspect. This might seem like a limitation, but prosecutions actually went on to run at a higher level between 1600 and 1620 than they had done before the panic. Evidently this edict was part of a negotiation between the two levels of authority, rather than the central authorities taking a stand against local witch-hunting. Even after the edict of 1600, the central authorities still confirmed most of the local sentences.[68]

Thus lessons from panics could produce ratchet effects either upwards or downwards. Successful panics taught one place after another about the importance of the witchcraft threat, and about how to carry out prosecutions. Witch-hunting could spread in an upward ratchet effect, and, in the period from about 1560 to about 1630, it clearly did so. On the other hand, failed panics – panics that were halted prematurely – could produce a downward ratchet effect, teaching one place after another that witchcraft prosecutions were a bad idea. The importance of the 1630 watershed should not be overstated, since both tendencies probably operated in some places both before and after that date, but there does seem to have been an overall downward trend thereafter. This will be discussed further in Chapter 10.

The end of a panic was not the same thing as the end of witch-hunting as a whole. Many panics raised no doubts about witch-hunting; indeed, many appeared to confirm the validity of witch-hunting. The community had been cleansed of witches for the time being, but who knew when the Devil might strike again? A panic that the authorities perceived as 'successful' could provide valuable lessons for the future: people now knew how to deal with witches. Places that had panicked once seem to have been prone to panic again – which suggests that not all panics were socially dysfunctional, or at least were not seen at the time as dysfunctional.

The witch-hunting experience

Witch-hunting touched the lives of large numbers of people in early modern Europe. As pointed out in the statistical discussion in Chapter 1, the total number of people executed for witchcraft was roughly 50,000. Probably that

The dynamics of witch-hunting   261

number could be doubled to take in the people who were formally accused but not executed – either they were tried and acquitted, or the charges were dropped, or there was some other outcome. Probably, too, many more people were identified as witches in their communities but not reported to the authorities; their numbers remain a matter for speculation.

Moreover, very many other people were involved in witch-hunting. For the trial itself, there would probably be a judge, a clerk of court, and one or more officers to act as messengers, doorkeepers and policemen. Some courts had more personnel, for instance 'assessors' (assistants) to the judge, a prosecutor or a defence lawyer. Some courts had juries – three, twelve or fifteen propertied men, usually from the accused witch's locality. Some courts consulted university law faculties. Schematically, something between five and twenty court personnel might be typical.

Then there were the people involved in imprisonment, interrogation and torture. Prisons had a small staff of gaoler and turnkeys. They might carry out torture themselves, or there might be one or more specialist torturers. There could be a pricker, or someone to search for the Devil's mark. Sleep deprivation required a rota of perhaps a dozen people to keep a suspect awake round the clock. We could be looking, again, at between five and twenty people involved in imprisonment.

Many trials involved input from the suspect's community, as witnesses and aggrieved victims. These numbers could vary widely, and during panics there might well be few or no such neighbours involved. One of the big unanswered questions about the European witch-hunt is what proportion of suspects had reputations as witches before their arrest. For a suspect with a reputation, between five and twenty people from the community would be entirely typical.

Burning a witch was a labour-intensive method of execution. Building a pyre required a large quantity of fuel to be carted or carried on people's backs. A stake was a heavy piece of timber that had to be specially carpentered and transported. There might well be a carpentered wooden framework round the pyre, or barriers to keep crowds under control. Perhaps another five to twenty people would be required to organise an execution.

So far we have between twenty and eighty people – say fifty as a rough average – as a typical number whose direct involvement was needed to execute one witch. There were also many more who contributed indirectly to the process. The men higher up the social scale, such as the judge, were attended by personal servants. Tradespeople supplied the court with candles and fuel, or the gaol with food and drink. The court officers might commission a banquet afterwards; even the executioner and his assistants would seek out a tavern to celebrate. Some of the carpenters, rope-makers and blacksmiths who made torture equipment must have known that it was for torturing suspected witches. To the fifty people directly involved we could easily add another fifty who were involved indirectly – a hundred in total. All these hundred had friends and families, whose connection to the witch-hunt was still more indirect but nevertheless real. And executions attracted crowds, which could easily run into the hundreds and sometimes thousands. Members of crowds need not have considered themselves as sharing responsibility for the execution, or even as welcoming the execution, but the execution certainly touched their lives in some way.

During panics, many witches were dealt with in groups. The same court officials, and the same gaolers, could try numerous witches. The numbers of people involved from the community would drop when evidence was sought mainly in the form of confessions rather than neighbours' statements, as often happened during panics. And one stake could have two or three witches tied to it. This means that, while each of the 50,000 executed witches typically had a hundred people contributing to their execution, this was not a hundred *different* people for each witch. Instead a lot of people were involved in multiple trials. Witch-hunting was part of the experience of life for very many people in early modern Europe, and for some the experience was intense.

Conclusion: Social attitudes towards witch-hunting

'Thou shalt not suffer a witch to live', said Exodus 22:18. The idea that witches should be executed may seem simple, but it was not an entirely normal or straightforward idea in early modern Europe. We need to understand the statement 'Witches should be executed' as an *ideological claim*. The idea of 'witches' was itself complicated and contestable. Were people thinking of workers of harmful magic (village witches), or of conspirators in league with the Devil (demonic witches)? As far as we can tell, the common folk thought primarily of village witches, and they did not usually regard execution as their preferred way of dealing with such people. The idea of demonic witches reached them, if at all, from the elite – via sermons, statements at executions, or popular prints. The common folk do not seem actively to have disagreed with these ideas, but it is questionable how far they ever embraced the idea of the demonic witch as their own. Questionable, also, is the extent to which the common folk embraced the idea that witches should be executed.

Did the elites of early modern Europe always agree that 'witches should be executed'? Many of them did, but others could easily be indifferent to the idea. It was argued above that keen central witch-hunting was unusual, while keen witch-hunting by local elites was much more typical. But even local elites were far from united in their support for witch-hunting. One central ruler, Karl, margrave of Burgau, Austria, tried to promote trials in the town of Günzburg, but was thwarted by the town council who ensured that no evidence was found. This pattern was repeated in several other towns in the area, as town councils sought to maintain their autonomy.[69] These councils may have thought that 'witches should be executed', but it was not a priority for them; protecting their own authority from outside interference was more important.

Peasants, too, can occasionally be found demanding that 'witches should be executed'. Such demands are rare, and fall into two main groups. First there were the witch-hunting committees of the Rhine-Moselle region, which, as we have seen, tended to be run by rich peasants. The committees may also have expressed the views of ordinary peasants, but this is not certain. The circumstances of these committees were unusual, and in them we may glimpse peasants learning more than they usually did about demonic witches and the need to execute them. The second group of peasants demanding witchcraft executions was formed by victims of the malefice of an individual village witch. Most victims did not demand the witch's execution; there were, however, some deathbed demands for vengeance, or similar demands by surviving kinsfolk. A witch who was seen to have killed a person was equivalent to a murderer, and murder was a crime for which the death penalty was universally accepted and indeed demanded (though the charge against witches was 'witchcraft', not 'murder'). By contrast, peasants were less likely to demand the execution of a witch who was not accused of having killed a human being. And they rarely if ever seem to have demanded that 'witches should be executed' for the thought-crime of *being* witches – the key demand of the demonologists.

More research is thus needed on popular attitudes to witchcraft executions. Peasants did not usually demand executions, but they did accept them. Did they accept them with reluctance or with enthusiasm? Or – remembering that the idea of the demonic witch was unfamiliar to them – with bewilderment? We know of many executions that were attended by crowds, but the attitude of those crowds remains enigmatic.

Notes

1 Quoted in Rolf Schulte, *Man as Witch: Male Witches in Central Europe*, trans. Linda Froome-Döring (Basingstoke, 2009), 78. Reproduced with permission of Palgrave Macmillan.
2 *Encyclopedia*, iii, 877.
3 Frédéric Max, 'Les premières controverses sur la réalité du sabbat dans l'Italie du XVIe siècle', in Nicole Jacques-Chaquin and Maxime Préaud (eds.), *Le sabbat des sorciers en Europe (XVe–XVIIIe siècles)* (Grenoble, 1993), 55–62, at p. 61.
4 K. Kozlowska, P. Walker, L. McLean and P. Carrive, 'Fear and the defense cascade: clinical implications and management', *Harvard Review of Psychiatry* (9 June 2015), electronic article.
5 Orlando Fernandes, Jr., Liana C. L. Portugal, Rita C. S. Alves, Rafaela R. Campagnoli, Izabela Mocaiber, Isabel P. A. David, Fátima C. S. Erthal, Eliane Volchan, Leticia de Oliveira and Mirtes G. Pereira, 'How you perceive threat determines your behavior', *Frontiers in Human Neuroscience*, 7 (2013), article 632.
6 Quoted in Julian Goodare, 'The Scottish witchcraft panic of 1597', in Julian Goodare (ed.), *The Scottish Witch-Hunt in Context* (Manchester, 2002), 51–72, at p. 63.

264   *The dynamics of witch-hunting*

7 Neil J. Smelser, *Theory of Collective Behavior* (London, 1962), 131, and ch. 6 ('The panic') generally.
8 Stanley Cohen, *Folk Devils and Moral Panics: The Creation of the Mods and Rockers* (3rd edn., London, 2002).
9 Barbara Rosen (ed.), *Witchcraft in England, 1558–1618* (2nd edn., Amherst, Mass., 1991), 72–82.
10 Martine Ostorero, *La chasse aux sorcières dans le Pays de Vaud (XVe–XVIIe siècles)* (Château de Chillon, 2011), 54.
11 Jonathan B. Durrant, *Witchcraft, Gender and Society in Early Modern Germany* (Leiden, 2007), 28, 84.
12 Durrant, *Witchcraft, Gender and Society*, p. xxii.
13 Wolfgang Behringer, *Witches and Witch-Hunts: A Global History* (Cambridge, 2004), 111–12.
14 Gábor Klaniczay, *The Uses of Supernatural Power: The Transformation of Popular Religion in Medieval and Early-Modern Europe*, trans. Susan Singerman (Princeton, NJ, 1990), 158–9.
15 H. C. Erik Midelfort, 'Witch hunting and the domino theory', in James Obelkevich (ed.), *Religion and the People, 800–1700* (Chapel Hill, NC, 1979), 277–88, at p. 284.
16 Victoria Carr, 'The countess of Angus's escape from the North Berwick witch-hunt', in Julian Goodare (ed.), *Scottish Witches and Witch-Hunters* (Basingstoke, 2013), 34–48.
17 William Monter, 'Witch trials in Continental Europe, 1560–1660', in Bengt Ankarloo, Stuart Clark and William Monter, *Witchcraft and Magic in Europe: The Period of the Witch Trials* (London, 2002), 1–52, at p. 49.
18 Marie-Sylvie Dupont-Bouchat, Willem Frijhoff and Robert Muchembled, *Prophètes et sorciers dans les Pays-bas, XVIe–XVIIIe siècle* (Paris, 1978), 129–32; Rita Voltmer, 'Witch-finders, witch-hunters or kings of the sabbath? The prominent role of men in the mass persecutions of the Rhine-Meuse area (sixteenth-seventeenth centuries)', in Alison Rowlands (ed.), *Witchcraft and Masculinities in Early Modern Europe* (Basingstoke, 2009), 74–99, at pp. 87–8.
19 Gary F. Jensen, 'Time and social history: problems of atemporality in historical analysis with illustrations from research on early modern witch hunts', *Historical Methods*, 30 (1997), 46–57.
20 Wolfgang Behringer, 'Weather, hunger and fear: origins of the European witch-hunts in climate, society and mentality', *German History*, 13 (1995), 1–27; Wolfgang Behringer, 'Climatic change and witch-hunting: the impact of the Little Ice Age on mentalities', *Climatic Change*, 43 (1999), 335–51.
21 Julian Goodare, 'Scottish witchcraft in its European context', in Julian Goodare, Lauren Martin and Joyce Miller (eds.), *Witchcraft and Belief in Early Modern Scotland* (Basingstoke, 2008), 26–50, at pp. 29–30.
22 Robert Muchembled, 'The witches of the Cambrésis: the acculturation of the rural world in the sixteenth and seventeenth centuries', in Obelkevich (ed.), *Religion and the People*, 221–76, at p. 240.
23 *Encyclopedia*, ii, 426.
24 Robert Walinski-Kiehl, 'Witch-hunting and state-building in the bishoprics of Bamberg and Würzburg, *c*.1570–1630', in Johannes Dillinger, Jürgen M. Schmidt and Dieter R. Bauer (eds.), *Hexenprozess und Staatsbildung: Witch-Trials and State-Building* (Bielefeld, 2008), 245–64, at pp. 258–9.
25 Alfred Soman, 'Le rôle des Ardennes dans la décriminalisation de la sorcellerie en France', *Revue historique ardennaise*, 23 (1988), 23–45, reprinted in Alfred Soman, *Sorcellerie et justice criminelle: Le parlement de Paris (16e–18e siècles)* (Aldershot, 1992).

26 Pedro Ciruelo, *A Treatise Reproving All Superstitions and Forms of Witchcraft*, ed. and trans. Eugene A. Maio and D'Orsay W. Pearson (Rutherford, NJ, 1977), 294.
27 Rainer Decker, *Witchcraft and the Papacy*, trans. H. C. Erik Midelfort (Charlottesville, Va., 2008), 83.
28 Christian Pfister, 'Climatic extremes, recurrent crises and witch hunts: strategies of European societies in coping with exogenous shocks in the late sixteenth and early seventeenth centuries', *Medieval History Journal*, 10 (2007), 33–73.
29 Dupont-Bouchat et al., *Prophètes et sorciers dans les Pays-bas*, 100–1.
30 Durrant, *Witchcraft, Gender and Society*, 20–1.
31 Franck Mercier, 'La vauderie de Lyon a-t-elle eu lieu? Un essai de recontextualisation (Lyon, vers 1430-1440?)', in Martine Ostorero, Georg Modestin and Kathrin Utz Tremp (eds.), *Chasses aux sorcières et démonologie: Entre discours et pratiques (XIVe–XVIIe siècles)* (Firenze, 2010), 27–44.
32 Midelfort, 'Witch hunting and the domino theory', 281.
33 Wolfgang Behringer, 'Witchcraft and the media', in Marjorie E. Plummer and Robin B. Barnes (eds.), *Ideas and Cultural Margins in Early Modern Germany* (Farnham, 2009), 217–36.
34 Alison Rowlands, *Witchcraft Narratives in Germany: Rothenburg, 1561–1652* (Manchester, 2003), 25–6.
35 Quoted in Johannes Dillinger, *Evil People: A Comparative Study of Witch Hunts in Swabian Austria and the Electorate of Trier*, trans. Laura Stokes (Charlottesville, Va., 2009), 150.
36 Quoted in Hans de Waardt, 'Witchcraft and wealth: the case of the Netherlands', in Brian P. Levack (ed.), *The Oxford Handbook of Witchcraft in Early Modern Europe and Colonial America* (Oxford, 2013), 232–48, at p. 237.
37 Quoted in Robert Muchembled, *Sorcières, justice et société aux 16e et 17e siècles* (Paris, 1987), 96–7.
38 Quoted in Gustav Henningsen, *The Witches' Advocate: Basque Witchcraft and the Spanish Inquisition, 1609–1614* (Reno, Nev., 1980), 18.
39 Quoted in Robert Muchembled, 'Satanic myths and cultural reality', in Bengt Ankarloo and Gustav Henningsen (eds.), *Early Modern European Witchcraft: Centres and Peripheries* (Oxford, 1991), 139–60, at p. 142.
40 Behringer, 'Weather, hunger and fear', 11.
41 Quoted in François Bordes, *Sorciers et sorcières: Procès de sorcellerie en Gascogne et pays Basque* (Toulouse, 1999), 64.
42 Quoted in Francis Bavoux, *Hantises et diableries dans la terre abbatiale de Luxeuil: D'un procès de l'Inquisition (1529) à l'épidémie démoniaque de 1628–1630* (Monaco, 1956), 129.
43 *Encyclopedia*, iii, 773–4.
44 Clive Holmes, 'Women: witnesses and witches', *Past and Present*, 140 (Aug. 1993), 45–78, at p. 56.
45 Muchembled, *Sorcières, justice et société*, 136–40.
46 Martine Ostorero, 'La chasse aux sorcières dans le Pays de Vaud (1430–1530): Bilan des recherches', *Schweizerische Zeitschrift für Geschichte/Revue suisse d'histoire/Rivista storica svizzera*, 52 (2002), 109–14, at pp. 112–13.
47 Martine Ostorero, *'Folâtrer avec les démons': Sabbat et chasse aux sorciers à Vevey (1448)* (2nd edn., Lausanne, 2008), 58–64.
48 William Monter, 'Toads and eucharists: the male witches of Normandy, 1564–1660', *French Historical Studies*, 20 (1997), 563–95, at p. 575.
49 Quoted in Edward Bever, *The Realities of Witchcraft and Popular Magic in Early Modern Europe: Culture, Cognition and Everyday Life* (Basingstoke, 2008), 387.
50 *Encyclopedia*, iii, 682–5.
51 Muchembled, 'Satanic myths and cultural reality', 145–6.

266 *The dynamics of witch-hunting*

52 Robin Briggs, *Witches and Neighbours: The Social and Cultural Context of European Witchcraft* (2nd edn., Oxford, 2002), 344.
53 Brian P. Levack, *The Witch-Hunt in Early Modern Europe* (3rd edn., Harlow, 2006), 186.
54 Levack, *Witch-Hunt*, 188.
55 Monter, 'Witch trials in Continental Europe', 9.
56 Briggs, *Witches and Neighbours*, 96–102 and *passim*.
57 Johannes Dillinger, 'Terrorists and witches: popular ideas of evil in the early modern period', *History of European Ideas*, 30 (2004), 167–82.
58 William G. Naphy, *Plagues, Poisons and Potions: Plague Spreading Conspiracies in the Western Alps, c.1530–1640* (Manchester, 2002).
59 The following discussion draws on numerous studies, including Tommaso Astarita, *Village Justice: Community, Family, and Popular Culture in Early Modern Italy* (Baltimore, Md., 1999); Michael J. Braddick and John Walter (eds.), *Negotiating Power in Early Modern Society: Order, Hierarchy and Subordination in Britain and Ireland* (Cambridge, 2001); Julian Goodare, *The Government of Scotland, 1560–1625* (Oxford, 2004), ch. 11; Mia Korpiola, '"Not without the consent and goodwill of the common people": the community as a legal authority in medieval Sweden', *Journal of Legal History*, 35 (2014), 95–119; Werner Rösener, *The Peasantry of Europe*, trans. Thomas M. Barker (Oxford, 1994), ch. 10; David Sabean, 'The communal basis of pre-1800 peasant uprisings in western Europe', *Comparative Politics*, 8 (1976), 355–64.
60 Bernd Roeck, 'Urban witch trials', *Magic, Ritual, and Witchcraft*, 4 (2009), 82-9.
61 E. W. Monter, 'Witchcraft in Geneva, 1537–1662', *Journal of Modern History*, 43 (1971), 179–204.
62 María Tausiet, *Urban Magic in Early Modern Spain: Abracadabra Omnipotens*, trans. Susannah Howe (Basingstoke, 2014), 17–18, 29, 124–42.
63 Alistair Henderson, 'The urban geography of witch-hunting in Scotland', in Goodare (ed.), *Scottish Witches and Witch-Hunters*, 177–95.
64 Muchembled, 'Satanic myths and cultural reality', 156–7.
65 Valerie Kivelson, *Desperate Magic: The Moral Economy of Witchcraft in Seventeenth-Century Russia* (Ithaca, NY, 2013); W. F. Ryan, 'The witchcraft hysteria in early modern Europe: was Russia an exception?', *Slavonic and East European Review*, 76 (1988), 56–74.
66 Briggs, *Witches and Neighbours*, 345–8.
67 Bengt Ankarloo, 'Sweden: the mass burnings (1668–76)', in Ankarloo and Henningsen (eds.), *Early Modern European Witchcraft*, 285–318.
68 Ostorero, *La chasse aux sorcières dans le Pays de Vaud*, 57–9, 68.
69 Dillinger, *Evil People*, 111–13.

9 Women, men and witchcraft

> Why there are more female witches than male witches.... Bodin says very clearly that it is not on account of the weakness and fragility of the sex, since some women were seen to endure torture more unswervingly than men ... It would thus be more the effect of the bestial cupidity [i.e. greed] that pushes and reduces woman to these extremes, into which she throws herself willingly to delight in her carnal appetites, to avenge herself, or for other novel and unusual experiences that are seen at these assemblies. This caused certain philosophers to locate woman between man and the brute beasts.
>
> Pierre de Lancre, France, 1612[1]

Introduction

Today we tend to think of witches as female, and there may even be a sense in which witches have always been thought of as female. However, men formed a majority of the small numbers tried for harmful magic in the middle ages, up to about 1350. After that date, women overtook them, and the proportion of women continued to rise in the fifteenth and sixteenth centuries. The fact that the great European witch-hunt was directed mostly at women is one of the single most important facts about it, and calls for careful examination.

A female majority and a male minority

No complete statistics exist for the great European witch-hunt, but overall the proportion of women was about 80 per cent – a huge female majority.[2] Yet the male minority of 20 per cent complicates the gender issue. We have to ask, not only why *most* witches were women, but also why *some* were men. Both questions must be pursued together; if we lose sight of either, we may go astray.

An understanding of the implications of '80 per cent' and '20 per cent' may begin by considering the few places where men formed a high proportion of witches, or even occasionally a majority. Two of the most notable were Normandy and Estonia. In Normandy, there were 278 recorded accusations against men, and 103 against women (73 per cent men); the authorities were particularly concerned about a tradition of shepherds magically misusing the Catholic sacraments.[3] In Estonia there were 116 accusations against men and 77 against women (60 per cent men).[4]

The fact that there were more male than female witches in Normandy and Estonia has been much repeated, and is sometimes used to argue against the importance of a female majority in the European witch-hunt. The argument tends to run: the female majority was usually 80 per cent, but sometimes there was a male majority – which reduces the importance of the female majority. However, this argument misunderstands these statistics. Witches were not 'usually' 80 per cent women: they were 80 per cent *on average*. An average, by definition, contains individual figures varying from it in both directions.

Thus, some areas prosecuted *more* than 80 per cent women, and these deserve full attention in understanding the 80 per cent average. There was a very high proportion of women in the Netherlands – between 90 and 95 per cent.[5] Strikingly, a few places prosecuted 100 per cent women, such as Holland in the Netherlands, the val de Lièpvre in Alsace, or Zagreb in Croatia.[6] Whenever we think of the men of Normandy and Estonia, we should think of the women of Holland, Lièpvre and Zagreb. No significant places had anywhere near 100 per cent male witches – even Normandy and Estonia prosecuted large female minorities; but it was possible to have only female witches.

Moreover, the areas with male majorities, like Normandy and Estonia, all prosecuted tiny numbers of witches. Proportionately, one of the largest male majorities was in Iceland, where 110 men were accused out of 120 in total – of whom only 22 were executed, 21 men and one woman. In percentage terms, this gives us a statistic of 95 per cent men executed – but the actual numbers are so small that, in Germany, some *villages* experienced a larger death toll. It may seem invidious to argue about numbers when the execution of even one witch can be recognised as a human tragedy, but it is worth studying these numbers if they can give us a clearer sense of causation.

Thus, a pattern can be identified in which it was possible to have a male majority among the witches in a given region – but only so long as the prosecutions remained at a low level. There were concerns in Normandy about shepherds practising magic, but otherwise relatively little concern about witchcraft. If the Normandy authorities had become more concerned about witchcraft in general, and had started to prosecute a large number of witches, it is inconceivable that men would have remained in the majority. Finland started off prosecuting mostly men, in small numbers, but switched to a female majority in the seventeenth century when numbers of witches grew and prosecutions came to be based on the demonic pact.[7] As for Normandy, large-scale prosecutions did in fact occur in one corner of it: the Channel Islands, culturally and linguistically part of the duchy of Normandy, but ruled by the English crown. The Channel Islands held chain-reaction trials based on pact and sabbat, in which women heavily outnumbered men; these women are omitted from the usual statistics for 'Normandy'. Overall, then, these Normandy statistics display two related patterns: mainland Normandy had light prosecutions and a male majority, while the Channel Islands had heavy prosecutions and a female majority. Other places had light prosecutions and a *female* majority – there was nothing inevitable about a male majority here. But the male-majority pattern was only ever found in areas of light prosecutions. The places that prosecuted *large* numbers of witches all, without exception, prosecuted a high proportion of women.

What this means is that there were social pressures all over Europe favouring the selection of women as witches – pressures that created the overall female majority. These pressures were not so strong as to exclude men altogether, but they created *probabilities*. These probabilities can be understood statistically. If you throw two dice, you will probably not get a double six. This statement is perfectly true even though people do sometimes get double sixes. (The chance of getting a double six, by the way, is not one in twelve as some might think, but one in thirty-six; the laws of probability are not simple.) The equivalent statement about witch-hunting is: if you examine the sex ratio of witches in any region, you will probably find a large female majority. This statement is perfectly true even though a small number of regions have male majorities. We should not describe these male majorities as 'exceptions to a rule', as if this somehow undermined the rule. They were *variations from an average*. An average, by definition, has variations from it in both directions; that is how averages work. So, having established that the female majority and male minority existed, the rest of this chapter will seek to explain them.

Patriarchy

Early modern Europe was a patriarchal society, in which men wielded almost all of the power – as husbands of subordinate wives, as fathers of deferential children, as masters of obedient servants, as lords and kings of deferential subjects, and as priests and pastors of anxious congregations. Men controlled all the courts which made decisions on crimes. Men preached all the sermons and wrote all the books. Men owned almost all of the property and occupied almost all of the prestigious jobs. Women's roles were largely restricted to acting as wives and mothers, organising domestic comforts for men, providing a labour force in subordinate occupations, and bearing sons to inherit the men's property and daughters to continue providing these services.

Patriarchy was not in itself a direct cause of witch-hunting. After all, patriarchy had existed long before, and continued long afterwards; it may be instructive to consider how much of it is still with us. Patriarchy, like village quarrels, is best seen as a vital background factor rather than a determining cause of the rise or decline of witch-hunting. It thus provided essential preconditions for witch-hunting. And, because witch-hunting occurred in a patriarchal society, patriarchy shaped the way in which it occurred.

Although patriarchy changed little during our period, there were one or two relevant developments. In particular, the third quarter of the sixteenth century was not only the period when mass witch-hunting took off: it was also a period of unprecedented female rule. After centuries of rule by kings, there now came to be queens ruling in their own right in England and Scotland, and women ruling as regents in France and the Netherlands. This led to some respectful treatises defending female rule, but also to criticism and dismay. The title of John Knox's 1558 tract said it all: *The First Blast of the Trumpet Against the Monstrous Regiment* [i.e. rule] *of Women*. And, while Knox's language was heated, his arguments were mainstream. Female rulers worried male elites. It would be hard to make a direct link between these worries and the rise of witch-hunting, but the issue may have been there in the background.

Patriarchy did not simply oppress women and exploit them; it also gave them recognised and manageable roles. These roles clearly subordinated women, but offered them some kind of livelihood and stability. This legitimised the whole system. The roles of wives and mothers were meaningful enough to provide women with at least some compensation for their subordinate position. The fact that some women valued their roles would be important in leading them to accuse other women of witchcraft – because witchcraft might be seen as threatening women's roles.

Although patriarchy was often assumed to be natural, it was fostered deliberately by political action. Laws and customs explicitly gave men preferential access to property, and kept women out of privileged occupations. Patriarchy was also deliberately defended. Demonologists like Krämer, Weyer and Bodin disagreed about much, but all agreed on this point: women needed to be controlled. The ways in which witch-hunting functioned to control women will need further attention.

Misogyny and stereotyping

Alongside patriarchy went misogyny – the deliberate denigration and negative stereotyping of women. Later in this chapter there will be more about stereotyping of witches themselves, but female witch stereotypes fitted within a broader pattern of stereotyping of women, so it is best to begin with a general discussion of stereotypes and how they functioned.

The leading Reformer, Martin Luther, exemplified the stereotyping of women when he remarked that it was obvious that women were meant to sit at home and be 'domestic', because they had narrow chests and broad hips. Men, by contrast, could be seen to possess 'wisdom', because they had broad chests and narrow hips.[8] Stereotyping involves generalising: do *all* women have broad hips? Stereotyping usually involves singling out the stereotyped group, so it is noteworthy that Luther commented on men's unusually narrow hips – to some extent he was stereotyping men as well. Stereotyping also involves limited thought: the connection with male 'wisdom' is far from apparent. Finally, stereotyping tends to confuse nature and social role: if women do most of the domestic work in a given society, that does not mean that they are *naturally* better at it.

Stereotypes are prejudices. A 'prejudice' is a 'pre-judged' opinion, reached without examining the individual circumstances. We tend to think of prejudices as being negative, probably because so many pre-judged opinions are indeed negative, but there can also be positive prejudices in favour of some groups. Social psychologists see the process of stereotyping as part of a broader process by which people divide themselves, and others around them, into 'ingroups' and 'outgroups'. Members of the ingroup think of themselves in positive terms, and define themselves by contrast to the negative terms in which they describe the outgroup. Both of these processes involve some stereotyping, but the outgroup attracts more stereotyping than the ingroup, because less is known about it. Statements about a person in an outgroup tend to be simple, generalised assumptions about the person's group, lacking detailed knowledge about the person as an individual. It is the stereotyping of outgroups that concerns us here.

When prejudices are linked to power, this leads to discrimination and oppression. Luther's wife, Katharina von Bora, may have held negative prejudices about men, but, if she did, she was not in a position to act on them. Luther had power, so his prejudices shaped society in a patriarchal way. Research has shown that those in power tend to rely more heavily on stereotypes – either because they have more need to categorise people in groups, or because stereotypes help them to maintain their power, or both.[9] The stereotyped ideas that we are considering here were ideas that were, in principle, shared both by the elite and by the common folk, though they could use them differently.

Stereotypes are thus, in a broad sense, political. Saying that an ingroup is good, or that an outgroup is bad, is an ideological claim. In practice, such claims are more often used to justify or enhance inequalities than to promote equality. An ingroup may be able to gain more resources by denigrating an outgroup with which it is in actual or potential conflict for those resources. This does not mean that people create a stereotype by cynically calculating that it is in their interest to do so: rather, they do so because they find the stereotype believable and meaningful. Unfortunately, we often find it easy to believe that people with whom we do not want to share our resources are bad people. This is particularly noticeable with misogyny, since men maintained their grip on material resources in part by denigrating women. Whether it applies directly to witchcraft stereotypes is not so clear; with the exception of the refusal-guilt syndrome (discussed in Chapter 4), witches were not thought of as people who had to be denied access to material resources. But, of course, most witches were women, and patriarchy did involve denying women access to material resources. And stereotypes do not have to be about material resources; they can be about moral purity or cultural deviance, for instance. Stereotypes of women inevitably fed into stereotypes of witches.

There were several different early modern stereotypes of women, and indeed several different ways of constructing such stereotypes. Women could be defined by negatives or absences of men's positive qualities, rather than by qualities of their own. Thus they were disordered, irrational, faithless, because men were thought of with positive human values: ordered, rational, faithful.[10] Or the stereotypes could be binary opposites of different women, with positive and negative poles. The most influential binary example was the Virgin Mary – virtuous, pure, loving, maternal, but not overtly sexual – as opposite to Eve – sinful, lustful and obviously sexual. When thinkers (mostly male) discussed what women were like, they tended to compare them to Mary or to Eve. The impossibility for real women of being like Mary made it easier to think of them as being like Eve. Like most women, Mary and Eve were not defined in their own terms, but in terms of their relationship to men. There were four main stereotypes of women in sixteenth-century literature, of whom one was positive – the Good Woman. The others were the Wanton (sexually promiscuous), the Shrew (argumentative) and the Witch.[11]

Men thought of women in sexual terms, because it was the sexual aspect of women's identity that marked them out as not-men. Women had unusual bodies – unusual to men, that is. The basis of women's unusual nature was their possession of a womb, which was certainly thought to be an unusual organ: it was a hungry and unpredictable thing that could wander physically around the body. To prevent this, the womb should be fed with sexual intercourse and pregnancy. The ancient Greek physicians, whose work underpinned medical knowledge in our period, had argued that a woman who retained her virginity as an adult was likely to become insane. If the womb started to wander, this would cause a woman to become hysterical; the term 'hysteria' derives from the Greek word for the womb. Related to the womb was menstruation, which could be used to explain the evil eye. Irregular periods caused malignant fluid to build up in the body, which in turn led to an emission of harmful matter from the eyes.

The woman's body connected her, not only with the mysteries of birth, but also with those of death. Physical, emotional displays of mourning and grief were expected from women, but not from men. This was relevant to witchcraft because one widely-discussed attribute of the witch was an inability to shed tears. Various demonologists commented on this, and inability to shed tears also surfaced in numerous trial records, especially in Germany. Although demonologists usually wrote about witches in a formally gender-neutral way, it seems clear that they were thinking here of women. And the individual witches who were accused of not having shed tears were virtually all women.

Although demonologists used negative stereotypes of women, they were usually mindful of the fact that witches were mostly women, rather than wholly women. Thus they sought to explain why witches were more likely to be women. They rarely produced binary arguments about why witches were always women and never men. They could argue that witches were irrational, and that women also tended to be irrational; but they had no difficulty with the idea that some women were rational, and indeed that some men were irrational.

This may be related to the standard intellectual way of understanding sexual difference in early modern times. Male and female were not seen as 'opposite sexes'; instead there was only one true model of humanity, the male one. Normal humans were men. Women were not a separate sex, but a weak and imperfect deviation from the male norm.[12] It could even be suggested that women were not fully human. Thinkers expressing this idea did so cautiously, because Christian theology was clear that women had immortal souls, while animals did not. Still, the idea of women as subhuman came up from time to time in demonology, as in the quotation from Pierre de Lancre at the head of this chapter. The extra teats with which some English witches suckled their animal familiars were partly an expression of demonic femininity, but also (separately) an expression of demonic animality.

Men stereotyped women in the way in which they thought about offences they committed. Men's offences did not define their entire identity, but once a woman had committed certain offences, they did. Once a woman was a 'scold', or a 'harlot', or a 'witch', then that was *all* she was. A study of the church courts in Canterbury, England, has shown that women accused of magical offences were called 'witches'; men accused of the same offences were not.[13] This illustrates the way in which stereotyping, especially of outgroups, involves simplification.

Overall, then, stereotypes did not simply convey a message that 'Women are like this'. The message was usually structured as 'Bad women are like this, good women are like that'. Most of the time, women as well as men could relate to the stereotypes; most women could assume (or hope) that they themselves were good, and that it was *other* women who were bad. One of the ways in which stereotypes assist the exercise of power is by dividing less powerful people among themselves. Here, the challenge for a woman was to prove, to herself and to others, that she really was good in patriarchal terms. In a man's world, women found it hard to fit in, but they mostly tried to do so.

Stereotypes of female witches

There were several different witch stereotypes, all of which were gendered in some way. Collectively, witches might be 80 per cent female, but, when people thought of the kind of person who might be a witch, they imagined someone with a specific gender – usually a woman. Indeed, as we shall see, they could imagine various different types of women as witches. There were also distinctly masculine witch stereotypes, which will be discussed in the next section. The present section will isolate the principal stereotypes of female witches – the standardised images that people thought of when they thought of a female witch. Here we should distinguish between stereotype witches and actual witches. Real individual witches did not necessarily display all the elements of any witchcraft stereotype – indeed, probably only a small minority did; but labels based on stereotypes could nevertheless be attached to them.

There were various different stereotypes of witches. Some earlier historians assumed that there was only one stereotype of a witch, and tried to group all cases around 'the witch stereotype'. It is better to see stereotypes as plural. These plural stereotypes could overlap; the idea that witches tended to be old women, for instance, was related to the idea that witches tended to be widows. However, it helps to keep such ideas separate for present purposes. Many widows were old, but that is a point about social profiles of actual witches, rather than about ideas of witches. The *idea* of the old woman, and the *idea* of the widow, were linked separately with the idea of the witch.

Let us begin with the most common stereotype, which was so common that it can be called the 'standard stereotype'. The standard stereotype of a witch was a quarrelsome woman who exercised magical power by harming her neighbours. This was the core of the idea of the village witch, as will be recognised from Chapter 4. Real village witches were not always women, but the idea of the woman who cursed her neighbours was a powerful, and gendered, idea.

The idea of the quarrelsome woman was constructed as an inverse of the ideal woman desired by men. For men, the ideal woman was submissively silent. Complaints about female 'unruliness' and 'disorder' were made whenever the subject of women came up. Women were notorious for 'scolding' – a term for disorderly public quarrelling. The term was used only about women; men might quarrel in public, but they were never 'scolds'. And quarrels, as we saw in Chapter 4, were often accompanied by curses. There were some overlaps between insults, threats and curses, but here we need to focus on curses, as it was these that were thought to wield magical power. Curses could be uttered in the heat of the moment, or could be deliberate, ritualised performances.

Public, ritual curses were carried out mainly by women – and were *thought* to be carried out by women. One can very occasionally find men who used curses, such as John Parry, in Wales, whose curse was blamed for the death of Mary Lloyd.[14] Men in Russia were also accused of cursing, apparently because of the prominence of malevolent but professional magical practitioners.[15] But there was no general idea that men's curses mattered. In a New England study, both men and women were shown as having been involved in quarrels, but only women's quarrelsomeness was taken as evidence of witchcraft.[16] Similarly, a Scottish study has indicated that the courts were not interested in men's curses.[17] Presumably this was because men were assumed to assault their enemies physically, or sue them in the courts. Only women were assumed to curse their enemies.

The dangers that people imagined from quarrelsome women went beyond open curses. Women's verbal aggression could be covert and indirect, spreading gossip to undermine a rival, rather than making frontal attacks. Another widely-feared form of covert attack was poisoning. Women were responsible for food preparation; everyone ate food that came from women. We tend to think of poison as a chemical substance, but pre-industrial ideas of poison were more magical. In Poland, poisoning was called 'giving the Devil'.[18] By extension, some people also feared giving food or drink *to* a suspected witch, since by doing so they were symbolically giving away something of themselves – which might give the witch power over them.

If the standard stereotype of the village witch was gendered, what about the demonic witch? Perhaps surprisingly, there was no stereotype of the demonic witch, gendered or otherwise, to parallel the stereotype of the village witch. The demonic witch was constructed around ideas about the Devil, not around ideas about particular kinds of people. Demonological theory did not point to women or men; the demonic pact could be made by anyone. The operative power of curses, too, came from the Devil, not from the witch's innate powers. Nevertheless, demonologists sometimes recognised the importance of women's curses in practice. The *Malleus*'s discussion of cursing was all about old women doing so.[19]

This leads on to the next gendered stereotype of the witch: the old woman as witch. Accusers of witches frequently used phrases like 'old witch' or 'old hag'. Whether or not these women really were old, they were being assimilated to a stereotype that assumed that they were.[20] The commonplace idea that old women were ugly was a logical component of misogynistic ideas about feminine 'vanity': young women were supposedly vain about their beauty, but soon they would be old and ugly. And, just as beauty was associated with virtue, ugliness was associated with wickedness.

Ideas of old women as witches were related to ideas about the menopause – another instance of women being stereotyped by their sexuality. Menopause was thought to occur between the ages of about 45 and 55, with fertility decline seen as a gradual process.[21] Menstruation was seen as the female body's way of ridding itself of impurities. After the menopause, these impurities were no longer released and could build up in the body, making an older woman into a cocktail of dangerous fluids. Moreover, patriarchal assumptions about women included the idea that their function was to bear children, thus making a post-menopausal woman anomalous because she could no longer do so.

Older women were often presented in court with reputations going back many years. This is a complex business, easily over-simplified. It was argued in Chapter 4 that some reputations were probably 'instant reputations', manufactured in retrospect. Another aspect of this may have been that a younger woman could not be such a credible witch because of her youth. Thus, she may have been involved in a quarrel that was followed by misfortune, but neighbours did not connect it so closely to witchcraft. This is discussed in some books as 'taking years to build up a reputation', which is fair enough as far as it goes – but the fact that a woman was younger at the beginning of this process and older at the end of it was an integral and relevant part of the process. A younger woman could not acquire a witchcraft reputation as easily as an older one.

The stereotype of the older woman became more sharply focused when the older woman was a widow – as many older women were in early modern Europe. But not all widows were old, so the stereotype of the widow as witch should be recognised as an independent one. The widow was a worrying figure for anxious men: they knew that she was sexually experienced, and also assumed that she was sexually frustrated and perhaps even predatory. Men's sexual potency was assumed to decline with age, but women's sexual desire – once awakened as the widow's was assumed to have been – was thought to continue and even increase. The widow thus sharpened men's fears of female sexuality.

The widow-as-witch stereotype could be used to attract attention, as in a pamphlet of 1652 about a group of trials in Maidstone, England. The pamphlet focused on six 'most notorious' widows, largely ignoring the fact that five married women and six men had also been arraigned.[22] This case is a good example of the need to distinguish between the recorded social profiles of those accused of witchcraft and the *ideas* that circulated about those accused. Stereotyping is a process of simplifying messy reality in order to create meaning from it.

One obvious fact about the widow was that she lacked a husband – a fact that she shared with women who never married. Patriarchy assumed that normal women were married; marriage was their natural, indeed virtually their only, social role. Wives were important as adjuncts to their husbands. In Mensfelden, Germany, in 1618, a fine of six florins was proposed for calling a married woman a witch.[23] Evidently the authorities did not think that slandering single women mattered – but slandering a married woman would damage her husband. Widows and never-married women were socially weaker; as we shall see, a husband was expected to defend his wife if she was accused of witchcraft. This, however, is a separate point that did not affect ideas about gender stereotyping. People did not think of witches as people who were socially weak – but they did normally think of them as female.

One gendered stereotype of the female witch even imagined her as a woman who was socially stronger than she should be, because she had inherited property. Patriarchal systems of marriage and inheritance meant that property normally went to sons. Women were not expected to inherit property; they were supposed to marry to secure a livelihood. However, inheritance rules rarely barred women altogether, so women did occasionally inherit property. There seems to have been a process of stereotyping at work in the way that such heiresses, socially anomalous, could attract a charge of witchcraft. Catherine David, in Draguignan, France, was accused in 1439 of having given her late father a magical potion that had caused him before his death to disinherit her three sisters in her favour. She had allegedly obtained the potion from a male magical practitioner, Monnet Sinhon, aided by a demon. Both were accused of heresy and witchcraft, though the case collapsed amid a welter of denials and counter-accusations.[24] Distinct patterns of accusations against heiresses have also been identified in New England and in Scotland.[25]

Finally, midwives formed a fearsome stereotype of female witches, at least according to several demonologists. Midwives were associated with magic, because their practical skills in delivering babies were usually accompanied by magical rituals, for instance to ease the pain of childbirth. They could also be called upon to perform emergency baptisms of sickly babies, which was allowed in the Catholic church but viewed with suspicion as an encroachment on the domain of male religious power. Above all, midwives were feared for their supposed association with the infanticidal rites of the witches' sabbat; demonologists assumed that babies stolen by midwives could end up in the cauldron, though they were vague about how this actually occurred. The *Malleus* inveighed against midwives: 'No one harms the Catholic Faith more than midwives.'[26] Midwife witches, it declared, prevented conception, caused miscarriages, stole babies for the sabbat, and dedicated babies to the Devil. Such stereotypical ideas contributed powerfully to the fear of female witches. Yet few actual midwives were prosecuted for witchcraft, for reasons that, as we shall see, help to explain the relationship between witchcraft stereotypes and actual witches.

Stereotypes of male witches

Some ideas about witchcraft pointed towards men, not women. There were various stereotypes of male witches. These were narrower in focus than the stereotypes of female witches. Many women, indeed most, might have been thought to be quarrelsome, while all had sexual attributes that men could find worrying. Male witchcraft stereotypes, by contrast, pointed only towards a few men. The ideas generated by these stereotypes nevertheless had their own importance in witchcraft discourse.

The first masculine stereotype to influence witchcraft was that of the heretic. As we saw in Chapter 2, witches were initially thought of in the fifteenth century as a 'new sect' of heretics. Heresies were imagined as being led by men, because nobody thought that women could be leaders, even though they could be followers. However, the stereotype of the heretical male witch declined in the sixteenth century, because the stereotype of the heretical witch declined. Witches were no longer a heretical sect called 'witches', they were simply witches. Catholics were confronted with Protestant heretics who were clearly not witches, while Protestants themselves rarely used the concept of heresy, preferring terms like 'papistry' or 'superstition'.

Another early masculine stereotype was the necromancer, a figure who had arisen in the late middle ages (as we also saw in Chapter 2). The Catholic church had many poor and under-employed priests, who were hard to supervise and who might turn to dubious activities in order to support themselves. The authorities knew that their knowledge of Latin rituals could be adapted into rituals for summoning demons, and the priest-necromancer became a recognisable male stereotype. Martín de Castañega, in Spain in 1529, complained that 'We see every day in our own experience how poor women and needy clerics take up the office of conjurors, witches, necromancers, and diviners in order to maintain themselves and have enough to eat'.[27] Rather than presenting the necromancer as a masterful figure, however, this seems to assimilate these downtrodden 'needy clerics' to a feminine stereotype. Related to the necromancer was the male magical practitioner with a book of spells (sometimes called a *grimoire*); in eighteenth-century Russia, 126 men and only 10 women were prosecuted for possessing such books.[28]

The witch-priest, though related to the necromancer, became a distinct male stereotype. Catholic priests had powers over the sacraments, and sometimes used their powers in non-approved ways, acting as magical practitioners in response to popular demand. Especially after the Counter-Reformation, the authorities sometimes sought to stamp this out even when they did not regard it as necromancy. Pierre de Lancre in France expressed concern about 'witch-priests', having executed three priests for witchcraft in 1609. He distinguished them from female witches, for whom their sexuality was more prominent.[29] Two priests from Normandy were caught in 1598 with 'a book of diabolical invocations and incantations, with figures, kept inside the breviary'; they were executed.[30] In Catholic countries where numbers of witches were low, like France and Italy, witch-priests could form a significant proportion of the total. They could also contribute demonological material; German witch-priests in Bamberg and Würzburg confessed to unusually detailed sabbats.[31]

Also related to the idea of the necromancer was the idea of the learned magician. Such a man was thought to have grand intellectual ambitions, and to be vulnerable to tempting offers of demonic assistance with his research project. Cornelius Agrippa, a German Renaissance intellectual who was mentioned in Chapter 3, gained a reputation as a stereotypical 'magician'. Even more influential was 'Dr Faust', a German contemporary of Agrippa about whom little is known for certain (not even his full name) – except that he was fiercely criticised for allegedly dealing with demons. Tales about him soon grew to make Faust into a legendary figure; increasingly the tales centred around his pact with the Devil. He was compared to Simon Magus, the wicked magician mentioned in the New Testament. By the late sixteenth century, 'Dr Faust' the learned magician was effectively a stereotype of a particular kind of male witch.

One sensational stereotype of the male witch was the werewolf. Wolves were dangerous predators that lurked in the forests near many a village. The idea that a man might transform himself into a wolf was an ancient one, but it gained fresh life in the sixteenth century. Demonologists all over Europe drew on accounts of werewolves in developing their ideas of shape-shifting witches. However, the *popular* belief in werewolves was confined to a few scattered regions, notably Franche-Comté. In its heartland, werewolf belief was largely assimilated into witch belief by about 1600. After that date, werewolf prosecutions became rare. For a time there were even some female werewolves, a development which seems to have been related to the disintegration of the distinctive male werewolf-witch stereotype.[32]

One stereotype male witch was the man in power. This statement should immediately be qualified: men in power were hardly ever accused of witchcraft. Nevertheless, there were some distinctive features about the few such male witches. Here we are concerned less with real elite men as witches, though there were a few of these, such as George Burroughs in Salem in 1692, the village's former minister. The point here is that the *idea* of powerful male witches was important. Bodin dwelt with horror on the male 'master sorcerer' Trois-eschelles du Maine, who was interviewed by King Charles IX of France. Du Maine allegedly claimed to have a hundred thousand accomplices.[33]

Politically powerful men were sometimes thought to orchestrate witches, which was related to being a witch. The earl of Bothwell, accused during the North Berwick panic in Scotland in 1590-91, was tried (though acquitted) for the crime of 'witchcraft', but the accusations against him were essentially about recruiting and organising witches; he was not said to have cast spells himself. The political power of the nobleman was not the same thing as the magical power of the witch; magical power was a technical skill rather than the ability to rule.

Ideas of patriarchy sometimes fed into stereotypical ideas about the witches' sabbat. When witches were thought of as mainly women, it was easier to imagine male witches if they had authority or some other special role at the sabbat. In Holstein, Germany, male witches were often described as 'captains' of groups of mainly female witches.[34] Musicians were also thought of as male. Bernhardt of Kenn, in Trier, Germany, in 1572, was accused of being the piper to a group of female witches.[35] Women too could imagine male witches having a special role; several female witches in Dieuze, Lorraine, in 1588–89, confessed that their group had a male 'captain' and a male 'fifer'. One woman from the Trier region, Maria, daughter of the mayor of Mertesdorf, was herself described as a 'captain' of witches in 1594, presumably because of her higher social status – but she herself denied being a 'captain', and would confess only to having been one of the cooks.[36]

A few masculine occupations were thought to be magical – notably blacksmiths, who worked closely with that mysterious and powerful thing, fire. Blacksmiths' work in shoeing horses sometimes extended into providing veterinary services of a more or less magical kind; some even healed humans as well. Shepherds and cattle-herders, also usually men, could also develop magical skills through their work with animals. Quite a few male witches were blacksmiths, shepherds or cattle-herders; whether men in these occupations bore a higher risk of accusation has not been proven statistically, but accusations against such men made sense in gendered terms. The same applies to male magical practitioners more generally; whether these formed a 'stereotype' of witches is not so clear, but they will be discussed later in this chapter when we move from discussion of stereotypes to discussion of actual witches.

Masculine witch stereotypes tended to be more unstable than feminine ones, possibly because of the smaller numbers involved. The masculine stereotypes could acquire feminine characteristics, or dissolve into broader concepts that were mainly feminine. The 'heretic' started as a masculine idea, but, once heretical witches began to be imagined in the fifteenth century, they progressively became more feminine. By the time further heresies arose in the sixteenth century, there was no possibility of overlap between witches and Protestants or Anabaptists. The 'werewolf', too, faded away, failing to maintain its distinct masculine identity once men became accused more straightforwardly of witchcraft. It has even been argued that male witches as a whole were conceived as slightly feminine, in the sense that they were seen as weak-minded or foolish – weak-mindedness being seen as a feminine characteristic.[37] This is probably more valid for village witches than for the specific stereotypes that we have been considering here, but it is still important.

Case study: Peasants and early inquisitors

Two neighbouring regions of Switzerland show that the female majority among witches was already well established in the fifteenth century – unless there was an unusual element. Trials in Lucerne, the first region, were carried out in lay courts and involved the suspects' neighbours in testifying against them.[38] Without exception the witnesses were concerned with malefice – against themselves personally, and against their families, farm animals and crops. The witnesses never mentioned the Devil. When the suspects made confessions (under torture), they usually confessed to making a pact with the Devil. The interrogators' knowledge of demonology was limited, however, and the sabbat was not mentioned in a confession until 1549. The witches were tried individually or in very small groups. Between 1398 and 1551 there were at least 69 trials; 63 of the suspects were women and only 6 men. Only about one-sixth of the women were widows, but most were older women. The witnesses saw the suspects as

(continued)

quarrelsome. It is hard to say who initiated the Lucerne trials, but there was clearly a large popular element, and probably the common folk already thought that witchcraft was something largely (but not entirely) practised by women.

Meanwhile, the records of nearby Lausanne show a strikingly different picture. The Lausanne court was an inquisitorial one, with inquisitors familiar with the stereotype of heretical cults. Between 1438 and 1498, 18 men were tried for witchcraft, and only 11 women. All the trials emphasised demonic witchcraft, with a detailed description of how the witch made a pact with the Devil and then attended the sabbat ('*sinagoga*') where the Devil was worshipped. Children were killed, cooked and eaten; promiscuous sex was indulged in, both between male and female witches and between demons and female witches. Allegations of magical harm played only a subordinate role. The female majority in Lucerne was a normal one, while the male majority in Lausanne arose from the inquisitors' specific concerns.

Scapegoating and deviance

Scapegoating theory aims to explain why people blame outgroups for social problems. Classic examples of scapegoating are blaming medieval Jews for the Black Death, or, in more recent times, blaming immigrants for unemployment. To the scholar, these accusations are obviously misguided. However, ordinary people in societies affected by these problems do not know this. Faced with a difficult problem with no immediately obvious cause, people persuade themselves that a distrusted outgroup is to blame. Scapegoating thus operates, not against individuals, but against groups – or, to be more precise, against people for whom their membership of a distrusted group is more important than their individual identity.

People blame a scapegoated group because it is better than doing nothing, and because there is – in their own terms if not in ours – some plausibility to the accusations against the group. The theory of scapegoating treats the beliefs of the community as rational in terms of the community's own knowledge and values, but does not endorse the beliefs. As we saw in Chapters 3 and 4, early modern people could have quite good reasons for thinking that witches caused illnesses or hailstorms – but the chain of reasoning that led them to this conclusion was an indirect one, and we, today, are not obliged to endorse it. Unfortunately, it is not obvious that more careful search for the 'real causes' of illnesses or hailstorms would have been helpful at the time; early modern people, no matter how 'rational' they were, did not know about bacteria or cumulonimbus clouds. Even if they had known about them, they would not necessarily have answered the 'Why did this have to happen to me?' question that lay behind many witchcraft accusations. Scapegoating has a real social function; it helps people make sense of an unfamiliar and threatening situation, and gives them a course of action.

Scapegoating is a response to hatred and fear. This is related to the theory of panic, discussed in Chapter 8. Here we need to ask: how does an excluded outgroup become hated or feared? In the social situation we are considering, the ingroup has more power of a conventional kind – but its members perceive the outgroup as having a grudge against them, loosely related to the fact of the outgroup's exclusion. The ingroup sees the outgroup as envious or resentful. The outgroup would be likely to want to get revenge. And, because they have less conventional power, the outgroup are likely to use unconventional means. Witchcraft is a credible weapon in these circumstances. Quarrelsome women were readily believed to use magic to harm others; it was seen as their natural weapon.

Some versions of scapegoating theory argue that people tend to fear an outgroup that is quite similar to themselves. They condemn in others the particular immoral desires that they consciously or subconsciously perceive in themselves, 'projecting' their own wicked thoughts onto the outgroup. Opposing participants in wars tend to assert their own country's virtue, and their opponents' wickedness, in quite similar ways. In psychological terms, this 'projection' of wickedness onto the enemy helps the community to justify itself: it's all the fault of the other lot. This does not apply to all scapegoating, however, and the similarity of accuser and scapegoat should not be over-emphasised. At an individual level, people who have specific immoral desires tend to empathise with people who put those desires into practice, and to seek milder, not harsher, punishments for them.[39] It seems clear, however, that witch stereotypes were sufficiently different from almost all men, and from most women most of the time, to enable these men and women to project their hostility onto such witches. Blaming witches could reassert control and reaffirm moral values.[40]

These ideas can be developed by relating them to sociological theories of 'deviance'. These theories describe the way in which a majority of conventional people relate to a minority of unconventional people – the 'deviants'. The deviants transgress the social norms of the majority, while more conservative people among the majority denounce the deviants and demand their punishment. This defines and reinforces social norms, underlines types of behaviour that transgress those norms, and labels and stigmatises individuals and groups who carry out the behaviour. Sometimes the behaviour is invented (either deliberately or through ignorant misunderstanding), and the individuals and groups are accused falsely; this usually happens when people perceive a pressing need to rally the pure community against the deviant, and do not stop to question the evidence. The social norms being defined and defended are often specific to one society – they are 'socially constructed' rather than universal traits of human behaviour.

Here it may help to compare ideas about witches with ideas about another 'deviant' group in early modern Europe: the Jews. Christians hated Jews, not because they harmed Christians directly, but because they were a visibly separate minority, affronting community values by attending their synagogue instead of the church. They were classic deviants. However, Christians did blame Jews for crimes, indeed horrific crimes – notably the 'blood libel', the accusation that Jews engaged in ritual child-murder. Now, people did not start with the idea of the blood libel (which was, after all, invented) and deduce from this that Jews were deviant. It was *because* Jews were deviant that people imagined that they would commit ritual child-murder. Similarly, it was *because* women were deviant – all fully normal humans were male – that people imagined that women were more likely to commit witchcraft.

A typical way in which this worked was that people gossiped about a quarrelsome woman, and identified her as a deviant. Meanwhile, misfortunes started to occur, and people decided that these formed a pattern and that the woman was responsible. Only then were the misfortunes defined as crimes rather than accidents. This pattern, familiar to us from Chapter 4, contrasts with the way in which conventional criminals were identified. When villagers wanted to identify the person responsible for a recent theft, they did not ask 'Who best fits the stereotype of a thief?' or 'Is there anyone I've offended recently, who might thus have a motive to steal my goods?' Instead they looked for the person who actually had the stolen goods, using short and direct chains of reasoning. But, when thinking about a recent bewitching, people did think about their relationship with their neighbours. One point of the present chapter is to show more clearly why it was that they tended to identify women – especially older women – as responsible for the bewitchings.

The godly state and gendered offences

The godly state, arising from the Reformation and Counter-Reformation, sought to prosecute a wider variety of offences that it believed to be antisocial. Several of these offences were gendered, usually being associated mainly with women. Mostly they were victimless offences – they transgressed social norms rather than harming individuals. The godly state and the courts have been discussed in Chapters 6 and 7; here we need to bring out the relevance of gender.

The rise of witchcraft prosecutions created a major women's crime – and this formed part of a broader pattern. Fewer women than men were convicted of crimes in the early modern period (a pattern that continues today); typically 10 per cent of convicted criminals were women, 90 per cent men. Their crimes also tended to be less serious: petty theft rather than homicides or robberies.[41] There can be a temptation to think of this as a straightforward reflection of real behaviour: fewer women really committed crimes.

284 *Women, men and witchcraft*

There may be an element of this, but 'crime' is ultimately something defined by the authorities, and here we are looking at the authorities' interest in crime. What we find is a rise in the prosecution of specific women's crimes, and in other moral offences with a gendered element.

This rise in gendered offences, along with the rise in witchcraft prosecutions, occurred in the sixteenth century. Late medieval authorities had done little to regulate sexual behaviour. Or, at least, the regulations they had were relaxed and liberal. Many towns had licensed brothels. Many parish priests lived openly with concubines. Extra-marital sex was not approved of, but it was not routinely punished. Now, however, this changed drastically. To begin with, marriage was more tightly regulated. This was partly because, with the Reformation, different jurisdictions began to have different rules on marriage. Protestants allowed divorce for adultery, for instance, while Catholics did not. As a result, each jurisdiction had to police its own rules more carefully – and this extended into a broader attack on ungodliness. The church courts became more active, as we saw in Chapter 6. Instead of waiting until people brought disputes before them, they started to seek out offences against what they saw as public morality.

Much of this policing activity was related to sexuality, and thus to gender roles. There were attempts to crack down on adultery, fornication, scolding, prostitution and sodomy. This was not simply about criminalising women, but it was about criminalising offences linked to sexuality. Increased concern over witchcraft was often linked to these. The early panic in Arras, in 1459–60, was linked to a concern over prostitution; most of the women arrested were prostitutes, and several of the men arrested were their clients. Several of the witches were accused of 'sodomy' with the Devil – sodomy usually meaning anal intercourse.[42] There was even a remarkable case in 1626 in Saragossa, Aragon, after two old women, Margalida Escuder and Juana Bardaxi, confessed in detail to demonic witchcraft and sex with the Devil. The inquisitorial judges declared them guilty of heresy – and sentenced them to one year's imprisonment in the city's House of Penance, an institution designed to reform former prostitutes.[43] These witches seem to have been assumed to be equivalent to prostitutes.

Infanticide was another offence comparable to witchcraft, with a significant gender dimension. Most people prosecuted for infanticide were women who had killed their illegitimate babies or allowed them to die; thus there was a link with the sexual offences of adultery and fornication. Infanticide attracted little official interest in medieval times, but the rise of the godly state saw a surge of infanticide prosecutions. A broad correlation between this and the rate of prosecution for witchcraft has been observed in Germany and in England.[44]

Another gendered offence was begging – though in this case the emphasis was on men. The early modern period saw a rise in begging, as a result of the sixteenth-century economic downturn and the destructiveness of seventeenth-century wars. Begging could be associated with witchcraft through the refusal-guilt syndrome, as we saw in Chapter 4; but it also had gendered implications. Wandering beggars were thought of as sexually promiscuous (partly because restrictive marriage regulations made it hard for them to marry). More beggars were men than women. In the seventeenth century, some authorities ordered crackdowns on beggars, and in a few places this led to beggars – mainly male beggars – being stigmatised as witches. In Carinthia, Austria, in the mid to late seventeenth century, witch-hunting grew although it was declining in nearby regions, and about two-thirds of the accused were male beggars.[45] Here, therefore, we see a state that was broadening its attack on gendered, deviant offences; usually such attacks were on women, but this one was on men.

Another male offence related to witchcraft was sodomy. In fifteenth-century Basel and Lucerne, Switzerland, prosecutions for witchcraft and for sodomy seem to have been linked: both were mild in Basel, both were intense in Lucerne. The link between these offences also appeared in language. The Swiss-German term '*ketzerei*', originally meaning 'heresy', extended its meaning in the fifteenth century so that it could also be used to mean sodomy, bestiality or witchcraft – a significant combination of terms.[46]

Women, men and magical practice

Everyday magical practices were gendered because of the broader gender division of labour in the village. Women bore and nurtured children, they prepared food and did other housework, they tended cows and did milking and dairying, and they harvested grain crops. Men did ploughing, building and carting, they looked after horses and sheep, and they carried out village crafts like carpentry. All these activities were supported by magical rituals, and all could be perceived as suffering interference through harmful magic. Magic was gendered but universal.

However, women's activities were more associated with harmful magic. The real charms that women recited over their butter churns, or murmured to their cows, thus became linked in everyone's minds – including their own – with the imagined spells that would turn butter sour, or cause cows to give blood instead of milk. Women preparing food or drink were even more closely linked to witchcraft, for it was through food or drink that magical poisons were feared. Women's knowledge of herbs for cooking came along with a knowledge of herbs for everyday household medicine – but healing knowledge could also be knowledge of how to harm. This was relevant to village witchcraft, and also to demonic witchcraft. Many interrogators, demanding details about the sabbat, focused heavily on feminine details, especially food and drink consumed there.[47]

Household knowledge of herbs could be connected with women's powers of cursing. Marguerite Touret, a magical practitioner in Quingey,

Franche-Comté, in the 1650s, prepared complex healing potions and ointments. For one client whose husband was ill, she advised her

> that she should say a novena [a Catholic prayer repeated nine times daily] and to this effect for nine days she should get up facing the rising sun and go to a certain herb without speaking to anyone, either in going or returning, and that on her knees she should curse the herb three times, then gather it and put it on the arm of her said husband, and at the end he would be cured.[48]

Cursing a herb may seem harmless, but it illustrates the way in which magical practitioners wielded power that could be used to harm – and, more significantly, could be *thought* or *feared* to be used to harm.

Some magical practices were more powerful than others. Ordinary folk knew some spells of their own, but some villagers, like Touret, were recognised as having special powers. They would help their neighbours as part of the regular process of village barter and co-operation. A few magical practitioners were fully professional, offering a wider range of services including 'unwitching' – identifying and removing the effects of bewitchment. These professionals were mostly men, whereas the amateurs were more often women, but this gender distinction was not clear-cut. Both female and male magical practitioners risked being accused of witchcraft, though the risk seems usually to have been a moderate one.

Male magical practitioners were prominent in the social profiles of witches in some regions where small numbers were prosecuted, such as Normandy, Iceland and Russia. However, as was argued in the introduction to this chapter, this reflects the fewness of *other* witches in these regions. Similar patterns can in fact be found in regions with more female witches. If we concentrate on the male witches in such a region, we often find that they were magical practitioners, as they were in Holstein.[49] Both male and female magical practitioners could be caught up in witch-hunts, but the women were less prominent because there were so many more *other* women. In Europe generally, magical practitioners might be accused of witchcraft, or might identify other people as witches. But the main role of magical practitioners, both male and female, was to underscore the pervasiveness of magic in everyday life.

This point can be developed further by returning to the question of midwives, who were all female. Although their work in delivering babies was mainly practical, they were often thought to use magic. Midwives formed a much-discussed female witchcraft stereotype, as we saw in the discussion of stereotypes above. Several demonologists wrote at length about how midwife witches stole babies for demonic rites. Midwives could also incur peasant worries through the perception that they had magical power. However, although there were some witchcraft accusations against midwives, there were fewer than their prominence in demonological literature would suggest. As with other areas of magical practice, the main way in which midwives were connected with witch-hunting was in the realm of broader ideas about magic. For the common folk, this tended to confirm that childbirth and the nurturing of infants involved magical forces – forces that operated within a gendered female sphere.

One highly gendered area of magical practice was love magic – magic aimed at obtaining a partner, either for marriage or just for sex. Most of those accused of love magic seem to have been women, but there were distinct dynamics here that involved both sexes in different ways. Here we shall examine, first, women's love magic (real or alleged), and then men's love magic.

Women were expected to get themselves husbands. A single woman found it harder to subsist than a single man, so women had a pressing economic motive to marry, and they might turn to magic in order to achieve this. In seventeenth-century Malta, cases of love magic formed half of all magical offences dealt with by the Inquisition. Most of the offenders were single women using magic to attract a partner, or to predict whether they would gain or regain the love of a partner.[50] In a case from Lucca, Italy, in the late fourteenth century, a woman concocted a potion from breastmilk and lochia (vaginal discharge in childbirth) mixed with flour. She then added religious power to the mixture by hiding it under the ornaments of an altar so that the priest saying mass would bless it unawares.[51] Such a powerfully-gendered spell might well be connected with witchcraft.

Men's love magic, by contrast, tended to aim at obtaining sexual partners without marriage. Miguel Melchor, in Saragossa, Aragon, in 1651, was married but determined to seduce another woman, so he acquired a book of spells and invoked demons. He succeeded in seducing the woman, but she then wanted to marry him. So he pretended to cast a spell that, he told her, would kill his wife, 'but he had had no other intent but to deceive her in order to get what he wanted'.[52] Other men used spells in the hope of seducing numerous women.

Women's and men's love magic thus differed in their objectives – marriage or short-term sex. They also differed in their methods. Men's magical spells often used consecrated objects or written words. Women used oral rhymes or adapted prayers, sometimes combined with giving magical food or drink. A particularly common women's ritual in Spain and Italy was bean-casting to predict future partners: dried beans were tossed and the patterns they made were interpreted. Overall, women's love magic seems to have been much more common than men's. The authorities also *thought* it was more common. The Roman Inquisition assumed that virtually all love magic was carried out by women.[53]

Most of these instances of love magic, both by women and by men, were treated by the authorities merely as superstitious magic, but they ran a risk of escalating into cases of actual witchcraft. This might happen if someone suffered a misfortune that could be explained as magical harm, or if the authorities decided that demons were involved. One way in which this escalation could occur was through the breakdown of a relationship, when disputes could give rise to damaging accusations. A man in particular might claim that his ex-partner had used magic to retain his affection, and then had turned to harmful magic when this failed.

Some ideas about magical practice, like some witchcraft stereotypes, focused on men. One distinct idea here was that of the man who wrote a pact with the Devil. This may seem surprising; after all, most witches were thought to make a pact with the Devil. However, these men were different because they did deliberately carry out a ritual to renounce God and give their allegiance to the Devil, and because their rituals usually involved writing, a skill usually associated with men. The accounts of these rituals had a believable individuality lacking in the stereotyped accusations against most witches. Ivan Zheglov, in Russian Siberia in the 1680s, wrote out a pact with the Devil; he also took off the cross that he wore, and wore it under his heel for thirteen days. He then saw a vision of the Devil.[54] A number of such cases have been found in eighteenth-century Sweden. These men had usually written their pact because they needed money badly and hoped that the Devil would provide it – though most admitted that they had been disappointed, and some remorsefully gave themselves up to the authorities. The pacts that they had written were usually produced in court. They received mild punishments for superstitious behaviour, and were not treated as witches.[55] The distinctiveness of these men lies in the way in which courts, even at the time, thought them misguided rather than wicked.

The idea of the Devil providing wealth was related to the idea of magical treasure-seeking. Treasure-seekers, who were almost entirely men, formed a distinct group. They tended to use magic in their search, and some even performed rites to summon the assistance of demons; but they were rarely prosecuted as witches. More often, their magical practices were seen as 'superstition', for which they received light punishments if any.[56] The same applies to the even more masculine pursuit of magic by soldiers, seeking spells to cure battlefield wounds or to become invulnerable to harm.[57] Men's magical practices formed part of a broader discourse of witchcraft and magic in the early modern world, but did not necessarily get the men themselves in trouble for witchcraft.

Gendered patterns of accusation

Although godly reformers could shape, direct and encourage them, witchcraft accusations were initiated – at least outside panics – by the common folk. Processes of village quarrels have been discussed in Chapter 4, but there are further issues related to gender that require attention here. Patterns of quarrelling were gendered. Women tended to interact with other women, and men with other men, so people's quarrels tended to be with people of the same gender. This in itself would not have produced the high proportion of women that we find, though, so this issue requires further investigation.

Patriarchal structures provided reasons for women to accuse other women of witchcraft. Women had, or aspired to having, particular social and domestic roles – roles that could be threatened by witchcraft. An established and successful village woman was typically someone who met various aspirations, but also had various worries as to how her status might be undermined. She was married – so she might fear the envy of disappointed rivals for her husband's hand, or might worry that he would be led astray (perhaps through magic) into unfaithfulness to her with another woman. She was a housewife – so the house, and particularly the hearth, were her domain. She was responsible for cooking – so she might worry when things went wrong with this. She was responsible for milking cows, and for making butter and cheese from milk – so she might worry when things went wrong with this, as they often did. She was expected to become a mother – so she might fear infertility. After the birth of a baby, most women had to breastfeed; difficulties with this could be attributed to witchcraft. As a parent, with primary responsibility for childcare, she would spend years worrying about her children's health and safety. Village witchcraft was a threat to the household and family – the woman's domain.

Accusations of magical harm could be gendered. In the German duchies of Schleswig and Holstein, 122 slander trials occurred in which someone complained to the courts that a neighbour had accused them of some kind of witchcraft. They fall into two distinct groups. Most women were accused either of interference with milk and butter, or of harming cattle, or of causing disease and death to humans. Most men were accused either of enriching themselves magically, or of being werewolves, or of harming horses. These divisions largely reflect gendered divisions of labour – women did dairy work, men looked after horses.[58]

Regional studies of slander cases have not all revealed consistent patterns, however. In Vollenhove, in the Netherlands, in slander cases involving witchcraft accusations there were 14 women insulted by women, one man insulted by a woman, 11 men insulted by men, and seven women insulted by men. Here one cannot say that the insult of 'witch' was mainly used by women.[59] In Lorraine, by contrast, men's accusations of witchcraft were taken more seriously than women's accusations. In cases of slander for calling someone a witch, 97 per cent of the convictions were of men.[60] No doubt women called other women witches, but the courts were evidently not interested when they did. Further study of slander cases is required.

Gendered witchcraft accusations were also made *within* families. Stepmothers were particularly at risk of being accused by their stepchildren, as in the case of Perrissone Gappit, in Vaud, Switzerland, in 1463. She quarrelled with her stepson Jordan dou Molard after he had hidden two of her kerchiefs, and became 'furiously and malevolently angered with him, such that she threatened him with bitter words, and told him that because of these hidden kerchiefs a misfortune would soon strike him'. He then feared to eat any food she prepared, and became ill with worry. He and his stepmother then had a reconciliation; he ate one of her meals and recovered. But stepmother and stepson quarrelled again, and eventually Gappit, the stepmother, was charged with witchcraft.[61]

It was argued in Chapter 8 that village leaders often orchestrated neighbours' accusations. This was to some extent an issue of class – it was the rich peasants, or members of the local elite, who took the lead. But gender was also relevant. These rich peasants and members of the local elite were all *men*. In Peney, Switzerland, in 1530, we can see Nicolas Balli acting as a village leader. He was a notary and a member of a wealthy local family. He not only accused eleven witches himself, he also marshalled numerous other witnesses to do the same.[62] In Lorraine, where many witnesses' statements about dated events have been studied, women's accusations tended to go back further into the past than men's.[63] This indicates that the women's accusations were taken less seriously: if a man accused someone, prompt action would be taken. Both class and gender were relevant to the accusation against Denis Deffontaines, a member of the village elite in Bouvignies, France, in 1679. After he was named by three confessing witches, another villager, Gaspard Verdier, accused Deffontaines publicly – but was ordered by the court 'to silence the wicked rumour concerning people of good reputation, as Denis Deffontaines is'. As a wealthy villager, Deffontaines was known as an 'honest man' and so *must* have a good reputation. His accuser was subjected to a ruinous fine.[64]

In a witchcraft panic, these gendered patterns could be partially or wholly swept away. If interrogators encouraged the making of accusations in really large numbers, then the resulting flood of names could seem sufficiently random for accusations to be made against women and men more equally. Between 1627 and 1629, during a panic in the prince-bishopric of Würzburg, the early accusations were mostly against women, but the proportion of men gradually rose.[65] Yet even this was not really random, for two further sub-patterns can be discerned within the panic. Firstly, over half of the accused men in the prince-bishopric as a whole were related by blood or marriage to a female witch. Secondly, however, in the town of Würzburg itself, the panic was more serious and also engulfed priests, bringing the proportion of men up to 43 per cent.[66] The witch-priest was of course one of the minor stereotypes.

Thus, many of the men who were caught up in the European witch-hunt did not fit any of the stereotypes of the male witch. Instead they were caught up in a chain-reaction trial beginning with women. Such a man could be the husband of a female witch, or otherwise connected to female witches. Typically he was named by a woman at a time when accusations even against men were credible. In the later stages of some larger panics, the proportion of men rose as the standard stereotype broke down. At this point, we need to consider further the issue of men who were secondary targets, named because they were connected to female witches.

Men as secondary targets

The variety of witchcraft stereotypes meant that many of the people executed for witchcraft – both women and men – can be considered as primary targets: they were identified because they themselves fitted one of the available stereotypes. But there were others, not noted as conforming to any stereotype, who were dragged in when they were named by another confessing witch. This could happen both to women and to men, but it has proved a particularly fruitful way of understanding how many men were accused. These men were secondary targets.

The secondary-target model indicates that a good deal of witch-hunting was primarily a hunt for women. In fact we can be more specific: much witch-hunting was primarily a hunt for *older* women, as the older, quarrelsome woman formed the standard stereotype of a witch. Witch-hunters thus tended to arrest older women, but they also dragged in some men (as well as some younger women, who will be discussed later), for two reasons. Firstly, some women were associated with specific men, such as their husbands or sons; either the woman named these men during interrogation, or else members of the community decided that the men shared the woman's guilt. These men were the most direct form of secondary targets, in which there was a clear individual link between the woman accused first and the man accused next. Secondly, though, during a more intense panic, the women being interrogated could name names more at random, as we saw in Chapter 7; these names could include names of men to whom they had no particular connection. During such a panic, women would also be named at random, but the proportion of men would be higher than usual.

The pattern of men as secondary targets has been found in several regional studies. In Lorraine, a high proportion of the men – almost half – were associated with a previous female witch.[67] Much the same pattern has been found in New England and in Holstein.[68] The pattern can also be found, and understood in more detail, in individual cases. In Württemberg, Germany, in 1653, the adulterous affair of Catharina Seeger and Michael Ellwein had a shocking outcome. Ellwein was convicted of poisoning his wife and child to death – but he was said to have done so at Seeger's instigation, with Seeger being tortured to confess to this. Seeger, the woman involved, was executed as a witch, Ellwein, less shamefully, as a poisoner.[69] It was the woman's witchcraft that attracted more attention.

Husbands whose wives were accused were in a difficult position. They would normally be expected to defend their wives, but they risked being accused themselves. A few husbands joined in the chorus of accusations. When Sarah Good in Salem (who was discussed in Chapter 7) was arrested, her husband William Good stated that he was 'afraid that she either was a witch or would be one very quickly'.[70] However, it was much more common for husbands to stand by their wives and defend them. The husband of Claudine Brevet, from Condé-sur-Noireau, Normandy, was asked 'if his wife hadn't taught him something', but he defended her stoutly; in the end, she was executed and he was condemned to row in the galleys for life.[71] Here we see a man as a secondary target even in Normandy, where male witches were in the majority.

It was thus generally easier to accuse a widow or an unmarried woman, because a married woman's husband might be expected to defend her. It is unlikely that accusations were deliberately made against easy targets; people accused someone of being a witch because they thought the person was a witch, not because they thought they were an easy target. But *successful* accusations may have been more common against widows or unmarried women; husbands often managed to fight off witchcraft accusations against their wives.

The model of primary and secondary targets also explains some of the accusations against younger women. During panics, accusations might begin with older women but then spread out to encompass some younger women as well. In New England, half of the younger women accused (those aged under 40) were brought in through association with an older female witch.[72] These young women, too, were secondary targets.

Children: Victims and victim-witches

Children played increasingly important roles as the European witch-hunt developed. They began as tragic victims of witches' malefice, then moved on to become actual accusers of witches. Eventually some children themselves were caught up in the witch-hunt. Executions of children were a notable feature of the later stages of witch-hunting. This section will concentrate on children as witches, but, since their role as witches grew out of their role as victims of witchcraft, it is necessary to begin with the latter.

It was easy to imagine children as victims of witchcraft. Their youth, vulnerability and innocence formed a contrast with old women, who were easiest to imagine as witches. Accusations that witches had caused the illness and death of children were frequently made throughout the witch-hunt. Rarer, but surfacing on several occasions, were accusations that witches carried children to the sabbat during the night; there were panics in Spain and Sweden about this. There were popular fears in Italy about witches visiting children at night and sucking their blood; these fears were related to, but still distinct from, the demonological idea of cannibalistic infanticide.

Children, like women, were particularly liable to be stereotyped in the patriarchal culture of adult men. Either they were pure and innocent – needing protection – or they were wild and destructive – needing discipline and punishment. Attitudes to children could swing widely between these two divergent stereotypes. As they did with women, men used stereotypes to understand children because children's individuality was less important to adult men than their social position.

In the early period, before these issues began to present themselves in practice through children's confessions, the *Malleus Maleficarum* laid out a few issues of theoretical demonology. It argued that children were unable to make a pact with the Devil, since this would involve renunciation of faith – faith that only an adult could possess. However, children could have the powers of witches (the power to raise storms was mentioned) if they had been dedicated to the Devil by their mother, or by the midwife, at birth. Such a child was still innocent, and could be rebaptised.[73]

In their confessions, children tended to present themselves as what may be called 'victim-witches'. They told stories of having been taken to the sabbat by an adult, in which they had themselves taken part in some of the rituals. Were they innocent victims, or guilty witches? The children themselves could emphasise one aspect or the other; their parents or interrogators could also emphasise one aspect or the other. The primary reason to question most of these children was not to establish their own guilt or innocence, but to elicit information about adults taking them to the sabbat or in attendance at it. Child witches often accused their mothers, implicitly or explicitly. Their stories were often full of detail, which was taken as an indicator of truthfulness. They generally emphasised the festive rather than horrifying aspects of demonic gatherings. We may see these stories as fantasies; that was not a standard view at the time, but there were some efforts to distinguish truth from fantasy. The councillors of Rothenburg ob der Tauber, often moderately sceptical about witchcraft, did not believe children who said that they had made demonic pacts or attended sabbats. But they did believe children who said that an adult had seduced them into witchcraft.[74]

Children as victim-witches appeared prominently in Spain in the early sixteenth century. The panic in Navarre in 1525, with two victim-witches who were accepted as mainly innocent, has been discussed in Chapter 8. In 1540, in Calahorra, the Inquisition encountered thirty 'witches' aged between ten and fourteen, and a further eight who were older but still regarded as children. They were all made to do penance.[75] Then the involvement of children in the panic of the 1580s in Trier, Germany, helped to fuel the general intensification of witch-hunting in this period.

Were these children, victim-witches in their own view, really innocent victims or guilty witches? Interrogators had a good deal of freedom to treat them as one or the other, and to pursue lines of questioning based on the assumption of innocence or the assumption of guilt. Some ambiguity remained for some time, probably because both innocent child victims and guilty child witches could be used to accuse adult witches who had visited the sabbat. Increasingly, however, in the last decades of the sixteenth century, the ambiguity about the children's own status was removed. Many authorities (though not all) decided that guilty child witches existed, and that they should be punished.

The emergence of children as witches was connected with broader issues to do with the godly state and the European economy. Official, published advice on child-rearing became harsher with the Reformation. Parents were warned more strongly that their children might be wicked, or become wicked. We do not know whether this advice led the average parent to treat children more harshly, but agencies of church and civil government were more likely to hold these views. Meanwhile, the sixteenth-century population upswing increased the proportion of children in the population as well as causing more widespread poverty. Gangs of vagrant children became a problem, and state authorities developed new policies against them. Vagrant beggars and witchcraft could be linked, as we have seen.

Once it was agreed that child witches existed, the question arose of how they should be tried and punished. Evidence of guilt seems to have been gathered from children's confessions under interrogation without torture, which makes sense when we reflect that children tend to co-operate with adults in authority.[76] In a panic in Molsheim, Alsace, in 1629–30, children were beaten by the schoolmaster to get them to confess.[77]

As to whether guilty child witches should be executed, no complete consensus was reached, but executions slowly spread. The legal minimum age of marriage, usually twelve for girls and fourteen for boys, was often taken as a minimum age for criminals to be executed. Peter Binsfeld, in Trier in 1591, recommended flogging, rather than execution, for witches aged under fourteen. Those aged fourteen and fifteen, he advised, should be held in prison until they reached the age of sixteen; then they should be re-examined and treated as adults.[78] Later demonologists, such as Rémy and Boguet, more often endorsed the execution of children.[79] Their guidance was not always followed, as a later (1629) case from Franche-Comté, Boguet's province, illustrates. Two child witches, aged seven and nine, were convicted along with both their parents; they were punished by making them each throw a bundle of sticks onto their parents' pyre.[80] Still, several courts, especially in the early seventeenth century, did execute children below the age of majority. In the Würzburg panic of 1627–29, 41 children were executed alongside 119 adults.[81] A related approach is illustrated by the case of Anne Hauldecoeur, a seven-year-old girl in the Spanish Netherlands; she was convicted of witchcraft in 1614, and the authorities kept her in prison until she reached the age of twelve in 1619. Then they executed her.[82] There could be embarrassment at executing children. The Alsace child witches, some of whom were as young as eight, were executed before daybreak to prevent crowds gathering.[83]

By the later seventeenth century, there were even a few panics that primarily involved children and young adults. The most notorious occurred in the Salzburg region of Austria between 1675 and 1690. These, which became known as the 'Zauberer-Jackl' trials ('sorcerer Jacob'), were directed at a supposed gang of vagrant witches led by one 'Jacob'. There were 124 executions or deaths in custody, mostly of boys and young men aged between ten and twenty.[84] A number of the beggars prosecuted for witchcraft in nearby Carinthia, mentioned earlier, were also young. In France, there were panics in Guyenne and Béarn in the late 1660s launched by boys aged between fourteen and sixteen, eventually halted by the king's council in 1672.[85] These instances of older children may indicate that there is more work to be done on the ages of male witches. Those in Normandy tended to be either adolescents or old men, for instance. A related issue here, to be discussed further in Chapter 10, is that the late emergence of these children and young men as witches seems to have been paralleled by the decline of the standard stereotype of the quarrelsome old woman witch.

Gendered images of witchcraft

Visual images of witches brought gender to the foreground. These images need careful study, not only because of what they tell us of the ideas of the artists themselves, but because many of the images achieved wide circulation. This was not an age of mass literacy, but it was an age of mass circulation of visual material. Printing, from the late fifteenth century, made visual images much more accessible – either as single sheets or as illustrations in books.

Unlike witchcraft texts, witchcraft images were highly gendered. Writers could write about generic, gender-neutral 'witches', but artists depicting witches had to depict their gender. Artists seized this opportunity, and produced a flood of images in which gender was not just acknowledged but highlighted.

One way of highlighting gender was by depicting female witches naked, as with Illustration 9.1. Nakedness was distantly related to the idea, found in some demonologies, that witches stripped naked in order to anoint themselves with the ointment that enabled them to fly to the sabbat. However, most pictures of naked female witches did not show them doing this, and some even showed naked women clustered improbably around a boiling cauldron. Many artists arranged the woman's body in a sexually-suggestive posture – with open legs, for instance – for the viewer's benefit.

Nakedness was sometimes combined with loose, flying hair. It may be hard, in today's hatless age, to realise how indecent it was for a woman's hair to be loose. But early modern women were expected to cover their heads as a sign of submission to male power. As a result, the uncovered female head was itself thought to be powerful; some women who uttered curses would ritually uncover their head in order to add to the power of the curse. The importance of loose hair in witchcraft images is underlined by the fact that even some of the naked witches manage to keep their hair bound up or covered.

Groups of naked female witches sometimes combined old and young women. These images were related to a tradition, current in the late middle ages, of juxtaposing images of old and young women in works against vanity. In these, a young, attractive woman would be shown next to an old, decrepit one. The respectable reason for these double images (or sometimes

Illustration 9.1 Imagining female witches, *c*.1514

This drawing, by Hans Baldung Grien, combines horror and sexual titillation. All the witches are naked women, ostensibly because nakedness was required for the witches to apply the flying ointment. The central figure is a young woman with her body provocatively arranged for the viewer. Her rolling eyes, flying hair and wild gestures suggest sexual ecstasy, but she is also being carried into the air by a purposeful older woman with a forked cooking-stick. The two women in the foreground make magical preparations; one reads from a manuscript and may be anointing her genitals with ointment, while the other holds aloft a jar that probably contains ointment. Body parts, the ingredients of the ointment, are scattered around.

triple images, when a skeleton was also included) was to warn young women that the beauty of which they were allegedly proud was a fleeting thing. Nevertheless, men probably welcomed the opportunity to look at images of naked women – an opportunity that was then rare. In these images they saw women being denigrated at the same time as they saw them presented as sexual beings. Much modern pornography is similar.

In witchcraft images, the combination of young and old women was unbalanced: the stress was very much on the young, sexually-alluring witches. This is remarkable, because written works on witchcraft more often either stressed old women, or (more commonly) omitted any discussion of age. The naked old women did have their own importance in these depictions; they were usually muscular, active and threatening. But the naked young women usually outnumbered the old women, were usually more prominently placed, and were sometimes depicted without any old women. Conventions of feminine sexual desirability have shifted since the Renaissance, so the young, naked witches of Albrecht Dürer or Hans Baldung Grien do not look exactly like today's bikini-clad 'celebrities'; in particular, Renaissance nudes tend to have rounded stomachs symbolising fecundity. The best of them are also original works of high art. They are, nevertheless, pornographic.

From the late fifteenth century onwards, pictures of witches usually depicted *groups* of women. These were not recognisable 'sabbats' until the 1590s, but for about a century it was conventional to depict witches working with other witches, rather than the solitary activity of the maleficent village witch. Often groups of three were shown. This allowed an age range to be depicted, often with one old and two young witches. Only rarely were male witches shown. Some of the triple images may have been influenced by the classical idea of Diana as a threefold goddess. A Renaissance interest in ancient texts is apparent in many of these images; they rarely come from the courtroom where actual witches were being tried.[86]

Artists also provided witches with accessories, developing a visual code that would identify the image of a given woman as a 'witch'. The witch's nakedness and loose hair were striking, but additional accessories might help to confirm her identity. This was particularly necessary for artists who shrank from depicting naked witches. The two most common witches' accessories were the cauldron and the forked cooking-stick, both of which alluded to feminine tasks. The cauldron was a standard piece of cooking equipment in a large household, but witches were depicted using it to brew up magical potions, often including human flesh. A typical witches' cauldron was shown with bones or body parts scattered around it. As for the forked cooking-stick, its normal domestic use was to hold a pot over a fire, but for many witches it was a vehicle for flight. Other witches simply brandished a cooking-stick to indicate their identity, and a few were depicted flying on an animal (such as a goat) while carrying a cooking-stick. The forked cooking-stick became a standard witch's accessory in German illustrations, which were the most common (Germany had the most printers as well as the most witches). One variant on the cooking-stick, sometimes found in French illustrations, was a broomstick – another feminine domestic item. Somehow it is the broomstick that has survived, along with the cauldron, to be used by modern illustrators.

Another witch's accessory was a demonic animal. The most common was a male goat, which was considered a highly-sexed creature. The goat also had classical connections, being linked to ancient Roman fauns or satyrs. In several illustrations (including Cranach's 'Melancholy' on the cover of this book), a witch rides *backwards* on a goat, denoting sexual disorder. A common community punishment for sexual misbehaviour was to be paraded through the street riding an animal backwards. Another sexualised accessory was the sausage, known to be a symbol for the penis. When female witches were depicted with collections of sausages, viewers could recognise a threat to male potency and dominance.

Artists failed to develop a visual code for the male witch. On the few occasions when male witches were depicted, they were simply shown as ordinary men in company with women identified as witches. Nakedness was absent, and witchcraft was usually indicated by depicting a demon. There were hardly any illustrations showing only male witches, whereas there were many showing only female ones.

There was, however, a visual code for the male learned magician. He was usually shown with a magic circle on the floor (used for summoning demons), and often had equipment like a wand, a book or a mirror (demons could be imprisoned in mirrors). He was richly dressed, as befitted his elite status. Thus the basic difference between men and women was reinforced by several other visual indicators relating to the man's education and social standing.

Sex with the Devil

It was the interrogators who insisted that witches provide stories about their sexual relationship with the Devil. The demonic witch was an elite concern. Nevertheless, the shape that these stories took was influenced by popular elements. Their gendered aspects go far to explain why women were thought to be witches. Men could engage with some aspects of demonology, but not this one. The prominence of sex between female witches and the male Devil made female witches normal.

Unmarried female witches, when asked about their relationship with the Devil, often shaped their stories like stories of courtship. Like any suitor, the Devil brought the woman small gifts, and made promises of long-term economic benefit. Peasant witches did not imagine that they themselves were worth a great deal to the Devil – they did not say that he promised them riches, merely that they would be 'given enough' or that they would 'never want'. And, as with a fickle suitor, the Devil's promises could prove unreliable. Once the woman had given him her soul – and of course her body – the coins he had given her often turned out to be dung or leaves. This was a folkloric motif in origin, though some interrogators encouraged it. The idea of the Devil as an unreliable boyfriend thus arose from women's own understanding of how their relationships with men could develop. As for married women, they sometimes shaped their pact stories like stories of seduction and adultery, in which again the Devil often failed to keep his promises.

In these narratives of encounters with the Devil, he rarely revealed himself immediately as the Devil. Suspects often told how they had originally thought that they were entering a relationship with an ordinary man, but later noticed – as in Illustration 9.2 – an unusual feature like a tail, a cloven hoof or a wooden hand. Walpurga Hausmännin, in Dillingen, Germany, in 1587, confessed that 'after the act of fornication she saw and felt the cloven foot of her whoremonger, and that his hand was not natural, but as if made of wood'.[87] This drew on a popular view that the Devil sought to counterfeit God, but could never make a perfect copy of God's creation. Symbolically, the unusual bodily feature was also related to the narrative of failed courtship. Women seeking partners knew that they had to be on their guard against men who seemed attractive but would later prove unsuitable. The revelation of the unusual feature symbolised the discovery that he was an unsuitable partner. But, by then, it was too late.

Versions of these narratives could be devised by accused men – but, without the sexual element, they lacked dramatic potency. For men, the courtship motif was replaced by that of the Devil offering solutions to other problems. The accused witch Pierre dou Chanoz, in Lausanne, Switzerland, told the following story in 1458: 'He met Antoine Aubremant in the mill of Torny-le-Grand, who said to him: "What, are you all melancholy because of your losses in the war of Fribourg? Ah well, if you wish to believe me, you will have a good vengeance on the Fribourgers who did you so much wrong."' Dou Chanoz related that he went to a mill with Aubremant and joined in a feast where they made 'good cheer' until he was frightened by noticing a pot containing the arm of a child. Nevertheless (his confession continued), at the next meeting he renounced God and worshipped the Devil in the form of a black cat.[88] As with most male witches, there was no sex here.

The idea of sex with the Devil or demons implied that the Devil or demons were humanoid. This was not, in fact, a straightforward idea in the Christian tradition. When the Devil was described in the Bible it was usually in the shape of an animal. Many medieval demons were depicted as fantastic beasts. The variety of shapes for the Devil was remarkable, as was the common ambiguity as to whether a singular Devil or plural demons were under consideration. However, by the time of the great European witch-hunt, the Devil had acquired a more or less human shape.

As well as being humanoid, the Devil was of course male. From a strictly theological point of view, it was not entirely clear that angels or demons had a gender – but, in practice, both angels and demons were definitely imagined

Illustration 9.2 The demonic pact as a narrative, *c*.1489

Confessing witches were expected to tell a convincing story about how they became witches. Women often told how they encountered a man who befriended them at a difficult time, but who then revealed himself as the Devil. Often, as in this illustration, the revelation was indirect: the woman noticed that he had an animal characteristic, such as a cloven hoof. This Devil has an animal's tail and bird's claws.

© INTERFOTO/Sammlung Rauch/Mary Evans

as male. And the Devil's maleness meant, by and large, that those witches with whom he was imagined as having a sexual relationship were female.

As a spirit, one thing that the Devil did not have was a physical body – which might have been a problem for his sexual prowess. However, demonologists agreed that he could fashion an imitation body out of condensed air. This body had no blood, and thus, according to contemporary medical theory, no heat. Not surprisingly, his sexual partners were expected to notice this, and quite a few interrogators asked female witchcraft suspects about the Devil's coldness. Sometimes the question was specifically about his semen; real semen was believed to be a form of blood, which carried the body's heat, so the coldness of the Devil's imitation semen was particularly noteworthy. Some demonologists carefully pointed out that demons, lacking real bodies, could not feel physical lust for women; their motive was to entrap human souls to damnation. This nevertheless made the Devil a sexual symbol, with sexuality being disapproved of because it impeded union with God.

Male witches rarely confessed to demonic sex, but, on the few occasions when they did, they usually described sex with a female demon. This idea was more plausible in folklore than in orthodox demonology; the common folk imagined both male and female nature spirits, after all. Some witches' confessions in Gascony, France, described the Devil accompanied by a '*diablesse*', apparently the Devil's wife.[89] And, while female witches were almost always restricted to a single demon as their sexual partner, men sometimes claimed relationships with several female demons.[90] Women were assumed to be more lustful than men, but also sexually passive; they had to wait for a partner to initiate sex. The male witch with several demons sounds like a man boasting of his sexual conquests. A related male idea is found in a small panic in Berry, France, in 1582–83. Two of the men prosecuted, Etienne Girault and Marin Semellé, both described a sabbat at which they, several other men and *one* woman had been present. First the Devil and then each of the men in turn had had sex with this woman. Girault and Semellé gave two different names for the woman – an indication (if we needed one) that their story was a fantasy.[91]

If the Devil was evil, might he transgress the norm of heterosexuality? Most demonologists did not raise this question, and, of those who did, most answered it negatively. The *Malleus* in particular insisted on the Devil's heterosexuality: homosexuality was so bad that even the Devil would not do it. The idea of demons' male homosexuality was nevertheless circulated by a few Italian writers, notably Gianfrancesco Pico della Mirandola in 1523. Male homosexuality was imagined here as part of a broader picture of transgressive sex. According to another such writer, Silvestro Prierias in 1521, the Devil had a two-pronged penis with which he engaged simultaneously in vaginal and anal intercourse with women.[92] As for female homosexuality, this was absent from demonology, no doubt because of the Devil's masculinity. Lesbian witches occasionally appeared in the courts. Elsbeth Hertner von Riehen, in Basel, Switzerland, in 1647, met spirits of the dead who advised her to have sex with a demonic woman.[93] Maud Galt, in Kilbarchan, Scotland, in 1649, was a real lesbian whose relationship with a female servant prompted a witchcraft charge, apparently because the shocked authorities found the idea of witchcraft easier to cope with than lesbianism.[94] Overall, though, homosexuality was uncommon in witchcraft cases.

Some early demonologists thought that women who had sex with the Devil did so 'in the manner of beasts' (that is, with the Devil entering from behind). This relates to a theological concern with the distinction between humans and animals; theologians were worried by anything that might undermine humanity's special status. This in turn relates to the idea that women might not be fully human, as discussed earlier in this chapter. These ideas were sometimes carried over into confessions, perhaps at the instigation of interrogators who had these concerns. Some women confessed to unusual positions for sex, or sex with a demonic animal or non-human being.[95] Sexual sins could be defined in terms of their interference with procreation; thus the 'missionary position' for intercourse (as it is called today) was recommended because it was thought necessary for conception to occur.[96]

Demons could swap genders, at least in theory. Behind some stories of demonic sex lay the ancient ideas of the incubus and the succubus. The incubus was a male demon that had sex with women at night; it tended to be reported in nunneries, and the idea perhaps originated with male priests hearing nuns' confessions of sexual fantasies. The succubus, a female demon that had sex with men, was rarely heard of in practice, and may have been invented for the sake of symmetry. As we saw in Chapter 3, William of Auvergne and Thomas Aquinas had developed the theory that demonic offspring could be engendered by a succubus demon stealing a man's semen, then transforming itself into an incubus and using the semen to impregnate a woman. The *Malleus* followed this line but insisted that incubus and succubus were two different beings; sex-change operations were too much for Krämer. Meanwhile Ulrich Müller, in 1489, argued that the stealing of semen would not work because the semen would lose its power in being transported.[97]

Some demonologies, including the *Malleus*, argued that women had more pleasure in sex with demons than with men, and that demons had larger penises which aided this. Others described demonic sex as painful and unpleasant. The Devil's penis could be as long and thick as an arm, or have barbed scales, or be made partly of iron. His semen could be not just cold, but painfully ice-cold. Confessions reflected this variety, with some women confessing to pleasurable sex, some to unpleasant sex. The idea of unpleasant sex may partly have been constructed from ideas of inversion: demonic sex would be the opposite of normal sex, which was assumed to be pleasurable. However, women could also be denigrated for taking excessive, lustful pleasure in sex, so the argument could go either way. Demonologists never reached a consensus view about it, though there seems to have been a gradual rise in the idea of unpleasant sex.

There was probably a complex two-way relationship between confessions and demonologies here. Some women will have taken the initiative in describing their sexual encounters (either positively or negatively), based no doubt on a combination of their own real sexual experiences and their fantasies. These confessions could then be used by demonologists. Some demonologists may have come across only one sort of confession in their region. However, by the mid sixteenth century at least, any reasonably well-read author could have come across reports of both pleasurable and unpleasant sex in the broader literature. If so, perhaps they believed only the ones from their region, or the ones that they themselves heard; or perhaps they deliberately ignored evidence that went against their view.

Some demonologists probably drew mainly on their own ideas and fantasies, rather than on confessions. Bearing in mind that demonologists were all men, this seems particularly likely for those accounts of demonic sex that focused on penises, usually a male preoccupation. Penises rarely featured in confessions, though cold semen was quite common. Interrogators, having read a particular book, might expect to find reports of a particular kind of sex, and would presumably shape their questions accordingly. Those who used the *Malleus*, for instance, would ask suspects to describe pleasurable sex. Unfortunately we rarely know much about the intellectual background of particular interrogators, so it is hard to be definite about the processes at work in any specific case.

Interest in demonic sex varied from region to region, depending largely on the views of the elite. There was a lot of demonic sex in the German heartland of witch-hunting. In France, too, demonic sex was common, though the rate of witch-hunting was far lower. In England, by contrast, demonic sex was rare, probably because prosecutions made little use of confessions and the law gave little importance to the demonic pact. In Russia, there was no demonic sex, because western demonology was not fully adopted and the Orthodox church gave little importance to the Devil.

Related to the idea of unpleasant sex was the idea of kissing the Devil's anus at the sabbat. Demonologists originated this idea, possibly as an imagined inversion of normal Christian worship, which was also carried out with the mouth (consuming the elements of communion). The idea remained more common in demonologies than in confessions, but witches in quite a few areas were expected to confess to it. Kissing the Devil's anus may have been linked to the idea that demons had a second face in that part of their bodies, depicted in a number of illustrations. Some Savoy witches confessed to kissing the Devil's 'second face'.[98] Another sexual idea appeared in the Cambrésis, Spanish Netherlands, where female witches were expected to confess that they had given the Devil 'a hair from their shameful parts'.[99] The links between witchcraft and sexuality, especially female sexuality, were manifold.

Malefices related to sex

As well as witches having deviant sex, there was a range of common ideas about witches interfering with *normal* sex. These ideas were partly shaped by demonology, but less driven by demonology than the ideas about sex with the Devil. The common folk, too, had their worries and fears about sex, and witchcraft could play a role in these.

When women suffered from sex-related malefices, this sometimes came in the form of infertility – the inability to bear children. If a couple were unable to produce children after intercourse, this was usually assumed to be the woman's fault. All five of the 'new sect' writers of the 1430s (discussed in Chapter 2) thought that witches impeded marriage and caused women to be infertile.[100] This idea seems to have faded in later demonologies, though it did not disappear. As for the common folk, a woman's failure to conceive seems less often to have been blamed on witchcraft than other fertility-related problems, such as failure to breastfeed or simply the illness and death of children. Children's illnesses were less directly sexual, though still related to gender roles.

One form of malefice, particularly feared by elite men, came in the form of witches' attacks on their sons, particularly their eldest sons. These sons represented the future of the dynasty. The witches of Lincoln, England, in 1619, turned out to have concentrated their attack on the eldest son of the earl of Rutland, and tried to prevent the earl and his countess from having further children.[101] The failure of an aristocratic lineage was a deeply troubling prospect.

When men suffered personally from sex-related malefice, this usually came in the form of 'impotence', meaning inability to achieve an erection. This was related to the popular idea of the 'ligature', a spell to 'bind' a man's penis.[102] Men with sexual problems could thus blame hostile magic for their failures and disappointments. Newly-married men were particularly vulnerable to the ligature, partly because of their inexperience, and partly because the binding spell was sometimes thought to be cast at the time of the wedding. In such cases, the perpetrator was often thought to be a jealous ex-partner, either of the man himself or of his bride.

Because the jealous ex-partner could be male or female, ligatures were not simply blamed on one sex. Most accusations seem to have been made against women, however. In Spain, male impotence was largely blamed on women.[103] This was probably the most common pattern, but there were at least some regional traditions focusing on men. Miners in Alsace had a tradition of using the 'art' of the ligature against rivals.[104] This may well be part of a broader pattern of variation in levels of fear of impotence. The ligature seems to have been rare in Poland, but Russian men at their weddings were terrified of it.[105]

Demonologists, characteristically, took the basic idea of the ligature and elaborated on it. Bodin claimed to have been told by 'a young noblewoman of good repute' that 'there were more than fifty ways to tie the codpiece-string: one to impede only the husband, the other to impede only the wife, so that the one frustrated with the impotence of his partner, will commit adultery with others.' However, 'it was usually only the man who was tied'.[106] These worries were male worries.

Even worse than failure to achieve an erection was another male fear: the complete disappearance of their penis. The *Malleus* gave a detailed description of how witches stole penises, solemnly explaining that the vanishing penis was purely a demonic illusion. The bizarre story of how witches kept stolen penises in a bird's nest may today be one of the book's most frequently-cited passages.[107] Yet this was not just a fantasy of the celibate Krämer; it occurred in real cases. In Württemberg in 1652, a young man, Jung Aberle, accused an older woman, Maria Schramm, of having taken his penis by witchcraft. She had walked past him when he was urinating in a herb garden, and made what may have been intended as a humorously flirtatious remark. When Aberle went home, he could no longer see his penis – and a witchcraft case ensued.[108] Witchcraft could mobilise people's deepest fears.

Women's experience of witchcraft prosecution

It was traumatic for anyone to be arrested on a charge of witchcraft, but the process had particular effects on women. Women were used to being subject to the authority of men, usually their fathers and husbands, but they were less used to being plunged into the public world of criminal courts and political authority. And male judges, interrogators and gaolers treated women in some distinct ways. In particular, women were often sexually abused by their gaolers during their sojourn in prison for interrogation.[109]

Searching for the Devil's mark involved strip-searches, and in some places this became standard. All seventeenth-century suspects in Savoy were stripped naked and shaved, in a search for the Devil's mark and to prepare them for torture.[110] In a few places, notably England and its colonies, strip-searches of women were carried out by specially-appointed groups of women, sometimes described as 'matrons'. But, in most places, such searches were done by men. These were usually the same men who administered torture. In Germany, the chief torturer was usually the executioner. Women thus feared the search for the Devil's mark as dishonourable – it involved being touched by the executioner, whose touch brought dishonour.[111] In some places, the Devil's mark was detected by pricking with pins; witch-prickers,

(*continued*)

too, were men. One Scottish witch-pricker actually turned out to be a woman disguised as a man, underlining the fact that pricking was a man's domain.[112]

Informal community processes could also abuse women. In the village of Elgorriaga, Spain, in 1611, a crowd of mainly young men seized two young women alleged to be witches, Juana de Echiverria and María de Echiverria, tied them to the ends of a ladder, and made them walk round the neighbourhood all evening and all night. The ostensible purpose of this charivari-like ritual was to keep the witches awake, since witches in this region were believed to abduct children to the sabbat in their sleep. At every village the two women were beaten, and taunted with insults including not only 'witch' but 'common whore'. The young men's leader was the village alderman, Juanes de Legasa, himself aged 22. Left alone in the darkness with the two women at one point, he first tried and failed to rape Juana and then did in fact rape María. For this, after the collapse of the region's witchcraft panic, he was banished from the village for two years.[113] This episode provides another illustration of links between witchcraft and sexuality.

Demonic possession

Demonic possession was a distinctive, often gendered, form of misfortune that generated a distinctive form of accusation. It occurred when a person, usually but not always a woman, behaved in strange ways that they claimed were caused by a demon. Typically they writhed and contorted their bodies, or made obscene gestures, or vomited strange objects such as wool or pins. They shrieked, blasphemed, or spoke in strange languages. This was not considered to be their fault; they were victims of the demon that was 'possessing' their body. Possession was identified and treated by expert churchmen; if they did not create it, they certainly orchestrated it and directed it into specific channels. Catholics had elaborate rites for dealing with demons, and 'exorcism' of a possessed person sometimes became a public battle between the exorcist and the demon, carried out over the body of a suffering woman. In a series of possession cases in Catholic countries, demons were made to confess that they were in league with Protestants. Protestants had their own possession cases but failed to gain so much propaganda mileage from them, owing to internal disagreements and a more limited range of exorcism techniques.

Possession is hard to explain. The best that can be done is to say that it was the manifestation of a psychological disorder. To say that it was 'psychological' ascribes the cause of the disorder to the inner workings of the human mind – thus denying the possessed persons' own key claim, that the cause of their behaviour was an external demon. Unfortunately, psychologists have not solved the problem of demonic possession, which manifested itself in culture-specific ways that are no longer readily accessible. For the purposes of historical interpretation, this is not crucial because we can take it as given that some people, then as now, were prone to psychological disorders (mental illnesses) of some kind. It was the *manifestations* of these disorders that constituted demonic possession – and the manifestations were specific to early modern culture. People attributed their problems to demons because early modern culture included a belief in demons.

The idea that the demon 'possessing' a victim had been sent by a witch was related to the idea that the witch might send their 'spectre' or 'apparition' to cause the victim to suffer. This occurred at Salem, Massachusetts, in 1692; thus Salem was not strictly an episode of *demonic* possession, but shared several characteristics with it from the point of view of witch-hunting dynamics.

All this had two connections with witchcraft. Firstly, intellectual discussion of demonic possession and exorcism was carried out within the same framework as intellectual discussion of witchcraft. Secondly, some possessed people blamed witches for causing their possession. It was a demon and not a witch that was doing the actual 'possessing', but, if a possessed person said that a witch had caused their problem, it was assumed that the witch had sent the demon. Possession could thus be a type of malefice – harm done by a witch. As such it was involved in some noteworthy witch-hunts, particularly in the seventeenth century. As an exotic and high-profile type of malefice, it was much discussed. Ultimately, as we shall see in Chapter 10, possession helped to discredit demonology.

Witchcraft and gender-related trauma

Early modern Europe could be a hard place to live. Quite a few people were involved in traumatic episodes of one kind or another during their lives, and suffered from guilt and psychological disturbance as a result. If such a person was accused of witchcraft, in their minds they might well link the accusation with their existing difficulties. They really felt guilty – not necessarily guilty of witchcraft, but guilty of something. Such feelings of guilt readily surfaced in confessions.

Patterns of trauma were often gender-related. Some troubled women experienced wicked thoughts, desires or fantasies. They felt angry, frustrated or inadequate in their relationships with their husbands or children. Some experienced fantasies of killing their husbands or children. Some experienced fantasies of killing themselves – a common symptom of depression. Such a woman might well understand, in terms recognised by her culture, that these wicked thoughts were inspired by the Devil. If she was then interrogated on suspicion of witchcraft, she might well say a good deal about her relationship with the Devil.

These wicked thoughts could be enough by themselves to make a woman feel that she had succumbed to the Devil's wiles, but some women went further and translated their thoughts into action. They really did kill their children, or tried to, and afterwards were racked with guilt. Priscilla Collit, in Suffolk, England, in 1645, confessed that twelve years earlier, in desperate poverty and in a 'sickness' that sounds like postpartum depression, she had laid her baby by the fire to burn it, but one of her older children pulled the baby away when its hair and clothes began to burn. What could have made her act so wickedly? Collit attributed her behaviour to 'temptation' by the Devil.[114] If someone suggested to such a woman that she was a witch, she might well accept this as an explanation of her guilt.

Other women felt guilty because of sexual problems or traumas. Zofia Fiertayka, in Korytkowo, Poland, was subjected to the swimming test and floated. Asked why the water had rejected her, she confessed that it was because she was suffering from a vaginal discharge, and because she had committed bad deeds in her youth that she had never confessed to a priest.[115] Barbelline Chaponey, accused in Alsace in 1604, had been raped by five soldiers in 1593; interrogated about her meeting with the Devil, she said that she had met him at the place where she had been raped.[116] Women could have traumatic relationships with their own bodies.

Curses, as we saw in Chapter 4 and earlier in this chapter, were gender-related; both men and women feared the power of the female curse. This was linked to gender-related trauma, because some women who uttered a curse saw their curse take effect – forcing them to look back in anguish at the harm they believed themselves to have caused. Goody Cross, after cursing a child in London, England, in 1628, remorsefully agreed to lift the curse after the child fell ill.[117] The 'refusal-guilt syndrome', discussed in Chapter 4, is usually considered from the point of view of the guilty feelings of the victim of witchcraft – the person who refused charity to the beggar, thus prompting the beggar's curse. But the beggar who saw their curse strike the victim did not necessarily feel pleased.

There may well have been a distinct pattern of adolescent trauma. Adolescence, then as now, could be a difficult time. Witchcraft loomed large in the fantasies of Margaretha Hörber, a troubled 13-year-old orphan lodged with a miller's family in Gebsattel, Germany, in 1627. She failed to learn prayers, then ran away but was sent back. When the miller and his wife threatened to beat her, Hörber claimed that the Devil was preventing her from praying. She then developed this into an elaborate sabbat narrative, including a claim that she had had sex with the Devil. A physical examination showed that she was a virgin, however, and her claims were dismissed.[118]

Thus, under interrogation, various traumas could become magnified and focused on witchcraft. Denise Prudhon la Mareschaude, one of the witches tried by Boguet in Franche-Comté in 1607, said this about herself and the three women who had accused her of having been at the sabbat: 'It is also necessary that I should be burned thus, for all four of us should be burned; I don't know how many times they took me there. I didn't kill anyone. I didn't do anything.'[119] Prudhon had clearly taken on board her accusers' idea that she was guilty, even though she was confused about what she was guilty of. Marguerite Touret, the Franche-Comté magical practitioner discussed above, felt that she was guilty of witchcraft 'because of my miserable youth'. She had long ago borne an illegitimate child and had made a wicked vow, 'renouncing her share of Paradise', in the hope of marrying the child's father. As a result, she lamented, 'she was lost'.[120]

A remarkable psychoanalytical interpretation has been offered of the young female witch-accusers of New England as they struggled with conflicting feelings towards their mothers. These daughters subconsciously separated out the loving feelings that they experienced from the aggressive feelings that they also experienced, and 'projected' the aggression onto others. The daughters, unable to allow themselves to feel angry or frustrated with their mothers, subconsciously turned these aggressive feelings round, experiencing a feeling that *someone else* – someone rather like their mother – was being aggressive against *them*. They did not accuse their actual mothers, though: instead they displaced the imagined aggression onto other older women who resembled their mothers. These adolescents thus made subconscious sense of their own internal troubles by perceiving aggression against them by other older women – the witches whom they accused of afflicting them.[121]

Research has not yet identified witch-related patterns of male trauma, or male fantasies of wicked magical power. Men's wicked fantasies may have been less related to gender-related offences. Documented infanticide, for instance, was largely carried out by women (about 90 per cent), and fantasies of infanticide may have been similarly gendered. Some of the men who made real pacts with the Devil (discussed above) may have suffered from depression. Andrzej Bocheński, in Poznań, Poland, in 1722, seems to have been issuing an indirect cry for help when he ran away from his master and left a written pact with the Devil on his brother's table, where it was sure to be found.[122]

Conclusion: Connecting witches and women

Many ideas about witchcraft were about sexuality. In a patriarchal society, that meant that they were predominantly about women, because women were thought of as sexual beings. Many other ideas about witchcraft were about fertility. These ideas too were predominantly about women, because women were thought of as fertile and nurturing beings. Witches were often opposed to fertility and nurturance, killing children instead of caring for them, offering food and drink that was poisonous instead of nourishing, interfering with dairying, and sometimes even bringing storms that devastated crops. To be socially accepted, women had to keep the sexual side of their natures under control, but keep the nurturing side constantly in view. Since the two were closely intertwined, this was a difficult balancing act.[123]

Connections between ideas about women and ideas about witches ran in two directions. When people thought about witches, they could identify characteristics of witches that would tend to associate them with women. Conversely, when they thought about women, they could identify characteristics of women that would tend to associate them with witchcraft. The connections were mostly indirect, but they existed.

As well as being a two-way relationship, connections between ideas about witches and ideas about women could also operate differently for the elite and the common folk. The relationship was one of ideas – or, if we prefer, of ideology – because it was *ideas* about people's nature or behaviour that were constructed as witchcraft, rather than their actual nature (whatever that was) or their actual behaviour. As far as we can tell, these ideas were shared by men and women, though it is hard to be sure, partly because women's ideas tended to be recorded in documents written by men. At any rate, we can break down these ideas into four categories: elite ideas about 'witches', elite ideas about 'women', popular ideas about 'witches', and popular ideas about 'women'. Let us take each of these categories in turn.

Members of the elite, when they thought about 'witches', knew that witches were not necessarily women. Their idea of the demonic witch foregrounded the demonic pact, the sabbat, and the idea of conspiracy, none of which were inherently gendered. Early demonological thinkers, indeed, might focus on *heretical* conspiracy, or on necromancers or learned magicians – ideas pointing towards men more than women. Several of the early demonologists of the 1430s did specify that women were involved in the 'new sect' of witchcraft, but their reasons for doing so were less explicit than their reasons for explaining the sect in other less gendered ways.

When members of the elite thought about 'women', by contrast, their ideas did point more clearly towards witchcraft. Women were seen as imperfect versions of men, lacking strength and reason, and so more open to the Devil's persuasions. Women were also thought of as sexual beings, because it was their sexuality that differentiated them from normal (male) humans. They were thus thought of as committing fornication and adultery, which was problematic for godly discipline. (Men also committed fornication and adultery, but were not blamed so heavily for it.) The realm of love magic, too, was a realm of illicit female power. Finally, women's sexuality also opened them to more intimate relations with the male Devil. Ideas focusing on sexual relations between witch and Devil inevitably foregrounded women.

As for the common folk: what gendered ideas did they have about 'witches'? Their main idea was that of the village witch. Village witches committed malefice, either against people's health – part of women's domestic sphere – or against aspects of their economic livelihood – which could be men's or women's responsibility. So far these ideas, like those of the elite, were only partially gendered. But the common folk also thought that witches cursed people – an idea that was closely related to malefice. Curses were things that women did, not men. And people believed in folkloric witches, who were not necessarily human but who were always female.

The common folk's ideas about 'women' could also point towards witchcraft. Women, they thought, tended to be quarrelsome and to curse people. In the realm of magical cursing we thus see a particularly strong two-way link between ideas about witches and ideas about women. The common folk also saw women as sexual beings, but this did not point so closely to witchcraft because the village witch was not as sexually active as the demonic witch. Women's contact with the physical but mysterious processes of birth and death might also point towards magical involvement.

Thus, the attack on witches was not simply an attack on 'women'. It was thought of as an attack on *quarrelsome* women, or *sexually-transgressive* women, or *superstitious* women. It was also an attack on some types of men, such as witch-priests or werewolves; but these were much narrower groups. Almost any woman might at some point in her life be considered quarrelsome, sexually-transgressive or superstitious. In early modern Europe, therefore, male witches were exceptional: female witches were normal. If you were a man, you could be confident that witches were other people; nobody would accuse you of witchcraft unless you fell within quite narrow categories. If you were a woman, you could not be so sure; a witch could easily be you.

Notes

1 Pierre de Lancre, *On the Inconstancy of Witches: Pierre de Lancre's Tableau de l'inconstance des mauvais anges et demons (1612)*, ed. and trans. Harriet Stone and Gerhild Scholz Williams (Turnhout, 2006), 80–1 (I.iii.2). Reproduced with permission of Brepols Publishers.
2 This figure derives from one of the most careful examinations of the statistics: Wolfgang Behringer, *Witches and Witch-Hunts: A Global History* (Cambridge, 2004), 158.
3 William Monter, 'Toads and eucharists: the male witches of Normandy, 1564–1660', *French Historical Studies*, 20 (1997), 563–95.
4 Maia Madar, 'Estonia I: werewolves and poisoners', in Bengt Ankarloo and Gustav Henningsen (eds.), *Early Modern European Witchcraft: Centres and Peripheries* (Oxford, 1991), 257–72, at p. 267.
5 Marijke Gijswijt-Hofstra, 'Six centuries of witchcraft in the Netherlands: themes, outlines, and interpretations', in Marijke Gijswijt-Hofstra and Willem Frijhoff (eds.), *Witchcraft in the Netherlands from the Fourteenth to the Twentieth Century*, trans. Rachel M. J. van der Wilden-Fall (Rotterdam, 1991), 1–36, at p. 33.
6 Willem de Blécourt, 'The making of the female witch: reflections on witchcraft and gender in the early modern period', *Gender and History*, 12 (2000), 287–309, at p. 300; Maryse Simon, *Les affaires de sorcellerie dans le val de Lièpvre (XVIe et XVIIe siècles)* ([Strasbourg:] Publications de la Société Savante d'Alsace, 2006), 8; T. P. Vukanovic, 'Witchcraft in the central Balkans (i): characteristics of witches', *Folklore*, 100 (1989), 9–24, at p. 10.

7 Raisa Maria Toivo, 'Male witches and masculinity in early modern Finnish witchcraft trials', in Marianna Muravyeva and Raisa Maria Toivo (eds.), *Gender in Late Medieval and Early Modern Europe* (London, 2013), 137–52.
8 Quoted in Susan C. Karant-Nunn and Merry E. Wiesner-Hanks (eds.), *Luther on Women: A Sourcebook* (Cambridge, 2003), 28.
9 Mario Weick and Ana Guinote, 'When subjective experiences matter: power increases reliance on the ease of retrieval', *Journal of Personality and Social Psychology*, 94 (2008), 956–70.
10 Sophie Houdard, *Les sciences du diable: Quatre discours sur la sorcellerie (XVe–XVIIe siècle)* (Paris, 1992), 43.
11 Lucy de Bruyn, *Woman and the Devil in Sixteenth-Century Literature* (Tisbury, 1979), p. xii.
12 Thomas Laqueur, *Making Sex: Body and Gender from the Greeks to Freud* (Cambridge, Mass., 1990).
13 Karen Jones and Michael Zell, '"The divels speciall instruments": women and witchcraft before the "great witch-hunt"', *Social History*, 30 (2005), 45–63.
14 Richard Suggett, 'Witchcraft dynamics in early modern Wales', in Michael Roberts and Simone Clarke (eds.), *Women and Gender in Early Modern Wales* (Cardiff, 2000), 75–103, at p. 91.
15 Valerie Kivelson, *Desperate Magic: The Moral Economy of Witchcraft in Seventeenth-Century Russia* (Ithaca, NY, 2013), 131–2.
16 Carol F. Karlsen, *The Devil in the Shape of a Woman: Witchcraft in Colonial New England* (New York, 1987), 117–52.
17 Julian Goodare, 'Men and the witch-hunt in Scotland', in Alison Rowlands (ed.), *Witchcraft and Masculinities in Early Modern Europe* (Basingstoke, 2009), 149–70, at pp. 157–8.
18 Wanda Wyporska, *Witchcraft in Early Modern Poland, 1500–1800* (Basingstoke, 2013), 56.
19 *Malleus*, 17A–C (I.2).
20 Karlsen, *The Devil in the Shape of a Woman*, 69.
21 Sara Read, *Menstruation and the Female Body in Early Modern England* (Basingstoke, 2013), 171–4.
22 Malcolm Gaskill, 'Witchcraft in early modern Kent: stereotypes and the background to accusations', in Jonathan Barry, Marianne Hester and Gareth Roberts (eds.), *Witchcraft in Early Modern Europe* (Cambridge, 1996), 257–87, at p. 261.
23 Johannes Dillinger, *Evil People: A Comparative Study of Witch Hunts in Swabian Austria and the Electorate of Trier*, trans. Laura Stokes (Charlottesville, Va., 2009), 79.
24 Roger Aubenas, *La sorcière et l'inquisiteur: Episode de l'Inquisition en Provence (1439)* (Aix-en-Provence, 1956).
25 Karlsen, *The Devil in the Shape of a Woman*, 77–116; Louise Yeoman, 'Hunting the rich witch in Scotland: high-status witchcraft suspects and their persecutors, 1590–1650', in Julian Goodare (ed.), *The Scottish Witch-Hunt in Context* (Manchester, 2002), 106–21.
26 *Malleus*, 64B (I.11).
27 David H. Darst, 'Witchcraft in Spain: the testimony of Martín de Castañega's Treatise on superstition and witchcraft (1529)', *Proceedings of the American Philosophical Society*, 123 (1979), 298–322, at p. 302.
28 Marianna G. Muravyeva, 'Russian witchcraft on trial: historiography and methodology for studying Russian witches', in Marko Nenonen and Raisa Maria Toivo (eds.), *Writing Witch-Hunt Histories: Challenging the Paradigm* (Leiden, 2014), 109–39, at pp. 123–4.
29 De Lancre, *On the Inconstancy of Witches*, 417–55 (VI.ii).

30 Monter, 'Toads and eucharists', 582.
31 Robert Walinski-Kiehl, 'La chasse aux sorcières et le sabbat des sorcières dans les évêchés de Bamberg et Würzburg (vers 1590–vers 1630)', in Nicole Jacques-Chaquin and Maxime Préaud (eds.), *Le sabbat des sorciers en Europe (XVe–XVIIIe siècles)* (Grenoble, 1993), 213–25, at pp. 221–2.
32 Rolf Schulte, *Man as Witch: Male Witches in Central Europe*, trans. Linda Froome-Döring (Basingstoke, 2009), 8–35.
33 Jean Bodin, *On the Demon-mania of Witches*, trans. Randy A. Scott, ed. Jonathan L. Pearl (Toronto, 1995), 113, 160 (II,4, III.5).
34 Schulte, *Man as Witch*, 215.
35 Lea, *Materials*, iii, 1192–5.
36 Elisabeth Biesel, 'Les descriptions du sabbat dans les confessions des inculpés lorrains et trévirois', in Jacques-Chaquin and Préaud (eds.), *Le sabbat des sorciers*, 183–97, at pp. 189–90, 192.
37 Lara Apps and Andrew Gow, *Male Witches in Early Modern Europe* (Manchester, 2003), 131–5.
38 Susanna Burghartz, 'The equation of women and witches: a case study of witchcraft trials in Lucerne and Lausanne in the fifteenth and sixteenth centuries', in Richard J. Evans (ed.), *The German Underworld: Deviants and Outcasts in German History* (London, 1988), 57–74.
39 Mario Gollwitzer, 'Do normative transgressions affect punitive judgments? An empirical test of the psychoanalytic scapegoat hypothesis', *Personality and Social Psychology Bulletin*, 30 (2004), 1650–60.
40 Zachary K. Rothschild, Mark J. Landau, Daniel Sullivan and Lucas A. Keefer, 'A dual-motive model of scapegoating: displacing blame to reduce guilt or increase control', *Journal of Personality and Social Psychology*, 102 (2012), 1148–63; Brock Bastian, Simon M. Laham, Sam Wilson, Nick Haslam and Peter Koval, 'Blaming, praising, and protecting our humanity: the implications of everyday dehumanization for judgments of moral status', *British Journal of Social Psychology*, 50 (2011), 469–83.
41 Trevor Dean, *Crime in Medieval Europe, 1200–1550* (Harlow, 2001), 77–8.
42 Franck Mercier, *La Vauderie d'Arras: Une chasse aux sorcières à l'automne du Moyen Âge* (Rennes, 2006), 99–107, 270.
43 María Tausiet, *Urban Magic in Early Modern Spain: Abracadabra Omnipotens*, trans. Susannah Howe (Basingstoke, 2014), 131–4.
44 Lyndal Roper, *Witch Craze: Terror and Fantasy in Baroque Germany* (New Haven, Conn., 2004), 132; Peter C. Hoffer and N. E. H. Hull, *Murdering Mothers: Infanticide in England and New England, 1558–1803* (New York, 1984), 28–30.
45 Schulte, *Man as Witch*, 218–45.
46 Laura Stokes, *Demons of Urban Reform: Early European Witch Trials and Criminal Justice, 1430–1530* (Basingstoke, 2011), 161–5.
47 Maryse Simon, 'Cuisine de sorcières entre France et Allemagne à l'époque moderne: remèdes et usages alimentaires de guérisseuses, faim et cannibalisme au banquet diabolique', *Food and History*, 6 (2008), 91–123.
48 Quoted in Francis Bavoux, *La sorcellerie en Franche-Comté (Pays de Quingey)* (Monaco, 1954), 122–3.
49 Schulte, *Man as Witch*, 216.
50 Carmel Cassar, 'Witchcraft beliefs and social control in seventeenth century Malta', *Journal of Mediterranean Studies*, 3 (1993), 316–34.
51 Christine Meek, 'Men, women and magic: some cases from late medieval Lucca', in Christine Meek (ed.), *Women in Renaissance and Early Modern Europe* (Dublin, 2000), 43–66, at p. 60.
52 Tausiet, *Urban Magic in Early Modern Spain*, 68–9.

53 Louise N. Kallestrup, *Agents of Witchcraft in Early Modern Italy and Denmark* (Basingstoke, 2015), 24–6.
54 Valerie A. Kivelson, 'Lethal convictions: the power of a Satanic paradigm in Russian and European witchcraft trials', *Magic, Ritual, and Witchcraft*, 6 (2011), 34–61, at p. 46.
55 Soili-Maria Olli, 'The Devil's pact: a male strategy', in Owen Davies and Willem de Blécourt (eds.), *Beyond the Witch Trials: Witchcraft and Magic in Enlightenment Europe* (Manchester, 2004), 100–16.
56 Johannes Dillinger, *Magical Treasure Hunting in Europe and North America: A History* (Basingstoke, 2012), 135–41.
57 B. Ann Tlusty, 'Invincible blades and invulnerable bodies: weapons magic in early-modern Germany', *European Review of History: Revue européenne d'histoire*, 22 (2015), 658–79.
58 Schulte, *Man as Witch*, 172.
59 Willem de Blécourt and Freek Pereboom, 'Insult and admonition: witchcraft in the land of Vollenhove, seventeenth century', in Gijswijt-Hofstra and Frijhoff (eds.), *Witchcraft in the Netherlands*, 119–31, at p. 126.
60 Robin Briggs, *The Witches of Lorraine* (Oxford, 2007), 70.
61 Alexandra Pittet, 'Derrière le masque du sorcier: une enquête sociologique à partir des procès de sorcellerie du registre Ac 29 (Pays de Vaud, 1438–1528)', in Martine Ostorero, Georg Modestin and Kathrin Utz Tremp (eds.), *Chasses aux sorcières et démonologie: Entre discours et pratiques (XIVe–XVIIe siècles)* (Firenze, 2010), 199–221, at p. 211.
62 Sophie Simon, *'Si je le veux, il mourra!' Maléfices et sorcellerie dans la campagne genevoise (1497–1530)* (Lausanne, 2007), 104–12.
63 Robin Briggs, *Witches and Neighbours: The Social and Cultural Context of European Witchcraft* (2nd edn., Oxford, 2002), 229.
64 Robert Muchembled, *Les derniers bûchers: Un village de Flandre et ses sorcières sous Louis XIV* (Paris, 1981), 73–5.
65 H. C. Erik Midelfort, 'Witch hunting and the domino theory', in James Obelkevich (ed.), *Religion and the People, 800–1700* (Chapel Hill, NC, 1979), 277–88, at pp. 282–3.
66 Roper, *Witch Craze*, 31–2.
67 Robin Briggs, 'Male witches in the duchy of Lorraine', in Rowlands (ed.), *Witchcraft and Masculinities*, 31–51, at pp. 40–2.
68 John P. Demos, *Entertaining Satan: Witchcraft and the Culture of Early New England* (Oxford, 1982), 60–2; Schulte, *Man as Witch*, 216.
69 Laura Kounine, 'The gendering of witchcraft: defence strategies of men and women in German witchcraft trials', *German History*, 31 (2013), 295–317, at pp. 306–10.
70 Quoted in Paul Boyer and Stephen Nissenbaum (eds.), *The Salem Witchcraft Papers*, 3 vols. (New York, 1977), ii, 357.
71 Monter, 'Toads and eucharists', 577.
72 Karlsen, *The Devil in the Shape of a Woman*, 65–6.
73 *Malleus*, 141B–D (II.i.13).
74 Alison Rowlands, *Witchcraft Narratives in Germany: Rothenburg, 1561–1652* (Manchester, 2003), 55.
75 Gunnar W. Knutsen, 'Topics of persecution: witchcraft historiography in the Iberian world', in Nenonen and Toivo (eds.), *Writing Witch-Hunt Histories*, 167–90, at p. 177.
76 This is not to say that children are necessarily more prone than adults to

developing false memories: C. J. Brainerd and V. F. Reyna, 'Reliability of children's testimony in the era of developmental reversals', *Developmental Review*, 32 (2012), 224–67.
77 Louis Schlaefli, 'Particularités relatives aux procès de sorcellerie intentés aux enfants à Molsheim au XVIIe siècle', *Revue d'Alsace*, 134 (2008), 213–27, at p. 220.
78 Hans Sebald, *Witch-Children: From Salem Witch-Hunts to Modern Courtrooms* (Amherst, NY, 1995), 42.
79 Nicolas Remy, *Demonolatry*, trans. E. A. Ashwin, ed. Montague Summers (London, 1930), 94–9 (II.2); Henri Boguet, *An Examen of Witches*, trans. E. A. Ashwin, ed. Montague Summers (London, 1929), 233–5.
80 Francis Bavoux, *Hantises et diableries dans la terre abbatiale de Luxeuil: D'un procès de l'Inquisition (1529) à l'épidémie démoniaque de 1628–1630* (Monaco, 1956), 160.
81 Midelfort, 'Witch hunting and the domino theory', 282–3.
82 Robert Muchembled, 'Satanic myths and cultural reality', in Ankarloo and Henningsen (eds.), *Early Modern European Witchcraft*, 139–60, at p. 143.
83 Schlaefli, 'Particularités relatives aux procès de sorcellerie', 219.
84 *Encyclopedia*, iv, 1000–1.
85 Robert Muchembled, 'Terres de contrastes: France, Pays-Bas, Provinces-Unies', in Robert Muchembled (ed.), *Magie et sorcellerie en Europe du Moyen Âge à nos jours* (Paris, 1994), 99–132, at pp. 122–3.
86 Margaret A. Sullivan, 'The witches of Dürer and Hans Baldung Grien', *Renaissance Quarterly*, 53 (2000), 333–401, at pp. 355–7.
87 Quoted in E. William Monter (ed.), *European Witchcraft* (New York, 1969), 76.
88 Georg Modestin, *Le diable chez l'évêque: Chasse aux sorciers dans le diocèse de Lausanne (vers 1460)* (Lausanne, 1999), 202–5.
89 François Bordes, *Sorciers et sorcières: Procès de sorcellerie en Gascogne et pays Basque* (Toulouse, 1999), 85–6.
90 Roper, *Witch Craze*, 90–1.
91 Nicole Jacques-Chaquin and Maxime Préaud (eds.), *Les sorciers du carroi de Marlou: Un procès de sorcellerie en Berry (1582–1583)* (Grenoble, 1996), 79, 126, 149, 161.
92 Tamar Herzig, 'The demons' reaction to sodomy: witchcraft and sexuality in Gianfrancesco Pico della Mirandola's *Strix*', *Sixteenth Century Journal*, 34 (2003), 53–72.
93 Roper, *Witch Craze*, 283.
94 Julian Goodare, 'Galt, Maud, fl. 1648/9', in Elizabeth Ewan, Sue Innes and Siân Reynolds (eds.), *The Biographical Dictionary of Scottish Women* (Edinburgh, 2006), 131.
95 Roper, *Witch Craze*, 91; Gustav Henningsen, *The Witches' Advocate: Basque Witchcraft and the Spanish Inquisition, 1609–1614* (Reno, Nev., 1980), 164.
96 Houdard, *Les sciences du diable*, 47–51.
97 Ulric Molitor (Müller), *Des sorcières et des devineresses*, trans. Emile Nourry (Paris, 1926), 77–8 (ch. 13).
98 Michèle Brocard Plaut, 'Le sabbat et sa répression en Savoie aux XVIIe et XVIIIe siècles', in Jacques-Chaquin and Préaud (eds.), *Le sabbat des sorciers*, 199–211, at p. 208.
99 Robert Muchembled, 'The witches of the Cambrésis: the acculturation of the rural world in the sixteenth and seventeenth centuries', in Obelkevich (ed.), *Religion and the People*, 221–76, at p. 261.

100 Michael Bailey, 'The medieval concept of the witches' sabbath', *Exemplaria*, 8 (1996), 419–39, at p. 439; *Encyclopedia*, iii, 647.
101 Barbara Rosen (ed.), *Witchcraft in England, 1558–1618* (2nd edn., Amherst, Mass., 1991), 319.
102 Emmanuel Le Roy Ladurie, 'The aiguillette: castration by magic', in his *The Mind and Method of the Historian*, trans. Siân Reynolds and Ben Reynolds (Chicago, Ill., 1981), 84–96.
103 Tausiet, *Urban Magic in Early Modern Spain*, 97.
104 Maryse Simon, 'Convergence d'intérêts ou conflits de juridictions? Jeux de pouvoirs dans les procès de sorcellerie entre Lorraine et Alsace', in Ostorero et al. (eds.), *Chasses aux sorcières et démonologie*, 45–65, at p. 51.
105 Wyporska, *Witchcraft in Early Modern Poland*, 141; Kivelson, *Desperate Magic*, 92–6.
106 Bodin, *Demon-mania*, 99–100 (II.1).
107 *Malleus*, 115A–118D (II.i.7).
108 Kounine, 'Gendering of witchcraft', 301–4.
109 Jonathan B. Durrant, *Witchcraft, Gender and Society in Early Modern Germany* (Leiden, 2007), 235.
110 Brocard Plaut, 'Le sabbat et sa répression en Savoie', 206.
111 Roper, *Witch Craze*, 54.
112 Lauren Martin, 'Caldwell, Christian, fl. 1660s', in Ewan et al. (eds.), *Biographical Dictionary of Scottish Women*, 59.
113 Gustav Henningsen (ed.), *The Salazar Documents: Inquisitor Alonso de Salazar Frías and Others on the Basque Witch Persecution* (Leiden, 2004), 67–73.
114 Louise Jackson, 'Women, wives and mothers: witchcraft persecution and women's confessions in seventeenth-century England', *Women's History Review*, 4 (1995), 63–83, at pp. 75–7.
115 Wyporska, *Witchcraft in Early Modern Poland*, 58.
116 Simon, *Les affaires de sorcellerie dans le val de Lièpvre*, 62–3.
117 Keith Thomas, *Religion and the Decline of Magic* (London, 1971), 611.
118 Rowlands, *Witchcraft Narratives*, 106–24.
119 Quoted in Houdard, *Les sciences du diable*, 122–3.
120 Bavoux, *La sorcellerie en Franche-Comté*, 130–1.
121 John Demos, 'Underlying themes in the witchcraft of seventeenth-century New England', *American Historical Review*, 75 (1969–70), 1311–26.
122 Wyporska, *Witchcraft in Early Modern Poland*, 66–7.
123 Clarke Garrett, 'Women and witches: patterns of analysis', *Signs*, 3 (1977–78), 461–70.

10 The end of witch-hunting

> We whose names are underwritten, being in the Year 1692, called to serve as Jurors, in court at Salem, on Tryal of many; who were by some suspected Guilty of doing Acts of Witchcraft upon the bodies of sundry persons:
>
> We confess that we our selves were not capable to understand, nor able to withstand the mysterious delusions of the Powers of Darkness, and Prince of the Air; but were for want of Knowledge in our selves, and better Information from others, prevailed with to take up with such Evidence against the Accused as on further consideration, and better Information, we justly fear was insufficient for the touching the Lives of any, Deut. 17. 6. whereby we fear we have been instrumental with others, tho Ignorantly and unwittingly, to bring upon our selves, and this People of the Lord, the Guilt of Innocent Blood.
>
> The apology of the Salem jurors, c.1696[1]

Introduction

Not long ago, historians studying witch-hunting used to consider that its decline was particularly hard to explain. As they researched witch-hunting from various angles, they discovered more and more reasons for why it occurred. Trials led on to more trials. It seemed as though the European witch-hunt was an unstoppable juggernaut. Why did it not hurtle onwards until it had engulfed everyone in its path?

The main answer to this question is that it is a badly-framed question. The European witch-hunt did engulf about 50,000 people. Many more were accused, and a climate of hatred and fear was stirred up to spread across Europe. It was a dark time. The foregoing chapters have indeed shown many reasons why witch-hunting occurred – enough reasons for 50,000 executions. So perhaps there were enough reasons for 50,000 executions *and no more*? Most people, most of the time, do not need a reason for not burning people at the stake.

The European witch-hunt in fact carried within itself some of the causes that would lead to its decline. There was often some doubt, some scepticism, and some protest. Moreover, there was often a good deal of indifference – indifference not perhaps to witch-hunting, but to the ideals of the witch-hunters. Not everyone wanted witch-hunting all that much. So we should not regard explaining the decline and end of witch-hunting as an insuperable problem.

There were three major causes of decline, all of which related mainly to the elite rather than the common folk. First, lawyers and judges became concerned about miscarriages of justice, and tightened up judicial standards. It became harder to achieve convictions in court, and people were discouraged from starting witchcraft prosecutions because they realised that the suspects were likely to be acquitted. Second, politicians lost interest in prosecuting witches, because their ideology began to accept religious pluralism. When religious wars ended, and states no longer proclaimed themselves as godly, there was less need to punish the enemies of godliness. Indeed, such punishments began to look like 'persecution', which was now agreed to be a bad thing. Third, intellectuals ceased to take demonology seriously, with the rise of the Scientific Revolution. The Devil was no longer necessary to explain strange events.

These three developments – judicial, ideological and intellectual – all interacted. If courts issued acquittals, that encouraged politicians to think that witches were ideologically unimportant. If politicians found witch-hunting to be ideologically unnecessary, lawyers would feel less need to achieve convictions of witches. If intellectuals circulated new scientific ideas, lawyers and politicians would feel that demonology was losing credibility. So it is hard to disentangle the three causes.

All three of these developments fed into a further trend in political culture: the decline of the Devil. Levels of fear are hard to measure with historical evidence, but the dethronement of the Devil as the great enemy of Christendom seems to have occurred during the seventeenth century – the crucial period during which witch-hunting went into a decline from which it would never recover. The chronology of the Devil's decline is hard to chart, but it will require attention, at least indirectly. Once the broader judicial, ideological and intellectual developments have been established, the remainder of this chapter will discuss the effects that these developments had on demonology and witchcraft prosecutions in an age of decline.

Patterns of decline

The decline of witch-hunting was a long, slow and uneven process. Complete statistics for executions over time have not yet been gathered, but it seems that a climax was reached in the 1620s. After that, the trend was uneven, but generally downwards for the next century and a half. Why was there a downwards trend? And why was it so slow and uneven? Before looking at the causes of decline, we need to establish the patterns of decline.

It is hard to chart a coherent long-term pattern, for two main reasons. The first reason is that short-term patterns predominate; much witch-hunting occurred in short bursts of panic. After each panic in a given region, there was a 'decline'. That 'decline' may seem to be a part of the overall decline of European witch-hunting, but this is misleading. We should regard the decline of an individual panic as no more than a regional and temporary phenomenon. After all, every individual panic declined, even when the overall trend of witch-hunting was upwards. Some regions had repeated panics.

A second reason why it is difficult to chart a long-term pattern is that there were different long-term patterns in different regions. For some regions, notably Italy, the overall long-term decline seems to have occurred as early as the early sixteenth century. For others, notably Hungary or Poland, witch-hunting increased in the later seventeenth century, and there is nothing that looks like 'decline' until the early eighteenth century. For most places, though, including the German heartland of witch-hunting, the decline of witch-hunting occurred in the seventeenth century. It is on that century that the present chapter will focus most of its attention. Particularly close attention should be given to the middle years of the century, from about 1630 to 1670, because it was during these years that the previous overall upward trend in witch-hunting seems to have reversed itself.

There was also a geographical shift. In the early seventeenth century, the heartland of witch-hunting was Germany, especially western Germany and its Rhineland neighbours: Luxembourg, Lorraine, Switzerland. In the later seventeenth century, the centre of gravity shifted eastwards: Hungary, Poland, Sweden. These were places that had not experienced serious witch-hunting before. Hungary, indeed, reached the peak of its witch-hunting as late as the early eighteenth century. This may be seen as an eastward movement, but it can also be seen as a movement towards the periphery. There were also very late panics in Portugal, and – across the Atlantic – in New England.

Was there a shift away from panics and towards individual trials? Possibly, but the evidence is not entirely clear. It is clear enough that the biggest panics were mainly confined to the peak period for witch-hunting, from about 1580 to 1630. We also know that the very last trials, in the middle decades of the eighteenth century, were mostly isolated events. But the period from about 1630 to 1730 does not show a single clear trend. There were few really big panics, but the really big panics had never been common. Small panics continued to occur during this century or so of 'decline', both in the German heartland and in the peripheries just mentioned. In many places, the very last trials occurred during this century, and they were often individual ones. In Geneva, Michée Chauderon was the last to be executed, in 1652; there had been no executions before hers since 1626. In northern France, the jurisdiction of the *parlement* of Paris, the last two executions were in 1691; at that date, there had been no executions since 1625.[2] On the other hand, some places continued to experience small panics right to the end. All the later witchcraft cases in Savoy occurred in linked chains.[3] Individual trials were always more common than panics; in the present state of our knowledge there is no reason to think that the ratio between the two changed during the period of decline. Future statistical studies may shed light on this, and also on a related question that seems to be unanswerable at present: whether the period of decline saw a higher proportion of acquittals. In some places we see many acquittals among the later cases, but in other places we simply see fewer trials.

Further important questions await statistical analysis. What was the likelihood of panics recurring? How common was the once-for-all panic, as opposed to the serial panic? A statistical analysis might, for instance, compare the incidence of panics in the 1590s and the 1620s: were the places that had panics in the 1590s more likely to panic again in the 1620s, or less likely? If repeat panics were more likely, we might call this the 'entrenched' model: witch-hunts, once they started, were likely to entrench and repeat themselves. If, by contrast, repeat panics were less likely than panics in new places, we might call this the 'forest-fire' model: witch-hunts, once they started, would spread to other places but would not repeat themselves in any given place.

Until such a study is undertaken, historians must rely on impressionistic evidence and educated guesses. Individual examples of both the 'entrenched' and the 'forest-fire' models can be found, so no simple either-or answer can be given. For what it is worth, it may be suggested that during the rise of large-scale witch-hunting – say from 1560 to 1620 – both models were in operation. Panics, once they occurred, were likely to entrench themselves, recurring in the same place – and they were *also* likely to spread like a forest fire to other places. Gradually, during the 1620s and 1630s, the entrenched model declined, as people in more places learned the disadvantages of panics and worked out means of avoiding them. But the forest-fire model continued after the 1630s; places that had not yet had panics could still have them. The late witch-hunting in Sweden, Poland, Hungary and Portugal illustrates this pattern. The forest-fire model may even apply to individual trials. Anna Göldi in Glarus (see the text box 'Anna Göldi, the last witch') was not just Europe's last witch; she was also Glarus's *first* witch.

In analysing the pattern of dwindling trials, we have the benefit of hindsight – but we must be careful not to misuse this. When Anna Göldi was executed in 1782, people knew that witchcraft executions had become rare, but they did not know that Göldi would be Europe's last witch. A regional comparison may illustrate this issue. England and the United Netherlands both had similar patterns of witch-hunting in the later sixteenth century; they were both Protestant countries that did not try very hard to build godly states. They both prosecuted increased numbers of witches in the 1580s and 1590s, followed by a decline in the years after about 1600. In the United Netherlands, hindsight shows the decline to have been terminal; the last witch was executed in 1603. England's decline at that point looks quite similar – but England went on to have a small panic in Lancashire in 1612, and a large panic in East Anglia in 1645–47. At one time these English panics were dismissed as unusual events, but they were no more unusual than most panics. So, if England was capable of having panics in the early seventeenth century, perhaps the Netherlands was too? At the time, England and the Netherlands had similar potential for witch-hunting, with a trigger waiting to be pulled to start panics. It is only with hindsight that we know that the trigger was pulled in England and not in the Netherlands.

Here we need to distinguish between *patterns* of decline and *causes* of decline. Various 'patterns' have been identified (though none with certainty) in the chronological and geographical distribution of later witchcraft cases. The best-known pattern of this kind may be the idea that large panics 'declined' earlier than individual trials. But these patterns are not *causes* of decline: they are *effects* of the actual causes. And the patterns are rarely clear enough for us to be able to say confidently that a specific pattern had a specific cause. The patterns may be clarified in the future by Europe-wide statistical analysis, but, even then, patterns and causes will still be separate. Causes of decline need to be identified in their own right. Most of the rest of this chapter will attempt to identify long-term shifts in the judicial, ideological and intellectual culture of seventeenth-century Europe – shifts that would gradually cause people to find it more difficult, and less necessary, to execute witches.

There is one final point to make about the chronology of the causes of decline. The predominance of short-term patterns – panics rising and falling – means that we do not necessarily need the long-term causes to take effect immediately after the decline of any given panic. With hindsight we see an overall long-term decline after the climactic panics of the 1620s – but those panics were likely to decline anyway through short-term causes, of the kind that were discussed in Chapter 8. Without input from long-term causes of decline, the short-term pattern that we would expect to see would be a recurrence of panics later – perhaps a generation later. Thus, the significant development that we need to explain by reference to long-term causes is not the immediate decline of panics in the 1630s, but the failure of panics to renew themselves on the same scale in the 1650s or 1660s. Long-term causes of decline only needed to arise in this later period. We shall see that there are reasons for thinking that, by the 1650s, several long-term causes of decline had indeed arisen.

Anna Göldi, the last witch

The last witch to be legally executed in Europe was Anna Göldi, in the canton of Glarus, Switzerland, in 1782.[4] Born in 1734, in the neighbouring canton of St Gallen, Göldi worked as a household servant. Like many young female servants she was vulnerable to the sexual advances of powerful men; she bore three illegitimate children, one of which was fathered by the son of her employer. Another of her children died immediately after birth, and she was banished for allegedly killing it. This dubious background probably did not help her reputation.

(continued)

> In 1781 Göldi was working for a local physician and judge, Johann Jakob Tschuldi. She had an argument with his daughter, Anne-Miggeli, whereupon pins were found in the daughter's breakfast milk. Tschuldi, blaming his servant rather than his daughter, immediately dismissed Göldi, who fled to another canton. But Anne-Miggeli then started to suffer convulsions, and claimed to have vomited pins, nails and wire. After a search for Göldi, she was arrested and brought back to Glarus, and urged to heal Anne-Miggeli. A reconciliation followed, and Anne-Miggeli's convulsions subsided. However, her father pressed for a witchcraft trial. Under the threat of torture, Göldi confessed that she had given Anne-Miggeli a poisoned cake to cause her convulsions. She was convicted by the Glarus parliament, the canton's highest judicial as well as political body, and beheaded on 13 June 1782. Her execution caused an outcry, particularly in Germany, where the trial was denounced as 'judicial murder'.

Judicial caution

Witches were executed through judicial processes, so bringing the executions to an end required changes in judicial processes. Judges had to find the evidence of neighbours' bewitchment less convincing, or had to be less keen to extract evidence of demonic witchcraft through interrogation and torture, or both. This does not rule out the ideological and intellectual developments to be considered later in this chapter, since judges can be influenced by ideological or intellectual considerations, but that influence did have to be felt in the judicial field. It helps, therefore, to investigate judicial developments. As with the short-term and long-term patterns identified in the previous section of this chapter, there were short-term and long-term patterns of judicial caution.

Judicial caution expressed itself in acquittals, procedural regulations and reluctance to prosecute, and only rarely in repeal of laws. Witch-hunting could in theory have been ended by a government abolishing the laws making witchcraft a crime. However, few governments did this while significant witch-hunting was still going on. Many states — in Germany, Italy and Spain, for instance — had no 'national' witchcraft statutes to repeal. When there were repeals, these usually came long after executions had ceased. The Irish witchcraft statute was repealed in 1821, over a century after the last execution. Witch-hunting usually ended in the courts, and repeals were unimportant. This is not to say, though, that politicians and judges had different views; as we shall see, their approach to the issues was usually similar.

Although judicial caution contributed to the decline of witch-hunting in the seventeenth century, most judicial caution was not actually new in that century. Rather, it was a kind of default position – something that any early modern judge would tend to adopt if he and his court were not embroiled in a witchcraft panic. Such a position can be seen in Rothenburg ob der Tauber, Germany, as soon as witchcraft became a significant issue – from the 1560s onwards.[5] The trouble with this kind of default position was that it was liable to be overridden in a panic. The magistrates of Rothenburg could maintain their cautious position because they were never involved in a panic. We cannot say for certain that their caution prevented a panic from occurring; other similarly cautious magistrates abandoned their caution when a panic broke out. Cautious judges may have helped to prevent panics breaking out; after all, there *could* have been more witchcraft panics in Europe than those that actually occurred. But, because most judicial caution was not new in the seventeenth century, it is best seen as a background factor rather than a precipitating cause of the seventeenth-century decline of witch-hunting.

Judicial caution could be learned, but it could also be forgotten or deliberately set aside. We often find judicial caution between panics, or just after panics. Crucially, we sometimes find judicial caution *before* panics, with the authorities lowering their previously high standards of evidence when they began to panic. When judges and courts felt a need to hunt witches, they would override their earlier procedural caution. Caution could return naturally once the panic was past. For example, Scotland experienced a series of five panics, often a generation or so apart, in 1590–91, 1597, 1628–31, 1649–50 and 1661–62. After some of these panics, notably those of 1597 and 1649–50, short-term lessons were learned about judicial caution, but those lessons were not remembered for long enough to prevent future panics.[6] Even the famous 'apology' of the Salem jurors, quoted at the head of this chapter, may be an instance of the learning of short-term lessons. Moving as it is in its admission of the wrongs that were committed in a mood of panic, the 'apology' remains rooted in a vision of a godly society – the kind of society to which the Devil and his witches continued to pose a threat. That society was changing in Salem, as we shall see, but for non-judicial reasons.

Caution of this kind, following panics, can be found even in the fifteenth century. During a panic in Arras, in the Burgundian Netherlands, in 1459–60, several dozen witches were arrested, and many executed. However, some wealthy and influential people were accused, and this led to opposition. There were appeals to higher courts, and popular ballads criticised the witch-hunters. A lesson had been learned, and the witches were pardoned by the *parlement* of Paris in 1468 – mostly posthumously, but the pardon did help to clear the name of one survivor, Huguet Aymery, who had fled into exile.[7] This caution, as far as it went, can be regarded as the same phenomenon that would eventually contribute to reining in witch-hunting. But, on its own, judicial caution following panics was insufficient to bring about a sustained decline in witch-hunting. To say that witch-hunting was 'declining' in the 1460s would stretch credibility; if the Arras authorities had wanted to panic again, they would have.

Judicial action to curtail witch-hunting often took the form of central intervention to restrain over-zealous local courts. This intervention could come from central courts, or from princes and their councils, or both – one reason for being aware of links between judges and politicians. First, though, the relationship between local and central courts needs to be clarified. Prosecutions usually began in local courts, because that was where witchcraft suspects and their accusers lived. The most likely role of a central court would be to hear an appeal if the suspect was convicted locally. Such appeals sometimes succeeded, but that does not mean that central courts were inherently more cautious. They could sometimes have been *less* cautious – but, if a suspect was *acquitted* locally, the prosecution could not appeal, so this was never put to the test. The other possible role of a central court would be to issue procedural regulations for witchcraft trials. Such regulations could well restrain over-zealous local courts – but, as we saw in Chapter 8, central regulations sometimes *facilitated* witchcraft prosecutions. Another point from Chapter 8 should be borne in mind: witchcraft prosecutions had to pass through several stages, even in the locality, so that there were various ways in which they could be curtailed.

The variety of local-central relationships can be illustrated by some examples. In Denmark, when a lower court convicted someone of witchcraft, this verdict *always* had to be appealed to the higher provincial court.[8] In France, the *parlement* of Paris was concerned for due procedure, not opposed to witchcraft trials as such. We shall see that it helped to restrict prosecutions in the seventeenth century, but in 1596 it reprimanded Rodolphe Faguet, a local judge in Perche, because he had not followed up the accusations that two confessing witches had made against others.[9] In Poland, we find an example of central restriction that proved ineffective. The central assessory court, between 1668 and 1673, issued a series of decisions forbidding small-town courts from trying witches, and ordering witchcraft cases to be held in the larger towns with more professional courts. However, Poland was such a decentralised state that the assessory court could not get its decisions implemented. The years after 1673 in fact saw a steep rise in the number of witchcraft trials.[10] Finally, in Germany, the Holy Roman Empire had two central courts of limited effectiveness, the imperial chamber court and imperial aulic court. The German princely states did not always recognise their jurisdiction in practice. Still, the imperial chamber court did hear many appeals, especially during the mass panics of the 1620s, and took a generally restrictive approach that may well have helped to slow the pace of witch-hunting; the imperial aulic court, similarly, intervened to halt the Bamberg panic in 1631.[11]

Some more detailed instances of central intervention may now be given, all of which turned out to contribute to a long-term downward trend in prosecutions. With all of them we have the problem of hindsight: only with hindsight do we know that the trend would be a long-term one. At the time, the absence of further panics in the region concerned may have been due merely to good fortune; circumstances might still have allowed a panic to break out if the trigger had been pulled. A Europe-wide statistical analysis might eliminate some of the uncertainty that arises from picking individual cases, but we also need to analyse social conditions in the region concerned to see whether further panics were likely. With these caveats in mind, let us now turn to instances of central intervention in Italy, France and Germany, followed by a counter-instance from the Netherlands.

In Italy, the Roman Inquisition in the 1590s adopted a procedural code, the 'Instruction Concerning Witchcraft Trials, Witches and Sorcerers', which included some highly restrictive procedures. In particular it insisted that nobody should be arrested, much less tortured, until the crime had been proven for certain and the only remaining question was who had committed it. This cut the ground from under almost all prosecutions based on interrogation and confession, since it was only by interrogating the suspect that it was possible to discover whether any witchcraft had been committed at all. The 'Instruction' was initially kept confidential, apparently for fear that secular criminal courts would object to its restrictive nature and demand that the Inquisition hand over jurisdiction to them. It was not always enforced rigorously, but there seems to have been a long-term trend towards its enforcement. It was finally published in 1657, and probably had more effect thereafter.[12]

In France, the growing caution of the *parlement* of Paris is instructive. The *parlement* was a professional supervisory court with jurisdiction over northern France – the most populous part of early modern Europe's most populous state, with eight to ten million inhabitants. The court, having encountered several instances of excesses in local courts, ruled in 1604 that all witchcraft cases were subject to appeal. This was not publicised, but the *parlement* then put pressure on individual lower courts to send in their cases. Most of the cases over the next two decades were from courts that had never had appeals heard before. Over 70 per cent were acquitted. Then, in 1624, the 1604 ruling was reissued and printed. By now most of the lower courts knew that there was no point in trying witchcraft cases; the result would be a forced appeal to Paris and an acquittal. The number of appeals declined from 20 per year to under 4 per year.[13]

The *parlement*'s jurisdiction did not cover southern France, but the royal council could intervene anywhere in France if it wished. A panic in 1670 in Navarre illustrates the restraining role now played by central authorities. The panic was sparked off by local Jesuits, who discovered a star witness with the ability to detect witches, an apprentice weaver called Jean-Jacques Bacqué. The local *parlement* of Navarre established a commission to tour the region; in thirty villages, the commission used Bacqué to identify no fewer than 6,210 witches. However, when the royal council heard of this, all the prosecutions were halted.[14]

The next step in France was a royal edict in 1682 which in effect abolished the crime of witchcraft, though only indirectly. It ordered the banishment of people who, 'under the empty claim of being diviners, magicians, witches or other such names', abused their clients.[15] Thus 'witches' were redefined as magical practitioners whose claims to exercise power were by definition false. The edict was mainly directed against poisoners, whether magical or otherwise. It was prompted, not by a witchcraft panic, but by a scandal at the French court in which numerous influential people were discovered to have consulted magical practitioners.

A German example of central intervention comes from the prince-bishopric of Trier, one of those states that had conducted intense witch-hunts. A newly-elected prince-bishop in 1652, Karl Kaspar von der Leyen, decided to end witchcraft trials completely, noting that such trials 'had resulted in all sorts of judicial excesses, fraud, wastefulness, and injustice'. Kaspar was trying to revive his shattered domains after the devastations of the Thirty Years' War (more on which later in this chapter), and evidently felt that witchcraft trials undermined good governance. He may have had broader ideological or even intellectual doubts about the trials, but his legal focus is clear. Ideologically, he could not be seen to criticise his predecessors, most of whom had taken an active part in the recent trials. Trier had even been the base for the suffragan bishop Peter Binsfeld, whose demonological treatise of 1589 was still being read. Kaspar's legal focus may have been sharpened by awareness of the work of Friedrich Spee (see the text box 'Friedrich Spee, critic of witch trials'), who had criticised witchcraft prosecutions on legal grounds and who had spent the last few years of his career in Trier. At any rate, it was the 'judicial excesses' of witch-hunting that Kaspar cited as his motive for ending the trials.[16]

The United Netherlands provides a counterexample to the idea that central intervention was necessary to halt local witch-hunting. It was a decentralised state in which the various provinces had much autonomy. The court system varied in different provinces. In Friesland it was centralised, and the central court discouraged prosecutions. In Asten, it was decentralised, but there was local opposition to prosecutions.[17] The main reason for the moderation and early termination of Dutch witch-hunting was the state's early adoption of effective religious pluralism. Most provinces were Protestant, but Catholic minorities were tolerated in practice – as were some other minorities, like Jews. There was no official religious fervour, and no authorities demanding witchcraft prosecutions, not even the Protestant pastors.

A deeper problem with attributing all the decline to courts is that courts may show us only the surface manifestation of the trend concerned, masking the underlying patterns. Witch-hunting *had* to end in the courts, simply because all witches were prosecuted in courts. But courts could be influenced by outside developments, and it can be tricky to work out whether the mainspring of the change was internal or external to the court. For instance, in Germany, the *Carolina* code of 1532 required that courts consult university law faculties in difficult cases. In the sixteenth and early seventeenth centuries, this often led to intensification of witch-hunting, as law faculties supported demonological ideas and encouraged their spread. In the later seventeenth century, however, jurists began to advise caution, so that these consultations now tended to discourage prosecutions.[18] What motivated these intellectual jurists to change their minds? They could have been exercising 'judicial caution', but they were certainly aware of the Scientific Revolution as it unfolded around them, which will be discussed later in this chapter. Nor is it likely that they were indifferent to ideological changes. But, before turning to these non-judicial developments, there is one more long-term judicial change to consider.

Friedrich Spee, critic of witchcraft trials

When witchcraft trials were at their height in Germany, their single most influential critic was Friedrich Spee.[19] Spee was born near Cologne in 1591, son of a minor nobleman. He entered the Jesuit order, the spearhead of the Counter-Reformation, and pursued a career as a preacher, teacher and hymn-writer. At the time when he wrote his famous book *Cautio Criminalis*, he was teaching moral theology at the Jesuit college of Paderborn, in the archdiocese of Cologne.

Spee published *Cautio Criminalis* ('Warning on Criminal Justice') anonymously in 1631. Subtitled *De Processibus Contra Sagas Liber* ('A Book on Witch Trials') and addressed 'to the magistrates of Germany in this time of necessity', the book was a detailed exposé of procedural abuses, especially torture. Spee described eloquently how chain-reaction trials could spiral out of control, and how the most innocent person would be forced to confess under the tortures currently in use. He made clear that the judges were at fault, and that it was the duty of ruling princes to intervene to halt their abuses. He also condemned the common people who demanded witch trials, and the princes who failed to correct them. Written in Latin, the book was soon translated into German, Dutch and French.

Spee's authorship of the book immediately became known, and he was much criticised within the Jesuit order, partly because he seemed to have published without the order's permission. (The book itself stated that it was being printed without the author's knowledge, which may or may not have been true.) His own superiors protected him, however, and he was able to issue a revised edition of his book in 1632, with his public anonymity wearing thin. While ministering to plague-stricken soldiers in Trier, Spee caught the disease and died in 1635, but his book continued to influence debate for the rest of the century.

The decline of torture and the death penalty

Torture had sustained most of the witchcraft panics of the sixteenth and seventeenth centuries, and it had its own history of decline. Without torture, there would be far fewer confessions. Without confessions, there would not only be far fewer witchcraft trials generally, but also the trials that remained would be likely to be individual ones rather than chain-reaction hunts. The decline of torture had causes extending well beyond witch-hunting, and this broader decline needs to be charted in order to understand the decline of witch-hunting. It was also, as we shall see, connected with the decline of the death penalty.

Torture went into general decline in the late seventeenth and early eighteenth centuries. Roman-law courts had previously required a confession for a conviction, and torture had been necessary in order to obtain confessions. Now, however, courts started to avoid torture by avoiding the need for confessions. They achieved this by developing alternative standards of proof and imposing lesser punishments that did not require a full conviction for a capital offence. Suspected criminals were now subjected to lighter punishments 'on suspicion', where a conviction could be imposed on lesser or circumstantial evidence – evidence that did not include a confession. The new lighter punishments were called *'poena extraordinaria'* ('extraordinary punishment'). For a judge to sentence a suspect to a non-capital 'extraordinary punishment', he still had to be convinced of the suspect's guilt, but he did not need to satisfy the demanding Roman law of proof. He could thus convict and sentence a criminal without having to use torture.[20] In this way, torture was not abolished directly; instead it became unnecessary, as a side effect of courts ceasing to need confessions.

The rise of 'extraordinary punishment' occurred only in Roman-law courts. Yet torture declined in customary-law courts too, for reasons that are less well understood. Legal scholarship was international, and the leading scholars in customary-law countries were influenced by Roman-law scholars. Scotland used customary law, but Sir George Mackenzie, writing in Scotland in 1678, drew extensively on Benedict Carpzov from Saxony and Giulio Chiari and Prospero Farinacci from Italy.[21]

There also emerged a new humanitarian objection to torture, to supplement the longer tradition of warning against excessive torture as ineffective. Friedrich Spee, though he had a clear humanitarian sympathy for those suffering under torture, essentially argued in the older tradition, that torture did not work: it failed in its task of separating the innocent from the guilty. He did not primarily argue as a humanitarian would: that torture, because it was cruel, should not be applied even if it worked. However, such arguments began to appear in Spee's time. Johannes Grevius, in the Netherlands in 1624, wrote that torture should be ruled out on grounds of Christian charity. There was a general shift of sensibility away from the idea of the infliction of pain. Alongside the direct humanitarian critique came an indirect but perhaps even more deadly line of criticism, also voiced by Grevius: torture was 'archaic', a relic of less civilised times.[22] Torturing judges might have shrugged at being told that they were cruel, but they now faced a worse prospect: being told that they were old-fashioned.

Execution, the normal punishment for witchcraft, became a less attractive idea. Seventeenth-century governments started to see criminals as a resource to be developed. Instead of being wastefully executed, they could be sentenced to serve in the state's galleys, or transported to the state's colonies, or set to work in municipal workhouses. The death penalty continued, but, like torture, it was now old-fashioned.[23] This may also reflect humanitarian concerns. Condemning someone to becoming a galley slave may not seem humane by today's standards, but it was distinct from traditional punishments that inflicted deliberate, physical pain.

National and local authorities, in the late seventeenth and eighteenth centuries, began to construct new institutions to process and control people, especially deviant or problematic people. Some of these institutions were intended as benevolent, but they could also be coercive. There were hospitals for the sick – including mental hospitals, clearly coercive institutions. Prisons were even more clearly coercive. It was at this time that imprisonment emerged as a punishment for crime; in earlier centuries it had been used largely for pre-trial detention. Barracks were established for soldiers, as a means of managing the new standing armies with which emerging states maintained their authority. Workhouses, poorhouses and foundling hospitals were established to control and manage the destitute poor in the growing cities. These institutions were expensive, but they expressed the new idea that deviant and problematic people were a resource for the state to develop. Witches, in this scheme of things, were no longer relevant; it was impossible to imagine them as a productive resource.

The decline of the godly state

For the ideological aspect of the decline of witch-hunting, we need to turn to the decline of the godly state. As an episode of state formation, the godly state was gradually succeeded during the seventeenth century by the less evangelical state of the early Enlightenment. We have to remember that the 'godly state' was a process of striving after godliness, not a static entity that had achieved godliness. The process of striving now slackened. Political systems stabilised, with less of the kind of 'disorder' that had prompted demand for divine-right monarchy to suppress it. After about 1650, states continued to develop their power and their demands on the people, but there were fewer tax revolts, religious wars or dissident religious movements. The 'struggle for stability', as it has been called, had passed its most critical phase.[24]

Pressure for godliness in these newer states reduced considerably, and was confined to a narrower range of offences. It is no coincidence that the decline of witch-hunting came, during the later seventeenth century, when states ceased to regard the enforcement of universal godliness as their business. Many states still punished 'superstition', as we shall see, but more because it was ignorant and offensive to public decency, less because it was feared as demonic.

The rise of witch-hunting had occurred in the later middle ages along with the idea that heretics should be hunted down and ultimately executed. Suppression of heresy and other forms of active religious dissent now became less important to the authorities. Executions for heresy peaked in the middle decades of the sixteenth century, earlier than executions for witchcraft; already by 1600 there were hardly any heresy executions still occurring. Persecution of active religious dissidents, when it continued in the seventeenth century, was carried out by means of fines, banishment or deprivation of political rights. It was harder to justify witches' executions when no other religious dissidents were being executed.

The political ideology that had sustained witch-hunting was the divine right of kings, which stressed the God-given power of the king to restore order and to combat demonic disorder. The divine right of kings declined in popularity from the 1620s onwards. An influential figure here was Hugo Grotius, from the United Netherlands, an expanding commercial state that practised religious toleration. In a series of publications, especially in the 1620s, Grotius argued that the basis of political authority was not Christian revelation but natural law. He introduced a concept of natural rights, especially rights to life and rights to property, which led to a new way of thinking about political authority – a way of thinking that did not require direct religious legitimation. In particular, warfare on religious grounds was illegitimate. Grotius's natural-rights ideas influenced other thinkers throughout Europe.

Natural-rights ideas succeeded partly because they drew on the existing constitutionalist tradition, ascribing authority to the political community rather than the divine ruler. Constitutionalist political thought had never asserted that the king possessed the kind of charismatic authority that enabled him to combat demons. Instead, constitutionalist thinkers put forward secular arguments to justify the kind of authority they favoured. From the 1620s onwards, these arguments could be based on concepts of property and natural rights. Thus, government was explained by saying that people had a natural right to liberty, but rationally surrendered some of their liberty to the government in return for protection and political stability. If divine-right theorists argued that their system also provided protection and political stability, that was merely an incidental benefit. They could not argue that divine-right monarchy was a rational choice, because their whole point was that people had no such choice.

A third tendency in political thought undermined the godly state in a different way. This was the ideology of 'reason of state', arguing that rulers should do whatever was necessary to maintain order, even if this transgressed normal ethical standards. Like divine-right ideology, reason-of-state ideology arose in response to political strife, but it was more pragmatic and secular-minded. Thinkers in this tradition tended to argue that religion – *any* religion – was a necessary tool to pacify the masses and keep them in subjection. They either ignored witchcraft altogether – as did the tradition's sixteenth-century founder, Niccolò Machiavelli – or disbelieved in it openly – as did Thomas Hobbes in *Leviathan* (1651). Reason-of-state arguments provided more direct support for strong government than the constitutionalist tradition. Rulers could now assert their authority, and seek to build orderly and powerful states, without these having to be *godly* states.[25]

Religious wars also declined. The Thirty Years' War (1618–48) was Europe's most destructive religious war ever – but its excesses helped to discredit the whole idea of religious war. The first phase of the war, up to about 1630, saw a series of Austrian Habsburg and Spanish victories against the Protestant states in Germany. Catholics were exultant and Protestants in despair; it seemed that the entire Protestant Reformation was about to be extinguished. It is no coincidence that the 1620s saw an upsurge in witch-hunting. In the early 1630s, however, Protestant Swedish armies stormed into Germany, and the Catholic gains evaporated. Yet the Swedes could not win either. Then, with the intervention of Catholic France on the Protestant side, the war was not only spreading but ceasing to be a meaningfully religious war. It was now merely about plunder, massacres and devastation of enemy territory. People began to realise that nobody was going to win outright, and that a compromise was necessary. Witch-hunters tended to be zealots, opposed to compromise.

Peace initiatives began as early as 1634, but it took many years to assemble a workable peace conference and negotiate the details of a satisfactory compromise settlement. What emerged was the Peace of Westphalia, in 1648. This provided a comprehensive settlement of all German disputes, and a workable set of legal arrangements to settle *future* disputes and prevent the renewal of religious war. The pope protested against the treaty, but was ignored by Catholics as well as Protestants. Westphalia turned out to provide a framework for international diplomacy that lasted until 1789.

After 1648, confessional boundaries often became more rigid, with individual territories becoming exclusively Catholic or Protestant. This process sometimes overrode existing informal local arrangements – but each territory achieved a more lasting understanding with its neighbours, so that religious war no longer occurred. Previous multiconfessional arrangements had often been assumed to be temporary. Now, such had been the success of earlier evangelisation, states had formed definite confessional identities that even a ruler could no longer overturn.[26] People increasingly recognised that neither side could ever crush the other, and they ceased to seek to do so.

One notorious episode after Westphalia showed how far the old-style godly state had changed. This was the French revocation of the Edict of Nantes in 1685, cancelling the limited toleration that France's Protestant minority had enjoyed since 1598. The revocation led, not to the mass conversions that the government expected, but to a mass exodus of prosperous

French Protestants to more tolerant states, damaging the French economy. The revocation of the Edict was widely condemned, illustrating how far the ideological goals of European states had shifted away from godliness and towards economic prosperity. Moreover, the revocation of the Edict did not trigger off religious warfare, unlike similar acts a century earlier. Most people did not *want* to tolerate religious opponents, even in a neighbouring state, but they more often accepted such toleration as a necessary evil. Persecution had failed, and toleration was the only alternative. Episodes of persecution were now more often criticised as 'persecution', and it was harder to justify them as law enforcement.

Even after that, religious war and sectarian conflict occurred occasionally in Europe. Notable later examples have been the Sonderbund War in Switzerland in 1847, the 'Troubles' in Northern Ireland in the late twentieth century, and the Bosnian War of 1992–95. But these modern conflicts have been ethnic as well as sectarian, linked to the modern idea that a 'nation' (defined as a people with a common ethnic identity) should have its own 'state'. Religion thus contributes to modern claims to ethnic identity and nationalism. This is distinct from the early modern claim that the state must enforce godliness on its people. It was the demand for the enforcement of godliness that led to witch-hunting.

Godly discipline itself declined during the seventeenth century. This was not a straightforward matter, since there continued to be a great deal of official encouragement of correct Christianity among the common people. But actual punishment of ungodly offences was reduced to a narrower range. There were fewer prosecutions for adultery and fornication. The newer official response to illegitimate births was to establish foundling hospitals, part of the institutional approach to criminality discussed above. Now that the authorities' interest in punishment of gendered offences was declining, it is not surprising that their interest in punishment of witchcraft – itself to a great extent a gendered offence – also declined.

States increasingly saw their role as promoting commerce and industry. Many commercial colonies were established during the seventeenth century, and many states devoted energies to colonial expansion. Instead of religious wars, there were now wars for trade and colonies. This shift in values is illustrated in microcosm by England's colony of Massachusetts, established in the 1620s as a godly commonwealth but increasingly permeated by profit-making. The Salem witchcraft panic of 1692 arose in part from resentment by a godly faction against this rising commercial tide – but people with anti-commercial values would never again hold the kind of political power that would enable them to prosecute witches.

There were new enemies for orthodox clergymen to worry about instead of witches. In the 1620s, the Spanish authorities condemned as heretical the spiritual movement of the '*Alumbrados*' ('Illuminated ones' or mystics), while there was a panic in France concerning an alleged sect of 'libertines' – atheists or freethinkers.[27] Atheism, occasionally real though more often imagined, emerged as a threat in several countries. There were a few prosecutions and even executions of people alleged to have denied religion as a whole.[28] These alternative enemies may have functioned like the sixteenth-century Anabaptists discussed in Chapter 6: a government could not easily devote its energies both to prosecuting witches and to prosecuting these alternative enemies, so that prosecutions of seventeenth-century atheists (or demands for their prosecution) distracted attention from witches. Another possibility is that the emergence of atheism as a threat produced a long-term shift, making the authorities less likely *ever* to return to witch-hunting. However, it is also possible that the threat of atheism confirmed the need for the godly state. The godly state, as long as it lasted, always had the potential for witch-hunting.

The fear of 'enthusiasm' became significant at this time. The concept of 'enthusiasm', more or less equivalent to the modern term 'extremism', came into use by mainstream theologians in the seventeenth century who came to see their faith as 'rational' and 'moderate'. The attack on 'enthusiasm' could undermine the traditional demonologists' claim to orthodoxy. Demonologists claimed to be upholding correct religion, but they themselves could look like 'enthusiasts'.

After the godly state, the new religious pluralism meant that some groups would continue to support witchcraft beliefs. The Pietist evangelical movement among German Lutherans, arising in the late seventeenth century, tended to challenge the 'moderate' and 'rational' orthodoxy of the establishment. The Methodists, an eighteenth-century English evangelical movement, are another example. The Methodist leader, Charles Wesley, wrote in his journal that 'Giving up witchcraft is, in effect, giving up the Bible'.[29] Wesley made no secret of his witch beliefs, and encouraged the providentialist view of an active God. (There is more on 'providentialism' later in this chapter.) However, neither Wesley nor other Methodists campaigned actively for witches to be punished. As we shall see, demonology had already become a theoretical issue, detached from any practical suggestion that witches should be executed. Meanwhile, the known association of Methodists with witchcraft beliefs meant that it was easier for non-Methodists – most of the elite – to reject them. If belief in witchcraft was seen as a tenet of Methodism, then it was by the same token an eccentric minority view. Illustration 10.1 shows how this was seen at the time. In it, the engraver William Hogarth mocked the Methodists' alleged religious extremism, using their belief in witches as a point of attack. 'Rational' religion now rejected all such beliefs.

One final point should be made. To speak of the decline of the godly state is not to say that the sixteenth and seventeenth centuries had been an age of especial piety; there had been piety before, and would still be piety afterwards. Thus, this is not an argument about 'secularisation', which has been extensively debated but which is only indirectly relevant to the present argument about the godly state. The godly state, in its operations, was not about general levels of religious belief or even religious commitment among the population: rather, it was about the ways in which the authorities punished specific types of religious deviance. Some historians have discussed

334 *The end of witch-hunting*

Illustration 10.1 Witchcraft is mocked as old-fashioned, 1762

This satirical English engraving by William Hogarth is entitled 'Credulity, Superstition and Fanaticism'. A fanatical Methodist preacher scares his credulous congregation with puppets of a witch and a demon. His wig slips, revealing him as a Jesuit in disguise. Old demonological books lie around. Superstitious events of the past are mocked, including Mary Toft, who had allegedly given birth to rabbits in 1726, and the Drummer of Tedworth, a poltergeist of the 1660s. This engraving, showing the witch with broomstick and cat, may have been influential in creating the modern image of a witch.

how far 'reforming' authorities succeeded in raising levels of religious commitment. But this is not relevant to witch-hunting; there is no point in discussing how far the authorities succeeded in stamping out witchcraft. Sadly, we have to recognise that the godly state had *created* the witches that it executed.

The Scientific Revolution

The dramatic intellectual changes of the seventeenth century had a profound effect on the thinking of educated elites. At one time, historians thought that these changes were all that was needed to explain the end of witch-hunting: people became 'rational' and 'enlightened', and naturally stopped carrying out 'barbarous' or 'superstitious' practices. Such ideas are no longer tenable, now that we have a better understanding of the sophisticated nature of demonology, and now that we realise that witchcraft trials had their own dynamics and were not simply caused by people reading books like the *Malleus Maleficarum*. The influence of the new scientific ideas was much more subtle, but still profound. This section will begin by outlining those aspects of the Scientific Revolution that were relevant to this process.

Older histories of the Scientific Revolution tended to tell a story of progress from ignorance to knowledge. They focused on knowledge that *later* science had accepted, asking a present-minded question: 'How did we acquire our present knowledge?' In the later twentieth century, historians reacted against this, urging that figures like Galileo or Newton needed to be understood in their own context. We should study all their ideas, not just the ones that had survived. Newton, for instance, was not just a mathematician who originated the theory of gravitation; he was also an alchemist (though he never published his alchemical researches) and a natural theologian. Some revisionist historians even questioned whether there was such a thing as a 'Scientific Revolution', preferring to emphasise continuity and randomness in scientific developments. However, scholarship has moved on, and more recent scholars have returned to the idea of a fundamental shift in understanding, mainly in the seventeenth century.

The revolution occurred partly because of the breakdown of traditional natural philosophy in the face of new theories and new data. This occurred in a number of fields. Explorers in the New World brought back a flood of information about new animal and plant species with no traditional cultural meanings, unlike (for instance) the story of the pelican discussed in Chapter 3. These animals and plants had to be interpreted in purely physical terms. In the field of human anatomy, a small revolution occurred in 1543 when Andreas Vesalius published an influential book exposing many errors in the ancient authorities traditionally used. Above all, traditional astronomy became unsustainable in the face of more detailed and accurate planetary observations. In 1577, Tycho Brahe tracked the path of a comet, showing that it must have passed between the orbits of the planets – so the planets could not be mounted on transparent crystal 'orbs'. It was a time of new ideas about the physical world, and of uncertainty about traditional ideas.

The scholastic Aristotelianism that was discussed in Chapter 3 thus went into decline. Numerous problems were already recognised in it during the sixteenth century, leading to competing attempts to revise it or patch it up. Then, between about 1600 and 1630, traditional Aristotelian university textbooks were replaced by a new generation of works which, while still 'Aristotelian', commented more directly on Aristotle himself. They moved away from the scholastic tradition deriving from the way in which Thomas Aquinas had Christianised Aristotle in the middle ages.[30]

Mathematics grew in importance. We may take it for granted that scientists use mathematics, but Aristotelian science was not particularly mathematical. Not only did it carry out few experiments, but it had little use for quantification or measurement. The new astronomy, and new ideas about motion generally, relied on mathematical calculations. When Copernicus argued in 1543 that the earth and other planets orbited round the sun, he was not just making a radical physical claim about the universe: he was also making a radical methodological claim about mathematics. The Aristotelian idea of planets mounted on rotating orbs had never fitted the observational data very well, because the planets periodically turned back in their observed paths. To solve this problem, the ancient scholar Ptolemy had devised a system of 'epicycles', lesser orbits within the main orbit; but thinkers in the Aristotelian tradition did not regard this as reflecting reality. The reality, in their view, was that the planets moved around the earth in regular, circular orbits, while Ptolemy's epicycles were just a hypothetical means to keep track of a planet's observed position. Now, Copernicus did not simply show that his heliocentric system could keep track of the planets' position without these epicycles; he also argued that, because his mathematical calculations fitted the observational data, the heliocentric system must be the reality. The planets really were where the numbers said they should be. It was not just a question of whether the earth moved or not: it was a question of whether observation and measurement were the way to prove it.

The proponents of the new science thus appealed to a different standard of authority. Instead of the authority of ancient texts (discussed in Chapter 3), they saw themselves as relying on 'experiment' – meaning, not only actual experiments as we understand them in today's science, but also direct observation of natural phenomena more broadly. They reconciled this with religion by arguing that God had created the world as a book to be read, and that by decoding it they were learning more about the Creation. Galileo took this claim too far in 1633 and was censured by the Catholic church, but this was an unusual episode. The Jesuits liked Galileo and his discoveries. His book *Siderius Nuncius* ('The Starry Messenger', 1610) was much used in Jesuit colleges. Some accounts of the Scientific Revolution portray a stark conflict between new science and traditional religion – but one of the noteworthy reasons for the success of the Revolution is that both sides, by and large, steered away from such a conflict. Mainstream practitioners of the new science usually insisted on their own piety, and were usually believed.

The system of thought that would replace scholastic Aristotelianism came to be known as the 'mechanical philosophy'. This offered explanations of the physical world in terms of its 'mechanical' qualities of shape, size and motion, rather than the Aristotelian qualities of hot, cold, wet and dry. These mechanical qualities, especially motion, could be measured and analysed mathematically. This was particularly damaging to demonology, because demonology often relied on the Aristotelian idea of action through 'occult' (hidden) qualities, which the mechanical philosophy discarded.

The main originator of the mechanical philosophy was René Descartes (1596–1650), who went back to first principles to analyse the workings of the human mind and its place in the world. His famous aphorism, 'I think, therefore I am', affirmed the mind's reality, as the solution to a thought-experiment in which he considered the possibility that an 'evil spirit' might have distorted all human perceptions of reality. Descartes concluded from this, not only that the 'mind' existed, but that everything else that existed in the world was inert 'matter'. This 'matter' was made up of moving particles that interacted 'mechanically'. Cartesianism did not explicitly abolish angels or demons (they could also be 'mind'), but it did abolish the 'occult' and the 'preternatural'. In practice, having dismissed his hypothetical 'evil spirit', Descartes showed no further interest in angels or demons. Spirits, as such, could not affect the physical world.

The mechanical philosophy came to be an influential and eventually dominant intellectual movement, eclipsing scholastic Aristotelianism. This was a gradual process, and the chronology is inevitably imprecise, but the decades between the 1630s and 1670s seem to have been crucial.[31] The mechanical philosophy provided an overarching way of thinking about the physical world, within which other practical themes could be pursued, notably mathematics and the experimental method. In Isaac Newton's theory, gravitation acted at a distance, which could make it an 'occult' force in Aristotelian terms. Newton was uninterested in this issue, however, simply regarding gravitation as real because its effects could be measured and predicted.

The mechanical philosophy undermined the older 'providential' world-view, on which demonology had relied. In 'providentialism', God and the Devil constantly intervened in the natural world in unpredictable ways. The mechanical philosophy, by contrast, tended to turn God into a retired engineer who had built the world as a machine, and now watched it run smoothly by means of the natural forces with which he had provided it. The workings of this machinery were not yet fully understood in every detail, but the mechanical philosophy promised to explain them without the need for 'providential' or 'preternatural' explanations.

Descartes' message was reinforced indirectly by one of his great successors, Baruch Spinoza (1632–77). Spinoza tackled some of the same questions as Descartes, and used a similar methodological approach from first principles, but came to even more radical conclusions. To him, God and nature were the same thing, the Divine Substance; and there was definitely no place for demons. These were shocking views, incompatible with conventional Christianity. Spinoza had few direct followers – but the depth and rigour of his thought forced later thinkers to define their views in relation to his. Cartesianism thus became an acceptable alternative to the even more radical Spinozism.

The idea of 'reason' became more important in the later seventeenth century. Before then, 'reason' had meant the rules of formal logic. Now, however, thinkers saw 'reason' as a human capacity to understand the world more generally. Using their 'rational' capacity, people were expected to recognise the basic ideas of Christianity, so this was not straightforwardly about religious freedom. But people were no longer expected to accept dogmas without question; human 'reason' acted as a kind of filter. It became easier to say that an idea was 'against reason'.[32] Demonology was just the kind of dogmatic idea that could fail to pass through this new filter.

The mechanical philosophy encouraged a focus on causation that tended to make bewitchment meaningless. To an Aristotelian philosopher, it made sense to say that a bewitchment worked because it had been brought about by a demon. But, to a mechanical philosopher, that was like saying that a telescope worked because it had been built by an instrument-maker. The relevant question was: '*How* does the telescope work?' The mechanical philosophers worked hard at answering such questions, often with the aid of their new mathematical or experimental techniques. But they were hardly ever interested in the question: '*How* does bewitchment work?' This was because the only available answer turned out to be an Aristotelian one: 'It was brought about by a demon.' This was so unsatisfactory as to make the question itself pointless.

There were, nevertheless, a few attempts to investigate bewitchments scientifically. The main such project was carried out in the middle to later years of the seventeenth century by the English group known as the 'Cambridge Platonists' – so called because they drew on the Neoplatonism of the Renaissance (which was discussed in Chapter 3). They aimed to put evidence of spirits on a scientific basis, stressing the reliability of their observational reports. This observational emphasis was new. Martin Delrio in 1599–1600 had related witch stories that were little more than fables, his justification for doing so being a Renaissance one of fidelity to the original text; this was no longer credible. By 1681, the leading Platonists Joseph Glanvill and Henry More carefully documented their observational sources for the strange occurrences that they related, and abandoned the Aristotelian framework that Delrio and others had relied on. This attempt to rejuvenate demonology may be compared with the way in which other leading proponents of the Scientific Revolution investigated other unusual phenomena such as astrology. With hindsight such an attempt may seem doomed to failure, but at the time it seemed plausible that astrology might only need to be 'reformed' rather than abandoned.

Thus, we know with hindsight that the junction of new demonology and new science would not last, but at the time it may have seemed promising. Glanvill presented his arguments in favour of witches as 'hypotheses' and as 'probable', testable by experiment, in contrast to earlier demonologists' dogmatic insistence on truth. One of his suggestions concerned 'vapours', which were then cutting-edge science as a result of experiments with air pumps: 'the evil spirit having breath'd some vile vapour into the body of the Witch, it may taint her blood and spirits with a noxious quality'.[33] He hoped that scientific experiments might detect this process of vapour transfer. No such experiments were carried out, however. The leading scientist in the field of 'vapours', Robert Boyle, was interested in Glanvill's ideas but cautious in practice, regarding most reports of witchcraft as false.[34] Meanwhile George Sinclair, another forward-thinking natural philosopher, drew heavily on Glanvill in his own demonological work of 1685, but some of Sinclair's case studies were less convincing, looking more like the unverifiable stories of Delrio. Sinclair even included the story of the Pied Piper of Hamelin.[35] Adapting demonology to the requirements of experimental science proved impossible to sustain.

Demonology in a sceptical age

Intellectual demonology entered the seventeenth century in a flourishing condition. The encyclopedic and highly successful work of Martin Delrio (1599–1600) was followed by further original treatises, notably those of Henri Boguet (1602), Francesco Maria Guaccio (1608) and Pierre de Lancre (1612). The details of demonology were being refined, and the consensus in its favour seemed to be complete. The sixteenth-century challenges to demonology mounted by Pietro Pomponazzi, Johann Weyer and Reginald Scot now had few defenders.

Yet demonology failed to maintain its forward momentum, and increasingly entered a sceptical age. After 1612, existing demonological treatises continued to be reprinted in fair numbers for another half-century or so, but no important new ones appeared. Writers still discussed demonology, but in a derivative and unoriginal way. Meanwhile, from the early seventeenth century onwards, fresh currents of scepticism started to appear. Before about 1650, few sceptics explicitly rejected the whole of demonology, but they did make the demonological project harder to sustain.

One early sceptic was Adam Tanner, a Jesuit, who influenced the debate in Bavaria in the early seventeenth century. He published a critique of prosecution as part of an encyclopedic work of theology in 1626. Tanner saw witchcraft as a wholly spiritual offence that needed to be met in a pastoral rather than punitive way. The witch should be converted with the aid of prayer, fasting and good works. Tanner criticised harsh trial procedures, but essentially saw trials as irrelevant to the task of making the witch into a good Christian.[36]

Shifting views can be detected in the publications of another German Jesuit scholar, Paul Laymann. He published three editions of his *Theologia Moralis* ('Moral Theology') in 1625, 1630 and 1634. This was an encyclopedic work with a large witchcraft section. Laymann was traditional in many respects, but, in discussing trial procedure, unlike earlier demonologists, he made no assumption that the accused was guilty, and urged the protection of the innocent. He discussed at length procedural details like whether a confessing witch had to repent before they could be asked about accomplices. He also had a number of differing authorities on which to draw, from Bodin and Delrio who encouraged severe procedure to Tanner who warned against it; and he gave full weight to them all, showing how much uncertainty there was. Laymann's 1634 edition was notably more cautious than his previous ones.[37]

These newly cautious views appeared just as witchcraft trials themselves were declining, from the 1630s onwards. This decline in trials seems to have had a dampening effect on demonological writing, with some writers showing awareness of the issue. In England, William Drage wrote in 1665 that 'we have not one Witch to one hundred that be in other Countreys, and fewer than formerly; and therefore the fewer are bewitched'.[38] Dutch lawyers in the seventeenth century, after trials for witchcraft had ceased, often congratulated themselves on being more enlightened than in other countries where witchcraft trials were still occurring. Even the idea that demonic witches existed in the Netherlands was criticised; there might have been some before the Reformation, but such 'superstition' had now vanished. Those who accused neighbours of witchcraft were under a false illusion – and might be guilty of slander, a crime which was still tried. These Dutch lawyers agreed that magical practitioners still existed and should be punished, but their offence was essentially that of deceiving their clients.[39]

The most important new development in seventeenth-century demonological writing was that writers ceased to demand the execution of witches. People continued to publish books saying that demons had preternatural powers and that humans made pacts with them – the basic argument for the existence of the demonic witch. But this was now an abstract intellectual point, not a political one. The classic demonological works had all demanded the punishment of witches, often including a section on how to prosecute them. This practical concern vanished from later works. One example is the French Catholic theologian Jean-Baptiste Thiers, whose influential four-volume *Traité des Superstitions* ('Treatise on Superstitions') was published and revised gradually between 1679 and 1704. Thiers endorsed the belief in demons and their powers, but knew that the French authorities no longer prosecuted witches. He showed no interest in witch-hunting, instead concentrating on cataloguing and reproving a vast range of lesser superstitions.[40]

While abandoning the demand to punish witches, later demonologists often treated witchcraft as a medical problem. This was not entirely new, since the case had been made by Weyer and others in the sixteenth century, but it now had more credibility. Nicolas Malebranche in 1674, in his *Recherche de la Vérité* ('Study of Truth'), sounded rather like Weyer a century earlier, but Cartesian science made his arguments more persuasive.

Malebranche treated witchcraft as a matter of stories that were believed by ignorant rustics and shepherds. He explained in scientific language how such people could come to believe that stories told to them were true:

> It is indubitable that real Witches deserve death, and that even those who do it only in imagination ought not to be treated as completely innocent; since ordinarily they are only persuaded to become Witches because they have a disposition of heart to go to the Sabbat, and have been rubbed with some drug to achieve their unhappy purpose. But by punishing all these criminals indifferently, common opinion is strengthened, imaginary Witches are multiplied, and so an infinity of people are lost and damned. It is thus right that many Parlements [in France] no longer punish Witches. There are many fewer of them in the lands of their jurisdictions; and the envy, hatred, or malice of evil men cannot use this pretext to destroy the innocent.[41]

Malebranche thus avoided provocative unorthodoxy, but his striking phrase 'imaginary witches' allowed his readers to recognise that witches were created by the process of community labelling.

During the seventeenth century, the concept of 'superstition' shifted its meaning. The traditional view was that 'superstition' was a false and dangerous belief, verging on heresy. God had prescribed correct forms of belief and worship, and anyone who deviated from these was superstitious. Moreover, if a 'superstitious' ritual worked, then it must have been the Devil who made it work. Such views were integral to demonology. However, when Gabriel Naudé in 1625 wrote of 'vain, Magical, superstitious and abhominable Ceremonies', he exemplified a shift in understanding: he assumed that the magic would *not* work.[42] Naudé's determinedly anti-demonological approach was close to a modern view of superstition as silly and harmless. Eventually, there was a further shift: radical thinkers turned back the charge of 'superstition' against the demonologists themselves. Eighteenth-century critics freely called believers in witches 'superstitious', their belief being unnecessary to the latest 'rational' religion.[43] There is more about such open attacks on demonology in the next section of this chapter.

The later seventeenth century was thus a period of decline for conventional demonology. The most original demonological thinkers had abandoned the subject's Aristotelian framework, as we saw in the previous section of this chapter. Meanwhile more mainstream demonologists, like Cotton Mather (see the text box 'A demonologist loses confidence'), were visibly failing to make their arguments effective. And demonology was declining in quantity. A study of demonological book collections in eighteenth-century French libraries shows that they consisted mostly of old, seventeenth-century books. There were fewer up-to-date demonological books for interested readers to buy.[44] The whole subject had become old-fashioned.

From then on, any continuing witch belief among the elite tended to be passive. People assented in principle to the existence of witches, but lacked any commitment to take action to deal with them. Committed witch belief required an active, providential God and an active, threatening Devil. The mechanical philosophy, by encouraging the idea of God as a retired engineer, encouraged passive witch belief. Dogmatic Christians could continue to insist on the reality of witchcraft and activity by demons. But they knew that they could no longer demand public action – witchcraft executions. Nor indeed did they generally *want* such executions. Such attitudes can be traced from the late seventeenth century up to the present day. One example is the article on 'witchcraft' in the 1913 *Catholic Encyclopedia*, stating that the reality of witchcraft 'can hardly be denied' – a tellingly passive formula – but mainly denouncing the 'delusion' that had led to witch-hunting in the past. We shall return in the next chapter to the idea of witch-hunting as a 'delusion'.

A demonologist loses confidence

Cotton Mather, an influential Boston minister, wrote *The Wonders of the Invisible World* in 1692 to justify the Salem trials of that year. But it got him into a lot of trouble – not just with his critics, but within his own mind. The problem was that many accusations at Salem were about 'spectral evidence', in which the 'spectre' of the alleged witch appeared to the victim. Mather had no doubt that demons had the power to cause spectres to appear, but it had occurred to him that demons might also have the power to impersonate innocent people. As he put it in a letter written during the trials: 'That the Divels have a natural power which makes them capable of exhibiting what shape they please I suppose nobody doubts, and I have no absolute promise of God that they shall not exhibit mine.'[45] But to say this publicly would have opened the door to too many other doubts. In his book, Mather tried to evade the issue. Demonology was on the defensive, and Mather's book was heavily criticised.

But this was a problem of loss of confidence. Mather could have had a ready-made escape route from his difficulty. The problem with 'spectral evidence' had already occurred to King James VI, a century earlier. In his 1597 treatise, James wrote simply that 'God will not permit Satan to use the shapes or similitudes of any innocent persons ... for then the devil would find ways anew to calumniate the best'.[46] Mather could no longer rely on such a simple argument; he knew that nobody would believe it, and he did not even believe it himself.

Open attacks on demonology

The decline of demonology as a credible intellectual topic is illustrated by the way in which its critics were increasingly able to mount open attacks on it. There had of course been sceptical voices raised against demonology in the sixteenth century and even before, as we saw in Chapter 3. But the sixteenth-century critics were expressing minority views, frequently marginalised as the demonological consensus took shape and gathered credibility. In the seventeenth century, one aspect of demonology's gradual loss of credibility was that a new generation of critics was able to attack it with more vigour and confidence than before.

Many of these new attacks expressed what can be called 'anticlerical' scepticism. Anticlericalism involved refusing to take clergymen as seriously as they took themselves, or demanding that clergymen reform their own lives before they criticised the sins of others, or arguing that some so-called sins were really just harmless fun. Demonologists were vulnerable to this kind of scepticism, because they made such heavy demands on their readers. Ultimately they were demanding that their readers should accept the necessity of burning people at the stake. During the seventeenth century, with the decline of the godly state, it became easier for anticlerical writers to refuse to take demonologists seriously.

Thus, Savinien Cyrano de Bergerac published an anticlerical essay in 1654, 'A Letter Against Witches', in which he mocked both witches and witch-beliefs. Witches were merely deluded peasants, and those who took them seriously – the demonologists – were pedantic fools. In this wholesale dismissal of demonology, he declared loftily that 'reason' alone would be his guide. He felt no need to argue against the demonologists point by point; to him, it was self-evident that their works were obscure, dogmatic and contrary to 'reason'.[47]

Some form of anticlericalism can be found in any age, but this anticlericalism was notable for its ability to link with new intellectual ideas. The Renaissance had promoted scepticism by making it easier for thinkers to question their immediate predecessors, but the Renaissance had sought to anchor its findings in classical or biblical antiquity. The mechanical philosophy sought to anchor its findings in experience and in logical reasoning, neither of which were any longer dependent on theology. The 'libertine' (freethinking) writer Charles Sorel, in the 1630s, made the direct attack on demonology that Descartes had not bothered to make. He dismissed the powers of demons simply by insisting that the laws of nature were fixed and universal. Even God could hardly change them; certainly demons could not. Sorel had in effect abandoned the category of the 'preternatural' – and, with it, the central claims of demonology.[48]

Related to the anticlerical attack was the satirical attack. Cyrano's essay, mentioned above, was making a serious intellectual point but used humour to do so. Writers whose primary purpose was humour also began to find witchcraft and demonology amusing. In the mid-1630s, a famous case of witchcraft and demonic possession erupted at Loudun in France; there is more about this later in this chapter. The exorcisms of Loudun became a celebrated if controversial media event – and one aspect of this was that a satirical novel was published, mocking the exorcists, in 1637.[49]

Another work appearing in 1637 was Johan van Heemskerk's *Batavian Arcadia*. This was a lighthearted introduction to the United Netherlands and its history – and witch-hunting was a part of Dutch history that could cheerfully be dismissed:

> It wouldn't surprise me if most of what has been said during the last hundred years in these lands about spirits, elves, ogres, *kollen, kolrijders*, male and female witches, were to have been foolish talk and frightening images. All the more since these days, now that the witchcraft charges are ceasing and are dismissed by the courts, one neither hears nor talks about such whims, nor the calamities and difficulties accompanying them. Whilst formerly not only houses and hamlets, but whole cities were in bad repute, and the annual felling of all the trees in Holland would scarcely have been enough to burn all those who had a bad name and were talked about in this connection.[50]

Here, the sceptical attitude was the modern attitude. Van Heemskerk had no sophisticated theory of why demonology was wrong, but he nevertheless expected his readers to see no meaning in it. Witchcraft was silly and out of date.

In France in 1690, Antoine Furetière's *Dictionnaire Universel* ('Universal Dictionary') added distancing phrases like 'it is believed that ...' to all the entries on witchcraft. Thus the 'sabbat' was defined as 'the nocturnal assembly that it is believed that witches hold on Saturdays, where they say that the Devil appears in the form of a goat ... the old women believe that they go to the sabbat on a broomstick'. Furetière did not expect his readers to believe any of this themselves; witchcraft was only for 'old women' to believe.[51]

The most sophisticated and notorious open attack on demonology came from the Netherlands. Balthasar Bekker, in his famous four-volume book, *De Betoverde Weereld* ('The Enchanted World', 1691–92), claimed to be completing the Reformation project to purge Christianity of medieval superstition. Like earlier Protestants he accepted the Bible as literally true and thus agreed that the Devil and angels existed. However, Bekker used Descartes' separation of mind and matter to argue that the Devil and other spirits consisted of 'thought', not matter, and thus could have no effect on the physical world. God could have such an effect, being beyond the mind-body distinction, and thus good angels could do so too at his command; but Bekker was cautious even here, pointing out that the Bible said little about angels' powers. Bekker dismissed most biblical accounts of demons as allegories of sinful human inclinations. Thus, the Devil did not really become a serpent in order to tempt Eve – she was simply tempted by her own sinful nature. Bekker counter-attacked against the notion of demonic power by arguing that it would be sinful to claim that God had allocated any of his power to the Devil.[52] He thus tilted the balance away from the demonologists' near-dualism, with God and the Devil as independent powers at war with one another; instead he emphasised the sole power of God. This had been a normal position for medieval theologians. In the 1690s, however, it no longer implied that God was in immediate control of all aspects of the world; rather it implied that God had created the world to function in accordance with natural law.

Bekker's work sparked a howl of protest from more orthodox theologians, and a more modest output of books and pamphlets, mostly by laymen, supporting him. *The Enchanted World* itself was a bestseller, but denunciations of him poured from Protestant presses in Germany and the Netherlands. Bekker's emphasis on 'philosophy' (Cartesianism) rather than theology was apparently popular with educated lay people, particularly students, but most feared to speak out and offend the church. One of Bekker's most outspoken supporters, Ericus Walten, derided his opponents as 'Devil-worshippers' and was imprisoned for blasphemy, dying in his cell in 1697.[53]

In assessing Bekker we have to pay attention to chronology, to geography, and to the content of his ideas. Bekker could obviously have no effect on witch-hunting in his home country, since that had ceased ninety years before he wrote. But his work attracted attention in Germany, where witch-hunting was continuing. In particular, Bekker inspired Christian Thomasius, a German intellectual whose published lecture *De Criminae Magiae* ('The Crime of Magic', 1701) was influential in discouraging German witchcraft trials. Thomasius was particularly effective in combining Bekker's 'philosophical' approach with Spee's practical critique of the excesses of torture.[54] However, the content of Bekker's ideas indicates that we should not just look at his subsequent legacy. The ideas that he expressed were already in circulation, having been put forward decades earlier by Descartes, Spinoza and others. And the controversy that he generated shows that traditional views still had supporters. However, most of the traditionalists just wanted to make an abstract intellectual point about the Devil's powers; they did not call actively for witches to be prosecuted. Moreover, the traditionalists were mostly clergymen, while laymen were more sympathetic. This was why Furetière could publish a dictionary with such open scepticism in 1690: a dictionary was not a theological work. The restricted world of intellectual theology formed the last refuge of demonology; beyond this refuge, it was no longer credible.

Witchcraft as fiction

It was argued in Chapter 3 that intellectual demonology was accompanied by other writings and illustrations about witchcraft that drew more on fiction. These works were effectively 'infotainment'. Some demonological authors included funny or exciting or erotic stories in their writings;

these were similar to other stories written mainly for their entertainment value. The serious works and the lighter ones complemented each other, encouraging a coherent view of witches as wicked and threatening. But could fictional works about witchcraft come to have the effect of undermining demonology?

The subject of witchcraft in fiction deserves fuller study than it can receive here. However, fictional stories about witches could, in the right circumstances, discourage witchcraft belief – or at least the kind of witchcraft belief that might promote witch-hunting. One way in which stories could do that was to present witches, or witch-hunters, or both, as comical figures. Another trend that would undermine witch-hunting was to move witch stories to a fairy-tale world.

In England around 1600, Shakespeare's witches were a blend of village witch, folktale witch and classical witch, which did not challenge witchcraft belief. Later English plays did. *The Late Lancashire Witches*, by Thomas Heywood and Richard Brome (1634), was a slapstick comedy of gender relationships that satirised, not only witches, but everyone else in sight – including witch-hunters. This is linked to the tendency towards humorous satire of demonology, discussed above. Fictional representations of witchcraft found it increasingly difficult to sustain the mood of high seriousness that was essential to witch-hunting.

In France in the early eighteenth century, a genre of literature arose laughing at 'superstitious' demonic beliefs, both of the elite and of the common folk. A leading example was a novel of 1710 by Laurent Bordelon, entitled *The Story of the Extravagant Imaginings of Monsieur Oufle, Caused by Reading Books about Magic, Necromancy, Demoniacs, Witches, Werewolves, Incubi, Succubi and the Sabbath; about Fairies, Ogres, Wanton Spirits, Genies, Phantoms and Other Ghosts; about Dreams, the Philosopher's Stone, Judicial Astrology, Horoscopes, Talismans, Lucky and Unlucky Days, Eclipses, Comets and Alamanacs; and about All Kinds of Apparitions, Divinations, Sorceries, Enchantments and Other Superstitious Practices.* Yes, that was the book's title. It was a satirical novel, in the vein of *Don Quixote*, about the comical scrapes into which Monsieur Oufle was led by his ridiculous belief in demonology. Oufle's name was an anagram of '*le fou*' ('the fool'). His library contained all the standard demonological works, which Bordelon dismissed as nonsense. Bordelon's book was so successful that some Enlightenment thinkers, who agreed with its sceptical message, even began to worry that it was encouraging interest in matters better forgotten.[55]

Witchcraft stories might also undermine demonology if they were presented as stories for children. Childhood was seen as a credulous age. Parents would scare their children with stories of monsters that would come and get them if they did not behave themselves. Part of the process of growing up was to reject childish beliefs. Part of the process of rejecting witchcraft would be to label it as a childish belief. This was not undertaken as a deliberate exercise in changing people's minds; rather, like many of these cultural developments, it was embedded in a broader shift of values.

Witchcraft first became childish in the late seventeenth century, with the emergence of the 'fairy-tale' as a literary genre. The common people had been telling folktales for centuries, but these new tales were intended to be literature, *read* by educated people. They were aimed at both children and adults, and adults who read them were thus encouraged to distance themselves from any factual content the stories might have. The most influential collection of fairy-tales, Charles Perrault's *Mother Goose Tales* (1697), provided what would become standard versions of 'Sleeping Beauty', 'Cinderella', 'Little Red Riding Hood', and others. There were only a few actual witches in these stories, but those witches appeared alongside 'fairy godmothers' who were witch-like crones, and other even more fantastic elements. As with Bordelon's story of Monsieur Oufle, these witches were now associated with an array of magical but improbable beings. Above all, the fairy-tale witches appeared in a fairy-tale setting – 'Once upon a time' – clearly different from real human society. Witches were thus symbolically removed from the everyday world.

Something similar happened to witches in the visual arts. These witches did not become childish, but they did become more clearly fantasy fiction. Arguably many witchcraft images had been created as fantasy fiction even in the Renaissance, but in that period they had been presented as plausibly realistic representations of demonological scenes. Now there was more extravagance and sheer entertainment, with artists treating 'witchcraft' as a repertoire of scary but also sometimes comical Gothic-horror motifs.

Shifting views of witches' malefice

Ideas about witches' activities shifted during the seventeenth century. Some traditional ideas of harm done by witches became less prominent. Meanwhile there was a rise in two new ideas that stirred up scepticism and controversy: demonic possession, and taking children to the sabbat.

The narrowing range of traditional malefice has not been studied systematically, but a few indications may be given. Shipwrecks could be attributed to witchcraft in Holland until the end of the sixteenth century, but not afterwards.[56] In England, accusations involving witchcraft and magic often featured in political trials and aristocratic disputes up to the early seventeenth century. For instance, the earl of Essex's alleged impotence with his wife was ascribed to bewitchment. By the 1630s, the elite were no longer willing to bring such accusations.[57] Courts also began to reject cases involving the killing or injuring of animals at this time; they would entertain prosecutions only if human death was involved. In Germany, there seems to have been a wholesale decline in cases of malefice attributed to older women.[58]

Meanwhile, there were new forms of malefice – forms that proved controversial. The later cases of witchcraft had a higher proportion of demonic possession, or of related phenomena such as witches inflicting 'fits' on their victims. Sixteenth-century possession cases had not usually involved witchcraft; exorcists simply conducted rituals commanding demons to depart from the possessed person. But, during the early seventeenth century, cases began to arise in which the possessed person claimed that a witch had sent the demon. This became a prominent feature of later prosecutions, such as the Salem panic of 1692. The last witch to be executed in Würzburg, Germany, was Maria Renata Singer, the elderly superior of a convent, accused of causing demonic possession in her nuns in 1749.[59] 'Fits' featured in the case of Anna Göldi in 1782.

Yet demonic possession was vulnerable to criticism. The magistrates of the *parlement* of Franche-Comté had doubts about possession and exorcism as early as 1629. During a witchcraft panic, they wrote to the archbishop of Besançon urging him to improve the quality of the parish clergy in order to make the people better Christians. In the first draft of their letter they also asked him not to send exorcists to the region, as exorcists' activities among possessed people would produce 'an infinity of malefices that are so occult that they would give the judges an incredible difficulty in discovering the truth'. They deleted this provocative passage from the letter before sending it, however.[60]

Demonic possession began to cause serious problems for the credibility of witchcraft in the 1630s, with the celebrated possession of the nuns of Loudun, France. The nuns' exorcisms became public spectacles that were discussed all over France and beyond. This led to the execution for witchcraft of a priest, Urbain Grandier, in 1634; the nuns claimed that he had caused their possession, although they had never met him. Illustration 3.1, above, shows Grandier's alleged demonic pact. People expected the execution to end the possessions, but the nuns' convulsions continued, sometimes for several years. Although Loudun's exorcists had supporters, the episode now attracted widespread condemnation, with many people claiming that the nuns' convulsions were faked. Jean-Joseph Surin, one of the exorcists at Loudun, later suffered from demonic possession himself. After his recovery he published a book in 1663 in which he argued that external, physical demonstrations of the demon's presence and activities should not be relied on. The essence of demonic possession was interior and inexpressible, invisible to outsiders.[61]

From the later seventeenth century onwards, the authorities often rejected witchcraft accusations if demonic possession was involved. Early eighteenth-century France saw numerous efforts to suppress unauthorised exorcists, mostly wandering priests, who claimed to be able to drive out demons, and who sometimes accused people of witchcraft. There was even an episode with a female exorcist, Marie de Lamarque, arrested in Béarn in 1734.[62] Ultimately, demonic possession survived longer than witch-hunting, with cases continuing to occur in the nineteenth century; but by then the phenomenon of possession was no longer blamed on witchcraft.

Along with demonic possession, a second theme that became more prominent in seventeenth-century malefice was the magical abduction of children to the sabbat in their sleep. The emergence of children as 'victim-witches' was discussed in Chapter 9; here we need to recognise that this was a transitional phenomenon that gave rise to scepticism. Eventually, panics involving child witches seem to have contributed to the decline of witch-hunting. In the early eighteenth century, a number of children were arrested in Augsburg, Germany, on suspicion of witchcraft; they were kept in prison for long periods and investigated in detail, but all were eventually released.[63] In the Canary Islands in 1781, an 11-year-old girl accused her mother of being a witch, making a statement full of detail about the sabbat and the Devil. The inquisitors noted it all down but took no action.[64] This association with children was probably related to the way in which, as we have seen, witchcraft itself sometimes came to be seen as 'childish'.

Continuing prosecutions for superstitious magic

Prosecutions for superstitious magic continued into the eighteenth century, while prosecutions for witchcraft declined. There was rarely any organised campaign against magical practitioners for being 'superstitious'. Practitioners were prosecuted only when someone complained – typically someone whom the practitioner had accused of theft or witchcraft. Such prosecutions had grown in number during the sixteenth century, along with prosecutions for actual witchcraft, but they now continued for about a further century after witchcraft prosecutions.

Some of these prosecutions for superstitious magic were substitutes for witchcraft prosecutions: someone who would have been prosecuted for witchcraft in the past was now being prosecuted for non-demonic 'superstition' instead. But prosecutions for superstitious magic had their own dynamics. The state of Siena, Italy, executed hardly any witches, but the Inquisition still followed a similar pattern. Prosecutions for illegitimate magical practice continued unabated through the seventeenth and early eighteenth century, while prosecutions for harmful magic dwindled after the 1670s. Yet Siena had hardly ever treated harmful magic as 'witchcraft', so this was not a decline of 'witchcraft' prosecutions.[65] Prosecutions for superstitious magic actually increased in some countries, such as Portugal, in the late seventeenth and eighteenth centuries.[66]

In the heyday of witch-hunting, prosecutions for superstitious magic had generally buttressed prosecutions for demonic witchcraft. However, once the two processes diverged, they no longer supported each other. Earlier, both witchcraft and 'superstition' had been the Devil's work; but, once demonic witchcraft declined in credibility, 'superstition' came to be seen as no more than popular ignorance. The police lieutenant of Paris complained in 1702 of the 'false diviners, the pretended witches' who, he said, 'abuse the simplicity of those who consult them'; he wanted them imprisoned.[67] Eighteenth-century witchcraft legislation in Austria effectively decriminalised witchcraft in order to eradicate 'superstition'.[68] This kind of attack on 'superstition' was intended to *prevent* people believing in witches.

These prosecutions were particularly characteristic of the 'enlightened absolutism' of eighteenth-century states like France and Austria. This was the supposedly benevolent governance provided by monarchical states that had become more stable and better organised since the witch-hunting period. Their 'enlightened' rulers, and indeed European elites generally, saw 'enlightenment' as a process unfolding through time: the present generation was more 'enlightened' than the last one, and so on. Educated men assumed that they were in the lead, but that the common people would eventually follow. There thus grew up a belief that popular 'superstitions' were declining. Anyone who discovered an instance of popular 'superstition' would express surprise or regret that people were 'still' superstitious.

Witchcraft's association with women now worked to undermine it. Elite men assumed that women were more superstitious than men; men were assumed to be more rational and to have been exposed to more 'enlightened' education. In the past, such assumptions had promoted witch-hunting by explaining why women were more open to temptation by the Devil. But, with the decline of fear of the Devil, women's association with magic and witchcraft showed only that they were 'superstitious' – and women's superstition, although deplorable, was now silly and harmless.

The collision of traditional and 'enlightened' beliefs can be seen in various individual cases. In the Central American colony of New Spain in 1704, Baltazar de Monroy claimed to be a witch and to have talked to the Devil. But the commissary of the Inquisition dismissed his case: 'such vices and superstitions are very widespread among the vulgar folk'.[69] In Sweden in 1753, a young man, Erik Olsson Ernberg, confessed voluntarily to having made a pact with the Devil. He described meeting the Devil on a moonlit night – but the authorities checked a lunar calendar and established that the moon had not been visible on that date. Ernberg's story was rejected as an illusion or dream.[70] Such disdain for 'vulgar superstition' would continue until the early nineteenth century, when the Romantic movement rediscovered popular culture as a source of literary and artistic inspiration. But that is a subject for the next chapter.

Village witchcraft after witch-hunting

Villagers in early modern Europe had ways of identifying witches, and such identifications continued long after witch-hunting ceased; so what changed after these witches could no longer be prosecuted? The main answer is: nothing much. Villagers never *needed* witch-hunting. They could live with witches, and had done so for centuries before the early modern witch-hunts began. Once the witch-hunts ended, villagers returned to much the same position as their medieval predecessors. They continued to believe in witches, and continued to cope with them, without the option of witchcraft trials.

The decline of witch-hunting is not normally explained through changes at village level, but there was one possibly relevant development in the seventeenth century. Community pressures for witch-hunting may have eased after the devastations of the Thirty Years' War. Many parts of Germany and adjacent areas, where the war was fought most fiercely, experienced massive numbers of deaths and population displacements. Some regions saw their populations halved. These upheavals probably erased many of the social memories that had allowed witchcraft reputations to form. Survivors and new immigrants did not remember who had been bewitching whom, nor did they care any more.

After witchcraft trials ended, it was still possible to have what Owen Davies has called 'reverse witch trials'. In these, one villager accused another of harmful magic, and it was the *accuser* who was prosecuted. Either the accused witch brought a case against their accuser for slander, or else the accuser assaulted the accused witch and was prosecuted for the assault. This pattern was not actually new; we saw in Chapter 4 that prosecutions for slander or for assault occurred even during the period of witch-hunting. After witch-hunting ended, the 'reverse witch trials' were the only ones that continued. Davies has particularly studied such trials in England in the eighteenth and nineteenth centuries. The people who were called witches had the same social profile as those earlier prosecuted for the crime: 91 per cent were women, about half aged over 50. Most of the few young women were associated with an older woman also thought to be a witch.[71]

Although village witchcraft continued, we should not assume that popular attitudes stood uniformly against witches. In Béarn, France, in 1746, Anne-Marie Dirette-Baringou was accused of various malefices, and a group of villagers dragged her to a grange near a precipice above a river. They may have intended to throw her over the precipice – but she was rescued by *other* villagers.[72] We do not know whether these other villagers thought that Dirette-Baringou was a witch, but they certainly disagreed sharply with her attackers. Her case is a reminder that, even during the witch-hunting period, village attacks on witches were often carried out by a faction rather than by universal consensus.

Did accusations of village witchcraft eventually die away? A full answer to this question would be well beyond the scope of this book, but a few points may be made. There does seem to have been a general trend of 'decline' of European witchcraft beliefs, but it was patchy, and such beliefs have certainly not disappeared from the whole of Europe. Prosecutions for slandering someone as a witch, or for assaulting someone said to be a witch, have not been reported in England since the early twentieth century. On the other hand, such cases were still occurring in small numbers in France as recently as the 1990s.[73] In Poland in 2004, a woman accused a man of stealing her cows' milk by witchcraft; the district court ordered her to apologise.[74] Even in England, although prosecutions may have ceased, many people retain a belief in harmful magic.[75]

As part of the overall decline of beliefs in harmful magic, the scope of magical harm seems to have narrowed. Long-lasting or unusual human illnesses, especially of children, continued to be attributed to witchcraft, but fewer other types of harm were mentioned. A number of cases have

352 *The end of witch-hunting*

also been found of witchcraft without a witch. Misfortune was blamed on 'witchcraft', but there was no attempt to trace the witch, and no suggestion that a specific individual was responsible.[76] Traditional witchcraft beliefs seem to decline with the break-up of traditional rural communities, the spread of universal state education, and the decline of churchgoing; such processes are still continuing.

One further question may be asked. In the next chapter, a global perspective on witchcraft will be introduced, and we shall see that African witchcraft beliefs have adapted to modern social and economic conditions. Magical harm in Africa can be used to explain essentially modern misfortunes. Did witchcraft's transition to modernity also occur in Europe? On the whole, the answer seems to be no, despite modern Europe's plethora of popular magical practices. There is a lively marketplace for 'alternative' healers, therapists, mediums and diviners. But such practitioners hardly ever encourage their clients to think that they have been bewitched by a named individual.

Conclusion: How witch-hunting became unnecessary

The first sections of this chapter have outlined broad judicial, ideological and intellectual developments that mostly undermined witch-hunting from the outside. Judicial caution was internal to witch-hunting, to the extent that it was something learned from the excesses of panics. But this was mainly a short-term phenomenon, found in all phases of witch-hunting, even in the fifteenth century. The decline of torture and the death penalty occurred through broader shifts in the practice of criminal justice, but still helped to bring witchcraft prosecutions to an end. Even more clearly, the decline of the godly state was an external shift. So were the big intellectual developments: the rise of the mechanical philosophy and other aspects of the Scientific Revolution. The history of witch-hunting cannot be understood in isolation from these broader developments.

So which of the broad developments was most influential? To tackle this question, it can be helpful to think about people becoming 'sceptical' about prosecuting witches. Connecting the idea of 'scepticism' with the judicial, ideological and intellectual developments, this indicates that there could have been three types of 'scepticism' – or indeed four, since intellectual scepticism can be subdivided into moderate and stronger versions. A sceptic would adopt one or more of these four positions:

1. *Judicial sceptic*: Witches definitely exist, but the evidence in any particular case is often inconclusive, and we shouldn't execute them unless we're really certain.
2. *Ideological sceptic*: Witches definitely exist, but they aren't important or threatening, so there's no need to take trouble to execute them.
3. *Intellectual sceptic (moderate)*: Witches probably exist, but we can't be certain that they do.
4. *Intellectual sceptic (stronger)*: Witches definitely don't exist.

Could these positions exist independently? If so, it should be possible to isolate the contribution made by each strand of 'scepticism' to the process of ending witchcraft prosecutions. For convenience, we can use the word 'commitment' to indicate the opposite of 'scepticism'.

Intellectual scepticism, if it arose, was particularly deadly to witch-hunting, because it was bound to lead to other types of scepticism also. Once you became even a moderate intellectual sceptic, you would have to agree with both the judicial and ideological sceptics on the crucial issues: there would never be clear evidence that a given person was a witch, and witches were certainly not important or threatening. However, it is unlikely that new scientific ideas spread far enough or fast enough for them to be the sole cause of the reversal of the upward trend in witch-hunting that occurred between the years 1630 and 1670. This is a difficult question, of course, since there were *some* new scientific ideas even in the sixteenth century. However, we should now turn to the other two types of scepticism, judicial and ideological, to see how they might exercise influence, either together or separately.

To show that judicial scepticism operated on its own, we would need to prove that a judge who restrained witchcraft prosecutions did so while still believing that witches existed (intellectual commitment), and that they were a threat, and that it was important to execute them (ideological commitment). Intellectual commitment was more or less a professional necessity for an early modern judge, since the law said that witches existed; a judge would not want to contradict the law in public, whatever he might think privately. But ideological commitment was another matter. Is it likely that a judge who believed that witches were a threat, and that it was important to execute them, would discourage prosecutions on the grounds of the uncertainty of the evidence? Such a judge would be in a worrying position, since he would in effect be declaring himself powerless to protect the community against a dangerous enemy. What is the evidence that any judges did that, or that any other public figures encouraged them to do it?

The search for such evidence is tricky, but it is reasonable to take Friedrich Spee as an example, since Spee is the best-known judicial sceptic. Could we read him as saying, 'Witches are a threat, and we need to execute them, but the evidence is often inconclusive'? Spee certainly began his treatise by stating that witches definitely existed and should be executed. He then devoted his efforts to proving that the evidence being presented in German courts was insufficient. Having called for improved judicial standards, did he conclude by saying that the courts should use these improved standards to identify and execute the real witches? No. He continued arguing against witchcraft trials right to the end of his treatise, concluding that witch-hunting was 'the catastrophe of Germany's zeal'.[77] Spee's opening statement that witches definitely existed and should be executed may have been sincere as far as it went, but he certainly did not think that witches were a threat, nor that it was important to execute them. He was both a judicial *and* an ideological sceptic. It is unlikely that pure judicial scepticism operated without ideological scepticism.

Could there have been ideological scepticism without judicial scepticism? A pure ideological sceptic would say, 'Witches definitely exist, *and we can identify them with certainty*, but they aren't important or threatening, so there's no need to take trouble to execute them.' In southern Europe, the position of the Roman, Spanish and Portuguese Inquisitions could well be described in these terms. Throughout the period they usually remained focused on the need to reclaim sinners for the Church, and were usually confident that they could do that even for witches. North of the Alps, such single-mindedly ideological scepticism was rare, though Adam Tanner in Bavaria expressed a similar wish to convert witches rather than burning them.

Let us return to the short-term and long-term patterns of what I earlier called 'judicial caution'. 'Caution' is not quite the same thing as 'scepticism', but the two are close enough for present purposes (the difference depends mainly on how openly controversial the question of witches was). This allows a further important conclusion to be reached. Not only did judicial scepticism and ideological scepticism usually operate together: they also constituted the normal 'default position' of early modern judges. Even at the height of witchcraft prosecutions, most judges took no active part in the process. Intense witch-hunting occurred only in a few countries or regions at a time. Most early modern judges seem to have been willing to prosecute a witch if a case came before them, but they would not take the kind of extraordinary panic measures that were described in Chapter 8. However, in some places and at some times, conditions were such that more intense prosecutions could arise. And such a short-term pattern could arise almost anywhere in Europe. Until the later seventeenth century, there were no long-term conditions in place that would prevent panics arising.

The importance of political ideology to early modern courts should be emphasised here. These courts were not autonomous institutions concerned solely with 'justice' as an abstract goal. They were agencies of government, and the 'justice' that they administered was often a matter of government policy. Courts were often administrative as well as judicial bodies. The *parlement* of Paris was not just a central court; it also concerned itself with taxation and even the maintenance of roads and bridges. Even with a narrower approach to 'justice', laws are not simple, and courts have to interpret what the law means. Studies of modern courts and judges show that, when faced with difficult or politically-controversial decisions, they sometimes make these decisions on the basis of political attitudes characteristic of their own social class, or of the perceived needs of the government, rather than on purely abstract considerations of 'justice'.[78] Today the political aspects of judicial processes are rarely made explicit, but central and local judges in early modern Europe were all fully aware that their role involved keeping the lower classes in their place. Godly discipline, in particular, was an overtly political matter.

We can now pull some of these threads together. The three developments outlined in the earlier parts of this chapter were judicial, ideological and intellectual. There were judicial changes in court procedures, ideological changes reducing the importance of the godly state, and intellectual changes with the Scientific Revolution introducing new ways of thinking about the natural world. All these changes related to Europe's elites. It might be thought that judges, politicians and intellectuals represented three different elite groups, but this would be misleading. The elites of early modern Europe formed a single group united by aristocratic values. Most of them were landlords, and those who were not landlords were the clients of landlords. There were urban elites, great merchants who had their own autonomy and were not directly beholden to landed aristocrats. But they shared similar values to the aristocrats on everything except the importance of commerce.

Was there a difference between central and local elites? Members of local elites were closer to the common folk, and less well educated. But they were still in touch with the shifts in values, because they were connected to greater men through ties of patronage. A local priest or pastor would owe his job to an aristocratic patron, either directly, or because the bishop to whom he answered was a member of an aristocratic family. A local judge required aristocratic patronage to obtain and to keep his job. Intellectuals in universities relied for their funding on town councils or aristocratic students. As for politicians, they were almost entirely aristocrats.

This is related to the question of how far down the social scale the new ideas spread. Most members of local elites were not university-educated. Could parish priests and pastors continue to promote traditional witch beliefs and witch-hunting? It seems that they now found it more difficult to do so. Moreover, traditional witch beliefs were a complex mixture of different elements, not all of which pointed towards witch-hunting. Beliefs in village witches recognised malefice, but tended to call for reconciliation. Beliefs in demonic witches recognised the pact and the sabbat, but were linked to more elaborate intellectual and ideological systems. It was argued in Chapter 8 that the idea that 'witches should be executed' was an ideological claim. When that claim no longer had the support of the intellectual elite, nor of the social superiors and political patrons of local elites, then the local elites on their own found it hard to act. They might feel inarticulate frustration that the sophisticated metropolitan elite no longer agreed with them about witches, but – like the common folk themselves – they were left with no coherent ideological alternative to the dominant view.

If there is a broader phase of history to which the rise and fall of witch-hunting can be linked, it is the rise and fall of the godly state. The ideological demand that the state must enforce godliness on its people was a distinct phenomenon arising in the sixteenth century and declining in the seventeenth century. Not only priests and pastors, but courts and other agencies of government, sought to spread a correct religious message and to punish those who failed to observe new, godly standards of behaviour. 'Reform', whether Protestant or Catholic, was needed to overcome wickedness inspired by the Devil. The divine plan called for active ideological commitment from everyone, even the common people. It also called for the crushing of God's enemies, whether these were neighbouring princes of a different persuasion, or the Devil's allies within the state – the witches. This ideological demand was undermined in the seventeenth century by a recognition that Christians of different persuasions could live together peacefully, at least in separate states. No longer was it necessary to make extraordinary public efforts to overcome a threat from the Devil. Fear of the Devil disappeared from the political agenda. Those who might have been identified as the Devil's human allies could now breathe more freely.

Notes

1 Quoted in Robert Calef, *More Wonders of the Invisible World* (London, 1700), 144. The 'Prince of the Air' was the Devil. Deuteronomy 17:6 said that criminals should be put to death on the testimony of two or three witnesses, but not of one witness.
2 Alfred Soman, 'Decriminalizing witchcraft: does the French experience furnish a European model?', *Criminal Justice History*, 19 (1989), 1–22, reprinted in Alfred Soman, *Sorcellerie et justice criminelle: Le parlement de Paris (16ᵉ–18ᵉ siècles)* (Aldershot, 1992).
3 Michèle Brocard Plaut, 'Le sabbat et sa répression en Savoie aux XVIIᵉ et XVIIIᵉ siècles', in Nicole Jacques-Chaquin and Maxime Préaud (eds.), *Le sabbat des sorciers en Europe (XVᵉ–XVIIIᵉ siècles)* (Grenoble, 1993), 199–211, at p. 205.
4 *Encyclopedia*, ii, 450–1.
5 Alison Rowlands, *Witchcraft Narratives in Germany: Rothenburg, 1561–1652* (Manchester, 2003), 60.
6 Julian Goodare, 'Witch-hunting and the Scottish state', in Julian Goodare (ed.), *The Scottish Witch-Hunt in Context* (Manchester, 2002), 122–45, at pp. 136–9; Michael Wasser, 'The privy council and the witches: the curtailment of witchcraft prosecutions in Scotland, 1597–1628', *Scottish Historical Review*, 82 (2003), 20–46.
7 Franck Mercier, *La Vauderie d'Arras: Une chasse aux sorcières à l'automne du Moyen Âge* (Rennes, 2006), 325–64.
8 Louise Nyholm Kallestrup, *Agents of Witchcraft in Early Modern Italy and Denmark* (Basingstoke, 2015), 2.
9 Alfred Soman, 'Trente procès de sorcellerie dans la Perche (1566–1624)', *L'Orne littéraire*, 8 (1986), 42–57, at pp. 45–6, reprinted in Soman, *Sorcellerie*.
10 Michael Ostling, *Between the Devil and the Host: Imagining Witchcraft in Early Modern Poland* (Oxford, 2011), 57–8.
11 Johannes Dillinger, 'The political aspects of the German witch-hunts', *Magic, Ritual, and Witchcraft*, 4 (2009), 62–81, at pp. 64–5; *Encyclopedia*, ii, 505–7.
12 Kallestrup, *Agents of Witchcraft*, 23, 29; *Encyclopedia*, ii, 559.
13 Soman, 'Decriminalizing witchcraft', 6–7.
14 François Bordes, *Sorciers et sorcières: Procès de sorcellerie en Gascogne et pays Basque* (Toulouse, 1999), 134–6.
15 Robert Mandrou, *Magistrats et sorciers en France au XVIIᵉ siècle* (Paris, 1968), 478–86.
16 Johannes Dillinger, *Evil People: A Comparative Study of Witch Hunts in Swabian Austria and the Electorate of Trier*, trans. Laura Stokes (Charlottesville, Va., 2009), 183–7; quotation at p. 183.

17 Marijke Gijswijt-Hofstra, 'Six centuries of witchcraft in the Netherlands: themes, outlines, and interpretations', in Marijke Gijswijt-Hofstra and Willem Frijhoff (eds.), *Witchcraft in the Netherlands from the Fourteenth to the Twentieth Century*, trans. Rachel M. J. van der Wilden-Fall (Rotterdam, 1991), 1–36, at pp. 31–2.
18 Brian P. Levack, 'The decline and end of witchcraft prosecutions', in Marijke Gijswijt-Hofstra, Brian P. Levack and Roy Porter, *Witchcraft and Magic in Europe: The Eighteenth and Nineteenth Centuries* (London, 1999), 1–93, at p. 18.
19 Friedrich Spee von Langenfeld, *Cautio Criminalis, or a Book on Witch Trials*, trans. Marcus Hellyer (Charlottesville, Va., 2003).
20 John H. Langbein, *Torture and the Law of Proof: Europe and England in the Ancien Régime* (Chicago, Ill., 1977), 45–60.
21 Sir George Mackenzie, *The Laws and Customs of Scotland in Matters Criminal*, ed. Olivia F. Robinson (Edinburgh: Stair Society, 2012), 414, 440–5.
22 Edward Peters, *Torture* (2nd edn., Philadelphia, Pa., 1996), 82–5.
23 Langbein, *Torture and the Law of Proof*, 27–44.
24 Theodore K. Rabb, *The Struggle for Stability in Early Modern Europe* (Oxford, 1975).
25 Stuart Clark, '"Feigned deities, pretended conferences, imaginary apparitions": scepticism in state theory and witchcraft theory', in Johannes Dillinger, Jürgen M. Schmidt and Dieter R. Bauer (eds.), *Hexenprozess und Staatsbildung: Witch-Trials and State-Building* (Bielefeld, 2008), 265–83.
26 Benjamin J. Kaplan, *Divided by Faith: Religious Conflict and the Practice of Toleration in Early Modern Europe* (Cambridge, Mass., 2007), 122.
27 Sophie Houdard, *Les invasions mystiques: Spiritualités, hétérodoxies et censures au début de l'époque moderne* (Paris, 2008), ch. 1.
28 Michael Hunter and David Wootton (eds.), *Atheism from the Reformation to the Enlightenment* (Oxford, 1992).
29 Quoted in Keith Thomas, *Religion and the Decline of Magic* (London, 1971), 681–2.
30 Stephen Gaukroger, *The Emergence of a Scientific Culture: Science and the Shaping of Modernity, 1210–1685* (Oxford, 2006), 117–18, 159.
31 Gaukroger, *Emergence of a Scientific Culture*, 253; Jonathan I. Israel, *Radical Enlightenment: Philosophy and the Making of Modernity, 1650–1750* (Oxford, 2001), 38–9.
32 Michael Heyd, *'Be Sober and Reasonable': The Critique of Enthusiasm in the Seventeenth and Early Eighteenth Centuries* (Leiden, 1995), 180–3.
33 Joseph Glanvil, *Saducismus Triumphatus, or, Full and Plain Evidence concerning Witches and Apparitions* (London, 1681), 17 (section III).
34 Julie A. Davies, 'Poisonous vapours: Joseph Glanvill's science of witchcraft', *Intellectual History Review*, 22 (2012), 163–79.
35 George Sinclair, *Satan's Invisible World Discovered* (Edinburgh, 1685), 165–6 (relation 27).
36 *Encyclopedia*, iv, 1106–7.
37 Lea, *Materials*, ii, 670–87.
38 William Drage, *Daimonomageia* (London, 1665), 4.
39 Herman Beliën, 'Judicial views on the crime of witchcraft', in Gijswijt-Hofstra and Frijhoff (eds.), *Witchcraft in the Netherlands*, 53–65, at pp. 62–3.
40 Euan Cameron, *Enchanted Europe: Superstition, Reason, and Religion, 1250–1750* (Oxford, 2010), 287–90.
41 Quoted in E. William Monter (ed.), *European Witchcraft* (New York, 1969), 124. Cf. Patrick Dandrey, 'De la pathologie mélancolique à la psychologie

de l'autosuggestion: l'herméneutique de la sorcellerie et de la possession au XVIIe siècle', *Littératures classiques*, 25 (1995), 135–59.
42 Gabriel Naudé, *The History of Magick, by way of Apology, for all the Wise Men who have Unjustly been Reputed Magicians*, trans. John Davies (London, 1657; first published in French 1625), 194.
43 Cameron, *Enchanted Europe*, 303–10.
44 Kay S. Wilkins, 'Attitudes to witchcraft and demonic possession in France during the eighteenth century', *Journal of European Studies*, 3 (1973), 348–62.
45 Quoted in M. Wynn Thomas, 'Cotton Mather's *Wonders of the Invisible World*: some metamorphoses of Salem witchcraft', in Sydney Anglo (ed.), *The Damned Art: Essays on the Literature of Witchcraft* (London, 1977), 202–26, at p. 211.
46 James VI, *Daemonologie* (1597), in Lawrence Normand and Gareth Roberts (eds.), *Witchcraft in Early Modern Scotland: James VI's Demonology and the North Berwick Witches* (Exeter, 2000), 423 (III.6).
47 Quoted in Monter (ed.), *European Witchcraft*, 114.
48 Isabelle Moreau, 'Diable voyageur et intelligence séparées, de la *Démonomanie* aux écrits libertins', in Holtz and Maus de Rolley (eds.), *Voyager avec le diable*, 271–88, at pp. 284–6.
49 Sophie Houdard, 'Les vagabondages comiques de la possédée du *Gascon extravagant* (1637), ou comment boucler le diable dans une fable', in Grégoire Holtz and Thibaut Maus de Rolley (eds.), *Voyager avec le diable: Voyages réels, voyages imaginaires et discours démonologiques (XVe–XVIIe siècles)* (Paris, 2008), 61–74.
50 Quoted in Beliën, 'Judicial views on the crime of witchcraft', 63–4.
51 Sophie Houdard, 'Quand les matous vont au sabbat ... Démons et sorciers dans le *Dictionnaire universel* de Furetière', *Littératures classiques*, 47 (hiver 2003), 149–66; quotation at p. 152.
52 Israel, *Radical Enlightenment*, 378–82.
53 Israel, *Radical Enlightenment*, 385–7.
54 Israel, *Radical Enlightenment*, 397–8.
55 Wilkins, 'Attitudes to witchcraft', 351–2.
56 Marijke Gijswijt-Hofstra, 'Witchcraft after the witch-trials', in Gijswijt-Hofstra et al., *Witchcraft and Magic in Europe: The Eighteenth and Nineteenth Centuries*, 95–189, at p. 177.
57 James Sharpe, *Instruments of Darkness: Witchcraft in England, 1550–1750* (London, 1996), 44.
58 Wolfgang Behringer, *Witchcraft Persecutions in Bavaria*, trans. J. C. Grayson and David Lederer (Cambridge, 1997), 337–8.
59 Brian P. Levack, *The Devil Within: Possession and Exorcism in the Christian West* (New Haven, Conn., 2013), 220.
60 Quoted in Francis Bavoux, *Hantises et diableries dans la terre abbatiale de Luxeuil: D'un procès de l'Inquisition (1529) à l'épidémie démoniaque de 1628–1630* (Monaco, 1956), 165–6.
61 Sophie Houdard, 'La possession et ses images: la scène équivoque de Loudun', in Ralph Dekoninck and Agnès Guiderdoni-Bruslé (eds.), *Emblemata sacra: Rhétorique et herméneutique du discours sacré dans la littérature en images* (Turnhout, 2007), 427–40.
62 Bordes, *Sorciers et sorcières*, 161–7.
63 Lyndal Roper, *Witch Craze: Terror and Fantasy in Baroque Germany* (New Haven, Conn., 2004), 204–21.

64 Francisco Fajardo Spinola, 'Des vols et assemblées des sorcières dans les documents de l'Inquisition canarienne', in Jacques-Chaquin and Préaud (eds.), *Le sabbat des sorciers*, 299–315, 303.
65 *Encyclopedia*, iv, 1035–6.
66 Timothy D. Walker, *Doctors, Folk Medicine and the Inquisition: The Repression of Magical Healing in Portugal during the Enlightenment* (Leiden, 2005).
67 Quoted in Robert Muchembled, 'Terres de contrastes: France, Pays-Bas, Provinces-Unies', in Robert Muchembled (ed.), *Magie et sorcellerie en Europe du Moyen Âge à nos jours* (Paris, 1994), 99–132, at p. 127.
68 Edmund M. Kern, 'An end to witch trials in Austria: reconsidering the enlightened state', *Austrian History Yearbook*, 30 (1999), 159–85.
69 Fernando Cervantes, *The Devil in the New World: The Impact of Diabolism in New Spain* (New Haven, Conn., 1994), 137.
70 Linda Oja, 'Responses to witchcraft in late seventeenth- and eighteenth-century Sweden: the superstitious other', in Owen Davies and Willem de Blécourt (eds.), *Beyond the Witch Trials: Witchcraft and Magic in Enlightenment Europe* (Manchester, 2004), 69–80, at p. 73.
71 Owen Davies, *Witchcraft, Magic and Culture, 1736–1951* (Manchester, 1999), 192–201.
72 Bordes, *Sorciers et sorcières*, 158.
73 Owen Davies, 'Witchcraft accusations in France, 1850–1990', in Willem de Blécourt and Owen Davies (eds.), *Witchcraft Continued: Popular Magic in Modern Europe* (Manchester, 2004), 107–32.
74 Ostling, *Between the Devil and the Host*, 60.
75 Thomas Waters, 'Maleficent witchcraft in Britain since 1900', *History Workshop Journal*, 80 (Autumn 2015), 99–122. Prosecutions still occur among recent immigrants.
76 Gijswijt-Hofstra, 'Witchcraft after the witch-trials', 177–9.
77 Spee, *Cautio Criminalis*, 219.
78 Sandra B. Burman and Barbara E. Harrell-Bond (eds.), *The Imposition of Law* (New York, 1979); William N. Eskridge, Jr., *Dynamic Statutory Interpretation* (Cambridge, Mass., 1994); J. A. G. Griffith, *The Politics of the Judiciary* (5th edn., London, 1997); Donald L. Horowitz, *The Courts and Social Policy* (Washington, DC, 1977).

11 Perspectives on the witch-hunt

> For the purposes of this Convention, the term 'torture' means any act by which severe pain or suffering, whether physical or mental, is intentionally inflicted on a person for such purposes as obtaining from him or a third person information or a confession, punishing him for an act he or a third person has committed or is suspected of having committed, or intimidating or coercing him or a third person, or for any reason based on discrimination of any kind, when such pain or suffering is inflicted by or at the instigation of or with the consent or acquiescence of a public official or other person acting in an official capacity. It does not include pain or suffering arising only from, inherent in or incidental to lawful sanctions.
> United Nations Convention against Torture, Article 1, part 1, 1984[1]

Introduction

Torture, as the United Nations reminds us, is very much part of today's world. This final chapter will assess the great European witch-hunt in a number of ways, one of which will be to place it in the context of other instances of persecution, past and present. In doing so it will also draw together some of the perspectives that have been developed in the previous chapters of this book – beginning with a reflection on the 'European' nature of the witch-hunt.

This chapter will also reflect on the various ways in which the European witch-hunt has been studied in the past. This will concentrate on the two great traditions, 'liberal' and 'romantic', that have inspired many scholars to seek a deeper understanding of it. Both the liberal tradition, focusing on persecution, and the romantic tradition, focusing on the witches' own experience, are alive and well in present scholarship, and have deep roots going back to the nineteenth century and beyond. Perhaps inevitably, some earlier scholars in these traditions took what can now be considered to be detours or wrong turns. And, because witchcraft and witch-hunting are topics of wide popular interest, some of these detours have fed into modern popular misconceptions. Everyone 'knows' something about the history of witch-hunting, but their 'knowledge' does not always come from the latest scholarship. As well as outlining these scholarly traditions, this chapter will also comment on the origins of modern witchcraft imagery, and on the darker subject of witch-hunting today in non-Western societies.

Within academic scholarship, witchcraft and witch-hunting are not just of interest to historians. Several other disciplines have concerned themselves with these topics, or with related topics. This chapter will thus explore the ways in which perspectives from other disciplines, notably anthropology and psychology, have enriched historical understanding and may do so further in future.

The witch-hunt as 'European'

The great European witch-hunt can be analysed, as it has been in this book, as a single phenomenon. However, it was also inescapably diverse. The book's central organising question has been: Why were 50,000 people executed for witchcraft in early modern Europe? However, there is no single answer to this question. The nearest one can get may be to relate witchcraft beliefs to pre-industrial peasant culture, and to relate the rise and decline of witch-hunting to the rise and decline of the godly state. As we saw in Chapter 6, the godly state was diverse, with some godly states allowing witch-hunting, or failing to prevent it, rather than leading it, and with other godly states decisively rejecting witch-hunting; nevertheless, the overall chronological boundaries of the godly state match the chronological boundaries of witch-hunting. Peasant culture, too, was diverse, with a variety of ways in which misfortune could be explained, and with regional traditions of folk belief and spirit cults. The level of peasant demand for witch-hunting also varied widely over time and place.

Nevertheless, witch-hunting was a single phenomenon, simply because witchcraft itself came to be recognised in the early modern period as a single phenomenon. From the various ideas about medieval magic, superstition, heresy, poisoning, dealing with spirits and other such matters, a single concept of 'witchcraft' emerged, as we saw in Chapter 2. It became clear that 'witches' were human beings who should be punished with death.

Variety thus manifested itself within this single concept. Partly this is because some linguistic diversity remained. The French-speaking parts of the Netherlands tended to call witches '*Vaudoises*', even after most other French-speakers had settled on the term '*sorcières*'. However, '*Vaudoises*' were treated the same as '*sorcières*'. The same applies to the German term '*Unholden*', which continued in south-eastern Germany even after other German-speakers had adopted the term '*Hexen*'. More importantly, the Inquisitions in Spain, Portugal and Italy remained resistant to the vocabulary of 'witchcraft', preferring terms like 'magic' or 'superstition' that allowed them to impose mild punishments on witch-like offenders.

There may be a geographical pattern here. The authorities in a few parts of Europe may have resisted, not only the vocabulary of 'witchcraft', but the central ideas that this vocabulary articulated – the ideas of harmful magic and the demonic pact. In southern Spain, the Inquisition mainly prosecuted 'superstitious' healing or love magic by recognised magical practitioners. Inquisitors recorded hardly any concern about harmful magic, let alone the demonic pact. This was partly because most rural people in southern Spain were 'Moriscos', forcibly-converted Muslims, who were unlikely to denounce their neighbours to the Inquisition.[2] In the Balkans, the Greek Orthodox church was mainly concerned about 'superstitious' healing; even when this involved demons, there was little or no recognition of harmful magic or the demonic pact.[3] The Balkans was unusual because its Muslim rulers, the Ottoman Turks, prevented witch-hunting, but it is still notable that some regions in the far south of Europe displayed a lack of official interest in witchcraft as it has been studied in this book – both village witchcraft and demonic witchcraft. In Russia, another peripheral region, most 'witches' who were prosecuted were recognised magical practitioners accused of magical harm, rather than village witches identified through neighbourhood quarrels.

Yet only Russia and the Balkans were really untouched by intellectual demonology. The *Malleus Maleficarum* was read in Spain, Portugal and Italy, just as it was in Scandinavia and Poland. Readers did not always agree with it, but they recognised that it carried a message for the whole of Europe. The transmission of demonological ideas was never complete, and different ideas were emphasised in different places, but a broad European consensus did emerge to recognise the key components of demonological witchcraft, as these were set out in Chapter 3 – the conspiratorial witch, usually female, who made a pact with the Devil and who practised harmful magic.

The age of European witch-hunting was also the age of European colonial expansion. Although the colonists did not prosecute witches among their newly-conquered peoples, their new awareness of ethnic diversity and danger sharpened their awareness of magical threats at home. English colonists in Massachusetts feared demonic forces among nearby native Americans. Norwegians expanding to the north encountered tribal Sámi people with unusual magical powers. Germans and even Scots worried about the 'barbarous North' (for the Scots this meant Orkney and Shetland). These fears operated only indirectly, and some may even have directed attention away from witch-hunting; this was certainly so with the Spanish Inquisition's campaigns among nominally-converted Jews and Muslims. Witch-hunting was mainly an attack on ungodliness, but this was linked in complex ways to European elites' perception of themselves as 'civilised' and their perception of non-Europeans as 'barbarous'.

Throughout Europe, people's engagement with witches was shaped by their social and political position. Most of the central rulers – the kings, dukes, councillors, popes and cardinals – took little or no interest in witch-hunting, as far as we can tell. They knew about witchcraft, of course, but they did not think that they should go out of their way to encourage the prosecution of witches. Some even disapproved of witch-hunting, at least when it involved panics. However, until the later stages of the witch-hunt it was unusual for central rulers to take action against witch-hunting, and it was normal for them to go along with it. Sometimes they issued regulations for prosecuting witches – regulations that could limit panics, but could also legitimise witchcraft prosecutions. At the other end of the social scale, most ordinary villagers were interested in village witches, and used witchcraft beliefs to structure their understanding of quarrels and misfortune. However, it was not normal for villagers to encourage witch-hunting. Their usual approach to witches in their village, as we saw in Chapter 4, was one of conciliation.

What about local elites? Priests, pastors, judges and officials in local courts not only spent longer thinking about witchcraft, but were also more likely to think that prosecution was a normal approach. They were in the front line of the campaign for godly discipline, as we saw in Chapter 6. If they thought that godly discipline was important, they might well think that it should include witch-hunting. The conversion of a state to Protestantism, or the active defence of Catholicism by a state, prompted the state to demand the active religious allegiance of its citizens. People could no longer treat their religion as an all-embracing community affair, in which everyone was assumed to believe the same thing. You had to know what you yourself believed; you were personally responsible for your beliefs, even if you were a peasant, even if you were a woman. Your state had a religious identity, and you had to fall into line with this. And if you believed the wrong thing, you could get into trouble. Local elites, both secular and ecclesiastical, formed the authority structures that attempted to enforce these orthodoxies on the common people of Europe.

Perspectives from the liberal tradition

Broadly speaking, there have been two dominant traditions of witchcraft scholarship: the liberal tradition, and the romantic tradition. To take the liberal tradition first, this has been an approach to the subject that favours freedom of worship and belief, and is hostile to persecution. This tradition initally arose from contemporary critiques of witch-hunting, but soon developed into a way of understanding witch-hunting as something that people of an earlier, less enlightened age had carried out.

As early as 1690, Robert Chouet, magistrate of Geneva, Switzerland, approached witch-hunting historically: 'Lately, as I was leafing through our archives, the trial of a Michée Chauderon, who was hanged and burned in 1652 for the crime of witchcraft, came into my hands.' He wrote that this was 'the last execution of this kind that has taken place in our city; and I hope that nothing like it will ever happen again.' Chouet knew, however, that outside Geneva witch-hunting was not yet history, adding: 'But judge, Sir, by this example, what we ought to think of the others.'[4]

Witch-hunting became history only gradually, as we saw in Chapter 10. But the leading thinkers of the eighteenth-century Enlightenment certainly thought that it was, or ought to be, history – a shocking example of the 'superstition' and 'barbarity' of recent centuries. The French philosopher Voltaire (1698–1778) was one of the most celebrated of these thinkers, bitterly and wittily combating what he saw as the obscurantism of Christian theology. He included numerous articles on witchcraft and magic in his *Dictionnaire Philosophique* ('Philosophical Dictionary') of 1764. Voltaire ridiculed witch beliefs as a combination of peasant ignorance and fantasy, and, above all, as a gross intellectual error. The Jesuit demonologist Martin Delrio incurred Voltaire's special condemnation as credulous and bigoted. Witch-hunting was everything that the Enlightenment thought of as unenlightened.

The Enlightenment was mainly an intellectual movement, but it also inspired creative artists interested in persecution and intolerance. One of these was the Spanish artist Francisco Goya (1746–1828), who in the 1790s produced a long series of paintings and prints on quasi-demonological themes. These were gloomy satires on the irrationalities and superstitions of his day, with the Catholic Church being a particular target. Like Voltaire, Goya articulated a crucial shift in the meaning of 'superstition'. During the witch-hunting period, the Church had defined what was 'superstitious', and had taken the lead in suppressing its version of 'superstition'. Now, with the Enlightenment, the Church itself was defined as 'superstitious'.

Goya's pictures included several witchcraft images – naked witches on broomsticks, and hags at gruesome sabbats. This was not because these were topical in the 1790s, but precisely because they harked back to an unenlightened past. These pictures are often used today to illustrate books on the history of witch-hunting, but Goya was not a contemporary; witch-hunting had ceased in Spain long before his lifetime. His 'enlightened' message was neatly summarised in the title of one of his famous prints: 'The Sleep of Reason Produces Monsters'. Goya's interest in 'monsters' also connects him with the romantic tradition, to be discussed in a moment.

With the rise of history as a distinct scholarly discipline in the nineteenth century, the liberal tradition developed a firmer grounding in documentary analysis. Wilhelm Soldan (1803–69), a German scholar, published the first scholarly history of European witch-hunting in 1843. Soldan coined the famous phrase 'witch craze' (*'Hexenwahn'*). The American scholar Henry Charles Lea (1825–1909) wrote about the Inquisition in an erudite but decidedly anticlerical way, and collected many documents on witchcraft that subsequent scholars have found invaluable. Lea's overall view was that witch-hunting arose from a 'delusion'. These interpretations thus combined moral condemnation, intellectual superiority, and a rudimentary sense of psychological derangement: witch-hunters were 'crazed' or 'deluded'. Such conclusions are no longer satisfactory in themselves, yet Soldan and Lea cannot be dismissed as wholly misguided. Their liberal approach remains valid – but we need fuller and better empirical data on which to base our moral judgements, and a more developed understanding of the social and psychological processes guiding human behaviour.

Thus, we can now see that the liberal tradition gave rise to a number of ideas that are no longer still current. Several of these ideas relate to the Inquisition. In the Enlightenment, the Inquisition became a symbol of religious obscurantism and oppression – an image that it has retained in popular culture ever since. This has led to several related misconceptions, such as the idea that the Inquisition was the main body responsible for witch-hunting, and that it burned witches to save their souls. In fact, although a few inquisitors helped to develop the witch-hunt in its early stages (for instance by writing the *Malleus Maleficarum*), the Spanish, Portuguese and Roman Inquisitions played a generally restraining role during the sixteenth and seventeenth centuries when most witches were executed. Most executions were the responsibility of secular criminal courts. The Inquisition was one of the main reasons why Spain and Italy had low rates of witchcraft prosecution. As for burning witches in order to save their souls: the Inquisition's preferred aim was to reclaim heretics to the true faith without burning them. Those whom it burned (or rather, whom it handed over to the secular authorities for burning) were the impenitent heretics. The burning, as such, did not save their souls but simply punished them for their crime.

Within scholarship, a particularly long-running idea was that the Inquisition was directly responsible for initiating the witch-hunt in the late middle ages. Soldan and Lea believed that the Inquisition, which had been established to persecute the Cathar and Waldensian heresies, moved on to hunting witches in order to keep itself in business after the Cathars, the most influential heretics, were suppressed in the early fourteenth century. They based this argument on documents describing mass witch-hunting in the early fourteenth century: the chronology fitted perfectly. It was not until the 1970s that these documents were revealed as forgeries, most of which had been concocted in 1829. It was argued in Chapter 2 that ideas about witchcraft developed slowly, piece by piece, during the middle ages. The combined concept of witchcraft – the idea of a heretical sect of witches who made pacts with the Devil and practised harmful magic – arose gradually during the fifteenth century, with key decades being the 1430s and 1480s.

Along with the emphasis on the Inquisition, the liberal tradition emphasised torture, as part of the 'barbarity' of witch-hunting and indeed of past ages as a whole. Torture was, of course, extremely important in the witch-hunt, so this is not entirely a misconception. However, the tortures that are reported in popular accounts of witch-hunting are often the most extreme and dramatic physical ones; the false implication is that these were normal. There is also today the false idea that torture was a punishment for crime; instead, as we saw in Chapter 7, torture was a means of obtaining evidence. The idea of torture leads on to the idea that trials of witches were so stacked against the defence that convictions were the only possible outcome. However, even during large-scale witchcraft panics, there were usually some acquittals, and other cases were dropped before trial. The idea of inevitable conviction is common because people are receptive to the idea that witch-hunting was cruel and barbaric.

The significance of the fact that most witches were women was rarely recognised before modern times. When scholars in the liberal tradition discussed the issue, they tended to say that women were more vulnerable to persecution – an easy target. Being hostile to the witch-hunters, they attributed bad motives to them. Thus we have the idea of the witch-hunter as a cad: he was so ungentlemanly as to attack women. As we shall see shortly, it has been the romantic tradition that has given more sustained and fruitful attention to the issue of women, though this has not been without its problems.

Finally, the liberal emphasis on the shocking enormity of witch-hunting also led to an inflation in the numbers of its victims. In the eighteenth century, Voltaire mentioned a speculative figure of 100,000 executions – quite close to modern estimates. However, in 1869, Gustav Roskoff studied the records of a local German panic and jumped to the conclusion that this sample represented a constant level of witch-hunting. He scaled his figures up to the whole of Europe and produced a figure of 9 million witches executed. This figure was repeated uncritically by many scholars for over a century, but can now be recognised as a wild exaggeration. The importance of witch-hunting is not just the numbers executed, but also the climate of fear that could be induced even by sporadic executions.

The liberal tradition continues today among scholars studying witch-hunters and the persecutions that they carried out. If today we see the limits of the early liberal understanding of the witch-hunt, we should also bear in mind that future generations may see the limits of our own understanding of it. And, as the modern world has become more secularised, we may need to remind ourselves of two things. First, religion mattered a great deal to people in the early modern world. Second, organised religions do not usually carry out witch-hunts; witch-hunting is problematic as a debating point for those who dislike today's religions.

Perspectives from the romantic tradition

The second tradition of witchcraft studies, arising with the romantic movement of the early nineteenth century, focused on the witches themselves. Scholars in this 'romantic tradition' concurred with the liberal account of oppressive persecution, but went beyond it to open up a series of ideas about the victims of persecution and about their cultural traditions.

Romantic writers tended to emphasise 'nature', believing that the deepest truths could be derived, not from artificial reason, but from a contemplation of humanity's essence and relationship with the natural world. The role of the imagination was crucial; the romantic movement as a whole was a creative endeavour, led by poets, novelists and painters. For studies of witchcraft, an influential romantic work was Johann Goethe's verse novel *Faust* (1808, 1832), celebrating the Renaissance necromancer as a flawed hero.

The romantic scholars moved beyond the liberal critique of Christian 'superstition' to develop positive ideas about the beliefs and practices of the common people. The 'fairy-tales' of the late seventeenth and eighteenth centuries had been consciously literary products, but those of the brothers Grimm in the early nineteenth century were presented as tales of the common folk. Popular culture was no longer simply vulgar superstition and ignorance: it was now interpreted as a rich storehouse of folk wisdom.

Two romantic works proved particularly influential in opening up the topic of witchcraft beliefs to scholarly study. Jacob Grimm, co-editor of the famous fairy-tales, also published *Deutsche Mythologie* ('German Mythology' or 'Teutonic Mythology') in 1835, a scholarly account of historical German culture that celebrated the witch as a 'wise woman', conserver of folk culture, oppressed by the political and ecclesiastical establishment. He was followed by Jules Michelet, who in 1862 published *La Sorcière* ('The Witch'), partly a novel, partly historical anthropology, that purported to reconstruct the imaginative world of the peasant woman oppressed by feudal lords and an overbearing church. Although Grimm's and Michelet's specific interpretations of their material are no longer accepted, they showed for the first time that it was possible to take popular witch beliefs seriously.

One legacy of the romantic movement has thus been an interest in folk culture and tradition. In the nineteenth and early twentieth centuries, folklorists collected a vast amount of information about traditional songs, dances, stories, beliefs and practices. In an age of emerging nationalism, some countries even established official 'folklore commissions' in order to discover, or assert, their national identity. Not all of the material they gathered was historical, but at its best it enabled scholars to understand the culture of past societies better – including the role of witchcraft in those societies. Unfortunately, these early folklorists often assumed that the 'oral traditions' they studied were ancient or even pre-Christian – which could lead witchcraft beliefs to be misinterpreted as 'pagan', as we saw in Chapter 5.

The romantic tradition's focus on the witches themselves led to a concentration on the idea of women as witches. This is the origin of the idea, popular today, that witch-hunting was an attack on women as such – a more or less conscious device by men for repressing women. Chapter 9 has argued that, although there was a clear relationship between women and witch-hunting, it was complex and indirect. Witch-hunters did not target women as such, they targeted witches. About 20 per cent of witches were men. Feminist scholarship has done much to bring these issues, which traditional anticlerical scholars had ignored, to the forefront of discussion.

Related to this is the idea that midwives were particularly targeted by witch-hunters, being blamed when babies died. As well as being a feminist idea this had an anticlerical element: the church was believed to have been hostile to midwives because they tried to reduce the labour pains ordained for women to punish the sin of Eve. Some demonologists did denounce midwives, believing that their access to babies gave them material for cannibalistic infanticide, but these denunciations were uncommon. Some midwives were indeed accused of witchcraft, but too few to suggest that they were being targeted; most midwives seem to have been well-respected people who were unlikely to be accused by their clients or neighbours.

Another idea popular in the late twentieth century was that an emerging male medical profession attacked traditional women healers, including midwives, by labelling them as witches. But the role of the medical profession in witch-hunting was peripheral; physicians were far less important than lawyers, for instance. Most witches were not folk healers, and witch-hunting was not an attack on folk healing as such. Healers sometimes encouraged witch-hunting, by diagnosing illnesses as witch-induced and helping clients to identify the witch responsible.

The romantic idea that was most influential in its time was that witchcraft was a surviving pagan cult. The witches who were hunted in early modern times were argued to have been practitioners of a pagan religion that had gone underground with the coming of Christianity. When their religion was discovered by the Christian church in the late middle ages, its members were persecuted for allegedly worshipping the Devil. Outline versions of this theory appeared occasionally in the nineteenth century, but it took its enduring and detailed form in 1921 with a book by the retired Egyptologist Margaret Murray, *The Witch-Cult in Western Europe*. According to Murray, the members of this 'witch-cult' worshipped a horned god, 'Dianus', and were organised in covens of thirteen. Her book appeared at the height of a vogue for 'pagan' survivals, and had a persuasive appearance of deep scholarship. This was in fact fraudulent – Murray's sources often did not say what she said they said – but this was not realised until later. Murray's theory became influential, particularly among folklorists, and gained a fresh vogue in the 1960s among historians interested in popular movements. It was frequently criticised by historians familiar with the records of witchcraft trials, but often they could say only that they had found no evidence for the theory in their own research. The painstaking work of exposing Murray's fraudulent use of sources was not undertaken until the 1970s.

But by then Murray's theory had been embraced by the modern Wiccan movement, whose founders wished to believe that they were inheriting an ancient tradition. This movement arose in England in the middle years of the twentieth century. It gradually created (or, as its founders saw it, recreated) a pagan religion that looked back to pre-Christian beliefs and practices. The key book by the movement's main founder, Gerald Gardner, was *Witchcraft Today* (1954), in which he announced that he was a member of a coven of witches that had survived since pre-Christian times. The book had an approving introduction by Murray herself. Murray's theory thus gained a new lease of life, and the witch-hunt became known as the 'Burning Times' among Wiccans believing that the witches who had been executed had been pagans like themselves. Some Wiccans still adhere to versions of this theory, but many others have recognised that the historical evidence provides no support for the existence of an organised or self-identified pagan movement in early modern Europe.

A comparable movement to create a pagan origin for the witches arose in Nazi Germany. The Nazi leader Heinrich Himmler created a special research group, the *H-Sonderkommando* (H for '*Hexen*'), to catalogue witchcraft trial records. They hoped to prove that the witches had been German pagans, with trials caused by the Catholic church having been infiltrated by Jews plotting to destroy the superior German race. They never got anywhere near proving this, but their tens of thousands of index card entries have been useful to subsequent scholars.

The broader romantic movement has sometimes been interested in the relationship between technological modernity and human nature. Mary Shelley's novel *Frankenstein* (1818) is a famous example. The late twentieth century saw an attempt to explain witchcraft in quasi-scientific terms, through the effects of the ergot fungus. This fungus grows on rye, and eating contaminated rye can bring on the disease known as ergotism, with symptoms that can include convulsions and hallucinations. It has occasionally been argued that ergotism was the cause of what was interpreted in early modern times as demonic possession. Those afflicted accused others of 'bewitching' them, thus causing witch-hunts. The idea was originally proposed specifically for the Salem panic, but it is sometimes extended to all cases of demonic possession or even all witch-hunting. However, the ergotism theory has been discredited at Salem for various reasons, including its inability to explain why the 'afflicted girls' were the only ones to suffer (ergotism affects entire households, and men as much as women), and why their symptoms were often brought on by the presence of the accused witches. Nor has ergotism succeeded in explaining European demonic possession. The idea's followers do not always realise that possession cases were rare exceptions to the normal pattern of witchcraft accusation based on neighbourhood quarrels and stereotyping. Nevertheless, the idea's 'scientific' appearance gives it high status in a world dominated by technology. The fact that ergot is the source of lysergic acid diethylamide (LSD) adds to the attraction: people are fascinated by the idea that people in past societies experienced drug-induced hallucinations. The theory was first popularised in 1976 by a *New York Times* article headed 'Salem Witch Hunts in 1692 Linked to LSD-Like Agent', and may safely be left there.

Many of these perspectives, both liberal and romantic, are attractive because they enable people to sympathise with the victims of witch-hunting – the romantic approach – and to feel indignant at those who inflicted their cruel fate – the liberal approach. It is perhaps natural to feel that there must have been some obvious fault in the witch-hunters: they were wicked, or ignorant, or both. Individualism, so pronounced since the twentieth century, has enhanced this tendency. The individual who does not fit in to the society around them, and who struggles to overcome collective prejudice in order to realise their true worth, is the hero of entire genres of fiction in modern culture. People identify with witches as misunderstood individuals of this kind: 'that could have been me', they think when they see witches persecuted. A related version of this identification is the wish to claim that one is descended from a witch. Such willingness to empathise with people of the past, particularly victims of persecution, is creditable. However, historians wish to extend the same understanding to all the people whom they study – witch-hunters as well as witches. Labelling witch-hunters as wicked or ignorant gets us no further in explaining what they did. We are not trying to endorse what they did; we are simply trying to understand it.

Perspectives from anthropology

The study of European witch-hunting entered a new era in 1970–71 with the publication of two books by Alan Macfarlane and Keith Thomas.[5] Working on English witchcraft and popular belief, they were influenced by anthropological studies, especially those of Edward Evans-Pritchard in Africa, on the role of witchcraft in community interactions. Macfarlane and Thomas explained English witchcraft accusations as part of a pattern of quarrels followed by misfortune, in which witchcraft functioned as an explanation for the misfortune. Coming at a time when history 'from below' was being opened up, their works were seized on with excitement, and have influenced studies of witch-hunting ever since.

There was, however, a problem. Macfarlane and Thomas had made clear that their work only covered England. Many Continental scholars, especially in Germany, continued to work in the liberal paradigm of persecution 'from above'. From the 1970s to the early 1990s it was often assumed that England was different from the Continent: English witch-hunting came 'from below', while Continental witch-hunting came 'from above'. This England/Continent dichotomy was particularly influential when it appeared to be accepted by scholars on both sides, but it can be seen in retrospect to have been unhelpful. The pioneering scholar of Scottish witchcraft, Christina Larner, wrestled with the problem of where to place Scotland in the England/Continent dichotomy. Writing in the 1970s, she saw Scottish parallels both with England and with the Continent, but did not realise that this was because the dichotomy was false.[6] However, one of the reasons why Larner's work remains influential may be that she grounded it in an analysis that took account, both of witch-hunting from below, and of witch-hunting from above.

Only in the 1990s did scholars, of whom the most influential was Robin Briggs, challenge the whole England/Continent dichotomy. Briggs showed that prosecutions in the duchy of Lorraine, the area in which he specialised, had much in common with prosecutions in England, as well as those in many other Continental countries. Briggs himself argued that witch-hunting came largely from below, pressing his case vigorously in order to overcome objections and win acceptance. His sophisticated analysis could take account of numerous other causes besides popular demand, while skilfully marginalising them or reducing them to the status of necessary preconditions.[7] Briggs's brilliant argument remains an essential perspective on witch-hunting, but it can be seen in retrospect to have been overstated. The welcome abolition of the England/Continent dichotomy surely allows us to see witch-hunting in European regions more clearly, with England and indeed Lorraine constituting variations on a broader theme. All over Europe, some witch-hunting came from above and some from below, as was argued in Chapter 8. The precise combination of these two patterns is still open to debate and to further research. Meanwhile, the anthropological approach to village witchcraft – now so mainstream among historians that they rarely maintain links with today's anthropologists – continues to bear fruit.

One promising approach here, pioneered by Ronald Hutton, is a global one.[8] Anthropologists have studied witchcraft beliefs in tribal societies on every continent, and it may seem as if all traditional societies have believed in witches. But, as Hutton shows, this is not so; there are several regions with no traditional witch beliefs, of which the largest and most paradigmatic is Siberia. Siberian tribes, with their shamanic ritual practices, have explained misfortune not through witchcraft but through angry spirits – spirits that it is the shaman's job to placate or neutralise. Hutton here was to some extent responding to an earlier broad interpretation of witch beliefs, that of Carlo Ginzburg. In the 1960s, Ginzburg had discovered the shamanistic cult of the *benandanti*, discussed in Chapter 5. He went on to construct an elaborate interpretation of the witches' sabbat, arguing that its core was found in an ecstatic journey to the realm of the dead. He traced this back to the ancient Celts, and, beyond them, to the Scythians.[9] The range of Ginzburg's learning was prodigious, but a scholarly consensus emerged that he had arbitrarily prioritised certain motifs and that it was hard to see reliable continuities across millennia. Thus, Hutton's approach also examines traditional beliefs but focuses more on broad sweeps of geography than chronology. It may in future be possible to trace cultural regions throughout the world in which misfortune has traditionally been explained in different ways. Witchcraft, from this perspective, is a common but not universal phenomenon of traditional society. There is more on global perspectives later in this chapter.

Anthropologists studying tribal magic have sometimes drawn a distinction between two types of harmful magic: one as a technique to be learned, the other as an inherent, inherited power. Magical techniques are described as 'sorcery', inherent powers as 'witchcraft'. This is not always a helpful distinction, and it is certainly not helpful in early modern Europe; villagers were little interested in the source of the witch's power, while demonologists saw the power as being granted by the Devil. This book has avoided the term 'sorcery' for this reason. Anthropologists' 'sorcerers' are often equivalent to what this book has called 'magical practitioners', especially when they are not entirely, or not at all, malevolent. Tribal magical practitioners have sometimes been called 'witch-doctors' if they cure the effects of witchcraft, but this term, little used in current anthropology, has also been avoided in this book.

Finally, although anthropologists usually study tribal societies, anthropological methods have also influenced the study of intellectual demonology in Europe. Stuart Clark, the leading scholar of demonology, has used anthropologically-influenced 'relativism' to argue that demonological writings should be studied on their own terms. Liberal scholars of previous generations had freely denounced demonology as a 'delusion' or 'superstition', but, Clark argued, this missed the point. Anthropologists studying tribal beliefs asked how these beliefs functioned and why they made sense to those who held them; the same approach should be taken to early modern demonology.[10] This is the approach that has been taken in Chapter 3.

Perspectives from psychology

It is under 'psychology', not under 'history', that books on the history of witchcraft are classified by standard library cataloguing systems. This should not surprise us. Psychologists study many aspects of human beliefs, behaviour and social interaction – though one may suspect that the old-fashioned ideas of 'craze' and 'delusion' may have influenced the cataloguing systems. How have recent historians drawn on perspectives from psychology – and how might they do so in future?

Early witchcraft scholars using 'psychology' mostly used the branch of it known as psychoanalysis – the tradition begun by Sigmund Freud, locating the origin of many psychological problems in childhood trauma. The work of John Demos on the traumas of adolescent accusers, discussed in Chapter 9, is an example. A broader psychoanalytical perspective argues that witch-hunters tended to find it difficult to integrate the good and bad aspects of the human personality. They could not admit, even to themselves, that they themselves were in any way bad, nor that the witches whom they accused were in any way good. This kind of black and white moral universe is common among young children. Most people grow out of it and develop a more sophisticated understanding of human motivation, but some revert to moral absolutes in stressful or threatening situations. Worse, they may react by denial when they find themselves feeling envy or anger in such situations; instead they blame others – their enemies – for their own destructive feelings. They rationalise their own upsetting emotions as good and correct reactions to the evil of others, thus making it all the more imperative to destroy those others. Lyndal Roper, in particular, has argued that witchcraft was an ideal topic to understand in terms of moral absolutes.[11]

Perspectives on the witch-hunt 373

People who felt violent impulses towards their enemies and oppressors seem to have acted these impulses out in fantasy. In real life they were relatively powerless, but in their imaginations they fantasised about how they might get even with those whom they hated and feared. They knew that hatred and vengeance were dubious or even wicked, so the fantasy character whom they imagined as assisting them was also dubious or wicked. In popular culture today, many violent 'heroes' are morally dubious, enabling them to act as credible vehicles for morally dubious aggressive fantasies. The most important such fantasy figure in pre-industrial times was the Devil. When people invoked the Devil in cursing their antagonists, they really meant what they said – in fantasy, at least. And the victims of these curses, who may themselves have felt violent impulses towards others, subconsciously felt the power of these curses, and may really have become ill as a result. The work of Edward Bever, who has opened up this subject, is discussed in Chapter 4.

Psychoanalysis is to some extent a specialised subdiscipline within psychology. Other branches of psychology have more to say about social circumstances, particularly social psychology, with its affinities with sociology. Research by social psychologists has moved on from the earlier idea of the 'authoritarian personality'. The propensity to apply negative stereotypes to others is not linked to any distinct personality type. Authoritarian moral absolutes arise, not from the psychology of individuals, but from social circumstances – times of warfare, economic crisis or ideological conflict. Witch-hunting was about the exercise of social power. These social and political stresses have been discussed in Chapter 8.

A psychological perspective may explain some of the strange phenomena reported by witches themselves or by their accusers. For instance, how should we understand reports of witches flying? Many suspects no doubt confessed to this under torture, but some accounts of flight seem too individualised to be simply standard responses to leading questions. Could out-of-body experiences, well documented in psychology, have something to do with these accounts? Bever has introduced this perspective to historical scholarship, and some of my own research has tried to develop it further.[12] Then there are the magical practitioners who encountered and worked with spirits; if they were accused of witchcraft and interrogated about when they had met the Devil, their answers were likely to draw on these encounters. This perspective has been discussed in Chapter 5, but future historians may understand it better by making links with psychologists. People who hear voices or see visions are well-recognised among the present-day population by psychologists, but the work of connecting the various conditions that cause such experiences with the material in witchcraft trials has barely begun.

Other aspects of witches' confessions can also be illuminated through a psychological perspective – notably the creation of false memory through suggestive questioning. It was argued in Chapter 7 that some tortured witchcraft suspects came to believe in their own guilt, and co-operated with their interrogators in constructing narratives of their relationship with the Devil. Lyndal Roper has played a leading role in reconstructing the negotiations in the torture chamber.[13] Earlier historians remained aloof from the details of confessions, believing that they were all 'stereotyped' answers to leading questions, and that nothing worthwhile could be learned from them about popular beliefs and practices. Close attention to suspects' individual stories has more recently brought, and continues to bring, insightful rewards.

Another relevant branch of psychology is cognitive psychology, which aims to explain human behaviour via mental processing. One assumption it makes is that the brain is made up of linked 'modules' performing specific functions – there is a module for classifying living beings, for instance. Could there be a module for identifying witches? Or, more precisely, could there be a module for detecting secret enemies within the community? Here it might be possible to use evolutionary psychology, which is related to cognitive psychology but focuses on explaining behaviour as the product of evolutionary development. We act in particular ways because our early ancestors took an evolutionary path in which they needed to be able to act in those ways. This idea is plausible, but it is hard to prove specific details. The earliest humans lived two million years ago. Fossil remains tell us little about how they behaved, let alone how they thought. If we do not know exactly what modules there are in our own brains, what chance do we have of understanding the brain of *Homo erectus*?[14]

Still, there is no need to be wholly negative about evolutionary psychology. We can work out that early humans must have needed to distinguish between predators and prey, and that in due course they evolved that unique human attribute, speech with syntax. Speech enabled humans to co-operate more effectively – but also to disagree in more elaborate ways. Some other animal species fight amongst themselves, but the fighting is usually ritualised and rarely causes serious harm. Human warfare, which involves the deliberate and large-scale killing of members of our own species, is highly unusual in biological terms. If the human species can express destructive hatreds against itself through warfare, we should perhaps look further at the origins of the human capacity for destructive hatred. Hatred seems to be rooted in fear, and fear is a much-studied biological mechanism, based in the amygdala region of the brain. The amygdala also acts to detect cheating and deceit among neighbours.[15] Is this the organ that people used to recognise the village witch? Again, further research is required.

Once early humans started expressing quarrels with their fellow humans in speech, they presumably started to develop pejorative words to describe those with whom they quarrelled. At some point, humans additionally began to develop magical beliefs and rituals. Once they came to believe in magic, they would believe that magic could be used in quarrels. What would we call someone who harmed their neighbour by magic in a quarrel? If we did not yet have a word for such a person, we would have to invent one.

The first person who called their neighbour a 'witch', whatever the language that they used in those far-off prehistoric times, was creating a compelling idea that would echo through millennia and that still has power to cause shock and fear.

Global perspectives

Witchcraft is a global phenomenon. In the modern world, witch-hunting itself continues to occur – mostly well beyond Europe, though modern Europe will also require attention. What can global perspectives add to our understanding of the great European witch-hunt? Was it a unique event, or an example of a much broader phenomenon? The following brief survey of witchcraft across the modern world cannot hope to be more than selective and partial, but it may point up some similarities with early modern Europe, as well as some differences. Similarities and differences may both be revealing.

It is mainly anthropologists who study witchcraft beyond Europe today. Have they found the whole of the fourfold concept of witchcraft, as this was outlined in Chapter 1? The answer is that they have found most of it, but not all. The demonic witch, in league with the Devil as a towering enemy of the human race, was unique to early modern Europe. Non-European witches may be said to contact spirits, but these witches are almost always individuals – village witches, accused of practising harmful magic – rather than members of groups. This removes one reason for panics over witchcraft, though we shall see that panics still occur. The folkloric witch, as a topic of folktales, certainly exists worldwide. So, probably, does the envisioned witch – the witch experienced through dream and trance. But it is the widespread occurrence of the village witch that particularly concerns us here.

Many non-Western societies, probably most, believe in witchcraft as magical harm, similar to the European beliefs about village witchcraft discussed in Chapter 4. The following global survey, though it cannot do justice to the complexities of witchcraft in any particular place, may help to set the beliefs and practices of early modern Europe in a broader context. One advantage of anthropological studies is that they can generate rich and well-focused evidence, which may help historians to take into account the gaps in surviving documentary sources.

Anthropologists studying 'witchcraft' do not usually focus on killings of witches – 'witch-hunting' as it has been called in this book. Such killings do occur, as we shall see, but there are many other discourses of witchcraft, with beliefs about magical power being used to structure and explain all sorts of events. This everyday discourse is easier for anthropologists to study; people who kill witches are rarely willing to talk about their actions to a Western-trained anthropologist. This is an opposing perspective on witchcraft from that usually encountered by historians. In historical documents, we rarely hear people's everyday discourse, whereas the unusual and dramatic killings of witches *are* more often recorded. This can remind historians that, although killings of witches were not everyday events in early modern Europe, ideas about witchcraft also structured people's everyday discourse.

Today, therefore, we see magical practitioners engaging in beneficial magic, advising people on counter-magic, and sometimes identifying witches. We find a common, though not universal, belief that witches are older women. The 'witchcraft' that is feared is village witchcraft – harmful magic. However, the early modern pattern of witches being identified through quarrels followed by misfortune seems less prominent today. Often, as in the case study of Guadeloupe in the text box ('Witches or spirits?', p. 381), people suffer a misfortune and then think about who might be envious of them; there does not have to have been a prior quarrel.

Witchcraft and witch-hunting in sub-Saharan Africa have been studied in particular detail and variety.[16] Tribal chiefs in Africa sometimes endorse witch-hunting, although state authorities do not. We may see here a parallel with the local elites who formed the mainspring of much witchcraft prosecution in early modern Europe. The laws of most African states make it an offence to accuse someone of witchcraft – a legacy of colonial 'witchcraft suppression' laws. In South Africa, there have been discussions of changing the law to recognise a 'reality' in witchcraft, but nothing has been done, and witchcraft remains within a realm of private discourse.[17] A few African countries do have laws criminalising witchcraft, in particular Uganda, Zimbabwe and Cameroon. These laws define witchcraft as harmful magic, with fines or imprisonment as penalties. Cameroon, which has been studied in most detail, adopted a criminal code in 1967 that made it a crime to commit 'any act of witchcraft, magic or divination liable to disturb public order or tranquillity, or to harm another person'. A few people were imprisoned under this law, but the attempt to enforce it was largely abandoned in 1985.[18] African witch-hunting occurs instead through unofficial processes.

State authorities sometimes take account of informal pressure for action against witches. South Africa and Ghana have established camps known as 'witch-homes' where people accused of witchcraft can be sent into internal exile. Residents of Ghana's witch-homes are almost all women. They are sent there semi-voluntarily, knowing that they are safer than in their own communities. African witch-homes may not directly legitimise attacks on witches, but they are certainly an admission of the authorities' inability to protect witches within their communities. The witch-home is both a refuge and a prison.[19]

What of the actual killing of witches? This occurs from time to time in several African countries (and elsewhere, as we shall see); we find both the killing of individual witches, and also panics in which large numbers are killed. Comprehensive statistics are hard to come by, but deaths in panics can run into hundreds or even, occasionally, thousands. Panics tend to be fostered by a travelling anti-witch specialist who puts himself at the head of a movement to rid the region of witches. Such a movement builds links with village leaders, and groups of young men are sent to kill the witches. The role of local elites forms a thought-provoking parallel to early modern Europe. Another parallel is that African witches are often burned, with the fire often coming from a burning car tyre. As for differences, African vigilante action is not very similar to early modern European legal processes, usually having little resembling a trial. Suspected witches may be tortured into confessing, but often the magical practitioners in the anti-witch movement simply announce that the person is a witch.[20] And the witches identified in panics, however large their numbers, remain individual village witches; there are no chain-reaction hunts in which one witch names others as members of a conspiracy.

Witch-hunting has attracted particular attention in Tanzania.[21] There were panics there in the 1980s and 1990s, some of which led to the killing of hundreds and very possibly thousands of witches. Widespread killings have continued since then. One study based on police data counted 2,585 killings in the five years up to 2009 – probably an underestimate because not all killings are reported to the police.[22] Although these are still not chain-reaction hunts in which one witch names others, Tanzania has a ready way of creating witches: witches are believed to have red eyes. Old women's eyes are indeed turned red by years of exposure to smoky cooking fires. Witch-hunting in modern Tanzania is comparable in scale to that in parts of early modern Europe.

Even in Tanzania, witches are not always killed. Few killings occur in the south of the country. There have been panics over witchcraft there, but their focus has been to encourage the ritual cleansing of people who *might* be witches. When witchcraft is feared, all sorts of people travel willingly to camps to take part in a cleansing ritual that removes any witchcraft that they might have had. They may or may not have been witches before, but once cleansed they definitely are not. The cleansing is a mass reconciliation ritual.[23] Reconciliations in early modern European villages often served as constructive alternatives to witchcraft trials; here we see a comparable process operating on a much larger scale. It has indeed been argued that, as in early modern Europe, witchcraft accusations in Africa are usually dealt with by negotiation and reconciliation.[24]

Witchcraft and magic function as part of a diffuse web of power, being invoked in various kinds of rivalries or interactions. Witchcraft has occasionally been invoked during political conflicts, as in Malawi in 1965 when Hastings Banda encouraged accusations of witchcraft against local opponents of his presidency.[25] Such accusations were occasionally found in early modern Europe too. Probably more common are the African rulers who employ magical practitioners themselves.[26]

In modern Africa, and indeed worldwide, the quarrels followed by misfortune that we find in early modern Europe are not particularly prominent. One modern pattern for identifying witches in Africa arises from the tension between successful migrants to cities and their impoverished kinsfolk back in the village. The migrants often help their kinsfolk to a certain extent, but witchcraft can be invoked both as an explanation for their economic success and as a reason why they do not help the kinsfolk as much as the kinsfolk expect. There can even be accusations that a successful person has magically 'sacrificed' one or more of their kinsfolk for their own gain. Nevertheless, these jealousies rarely lead to accusations that a particular person is a 'witch'.

African witch beliefs are not just about simple material harm; they are embedded in complex religious traditions. Indigenous religions focusing on ancestral spirits have sometimes been modified in contact with organised religions – Islam, and, in particular, modern evangelical Christianity. Christian Pentecostalist pastors have encouraged the demonisation of traditional spirits, rather in the way that nature spirits were reinterpreted as demons in early modern Europe. The 'providential' world-view of Pentecostalism gives demons an active role. Demonic possession and exorcism allow the identification of innocent possessed people – it is not their fault that the demon is assaulting them. Also, however, there are guilty witches who have allowed demons to take control of them. This can even lead to the idea of witches' sabbats; those accused of witchcraft can be tortured and made to confess to attending a sabbat. In early modern Europe, such practices sometimes spiralled outwards, with courts arresting those named in confessions. However, in Africa, tortures and interrogations are carried out in private and lack legal sanction. A family, or a prayer group, can torture one of its own members, but does not have ready access to others. Lack of access to state power may explain the emphasis on witchcraft within families that we see in many countries.

Pentecostalism has played a role in two further developments. In South Africa, there is a movement of 'born again' young women who confess publicly to having *formerly* been witches. Their stories of amazing witchcraft adventures and fantastical malefices bear comparison with the exotic witchcraft confessions of early modern Europe. However, because these women have now been saved from witchcraft, they have a positive status, at least within the church.[27] More negatively and even tragically, child witches are a growing problem in central Africa. Parents come to believe that their children have become witches through being taken over by demons, and blame their misfortunes on the children. This leads to abuse of the children and ultimately to their being expelled from the family. In several African countries, there are thousands or even tens of thousands of abandoned street children, rejected for being witches.[28] There were child witches in early modern Europe, as we saw in Chapter 9, but not on anything like this scale; nor were European child witches accused primarily by their own parents.

At this point we can turn more briefly to examine some relevant examples from other parts of the world, beginning with Indonesia. Here we find

Perspectives on the witch-hunt 379

'reverse witch trials' (as these were called in Chapter 10): prosecutions of someone who has assaulted a witch. Indonesian law does not recognise witchcraft as an offence, but judges may be swayed by their own belief in witchcraft, or by their wish to respect villagers who believe in it. They sometimes issue unusually lenient sentences to those convicted of assaulting witches. They may also prosecute witches themselves – not for witchcraft as such, but for 'disturbing the peace' with their magical activity.[29]

Another country with witch-killings is India. India's witches are mainly found among its tribal peoples. Killings may occur on a considerable scale, though little research has been done to quantify this. Witches are mainly women, often widows. One study shows some of the witches being identified through quarrels between women followed by misfortune to one of the parties – the classic pattern from early modern Europe.[30] Another stresses the role of magical practitioners in identifying witches, and of village headmen in sanctioning attacks on them.[31] Killings of witches occur today in various parts of the world.

The killings of witches that have been discussed so far are all extra-judicial lynchings. There was a law in Papua New Guinea, between 1971 and 2013, that encouraged killings indirectly: penalties were reduced for killers who said that they were acting to stop witchcraft. How much influence this had is unclear. In practice, killers of witches were rarely prosecuted at all, and killings have continued since the repeal of the law.[32] Witches are mostly women believed to have carried out harmful magic. Even in Papua New Guinea, though, witchcraft is mainly used in an indirect way, to explain misfortune and lack of prosperity, rather than to attack individual witches.[33]

Closer parallels to the great European witch-hunt can be found in the Middle East. Several Middle Eastern states aim to enforce religious laws, in ways comparable to the 'godly states' of early modern Europe. In these states, people can be legally convicted of witchcraft and punished. Those convicted are mostly magical practitioners, or people believed to have cast spells. They do not have to have committed harm. Non-capital punishments like flogging or imprisonment are the most common, but some actual executions for witchcraft take place in Saudi Arabia.[34]

In the Middle East, therefore, we come closest to the early modern European witch-hunt: the authorities themselves are punishing witchcraft, sometimes using the death penalty. Some differences should also be noted. There is nothing directly comparable to the early modern concept of the demonic witch, in which people were defined as witches simply for having made a pact with the Devil. Islam gives little importance to a being comparable to the Christian Devil.[35] Islam has angels and demons, the latter known as 'jinns'. Unlike in Christianity, jinns can be either good, bad or ambivalent. Islamic authorities, like Christian ones, have long debated how to distinguish legitimate religious practices from illegitimate 'magic' or 'superstition'.[36] The Moroccan jinn beliefs discussed in the text box ('Witches or spirits?') have no apparent engagement with modernity, and would be regarded as 'superstitious' by reforming Muslims.[37] The Saudi authorities treat dealings with jinns as 'idolatry' – an approach comparable with Protestant and Catholic 'reforming' efforts to stamp out popular magical practices in early modern Europe.[38] But Middle Eastern witches are always thought of as individuals, not as members of a conspiracy. No modern state authority seems to have had a *panic* about witches.

Global perspectives, then, underline the uniqueness of the early modern demonic witch, and of the chain-reaction panics and multiple executions that were so destructive in early modern Europe. Such perspectives, though, also underline the pervasiveness of the idea of the village witch, and of the coping strategies that people usually adopt towards such a person. Killing was not a normal solution to the problem of the early modern village witch, nor is it normal today; but witchcraft was, and is, viewed so seriously that killing a witch can be thought justifiable.

Finally, a global perspective on the modern world should not omit modern Europe itself. As was pointed out in Chapter 10, traditional witchcraft beliefs have continued in some parts of Europe at least. An influential study of French villagers in the 1970s showed witchcraft very much alive as an explanation for misfortune, with magical practitioners conducting 'unwitching' rituals similar to those used in the early modern period.[39] A comparative study of popular beliefs in Slovenia and Macedonia in the early 2000s, by Mirjam Mencej, revealed some thought-provoking contrasts. Slovenia had a Catholic tradition, and had been ruled by the Austrian Habsburgs during the witch-hunts of the early modern period. Macedonia had an Orthodox tradition, and had escaped witch-hunting because it had been ruled by the Ottoman Turks. Slovenian villagers were readily able to identify village witches and to blame harmful magic on them, much as their early modern predecessors had done. Macedonians, by contrast, had a word for witch (*'vešterka'*), but were rarely able to identify actual witches; moreover, when they talked about harmful magic, they rarely blamed this on witches.[40] Does this indicate the continuation of traditions from early modern times?

Another study by Mencej is perhaps even more remarkable, showing the survival of envisioned witchcraft. She found that many people had had nocturnal encounters with 'witches' who were generally not human.[41] In Sicily, the cult of the *donas de fuera*, discussed in Chapter 5, was found in the 1980s to be still in existence.[42] Indeed, early modern witch-hunting may have left quite specific cultural legacies in particular localities. Jersey, in the Channel Islands, provides an example. In the early twentieth century, parents would scare naughty children by threatening to send for a traditional bogeywoman, a frightening witch called 'Marie Tourgis'. In 1938 it was found that Marie Tourgis had really existed: she was a young woman from the village of Grouville, who had been executed for witchcraft in 1618. Her memory had survived in oral tradition for three centuries.[43] Thus our global survey returns us to a point at which we are reminded of the local and indeed unique human experience of every individual witch.

Witches or spirits? Two case studies

Witchcraft is a common explanation for misfortune worldwide, but not a universal one. Our first case study to illustrate this is the island of Guadeloupe in the West Indies.[44] People there sometimes explain misfortune, especially the unusual illness of a child, as the result of witchcraft. The witch is someone else in the community, often a near neighbour or a member of the extended family, who causes harm through maleficent magic. Often, though not always, it is an older woman who is identified as a witch; witchcraft tends to be part of a discourse among women. People who suspect themselves to have been bewitched may visit a magical practitioner who can help them to confirm their suspicions and guide them towards identifying the witch. If they accuse the witch publicly, this can lead to bitter and long-lasting conflict, though there are possibilities for reconciliation. So far this is much like the village witchcraft of early modern Europe.

There are also a few differences. One is that the witch is not usually identified through an overt quarrel with the victim. Instead, victims tend to be people who have been successful in acquiring consumer goods and economic security. When they suffer a misfortune, they identify their enemy by asking themselves who might be jealous of their perceived success. In this way, witchcraft feeds into a discourse of modernity. Another difference from early modern Europe, perhaps more obvious, is that the French authorities in Guadeloupe do not recognise witchcraft as a crime, so there is no option to prosecute a witch.

A case study from Morocco, part of the Islamic world, illustrates a contrasting pattern. Many illnesses are attributed to spirits known as jinns. For a cure, the sufferer visits a shrine staffed by healers who invoke the power of a traditional saint. The jinns appear vividly; there are various tribes of jinns with different personalities, not all of which are simply evil. The healer uses the saint's power to identify the jinn, negotiate with it and banish it. The focus on the jinn itself as the source of harm means that there is hardly any interest in the question of whether another human might have sent it.[45] It is only that question that would give rise to witchcraft accusations. In Morocco, therefore, we see evil spirits as an alternative to witchcraft in explaining misfortune (see the previous text box 'Making sense of misfortune', in Chapter 4, pp. 90–1).

Modern Western images of witches

In the industrial Western world today, popular images of 'witches' do not derive from today's African or Saudi Arabian witches, but from the witches of early modern Europe who have been the subject of this book. However, these images have been shaped to modern purposes, and we can hardly expect historical accuracy to be an overriding priority for modern storytellers, illustrators and film-makers. We tend to view early modern witches through these well-known modern images, which may distort our perspectives. A comprehensive account of modern imagery would be well beyond the scope of this book, but a few points may be made about the way in which ideas of witchcraft have developed since early modern times. Some early modern ideas have continued, while others have been dropped, and still others have been transformed.

The image of the witch in modern Western popular culture seems well entrenched. The old woman in cloak and pointed hat, riding a broomstick, is universally recognised. Often she has a cat, an echo of the English witch's familiar. Early modern familiars also included toads, insects and fantasy creatures, but the cat has survived because we can readily imagine cats as pets. The pointed hat is also English; it became part of the popular image of a witch in the eighteenth century, when such hats, like witches, came to be seen as old-fashioned. The broomstick, by contrast, is originally French; historical English witches were rarely described as flying. It is surprising that the broomstick survived, since many more witches were accused in Germany, where witches flew on forked cooking-sticks. Today's old-woman witch is thus a composite image. She usually grins cheerfully, and is rarely malevolent or frightening, except to young children. She does not belong to the everyday world; when airborne, for instance, illustrators show her from an imaginary sideways viewpoint, rather than from the point of view of a real observer on the ground. One thing is certain, though: unlike the historical witches, she is always female. The idea that men could ever have been witches has largely vanished.

Perhaps as a result, another image of the witch has gained prominence: that of the young, sexy female witch. Unlike her early modern predecessor, she is presented as a largely positive role model. Practising 'teen witches', mostly female, find themselves navigating between commercial imagery in films, magazines and websites, and the more serious spirituality of Wicca.[46] The image of the young, sexy witch has arisen from the commercialisation of culture, the promotion of glamorous 'celebrities', and the emphasis on young adulthood as an ideal state. For commercial artists, there is no money to be made from depicting old women, but a great deal to be made from exploitative images of young women. The young, sexy witch is still partly dependent on her elderly relative; she may need a pointed hat, for instance. But her sexuality can be emphasised in a way that an older woman's no longer can – and sex sells. The power of sex in modern culture even helps to make the young, sexy witch a particularly convincing 'magical' figure. 'Magic' is almost as large a part of the stock-in-trade of the advertising copywriter as sex itself. A young female witch can readily wield magical power. She is 'enchanting', or 'glamorous' (a word originally meaning 'magical'), or even 'bewitching'.

The young, sexy witch is not actually new. As we saw in Chapter 9, Renaissance artists delighted in depicting her, and probably for some of the same sexist reasons. But then she was typically depicted *alongside* older women. A late literary example of this is Robert Burns's comic poem 'Tam o' Shanter' (1791), in which Tam drunkenly stumbles across a witches' sabbat. Most of the witches are old hags, but Tam's – and the reader's – attention falls on the one young woman in the group, a 'winsome wench' invitingly dressed in nothing but a short chemise (a 'cutty sark').

This leads on to another shift in the image of the witch: the abandonment of the witches' sabbat. Burns depicted it with gusto, and in 1867 the Russian composer Modest Mussorgsky created a musical portrait of a St John's Eve witches' sabbat in his orchestral tone-poem 'A Night on Bald Mountain'. But, in 1940, when Walt Disney added pictures to Mussorgsky's music in the film *Fantasia*, the witches were replaced by demons and ghosts. The disappearance of the sabbat is probably related to the general positive revaluation of the witch during the twentieth century.

What then is left today of the idea of the evil witch? Disney has provided some pointers to where the idea has gone. In *Snow White and the Seven Dwarfs* (1937) the wicked queen was effectively a witch, complete with cloak and pointed hat. However, she developed her spells in a laboratory, evidently a nod to the prestige of modern science and technology. The evil laboratory is one way in which imagery of evil has shifted away from the witch; the renegade scientist whose inventions threaten the world is a powerful figure in popular fiction, but the scientist is almost always male, and his inventions are not presented as 'magical'.

Magic has nevertheless returned by the back door – if indeed it ever left; but evil magic is rarely associated with witches. Along with the rise of science has come a blurring of the separation between science and magic in popular culture. Cartoon heroes, from Superman onwards, wield amazing powers that are supposedly 'scientific' (with much reference to space travel, radioactivity and so on) but are often in effect magical. Horror films use 'magic' more overtly – but they tend to use a broader concept of the 'supernatural', with actual witches being absent (*Carrie*, 1976) or peripheral (*The Blair Witch Project*, 1999). Some films use elements of traditional Christian demonology (*The Exorcist*, 1973), but the combined concept of the demonic witch seems to have vanished. The demons in some horror films are clearly non-Christian (*The Evil Dead*, 1981, 2013). There are some remnants of the evil witch among the plastic paraphernalia of the modern Hallowe'en, but they are not really threatening, except perhaps to small children.

Meanwhile, however, awareness of historical witch-hunts remains important. How do people use the idea that witches were persecuted in the past? They usually seem to do so constructively and sensibly. Most people today are not expert historians, and there is no point in criticising them for this. Some popular ideas on witch-hunting seem to arise from present-day common-sense – which is well worth commending, even though it may not be enough to get beyond present-day values.

One modern idea seems unnecessarily condescending to the people of the past: the popular story of how the swimming test was conducted. It is commonly related that those who floated were executed, while those who sank were drowned although they were innocent. In fact, as we saw in Chapter 7, ropes were tied to the suspect to pull them out of the water. The popular version of the story functions as an affirmation of our own cultural superiority: we, today, are cleverer or more sensible than the ignorant witch-hunters. An early instance of this comes from the missionary David Livingstone in the 1850s, who explained the swimming test in this way to his African followers as part of 'the wisdom of my ancestors' in order to criticise some of their own traditional customs.[47] Livingstone's celebrated writings may have originated the idea, but it is the kind of story that could have arisen in more than one place independently.

Many people have told me that a witchcraft accusation was a means of 'getting rid of anyone you didn't like'. This seems to mean that the accusation was hypocritical: the accuser named someone as a witch, not because they thought they were a witch, but for some other motive. In modern fiction, the motive is often sexual jealousy; accusations come from a rejected suitor or lover. Arthur Miller's celebrated play about Salem, *The Crucible* (1953), includes an accusation of this kind. Although much of *The Crucible* is believable historically, this theme strikes a false note. A person who rejected a suitor or lover was not behaving like a witch – there was no indication of harmful magic or dealings with the Devil.

A related popular idea focuses, not on sex, but on money. In this account, the accuser was jealous of the witch because of the witch's economic success. Typically, the idea is that the witch's crops grew better than the accuser's, which the accuser resented. Historically, there were occasional accusations against suspects who had prospered unaccountably, but such suspects were usually men, and this pattern of accusation was rare even for men. Witches were more often getting poorer than getting richer. The 'getting rid of anyone you didn't like' idea, and the economic jealousy idea, seem to arise today among people who sense that community relationships were important, but who know little of pre-industrial society.

What of the popular idea that witches were accused in order to *make* money? Usually it is said that the authorities themselves stood to profit, but sometimes accusations by neighbours are said to have been motivated by the neighbour's desire for the alleged witch's goods. We saw in Chapter 7 that some courts could confiscate a criminal's goods, but many other courts did not do this, and most witches were too poor to have possessions worth coveting. A few active witch-hunters like Matthew Hopkins received payment, but even he received only modest fees plus expenses; it was certainly not desire for money that made him a witch-hunter. A handful of rich witches were accused because of resentment at their inheritance of property, but they were a tiny minority. The idea of witch-hunting for money is attractive because it attributes to the witch-hunters a motive that is readily understood in the modern world. In origin it is probably a modern fantasy.

These ideas also display an inability to take witchcraft itself seriously. People tend to think that witchcraft is not (and was not) real, so they jump to the conclusion that witchcraft accusations must 'really' have been about something other than witchcraft. The idea that accusations were really about money or sex is readily grasped because people today take money and sex seriously.

Some accusers certainly had ulterior motives – or perhaps they should be called additional motives – for their accusations. At Salem, accusations were made by one political faction in the village against its enemies, but there is no evidence that this was done cynically. On the contrary, the leading accusers were desperately upset by the demonic tormenting of their daughters; it seemed clear that witchcraft was the cause, and it seemed logical that it would be their enemies – those who were believed to hate them – who would be behind the tormenting. The worst interpretation we can put on this is to say that the accusers psychologically projected their own anger onto those whom they accused, believing that it was the accused who were really angry and destructive. Occasionally, they also faked evidence, especially when prosecutions seemed to be going badly. But they did not deliberately invent accusations that they knew to be false.

There are in fact no grounds for thinking that accusers' beliefs differed from those of the general population. People believed in witchcraft, and that includes the witches' accusers. A witchcraft accusation was not 'really' about something else: it was really about witchcraft. The overwhelming majority of witchcraft accusations occurred, not because of sexual or economic jealousy, but because the suspect simply appeared to have been behaving like a witch or to fit one of the stereotypes of a witch. If witches of the past are discussed in modern culture, it is better for historical understanding if the past belief in witchcraft is taken seriously.

Remembering the witches

After persecutions and atrocities have ceased, people sometimes feel a need to say something publicly about what has happened, to learn what went wrong and to commemorate the victims. Particularly since 1945, memorials have been erected, not just to the great and good of the past, but also to the victims of injustice and suffering. And when the injustice and suffering was inflicted by the authorities of the past, it can seem appropriate for today's authorities to issue some kind of statement about it, such as an apology, or – in legal cases – a pardon.

(continued)

Pardoning witches is usually urged on grounds such as 'rectifying injustice' or 'setting the record straight'. Most modern pardons are for individuals, though there are occasional demands for a country to pardon all its witches. There are also occasional demands for retrials – a slightly different legal concept, since a pardon removes the effects of a criminal conviction whereas only a retrial can declare someone innocent. This distinction seems unimportant to those who campaign for pardons of witches; they usually treat a pardon as a declaration of innocence, perhaps because there seems, today, little reason to doubt the innocence of the executed witches.

Pardoning witches is not new. The witches of Arras, executed in 1459–60, were pardoned in 1468, as we saw in Chapter 10. The witches of Salem, executed in 1692, received a general amnesty in 1711 under which financial compensation was offered to surviving relatives. Modern pardons are more symbolic and commemorative. Since 1957, various state governors of Massachusetts have pardoned individual Salem witches. In 2006, the governor of Virginia pardoned the state's one witch, Grace Sherwood, though she had not been executed and it was not certain that she had ever been convicted. These pardons carry a danger of trivialisation. They tend to be made public around Hallowe'en, to catch the media's demand for entertaining witch stories at this season. Thus, on 31 October 2004, a pardon for eighty-one witches 'and their cats' was issued by a Scottish baron court – a private, ceremonial body that had never exercised jurisdiction over witchcraft and had indeed possessed no jurisdiction at all since the eighteenth century.[48] In Switzerland, more seriously, Anna Göldi, the last witch, was pardoned in 2008 by the Glarus parliament, the body that had convicted her in 1782. These modern pardons are well meant, but they are questionable, at least to a historian, in their apparent attempt to *change* the past.

Memorials to witches are another way of remembering them publicly. These are more costly than pardons, but have a wider and more lasting public impact. If designed in a historically informed way, they may also have a more positive relationship with the past. A memorial was erected at Salem in 1992. Cologne in Germany has erected an impressive double memorial – to Friedrich Spee, critic of the witch trials, and Katharina Henot, a witch executed in 1627. Grace Sherwood, as well as being pardoned, has received a statue depicting her, improbably, with a raccoon. More historically informed is the large and striking Steilneset Witch Memorial at Vardø, Norway, commemorating the ninety-one witches who died in the country's sparsely-populated Arctic province. Art, architecture and history combine at Steilneset, the windswept execution spot.

Conclusion: Power, persecution and the lessons of the witch-hunt

It can be a strange experience to sit calmly in an air-conditioned library and read the records of witchcraft panics. Details of torture are rarely recorded, and we do not hear the cries of pain. Not only that, but the relentless similarity of many of the confessions – not to mention their relentless weirdness – tends to induce a sense of incredulity. Surely nobody could have believed these stories of demonic encounters and nocturnal assemblies – stories at once gruesome, fantastic and stereotyped? Yet the grim fact is that witch-hunters at the time did believe these stories. They were so convinced of the suspects' guilt that they accepted even stereotyped answers to leading questions as proof. The escalating numbers of confessions provided further evidence of the terrifying scale of the witchcraft conspiracy. They were angry and fearful: and they panicked.

Persecution differs from law enforcement by pushing the prosecution evidence too far. 'Panic' is important here, but is not the sole explanation for persecution. Determination to wield power, regardless of the consequences, is also important. In early modern Europe, such a determination was found in those enforcing the programme of the godly state. Witches could be a 'target' (like the Jews in Nazi Germany) for the godly state, though they were not the only one. This is where the sociological idea of 'scapegoating' comes in. In difficult times, political movements may be able to gain power by blaming a marginal group for the problems. Give us more power, and we'll sort out your problems by dealing with these wicked people. It may sound cynical, but the persecutors are usually sincere in their beliefs.

As well as sincere commitment, persecutors also need to avoid facing up to what they are really doing. Studies of modern atrocities and persecutions show that smokescreens of secrecy and strategies of wilful ignorance are incorporated into the proceedings as they occur. Those at the top make sure that they are not told the operational details. Those at the bottom make sure that they do not find out the big picture. Everyone can say, and even think, that they are not personally responsible. Euphemisms are used: breaking rules is 'flexibility', killings are 'special actions'. Such euphemisms can readily be recognised in the witch-hunt, such as 'putting to the question' as a term for torture. All this is partly to aid subsequent cover-up and deniability, but mainly to make the atrocities palatable at the time for the perpetrators themselves.[49]

One familiar justification for modern atrocities is particularly relevant to witch-hunting: denial of victimhood. They are not victims, they are guilty criminals, they started it, look what they've done to us.[50] This is relevant because it puts ideology in the foreground. To the authorities at least, witchcraft was an ideological crime. Critics saw witch-hunting as directed against poor old women, helpless to resist persecution; seeing them like that was seeing them as victims. The witch-hunters, however, saw the terrifying power of the Devil behind the witchcraft conspiracy; they certainly did not see victims when they executed witches.

So witch-hunting was about power. Deliberately burning people to death was a dramatic and gruesome demonstration of power over them. But who, exactly, was wielding the power? The first and simplest answer is that it was the authorities who wielded power over the common folk. With very rare exceptions, witches were not lynched; they were executed by due legal process. Witch-hunting was also about religious power over deviant belief and practice, and again this highlights the role of the authorities – religious rather than secular – who sought to enforce orthodoxy. This 'top-down' view of witch-hunting, however, is not the whole answer to the question of power. Witch-hunting to some extent attempted to express the whole community's power over the uncanny magical threats that lurked in an uncertain world. Peasants sometimes demanded the execution of witches, though larger numbers of witches seem to have been dragged in without having angered the community. A further strand in the web of power is that witch-hunting was to some extent about male power over women.

There was a tragic convergence between these different strands of power. The peasants' desire for protection and vengeance meshed with the authorities' desire for control. While ordinary folk complained about magical harm, educated elites saw magical harm as stemming from the Devil, and feared a conspiracy. Peasants generally envisaged only one witch at a time, but they had their own beliefs in the Devil, and their own ideas about transmission of witchcraft (from mother to daughter, for instance). When peasants were told that their witches were part of a larger conspiracy, they do not seem to have disagreed. Similarly, when women were told that their curses were demonic, other women do not seem to have disagreed.

Following these lines, it is easy to paint a picture of witch-hunting as something that enhanced social stability. In this picture, different people, for different reasons, found that witch-hunting was something that they could agree on; it reaffirmed consensual values. Such a picture contains much truth, but not the whole truth. The consensus over witchcraft was not automatic or complete. Demonologists generally agreed that witches existed and that it was important to punish them – but they had to keep working at the task of persuading people. There were always sceptics. Many people in authority were reluctant to prosecute, and a few were sceptical even of some of the essentials of witchcraft belief. Witch-hunting was certainly not *necessary* to social or political stability. In parts of Europe, particularly southern Europe, there was little witch-hunting, and in a few places hardly any. Even in the German heartland of witchcraft prosecution, there were individual territories that prosecuted few or even no witches. Only a minority of Europe's villages had their own witchcraft cases. Witch-hunting was normal, but not universal.

Witch-hunting was sometimes actively destabilising. Some prosecutors went too far, and miscarriages of justice were seen to occur. The execution of an individual witch did not usually cause adverse comment, but large-scale panics often got out of hand and led to recriminations afterwards. There is a sense in which witch-hunting ended because people eventually learned from their predecessors' mistakes and decided to ensure that they would not be repeated. Perhaps it is encouraging to think that we can learn lessons from history.

What lessons, therefore, can we learn from the great European witch-hunt? Historians these days rarely moralise about their findings, but some of the issues raised by witch-hunting are still with us. I have argued here that witch-hunting was about power. There is a sense in which we can recognise that it was an abuse of power. Witch-hunting was cruel and unjust. If early modern Europeans had been able to treat their fellow humans more kindly, not only would thousands of needless killings have been avoided, but *everyone* would have been happier.

Here we have to be careful not to apply anachronistic standards to the past. Today we do not usually believe in witches, but it is unreasonable to criticise early modern Europeans for believing in witches. However, believing in witches is not the same as hunting witches. Even historical societies that have believed in witches have not usually hunted them – certainly not on the scale seen in early modern Europe. Very few witches were executed in the middle ages. And throughout the early modern period that we have been studying, some people raised their voices to criticise witch-hunting. In the sixteenth century, Pietro Pomponazzi and Reginald Scot argued powerfully that the Devil did not have the powers with which he was widely credited. Johann Weyer and Michel de Montaigne empathised with the accused witches and sensed that they were being condemned unjustly. They failed to convince a majority of Europe's articulate thinkers; Weyer in particular attracted a storm of criticism, and Montaigne kept his remarks on the subject brief. But their world-view was surely, *in sixteenth-century terms*, as coherent and convincing as that of the committed witch-hunters. In the seventeenth century, criticism of witch-hunting gathered pace, and Friedrich Spee – a gentle hymn-writer whose hair reportedly turned white as a result of hearing the private confessions of condemned witches in Paderborn – spoke for many when he exposed the abuses of the torturers in 1631. We can say that witch-hunting was understandable, but we do not have to accept that it was necessary.

So the question about 'lessons of the witch-hunt' is worth asking. The question can perhaps be restated in the following ways. First: If we can recognise witch-hunting as an abuse of power, can that help us to recognise abuses of power today? Second: Are thousands of needless killings occurring today? My own answers to these questions would be yes and yes, and I would add that everyone – including the abusers and killers – would be happier if they could find ways of treating their fellow humans more kindly. Where witch-hunting, specifically, has something to teach us here is in the related issues of fear, panic and crusading zeal. Early modern Europe was a fearful society, living with all sorts of hidden dangers both real and imagined. In order to cope, people sometimes felt a need for someone to blame. Fear leads to panic, and to anger and aggression; because people feared witches, they hated them. Hate leads to crusading zeal; because people hated witches, they convinced themselves that killing witches was the right thing to do, and that extraordinary efforts needed to be made to identify and eliminate them. Crusading zeal against our human enemies – any enemies – blinds us to the common humanity we share with them. You or I may not be a Spee, or even a Montaigne, but perhaps an understanding of the great European witch-hunt may help us to recognise abuses of power, and to value the common humanity that we share even with those whom we are told to hate and fear.

More lessons can be learned about witch-hunting by comparing it with other persecutions. Those who wrote about the great European witch-hunt in the second half of the twentieth century knew this well, living as they did in the shadow of other more recent episodes of persecution. There were the anti-Communist 'red scares' in the United States in the late 1940s and early 1950s, during which the actual phrase 'witch-hunt' first entered common usage in English. There were Stalin's persecutions of his opponents in the Soviet Union, notably the 'show trials' of the 1930s. Above all there was the Nazi persecution of the Jews between 1933 and 1945. Political culture in the aftermath of this dreadful period made strenuous efforts to ensure that such horrors would not recur. The United Nations adopted the Universal Declaration of Human Rights in 1948. With the fading of post-war optimism, people gradually realised that persecution had not ceased. In 1961, Amnesty International was formed to campaign against the imprisonment and torture of political and other dissidents. Amnesty encouraged the United Nations' adoption of a Convention against Torture in 1984, quoted at the head of this chapter. Today, Amnesty International still finds plenty of work.

One particular episode of persecution, in the 1980s and 1990s, displayed parallels with early modern demonology. This was the series of panics, mainly in the United States and Britain, over 'Satanic ritual abuse'. The idea was that an organised network of Satan-worshippers was conducting criminal rituals. Attention fell mainly on the alleged sexual abuse of children by Satan-worshippers, though other rituals were also mentioned, some involving blood sacrifices. 'Satanic ritual abuse' is now generally recognised to have been non-existent in itself, though partly constructed in a few cases from evidence of real child abuse. During the panics, investigators pursuing alleged child abuse tended to assume that the alleged abusers were members of a 'Satanic cult'. Here is a passage from a manual for therapists, published to enable them to identify such cults:

> The power that exists in Satanic (and Luciferian) cults is reportedly reflected in an organized hierarchy with incremental ranks. These positions may vary somewhat from one group to another, but some which appear common include the following: page, knight, priest (or priestess),

prince (or princess), high priest (or high priestess), king (or queen), savior, and god (sometimes goddess).[51]

Does this sound familiar? These details of 'Satanic cults' were developed and elaborated very much in the same way that early modern demonologists developed and elaborated their own ideas about witches. The word 'reportedly' is noteworthy. The early modern witch cult was imaginary, and so was the modern 'Satanic ritual abuse'. One legacy of these panics may have been an improved understanding of real child abuse (most of which is carried out by individuals rather than organised groups), and of the ways in which children may tell true or false stories in courtrooms.[52]

There may be problems with the term 'witch-hunting' as it is commonly used today. It can be devalued by being applied to individuals; some politicians say 'I'm being witch-hunted' when all they mean is 'I'm being unfairly criticised'. But even when the term is applied to persecuted groups, a historian may notice a certain lack of symmetry. Vigilante campaigns against alleged paedophiles are 'witch-hunting'; the McCarthy prosecutions were 'witch-hunting'; and the witch-hunt itself was – 'witch-hunting'. By using the term 'witch-hunting' to mean persecution in general, we run the risk of depriving ourselves of a specific term for the events described in this book. Still, maybe it is worth blurring some of the specificities of historical witch-hunting if it allows this powerful phrase to be invoked in the struggle against present-day cruelty, intolerance and oppression.

So I hope that readers of this book will appreciate, both the differences between episodes of persecution, and the similarities between them. Only thus can we fully understand modern persecutions, let alone historical ones. The European authorities hunting witches in early modern times targeted people who could be found in any village in their own territories. The recent panics over 'Satanic child abuse' were similar in that they targeted an enemy within the community. By contrast, present-day Western authorities sometimes practise cruelty, intolerance and oppression on a large scale – indeed in some ways on a scale unimaginable in early modern times; but they do it mostly at a distance and by proxy. Western dependence on the resources of the rest of the world leads to the fostering of undemocratic and illiberal client regimes there, and it is those regimes – answerable to Western corporate interests rather than their own people – that practise most of the torture, imprisonment without trial and extrajudicial killing that occur in the world today. Among the undemocratic and illiberal regimes are some anti-Western ones (some of them answerable to Chinese or Russian corporate interests), so that both sides can justify their persecutions by citing the misdeeds of the other side. We recognise ties of human kinship with the persecuted European witches of four centuries ago; so, to take just one example, perhaps we can recognise ties of human kinship with those imprisoned in present-day Turkey for the crime of 'public denigration of the

Turkish nation'. This crime, under Article 301 of the Turkish Penal Code, has been interpreted to include publicly mentioning the fact that a million Armenians were massacred in Turkey in 1915–16. The Turkish government denies that this genocide occurred.[53] Many other examples of modern abuse of human rights could be cited from all over the world, including some places nearer to home than we might think.

Ties of human kinship bind us, in our imaginations, to persecuted people of earlier centuries. Many women have said to me, 'If I'd lived in those times I might have been accused of witchcraft.' Such empathy with the persecuted may well help people understand, and resist, persecution. This is important; but it is not enough. Nobody of either sex has ever said to me, 'If I'd lived in those times I might have accused someone else of witchcraft.' I sometimes wish they would. Righteous indignation against the persecutors of witches is easy enough at a distance of four centuries; but can we be sure that we, today, are always the persecuted and never the persecutors?

Today's persecutors can be harder to identify than early modern witch-hunters, because they are enmeshed in a global system. The Turkish government is only a small example, and it is certainly not singled out here because it is unusual – far from it. Like many other governments, it is a client of the United States, political and economic leader of the industrialised world. Many readers of this book may be beneficiaries of US global hegemony; if you are one of those beneficiaries, does that make you complicit in its misdeeds? The question at least calls for careful thought. But you are probably unlike the peasant accusers of witches in one way, since they named people well known to them as neighbours. Today we probably feel that we are unlikely to persecute our neighbours – as witches, or as anything else – because in suburbia we do not know our neighbours well enough. The classic case of persecution for modern times is the Nazi Holocaust: industrial, impersonal and bureaucratic. Yet even the Gestapo relied on neighbours to inform them about the Jews and others whom it hunted.

The great European witch-hunt still has much to teach us about modern persecution, and not only by being different from it in some ways. Peasants may have accused neighbours, but the educated judges and demonologists were responsible for the chain-reaction witch-hunts that claimed most of the lives. Readers of this book are, or hope to be, very well educated. We may well ponder the moral certainties that led educated people in early modern Europe to set aside ties of human kinship with those accused of witchcraft, and to inflict suffering and death on them in the name of a greater good. Their greater good was the godly society; what is ours? Moral certainties that cast our enemies as wholly evil – and, by extension, cast ourselves as wholly good – are still very much with us, and still encourage us, or our agents, to treat alleged enemies unjustly. If the European witch-hunt has a lesson for us today, the idea that we could have been the victims is an easy lesson. The harder lesson to learn is that we could have been the persecutors.

Notes

1 UN document A/RES/39/46, at <www.un.org/documents/ga/res/39/a39r046.htm>, accessed 21 June 2013. From The United Nations Convention Against Torture by the UN General Assembly, © 2016 United Nations. Reprinted with the permission of the United Nations.
2 Gunnar W. Knutsen, *Servants of Satan and Masters of Demons: The Spanish Inquisition's Trials for Superstition, Valencia and Barcelona, 1478–1700* (Turnhout, 2009).
3 Adelina Angusheva, 'Late medieval witch mythologies in the Balkans', in Gábor Klaniczay and Éva Pócs (eds.), *Witchcraft Mythologies and Persecutions* (Budapest, 2008), 83–98.
4 Quoted in E. William Monter, *Witchcraft in France and Switzerland: The Borderlands during the Reformation* (Ithaca, NY, 1976), 38.
5 Alan Macfarlane, *Witchcraft in Tudor and Stuart England* (London, 1970); Keith Thomas, *Religion and the Decline of Magic* (London, 1971).
6 Christina Larner, *Enemies of God: The Witch-Hunt in Scotland* (London, 1981), 201–2 and *passim*.
7 Robin Briggs, *Witches and Neighbours: The Social and Cultural Context of European Witchcraft* (2nd edn., Oxford, 2002), 343–56 and *passim*; Robin Briggs, '"Many reasons why": witchcraft and the problem of multiple explanation', in Jonathan Barry, Marianne Hester and Gareth Roberts (eds.), *Witchcraft in Early Modern Europe* (Cambridge, 1996), 49–63. English exceptionalism was also challenged by James Sharpe, *Instruments of Darkness: Witchcraft in England, 1550–1750* (London, 1996).
8 Ronald Hutton, 'Anthropological and historical approaches to witchcraft: potential for a new collaboration?', *Historical Journal*, 47 (2004), 413–34.
9 Carlo Ginzburg, *Ecstasies: Deciphering the Witches' Sabbath*, trans. Raymond Rosenthal (London, 1991; first published in Italian as *Storia notturna* in 1989). For a detailed analysis and critique see Willem de Blécourt, 'The return of the sabbat: mental archaeologies, conjectural histories or political mythologies?', in Jonathan Barry and Owen Davies (eds.), *Palgrave Advances in Witchcraft Historiography* (Basingstoke, 2007), 125–45.
10 Stuart Clark, *Thinking with Demons: The Idea of Witchcraft in Early Modern Europe* (Oxford, 1997), 8–10.
11 Cf. Lyndal Roper, *Witch Craze: Terror and Fantasy in Baroque Germany* (New Haven, Conn., 2004), 63.
12 Edward Bever, *The Realities of Witchcraft and Popular Magic in Early Modern Europe: Culture, Cognition and Everyday Life* (Basingstoke, 2008), 124–9; Julian Goodare, 'Flying witches in Scotland', in Julian Goodare (ed.), *Scottish Witches and Witch-Hunters* (Basingstoke, 2013), 159–76.
13 Roper, *Witch Craze*, 44–66.
14 William M. Reddy, 'Neuroscience and the fallacies of functionalism', *History and Theory*, 49 (2010), 412–25.
15 Niek Koning, 'Witchcraft beliefs and witch hunts: an interdisciplinary explanation', *Human Nature*, 24 (2013), 158–81.
16 The following account is drawn from a number of sources. In addition to those cited below, see John A. Cohan, 'The problem of witchcraft violence in Africa', *Suffolk University Law Review*, 44 (2011), 803–72; Mohammed A. Diwan, 'Conflict between state legal norms and norms underlying popular beliefs: witchcraft in Africa as a case study', *Duke Journal of Comparative and International Law*, 14 (2004), 351–87; Peter Geschiere, *The Modernity of Witchcraft: Politics and the Occult in Postcolonial Africa*, trans. Peter Geschiere and Janet Roitman (Charlottesville, Va., 1997); Peter Geschiere,

Witchcraft, Intimacy, and Trust: Africa in Comparison (Chicago, Ill., 2013); Erich Leistner, 'Witchcraft and African development', *African Security Review*, 23 (2014), 53–77; and Henrietta L. Moore and Todd Sanders (eds.), *Magical Interpretations, Material Realities: Modernity, Witchcraft and the Occult in Postcolonial Africa* (London, 2001). There is an overview of the subject up to 2004 in Wolfgang Behringer, *Witches and Witch-Hunts: A Global History* (Cambridge, 2004), 196–228. A recent non-academic survey is HelpAge International, *Using the Law to Tackle Allegations of Witchcraft: HelpAge International's Position* (2011), downloadable from <www.helpage.org>.

17 Isak Niehaus, 'Witchcraft as subtext: deep knowledge and the South African public sphere', *Social Dynamics: A Journal of African Studies*, 36 (2010), 65–77.

18 Cyprian F. Fisiy and Peter Geschiere, 'Witchcraft, development and paranoia in Cameroon', in Moore and Sanders (eds.), *Magical Interpretations, Material Realities*, 226-46; quotation at p. 234.

19 Paul Thomas, 'Religious education and the feminisation of witchcraft: a study of three secondary schools in Kumasi, Ghana', *British Journal of Religious Education*, 34 (2012), 67–86, at pp. 82–4.

20 Adam Ashforth, *Witchcraft, Violence and Democracy in South Africa* (Chicago, Ill., 2005), 258–9.

21 Edward Miguel, 'Poverty and witch killing', *Review of Economic Studies*, 72 (2005), 1153–72; Simeon Mesaki, 'Witchcraft and the law in Tanzania', *International Journal of Sociology and Anthropology*, 1 (2009), 132–8; HelpAge International Tanzania, *NGO Thematic Report on Older Women's Rights in Tanzania* (2008), online at <www2.ohchr.org/english/bodies/cedaw/docs/ngos/HAITanzania41.pdf>.

22 Legal and Human Rights Centre, *Tanzania Human Rights Report 2009* (2010), 19–23, online at <www.humanrights.or.tz/downloads/tanzania-human-rights-report-2009.pdf>.

23 Maia Green, 'Witchcraft suppression practices and movements: public politics and the logic of purification', *Comparative Studies in Society and History*, 39 (1997), 319–45; Maia Green, *Priests, Witches and Power: Popular Christianity after Mission in Southern Tanzania* (Cambridge, 2003), 120–40; Maia Green and Simeon Mesaki, 'The birth of the "salon:" poverty, "modernization," and dealing with witchcraft in southern Tanzania', *American Anthropologist*, 32 (2005), 371–88.

24 Adam Ashforth, 'Witchcraft, justice, and human rights in Africa: cases from Malawi', *African Studies Review*, 58 (2015), 5–38.

25 A. C. Ross, 'The political role of the witchfinder in southern Malawi during the crisis of October 1964 to May 1965', in R. G. Willis (ed.), *Witchcraft and Healing* (Edinburgh, 1969), 55–70. For references to more recent examples see Dirk Kohnert, 'On the renaissance of African modes of thought: the example of the belief in magic and witchcraft', in Burghart Schmidt and Rolf Schulte (eds.), *Hexenglauben im modernen Afrika: Hexen, Hexenverfolgung und magische Vorstellungswelten / Witchcraft in Modern Africa: Witches, Witch-Hunts and Magical Imaginaries* (Hamburg, 2007), 32–54, at pp. 42–3.

26 Jean-François Bayart, Stephen Ellis and Béatrice Hibou, *The Criminalization of the State in Africa*, trans. Stephen Ellis (Oxford, 1999), 38.

27 Jennifer Badstuebner, '"Drinking the hot blood of humans": witchcraft confessions in a South African Pentecostal church', *Anthropology and Humanism*, 28 (2003), 8–22.

28 Mensah Adinkrah, 'Child witch hunts in contemporary Ghana', *Child Abuse and Neglect*, 35 (2011), 741–52; Emilie Secker, 'Witchcraft stigmatization in Nigeria: challenges and successes in the implementation of child rights', *International Social Work*, 56 (2012), 22–36.

29 Herman Slaats and Karen Porter, 'Sorcery and the law in modern Indonesia', in C. W. Watson and Roy Ellen (eds.), *Understanding Witchcraft and Sorcery in Southeast Asia* (Honolulu, Hawaii, 1993), 135–48.
30 Soma Chaudhuri, 'Violence against women: targets in tea plantations of India', *Violence Against Women*, 18 (2012), 1213–34.
31 Puja Roy, 'Sanctioned violence: development and the persecution of women as witches in South Bihar', *Development in Practice*, 8 (1998), 136–47.
32 Amnesty International report, 'Papua New Guinea repeals Sorcery Act while moving closer to executions', 28 May 2013, online at <www.amnesty.org/en/latest/news/2013/05/papua-new-guinea-repeals-sorcery-act-while-moving-closer-executions/>.
33 Ryan Schram, 'Witches' wealth: witchcraft, confession, and Christianity in Auhelawa, Papua New Guinea', *Journal of the Royal Anthropological Institute*, 16 (2010), 726–42.
34 Detailed academic studies are hard to find, but see Dawn Perlmutter, 'The politics of Muslim magic', *Middle East Quarterly*, 20:2 (Spring 2013), 73–80; Ryan Jacobs, 'Saudi Arabia's war on witchcraft', *The Atlantic*, 19 August 2013, online at <www.theatlantic.com/international/archive/2013/08/saudi-arabias-war-on-witchcraft/278701/>; Amnesty International, *Death Sentences and Executions in 2014* (Amnesty International report, 2015), 8.
35 Constant Hamès, 'Problématiques de la magie-sorcellerie en islam et perspectives africaines', *Cahiers d'études africaines*, 189–90 (2008), 81–99.
36 Toufic Fahd, 'La connaissance de l'inconnaissable et l'obtention de l'impossible dans la pensée mantique et magique de l'Islam', *Bulletin d'études orientales*, 44 (1992), 33–44.
37 Mohammed Maarouf, *Jinn Eviction as a Discourse of Power: A Multidisciplinary Approach to Moroccan Magical Beliefs and Practices* (Leiden, 2007), 251–2.
38 Yusuf Muslim Eneborg, 'The quest for "disenchantment" and the modernization of magic', *Islam and Christian-Muslim Relations*, 25 (2014), 419–32.
39 Jeanne Favret-Saada, *Deadly Words: Witchcraft in the Bocage*, trans. Catherine Cullen (Cambridge, 1980).
40 Mirjam Mencej, 'Witchcraft in eastern Slovenia and western Macedonia: a comparative analysis', in Zmago Šmitek and Aneta Svetieva (eds.), *Post-Yugoslav Lifeworlds: Between Tradition and Modernity* (Ljubljana, 2005), 37–67.
41 Mirjam Mencej, '"The night is yours, the day is mine!" Functions of stories of night-time encounters with witches in eastern Slovenia', *Estudos de Literatura Oral*, 13–14 (2007–08), 189–206.
42 Gustav Henningsen, 'The witches' flying and the Spanish Inquisitors, or how to explain (away) the impossible', *Folklore*, 120 (2009), 57–74.
43 G. R. Balleine, 'Witch trials in Jersey', *Société jersiaise: bulletin annuel*, 13 (1939), 379–98, at p. 389.
44 Christiane Bougerol, *Une ethnographie des conflits aux Antilles: Jalousie, commérages, sorcellerie* (Paris, 1997).
45 Maarouf, *Jinn Eviction*, 216 and *passim*.
46 Denise Cush, 'Consumer witchcraft: are teenage witches a creation of commercial interests?', *Journal of Beliefs and Values*, 28 (2007), 45–53.
47 David Livingstone, *Missionary Travels and Researches in South Africa* (London, 1857), 622.
48 Julian Goodare, 'Remembering Scottish witches', *The Bottle Imp*, no. 14 (Nov. 2013), online at <www.thebottleimp.org.uk>.
49 Stanley Cohen, *States of Denial: Knowing about Atrocities and Suffering* (Cambridge, 2001), 64–80 and *passim*.
50 Cohen, *States of Denial*, 96–7.

51 Quoted in David Frankfurter, *Evil Incarnate: Rumors of Demonic Conspiracy and Satanic Abuse in History* (Princeton, NJ, 2006), 126.
52 J. S. La Fontaine, *Speak of the Devil: Tales of Satanic Abuse in Contemporary England* (Cambridge, 1998); Ross E. Cheit, *The Witch-Hunt Narrative: Politics, Psychology, and the Sexual Abuse of Children* (Oxford, 2014); Mark L. Howe and Lauren M. Knott, 'The fallibility of memory in judicial processes: lessons from the past and their modern consequences', *Memory* (online 2015); Thomas D. Lyon and Stacia N. Stolzenberg, 'Children's memory for conversations about sexual abuse: legal and psychological implications', *Roger Williams University Law Review*, 19 (2014), 411–50.
53 *Turkey: Decriminalize Dissent* (Amnesty International report, 2013), 10–11.

Further reading

Introduction

This is a bibliographical essay discussing books that have been published in English on aspects of the European witch-hunt. For the sake of brevity it excludes articles in scholarly journals. However, it does include some books that are not 'about witchcraft' but that those studying witchcraft sometimes need to understand – works about early modern courts, or about political theory, for instance. If you are interested in a particular topic, you can begin with the books recommended here, and then follow up the references that these books give.

The bibliography is divided into thematic sections that mostly follow the chapters of this book, from Chapter 2 onwards. There is also an introductory section of 'Overviews and reference works'. At the end are two sections of 'Regional studies' and 'Primary sources'. Dividing up the subject like this is an imprecise exercise. In particular, the division between the thematic sections and the regional section is imprecise; studies of a region may also focus on a theme. A few works are mentioned in more than one section.

There is a great deal of material about witch-hunting on the Internet. Be warned: the academic value of witchcraft websites is generally low, and they can be seriously misleading. Many are produced by non-experts, and a worse problem is that they often have non-historical agendas. Searching the Internet for information about the European witch-hunt thus produces large quantities of unsatisfactory or misleading material, as well as some material that may be good but is hard to evaluate. Serious academic scholars mostly publish books and scholarly articles rather than websites. Fortunately, there are many good books on this subject.

Please pay attention to when books were published. Chapter 11 discusses the way in which scholarly understanding of the subject of the European witch-hunt has developed over the years. There have been different phases of debate, and some interpretations that were once common are now no longer accepted. All the books listed here have something to teach us today, but some of the older ones are partly out of date and should be supplemented by more recent ones. The oldest book here (except in the 'Primary sources' section) was published in 1970, and more than half of the books were published after 2000.

Overviews and reference works

If a reader of the present book were to read one further book on the topic, it should probably be Brian P. Levack (ed.), *The Oxford Handbook of Witchcraft in Early Modern Europe and Colonial America* (Oxford, 2013). This is a large, recent and important work, divided into three sections: 'Witch Beliefs', 'Witchcraft Prosecutions', and 'Themes of Witchcraft Research'. The first and third of these cover general themes that are important for the whole of Europe; the 'Witchcraft Prosecutions' section is a series of chapters on individual countries and regions. Contributors were asked both to provide an overview of the current state of knowledge in their field, and to survey the historiography of the field. The lists of further reading at the end of each chapter can be useful research tools.

Two single-author studies of the European witch-hunt, and one further collection of essays, are particularly worth mentioning. Brian P. Levack, *The Witch-Hunt in Early Modern Europe* (4th edn., London, 2015), is a clearly-expounded analysis that has been highly successful with students ever since the first edition appeared in 1987. Wolfgang Behringer, *Witches and Witch-Hunts: A Global History* (Cambridge, 2004), sets early modern Europe in a broader chronological and geographical context. Much of the book consists of non-stop narratives of major panics, which can be hard to follow, but Behringer is one of the most influential scholars of witch-hunting, especially in the German heartland; his book is thoroughly researched and packed with information. As for the collection of essays, this is Bengt Ankarloo and Gustav Henningsen (eds.), *Early Modern European Witchcraft: Centres and Peripheries* (Oxford, 1990), an older but high-quality volume, combining important thematic overviews with regional studies.

There is a six-volume series, 'Athlone History of Witchcraft and Magic in Europe', general editors Bengt Ankarloo and Stuart Clark. Each volume has three or four sections that together aim at comprehensive coverage of the topic. Individual volumes in the series are: Frederick H. Cryer and Marie-Louise Thomsen, *Witchcraft and Magic in Europe: Biblical and Pagan Societies* (vol. 1; London, 2001); Valerie Flint, Richard Gordon, Georg Luck and Daniel Ogden, *Witchcraft and Magic in Europe: Ancient Greece and Rome* (vol. 2; London, 1999); Karen Jolly, Catharina Raudvere and Edward Peters, *Witchcraft and Magic in Europe: The Middle Ages* (vol. 3; London, 2002); Bengt Ankarloo, Stuart Clark and William Monter, *Witchcraft and Magic in Europe: The Period of the Witch Trials* (vol. 4; London, 2002); Marijke Gijswijt-Hofstra, Brian P. Levack and Roy Porter, *Witchcraft and Magic in Europe: The Eighteenth and Nineteenth Centuries* (vol. 5; London, 1999); and Willem de Blécourt, Ronald Hutton and Jean La Fontaine, *Witchcraft and Magic in Europe: The Twentieth Century* (vol. 6; London, 1999). Volumes 3, 4 and 5 are particularly relevant to early modern witch-hunting.

There are several useful collections of reprinted journal articles, some of which also contain reprinted book chapters. Three single-volume collections are: Darren Oldridge (ed.), *The Witchcraft Reader* (2nd edn., London, 2008); Merry E. Wiesner (ed.), *Witchcraft in Early Modern Europe* (Boston, Mass., 2007); and Elaine G. Breslaw (ed.), *Witches of the Atlantic World: A Historical Reader and Primary Sourcebook* (New York, 2000), which also contains some primary documents. There is also a six-volume collection of reprints: Brian P. Levack (ed.), *New Perspectives on Witchcraft, Magic and Demonology*, 6 vols. (London, 2001). The individual volumes are as follows: vol. 1, *Demonology, Religion, and Witchcraft*; vol. 2, *Witchcraft in Continental Europe*; vol. 3, *Witchcraft in the British Isles and New England*; vol. 4, *Gender and Witchcraft*; vol. 5, *Witchcraft, Healing, and Popular Diseases*; and vol. 6, *Witchcraft in the Modern World*.

The most comprehensive reference work is Richard M. Golden (ed.), *Encyclopedia of Witchcraft: The Western Tradition*, 4 vols. (Santa Barbara, Calif., 2006). This is a valuable research tool, with articles on a multitude of relevant topics, all of which have short lists of further reading at the end. Jonathan Durrant and Michael D. Bailey, *Historical Dictionary of Witchcraft* (2nd edn., Lanham, Md., 2012), has a similar scope to Golden but is much less detailed.

Two specialist academic journals have begun publishing in recent years. Not only their articles but also their book reviews show how the subject has developed and continues to do so: *Magic, Ritual, and Witchcraft* (University of Pennsylvania Press, 2006 onwards), and *Preternature: Critical and Historical Studies on the Preternatural* (Penn State University Press, 2012 onwards).

Towards witch-hunting

The framework for the understanding of the development of witchcraft stereotypes was provided in 1975 by the first edition of Norman Cohn, *Europe's Inner Demons: The Demonization of Christians in Medieval Christendom* (3rd edn., Chicago, Ill., 2000). This is a brilliant and influential reconstruction. The context of medieval 'persecution' can be seen in Robert I. Moore, *The Formation of a Persecuting Society: Power and Deviance in Western Europe, 950–1250* (Oxford, 1987).

Further studies of learned witch beliefs in the late medieval period are Edward Peters, *The Magician, the Witch and the Law* (Philadelphia, Pa., 1978); Walter Stephens, *Demon Lovers: Witchcraft, Sex, and the Crisis of Belief* (Chicago, Ill., 2001); Hans P. Broedel, *The Malleus Maleficarum and the Construction of Witchcraft: Theology and Popular Belief* (Manchester, 2003); and Michael D. Bailey, *Fearful Spirits, Reasoned Follies: The Boundaries of Superstition in Late Medieval Europe* (Ithaca, NY, 2013).

Actual witch trials in the middle ages have been surveyed by Richard Kieckhefer, *European Witch Trials: Their Foundation in Popular and Learned Culture, 1300–1500* (London, 1976). Kieckhefer analyses the ideas contained in trial documents and outlines a method of distinguishing 'popular' and 'learned' elements of belief.

Witchcraft and the intellectuals

Stuart Clark, *Thinking with Demons: The Idea of Witchcraft in Early Modern Europe* (Oxford, 1997), is a huge and important book on intellectual demonology. Reading it can be a major intellectual effort, but it contains handy introductions to each of its five sections. Clark also contributed a demonological section to volume 4 of the 'Athlone History' series (see above), which is a more accessible narrative of developing ideas. Several witchcraft ideas developed in the later middle ages, so some of the books in the 'Towards witch-hunting' section above are also relevant here.

Many intellectual ideas of witchcraft tended to organise themselves around the concept of 'superstition', meaning unnecessary and therefore false Christian belief. There is a magisterial study of this: Euan Cameron, *Enchanted Europe: Superstition, Reason and Religion, 1250–1750* (Oxford, 2010). Cameron covers some similar ground to Clark's *Thinking with Demons*, but focuses more on historical change. Witchcraft can be studied within the broader context of magic, for which there is a useful general survey: Richard Kieckhefer, *Magic in the Middle Ages* (2nd edn., Cambridge, 2014).

On witchcraft in the visual arts, two books cover the early part of the period: Charles Zika, *The Appearance of Witchcraft: Print and Visual Culture in Sixteenth-Century Europe* (London, 2006), and Linda C. Hults, *The Witch as Muse: Art, Gender, and Power in Early Modern Europe* (Philadelphia, Pa., 2005). Lyndal Roper, *The Witch in the Western Imagination* (Charlottesville, Va., 2012), is a wide-ranging collection of essays, of which the title essay is particularly important in linking demonology with other genres of elite culture.

Witches in the community

The essential work here is Robin Briggs, *Witches and Neighbours: The Social and Cultural Context of European Witchcraft* (2nd edn., Oxford, 2002). This celebrated book covers the vital topic of neighbourhood witchcraft relationships. Few other books focus exclusively on village witchcraft, but it has been a theme of many of the books in the 'Regional studies' section below. For more on the early modern village generally, see David Sabean, *Power in the Blood: Popular Culture and Village Discourse in Early Modern Germany* (Cambridge, 1984), which includes a witchcraft chapter.

Edward Bever, in a large, important and densely-written book, has used studies of psychology to argue that the curses of quarrelsome witches could really take effect on their victims through stress-related trauma: Edward Bever, *The Realities of Witchcraft and Popular Magic in Early Modern Europe: Culture, Cognition and Everyday Life* (Basingstoke, 2008).

Witchcraft and folk belief

Here it is best to begin with some works about the context of folk belief, rather than about witch beliefs as such. Peter Burke, *Popular Culture in Early Modern Europe* (3rd edn., Farnham, 2009), has been recognised as a classic since the first edition appeared in 1978. Stephen Wilson, *The Magical Universe: Everyday Ritual and Magic in Pre-Modern Europe* (London, 2000), is a large if uncritical compilation of popular beliefs and practices. For popular magic, see also Jonathan Roper (ed.), *Charms and Charming in Europe* (Basingstoke, 2004).

The use of popular beliefs in witchcraft confessions is one of the important topics in Lyndal Roper, *Witch Craze: Terror and Fantasy in Baroque Germany* (New Haven, Conn., 2004). Based on case studies from southern Germany, but proposing interpretations that are relevant for the whole of Europe, Roper shows how witches' confessions were shaped by a combination of elite and popular fears and fantasies. Kathryn A. Edwards (ed.), *Werewolves, Witches, and Wandering Spirits: Traditional Belief and Folklore in Early Modern Europe* (Kirksville, Mo., 2002), looks at elite encounters with ghosts, werewolves and other aspects of popular belief.

The transmission of deep folkloric beliefs through millennia is the subject of Carlo Ginzburg, *Ecstasies: Deciphering the Witches' Sabbath*, trans. Raymond Rosenthal (London, 1991). This book was partly a follow-up to Carlo Ginzburg, *The Night Battles: Witchcraft and Agrarian Cults in the Sixteenth and Seventeenth Centuries*, trans. John and Anne Tedeschi (London, 1983), a much-cited study of the *benandanti* ('good walkers'), an extraordinary shamanistic cult in northern Italy. Although Ginzburg's work has attracted much interest, most scholars have remained sceptical of *Ecstasies*, or at least of the specific interpretative scheme that it propounds. However, the importance of the general topic of deep folkloric beliefs and practices has been established. Further works on this topic include Gábor Klaniczay, *The Uses of Supernatural Power: The Transformation of Popular Religion in Medieval and Early-Modern Europe*, trans. Susan Singerman (Princeton, NJ, 1990); Éva Pócs, *Between the Living and the Dead: A Perspective on Witches and Seers in the Early Modern Age*, trans. Szilvia Rédey and Michael Webb (Budapest, 1999); and Gábor Klaniczay and Éva Pócs (eds.), *Communicating with the Spirits* (Budapest, 2005). Two important case studies are Wolfgang Behringer, *Shaman of Oberstdorf: Chonrad Stoeckhlin and the Phantoms of the Night*, trans. H. C. Erik

Midelfort (Charlottesville, Va., 1998), and Emma Wilby, *The Visions of Isobel Gowdie: Magic, Witchcraft and Dark Shamanism in Seventeenth-Century Scotland* (Brighton, 2010).

Witches and the godly state

Theodore K. Rabb, *The Struggle for Stability in Early Modern Europe* (Oxford, 1975), is a classic essay on the political and social instability of this period, and on the efforts of governments and others to come to terms with it. Instability and the search for control are also themes in a wide-ranging study of European culture as a whole: John Hale, *The Civilization of Europe in the Renaissance* (London, 1993).

The Reformation is covered by many studies including Euan Cameron, *The European Reformation* (2nd edn., Oxford, 2012). The changing nature of early modern Christianity is discussed by John Bossy, *Christianity in the West, 1400–1700* (Oxford, 1985), a remarkable study that gets beyond the issue of what divided Catholics and Protestants. An innovative study of divisions is Benjamin J. Kaplan, *Divided by Faith: Religious Conflict and the Practice of Toleration in Early Modern Europe* (Cambridge, Mass., 2007). The divine right of kings, the political theory of the godly state, is explained and contextualised by J. H. Burns (ed.), *The Cambridge History of Political Thought, 1450–1700* (Cambridge, 1991).

Witches in court

Richard van Dülmen, *Theatre of Horror: Crime and Punishment in Early Modern Germany*, trans. Elisabeth Neu (Oxford, 1990), is an introduction to criminal courts and their procedures, stressing that this was a period of harsh treatment for criminals in general. Standard works on torture are John H. Langbein, *Torture and the Law of Proof: Europe and England in the Ancien Régime* (Chicago, Ill., 1977), and Edward Peters, *Torture* (2nd edn., Philadelphia, Pa., 1996).

The Spanish, Portuguese and Roman Inquisitions usually restrained witch-hunting. For overviews see Henry Kamen, *The Spanish Inquisition: A Historical Revision* (London, 1997) and Rainer Decker, *Witchcraft and the Papacy*, trans. H. C. Erik Midelfort (Charlottesville, Va., 2008).

Modern psychological studies help to illuminate how and why people confess. In particular see Gisli H. Gudjonsson, *The Psychology of Interrogations and Confessions: A Handbook* (Chichester, 2002). Witness testimony, too, is affected by psychological factors, for which see Anthony Heaton-Armstrong, Eric Shepherd and David Wolchover (eds.), *Analysing Witness Testimony: A Guide for Legal Practitioners and Other Professionals* (London, 1999). Concepts like suggestibility and false memory, discussed in these works, are important for witchcraft trials.

The dynamics of witch-hunting

Most of the information for this chapter comes from works categorised as 'Overviews and reference works' (see above) or 'Regional studies' (see below). Two classic sociologial studies of 'panics' are Neil J. Smelser, *Theory of Collective Behavior* (London, 1962), and Stanley Cohen, *Folk Devils and Moral Panics: The Creation of the Mods and Rockers* (3rd edn., London, 2002). For a sociological analysis of the witch-hunt itself see Gary Jensen, *The Path of the Devil: A Study of Early Modern Witch Hunts* (Lanham, Md., 2007), which displays a particular interest in statistics, correlations and social-science theory.

Women, men and witchcraft

Traditional accounts of witch-hunting paid little attention to gender, but it is now discussed intensely. Many recent works in the 'Regional studies' section below have some discussion of gender. Anne L. Barstow, *Witchcraze: A New History of the European Witch Hunts* (San Francisco, Calif., 1994), is an early overview of the subject from a feminist perspective. It has several weaknesses, notably a lack of attention to male witches, but its material on misogynist brutality remains relevant. On gendered aspects of the godly state, there is Merry E. Wiesner-Hanks, *Christianity and Sexuality in the Early Modern World* (London, 2000). There are influential essays in Lyndal Roper, *Oedipus and the Devil: Witchcraft, Sexuality and Religion in Early Modern Europe* (London, 1994). On demonic possession, often a gendered topic, see Brian P. Levack, *The Devil Within: Possession and Exorcism in the Christian West* (New Haven, Conn., 2013).

Some regional case studies focus on gender: Carol F. Karlsen, *The Devil in the Shape of a Woman: Witchcraft in Colonial New England* (New York, 1987); Sigrid Brauner, *Fearless Wives and Frightened Shrews: The Construction of the Witch in Early Modern Germany* (Amherst, Mass., 1995); Jonathan B. Durrant, *Witchcraft, Gender and Society in Early Modern Germany* (Leiden, 2007); and Raisa Maria Toivo, *Witchcraft and Gender in Early Modern Society: Finland and the Wider European Experience* (Aldershot, 2008).

Some studies of women as witches also mention the issue of men as witches. Men are also the focus of two important books. Alison Rowlands (ed.), *Witchcraft and Masculinities in Early Modern Europe* (Basingstoke, 2009), has case studies of a number of countries and a wide-ranging introduction; Rolf Schulte, *Man as Witch: Male Witches in Central Europe*, trans. Linda Froome-Döring (Basingstoke, 2009), is an in-depth study of several German regions. For children as accusers of witches there is Hans Sebald, *Witch-Children: From Salem Witch-Hunts to Modern Courtrooms* (Amherst, NY, 1995).

The end of witch-hunting

This is another chapter for which most of the information comes from works categorised as 'Overviews and reference works' (see above) or 'Regional studies' (see below). Judicial caution, the decline of judges' willingness to prosecute, is discussed in some of the works in the 'Witches in court' section above. Intellectual scepticism concerning witches is related to the Scientific Revolution and other intellectual currents. One major study, though now a little dated, is Brian Easlea, *Witch-Hunting, Magic and the New Philosophy: An Introduction to Debates of the Scientific Revolution, 1450–1750* (Brighton, 1980). For a more recent brief introduction to the Scientific Revolution, see John Henry, *The Scientific Revolution and the Origins of Modern Science* (3rd edn., Basingstoke, 2006). Henry has a chapter on magic, but his chapter on the 'mechanical philosophy' is particularly relevant. There is more detail in Stephen Gaukroger, *The Emergence of a Scientific Culture: Science and the Shaping of Modernity, 1210-1685* (Oxford, 2006), and in Jonathan I. Israel, *Radical Enlightenment: Philosophy and the Making of Modernity, 1650–1750* (Oxford, 2001).

Two important works on the eighteenth century and after are Owen Davies and Willem de Blécourt (eds.), *Beyond the Witch Trials: Witchcraft and Magic in Enlightenment Europe* (Manchester, 2004), and Willem de Blécourt and Owen Davies (eds.), *Witchcraft Continued: Popular Magic in Modern Europe* (Manchester, 2004). Most of the essays primarily concern aspects of popular culture and belief, but they also contain information on the way in which this was treated by the authorities.

Perspectives on the witch-hunt

Jonathan Barry and Owen Davies (eds.), *Palgrave Advances in Witchcraft Historiography* (Basingstoke, 2007), is an innovative companion to conventional textbooks. Rather than focus directly on early modern witchcraft, it mainly discusses how scholars and others have attempted to make sense of early modern witchcraft at different periods, and from different genres and intellectual disciplines. It thus reviews the state of the debate, or indeed the state of a number of debates. A more recent collection of essays along these lines, including several regional studies, is Marko Nenonen and Raisa Maria Toivo (eds.), *Writing Witch-Hunt Histories: Challenging the Paradigm* (Leiden, 2013).

There is a major sociological study of persecution: Stanley Cohen, *States of Denial: Knowing about Atrocities and Suffering* (Cambridge, 2001). For the question of why people believe in evil conspiracies, David Frankfurter, *Evil Incarnate: Rumors of Demonic Conspiracy and Ritual Abuse in History* (Princeton, NJ, 2006), ranges widely and provides comparative material. Actual modern witchcraft, far more benign, is the subject of Ronald Hutton, *The Triumph of the Moon: A History of Modern Pagan Witchcraft* (Oxford, 1999); this is mainly relevant to early modern witchcraft by discussing aspects of the development of modern scholarly ideas. A twentieth-century anthropological study from France has been influential: Jeanne Favret-Saada, *Deadly Words: Witchcraft in the Bocage*, trans. Catherine Cullen (Cambridge, 1980). This is worth looking at to see whether the 'traditional' beliefs that it reveals can shed any light on earlier periods.

Regional studies

Germany and the Netherlands

The most important single book on Germany in English is Lyndal Roper, *Witch Craze: Terror and Fantasy in Baroque Germany* (New Haven, Conn., 2004). Wolfgang Behringer, *Witchcraft Persecutions in Bavaria*, trans. J. C. Grayson and David Lederer (Cambridge, 1997), is another major work covering south-eastern Germany. A pioneering book by H. C. Erik Midelfort, *Witch-Hunting in Southwestern Germany, 1562–1684* (Stanford, Calif., 1972), hardly seems to have dated and is a classic study of a region that had major panics. Two separate regions are compared by Johannes Dillinger, *Evil People: A Comparative Study of Witch Hunts in Swabian Austria and the Electorate of Trier*, trans. Laura Stokes (Charlottesville, Va., 2009). Jonathan B. Durrant, *Witchcraft, Gender and Society in Early Modern Germany* (Leiden, 2007), is about Eichstätt, one of the Catholic prince-bishoprics that produced some of the most intense witch-hunting that Europe ever experienced. By contrast, Alison Rowlands, *Witchcraft Narratives in Germany: Rothenburg, 1561–1652* (Manchester, 2003), focuses on a town that prosecuted few witches but preserved detailed records of them. Two even more detailed case studies are Thomas Robisheaux, *The Last Witch of Langenburg: Murder in a German Village* (New York, 2009), and Peter A. Morton and Barbara Dähms (eds.), *The Trial of Tempel Anneke: Records of a Witchcraft Trial in Brunswick, Germany, 1663* (Toronto, 2005). For the Netherlands, the main book is Marijke Gijswijt-Hofstra and Willem Frijhoff (eds.), *Witchcraft in the Netherlands from the Fourteenth to the Twentieth Century*, trans. Rachel M. J. van der Wilden-Fall (Rotterdam, 1991).

France, Lorraine and Switzerland

France has not been well served by books in English, but an influential collection of essays on witch-hunting in northern France includes three essays in English: Alfred Soman, *Sorcellerie et justice criminelle: Le parlement de Paris (16ᵉ–18ᵉ siècles)* (Aldershot, 1992). For French demonology see Gerhild S. Williams, *Defining Dominion: The Discourses of Magic and Witchcraft in Early Modern France and Germany* (Ann Arbor, Mich., 1995), and Jonathan L. Pearl, *The Crime of Crimes: Demonology and Politics in France, 1560–1620* (Waterloo, 1999). Lorraine is comprehensively covered by Robin Briggs, *The Witches of Lorraine* (Oxford, 2007).

Coverage of Switzerland is patchy, but see Laura Stokes, *Demons of Urban Reform: Early European Witch Trials and Criminal Justice, 1430–1530* (Basingstoke, 2011), on three towns, Lucerne and Basel (in Switzerland) and Nuremberg (in south Germany). E. William Monter, *Witchcraft in France and Switzerland: The Borderlands during the Reformation* (Ithaca, NY, 1976), is an important regional study of Savoy, Franche-Comté and western Switzerland. William G. Naphy, *Plagues, Poisons and Potions: Plague-Spreading Conspiracies in the Western Alps, c.1530–1640* (Manchester, 2002), is about prosecutions for plague-spreading (real or imaginary), but those prosecuted were sometimes thought to be witches or to have made a demonic pact like witches.

Italy, Spain and Portugal

These countries have not been covered comprehensively, but there are studies of witchcraft in several Italian regions: Matteo Duni, *Under the Devil's Spell: Witches, Sorcerers, and the Inquisition in Renaissance Italy* (Syracuse, NY, 2007); Ruth Martin, *Witchcraft and the Inquisition in Venice, 1550–1650* (Oxford, 1989); Jonathan Seitz, *Witchcraft and Inquisition in Early Modern Venice* (Cambridge, 2011); and Louise Nyholm Kallestrup, *Agents of Witchcraft in Early Modern Italy and Denmark* (Basingstoke, 2015). Witchcraft is set in a wider system of popular belief by David Gentilcore, *From Bishop to Witch: The System of the Sacred in Early Modern Terra d'Otranto* (Manchester, 1992). Italian demonology is analysed by Armando Maggi, *Satan's Rhetoric: A Study of Renaissance Demonology* (Chicago, Ill., 2001), and Armando Maggi, *In the Company of Demons: Unnatural Beings, Love, and Identity in the Italian Renaissance* (Chicago, Ill., 2008).

For Spain there is a classic and wide-ranging study of how a sceptical inquisitor halted a witchcraft panic: Gustav Henningsen, *The Witches' Advocate: Basque Witchcraft and the Spanish Inquisition, 1609–1614* (Reno, Nev., 1980). Gunnar W. Knutsen, *Servants of Satan and Masters of Demons: The Spanish Inquisition's Trials for Superstition, Valencia and Barcelona, 1478–1700* (Turnhout, 2009), compares two contrasting regions, while María Tausiet, *Urban Magic in Early Modern Spain: Abracadabra Omnipotens*, trans. Susannah Howe (Basingstoke, 2014), is an in-depth study of Saragossa. For Portugal there is Timothy D. Walker, *Doctors, Folk Medicine and the Inquisition: The Repression of Magical Healing in Portugal during the Enlightenment* (Leiden, 2005).

England and Scotland

James Sharpe, *Instruments of Darkness: Witchcraft in England, 1550–1750* (London, 1996), is a carefully-researched and well-rounded account. Two classic studies are Alan Macfarlane, *Witchcraft in Tudor* and *Stuart England* (London, 1970) and Keith Thomas, *Religion and the Decline of Magic* (London, 1971). These works are related, and both should be read. Macfarlane's book was reprinted in 1999 with a new introduction by James Sharpe. Thomas's book is quite simply one of the most celebrated and influential history books written in the twentieth century.

England has provided several studies of the issue of women (which Macfarlane and Thomas have been criticised for neglecting). See Deborah Willis, *Malevolent Nurture: Witch-Hunting and Maternal Power in Early Modern England* (Ithaca, NY, 1995), and Diane Purkiss, *The Witch in History: Early Modern and Twentieth-Century Representations* (London, 1996). England's two main panics are covered by Philip C. Almond, *The Lancashire Witches: A Chronicle of Sorcery and Death on Pendle Hill* (London, 2012), and Malcolm Gaskill, *Witchfinders: A Seventeenth Century English Tragedy* (Cambridge, Mass., 2005). On English intellectual attitudes in the period of decline, see Ian Bostridge, *Witchcraft and its Transformations, c.1650–c.1750* (Oxford, 1997). Popular beliefs after witch-hunting ended are the subject of Owen Davies, *Witchcraft, Magic and Culture, 1736–1951* (Manchester, 1999).

On Scotland, Christina Larner, *Enemies of God: The Witch-Hunt in Scotland* (London, 1981), is a much-cited classic though now rather dated. Four collections of essays bring the subject up to date: Julian Goodare (ed.), *The Scottish Witch-Hunt in Context* (Manchester, 2002); Julian Goodare, Lauren Martin and Joyce Miller (eds.), *Witchcraft and Belief in Early Modern Scotland* (Basingstoke, 2008); Brian P. Levack, *Witch-Hunting in Scotland: Law, Politics and Religion* (London, 2008), a collection of Levack's own essays (new and reprinted); and Julian Goodare (ed.), *Scottish Witches and Witch-Hunters* (Basingstoke, 2013). Finally, there is a comparative study making innovative use of a close reading of confessions: Liv Helene Willumsen, *Witches of the North: Scotland and Finnmark* (Leiden, 2013).

Hungary, Poland, Russia and Scandinavia

Two works focusing on popular belief are based partly on studies of Hungary and neighbouring regions: Gábor Klaniczay, *The Uses of Supernatural Power: The Transformation of Popular Religion in Medieval and Early-Modern Europe*, trans. Susan Singerman (Princeton, NJ, 1990); Éva Pócs, *Between the Living and the Dead: A Perspective on Witches and Seers in the Early Modern Age*, trans. Szilvia Rédey and Michael Webb (Budapest, 1999). Poland is covered by Michael Ostling, *Between the Devil and the Host: Imagining Witchcraft in Early Modern Poland* (Oxford, 2011), and Wanda Wyporska, *Witchcraft in Early Modern Poland, 1500–1800* (Basingstoke, 2013). On Russia see Valerie Kivelson, *Desperate Magic: The Moral Economy of Witchcraft in Seventeenth-Century Russia* (Ithaca, NY, 2013), and W. F. Ryan, *The Bathhouse at Midnight: An Historical Survey of Magic and Divination in Russia* (Stroud, 1999). There are several

Scandinavian chapters in Bengt Ankarloo and Gustav Henningsen (eds.), *Early Modern European Witchcraft: Centres and Peripheries* (Oxford, 1990). On Sweden see Per Sörlin, *Wicked Arts: Witchcraft and Magic Trials in Southern Sweden, 1635–1754* (Leiden, 1998). On Finland see Raisa Maria Toivo, *Witchcraft and Gender in Early Modern Society: Finland and the Wider European Experience* (Aldershot, 2008). On Denmark see Louise Nyholm Kallestrup, *Agents of Witchcraft in Early Modern Italy and Denmark* (Basingstoke, 2015). For the distinctive trials in Finnmark, northern Norway, see Liv Helene Willumsen, *Witches of the North: Scotland and Finnmark* (Leiden, 2013).

America

Attention is usually focused on witch-hunting in the seventeenth-century English colonies in New England. John P. Demos, *Entertaining Satan: Witchcraft and the Culture of Early New England* (Oxford, 1982), is an important book combining narrative, psychological interpretation and social science analysis. Carol F. Karlsen, *The Devil in the Shape of a Woman: Witchcraft in Colonial New England* (New York, 1987), has been influential on the issue of women.

The Salem panic of 1692 is well-documented and much studied. The classic account is Paul Boyer and Stephen Nissenbaum, *Salem Possessed: The Social Origins of Witchcraft* (Cambridge, Mass., 1974), an extremely influential book. Other works on Salem include Bernard Rosenthal, *Salem Story: Reading the Witch Trials of 1692* (Cambridge, 1993); Larry Gragg, *The Salem Witch Crisis* (New York, 1992); Mary B. Norton, *In the Devil's Snare: The Salem Witchcraft Crisis of 1692* (New York, 2002); and Emerson W. Baker, *A Storm of Witchcraft: The Salem Trials and the American Experience* (Oxford, 2014).

The other major European colonies were in Spanish and Portuguese America. Hardly any witches were executed, but for broader issues see Fernando Cervantes, *The Devil in the New World: The Impact of Diabolism in New Spain* (New Haven, Conn., 1994); Andrew Redden, *Diabolism in Colonial Peru, 1560–1750* (London, 2008); and Laura de Mello e Souza, *The Devil and the Land of the Holy Cross: Witchcraft, Slavery, and Popular Religion in Colonial Brazil*, trans. Diane Grosklaus Whitty (Austin, Tex., 2004).

Primary sources

Many primary sources on witchcraft have been published, either in full or in extracts. The main types of source are demonological writings and trial documents. The most remarkable compilation of sources is Henry C. Lea,

Materials Toward a History of Witchcraft, 3 vols., ed. A. C. Howland (Philadelphia, Pa., 1939). This is a collection of extracts, some transcribed in full and others summarised, which is basically Lea's notes for a book he never wrote. It covers all aspects of the subject and has proved a goldmine of information for subsequent scholars, though it can be hard to follow and does not translate everything. More accessibly, there are several modern one-volume collections of primary sources, notably Brian P. Levack (ed.), *The Witchcraft Sourcebook* (2nd edn., London, 2015). For other collections see Alan C. Kors and Edward Peters (eds.), *Witchcraft in Europe, 400–1700: A Documentary History* (2nd edn., Philadelphia, Pa., 2001); P. G. Maxwell-Stuart (ed.), *The Occult in Early Modern Europe: A Documentary History* (Basingstoke, 1999); P. G. Maxwell-Stuart (ed.), *The Occult in Medieval Europe, 500-1500* (Basingstoke, 2005); P. G. Maxwell-Stuart (ed.), *Witch Beliefs and Witch Trials in the Middle Ages: Documents and Readings* (London, 2011); and Elaine G. Breslaw (ed.), *Witches of the Atlantic World: A Historical Reader and Primary Sourcebook* (New York, 2000), which also contains reprints of some modern essays.

For modern scholarly editions of individual demonological works, see *Hammer of Witches: A Complete Translation of the Malleus Maleficarum*, 2 vols., trans. Christopher S. Mackay (Cambridge, 2009; original publication 1486); Johann Weyer, *Witches, Devils, and Doctors in the Renaissance: Johann Weyer, De Praestigiis Daemonum*, trans. John Shea, ed. George Mora (Binghamton, NY, 1991; original publication 1563); Jean Bodin, *On the Demon-mania of Witches*, trans. Randy A. Scott, ed. Jonathan L. Pearl (Toronto, 1995; original publication 1580); Lawrence Normand and Gareth Roberts (eds.), *Witchcraft in Early Modern Scotland: James VI's Demonology and the North Berwick Witches* (Exeter, 2000; *Daemonologie* original publication 1597); Martín Del Rio, *Investigations into Magic*, trans. P. G. Maxwell-Stuart (Manchester, 2000; original publication 1599–1600); Pierre de Lancre, *On the Inconstancy of Witches: Pierre de Lancre's Tableau de l'inconstance des mauvais anges et demons (1612)*, trans. Harriet Stone, ed. Gerhild Scholz Williams (Tempe, Ariz., 2006; original publication 1612); Friedrich Spee von Langenfeld, *Cautio Criminalis, or a Book on Witch Trials*, trans. Marcus Hellyer (Charlottesville, Va., 2003; original publication 1631); and Christian Thomasius, 'On the crime of sorcery', in his *Essays on Church, State, and Politics*, ed. Ian Hunter, Thomas Ahnert and Frank Grunert (Indianapolis, Ind., 2007; original publication 1701). Finally, mention should be made of Jean-Pierre Coumont, *Demonology and Witchcraft: An Annotated Bibliography: With Related Works on Magic, Medicine, Superstition, &c* (Utrecht, 2005), a detailed list of relevant books from the dawn of printing up to modern times. It is particularly useful for its careful lists of editions of early modern demonological works.

Appendix
Intensity of witch-hunting in Europe

This appendix gives basic statistical information about rates of execution for witchcraft in early modern Europe. It supplements the map by tabulating and explaining the data on which it is based.

The table, below, lists the main countries of Europe, showing the numbers of executions and the population in 1600. Dividing the first figure by the second one provides a simple measure of the intensity of witch-hunting in the country concerned. The overall average comes out as just below 0.5 executions per thousand of population in 1600 – which should not, of course, be taken to imply that all the executed witches lived in 1600. An individual country can thus be categorised in relation to that average figure.

The right-hand column of the table shows which of five categories each country has been placed in: Extreme (2.0 or over), Intense (between 0.8 and 1.99), Average (between 0.3 and 0.79), Moderate (between 0.1 and 0.29) and Mild (below 0.1). These categories, and the figures behind them, provide a way of comparing different countries. For instance, Switzerland, in the 'Extreme' category with 3.5 executions per thousand of population in 1600, executed 66 times more witches *per capita* than France, in the 'Mild' category with 0.053 executions per thousand of population in 1600. Looked at another way, Switzerland's execution rate was seven times the European average, whereas France's was one-tenth of that average.

Intensity of witch-hunting in European countries

Country	Executions	Population (millions) 1600	Rate per capita 0/00	Category
Austria	1,900	2.0	0.95	Intense
Bohemia	400	2.3	0.174	Moderate
Denmark	240	0.58	0.414	Average
England	500	4.4	0.114	Moderate
English colonies	40	0.094	0.426	Average

Appendix 411

Country	Executions	Population (millions) 1600	Rate per capita 0/00	Category
Estonia	50	0.06	0.833	Intense
Finland	70	0.4	0.175	Moderate
France	1,000	19.0	0.053	Mild
Franche-Comté	400	0.4	1.0	Intense
Germany	27,500	16.0	1.72	Intense
Hungary	1,110	4.4	0.252	Moderate
Iceland	22	0.05	0.44	Average
Ireland	8	1.4	0.006	Mild
Italy	546	13.1	0.042	Mild
Lorraine	1,600	0.3	5.33	Extreme
Luxembourg	1,600	0.3	5.33	Extreme
Norway	330	0.44	0.75	Average
Poland	2,000	3.4	0.588	Average
Portugal	4	1.1	0.004	Mild
Russia	200	12.0	0.017	Mild
Savoy	900	0.88	1.023	Intense
Scotland	2,500	1.0	2.5	Extreme
Slovenia	265	0.3	0.883	Intense
Spanish Netherlands	250	1.6	0.156	Moderate
Spain	300	8.1	0.037	Mild
Sweden	400	1.0	0.4	Average
Switzerland	3,500	1.0	3.5	Extreme
Transylvania	20	0.67	0.03	Mild
United Netherlands	150	1.5	0.1	Moderate
TOTAL	47,805	97.774	0.489	

Source: Based initially on Richard M. Golden, 'Satan in Europe: the geography of witch hunts', in Michael Wolfe (ed.), *Changing Identities in Early Modern France* (Durham, NC, 1997), 216–47, updated with reference to other sources, particularly *Encyclopedia*.

The table omits the Balkan states, and the Spanish and Portuguese colonies, because they had no executions. However, it does include the English colonies, although they are not on the map.

Not all these countries were fully independent. Some were ruled by other countries or politically joined to them. For instance, Estonia and Finland were ruled by Sweden, Norway and Iceland were ruled by Denmark, and Naples was ruled by Spain, as was Portugal for part of our period. However, the components of these multiple monarchies retained their own identity. The areas called 'Germany' and 'Italy' were not single states, but conglomerations of autonomous territories of widely-varying size and (especially in Germany) with different intensity of witch-hunting. In future it would be desirable to disaggregate the figures for 'Germany' and 'Italy'.

Some of the figures for individual countries are best-estimate figures (for instance those for Germany and Scotland), attempting to take account of missing data or incomplete research. Others are minimum figures (for instance those for Italy and Russia), where data are probably missing but there is no reliable way of estimating how much, at least in the current state of research. The figure for Poland is an example of a hybrid: a best estimate of a minimum. Best-estimate figures should aim to avoid the exaggerated estimates that have sometimes been circulated in the past. Ideally we would want a sense of how reliable a given estimate is, and perhaps a range of possible figures. As for minimum figures, they are less than ideal because they do not even attempt to show the full extent of witch-hunting; in future it would be desirable to replace them with best-estimate figures if this could be done without distortion.

Because some of the figures are minimums, the overall total of 47,805 should be recognised as an underestimate. Its appearance of precision is also misleading, since many of the figures that have gone into it (including that for Germany, making up over half the total) have no such precision. Elsewhere in this book, the figure of 50,000 is used as a best-estimate figure for the overall number of executions in Europe.

The figure for 'English colonies' comprises the two colonies where witchcraft executions occurred: New England and Bermuda. These colonies existed for less than half of the witch-hunting period, and their population is given as it was in 1700 rather than 1600 (it would have been nil in 1600). This has not been taken into account in calculating their intensity of witch-hunting, but it could be noted that their average intensity *per year* was over twice the figure given here.

When data are presented country by country, this tends to give the impression that 'countries' were what mattered. Countries did matter, but so did regions within countries. Especially within the larger countries, executions were unevenly distributed, often being concentrated in smaller regions; the data as presented cannot show this. A related problem is that countries were different sizes. France, the most populous country, had nearly four hundred times the population of Iceland, the least populous. In comparing the two, we are not comparing like with like.

Figures for executions do not tell the whole story of the European witch-hunt. In Italy, Spain and Portugal, for instance, the Inquisition punished large numbers of people for superstitious magic that was sometimes regarded similarly to witchcraft. Few were executed, but these people should not be ignored altogether just because they escaped with their lives. Some countries, such as England, had high acquittal rates in trials for actual witchcraft; those who were acquitted do not show up in these figures either. Ultimately, statistics can help us to explain witch-hunting, but they will never capture the full range of experience that witch-hunting represented for the people of early modern Europe.

Index

People who wrote about or depicted witchcraft or demonology are denoted by '(d)'; other early modern intellectuals and writers are denoted by '(i)'; neighbours or accusers of witches are denoted by '(n)'; modern scholars are denoted by '(s)'; people accused of witchcraft are denoted by '(w)'.

Aberdeenshire 103
Aberle, Jung (n) 305
Abundia 142
accomplices 16, 151, 162, 230, 235
Acre 37
Ada, Catharina (w) 99
Adamites 171
Adamo, Laura de (w) 211
Adeline, Guillaume (w) 46
adolescents 295, 308–9, 372
Africa 4, 352, 370, 376–8, 382, 384; African slaves 174, 175
Agrippa, Cornelius (d) 63, 278
alchemy 64, 170, 335
Alciati, Andrea (d) 80–1
Alençon 248–9
Alessandra (n) 107
Alexander V, pope 31
aliens 140, 146–7
Alps 39, 40–2, 45, 47, 179, 215
Alsace 23, 98, 268, 294, 304, 308
Alumbrados 332
Amadeus VIII, duke of Savoy 40
Amazonia 143
America 173–6, 408 (further reading); native Americans 140, 173, 174–5, 362; *see also* United States of America
Amnesty International 390
Anabaptists 170–1, 185, 280, 333
anatomy 335

Angelica (w) 107
angels 56, 57, 127, 129, 140, 299, 337, 344
anger *see* fear and anger
Angus, earls of 239–40
animism 125–6 (text box)
anthropology 1, 4, 361, 367, 370–2, 375–6
Anyo, Jeannette (w) 213
Apafy, Mihály, prince of Transylvania 239
Aquinas, St Thomas (d) 60–1, 69–71, 80, 302, 336
Aragon 218, 253, 284, 287
Arctic 200, 386
Arians 33
Aristotle, Aristotelianism 60–1, 64, 79–80, 335–7, 338
Armenians 392
Arras 47, 284, 323–4, 386
Artois 254
Asten 326
astrology 64, 338
atheism 332–3
Atlantic 174, 319
atrocities 206, 385, 387
atropine 145
Aubremant, Antoine (w) 299
Augsburg 349
Augustine, St (d) 59, 68–9
Auldearn 143
Austria 29, 85, 140, 195, 240, 262–3, 294, 349–50, 380; *see also* Carinthia
auto da fe 15
Avignon 38, 84
Aymery, Huguet (w) 323

baba-iaga 134
bacchanalia 173

Bacqué, Jean-Jacques (n) 325
Baden 14, 16, 150
Bain, Margaret (w) 103
Bald Mountain 136, 383
Baldung Grien, Hans (d) 296 (illustration 9.1), 297
Balkans 86, 192, 362
Balli, Nicolas (n) 290
Ballini, Pierre (w) 113
Baltic states 158
Bamberg 85, 162, 180, 210–11, 237, 238–9, 242, 324; witch house 234 (illustration 8.1), 239
Banda, Hastings 377
Barcelona 203
Bardaxi, Juana (w) 284
Barnes, Elizabeth (n) 109
Baroque 83
Basel 285, 301–2; Council of 45
Basque country 152, 174, 212, 215–16; *see also* Labourd; Navarre
Bavaria 178, 183, 247
Bazuel 201, 248
bean-casting 287
Béarn 247, 295, 348, 351
beggars 94–5, 251, 284–5, 294, 308; *see also* refusal-guilt syndrome
Behringer, Wolfgang (s) 242
Bekker, Balthasar (d) 344–5
Béldy, Pál 239
belief, nature of 2–3, 82 (text box), 116–17 (text box), 124–5
benandanti 142–3, 371
Benevento 136
Bermuda 175, 200
Bernadino of Siena (d) 39–40, 45
Bern 260
Berry 115–16, 301
Besançon 348
Besançon, Jean (w) 113
Bettenfeld 96
Bever, Edward (s) 101, 373
Bible 5, 18, 58, 59, 61, 67–8, 69, 82, 158, 190–1, 262, 333; and Reformation 164; *see also* Lord's Prayer; Ten Commandments
Binsfeld, Peter (d) 74, 85, 214, 294, 326
birds 138; *see also* chickens; pelicans
Bisa, Diamante de (w) 169
Blå Jungfrun 136
Black Death 35, 146, 243, 281
blacksmiths 144, 261, 279–80
Blåkulla 136, 210, 258–9
Blankenstein, Chatrina (w) 104

Blocksberg 75 (illustration 3.2), 133, 136
blood-sucking 174; *see also* children, blood-sucking
Bocage 18–19
Bocheński, Andrzej (w) 309
Bochet, Claude (w) 215
Bodenham, Anne (w) 195
Bodin, Jean (d) 62, 86, 155, 226, 279, 304–5; and law 202; and sabbat 74, 173; in controversy 81, 182, 270, 340; translations 74, 162
Boguet, Henri (d) 62, 82, 163, 208, 247, 294, 308, 339
Bohemia 40
bone miracle 141
Bora, Katharina von 271
Bordelon, Laurent (d) 346, 347
Bosnian War 332
Boston 342
Bothwell, earl of (w) 239–40, 279
Bouchain 247
Bouillon 244
Bouvignies 105, 290
Boyle, Robert (i) 339
Brahe, Tycho (i) 335
Braunsberg 150
Brazil 173, 174
Bregenz 163
Brevet, Claudine (w) 291–2
Briggs, Robin (s) 249–50, 255, 370–1
British Isles 194; *see also* England; Ireland; Scotland; Wales
Brocken *see* Blocksberg
Brome, Richard (d) 346
broomsticks 45, 78, 137, 298, 334, 344, 364, 382; *see also* cooking-sticks
Browne, Sir Thomas (i) 60
Bruges 170
Brzeżański, Stanisław (d) 167
bubonic plague 97, 146, 251; *see also* Black Death
Buda 136
bufotenin 145
Bugs Bunny 212
Burg 96
Burgau 262
Burgundian Netherlands 47, 323–4
Burnett, John (n) 103
Burns, Robert 383
Burritaz, Claude (n) 248
Burroughs, George (w) 279
Bury St Edmunds 201
Byser, Urban (w) 150

416 Index

Calabria, Felipa la (w) 14, 15 (illustration 1.1)
Calahorra 293
calendar rituals *see* equinox; Hallowe'en; St John's Eve; St Walpurgis Eve
Calvin, John 164; Calvinism 162, 164, 170
Cambrésis 242, 303
Cambridge Platonists 338–9
camels 138
Cameroon 376
Canary Islands 134, 138, 151, 211, 215, 349
cannibalism 7, 173; *see also* children, eating of
Canon *Episcopi* 71–3, 141, 144
Carinthia 211, 285, 294
carnival 169–70
Carolina code 189, 190, 205, 216, 219, 326–7
Carpzov, Benedict (i) 328
Cartesianism 337, 340, 345
Castañega, Martín de (d) 278
Catalonia 218
Cathars 33–5, 365
Catholic church 33, 59, 336, 364, 369; papacy 156, 331
cats 131, 139, 146, 299, 334, 382, 386; shape-shifting into 109, 117, 135, 138, 147
cauldrons 295, 297–8
cauls 143
Cavalinhos, Val de 136
Celestina 84
Celts 371
Chaderton, Laurence (d) 166–7
chain-reaction witch-hunts 50, 53, 195, 205, 219, 328, 377, 380, 392; and gender 269, 290; in specific places 225, 245, 249, 319; and nature of panics 229–31, 235, 236–8, 246; criticism of 249, 327; proportion of executions in 116, 118, 225, 250; *see also* accomplices
Chamonix 218
Champagne-Ardennes 242
Chandler, R. (n) 195
changelings 130
Channel Islands 93, 218, 268–9; *see also* Guernsey; Jersey
Chanoz, Pierre dou (w) 299
Chaponey, Barbelline (w) 308
charivari 170, 306

Charles V, Holy Roman Emperor 190
Charles, duke of Gelderland 246
Chauderon, Michée (w) 319, 363
Chavaz, Pierre (w) 127, 211
Chelmsford 233
Cherkes 176
Cherry Tree Carol 126
Chiari, Giulio (i) 328
chickens 91, 131
child abuse 231, 378; alleged Satanic abuse 390–1
children 103, 105, 107, 121–2, 165, 213, 216, 269, 289, 308, 309; abduction to sabbat 135, 152, 201, 258, 306; as accusers of witches 152, 258–9, 292; as victim-witches 292–5; blood-sucking 40, 65, 134, 215, 292; childbirth 166, 275, 277, 285, 287; death of 12, 98, 104, 122, 169, 212, 218, 248, 291, 304; demonic offspring 69, 135; eating of 10, 11, 12, 39, 42, 45, 53, 64–5, 76, 78, 134, 135, 143, 211, 281, 299; host as child 163; in modern Africa 378; stealing of 10, 11, 77, 78, 134; stories for 24, 124, 129, 133, 346–7; unbaptised babies 12, 127, 166; *see also* adolescents; changelings; child abuse; infanticide; Jews, blood libel; midwives; sabbat, abduction to
Chouet, Robert 363
Christian IV, king of Denmark 246
Christianity 2, 31, 32–3, 58, 126–8, 337, 338, 364; *see also* Catholic church; heresy; Orthodox church; Pentecostalism; Reformation and Counter-Reformation
chronology of witch-hunting 27–8, 30, 38, 39–48, 51–3, 74, 85–6, 157, 163–4, 170–1, 179, 193; and prosecution of children 292–5; *see also* decline of witch-hunting; panics, chronology of; panics, decline of
church courts 49, 96, 109, 167, 189, 190, 284
churchyards and burials 134, 218
Circe (w) 84
Ciruelo, Pedro (d) 81, 243
Clark, Stuart (s) 372
Cohen, Stanley (s) 232, 247
Collit, Priscilla (w) 308
Cologne 23, 179, 180–1, 239, 247, 327, 386

comets 61, 335
Condé-sur-Noireau 291–2
Condurier alias Chaillot, Jacques (w) 105
confessions 7, 80–1, 85, 124, 136, 208–16, 240; *see also* memory; repentance; torture
conspiracy *see* demonic witchcraft; heresy
Constantine, Donation of 158
constitutionalism 160–2, 330
cooking-sticks 78, 137, 139, 215, 296–7 (illustration 9.1), 382
Cooper, Thomas (d) 163
Copernicus, Nicholas (i) 55, 79, 336
Corsica 143–4
Cosme (w) 211
cosmos, structure of 55–6, 79, 335–6
counter-magic 89, 90, 111–13, 117, 134, 376
Counter-Reformation *see* Reformation and Counter-Reformation
courts *see* church courts; criminal courts; Inquisition
crafts 144
Cranach, Lucas, the elder (d) 138–9, 298
Creed 200–1
crimen exceptum see exceptional crime
criminal courts 49, 52, 167–9, 189, 191, 261, 347, 402 (further reading); accusatorial and inquisitorial procedure 194; costs and profits of trials 216–17; judicial caution 318, 322–7, 352–5; local courts 156, 164, 324–6; miscarriages of justice 220–1, 318, 388–9; professionalisation of 185; *see also* evidence; exceptional crime; imprisonment; interrogations; judges; lawyers; punishments; sentences; trial records; verdicts
Croatia 143, 268
Cross, Goody (w) 308
Crusades 33; *see also* Templars
cults 125, 136, 140–5, 361; *see also benandanti; donas de fuera; kresniki; mazzeri;* seely wights; *táltos; vilenicas; zduhačs*
cunning folk 24
Cunningham, John 86
Curran, Jonathan 216
curses 17, 92–3, 99–101, 110, 373; and gender 49–50, 285–6, 308, 388; identifying witches through 12–13, 14, 52, 95
Cyrano de Bergerac, Savinien (d) 343

Dadd, Helen (w) 114–15
Daneau, Lambert (d) 62
Danielsdatter, Bodill (w) 206
Dauphiné 40, 47
David, Catherine (w) 277
Davies, Owen (s) 351
deadly nightshade 145
deathbed speeches 115
decline of witch-hunting 317–56, 404 (further reading); *see also* scepticism
Deffontaines, Denis (w) 290
Deffontaines, Marie (n) 105
Delaware 176
Delrio, Martin (d) 73, 85–6, 129, 203, 339; in controversy 162, 183, 214, 338, 340, 364
Delvaux, Jean (w) 85
demonic pact 3, 10, 24, 70 (illustration 3.1), 88, 140, 163, 167, 219, 300 (illustration 9.2), 303, 385; explicit and implicit pact 71; folkloric pacts 127, 128–9, 131, 150; in confessions 194, 198, 208, 213–14, 215, 280–1, 298–9; in demonology 14, 48, 51–2, 63, 67, 77 (diagram 3.1), 199, 275, 278, 293, 310, 340, 355, 362; in panics 13, 235, 268–9; origin of 37, 38, 39–40, 44; real pacts 145, 288, 309, 350
demonic possession 181, 238, 306–7, 348–9, 369, 378; *see also* exorcism; spectral evidence
demonic witchcraft, definition of 10, 12, 13, 50–3, 77 (diagram 3.1), 310, 375
demonology 7–8, 55–87, 173–4, 214–15, 372, 400 (further reading), 409 (further reading); decline of 339–45 (text box); development of 39–53, 399–400 (further reading); *see also* cannibalism; demonic pact; demonic witchcraft; Devil; divine permission; flight by witches; impotence and infertility; providence; sabbat; storms
demons 12, 43, 56, 90, 111, 174, 337; appearance of 139, 211, 299, 383; fairies seen as 123 (illustration 5.1); hierarchy of 85; Island of Demons 173; noon-tide demon 134; personal demons 131
Demos, John (s) 372
Denmark 86, 131, 195, 246, 249, 324
Descartes, René (i) 337, 343, 344, 345; *see also* Cartesianism

418 *Index*

Devil 9, 12, 13, 24, 387–8; and godly state 157, 159–62, 168, 256; appearance of 128, 200, 299; decline of fear of 318, 330, 350, 355–6; folklore about 123–4, 127–9, 130; powers of 5, 56, 67–71, 74, 208, 230, 344–5, 389; sex with 7, 50, 74, 127, 210, 284, 298–303, 308; *see also* demonic pact; demonic possession; demons; Devil's mark; Satan
Devil's mark 62, 77, 199, 261, 305; *see also* pricking
Diana 71–2, 141, 144, 297
Dietherich, Susanna (w) 212
Dieudegnon, Claude (n) 104–5
Dieuze 279
Dillingen 218, 299
Dirette-Baringou, Anne-Marie (w) 351
Dishypatos, Michael (w) 40
Disney, Walt 383; Disneyland 212
divine permission 8, 9, 49, 69, 77, 243, 342
divine right of kings 159–62, 184, 329, 330
dogs 131, 138, 143, 150
Dôle, *parlement* of 247
Domen 136
donas de fuera 127, 141–2, 143, 380
Dornhan 249
Drage, William (d) 86, 340
Draguignan 277
dreams 209, 350; *see also* nightmares
dreng 131
Dufosset, Marie-Anne (w) 105
Duncan, Geillis (w) 239
Dürer, Albrecht (d) 297

East Anglia 172, 240, 247, 320
East Barns 98
Echiverria, Juana de (w) 306
Echiverria, María de (w) 306
economics 4; *see also* village economy
Eden, Garden of 56, 68; *see also* Eve
Edinburgh 253
education 12, 184, 298, 350, 351; *see also* literacy; printing; universities
Eggers, Anna (w) 96
Eichstätt 180, 208–9, 216, 225, 237, 244
Elben 131
Elgorriaga 306
elite, definition of 24–6, 250–1; *see also* local elites; rich peasants

Ellwangen 180–1, 213
Ellwein, Michael 291
elves 123 (illustration 5.1), 344; elf-arrows 144
emotions 230, 272, 372; *see also* envy; fantasy; fear and anger; greed; jealousy; lust; melancholy; psychology; refusal-guilt syndrome; repentance; trauma; vengefulness
England 23, 29, 40, 86, 250, 252, 270, 284, 303, 370–1, 406–7 (further reading); Civil War and Revolution 171, 172, 240; courts in 7, 172, 195, 200, 201, 218, 240, 247–8, 305; decline of prosecutions 320–1; familiars in 131, 382; individual cases in 114–15, 233, 276, 304, 308; later beliefs in 351; Reformation in 158, 163, 166–7; refusal-guilt syndrome in 88, 95; *see also* East Anglia; English colonies; Essex; Lancashire
English colonies 7, 29, 175; *see also* Bermuda; Massachusetts; New England; Salem; Virginia
Enlightenment 329, 346, 350, 364–5
enthusiasm 333
envisioned witchcraft, definition of 10, 11, 13, 149 (diagram 5.2), 375
envy 112, 282, 289, 341, 372
Enzensbergerin, Anna (w) 108
Epicurus 79
epidemics 32, 97; *see also* Black Death
equinox 137
Erasmus (i) 79
Erastus, Thomas (d) 81
ergotism 369
Ernberg, Erik Olsson (w) 350
Errores Gazariorum 46, 47
Escuder, Margalida (w) 284
Essex 102; earl of 347
Esslingen 242
Estonia 267–8
Evans-Pritchard, Edward (s) 370
Eve 272, 344–5, 368
evidence 197–201; *see also* confessions; deathbed speeches; Devil's mark; tears, inability to shed; reputations; spectral evidence; swimming test; witnesses
evil eye 99, 112, 199, 272
Evreux 46
exceptional crime 202 (text box)
executions 16 (illustration 1.2), 216, 217–20, 261–2; decline of death

penalty 329; executioners 210, 219–20, 261, 305; *see also* lynchings of witches
exorcism 36, 306–7, 344, 348

Faguet, Rodolphe 324
fairies 11, 13, 102, 123, 130–1, 140, 150, 209; fairy-tales 24, 347, 367; fairy cults 65, 141–2; *see also* changelings
familiars 131, 218, 233
fantasy 3, 34, 209, 293, 301, 305, 307–8, 373, 385
Farinacci, Prospero (i) 328
farming *see* peasants; village economy
fate women 132
fauns 298
Faust, Dr (w) 278, 367
fear and anger 229–30, 232, 236, 241, 282, 372–3, 374–5, 389–90; *see also* Devil, decline of fear of
Fessler, Anna (n) 114
feuds 95–6, 106
Feugeyron, Ponce (d) 31, 41–2, 44–5, 47
Ficino, Marsilio (i) 63–4
Field, Elizabeth (n) 247–8
Fiertayka, Zofia (w) 308
Finland 95, 176, 268
Finnmark 86, 150, 177, 200, 206
Fischart, Johann (d) 74
Flade, Diederich (w) 85, 239
Flanders 254
flight by witches 4–5, 7, 8, 38, 40, 61, 80, 297; in confessions 137, 143–4, 209, 211; in demonology 43 (illustration 2.1), 45, 51, 67, 71–3 (text box), 74, 77–8, 86, 295; in popular belief 11, 135, 136–9 (text box), 149–50, 373; *see also* cooking-sticks; ointments and powders; sleep paralysis; spirit voyages
Flower, Joan (w) 218
folkloric witchcraft, definition of 10, 11, 17, 135 (diagram 5.1), 375, 401–2 (further reading)
folktales 24, 128–9, 347; folktale witches 133–5, 143
Forfar 201
Förner, Friedrich (d) 162, 238–9
Francavilla Fontana 211
France 29, 249, 252, 270, 380, 405 (further reading); beliefs in 133, 278, 297–8, 303; courts in 194, 205;
decline of prosecutions 324–6, 332, 341, 350, 351; Edict of Nantes 331–2; individual cases in 277, 290; law code 190; medieval prosecutions 36, 37, 39; religious wars 158, 172, 182; state structure 156, 177, 178; *see also* Béarn; Berry; Bocage; Champagne-Ardennes; Dauphiné; Gascony; Guyenne; Loudun; Normandy; Paris
Francesco, Matteuccia di (w) 40, 136
Franche-Comté 29, 138, 200, 203, 247, 348; individual cases in 137, 285–6, 294, 308–9; *see also* Boguet, Henri
Franconia 253
fraudulent accusations 114–15, 385
Frérot, Isabeau (w) 208
Freud, Sigmund (s) 372
Fribourg 41, 299
Friesland 326
Friuli 142, 143
Fründ, Hans (d) 42, 44–5, 47
Fuchs von Dornheim, Johann Georg 234
Furetière, Antoine (d) 344, 345

Gabler, Paul 237
Gackstatt, Leonhard (n) 96
Galileo (i) 31, 335, 336
galleys, as punishment 292, 329
Galt, Maud (w) 302
Gappit, Perrissone (w) 289–90
Gardiner, Jean (w) 200
Gardner, Gerald 368
Gascony 46
Gaudry, Suzanne (w) 205
Gebsattel 308
Geiler, Johannes (d) 23, 73
Gelderland 95, 246
Geneva 97, 105, 150, 162, 253, 319, 363
geography of witch-hunting 28–9 (map), 30, 176–9, 225, 252–3, 319–21, 361–3, 380, 410–13
Gerlingen 215
Germany 9, 175, 251, 252, 276, 366, 405 (further reading); beliefs in 75, 85, 131, 133, 136, 303, 345, 361, 362; courts in 194, 195, 197, 200; decline of prosecutions 319, 322, 324, 351; individual cases in 104, 105, 212, 218, 299, 308; Nazi research group 369; neighbourhood panics in 231, 240–1;

political fragmentation of 29, 156, 172, 176–9, 239, 257; prince-bishoprics 180–1 (text box), 183, 234; printing industry in 245, 297; Reformation and Counter-Reformation in 158, 163, 165, 168, 171, 172; rise of prosecutions 45–6; scale of witch-hunting in 29, 176–9, 241, 268, 284; *see also* Augsburg; Austria; Baden; Bamberg; Bavaria; Cologne; Eichstätt; Ellwangen; Franconia; Holstein; Holy Roman Empire; Langenburg; Liège; Mainz; Nördlingen; Palatinate; Rhine-Moselle region; Rothenburg ob der Tauber; Rottenburg; St Maximin; Saxony; Schleswig; Swabia; Trier; Wiesensteig; Württemberg; Würzburg
Gerson, Jean (d) 39
Ghana 376
ghosts 13, 63, 123, 132–3, 150, 383; *see also* revenants; vampires
giants 11, 123, 143, 344
Gifford, George (d) 88, 97
Ginzburg, Carlo (s) 371
Girault, Etienne (w) 301
Glanvill, Joseph (d) 338–9
Glarus 320, 321–2 (text box), 386
global perspectives 13, 30, 173–6, 352, 371, 375–81
Glöckner, Valerius 129
goats 43 (illustration 2.1), 75 (illustration 3.2), 136, 137, 139, 151, 297–8, 344
goblins 130, 133
Godelmann, Johann Georg (d) 129
godly state *see* Reformation and Counter-Reformation; state formation
Goethe, Johann 367
Göldi, Anna (w) 320, 321–2 (text box), 348, 386
Good, Sarah (w) 201, 216, 291
Good, William (n) 291
Gowdie, Isobel (w) 143–4
Goya, Francisco (d) 364
Grady, Mother (w) 176
Grandier, Urbain (w) 70, 71, 348
grapes 241, 242
Greece 86, 362
greed 267
Grelant, Jean (w) 218
Grevius, Johannes (d) 328–9

Grimm, Jacob (s) 367
grimoires 278
Grotius, Hugo (i) 330
Grouville 380
Guaccio, Francesco Maria (d) 83, 148, 339
Guadeloupe 376, 381 (text box)
Guernsey 218
Gui, Bernard (d) 36
Günzburg 262
Guthrie, Helen (w) 210
Guyenne 295

Haan, Georg (w) 238–9
Habsburgs 380
hailstorms *see* storms
Hainaut 254
Hallowe'en 136, 383, 386
hallucinations 145–6, 369, 373; hallucinogenic drugs 145, 341, 369
Hamelin, Pied Piper of 339
Hansen, Joseph (s) 65
hares 129, 138
harmful magic 17, 32, 100 (illustration 4.1), 371–2, 374–5, 384; and 'new sect' of witches 44–7, 52–3; and poisoning 23; relationship with demonic conspiracy 35–6, 38–9, 362; *see also* malefice
Harz Mountains 136
Hathorne, John 216
Hauldecoeur, Anne (w) 294
Hausmännin, Walpurga (w) 218, 299
heaven 56–7, 61, 122, 212, 218, 309
Heemskerk, Johan van (d) 344
hell 56–7, 61, 122, 211, 218
Hellequin 132–3
henbane 145
Henot, Katharina (w) 239, 386
Henry IV, king of France 182
heresy 10, 23, 33–5, 40–1, 77, 139, 280, 330, 361; heretics' alleged horrifying rites 34, 36, 37, 39, 46, 47, 51–2, 171; *see also* Adamites; Arians; Cathars; Hussites; Lollards; Luciferians; 'new sect' of witches; Waldensians
Hermes Trismegistus 63–4
Herod Antipas 142
Herodias 142
Hertford 247–8
Hertner von Riehen, Elsbeth (w) 301–2
Hewat, Isobel (w) 210
Heywood, Thomas (d) 346

Himmler, Heinrich 369
Hobbes, Thomas (d) 331
Hogarth, William (d) 333, 334 (illustration 10.1)
Hogbin, Thomas (n) 114–15
Hohenberg 195
Holden 131
Holl, Maria (w) 206, 207, 213
Holland 268, 344, 347
Holstein 279, 286, 289, 291
Holy Roman Empire 156, 160, 190, 207, 216, 239, 324
homosexuality 34, 37, 301–2; *see also* sodomy
Hoogstraten, Jacob van (d) 23
Hopkins, Matthew (d) 97, 247, 384–5
Hörber, Margaretha (w) 308
Horn, Margaretha (w) 96
horses 138, 143, 279
Horst, Gerhard de 240
Hös, Anna (n) 148
Houffalize 207
Hougham 114–15
human and non-human witches 11, 133–5; *see also* folktale witches; legendary witches; night witches
human nature 1, 125, 366–7; *see also* psychology
Hungary 158, 172, 319, 407 (further reading); beliefs in 131, 136, 143, 149; courts in 194, 207–8
Hupricht, Treyn (w) 206
Hussites 40
Hutton, Ronald (s) 371

Iceland 138, 268, 286
idolatry 168, 173
illness and disease 12, 32, 61, 76, 96–9, 122, 281; mental illness 210, 307–9; *see also* epidemics; impotence and infertility; physicians; trauma
image-magic 99–101, 200
impotence and infertility 38, 42, 215, 304–5
imprisonment 205–6, 207, 216, 234 (illustration 8.1), 261–2, 329
Incas 175
incubus and succubus 69, 134, 147, 302
India 379
Indonesia 378–9
infanticide 219, 284, 309
Ingolstadt 183
Inich, Diederich (w) 105
Innsbruck 48, 49, 85

Inquisition 34–6, 39, 49, 52, 114, 192, 287, 349; and Counter-Reformation 164–5; Roman 7, 192, 287, 325, 361, 365; Portuguese 171, 361, 365; Spanish 15, 171, 293, 350, 361–2, 365
insects 131, 138, 382
interrogations 13, 14, 16–17, 130, 147; leading questions 198, 204–5, 212, 214, 215, 221, 387; *see also* confessions
inversion 60, 74
Ireland 37–8, 39, 131, 181–2 (text box), 322; Northern Ireland 332
Islandmagee 181
Italy 31, 45, 114, 158, 172, 252, 253, 278, 362, 406 (further reading); beliefs in 102, 134, 136, 142, 143, 175, 230, 287, 292, 301; courts in 7, 194, 328; early prosecutions 39–40; decline of prosecutions 319, 322; individual cases in 107, 128–9, 211, 215; political fragmentation 156, 178–9; *see also* Friuli; Inquisition, Roman; Lucca; Modena; Naples; Sicily; Siena; Venice

Jacquier, Nicolas (d) 46, 47
James VI, king of Scotland (d) 85, 160, 161 (illustration 6.1), 231, 239–40, 242
Japan 174
jealousy 112, 304, 378, 381, 384–5
Jersey 93, 206, 218, 380
Jesuits 158, 173, 182, 325, 327, 336, 339
Jesus 5, 56, 68, 126, 213; mentioning name of 127, 137
Jews 14, 32, 33, 44, 67–8, 125, 248, 326; alleged conspiracies by 31, 35, 163, 185, 281, 369; blood libel 171, 283; *conversos* 171, 362; Nazi Holocaust 387, 390, 392
jinns 380, 381
Joan of Arc 44
Job 67–8
John XXII, pope 36
Josiah 159
judges 83, 117, 156, 160, 182, 204, 231, 379; as demonologists 85; individual judges 42, 62, 183, 215, 247, 249, 324, 363
Junius, Johannes (w) 210–11, 237, 239
juries *see* verdicts

422 Index

Karin the Finnish woman (w) 176
Karl, margrave of Burgau 262
Käserin, Ann (w) 208–9, 215
Kaspar von der Leyen, Karl 326
Kenn, Bernard of (w) 279
kikimora 131
Kilbarchan 302
Kilkenny 38
king's evil 160
Kiskunhalas 148
Knadel, Margarete (w) 96
Knapiusz, Grzegorz (d) 134
Knox, John (i) 270
kolduny 110
Korytkowo 308
Krämer, Heinrich (d) 48–50, 66, 72, 85, 270, 302: *see also Malleus Maleficarum*
kresniki 143
Kyteler, Alice (w) 37–8, 39

Labourd 177, 220
Labrador 173
Lageret, Jean (w) 40
Lamarque, Marie de 348
lamiae 64–5, 134, 137
Lancashire 176, 320, 346
Lancre, Pierre de (d) 55, 62, 67, 72, 84, 85, 174, 220, 278, 339
Lanechin, Marie (w) 201
Langenburg 114
Langjahr, Agnes (w) 99
Larner, Christina (s) 370
Lasse the Finn (w) 176
Latvia 143
Lausanne 41, 213, 215, 248, 280–1 (text box), 299
law codes 65, 137; *see also Carolina code*
laws on witchcraft 190–1, 322
lawyers 180, 201, 214, 216, 252, 318, 340, 368; defence lawyers 98, 197, 261; individual lawyers 247
Laymann, Paul (d) 339–40
Le Franc, Martin (d) 42, 44–5, 47–8
Le Poyne, Françoise (w) 248–9
Lea, Henry Charles (s) 364–5
learned magicians 63, 278, 298, 310; *see also* Neoplatonism
Ledrede, Richard 38, 39
leg brace 203
Legasa, Juanes de (n) 306
legendary witches 133–5, 143
Lent 170

Leonardo da Vinci (i) 31
lepers 14, 34, 35
Levack, Brian (s) 250
liberal tradition 360, 363–6, 369–70, 372
lidérc 131
Liège 85
Lièpvre, val de 98, 268
ligatures 304–5
Lincoln 304
Lindau 163
Lisbon 136
literacy 114, 164, 256, 288
Lithuanians 176; Lithuania *see* Poland-Lithuania
Livingstone, David 384
lizards 131, 215
Łobżenica 200
local elites 228, 236–7, 247–8, 256–7, 262–3, 363, 376
Logroño 101
Lollards 40
London 254, 308
Lord's Prayer 200–1
Lorraine 29, 62, 131, 133, 151, 225, 247, 317, 370–1, 405 (further reading); individual cases in 104–5, 106, 279; slander in 289; torture in 206; witnesses in 290; women and men in 291
Loudun 174, 344, 348; *see also* Grandier, Urbain
Loue, river 137
love magic 21, 84, 287–8, 310
Lucca 178, 287
Lucerne 47, 280–1 (text box), 285
Luciferians 41
Lugrezia (w) 99–101
lust 272, 301–2
Luther, Martin (d) 129, 158, 162, 270–1
Luxembourg 29, 195, 206, 207, 208, 240, 244, 319
Luxeuil 203
Lymousin, Romble (n) 115–16
lynchings of witches 113, 155, 231, 249, 388
Lyon 45, 245
Lyon, Jean (w) 240

Macarella, Antonia 128–9
Macbeth 132
Macedonia 380
Macfarlane, Alan (s) 95, 370
Machiavelli, Niccolò (i) 331

Mackenzie, Sir George (i) 328
Madrid 182
magic, definition of 19–22, 121–2; *see also* counter-magic; harmful magic; learned magicians; love magic; magical practitioners; Neoplatonism; protective magic
magical practitioners 14, 23, 89, 102–3 (text box), 108, 286, 349–50, 368; and religious services 14, 81, 165–7; diagnosing bewitchment 97, 376–7; harmful magic by 110, 169; in modern world 376–7, 379–81; in tribal societies 371–2; *see also* blacksmiths; learned magicians; midwives; shamanism; shepherds; spells
magicians *see* learned magicians
Magnus, Olaus (d) 123
Maidstone 276
Maine, Trois-eschelles du (w) 279
Mainz 180
Malawi 377
Malebranche, Nicolas (d) 340–1
malefice 86, 112, 192, 201, 235, 242, 263, 292; and combined concept of witchcraft 39, 51, 66, 71; and decline of witch-hunting 347–9, 351; and different types of witch 11, 12, 24; by familiars 131; in confessions 150–1, 208–9, 233; in demonology 77–8, 80, 81, 307; in folklore 134, 149; in village witchcraft 97–9, 105, 116, 194, 198, 280, 297, 310–11, 355; related to sex 304–5
Malleus Judicum 205
Malleus Maleficarum 52, 69, 74, 83, 84; and development of demonology 47, 66–7, 76; and rise of witch-hunting 85, 156; influence of 86, 162, 335, 362; on aspects of witchcraft 71–2, 130, 293; on court procedure 83, 202, 203, 207; on women 18, 44, 277, 301, 302–3, 305; overview 48–50 (illustration 2.2)
Malta 287
Mansenée, Desle la (w) 203, 209
Máramos 148
Maria (w) 279
marriage 276, 284, 285; *see also* impotence and infertility
Mary Queen of Scots 254
Mary, Virgin 56, 126, 129, 130, 163, 272

mascae 65
Massachusetts 96, 240, 332, 362, 386
mathematics 335, 336–7
Mather, Cotton (d) 175, 341, 342 (text box)
Maximilian I, duke of Bavaria 170, 183
Mayen 105
mazzeri 143–4
McCarthy, Joseph *see* red scares in USA
Meath, Petronilla of (w) 38
mechanical philosophy 336–8, 342, 343
Medea (w) 86
melancholy 81, 138–9, 145
Melchor, Miguel (w) 287
Mellingen 204
memorials to witches 385–6 (text box)
memory 198; false memory 147, 211–12, 373–4
men 267; as majority of witches 254, 267–9; as secondary targets 291–2; stereotypes of 277–80; *see also* patriarchy
Mencej, Mirjam (s) 380
Mensfelden 276
Mercator, Gerhard (i) 173
Mertesdorf 279
Methodism 333, 334 (illustration 10.1)
Mexico 174
Michelet, Jules (s) 367
Middle East 379–80
Middleton, John (w) 200
midwives 103, 144, 218, 277, 286–7, 293, 367–8
milk witches 95
Miller, Arthur 384
miracles 61
misfortune 10–11, 14, 50, 76, 81, 88–9; explanations for 90–1 (text box), 371, 381 (text box); *see also* children, death of; illness and disease; impotence and infertility; village economy
Mjölnare, Nils (w) 98
Möden, Johann 247
Modena 169, 178
modernity 352, 369, 379–80
Molard, Jordan dou (n) 289–90
Molsheim 294
Monroy, Baltazar de (w) 350
Montaigne, Michel de (d) 80, 82, 389–90
Monter, William (s) 250
mora witches 148
moral panics 2, 6, 232, 247

Mordvins 176
More, Henry (d) 338
Morocco 379–80, 381 (text box)
Moses 64
mothers and daughters 12, 151, 204, 210, 212, 349, 388
mountains 136, 176
Müller, Ulrich (d) 59, 135, 302
Munier, Pierre (w) 44
Murray, Margaret (s) 125, 368
Muslims 33, 86, 125, 192, 207, 379; jinn beliefs 379–80, 381; Moriscos 171, 362; reforming Islam and godly states 379–80
Mussorgsky, Modest 383
mystery plays 127

Napier of Merchiston, John (i) 58
Naples 136, 253
natural philosophy 60–4
nature spirits 122, 301, 378; *see also* elves; fairies; giants; goblins; trolls; water-spirits
Naudé, Gabriel (d) 341
Naumburg 104
Navarre 131, 152, 177; panics in 238, 240, 293, 325
necromancy 36–7, 40, 44, 63, 71, 81, 110, 170, 239, 278, 310, 367; *see also* exorcism
neo-pagan witches 26, 368–9, 384
Neoplatonism 63–4, 338
Netherlands 162–3, 172, 361; *see also* Burgundian Netherlands; Gelderland; Spanish Netherlands; United Netherlands
Neuchâtel 151
Neuerburg 212
New England 175, 277, 291, 319; *see also* Massachusetts; Salem
New Granada 174
'new sect' of witches 41–8 (text box), 50, 57, 67, 80, 277, 310
New Sweden 176
Newfoundland 174
Newton, Isaac (i) 31, 335, 337
Nicaea, Council of 33
Nicaise, Antoine (n) 201
Nider, Johannes (d) 42, 44–5, 47–8
night phantoms 140
night witches 134, 380
nightmares 11; nightmare experience *see* sleep paralysis
Nogaret, Guillaume de 37

Nördlingen 206
Normandy 207, 267–9, 278, 286, 291–2, 295; *see also* Rouen, *parlement* of
North Berwick 160–1, 239–40, 279
North, barbarous 362
Norway 86, 136, 138, 195, 362, 386; *see also* Finnmark
nunneries 302, 348
Nuremberg 253

Oberstdorf 140
occult 61–2, 337
Offenburg 150
ointments and powders 76, 77, 148; as evidence 200; flying ointment 73, 78, 139, 215, 296 (illustration 9.1), 341; for malefice 78
Öland 98
ordeals *see* swimming test
Oria 215
Orkney and Shetland 362
Orleans 33
Orthodox church 33, 86, 192, 362
Ortobello 114
Ossory 38
Ottoman Empire 27, 29, 86, 192, 207, 362, 380
Oudewater 109–10

Paderborn 327, 389
paganism 32, 68, 125–6 (text box), 167, 367, 368; *see also* Diana; neo-pagan witches
Palatinate 46, 178
Palermo 15
panics 14, 104, 118, 185, 201, 225–6, 229–49, 290, 387, 403 (further reading); chronology of 260; decline of 318–21; entrenched and forest-fire models 320; in modern world 375, 376–7, 380; opposition to 259–60, 363; sociological models 232 (text box); *see also* chain-reaction witch-hunts; moral panics
papacy *see* Catholic church
Papua New Guinea 379
paranormal 4–6
pardons 323, 385–6 (text box)
Paris 37, 39, 193, 252, 254; *parlement* of 319, 323, 324, 325
pastors *see* priests and pastors
patriarchy 8, 44, 269–70
Patrimia, Caterina (w) 215

Pavia, Lauria de (w) 137
peasants 8, 10–13, 66, 76, 88–9, 111, 133, 341; as members of witchcraft sect 41, 44, 46, 49–53; *see also* rich peasants; village economy
Pedrosa, Francesco 114
pelicans 60, 335
Peney 105, 113, 290
Penmaenmawr 176
Pentecostalism 378
Perauer, Lorenz (w) 211
Perche 324
Percheval, Reyne (w) 242, 248
Perdomo, Ana (w) 215
Perkins, William (d) 23, 82
Perrault, Charles (i) 347
Perroz, Françoise (w) 137
persecution 318, 330, 332, 360, 364, 370, 387–92; *see also* atrocities; liberal tradition
Peru 174
Peter of Bern 215
Philip IV, king of France 37
philosophy 4, 82; *see also* natural philosophy; relativism
physicians 97–8, 200, 204, 215, 272, 368
Pico della Mirandola, Gianfrancesco (d) 301
Piedmont 40, 41
Pietism 333
pilgrimages 122
planets *see* cosmos, structure of
Plato 63
Plotinus 63
poisoning 32, 82, 91, 291, 361
Poland 86, 156, 158, 171, 179, 249, 319, 407 (further reading); beliefs in 131, 136, 167, 175, 275, 304, 362; courts in 194, 196, 200, 324; individual cases in 308, 309, 351; Poland-Lithuania 178
political ideology *see* constitutionalism; divine right of kings; reason of state
Pomponazzi, Pietro (d) 80, 81, 339, 389
Portugal 29, 136, 319, 362, 406 (further reading); Portuguese colonies 125, 173–5; *see also* Brazil; Inquisition, Portuguese
possession *see* demonic possession
powders *see* ointments and powders
power and negotiation 226–9
Poznań 309
Praetorius, Johann (d) 85

Prättigau 240
preaching 23, 39, 46, 84, 129, 219, 242, 262; and religious reform 128, 157, 159, 166–8, 174, 181; by Devil 78, 84
preternatural *see* supernatural and preternatural
pricking 199, 261, 305–6
Prierias, Silvestro (d) 301
priests and pastors 13, 20, 81, 166, 212, 248, 252, 258, 269, 308, 326, 355; priests as witches 237, 278, 290; shortcomings of 126, 182, 284, 348; *see also* preaching
printing 47, 48, 49, 245, 256, 262
prostitution 284
protective magic 89, 111–12, 117, 134–5
providence, providentialism 56, 333, 337, 342, 378
Prudhon la Mareschaude, Denise (w) 308–9
Prussia 150
psychology 1–2, 4, 101, 209, 230–1, 282, 309, 360, 372–5, 385; *see also* fantasy; memory; trauma
Ptolemy (i) 336
punishments 190; of children 294; *see also* executions; galleys; imprisonment
purgatory 57, 132, 140
Pyrrho 80

Quakers 171
quarrels 11, 32, 49, 52, 77, 92–6, 198, 311, 369; *see also* curses; feuds; reconciliations; refusal-guilt syndrome; scolding; vengefulness
Quiévy 216
Quingey 137, 285–6

rack 203
Raimbault, Nicolas (w) 104–5
Ramée, Pierre de la (i) 79
rape 206, 305, 306, 308
reason of state 330–1
reconciliations 93, 106–10, 111, 113, 115–16, 250, 256, 290, 377
red scares in USA 390, 391
Reformation and Counter-Reformation 8, 22, 23, 155–88, 216, 248, 254, 263, 402 (further reading); and popular belief 127–8; decline of godly state 329–34, 355–6; *see also* preaching; religious pluralism and toleration; religious wars

426 Index

refusal-guilt syndrome 88, 95, 110, 308
Reillon 104
relativism 3–4, 372
religion, definition of 19–22; *see also* animism; atheism; Christianity; Jews; Muslims; paganism; religious pluralism and toleration
religious pluralism and toleration 318, 326, 331–2, 356
religious wars 58, 82, 158, 171–2, 329, 330; *see also* Thirty Years' War
Rémy, Nicolas (d) 62, 74, 86, 133, 247, 294
Renaissance 8, 24–5, 338, 367; and Reformation 158; and ideas of witchcraft 83–4, 173, 278, 297, 347, 383; and scepticism 61, 79–80, 343; *see also* Neoplatonism
repentance 192, 197, 208, 212–13, 219
reputations for witchcraft 92–4, 103–4, 129, 227, 235, 237, 290; instant reputation 104–6; *see also* quarrels; reconciliations; refusal-guilt syndrome
revenants 123, 132
reverse witch trials 351, 379
Rhine, river 29, 144
Rhine-Moselle region 116, 240–1, 254, 255, 263
rich peasants 93, 114, 151, 248, 252, 256, 263, 290
Rieux 205
Rojas, Ferdinando de (d) 84
Romania 142
Romantic movement 350, 366; romantic tradition 360, 364, 366–70
Rome 58; Roman Empire 21–3, 194, 196; *see also* Holy Roman Empire
Roper, Lyndal (s) 372, 374
rosary beads 163, 164, 200
Rose, Antoine (w) 46, 135
Rose, Michel (n) 135
Roskoff, Gustav (s) 366
Rothenburg ob der Tauber 114, 205, 293, 323
Rottenburg 168, 245
Rouen, *parlement* of 207, 249
Russia 86, 175, 176, 178, 239, 407 (further reading); beliefs in 131, 134, 136, 303, 304; courts in 7, 114, 192, 194, 254; magical practices in 110, 254, 286, 288, 362
Rutland, earl and countess of 304

sabbat 3, 10–13, 14, 277, 297, 344, 364; abduction to 149, 201, 292–3, 306, 347, 349 (*see also* children, abduction of); and cumulative concept of witchcraft 66–7; dancing at 10, 74, 75 (illustration 3.2), 77, 78, 86; development of 42–3, 45–6, 50–3, 134; disappearance of 137; extent of 86–7; in chain-reaction trials 226, 229, 236; in confessions 16–17, 85, 136, 150–1, 194, 198, 201, 205, 208–9, 211, 212, 215, 278, 285, 301, 308–9; in demonology 55, 72, 77 (diagram 3.1), 78, 84, 85, 134, 163, 173, 243, 280–1, 303, 310, 341, 355; in folk belief 124, 133, 135 (diagram 5.1), 150–2, 216; in modern world 378, 383; musicians at 279; reports of harm at 62; revival of 73–6, 77–8; *see also* flight
sagas 137, 138
Sainte-Croix 127
St Gallen 321
Saint-Gellert 136
St John's Eve 111, 136
St Maximin 181
St Walpurgis Eve 135
saints 59, 126, 129, 163, 169, 381
Sala de Juxue, Jeannette de (w) 46
Salem 7, 96, 175, 181, 201, 240, 245, 342 (text box), 348, 408 (further reading); apology of jurors 317, 323; ergotism theory 369; factions in village 332, 385; individual cases in 201, 216, 279; memorial to witches 386; pardons of witches 386
Salian Franks 65
Salisbury 195
Saluces, Georges de 248
Salzburg 294
Sámi people 125, 141, 362
Saragossa 182, 253, 284, 287
Satan 67–8; alleged Satanic abuse *see* child abuse
Sattler, Gottfried 183
satyrs 123, 298
Saudi Arabia 379–80, 382
sausages 298
Savoy 29, 40, 41, 46, 47, 162, 178, 303, 319
Saxony 96, 328
Scaedeli (w) 215

Scandinavia 123, 136, 158, 194, 362, 407–8 (further reading); *see also* sagas; Sámi people
scapegoating 281–3, 387
scepticism 79–82, 202, 317, 334 (illustration 10.1), 339–45, 346, 347–9, 352–4, 388
Schaffhausen 45
Schleswig 289
Schmeig, Anna (w) 114
scholasticism 58–9, 68, 83
Schongau 247
Schramm, Maria (w) 305
Schweistal, Johann (w) 240
science 5, 19, 21, 60; *see also* natural philosophy; Scientific Revolution
Scientific Revolution 8, 21, 64, 218, 327, 335–9; *see also* Cartesianism; cosmos, structure of; mathematics; mechanical philosophy
scolding 96, 273
scopolamine 145
Scot, Reginald (d) 80, 81–2, 339, 389
Scotland 29, 270, 277, 362, 370, 386, 407 (further reading); beliefs in 86, 121, 132, 242, 275; individual cases in 98, 103, 127, 143, 210, 279, 302; Irish connection 181; law in 167, 328; panics in 231, 239–40, 323; Reformation in 158, 162, 167; towns in 253; witch-pricking in 306; *see also* James VI; North Berwick; seely wights
Scythians 371
seasons 122–3; *see also* calendar rituals
Secretain, Françoise (w) 163
Seeger, Catharina (w) 291
seely wights 142, 143
Semellé, Marin (w) 115–16, 301
Seneca 86
sentences 197, 227–8; *see also* executions; imprisonment; pardons; punishments
Serbia 143
sermons *see* preaching
Seven Deadly Sins 168
sexual offences 164–5, 185, 194, 332; gendered offences 283–5
Shakespeare, William (i) 31, 132, 346
shamanism 65, 108, 140–5, 371
shape-shifting 40, 61, 74, 109, 129, 137–8; *see also* cats; hares; werewolves
Shelley, Mary 369

shepherds 268, 280, 341
Sherwood, Grace (w) 109, 386
shipwrecks 347
Siberia 140, 288, 371
sibyls 143
Sicily 15; *see also donas de fuera*
Siena 107
sieve and shears 112
Simon Magus 278
Sinclair, George (d) 339
Singer, Maria Renata (w) 348
Sinhon, Monnet (w) 277
slander 96, 109, 276, 289, 351
sleep deprivation 147, 203, 261
sleep paralysis 146–50 (illustration 5.2)
Slovenia 143, 380
Småland 98
Smelser, Neil (s) 232
Smith, George (n) 98
Smith, William (n) 98
sociology 1–2, 4, 232, 282–3, 373
sodomy 193, 284, 285
Soldan, Wilhelm (s) 364–5
soldiers, magic by 288
sorcery 38, 39, 371–2
Sorel, Charles (d) 343
South Africa 376, 378
Spain 29, 33, 158, 172, 331, 362, 406 (further reading); beliefs in 81, 137, 215–16, 243, 278, 287, 304; courts in 194, 203; decline of prosecutions 322, 332; individual cases in 101, 203, 212, 306; law code 190; panics in 238, 240, 292, 293; Spanish colonies 125, 174–5, 350; *see also* Aragon; Catalonia; Inquisition, Spanish; Navarre
Spanish Netherlands 170–1, 216, 246, 247, 249, 254, 270, 303; individual cases in 105, 201, 242, 248, 294
spectral evidence 11, 201, 307, 342 (text box)
Spee, Friedrich (d) 202, 206, 214, 219–20, 326, 327 (text box), 328, 345, 386, 389–90
spells 5, 12, 19, 71, 89, 91, 201, 209, 213, 254; and curses 93, 99–101, 285–6; for flight 78; *see also grimoires*; image-magic; love magic
Spina, Bartolomeo della (d) 178, 230
Spinoza, Baruch (i) 337, 345
spirit voyages 10, 76, 125, 140–5, 373; *see also* shamanism

Sprenger, Jacob 48
Stalin, Joseph 390
state formation 156–7, 183–6, 192–3, 256–7; types of state 176–9
statistics on witch-hunting 27–9, 118, 176–7, 229, 260–2, 267–9, 319–20, 366, 410–13
Steilneset 386
stereotypes 10, 11, 17, 239, 273–80, 290, 292, 369, 373
Stockholm 210, 258
Stoeckhlin, Chonrad (w) 108, 140–1
storms 9, 36, 97, 99, 122, 133, 151, 201, 281; and demonology 12, 45, 77–8, 80, 242–3, 293; and panics 180, 241, 242
strappado 203, 204 (illustration 7.1), 211
Strasbourg 23
striae, striges 65, 134
succubus *see* incubus and succubus
Suffolk 308
Sugny 244
suicide 206
Summers, Montague (s) 48
supernatural and preternatural 60–2, 81–2, 96–7, 200, 337, 343
superstition, definition of 2, 22–4; superstition after witch-hunting 340–1, 349–50; superstition and godly state 167, 169–70, 184–6, 288, 362
Surin, Jean-Joseph (d) 348
Swabia 242; Swabian Alps 136
Sweden 98, 137, 152, 176, 201, 210, 288, 319, 350; panic in 234, 258–9 (text box), 292
swimming test 109–10, 199–200, 308, 384
Switzerland 29, 137, 151, 158, 171, 172, 178, 193, 280–1 (text box), 319, 406 (further reading); individual cases in 127, 204, 211, 218, 290; Sonderbund War 332; *see also* Alps; Basel; Fribourg; Geneva; Glarus; Lucerne; Lausanne; Prättigau; Schaffhausen; Valais; Vaud
Szeged 207–8

táltos 143
Tambora 244
Tanner, Adam (d) 183, 214, 339
Tanzania 377
Tatars 175, 176

tears, inability to shed 272
Tedworth, drummer of 334 (illustration 10.1)
Tembley, Richard de (n) 105
Templars 37–8
Ten Commandments 12, 167, 168
Teresa of Ávila, St 141
terrorism 231
Theophilus 129
Thiers, Jean-Baptiste (d) 340
Thirty Years' War 172–3, 239, 326, 331, 351
Tholosan, Claude (d) 42, 44–5, 47
Thomas the Rhymer 121, 130
Thomas, Keith (s) 95, 370
Thomasius, Christian (d) 345
thumbscrew 203, 210
Tisza, river 207
toads 131, 145, 242, 382; dressed toads 215–16
Todi 40, 136
Tofts, Mary 334 (illustration 10.1)
Torny-le-Grand 299
Torrent, Pere (w) 203
Torrenté, Ulric de 41
torture 189, 195–6, 202–9 (illustration 7.1), 210–13, 220, 235, 258, 261, 365, 373–4, 387; decline of 328–9, 389; in modern world 360, 377, 378, 387, 390–1; *see also* atrocities
Toulouse 34
Touret, Marguerite (w) 285–6, 309
Tourgis, Marie (w) 380
towns 89, 189, 191, 252–3, 259
trances *see* spirit voyages
Transylvania 239
trauma 3, 230, 305, 307–9, 372
treasure-seeking 288
Trembley, Conrad de (n) 113
trial records 6–7, 105, 108–9, 114, 128, 206, 242, 255, 408–9 (further reading)
Trier 167, 180, 239, 245–6, 279, 293, 294; decline of prosecutions 326
trolls 24, 130, 137
Tschuldi, Anne-Miggeli (n) 322
Tschuldi, Johann Jakob (n) 322
Tupí Indians 174
Turkey 391–2

Uganda 376
Ukraine 134

United Nations 360, 390
United Netherlands 82, 109–10, 178, 268, 405 (further reading); decline of prosecutions 320–1, 326, 328–9, 330, 340, 344, 345; *see also* Asten; Friesland; Holland; Vollenhove
United States of America 390, 392
universities 33, 58–9, 86, 95, 129, 251; advice to courts 183, 193, 228

Valais 41–2, 47
Valla, Lorenzo (i) 158
vampires 132
Van der Camere, Charles 247
van Dyck, Anthony 15
Vardø 200, 386
Vaud 41, 248, 260, 289–90
Vaudoises 41–2, 43 (illustration 2.1), 45, 361
ved'ma 134
vengefulness 76, 91–2, 94–5, 103, 198, 373
Venice 97, 99, 131, 136, 200, 205–6
Venusberg 143
verdicts 197, 206, 227, 261; customary and Roman systems 194–6, 258, 328; *see also* judges; sentences
Verdier, Gaspard (n) 290
Vesalius, Andreas (i) 335
vilenicas 143
village economy 88–9, 241–3, 251–2; and gender 285; and Little Ice Age 243–4 (text box); *see also* beggars
village witchcraft, definition of 10–11, 90 (diagram 4.1), 310–11, 375, 400–1 (further reading)
Virginia 109, 386
visionaries *see* spirit voyages
visual images of witchcraft 14–15, 74, 84–5, 138–9, 295–8, 347, 364; in modern world 382–3
Vitéz, Zsuasanna (w) 239
volcanic eruptions 243–4
Vollenhove 289
Voltaire (d) 364, 366
Vuiteboeuf 211

Waldensians 33–5, 40, 41–2, 170, 174, 365; *see also Vaudoises*
Wales 176, 274
Walten, Ericus (d) 345
water ordeal *see* swimming test
Waterhouse, Agnes (w) 233

Waterhouse, Joan (w) 233
water-spirits 135
Wattelier, Pierre (n) 248
weather magic *see* storms
Weissenbühler, Anna Catharina (w) 214–15
Weixler, Magdalena (w) 213
Wenham, Jane (w) 247–8
werewolves 62, 137, 138, 143, 279, 280
Wesley, John (d) 333
Westerstetten, Johann Christoph von 216
Westphalia, peace of 331
Weyer, Johann (d) 80, 81–2, 86, 270, 339, 340, 389
whales 138
Wiccans *see* neo-pagan witches
Wiesensteig 245
Wild Hunt 65, 132–3, 140
Wilhelm V, duke of Bavaria 183, 245
William of Auvergne (d) 69–71, 302
Wilverdange, Isabeau (w) 207
wine cellars, visits to 141, 215
witchcraft: combined concept of 51–3, 365; cumulative concept of 65–7; definitions of 9–13, 38; elaborated concept of 76–9; *see also* demonic witchcraft; envisioned witchcraft; folkloric witchcraft; human and non-human witches; village witchcraft; words for witches
witch-doctors 372
witch-homes 376
witch-hunting, definition of 26–7; *see also* chronology of witch-hunting; decline of witch-hunting; geography of witch-hunting; statistics on witch-hunting
witnesses 194, 248, 261; star witnesses 219, 238, 325; witness statements 12, 98, 115–16, 124
Wittenberg 129
wolves 91, 137; *see also* werewolves
women 8, 31–2, 38, 39–40, 44–6, 267–311, 350, 366, 367–8, 403 (further reading); and demonic pact 300 (illustration 9.2); and food preparation 91, 285, 309; and Inquisition 280–1 (text box); as subhuman 267, 273, 302; experience of prosecution 305–6 (text box); in shamanistic

cults 144; nakedness in imagery 139, 295–7 (illustration 9.1), 364; older women 237, 275–6, 297, 347, 351, 376, 377, 382, 387; widows 274, 276, 280, 292, 379; younger women 276, 291, 292, 295–7, 382–3; *see also* Devil, sex with; men; mothers and daughters; patriarchy; rape; scolding; sexual offences; visual images of witchcraft
Wood, Janet (w) 127
words for witches 17–19 (text box), 36, 45–6, 47–8, 52, 65, 134, 192, 285, 361, 374–5

Württemberg 169, 178, 249; individual cases in 99, 214–15, 291, 305
Würzburg 85, 180, 225, 290, 294, 348

Young, Isobel (w) 98
Yriarte, María de (w) 212

Zagreb 268
zână 142
Zaragoza 174
Zauberer-Jackl trials 294
zduhačs 143
Zheglov, Ivan (w) 288
Zimbabwe 376
zirokhvatka 134